Rosmini's Suspended Middle

Rosmini's Suspended Middle

The Synthesistic Performativity of Genius and Interdisciplinary Thinking

EDITED BY
FERNANDO BELLELLI

Translated from Italian by Katherine M. Clifton
Foreword by Antonio Staglianò
Afterword by John Milbank

⌒PICKWICK Publications · Eugene, Oregon

ROSMINI'S SUSPENDED MIDDLE
The Synthesistic Performativity of Genius and Interdisciplinary Thinking

Copyright © 2024 Wipf and Stock Publishers. All rights reserved. Except for brief quotations in critical publications or reviews, no part of this book may be reproduced in any manner without prior written permission from the publisher. Write: Permissions, Wipf and Stock Publishers, 199 W. 8th Ave., Suite 3, Eugene, OR 97401.

Pickwick Publications
An Imprint of Wipf and Stock Publishers
199 W. 8th Ave., Suite 3
Eugene, OR 97401

www.wipfandstock.com

PAPERBACK ISBN: 978-1-6667-5427-8
HARDCOVER ISBN: 978-1-6667-5428-5
EBOOK ISBN: 978-1-6667-5429-2

Cataloguing-in-Publication data:

Names: Bellelli, Fernando, 1977– [editor]. | Clifton, Katherine M. [translator].

Title: Rosmini's suspended middle : the synthesistic performativity of genius and interdisciplinary thinking / Fernando Bellelli ; with a foreword by Antonio Staglianò and an afterword by John Milbank.

Description: Eugene, OR: Pickwick Publications, 2024 | Includes bibliographical references and index.

Identifiers: ISBN 978-1-6667-5427-8 (paperback) | ISBN 978-1-6667-5428-5 (hardcover) | ISBN 978-1-6667-5429-2 (ebook)

Subjects: LCSH: Rosmini, Antonio, 1797–1855 | Philosophical theology | Catholic Church—Italy—Clergy | Philosophers—Italy |

Classification: B3647 B52 2024 (paperback) | B3647 (ebook)

01/09/24

Unless otherwise indicated, emphases in quotations are original and not added.

Front cover: Francesco Hayez, *Ritratto di Antonio Rosmini*, 1853, public domain.

Back cover: Wiligelmo, *L'Eterno in mandorla e la Creazione di Adamo. Prima lastra con storia del Genesi*. Modena (Italy), Duomo. The photo is from: Archivio fotografico del Museo Civico (foto G. Roli), Modena (Italy).

To Giovanna, at the Sodality
of Ascribed Members "Plenitudo Charitatis,"
to all the Ascribed Rosminian Members of the Istituto della Carità,
and to all friends of Rosmini, past, present and future.

"In the ineffable plan of the Incarnation and Redemption, Charity is the *end*, Charity is the *beginning* that works in Christ to attain this end; the actions of Christ, as *means* of connecting this beginning with the end are also Charity. . . . Since only Charity can fully comprehend itself and *know that which surpasses science*, so only Charity can accomplish Charity. This is the *beginning* of acting according to God, its *means* and its *end*, that is eternal glory."

Antonio Rosmini, "Lo spirito dell'Istituto della Carità," in *Operette spirituali*, edited by Alfeo Valle, ENC 48, 71–72 (Rome: Città Nuova, 1985). Translated by Katherine M. Clifton.

Contents

Permissions	xi
Curator's Note	xiii
Acknowledgments	xv
List of Abbreviations	xvii
List of Contributors	xix
Foreword by Antonio Staglianò	xxi
Introduction	1
Fernando Bellelli	

Part 1 | Rosmini's Purification of the Scotist Aporias of Phenomenology (between Analogy and Paradox) and the Division of Being: Metaphysics and Ontology

1. Rosmini's Ontology   41
   Umberto Muratore

2. Identity "as" Difference: "A-dialectical" Denial in the Rosminian God   59
   Massimo Donà

3. Laicity of Rosminian Theoresis   74
   Samuele Francesco Tadini

4. In Search of a Metaphysical Rooting of Phenomenology: Rosminian Perspectives on Purifying Hermeneutical Reductionism   89
   Alberto Peratoner

Part 2 | Rosmini's Trinitarian Ontology and His *Suspended Middle*: The Primality of the Moral Form of Being in Synthesism with the Real and Ideal Forms

5 Knowledge and Justice of Pro-Affection   103
PIERANGELO SEQUERI

6 Beyond Extrinsecism between Philosophy and Theology, in a Solid Circle in Rosmini Theology: Twenty Years after the Doctrinal Note   114
ANTONIO STAGLIANÒ

7 Antonio Rosmini in *Veritatis Gaudium:* Unity of Knowledge and Trinitarian Ontology   133
PIERO CODA

8 Between "Theosophy" and "Philosophy of Law": Intersubjectivity as a Way to the "Other" in Rosmini   150
EMANUELE PILI

9 Thinking about Faith in Time of Its "Foaming" Relevance: Notes from *Supernatural Anthropology*   166
GIAMMARIA CANU

Part 3 | Rosmini's *Suspended Middle* (and the Comparable Social Theory of Radical Orthodoxy's *Suspended Middle*): Possible Pedagogical Implications

10 Notes on the Rosminian Pedagogical Method   183
FULVIO DE GIORGI

11 Pedagogical Parallels between Saint Augustine and Rosmini   198
JACOB BUGANZA

12 Philosophical Anthropology of Antonio Rosmini Compared to the One of Viktor Emil Frankl   212
DOMENICO CRAVERO

13 Affection and Intersubjectivity in the Thought of Antonio Rosmini and Edith Stein   234
MARTINA GALVANI

14 *Affection* of *Cognition* in the Method and Methodology of Antonio Rosmini   252
FERNANDO BELLELLI

Part 4 | Rosmini's *Suspended Middle* (and the Comparable Social Theory of Radical Orthodoxy's *Suspended Middle*): Possible Political Implications

15 Philosophy of Politics and Philosophy of Right and Law in Rosmini 273
   MARTA FERRONATO

16 Ethics and Society in the Political Thought of Antonio Rosmini 289
   CHRISTIANE LIERMANN

17 Can Rosminian Thinking Have Meaning within the *Italian Theory*? 298
   LUCIANO MALUSA

18 Antonio Rosmini: Spirituality of Justice and Anthropological Conception 319
   PIERLUIGI GIROLI

Part 5 | Rosmini's *Suspended Middle* (and the Comparable Social Theory of Radical Orthodoxy's *Suspended Middle*): Possible Juridical Implications

19 Consuetude and Neuroscience? Elements for an Affective Reading of Rosmini's Thought 345
   PAOLO HERITIER

20 Philosophy and Theology of Law: Rethinking the Legal Systems in the Light of Rosmini's Ideas 364
   MARIO CIOFFI

21 Antonio Rosmini: Ascetic and Mystic 379
   VITO NARDIN

22 Rosminian Suggestions on Ecclesiology 402
   ALESSANDRO ANDREINI

23 Spiritual Theology of Desire and Intellectual Charity in Antonio Rosmini 412
   WILLIAM ABBRUZZESE

24 Conclusion 428
   FERNANDO BELLELLI

Afterword 457
   JOHN MILBANK

Index 463

Permissions

THE ESSAYS IN THIS volume were translated from the following publications, and formal release was given by the publishing houses for translation and publication with W&S.

Fernando, Bellelli, ed. *La metodica di Rosmini tra filosofia, teologia e pedagogia. Prospettive interdisciplinari.* Milan: Mimesis 2022.

Fernando, Bellelli, ed. *Rosmini filosofo e teologo con Tommaso: unità di scienza e santità. Divus Thomas* 1 (2023).

Donà, Massimo. "Identità 'come' differenza. Negazione 'a-dialettica' nel Dio rosminiano." *Sophia* 2 (2021) 233–47.

Scripture texts in this work are taken from the New American Bible, Revised Edition, © 2010, 1991, 1986, 1970 Confraternity of Christian Doctrine, Washington, DC, and are used by permission of the copyright owner. All rights reserved. No part of the New American Bible may be reproduced in any form without permission in writing from the copyright owner.

Curator's Note

ROSMINI'S WORKS PRESENTED IN the volume were consulted in the language in which they are quoted, and as such they are listed in the bibliography.

We have tried to keep the quotation of the titles of works by Antonio Rosmini unform. The titles of works by Rosmini are to be found in Italian in the bibliography of each contribution.

In each contribution, in the body of the text, they are given in English the first time, followed by the original Italian title. In the notes they are given in Italian to facilitate consultation of the bibliography.

The contribution of Marta Ferronato follows precise rules set down by the author. As requested by the publisher's style guide, the page numbers of the works quoted in the notes are not preceded by any particular acronym.

The works of Antonio Rosmini in the original editions are often divided into paragraphs in order to facilitate consultation also in different editions. When the author has quoted a paragraph rather than the page, the number of the paragraph is preceded by "para."

Some of Rosmini's works are abbreviated, as indicated in the table of abbreviations. The abbreviations of the biblical quotations are given in a table on xviii

Acknowledgments

THANKS FOR HIS SUPPORT, encouragement, and assistance go to Father Vito Nardin, Father General Emeritus of the Rosminian Istituto della Carità and now Collaborator at Sacro Monte Calvario in Domodossola, Italy.

Among all those who have assisted me in this work of intellectual charity, particular thanks go to Giovanna Gabbi, Rosminian Ascribed Member, without whose untiring dedication and competence this volume would never have been completed.

Thanks to Spei Lumen APS-Cenacolo Rosminiano Emiliano Romagnolo and to the Sodality of Ascribed Members "Plenitudo Charitatis."

List of Abbreviations[1]

Books by Rosmini

AAMS	*Antropologia in servizio della scienza morale* (Anthropology as an aid to moral science)
CSJ	*La Costituzione secondo la giustizia sociale* (The constitution under social justice)
EN	Edizione nazionale delle opere edite e inedite di Antonio Rosmini
ENC	Edizione nazionale e critica delle opere di Antonio Rosmini
FW	*Delle cinque piaghe della Santa Chiesa* (The five wounds of the holy Church)
IP	*Introduzione alla filosofia* (Introduction to philosophy)
NE	*Nuovo Saggio sull'origine delle idee* (A new essay concerning the origin of ideas)
PL	*Filosofia del diritto* (Philosophy of law)
PMS	*Principi della scienza morale* (Principles of moral science)
Pp	*Filosofia della politica* (Cedam, It.: Padova) (Philosophy of politics)
PY	*Psicologia* (Psychology)

1. The table does not include all the works by Rosmini mentioned in the text, since they appear in the bibliographies of the individual essays, but only those whose titles were abbreviated on request of the authors.

LIST OF ABBREVIATIONS

RPMAE   "Del principio supremo della Metodica" (The ruling principle of method applied to education)

SA   *Antropologia soprannaturale* (Supernatural anthropology)

T   *Teosofia* (Theosophy) (edited by Samuele F. Tadini)

Th   *Teodicea* (Theodicy)

Theos   *Teosofia* (Theosophy) (edited by Maria A. Raschini and Pier P. Ottonello)

TL   *Il linguaggio teologico* (The theological language)

Scripture Abbreviations

Old Testament

Genesis	Gen	Sirach/Ecclesiasticus	Sir
Eccl (or Qoh)	Ecclesiastes (or Qoheleth)	Song of Songs	Song
		Isaiah	Isa
Psalms	Ps	Jeremiah	Jer
Proverbs	Prov	Wisdom of Solomon	Wis

New Testament

Matthew	Matt	Ephesians	Eph
Romans	Rom	1 Thessalonians	1 Thess
1–2 Corinthians	1–2 Cor	Hebrews	Heb
Galatians	Gal	James	Jas
Philippians	Phil	Revelation	Rev
Colossians	Col		

Church Documents Abbreviations

Veritatis Gaudium	VG
Evangelii Gaudium	EG

List of Contributors

UMBERTO MURATORE, deceased 2022, previously Director of the Centro Internazionale di Studi Rosminiani in Stresa, Italy

MASSIMO DONÀ, Ordinary Professor of Theoretical Philosophy at the Faculty of Philosophy, Università San Raffaele, Milano, Italy

SAMUELE F. TADINI, Researcher at the Centro Internazionale di Studi Rosminiani in Stresa (Italy) and Lecturer at the Faculty of Theology in Lugano (Switzerland), Director of the *Rivista Rosminiana*, journal of philosophy and culture

ALBERTO PERATONER, Professor at the Facoltà Teologica del Triveneto, President of the Cenacolo Rosminiano Triveneto, Italy

PIERANGELO SEQUERI, previously Dean of the Facoltà Teologica dell'Italia Settentrionale, Milano (Italy), and of the Pontificio Istituto Teologico Giovanni Paolo II for Matrimonial and Family Sciences, where he is currently the Director of the "Cattedra Gaudium et spes." Consultant to the Synod of Bishops and Consultant to the Pontificia Accademia for life

ANTONIO STAGLIANÒ, Bishop, Dean of the Pontificia Accademia di Teologia, Bishop Emeritus of the Diocese of Noto (Italy)

PIERO CODA, Ordinary Professor of Trinitarian Ontology at the Istituto Universitario Sophia di Loppiano (Italy), of which he was the first Dean; General Secretary of the International Theological Commission; Consultor of the Dicastero per la Dottrina della Fede

EMANUELE PILI, Researcher in History of Philosophy at Università degli Studi di Perugia, Italy

GIAMMARIA CANU, Priest of the Diocese of Ozieri (Sardinia), Italy; PhD in Fundamental Theology from the Pontificia Università Lateranense

LIST OF CONTRIBUTORS

FULVIO DE GIORGI, Ordinary Professor of History of Education at Università di Modena e Reggio Emilia and President of the CIRSE (Centro Italiano per la Ricerca Storico-Educativa), Italy

JACOB BUGANZA, Ordinary Professor at Universidad Veracruzana, Mexico

DOMENICO CRAVERO, Parish Priest in Poirino (TO), psychologist, currently studying for a PhD in Humanistic Sciences at Università di Modena e Reggio Emilia, Italy

MARTINA GALVANI, PhD in Philosophy from the Consorzio FINO, Università di Genova, Italy

FERNANDO BELLELLI, PhD in Humanities and ThD in Fundamental Theology, Founder and Coordinator of the Cenacolo Rosminiano Emiliano-Romagnolo, Lecturer at Università di Modena e Reggio Emilia and at Università di Verona, Italy

MARTA FERRONATO, Associate Professor of History of Political Thought at the Department of Political and Juridical Sciences and International Studies, Università di Padova, Italy

CHRISTIANE LIERMANN, PhD in Political Philosophy, General Secretary of Villa Vigoni–German-Italian Centre for European Dialogue, Italy

LUCIANO MALUSA, previously Ordinary Professor of History of Philosophy, Università di Genova, and before of this Professor at Università di Padova and Università di Verona, Italy, one of the most important experts on the history of Rosminian philosophical thought

PIERLUIGI GIROLI, Rosminian Father, PhD in Spiritual Theology from the Pontificia Università della Santa Croce, Rector of the Basilica dei Santi Carlo e Ambrogio, Roma, Italy

PAOLO HERITIER, Ordinary Professor of Philosophy of Law at Università del Piemonte Orientale, Italy; Co-Director of the journal *Theory and Criticism of Social Regulation*

MARIO CIOFFI, graduate in Jurisprudence and Cassation Lawyer in Italy

VITO NARDIN, Rosminian Father, General Provost Emeritus of the Istituto della Carità, Collaborator at Sacro Monte Calvario in Domodossola, Italy

ALESSANDRO ANDREINI, PhD in Philosophy; Priest and Member of the Comunità di San Leolino, Parish Priest of Panzano in Chianti (FI), Italy

WILLIAM ABBRUZZESE, Licentiate in Spiritual Theology from the Facoltà Teologica dell'Italia Settentrionale di Milano, Priest of the Archdiocese of Milano

JOHN MILBANK, Emeritus Professor of Theology, Philosophy, and Ethics at the University of Nottingham, founder of the radical orthodoxy movement

Foreword

ANTONIO STAGLIANÒ

WHAT IS ROSMINI'S SUSPENDED *middle*? In its original capacity, it gives life to a theological-philosophical *and methodological* rethinking—with implications in the sciences, in particular, pedagogical, political, and juridical—of the relationship between the *natural* and the *supernatural* (anticipating in this the operation carried out by the *nouvelle théologie*). And what, therefore, would be the connection between *Pop-Theology* and Rosmini's suspended middle, documented and developed in this substantial and significant volume? *Pop-Theology* is the performative communication of Rosmini's *suspended middle*, regenerative of ethos (*moral form of being*), pathos (*real form of being*), and logos (*ideal form of being*), the inter-multi-trans-discipline of *culture* and *cultures*. Rosmini starts from the person, as *the* right and subsisting relationship, to reach God: people, as it is civil society that is an expression of the bonds between people, are the reality in which Rosmini's *suspended middle* is in place. *Pop-Theology* is, therefore, Rosmini's *suspended middle* in action.[1]

1. Here is the manifesto of Pop-Theology: (1) Pop-Theology is "intellectual charity" (A. Rosmini): the ethical commitment to translocate the discoveries of theological science into sensible words that reach the very heart of common sense, therefore to everyone. (2) Pop-Theology develops with the imagination of reason; therefore, it delves into the languages of art to achieve the popular goal of communicating the intelligence of the Christian faith to anyone. (3) Pop-Theology is a choice of field (popular culture) and a preferential option of one's interlocutor (ordinary people); hence its inalienable pop or "popular" character. (4) Pop-Theology occupies the space of the eighth functional specialization of Bernard Lonergan's transcendental method, communication: it is the space without which all the work of professional theologians is practically useless. (5) Pop-Theology is not so much quoting the singer's song, but rather responding critically to questions that challenge the popular experience of the Christian faith. (6) Pop-Theology is daring on the path of paradox, to educate every believer to critical reflexivity,

FOREWORD

Let us concentrate on the fundamental nucleus of the essential intuition carried out by Rosmini in his encyclopedic scientific and literary production.

Serving the gospel, spreading the truth of Christ in the world: it can also be done philosophically and it would be a "great service" to theology, which should certainly do it by "natural right" (for a question that pertains to its very nature or definition). Is it, however, something that philosophy can do at a prejudicial distance or separation from theology? Rosmini replies: *absolutely not*. It seems to me that I documented this response "scientifically" in my doctoral work in theology that I published with Morcelliana in 1988 (coincidentally exactly one hundred years after the *Post Obitum*) under the title *La "teologia" secondo Rosmini. Sistematica-critica-interpretazione del rapporto fede e ragione*. It is a work that has been completely ignored by *philosophical* Rosminianism up until today, and for (good!) reasons: *because it dared to ask for a rethinking of Rosminian philosophizing that would epistemologically, and more directly, link it back to the original way in which Rosmini himself thought about in his freedom of philosophizing, unpolluted by reference to Catholic dogma and the Christian faith*. Even as a young man, Rosmini overcame the Enlightenment prejudice that excludes faith from knowledge, and which grants knowledge only and exclusively to reason (moreover reduced to unnatural/impure limits for reason itself and, in this unnaturalness, considered by Immanuel Kant "pure"). In Rosmini's time philosophy still functioned as a "handmaid" of theology—considered the "queen of all sciences"—despite the fact that Immanuel Kant had overturned the scheme of knowledge with *The Conflict of the Faculties* and Auguste Comte in his *Course of Positive Philosophy* had relegated theology to the infantile stage of humanity. It is well known how philosophy—in the

---

with a nonnegligent dissemination of the truths of faith, beyond the misunderstandings about God of ordinary believing practice. (7) Pop-Theology is hermeneutics of the Christian obvious: it shows the incompatibility of Christianity with the obvious with which it is often masked. (8) Pop-Theology is an exercise of the critical intelligence of the counter-intuitive gaze in Christian life: it shows that in the practiced rites, in religious appearances, and even in ideas about God, all that glitters is not gold. (9) Pop-Theology is a cure for the "difficult beauty" of the gospel, in addition to and against the many forms of aestheticization of Christian living that anesthetize the ecclesial body, extinguishing its vitality and missionary ardor. (10) Pop-Theology proposes itself as a true theology attentive to the "other words of the differently believer or non-believer" in the profound conviction that every man is, in his humanity, like a grammar of a possible self-communication of God (K. Rahner). See Antonio Staglianò, *Dibattito pubblico e inculturazione della fede*, Pop-Theology 5 (Rosolini, It.: Santocono, 2021), 27–29. In addition to the manifesto, I also refer to my decalogue on Rosmini the thinker, prophet and holy, in *Il Beato Antonio Rosmini patrono della Pop-Theology*, Pop-Theology 7 (Rosolini, It.: Santocono, 2021), 86–87.

modern period—separated from theology and established itself in full autonomy and autarchy.

Differently and inversely, Rosmini believed that faith was his knowledge and that it was necessary to find the appropriate language of this knowledge to be able to "critically" (i.e., philosophically) communicate it to the men of his time. *With a theological intentionality* (we could say, without any "apologetic" fear) *he undertook the work of refounding all of philosophy* so that the knowledge of the faith (the gospel and the dogmas of the Catholic Church) could be accessible to all, at least by removing—and here is the action of "intellectual charity" or even of evangelically enlightened pastoral action—"what is obscure and contrary to reason, every absurdity for reason." *There is no rationalistic blunder, rather there is an account of the hope of faith and dogma.*[2]

What is the fundamental theoretical-speculative device of Rosmini's suspended middle? The *Rosminian theory of synthesism*. This *theory* appears *capable* of overcoming both the separating extrinsecism of faith and reason, and the confusing intrinsecism: *it is in the Rosminian synthesism that we can imagine the possibility of a "being-in" of each of the forms of being in the other*, remaining absolutely oneself, without confusion and without separation, but "inside" intimately nested. In line with all the Catholic tradition—which has always spoken of a healing and elevating exercise of faith with respect to human reason as such—the methodological perspective of Rosmini, after adequately distinguishing between reason and faith, is that of *uniting*, showing by action the fecundity of the "salvific" union of the faith with reason: in a solid circle that helps reason and does not impoverish the faith; rather it justifies and gives credibility to the faith, because it shows the reason since it shows itself to reason "as a teacher, who unfolds before them and delivers the secrets of wisdom," so that reason can also be called "a child of faith" or "the constant guard of human reason," as Rosmini would say in *Teodicea*, where he says that it is possible to treat the Trinitarian truth as "a scientific proposition like the others," without taking from the dogma its mystery and its transcendence (faith is faith and remains such). The emanationism of the unitary systems, ancient and modern (Plotinus and Hegel) is a philosophical error of considerable range, because it does not provide solutions to the problem par excellence that regards first "how the perfect unity of the first being is reconciled with that sort of multiplicity which is necessary for it to be full, active and the cause of things." This problem presents an antinomy "that has vexed . . . philosophy for centuries, which Christ satisfied, but

---

2. See Stagliano, *Dibattito pubblico*, 20–22.

revealing the mystery." In this sense it is no wonder that the Trinity of the divine persons lies "at the root of Theosophy as the mysterious foundation."[3]

The "intellectual charity" of Antonio Rosmini or the "intellectual patience of charity" of Marie-Dominique Chenu is similar and in profound harmony with what Pope Francis requires. It is perhaps time to be more daring, patiently and charitably, on the vast grounds of the scientific vision of the world, to rediscover *new synergies between science and faith*.[4]

The Blessed Antonio Rosmini is the patron of *Pop-Theology*.[5] The theological redemption of his thought is essential if we are to appreciate the importance of his contribution for the purposes of understanding how and why faith reclaims the reason that makes faith human. In order to allow theology to leave its marginality behind, it is necessary for the performative and *imaginative* theology of the multi-inter-trans-disciplinarity of Rosmini's thought—also and specifically as a possible "handmaid" to all sciences (see Giuseppe Tanzella-Nitti's works on the topic) —to be welcomed, appreciated, and put to use on the new frontlines of science itself. The return from exile of both Rosmini and of theology, a return that creates a new dialogue with all, has provoked amazement and new wisdom: this is why *Pop-Theology* transfigures theology: because in being *popular* theology, it embodies the *kerygma* of the *justice of agape*, which always comes from the *missio* of the Word, which is his eternal intra-Trinitarian *generation* of his being a *subsisting relationship* that became flesh and *history*.

In the present historical period, in which we are seeing the travails of social, cultural, and spiritual metamorphism, Christian theology must also be *provided with an unprecedented criteriology* through which it can rethink and develop, facing with awareness and trust the looming future. From the *proemio* of the *Veritatis Gaudium* we draw some of the criteria capable of reconfiguring—in view of futurity—the epistemological profile of theology. In para. 3 of the *proemio*, Pope Francis points out to the theological academies the urgent need for "a radical change of paradigm" and for "a courageous cultural revolution." It seems to us that we can interpret this indication as an encouragement to organize theological research—and therefore theological knowledge—*not on the basis of a deductive method, but rather on the basis of an inductive method*. And this is a promising trait that could impress on Christian theology the features of its future face.

3. See Antonio Staglianò, *Fede cattolica e cultura, letteratura e scienza, in circolo solido*, Pop-Theology 9 (Rosolini, It.: Santocono, 2022), § 6, "'Senza confusione' e 'senza separazione.'"

4. See Antonio Staglianò, *Oikos. Per una ecologia umana e integrale verso un decalogo teologico* (Rosolini, It.: Santocono, 2017), 29.

5. See Staglianò, *Beato Antonio Rosmini*.

The *technological change* will have to involve first of all the "theological method" (see not only Rosmini but also Bernard Lonergan, whose respective methods can be usefully placed in dialogue with each other), emphasizing the utmost importance of the context. The contextualization of theology, moreover, is by no means equivalent to the extrinsic and artificial adaptation of its content to some new situation. Nor does it mean a linguistic transposition of typically Western concepts, or the mere translation of its classical language for a new audience in the rest of the world. *Instead, the contextualization of theology finds its archetype in the incarnation of the eternal Logos:* it is not to be reduced to a mere terminological adaptation, but consists of a profound inclusion and a serious search for the truth of God, revealed in Christ, in the horizon that safeguards the *culture of a people, their vision of the world, their religious tradition.*

In his speeches dedicated to the renewal of theology held here and there around the world (also here in Italy, at the Facoltà Teologica dell'Italia Meridionale (Theological Faculty of Southern Italy) in Naples in June 2019. Theology can then *stop being only a theoretical speculation and can finally allow itself to seriously question the substantiality of the reality*, to also become discerning of the "signs of the times" and to question the response that the Church is struggling to give—or cannot give—to their urgency and their more uncomfortable projections. In other words, in this change of era, theology awaits the decisive provocations in order to reorganize itself as *intellectus caritatis*. For centuries it has—rightly—thought and structured itself as *intellectus fidei,* from the fathers of the church to the *Fides et Ratio*, passing through the *Aeterni Patris* (which has marked the last hundred and fifty years, approximately). The time has come to express also the awareness of being called on to take form as a *theologia amoris*. Charity and love are no less constitutive of the theological knowledge than faith, both because it is necessary to consider the theological circularity between faith, hope, and charity, and because an echo typically theological of the evangelical announcement remains unescapable: "The one who does not love does not know God, because God is love" (1 John 4:8).[6]

The prophecy of Joachim da Fiore, but also the vision of Rosmini, materialized in the Vatican Council II, in the path of renewal that has begun: it is in fact well known that the *Cinque piaghe* was accepted by the *Sacrosantum concilium*. Therefore, Saint Paul VI could say, "This difficulty of having to love the Church in her human reality has diminished today. Today the Church presents a face more worthy of admiration than of reproach and

---

6. See Antonio Staglianò, *Il ritorno dall'esilio. La Theo-logia futura, umile Teo-sofia a servizio del Vangelo e di tutti i saperi*, Pop-Theology 11 (Rosolini, It.: Santocono, 2023), 29–34.

commiseration. Today throughout the Church there are magnificent efforts of authenticity, of renewal, of Christian vitality, of holiness; a less habitual and environmental holiness, if you like, than that of other times, but more personal and conscious, also more community oriented and more industrious. . . . *The Christian knows that the Church is not a purely historical institution entrusted to the care of man*, but is and always remains a mysterious reality supported and guided by the Spirit of God himself. Present evils, provided that it is done in the right way and only in the face of the "manifest Will of the Lord."[7]

Hence the urgency that Rosmini's theology be freed—through philosophical Rosminianism of Rosmini's *suspended middle*—from the philosophical prejudice that relegates it to the periphery of Rosmini's thought, "finally free to think freely," perhaps as an "intellectually equipped form of catechesis or Christian preaching" and not instead as "critical knowledge of the faith" and therefore "a believing episteme that encourages thinking and makes one think in freedom, even philosophically." From this angle—of a distinction without separation or of a unity without confusion between the theological and philosophical in Rosmini—the goal that a Pop-Theology society, an "Association of Friends of Pop-Theology" would like to propose, could be achieved: *intellectual charity at the service of the joy of the gospel.*[8] This publication stands rightly in this *"erigenda"* Association of Friends of Pop-Theology, and in its own right makes the already visible operativity tangible, assisting in its development.

In a hypothesis of scientific work, on the possibility that Rosmini was an *ante litteram* pop-theologian, it would not be enough, for this purpose, just to investigate his catechism (arranged "according to the order of ideas") or even to evaluate his ability-incapacity to be a pastor of souls in the year in which he was parish priest. It would not suffice for truly unprejudiced philosophical inquiry. In fact, we should go to the heart of the matter: and, therefore, ask ourselves why the Italian Kant (what a "frightening" banality!) decided to undertake the great project of the "refoundation of all philosophy," discovering his "system of truth," which already in the *Nuovo Saggio dell'origine delle idee* he presented as a grandiose "theory of

---

7. See Staglianò, *Beato Antonio Rosmini*, 110–11.

8. See Staglianò, *Dibattito pubblico*, 18–19. There are therefore two words in which the school of God, made teacher of men, is summed up: *truth* and *charity*; although these two words mean different things, but each of them includes the other: in each is the whole; but in truth there is charity, and in charity there is truth: if each one did not have the other with it, it would no longer exist. (See Antonio Staglianò, who quotes Rosmini, *Apologia dell'idea. Ritornare a pensare per ricominciare a credere e credere veramente per pensare nella verità* [Rosolini, It: Santocono, 2019], 52).

the gospel." *Serving the gospel, spreading the truth of Christ in the world*: it can also be done philosophically and it would be a "great service" to theology, which should certainly do it by "natural right" (a question that pertains to its very nature or definition). Is it, however, something that philosophy can do in prejudicial distance or separation from theology? Rosmini replies: *absolutely not*.[9]

A Pop-Theology association could then, by design, contribute—as this book, which could rightly be considered an expression of this Pop-Theology association, explains and exemplifies—to the dissemination of theology among the people, so that faith becomes lived "in an adult way." Several years ago, the Italian bishops wrote that the Catholic faith is adult also because it is "thought" and, therefore, not only because it is a theological faith, but also because it is theologizing. From this point of view, pastorally speaking, the always-inextricable and always-to-be-interpreted knot of the relationship between faith and culture, between reason and faith (see the project *Fides et Ratio* project of John Paul II, but also *Lumen Fidei* of Pope Francis). An Association of Friends of Pop-Theology could move, both theoretically and pastorally, in the vast semantic field opened up by the ten points established in the Pop-Theology Manifesto (see above).[10]

Catechetical discourse arises (by itself and in itself) in relation to the question and the educational challenge. Rosmini, in addition to being a theologian, is not only an all-round philosopher, but a political philosopher as well as a jurist and an educator (and pedagogue). *Pop-Theology*, therefore, also and in particular in the light of the *multi-trans-disciplinarity of Rosmini's thought and work*, effectively places itself specifically between spiritual theology and pedagogy, intercepting the theological needs and proposals available both in the crucial questions of the current educational emergency (including that of digitization, which, just as it can be a great resource, can also suffocate the human in a shattering multiplicity of forms of alienation and technical reduction of the quality of the spiritual to pure dehumanization) both in the resources and in the new possibilities that, also in terms of globalization, are offered to us today by the possible rereading and reunderstanding of the Christological *kerygma* propitiated by the context in which we find ourselves.[11]

In order to better understand all this, years ago people began to reflect on theology and philosophy, on the "Trinitarian ontology," or on the "metaphysics of charity," or on the "metaphysics of agape," or on the "affective

---

9. See Staglianò, *Dibattito pubblico*, 19–20.
10. See Staglianò, *Dibattito pubblico*, 23–24.
11. See Staglianò, *Beato Antonio Rosmini*, 38.

turn of metaphysics." The truth of the Christian faith—God-Trinitarian-agape—establishes the possibility of thinking of being not only in a "triadic" sense, but even in a Trinitarian sense, placing—as Rosmini did in his *Teosofia*—the mystery of the Trinity as the "foundation of metaphysics." In fact, Rosmini was the first to think of the three constitutive forms of being (real, ideal, moral), interpreting their relationship in a Trinitarian way, with a philosophical reasoning that objectively advances (thanks to and) within the epistemic horizon of faith. Thus, he even hints at a rational demonstration of the Trinity, not because he claims to "demonstrate" the Trinitarian mystery of God starting from the three forms of being. The triune God cannot be deduced from any human experience and from any conceptual reflection. However, the Rosminian proof is called "deontological," because it refers "to how God must be" if the Christian revelation, applied as light, vision, intelligence, and as an episteme, helps to definitively resolve the problems of being, the fundamental theosophical ones that concern the unity and multiplicity of entities.[12] The "deontology of the foundation" (see Pierangelo Sequeri) is, therefore, one of the main points of reference—also in an inter-multi-trans-disciplinary key—of the pop-theo-ontological and triadic-Trinitarian and christological dimensions—pneumatologic of the "affective turn of metaphysics," "agapic metaphysics," "metaphysics of charity," "Trinitarian ontology."

The Holy Spirit is really present, through baptism, in man's life as his "objective form," that is, immanent and transcendent at the same time, not confused or even "limited" by man's finite creaturehood. Since his creation, man has been unnecessarily available to be, by grace, Christiform, spiritiform, deiform: that is, implemented by the form of God, of Christ, of the Spirit. Obviously, there is nothing magical and anything can happen in the grammar of human freedom, in which the grace of God, if freely accepted, liberates freedom, manifesting it "in fullness and in truth," in the actions of those who newly live "according to the Spirit," "according to the Spirit of Christ," that is, live in the regenerating truth of the Risen One.[13]

I am very pleased to introduce the English translation of the proceedings of the 2021 international conference, in which I was pleased to participate as a speaker, twenty years after the doctrinal *Note* on Rosmini's thought, since the qualified work of organization and curatorship by Fernando Bellelli allows us to arrive at a significant internationalization of Rosmini's thought and work, which—as already underlined above—is

---

12. See Staglianò, *Fede cattolica e cultura*, point 8, §2, "Fede cattolica e cultura dell'umano in circolo solido."

13. See Antonio Staglianò, *Sarx. Credere nell'umanità di Gesù per accogliere la novità radicale dell'incarnazione* (Rosolini, It.: Santocono, 2016), 65.

greatly needed in order to bring both Rosmini and theology out of the exile in which they found themselves until recently. Rosmini is to all intents and purposes the one who, adequately understood, was able to elaborate a complete synthesis between modernity and Christianity, precisely at the moment in which he indicated the way by which Christianity can (and must) overcome modernity. The coordinates can be found in the five parts into which this volume is divided, with its contributions (which at the same time propitiate, in addition to innovative and correct understanding and valorization of the Catholic orthodoxy of Rosmini's thought, also its participation in the current ecumenical and interreligious debate, from a multidisciplinary perspective): (1) Rosmini's purification of the Scotist aporias of phenomenology (between analogy and paradox) and the division of being: metaphysics and ontology; (2) Rosmini's Trinitarian ontology and his suspended middle: the primality of the moral form of being in synthesism with the real and ideal forms; (3) the pedagogical implications of Rosmini's suspended middle in the "synthesism within the synthesism" of affection, intellection, volition, cognition, and reflection; (4) the political implications of Rosmini's suspended middle in his theory—also and specifically theological—of fulfillment; (5) the juridical implications of Rosmini's suspended middle in terms of the developments under development and to be developed both of his "integrated theory of human dignity" and of his "legal pedagogy."

The appreciation, the auspice, and the recommendation, with regard to this achievement, are that this work is recognized and employed as it deserves, as an important, authoritative, and innovative reference and tool for the journey in and with it already profitably undertaken, also in the context of the Rosminian mission of intellectual charity of the Pop-Theology society—the Association of Friends of Pop-Theology in particular.

BISHOP ANTONIO STAGLIANÒ
Dean of the Pontificia Accademia di Teologia (PATh)

Introduction

FERNANDO BELLELLI

THIS VOLUME CONTAINS THE English translation of the proceedings of the conference, which were published in Italian in two separate volumes: in the journal *Divus Thomas* 1 (2023)[1] and in the editorial section of pedagogical Rosminianism.[2]

---

1. See Bellelli, "Rosmini filosofo." Rosmini was a theologian and philosopher *with* Thomas Aquinas by virtue of the respective original (and compatible) way in which both combine *ab origine* (and develop) in unity *science* and *holiness*. The word *with* is to be understood in a twofold sense: *first of all*, Thomas was, as such, correctly and globally Rosmini's reference author in the configuration of his philosophy and theology (and of the other knowledge he dealt with); *second*, for Rosmini (and for Rosminianism), Thomas (and Thomism) was the main reference for a direct, articulated and fruitful confrontation also and in particular in the *original* elaboration of his thought, which makes him *ante litteram* an *orthodox creative Thomist sui generis*. This curatorship explores the reference and comparison between (and on) Rosmini and (on) Thomas, focusing not only on the historical-cultural and epistemological aspects of the mutual *inseparable* interaction of their philosophy and their theology, but also analyzing and developing the Rosminian pedagogical-spiritual and juridical-cultural foundations (and some of their implications). What emerges from the contributions offered in the three sections of this volume is, at the same time, the *fidelity* and *genius* with which Rosmini assimilated and made his own the thought of the *Doctor Communis, Angelicus et Humanitatis*, starting from the reference to which Rosmini, through the synthesism of the three forms of being, impressed on his speculation and theoresis such an originality that the indelible Thomasian imprint and inspiration allowed him to effectively explore his *own* organic and paradigmatic proposal for overcoming modernity, providing (also) to the theology and philosophy he produced and practiced—and with him producible and practicable—the epistemological references necessary both to *synthesistic* recomposition in ecological-integral unity of the (new) knowledge and (new) sciences, both to them possible and desirable organic open and *humanistic* reconfiguration, and all this especially in relation to *scientia Dei et beatorum*.

2. See Bellelli, *Metodica di Rosmini*. The necessity, not only methodological but also epistemological, of the contemporary affective turn of the humanities, in the

INTRODUCTION

In setting out the aspects of the problem of translating into English the fundamental concepts of Rosmini's thought and Rosminianism, we worked with a professional translator, a decision made following my consultations of English translations of Rosmini's works, which I have read over the years, having also explored the history of translations of his works, carried out during his lifetime and more recently. On the question of the translation into English of Rosmini's works, I do not intend to say the last word regarding the criteria and the choices to be made, but I intend to present the problem with scientific rigor and to suggest the feasibility of standards for translation that are particularly valuable and effective, also through the fruitful dialogue between the translator, myself, and the authors of the essays in this volume.[3] The translations into English of Rosmini's works (and the ones of the other authors' works) in this book are ours.

---

multiplicity of their approaches, can find some of its most significant coordinates in the (re)discovery and *performative* resumption of at least two central aspects of Rosminianism, intrinsically related to each other: the political-moral theoresis of logic—natural and supernatural—of *fulfillment*, and the philosophical-theological theoresis—mainly pedagogical-juridical—based on the orders of *affection* of *cognition* (and, consequently, of *reflection*), proper to the "synthesism within synthesism" of affections (real being), intellections (ideal being) and volitions (moral being).

3. Rosmini's vast production has not yet been translated into English with a global and comprehensive program, complete with a critical edition. Such a project should definitely be promoted and this publication is intended to be a contribution in this sense, a synchronic and diachronic study to organize a wide-ranging translation project, in particular into the English language—with both scientific and popular editions—of Rosmini's works, dealing through shared synergy with both the theoretical questions and linguistic ones. The first translations of his works appeared in the nineteenth century, when the Istituto della Carità was established also in Great Britain; they were above all of a spiritual and catechetic nature and it was only in 1882 that the first English translation of a work of a philosophical nature was published, edited by Thomas Davidson. Tadini has carried out research into the translations of Rosmini's works into English under the title "Il Rosminianesimo in Gran Bretagna nel XIX secolo" but, as the title suggests, it is limited to the nineteenth century and to Great Britain. For the twentieth and twenty-first centuries, this writer has carried out a review of the translations, including the various editions in English through the volume *Bibliografia rosminiana degli scritti editi di Antonio Rosmini Serbati* by Cirillo Bergamaschi, which ends with the year 2010 and is available from the major research centers and libraries, and on the website http://rosminipublications.com/, which shows also the more recent translations. This task was not easy, given the fragmented nature of these sources, even in terms of presentation. From this review, which deserves to be presented in detail in an ad hoc study that we decided not to carry out here, postponing it to further researches, it is evident that in addition to new translations of *Costituzioni* and of *Massime di perfezione Cristiana*, and translations of some excerpts from *Manuale dell'esercitatore*, entitled *Meditations* are available. *Nuovo Saggio sull'origine delle idee* has been published in two volumes under the titles *The Origin of Thought* and *Certainty* and subsequently in three volumes entitled *A New Essay Concerning the Origin of Ideas*. Another translation of *Nuovo Saggio* appears in translation in excerpts entitled *Fundamentals of Rosmini Epistemology*. We have also noted the translation of *Principi*

INTRODUCTION

The Three Forms of Being and Their Synthesism: Anagogical Thomism (Ideal Being), Absolute Realism (Real Being), and the Ethics (Also Juridical) of the Foundation (Moral Being).

The purpose of this work is to illustrate, as a criterion for reading the essays of this curatorship, in its theoretical structure, the epistemological device underlying Rosmini's thought. Since it is a multidisciplinary device,[4] it is necessary to emphasize the connection between the logic, the method, and the methodology of its speculation. The heart of all this is Rosmini's theoresis, within synthesism, on the act.

One of the most effective and complete passages in which Rosmini describes the synthesism of the three forms of being, in the perspective of unity, is the following:

> Therein lies the *scientific synthesism* (Psicol. 34–44, 1337–1339); to which the need for *ontological synthesism* must respond. Since, if we accept the principle of cognition, which is the most

---

della scienza morale with the title *Principle of Ethics*; *Delle cinque piaghe della Santa Chiesa*, entitled *The Five Wounds of the Church*; *Filosofia della politica*, in two volumes entitled *The Summary Cause for the Stability or Downfall of Human Societies* and *Society and Its Purpose*; *Antropologia in servizio della scienza morale* with the title *Anthropology as an Aid to Moral Science*; *Trattato della coscienza morale* entitled *Conscience*; *Filosofia del diritto* in six volumes with the title *Philosophy of Right*; part of *Introduzione alla filosofia*, specifically *Degli studi dell'Autore*, with the title *Introduction to Philosophy—About the Author's Studies*; *Linguaggio teologico* with the title *Theological Language*; a selection from *Epistolario ascetico* with the title *A Selection from Ascetical Letters*; *Psicologia*, entitled *Psychology*, in four volumes; *Dell'educazione Cristiana*, with the title *On Christian Education*, part of *Teosofia*, entitled *Theosophy*; *Teodicea*, with the title *Theodicy*, a publication of the first part of *Antropologia sopranaturale* with the title, *Supernatural Anthropology*; *Introduzione al Vangelo secondo Giovanni Commentata*, entitled *A Commentary to the Introduction of the Gospel According to John*. We also call attention to the translation of Rosmini's mathematical thought, entitled *Edited Translation of Rosmini's Mathematics*. We found American translations of three of Rosmini's works. The first is *Del principio supremo della Metodica*, under the title *The Ruling Principle of Method Applied to Education*, editions from 1887–1893–1895 and 1905. The second includes part of *Doveri ecclesiastici* and is entitled *Talks to the Priest*; the third, published recently, *La Costituzione secondo la giustizia sociale*, appeared in English with the title *The Constitution under Social Justice*. The bibliographical details of the translations briefly listed here are to be found in the bibliography at the end of this volume. With regard to the "Rosminian bibliography" of studies on Rosmini, another monumental work by Cirillo Bergamaschi in addition to *Bibliografia degli scritti di Antonio Rosmini* and *Grande dizionario antologico del pensiero di Antonio Rosmini*, see also the English translation from 1907 of *Vita di Antonio Rosmini Serbati*, by Giambattista Pagani.

4. For the chrono-theoretical reconstruction of its composition both—diachronically—in Rosmini's thought and in the history of the Rosminian question, reference is made to what is progressively offered by the journal *The Rosmini Society*.

evident (*Ideol.* 559–574; *Psychol.* 1294–1302) that is, if we accept that being is the object of thought, how and why does the mind not settle down in the one? How and why does the mind not settle in many? Every power, when it is fully united with its object finds quiet and full satisfaction, there being no other activity left to explain (*Ideol.* 515). If therefore the mind which has being as its object does not settle down in the one, it must be said that being as one is not fully being. And if it is not quiet in the many, without unity, it is appropriate to say that the many without unity are not fully being. But if it is quiet in the one-many, so that it knows that in this antinomy there is no contradiction, it is better to conclude that being is one-many; that is that both unity and multiplicity coexisting in it without discord and is essential to being. Therefore, the one and the many form an ontological synthesism in being. They are both necessary conditions for being, the object of all intelligence. And this receives an irrefutable confirmation from the previous book, in which we searched for the categories, for by moving us from a multitude of entities that, like a nebula, appears at first glance to the speculator, and laboring to reduce them to the smallest possible number, we have finally come to know that they cannot be gathered in a number of classes smaller than three, having as their foundation the three concepts of objectivity, of subjectivity and of holiness. But then, examining the content of these three concepts, we have understood that they constitute three primitive forms of being and not three parts of being. For each of them, the whole being can be contained, but in such a way that the being cannot dwell whole in one of those forms without thought being obliged to believe that it also dwells whole in the other two. Thus, we found the first and essential synthesism of being.[5]

---

5. Rosmini, *T*, para. 199. To put this definition in context, it may also be useful to read the previous issues which, for the sake of brevity, I put here in a footnote: "197. *Being*, conceived as the act of existence, is simple and one. Wherefore, if the speculator stopped at this concept, he could not give movement to his thought, and all science would end in one word, in the word *being*. The movement of thought, therefore, and the form of doctrine that derives from it, needs a multiplicity. And this is found in being, when it is not halted by our thoughts at the beginning of its activity, but it is allowed to reach the end. Being one, therefore, is not the object of a science, except when it is considered in relation to multiplicity. Ontology then cannot deal with being one except in this relation. 198. But how does he who approaches philosophizing find multiplicity? This is that which is given to him by the natural development of man, a jumble of varied feelings and concepts of which every adult man is provided and which are present from the first moment, about which he begins to speculate, and which oppresses and almost attacks him because of their multiplicity, or, to convey to use the much more sublime

INTRODUCTION

In the perspective of the synthesism of the three forms of being within the theoresis on the ideal form of being, *anagogical Thomism*[6] is placed, to all intents and purposes, as a speculative exploration of Aquinas's thought, compatible with the interpretation offered by Rosmini; in this sense this compatibility propitiates both the necessary and possible historical-cultural reconstruction and the analysis and rereading of the debate on Thomism present within the "Rosminian question," particularly and emblematically precisely in the journal *Divus Thomas*. Below is one of the fundamental passages in which Rosmini deals with anagogy, within his reflection on the ontological chain:

> Therefore, if we want to observe all the links in this chain of the etic actions, let us keep an eye on the twelve links of which it is composed and continues, which are: 1. Principle, 2. Word, 3. Holy Spirit 4. Final Cause, 5. Exemplary case, 6. Efficient cause, 7. Real finished, 8. Intelligible form, 9. Final appetite 10. Operation of the Holy Spirit by which he is incarnated 11. the revelatory Word, 12. the Father. We see here that the first three rings demonstrate the eternal constitution of the infinite Entity, the second three the eternal constitution of the Cause, the next three the constitution of the Caused, that is, of the finite entity,

---

words of Plato, makes him stupid, like those who are touched by a stingray. For the man who wants to understand speculatively and suddenly sees himself faced with so many different entities, no longer knows what to say, and is persuaded not to understand anything. The speculative mind believes that it does not understand, if it does not understand the *reason* of things, and of the multitude of individual things, from the start it does not see any reason: this then appears to be a mystery, dark chaos. When it recovers from its stupor and finds the strength to discover the reason that enlightens, what does it seek, what does it expect from this attempt? Nothing more than to arise from the multitude to the unity that it contains and that gives it order, proving it to be relevant to the nature of being, as was shown in the book on the problem of Ontology (c. I–III). Thus, the need and desire for science does not allow man to accept being one, but from this he is driven towards multiplicity: however, multiplicity rejects him from this need or desire and makes him go back to being one, in which he already sees that multiplicity contained. This shows that neither the one taken separately from the many, nor the many taken separately from the one are sufficient to satisfy that twofold need of the human mind, or to constitute some science. At the point where the speculative mind can descend from the one, without any leap, to the many, finding in the same one the reason and cause of this passage; and when it is likewise given to it to ascend from the many to the one, which contains them and explains them; then it calms down and is satisfied, and thinks it knows. In this twofold movement, therefore, or rather, in this twofold action of thought, which goes incessantly from many to one, and from one to many, without will, but for a continuous necessity of reason, consists the intellectual life of the speculator. Science then consists in seeing the many in the one, and the one in the many without contradiction, neither confusion nor destruction of the two terms."

6. See Barzaghi and Salvioli, *Che cosè la storia?*

and the last three the sublimation of the Caused or finite entity to the Infinite; that is, the supernatural order through which creation is accomplished according to the eternal preestablished design. We see again that each of these four triads successively holds an inverse order from that of the previous one. Thus, the second triad adheres with its first link, which is the final Cause, to the last of the previous triad, that is, to the Holy Spirit to whom the end is appropriated, and then comes the exemplary cause that appropriates the Word, then the efficient cause that appropriates the Father. The first link of the third triad that represents what is first conceived in the Caused or in the effect joins with the last link of the previous triad, that is, with the efficient cause corresponding to the Father, the second, the intelligible form is the realization of the model corresponding to the Word, the third and the final appetite is derived from the final cause corresponding to the Holy Spirit. And from this begins again the fourth triad, since the final appetite is sublimated by the Spirit to the supernatural order that gives the Word to the world, so that the world receives the revelation of the Father who, inasmuch as it is manifested to men, constitutes the *last link and the fulfillment of the constitution of the supernatural order in creation: which once constituted begins the blessed infinite anagogical circle, of which it is not for us to speak* [emphasis added]. In this quadruple triad, where the following series reverses the order of the previous one, only the middle term, never changes place; for the *Word*, the *Model*, the *Intelligible Form*, and the *Incarnate Word* are always found occupying the middle place of every triad, as an unchanging mediator. These twelve links therefore abide by and continue to each other and demonstrate a continuity of life and action in all being, in whatever way it may be, in the university of the whole.[7]

The blessed infinite anagogical circle that Rosmini speaks of is wholly compatible with the *anagogical Thomism* of Giuseppe Barzaghi,[8] the relevance of the comparison and development of which undoubtedly deserves to be carried out with in-depth ad hoc studies.

The key to understanding the articulation of both ontological and scientific synthesism is cognition and its beginning. For Rosmini, therefore, understanding what cognition is constituted the sine qua non for understanding his theory on the act, which, in gnoseological terms, is closely

---

7. Rosmini, *T*, para. 1403.

8. With regard to the *anagogical Thomism* of Father Giuseppe Barzaghi OP, see Barzaghi: *Anagogia*; *Sguardo di Dio* (both vols.); "Anagogia"; and "Mistica anagogica."

connected with the notion not only of essence but also of subjectum. The act as a fundamental metaphysical notion of the entire Rosminian theory is tackled, analyzed, and described by the Rosmini in a variety of ways, among which its relationship with the terms-concepts of subjectum is functional to the present study, due to their centrality for the epistemological-gnoseological-ontological device underlying his thought. In light of the perspective of synthesism, this is how Rosmini defines the act in a perspective of connection with his anthropological reflection:

> We see therefore how the human mind distinguishes between being the *subjectum*, the *act*, and the *essence*. The subjectum "is a primary act, which is considered independent, and on which other acts depend." The word *act* applies as much to the first and independent acts as to the subsequent and dependent ones, whence it is more universal than the word subjectum; on the contrary, it is so universal that it cannot be defined, and it must be placed among the things known *per se*, knowing itself immediately in being, which is absolutely the first act. But when it is opposed to subjectum, saying, for example, "the act of the subjectum," then it takes the form of a second act, and is a particular meaning of the word act. Hence, just as the subjectum indicates a first act which has a causal relationship with a second act, so an act does not involve any similar relationship in its concept. Essence then indicates everything for which a given subjectum is what it is, an abstraction made by the subjectum itself which remains understood as an implicit condition. Therefore, the essence of a given thing always determines the subjectum to be that thing; but this determination can be conceived by the mind either prior to the actual determination, as an essence capable of determining and not yet determining, or in the act itself which determines the subjectum. Thus, in the expression, "human being," being takes the place of subjectum, and human that of act, and here the essence, that is, humanity, belongs to the act, because it is an act which determines the being: in the expression then, "the man is," man is the subjectum to which humanity belongs, where 'is' is the act of the subjectum, but not the act that determines it. When, therefore, the essence is considered as the quiddity of the subjectum, the subjectum remains immersed in the essence, which is only relative to the mind, which does not consider it, but implicitly thinks it in the object. When then the essence is considered as the quiddity of the act which determines the subjectum, then the act is disregarded in this sense, it remains immersed in the essence, that is, the mind

thinks it as potential in the essence itself; since essence, for example humanity, is understood as that which can receive the act with which it changes itself into man.⁹

The semantization conferred by Rosmini to the subject and the subjectum is one of the most characteristic traits through which he, on the one hand, measures himself against the anthropological shift of the subject brought about by modernity and assimilates all the theoretical traits that appear to him to be an essential theoretical escalation to be acquired for the development of thought; on the other hand he introduces conceptual-terminological distinctions such as the following to offer his hermeneutics of modernity, lately emerging as its fulfillment and overcoming, here particularly exemplified in the distinction between subject and subjectum:

> *Observation II.* The principle of feeling is also called subject or subjectum (12). (12) It would be desirable to always observe the distinction that I make in some places in the use of these two words, prevailing with the first to indicate that principle of feeling or acting which is substance;¹⁰ and of the second to indicate that special principle of feeling or acting which is a simple faculty.¹¹ Having two words at hand, which distinguish these

---

9. Rosmini, *T*, para. 770.

10. See Rosmini, *PY* 1, para. 56: "*Nature* is all that constitutes and implements an entity. Corollary—Hence the difference between *substance, nature* and *subject*. Substance is the first act by which an essence subsists [para. 52]. But nature embraces all that is necessary for the subject to subsist, and therefore also embraces the necessary term of the act whence he subsists. For example, the act where a brute body subsists is the force, and in this lies the *substance* of it. But the *nature* of the body also embraces the extent to which that act called force can spread. Nature embraces accidents not taken individually, which can be missing, but taken as a whole when they are necessary. For example, a body can exist without it having a round shape, but this single accident does not constitute [p. 58] its nature. But the same body cannot exist without some form, and so form in general enters the *nature* of the body although it does not belong to its substance. The *subject* is the commencement of sentient substance. It is therefore necessary, for a substance to be called a subject, 1st that it be a feeling; 2nd that it considers itself a commencement. And this second characteristic distinguishes the *subject* from the *sensory nature*; because the sensory nature also embraces what is *felt*, necessary for there to be a substantial feeling; but the *subject* is no more than the *sentient*; because the sentient alone has the right to commence."

11. See Rosmini, *Logica* (Logic), 132: "We use the word faculty in a broader sense than the word power. Every power is a faculty, and not vice versa. Power is a special force or virtue of the subject. But the subject himself can move all of himself and not his special virtue: this is called by us the faculty of the subject, not power. Therefore, there is the faculty of assent, that is, the subject has the faculty to give it, but does not give it by means of a special power, or virtue, but by moving everything himself."

two operating principles, would often reduce philosophical reasoning to a shorter and clearer state.[12]

Introducing the distinction between *subject* and *subjectum*, respectively as the principle of feeling or acting and as the principle of *special* feeling or acting, Rosmini assimilates, criticizes, and re-elaborates the theoretical-speculative approach of the thinking of idealism and modernity. This aspect of Rosmini's speculation fits within his open system of truth, in which the central notion is that of *order*. The entire Rosminian theoresis and thought, in fact, has the notion of *order* as its hub and interpretive key, markedly, in the specific case, in relation to the connection between theological-Trinitarian synthesism and anthropological-triadic synthesism. The theoretical device that acts as a link between these two concepts, is precisely the general definition of *order* given by Rosmini: "Two entities that have a relationship already form an order."[13]

The act of the relation of the (natural and supernatural) orders of being and knowing, an act of the unity and multiplicity of the three forms of being, is therefore de-composable and re-composable in the "synthesism within the synthesism of affection, intellection, volition, cognition and reflection-judgment." Order, therefore, is applicable to all these concepts and realities, since the entities that have a relationship between them are, from time to time, starting from the real being, affection and intellection, intellection and volition, volition and cognition, cognition and reflection-judgment.[14]

As can be seen from Rosmini's reflection on "synthesism within synthesism,"[15] volition and its orders are acted by reflection and its orders. Reflection, in turn, is closely linked to the act of judgment, which cannot occur without the relationship between volition and reflection being mediated by cognition. Here is how Rosmini defines cognition and its commencement: "The commencement of cognition means that intelligence does not conceive in any entity other than being, or an act of being, and therefore a thing can only be thought of if it has being";[16] and again: "an antecedent commencement, which I call the *commencement of cognition*, and that I express in this proposition: 'The object of thought is being or the entity.'"[17] The importance of the commencement of cognition is not only

---

12. Rosmini, *PY* 1, para. 154 and note.
13. Rosmini, *T*, para. 970.
14. See Bellelli: "Genesi e ricezione"; "Importanza"; "*Affezione* della *cognizione.*"
15. See Bellelli, *Etica originaria* monograph, in which I introduce for the first time this syntagma, 113–31.
16. Rosmini, *Logica*, para. 340.
17. Rosmini, *NE* 2, para. 466.

such for theoresis and ontological-metaphysical-gnoseological speculation, but it is also such for the pedagogical, juridical and political sciences. In this sense, the logic, method, and methodology of Rosmini are intrinsically connected; with regard to the philosophical method, he expresses himself on the commencement of cognition, determining its importance as the first of the beginnings of reasoning: "What gives intuition are the commencements of reasoning, and mainly cognition, contradiction, substance and cause."[18] In next paragraphs of this introduction I will present in a concise and reasoned way the essays of the five parts of this book.

Rosmini's "Synthesism within Synthesism" (and the Order of Being): His Suspended Middle[19]

On cognition and its orders Rosmini bases not only his theoresis, his anthropology and his moral philosophy, but also his theology, both natural and revealed-supernatural. As S. F. Tadini has exhaustively and brilliantly said, it is precisely on the basis of cognition and its theoretical-metaphysical principle that Rosmini illustrates the rational demonstrability of the existence of God, who is knowable in his existence as *absolute cognition* (human intelligence being precluded from knowing in itself such *absolute cognition*).[20] "One can begin by distinguishing the introduction of philosophy from philosophy itself. That leads to ascertaining whether we have

---

18. Rosmini, "Del metodo filosofico," lesson 8.

19. The reference to one of the principal texts of radical orthodoxy is deliberate, it is intended to refer to the overall thinking and to the founder of this school of thought: Milbank, *Suspended Middle*. The access point for the comparison of Rosmini's *Suspended Middle* and that of Milbank is constituted by M. Salvioli, "Beyond 'Philosophy' and 'Theology'": "Starting from the recovery of Blessed Antonio Rosmini's thinking, implemented by Roman Magisterium, and inspired by the main assumptions of the Radical Orthodoxy, the paper aims to describe the proposal of this Italian thinker as a very fruitful example, of how to renew the way in which we understand the relationship between Philosophy and Theology. In particular, the paper examines the relationship between nature and grace to show the real basis for comprehending the more studied relationships between Philosophy and Theology *and* Reason and Faith. The phenomenological-metaphysical sensibility of Rosmini's argumentation, the fidelity to the Augustinian and Thomistic tradition and the dialogue with modern philosophers—in the perspective to overcome their conclusions—are the main characteristics of this important witness of the Christian thinking for postmodern and, possibly, post-secular age. Because of this potentiality, the paper finally stresses that it can be challenging to read the works of the Blessed Rosmini through the lenses of Radical Orthodoxy's hermeneutics, which aims to deconstruct the modern literary genres, called 'Philosophy' and 'Theology'" (376–77).

20. See Tadini, *Problema di Dio*.

absolute cognition; this speaks of this *absolute cognition*; or rather this is *absolute cognition*. Absolute cognition shows that all things are knowable in an absolute way considered as entities: now insofar as they are knowable, they are called *ideal entities*."[21] When we want to grasp the development of the order of cognitions in relation to the orders of the reals, the importance of which is covered because of the passage between cognitions and reflections, the following words of Rosmini are exemplary:

> A distinction should therefore be made between the *order of knowledges* and the *order of the realities*. In our mind, real objects are nothing other than their cognition. The order, therefore, of the cognitions and of the ideas precedes the *order of the real objects*. It is therefore advisable to move from the problem of the validity of cognitions, before reasoning on any real object, even if it is the same absolute.[22]

The next step involved in the Rosminian epistemological device that is reconstructed and composed here is that inherent in reflection and its orders: reflection is "the faculty of applying the idea of being to our cognitions and their objects."[23]

Specifying in detail the reflections that underlie the determination of the judgment, which is the final and contextual step, we read:

> Therefore we have three kinds of acts of reflection: namely, there is a kind of reflection that is nothing but an immobile contemplation of things already known; this neither produces new cognition, nor is it directed towards volition: there is a kind of reflection that analyzes, unites, and integrates the things cognited; this produces new cognition, but it is not a volition: finally, there is a kind of reflection, which in the time that looks at a cognitive object, willingly draws pleasure from it, enjoys it, enjoys the delight that abounds in the intelligent being, when it fully recognizes the good of cognitive things, not setting up obstacles, indeed promoting in itself this delight, and abandoning itself to it, or lending itself to that pleasant action, which everything well-liked causes in the mind; and this is a volition.[24]

Reflection, therefore, in its third form, applying the idea of being to elaborated cognitions and their objects, makes "synthesism within

---

21. Rosmini, "Frammenti," 495.
22. Rosmini, *NE* 3, para. 1408.
23. Rosmini, *PY* 2, para. 1182.
24. Rosmini, *PMS*, para. 121.

synthesism" pass from one order of reflection to another, specifically because a volition is determined which, by virtue of the interaction between the moral form and the real form of being, makes the *affection* of *volition* interact with the *affection* of the *fundamental bodily feeling*, which, in turn, can be both *intra-corporeal* and *extra-corporeal*. The real form of being—or real being—is such that the supernatural grace of christological-Trinitarian revelation is communicated to the human person through the *supernatural fundamental sentiment*, which, in the "synthesism within synthesism" in the supernatural order, determines corresponding supernatural *affections, intellections, volitions, cognitions, reflections,* and *judgments*.

After defining reflection as that particular human act through which we arrive at the application of the idea of being to the objects of cognitions and to the cognitions themselves—since cognitions are the result of the gnoseological-ontological process derived from affection (understood as the action of the extra-corporeal being on the fundamental bodily feeling) up to volition—with regard to the orders of reflection, the following definitions given by Rosmini are useful:

> 163. That if we want to see the relationship that these formulas [Editor's note: formulas concerning entities in relation to each other] have with the faculty to reflect, so as to distribute them according to the *orders of reflection*, it is necessary that we simplify all this doctrine by seeking a principle that directs us in classifying these duties according to the orders of reflections: and the principle will be as follows: "the relations of the entities, which are the basis of moral obligations, all refer to two concepts, to *being* and *doing* things." 164. So the moral formulas that originate from those relationships 1st. either look at their respective cost, 2°. or their immediate or mediated actions, good or bad in their effects.[25]

Judgment is that particular form of reflection through which moral obligations become human actions, which, intrinsically, in turn, produce good or bad effects, based on the correct (or incorrect) application of the evaluation of the moral value of relations between entities, which, in doing and being, found moral obligations.

> It would be long to prove this by deduction in all kinds of judgments, but it can always be done exactly; and consequently it is possible to show that a judgment is nothing other than the operation by which we unite a given predicate to a given

---

25. Rosmini, *Trattato della coscienza morale* (Treatise on moral conscience), paras. 163–64.

subjectum; and therefore that in this operation of our mind 1st we take the subjectum and the predicate separately as two mentally distinct things, that is, such things on which we can fix our attention exclusively, and thus distinguish one from the other; 2nd we recognize that these two entities are united in nature, that is, we fix our attention not on each of the two terms separately, but on their relationship of union in the subjectum.[26]

What the judgment does most is to fix the attention on the relationship of union in the subjectum—even in nature—between the subjectum itself and the predicate. Now, for Rosmini, the judgment can be of different types, possible according to certain characteristics: practical judgment, speculative judgment, practical judgment of a practical judgment, speculative judgment of a speculative judgment, speculative judgment of a practical judgment, or practical judgment of a speculative judgment. For Rosmini, reflected consciousness arises in the act of speculative judgment of a practical judgment, at least of the second order of reflection. This means that judgments are made within the orders of reflection, and that, for each order of reflection, there are capabilities and possibilities to formulate, express and determine specific and personal judgments, through which the capacities of feeling, intellect, and human will are formed. The formation of consciousness and the formation of conscience are, therefore, distinct but interrelated processes and dynamics, both as regards conscience as a moral act,[27] and as regards the progressive constitution of orders of reflection innate in the formation of law as such, of natural law and human rights.[28] The human person, in this sense, appears in Rosmini as a new humanism that springs from the fulfillment of the project of Renaissance humanism through the overcoming of Enlightenment modernity.

26. Rosmini, *NE* 1, para. 42. See also: "Therefore, the affirmation of a real entity deserves the appellation of judgment when it is formed and not before. Now reflection *distinguishes the predicate* and the *subject* in any judgment, analyzing the judgment already formed, because if it were not formed, it could not be analyzed and broken down. By means of this analysis or de-composition, by which the predicate is distinguished from the subject, one also comes to form the definition of judgment, saying that *judgment is the logical union of a predicate with a subject*. Now this definition is analytical, it is the work of reflection on the statement. Therefore the qualification of judgment that is given to any affirmation, is a qualification subsequent to it, it does not express its primitive origin, but expresses its nature as it appears to analysis and reflection: these conceive the affirmation in their own way, with certain modification that comes from the laws of their work; and this modification is what makes the affirmation acquire the appellation of judgment" (Rosmini, "Sistema filosofico" (Philosophical system), para. 46).

27. See Staglianò, *Ecce homo*.

28. See Bellelli, *Percorsi storici*, 252–65.

INTRODUCTION

The essays contained in this volume have in this introduction and in the conclusion a real chiasmus: the three sections, philosophical, theological, and spiritual, investigate and analyze Rosmini's thought having as their *focus* the human person and the Persons of the Trinity, consequently having among the main criteria of inspection the *esse ut actus* and the P/persona as intersubjective *relatio-ius subsistens*. They must be read within the reference coordinates of the synthesism of the three forms of being, as has been briefly explained in this introduction. As a result, the reader who has the benevolence to read the entire volume in the light of the perspectives of investigation that I have indicated will be able to find the relevance of the theoretical-speculative hypothesis that arises from it, which I anticipate here and which I present in more detail in the conclusion. The path of *anagogical Thomism* constitutes a theoretical-speculative increase of the philosophical-theological dimension of the ideal form of the synthesism of being; *absolute realism*[29] (and ontoprismaticism) constitutes a theoretical-speculative increase of the philosophical-theological dimension of the real form of the synthesism of being; the *deontology of the foundation* in *Trinitarian* ontology constitutes a theoretical-speculative increase of the philosophical-theological dimension of the moral form of the synthesism of being. It is worth reading the entire volume because, since the T/truth is symphonic, it is in the synthesistic resonance of the three forms of being that all the ontoprismatic implications of the *unity* of *science* and *holiness* in and of Thomas Aquinas in Rosmini's work can be appreciated.

Part 1: Rosmini's Purification of the Scotist Aporias of Phenomenology (between Analogy and Paradox) and the Division of Being: Metaphysics and Ontology

Rosmini's thought included the solution to the problem of how being, thought (not a genus) should be divided. Analogy and paradox are suitable criteria for properly understanding the Rosminian synthesism of three forms of being. This first part describes Rosminian ontology and metaphysics (also in this "Milbankian" point of view). This perspective includes not only an illustration of the compatibility of this line of research with that derived from the Rosminian studies of (and on) Vincenzo La Via, but also the possibility of comprehending the purification of Rosmini's thought—internal to it—from the reductionism implicit in the Scotus's solution, thus

---

29. See Brancaforte, *Portata metapolitica dell'assoluto realismo* and *Laicità dell'idea di Dio*. The journals that develop this perspective are *The Rosmini Society* and *Teoresi*; the first issue of a new series of *Teoresi* is forthcoming.

providing the hermeneutics of this purification as a Rosminian critical anticipator of the aporias of phenomenology.

Father Umberto Muratore, previously the director of the Centro Internazionale di Studi Rosminiani in Stresa, who died on December 28, 2022, is to be considered one of the utmost experts in Rosmini's thinking. In his contribution to this volume, he offered a summary of the fundamental points of Rosminian ontology, together with indications that, in his opinion, should be a fecund and important basis for future research into, and understanding of, Rosmini's thought. Among the topics he mentioned, the ontological chain is particularly significant: it was, in fact, Rosmini himself who indicated the relationship between *Theosophy (Teosofia)* and *anagogy*, precisely when he dealt with the *ontological chain*. Muratore, in agreement with other authors and above all with Sequeri, showed the agapeic dimension of Rosmini's triadic-Trinitarian ontology as an element of great importance to be considered in philosophical and theological research. The convergence between Muratore and Sequeri is an encouraging sign of a turning point in contemporary theological and metaphysical sciences in the emphasis on the plexus of agape justice.

Donà's contribution concentrates our attention on the central point where Rosmini inscribed perfect unity and relationship (multiplicity) in divine reality without denying either, and in his theory, he did not make unity multiple or transform the composite of multiplicity into simplicity. Indeed, he carried out this theoretical operation also by virtue of the distinction between the absolute and absoluteness, distinguishing what is absolute from the "absolute being," of what is precisely posited as absolute. The essay delves theoretically into the speculative reasons for Rosmini's ingenious solution (synthesism) to one of the thorny questions—that of the relationship between unity and multiplicity—to which his thought would constantly be subjected, and which only the Trinitarian dogma could transform into a surprising explanation of the ability of identity and difference to be "perfectly identical" precisely in constituting themselves as perfectly distinct, indeed, as absolutely opposite.

It is appropriate to underline the theoretical convergence between Rosmini's theory and Barzaghi's anagogical Thomism, which is certainly among the objectives of future Rosminian studies on the subject. The ascribability of anagogical Thomism to Rosmini's theological theory regarding the ideal form of being ensures (in the perspective of Rosminian synthesism of the three forms of being, the convertibility of anagogy, as far as the real form of being is concerned) that the ontoprism of S. F. Tadini's speculative research and absolute realism is one of the main research areas of the Rosmini Institute.

INTRODUCTION

Tadini's contribution delves into the logical-theoretical structure of ontoprism, which is expounded and studied in the light of a chrono-theoretical analysis of Rosmini's thought and focuses, in particular, on the identification of the *logic* elaborated by Rosmini and applied and used in all the sciences he dealt with. This interesting speculative itinerary briefly explores the real form of being in Rosmini's thought, bearing in mind that its elaboration is the great unfinished element of *Theosophy*, and, with significant results and in a wholly believable way, derives it from the argumentative development offered by the publication of texts starting from the concentration on Rosminian theoretical production on the ideal and moral form of being.[30] The theoretical production offered in this sense by Tadini and the research group orbiting around the Rosmini Institute, is already amply documented by the Rosminian resumption of the *absolute realism* of Vincenzo La Via, who identified this phrase in his studies on Rosmini.

A turning point—in the relationship between ancient-medieval philosophy and modern philosophy, within the studies on the thought of Thomas Aquinas, and within the studies on the thought of Rosmini—is the theoretical formulation of the relationship between phenomenology and metaphysics, based on the resolution of the speculative problems posed by the question inherent in the terms of the interaction between them.[31]

Peratoner's essay deals precisely with this turning point, providing a speculative framework justifiably illustrating the mutual non-exclusion of metaphysics and phenomenology. Peratoner indicates comparison between the thought of Rosmini and that of Edith Stein as the way to achieve significant results, in addition to the "reconciliation" between phenomenology and metaphysics, in order to find argumentative structures and ontological and theoretical convergences.[32] Indeed, both Rosmini and Stein found in Thomas Aquinas one of their main masters of reference. Another very stimulating research path is the comparison between Rosmini's Thomas and the Thomas of John Milbank's radical orthodoxy. Confronted with these two perspectives, Peratoner's essay highlights a characteristic of great importance for the proto-phenomenologist Rosmini: to all intents and purposes,

---

30. See La Via, *Coscienza e libertà* and La *Idealismo attuale di Giovanni Gentile*.

31. In the synthesistic perspective of the ideal form of being proper to *anagogic Thomism*, see Salvioli, "Misericordia invisibile del Padre."

32. See Galvani, *Sguardo sull'umano*. Galvani is a member of the Cenacolo Rosminiano Emiliano-Romagnolo, who, on Dec. 15, 2021, held a seminar at the Biblioteca dei Padri Cappuccini di Reggio Emilia, on his book (https://www.youtube.com/watch?v=_sBzYWWL2BU&t=109s). The journal *Divus Thomas* has often hosted articles on the comparison of the thought of Saint Thomas Aquinas and E. Stein; see, for example, Salvioli, "Struttura della persona."

INTRODUCTION

Rosmini's work contains the metaphysical and phenomenological criteria for the purification of phenomenology from those elements that make it incompatible with the affective turn of metaphysics that Rosmini himself propitiates and inaugurates. Starting from this last aspect, the compatibility between John Milbank's critique of the Scotist drift of a certain contemporary univocal phenomenology[33] and the perspective of the affective turn of metaphysics and the deontology of Rosmini's foundation is recognizable—and to be explored and developed—in keeping with the elaboration that P. Sequeri and P. Heritier offer on the same topic.

It appears to me that the present volume contributes to clarifying that the Scotist interpretation of Rosmini's thought not only does not correspond to his thinking, but also risks preventing an appreciation that in Rosmini's work there is a critical response to the degenerations of Scotism which came about before and after him (and which cannot be carried forward and developed in his name). In any case, it is true that there should be some currents of interpretation of Rosmini's thought (and of his delicate "question") that in my opinion are running the risk of mystifying the purification carried out by Rosminianism—and within it—concerning the degenerations of Scotism: above all I reiterate and emphasize that these degenerations are not *in* Rosmini's thought and that in turn I am far from wanting to create (an intent that in any case I would not be able to pursue) a Rosminian *scholasticism*. On this matter, in particular, careful analysis of the studies of Rosmini's thinking on the question is required, which the most recent criticism seems to have forgotten.[34]

33. See Milbank, "Trinitarian Ontology."

34. One example is the not-recent brief criticisms by Giulio Bonafede, certainly to be read and commented upon: Bonafede, *Rosmini e la scolastica*: "b) *Rosmini e Duns Scotus*. While Rosmini's *being* does not coincide with the *being* of Saint Bonaventura, it certainly does not seem that it can be identified with the *being* of which Duns Scotus speaks. . . . *L'essere univoco*—Rosmini does not renounce either the innatism of being, nor its divine nature, its function as a link between the finite and the infinite, that is *univocal* preaching. . . . The struggle between the Scotists and the Thomists, insists Rosmini, derives from the fact that two very different issues were confused, because it is one thing to ask a reality whether *it exists*, it another to ask *what it is*. . . . By clearly distinguishing between the two questions, it seems to Rosmini that it is possible to answer affirmatively the question of whether the ideal being preaches of God and creatures in a univocal way; and therefore, thinks that the Thomists and the Scotists can be easily reconciled. This is what he says in *Introduzione alla filosofia*. In *Teosofia* he says that denying this univocal preaching would make all theology impossible, because the doctrine of the analogy presupposes something common between God and the creature, and this common element is *being*. To Rosmini the question between Scotists and Thomists appears complicated also because, in his opinion, the two movements were headed by Aristotle, who reduced metaphysics to anguish, because he started from the consideration of the finite entity and did not know how to rise to the consideration of

INTRODUCTION

A turning point—both in the relationship between ancient-medieval philosophy and modern philosophy and within the studies on the thought of Thomas Aquinas, and of Rosmini—is the theoretical formulation of the relationship between phenomenology and metaphysics,[35] based on the resolution of the speculative problems posed by the question inherent in the terms of the interaction between them. Peratoner's essay deals precisely with this turning point, providing a speculative framework justifiably illustrating the mutual non-exclusion of metaphysics towards phenomenology and phenomenology towards metaphysics. Peratoner indicates in the comparison between the thought of Rosmini and that of Edith Stein the way to achieve significant results, in addition to the "reconciliation" between phenomenology and metaphysics, to find argumentative structures and ontological and theoretical convergences. Both Rosmini and Stein, in fact, saw in Thomas Aquinas one of their main teachers of reference. Another very stimulating research track is the comparison between Rosmini's Thomas and John Milbank's radical orthodoxy Thomas. Compared with these two perspectives, Peratoner's essay highlights a characteristic of great importance within the proto-phenomenologist Rosmini: Rosmini's work, to all intents and purposes, contains the metaphysical and phenomenological criteria of the purification of phenomenology from those elements that make it incompatible with the affective turn of metaphysics that Rosmini himself propitiates and inaugurates. Starting from this last aspect, the compatibility between John Milbank's critique of the Scotist drift of a certain contemporary[36] univocal phenomenology and the perspective of the affective turn

---

the entity as such. But the differences between Rosmini's solution and that of Duns Scotus are evident. Duns Scotus has no sympathy for the doctrine of enlightenment of Henry of Ghent or for that of Augustine, which he reduced to minimum terms; he does not accept innatist solutions to the problem of knowledge but fights the Thomist solution to the problem of the object of the intellect and gives his own, different, solution. . . . The differences between Rosmini and Duns Scotus are market, above all with regard to the gnoseological assumptions that the doctrine of being poses. They agree on the results, but the basis differs. We could also advance the hypothesis that the Rosminian solution is a useful and necessary integration of the Scotist position, since the possibility of Scotist metaphysical affirmations would be justified by the innatism of being, by the fact that being is an intelligible element, susceptible to being applied to the finite and the infinite because it is not coerced either to the sensitive, nor to the intelligible, because it is open, indifferently, to both the sensitive and the insensitive. However, this integration . . . does not justify the affirmation of the identity between the two, both because of the differing assumptions and because the common being—*ens in comuni*—could not have for Duns Scotus the divine character that Rosmini recognizes" (29–31).

35. In the synthetistic perspective of the ideal form of being proper to the *Anagogic Thomism*, see Salvioli, "Misericordia invisibile del Padre."
36. See Milbank, "Trinitarian Ontology."

of metaphysics and the deontology of Rosmini's foundation is recognizable—and to be explored and developed, in line with the elaboration that P. Sequeri and P. Heritier offer of the same.

Part 2: Rosmini's Trinitarian Ontology and his Suspended Middle: The Primality of the Moral Form of Being in Synthesism with the Real and Ideal Forms

Rosmini's Trinitarian ontology is valued at its best if the specific meaning of the moral form of being in relation to the other two, real and ideal, is comprehended as a primality (which is not primacy). In fact, the synthesism of the three forms of being effectively instructs not only a fundamental theology and/or a Trinitarian theology, but also a specifically Rosminian Christology and pneumatology. From these, the originality of Rosmini's *Suspended Middle*, the basis of his fundamental anthropology, can be properly understood and fully comprehended in its performativity through the device of synthesism within the synthesism of affection, intellection, volition, cognition, and reflection.

It is precisely with the ethics of the foundation of the *justice of agape* that the second section opens, dedicated to the theological implications of the thought elaborated by Rosmini with reference to Thomas Aquinas; Sequeri's contribution in this sense plays a leading role. Knowledge and the justice of *pro-affection* are among the main constitutive criteria of the ethics of the foundation. If we consider the philosophical need to reflect on the foundation of being and the theory of foundation, these words from Rosmini, referring to Thomas Aquinas, are a perceptive link between the theoretical foundation of the Thomist synthesis[37] and Rosmini's thought:

> When Saint Thomas spoke of the divine essence: *potest autem cognosci non solum secundum quod in se est sed etiam secundum quod est participabilis secundum aliquem modum similitudinis a creaturis* (S. I, XV, II) he too used it to explain the *possible*, that is the divine ideas, in relation to the *creatures*. In the logical order, therefore, these are supposed to be in some way preexisting, such as the foundation of the relationship with the divine essence, from which ideas are born, that is *plures rationes proprias plurium rerum*. Therefore, in order to conceive the specific ideas of worldly things in God, it is wise to suppose not that things exist in time, but that the creative act exists *ab aeterno*, the divine

---

37. See Barzaghi, *Fondamento teoretico*, and Barzaghi et al., *Ai confini della contraddizione*.

imagination of the real with which the real is created *ab aeterno* over time.[38]

In Rosmini's elaboration the *divine imagination* of the real, seen from a deontological standpoint, that is, of the moral form of being, leads to the description and definition of the deontological demonstration of the existence of God, philosophically applied triadically also to and in theology (fundamental and systematic, in particular, Trinitarian):

> Now the demonstration that we will give of the proposition that "God subsists in a Trinity of persons" will be this (and here we can only outline it): "If that trinity were denied, clearly absurd consequences would follow, and the doctrine of being would become ultimately become a chaotic mass of manifest contradictions." This proof will be gradually illuminated by the whole theory of being, which we will set out, and in theology it will receive its complete form. There we will have only to recapitulate what has already been said and show that there is no other option, either it is better to admit the divine triad, or to leave the theosophical doctrine of pure reason not only incomplete, but fighting against every part of itself, shredded and completely annulled by the inevitable absurdities. This is certainly an indirect proof, just as the proofs that mathematicians conduct from the absurd are indirect, and they are no less effective for this (*Logica* (526)): it is a deontological demonstration, because it shows not that the thing is so, but that it *must* be so, it cannot be anything other than so, and this way also, if it is in order, gives an irrefutable certainty.[39]

The intrinsic connection between the deontology of the foundation and the moral form of being, in the perspective of the affective turn of metaphysics, is further found in Rosmini in this emblematic and exemplary argumentative passage, which combines similarity and analogy with the argumentative form of "deontological apodictic reasoning" on which P. Sequeri[40] and P. Heritier base the developments of their own originality:

> *Morality* is also to be considered in the absolute being; and in the human entity, as we have done in the two preceding sections on the subjectum and the object; and it is to be seen how in both entities the three forms are found in the connected morality. But not having experience of the absolute Being it is better

---

38. Rosmini, *T*, para. 468n10.
39. Rosmini, *T*, para. 194.
40. See Sequeri, *Iscrizione e rivelazione*.

to argue about him from what we know from experience that comes about in man. And this we have done in previous discussions. Nor for this reason are the conclusions drawn from it less firm, because we do not already move from the human to the divine by simple similarity or analogy, but by a deontological apodictic reasoning that has this form: "This is what happens in the finite entity, therefore it must necessarily happen in the same way in the infinite entity." And the reason on which such a way of arguing is based can be formulated thus: "if this given conclusion were not true, the being would not be infinite, in contrast to the hypothesis of argumentation" and even more: "If this given conclusion were not true, being would not be being." Everything that does not admit this form, does not belong to science that we expound.[41]

In this argumentative context, the epistemological framework of the relationship between faith and reason that emerges in Rosmini's thought is explored with speculative rigor by Antonio Stagliano in his contribution. Dispelling any misunderstanding regarding the fact that Rosmini's philosophy is drawn from the viscera of Christianity and is therefore autonomous, in that it fully responds to the freedom of reason, still it can never be separated from his theology, since the speculation in the philosophical thought applied to the christological Trinitarian revelation[42] is not extrinsic to the revealed truth, just as the contribution of theology to philosophizing is not perceptible as an undue intrusion of a knowledge that violates the rights of reason, but rather as a knowledge having its own epistemological statute, which enriches reason and philosophy and provides them with useful and significant stimuli in their search for the only truth. Stagliano is an authoritative expert and scholar on Rosmini, in particular with regard to his relationship with philosophy, from which he also elaborated and is exploring pop theology (regarding which he invoked the intercession of Blessed Rosmini as its patron). This is a *science* constituting a *unicum* with *holiness* (among the authors who have very similar perspectives on this point, in addition to that of the absolute transcendence of love, one cannot fail to mention Hans Urs von Balthasar).

It is in the field of education that P. Coda's essay on the unity of knowledge and Trinitarian ontology engages the theme of unity of *science* and *holiness* in Rosmini. Coda masterfully explores and discusses the reference of the Apostolic Constitution of Pope Francis *Veritatis Gaudium* to Rosmini (specifically para. 4c) and to the pillars of education on which his thought

---

41. Rosmini, *T*, para. 866.
42. See Pagazzi, *Singolarità di Gesù*.

is based, set out in the work *Delle cinque piaghe della Santa Chiesa*: "the uniqueness of science, the communication of holiness, the habit of life, the exchangeability of love." The unity of the principle refers to knowledge, which is one with the practical form of ecclesial reform proposed, also in a political and juridical sense, by Rosmini. He fully showed the overall and integral goodness of this project of ecclesial reform precisely through his holiness: in fact, he was able to make his *spirituality* the principle and the organizational and expressive foundation—concisely and prospectively—of that unity of science and holiness, which, in addition to being brilliantly elaborated by him in theoretical and practical terms (think of the religious order he founded), was also heroically and admirably witnessed in the first person with the offering of his life's work. It will be necessary to carry out studies that explore these aspects of correlation between the deontology of Rosmini's beliefs and his idea of reform—also political and juridical—of the church and of the other two societies he dealt with (civil society and domestic-parental society) in the epistemological framework of the relationship between theology and philosophy in his writings, and, for example, in comparison with more than significant authors who dealt with these topics in the twentieth century, such as H. de Lubac, Y. Congar, and L. Milani.

Rosmini is also recognized as a philosopher and theologian who contributed and can increasingly continue to contribute to the delineation of a triadic-Trinitarian ontology (see Michele Federico Sciacca), dialogically related with the theses of Trinitarian ontology by Klaus Hemmerle: in the project *Dizionario dinamico di ontologia trinitaria*, a scientific enterprise that is seeing the light and taking its first steps under the guidance of Piero Coda.[43] In his essay, Emanuele Pili, a participant in this project, offers the criteria for a study, also from a juridical perspective, of intersubjectivity, anthropologically understandable and understood in terms of recognition. While, in fact, the synthesism of the three forms of being resolves in terms of Trinitarian ontology the *magna quaestio* of the relationship between the one and the many, it is true that it is necessary to concentrate not only on the *form* of each of the three forms of being, but also on the *dynamic principle* of their unity. The Trinitarian ontology of the *Dizionario dinamico di ontologia trinitaria* focuses precisely on the *dynamic principle (and its form) of the forms* of being. The relationship with the thought of Thomas Aquinas is of incisive importance also in this field, in particular in the configuration that has been offered by the dynamic realism of T. Demaria.[44] Among the questions dealt with in Pili's essay, and worthy of a resumption in the

---

43. See Donà et al., *Unità*.
44. On the ideas of Demaria, see Mantovani et al., *Oltre la crisi*.

analysis offered here, mention should be made of the genetic locus of the correlation between the purely moral dimension of relational experience and the establishment of its ontological-juridical status.

The contribution of G. Canu, with regard to the act of faith as a form of knowledge, focuses on this theological virtue and, pitting itself against the "provocations" of Peter Sloterdijk to the Christian West, dialogically assumed within the framework of Rosmini's theology, and identifies from this trial the following results, which also constitute a starting point for both research and practice: thinking of the interior dimension of the act of faith, thinking of the "sensible reality" of the act of faith, thinking of the "soteriological ministry of theology." Rosmini's thought, in all this, proves, also from this point of view, very stimulating and fruitful; moreover, the style and terms of philosophy and theology of the act of faith with which Canu carries out this theological-philosophical operation assume the traits of an emblematic modality to be applied other topics of Rosmini's thought and of the contemporary theological-pastoral debate, also in contiguity and continuity with the practical form of reform of the church of which, in particular with regard to intersubjectivity, they deal with Coda and Pili.

Part 3: Rosmini's Suspended Middle (and the Comparable Social Theory of Radical Orthodoxy's Suspended Middle): Possible Pedagogical Implications

Rosmini's *Suspended Middle* propitiates a real *social theory*, having implications also and especially in the fields of pedagogical science, political science, and legal science. In this third part of the volume, the implications in the field of pedagogical sciences are explored. The fruitful contribution of Rosmini's thought is highlighted, underlining the value of his method and his methodology, by comparing them with the main contemporary sociopsycho-pedagogical approaches (for example, the cognitive behavioral one of the analytic area) and with the thoughts on the subject of some very important authors of the Christian tradition, not only ancient (Augustine) but also modern (Stein), and other significant authors (Frankl).

In his contribution F. De Giorgi focuses on the three concise ideas of Rosminian pedagogy: the perspective of grading, the preventive dimension,[45] and the primary importance of language teaching. In particular, De Giorgi emphasizes Rosmini's attention to the following aspects: *purpose of education*, *means of education*, *methods*. Thanks to the resumption

---

45. See De Giorgi: *Educare Caino*; *Scuola italiana di spiritualità*; "Antonio Rosmini."

of this Rosminian subdivision it is clear that the pedagogical science in his considerations cannot be attributed only to philosophical science, but is also a science with its own epistemological status, in which, in addition to the theoretical component (philosophy of education), a practical-experimental component identified by Rosmini in what he calls the *art* of education can also be found. Finally, the development and application of Rosminian synthesism to the three forms of being that De Giorgi presents, in analogy with the synthesism within synthesism that I propose, is particularly interesting: the correspondence of the ideal being with the master, that of being real with the student, and that of moral being with the community. It would be particularly productive, from the point of view of juridical pedagogy, to make the anthropological synthesism of teacher-student-community interact not only with the synthesism of the three forms of charity (intellectual, temporal, spiritual morality) but also with the synthesism of the three societies, the domestic-parental, the civil, and the ecclesial. In particular, the morality of the community, in this sense, would be read not only in a perspective of philosophical anthropology but also of theological anthropology: the civil community does not exhaust the totality of morality, which is measured with the demand for transcendence and therefore interacts with what Christian theology calls the church.[46]

It is precisely on the cusp between the juridical dimension and the educational dimension of Rosmini's spiritual charity that J. Buganza's essay stands. Augustine was the leading theologian of the (Western) patristic era, Thomas Aquinas was the leading theologian of the medieval era, and Rosmini is progressively being recognized as the leading theologian of the modern era. One cannot therefore understand Rosmini's Thomas if one does not first understand Thomas's Augustine. Well aware of this, Buganza highlights the theological and catechetical characteristics of Rosminian pedagogy that resonate, in particular, in his reading of Augustine. For the latter, in fact, the spiritual dimension of education (also of faith) has an intrinsic ethical-moral characterization based on the Thomist conception of law and on the education of freedom and will that receive, assimilate, and apply the universal law in practical situations, whether natural or supernatural. Buganza also moves masterfully within the theoretical device of the synthesism of the three forms of being, highlighting the aspects of Rosminian pedagogy attributable to the moral form of being (form and substance of the christological-Trinitarian revelation), to the ideal form of being (the contents of the only creatural and supernatural truth and the ways it is communicated and assimilated), to the moral form of being (the

---

46. See Campanini, *Antonio Rosmini*.

loving and fond adherence to the amiability of the beauty of truth, to which conscience as a speculative judgment of a practical judgment, at least of the second order of reflection, adheres with the freedom of the will in the [theological] ethics of truth).

The contribution of D. Cravero also has its center of gravity in philosophical anthropology, and makes a comparison between Rosmini and another significant author of the twentieth century, Viktor Emil Frankl who, like Edith Stein, was Jewish. In the case of this author, philosophical anthropology was urged to measure itself against the humanities, up to the intersection between philosophy, psychology, psychiatry and neuroscience. The epistemological-disciplinary hiatus that undoubtedly separates Rosmini and Frankl is the birth, after Rosmini's death, of disciplines such as experimental psychology, psychiatry, and neuroscience. The distance between the two authors, rather than constituting the definitive impossibility of comparison between their philosophical anthropologies, paradoxically, allows us to verify the analogies between Rosmini's triadic-Trinitarian philosophical-theological anthropology and Frankl's three-dimensional philosophical anthropology of (theocentric) self-transcendence. By emphasizing the differences between these two perspectives, the similarities and complementarities between them are highlighted, in the perspective of the fruitful interaction between neuroscience and anthropology, always in phenomenological, theological, and metaphysical synergy, whose contribution bears enrichments that allow us to grasp aspects that otherwise would remain in the shadows.

The contribution of M. Galvani, agreed on with the organizer of the conference and editor of the proceedings, focuses on the theme of *affection*, presenting with theoretical accuracy and an abundance of details and bio-bibliographical documentation the presence of this term and what it theoretically entails both in Rosmini and in Stein. He also carries out an initial comparison of the systems of thought of the two authors, precisely in the light of *affection*. Galvani specifically focuses on affection as a fundamental component of Rosmini's reflections on the real form of being. With regard to Rosmini, the contribution deals almost exclusively with the configuration that the affection as a real being receives in the structure of the human person: in other words, in Rosmini's work affection is considered an intra-subjective and anthropological dimension (mainly on the philosophical side, although there is no lack of ideas on the theological side). Rosmini's "affection" is compared with the configuration in Edith Stein's phenomenology in the light of the Jewish and Carmelite philosopher's treatment of empathy, probed in both phenomenological and metaphysical perspectives. The importance of the introspective and intersubjective dimension of the person is a characteristic trait of both Rosmini and Stein, an undoubtedly interesting attribute that deserves further study.[47]

My own contribution, which can be read in the light of the ethics of education, with which to consider the orders of reflection (both genetic of reflected consciousness, and genetic of law and human rights), allows us to focus awareness on the fact that the latter have their fulcrum in "synthesism within synthesism," and in particular in the *affection* of *cognition*.

Part 4: Rosmini's Suspended Middle (and the Comparable Social Theory of Radical Orthodoxy's Suspended Middle): Possible Political Implications

Rosmini's *Suspended Middle* propitiates a real *social theory*, having implications also and especially in the field of political science, that are explored in this fourth part.

Rosmini was a very important character of the Italian *Risorgimento*, developing a political theory, and undertaking diplomatic missions to the Holy See, in particular for the kingdom of Savoy. Rosmini's liberal Catholicism was connoted by his use of the word *liberalesimo*, to define his position on the matter, and he greatly admired the political-democratic process of the American Revolution. Among the authors with whom he wove a critical intellectual confrontation are John Locke and Alexander de Tocqueville.

This chapter intends to express the fruitfulness of Rosmini's political thought, as proponent of a very significant theological-political path based on the three societies (parental-domestic, civil, and ecclesial) alternative to both liberalism and socialism, and to introduce it into the contemporary debate on these topics.

In her essay, Marta Ferronato makes one of the first and few attempts to deal with the possible implications between the philosophy of law and the philosophy of politics in Rosmini in a focused way. On these topics the ethics of education makes it possible to effectively determine the interaction of juridical pedagogy in its possible dual disciplinary status as a specific pedagogy and as a political philosophy, having in the theory of *fulfillment*[48]

---

47. See Galvani, *Sguardo sull'umano*, and Fornari et al., *Pensiero virtuoso*.

48. For a spiritual reading of Rosmini's theory of contentment, see De Giorgi, *Scuola italiana di spiritualità*, 660–62: "And so for Montini unsatisfactory happiness, when only human, can fall into despair, Christian hope, instead, is satisfied in the love of God, but not in a fideistic and abstract immediacy, that is, inhuman, but assuming fully in itself the not human satisfaction. Paul VI therefore said: 'And with regard to hope there is a difference between the Christian and the modern profane man: the latter is a *vir desideriorum*, the man of many desires (between desire and hope there

one of its main characteristics, consequent and preparatory to the philosophy and theology of the person as a right subsisting in law.

Christiane Liermann's contribution deals with the relationship between the law of cyclicality and the three societies in the perspective of Rosminian theology of philosophy and political theology. From the argument developed by Liermann we can deduce, in addition to the centrality of the relationship between the philosophy of revelation and fundamental theology, the need for the resumption in new interpretative keys of both social theodicy and the elaboration and development of a true and proper ecclesial theodicy. The Rosminian ethics of education is embedded in all its significance in the relationship between ethics and politics, where philosophical anthropology and theological anthropology interact in the determination of social laws capable of orienting the cyclicality of the processes of civil societies not towards their decay, but towards their regeneration. With a possible reference to Malusa's contribution, it must be emphasized that one of the most significant specificities of Rosmini's political philosophy can be recognized in the relationship between personal reflected consciousness as a speculative judgment of a practical judgment at least of the second order of reflection and the art of government as an interaction between the speculative reason of the individual and the practical reason of the masses.

According to Luciano Malusa, one of the leading experts in the philosophical history of Rosminian thought, educational ethics in political philosophy could lead to the restitution and reentry into the current debate, in an international perspective, of Rosmini's philosophy of politics, placed

---

is close kinship: the former is one of the instincts of strength, the latter an instinct of enjoyment, but both tend to future benefits); and it is man who seeks to reduce the distance between himself and the benefits to be achieved; He is a man of short-term hopes, he wants them soon fulfilled, and the sensitive, economic and temporal ones are more quickly attainable, and therefore, once exhausted, leave the heart of man tired, empty, and often disappointed. It is his hopes that do not make his spirit great, and do not give life its full meaning, directing the path of life itself on routes of questionable progress. The Christian, on the other hand, is the man of true hope, the one who aspires to the attainment of the highest good (see S. Aug., *Conf.* 1,1: *Fecisti nos ad Te*), and who knows that he has for his desire and his effort the help of that same supreme Good, who infuses hope with the confidence and grace to attain it (see *Summ. Theol.*, I–II, 40, 7). Both the profane and the Christian hopes draw impetus from a deficiency of our present condition of life, from pain, poverty, remorse, need, discomfort; but a different tension sustains them, although the Christian tension can make its own all the truly human and honest tension of profane hope: is this not the inspiring idea of the great Pastoral Constitution *Gaudium et Spes* of the recent Council? 'There is nothing genuinely human that does not find an echo in the heart of Christ's disciples' (*Gaudium et Spes*, 1; see Ter.: "*Humani nihil a me alienum puto*").' In other words, the human aspiration to perfection, to a fullness of humanity, had to be completely accepted: the Christian was aware of its weaknesses. This is why his humanism had other bases."

in critical dialogue with *Italian theory*, because precisely the ethics of education is capable of reflecting the fruitful and indispensable requirement proper to the most complete and successful Italian conception of political philosophy.[49] It is emblematically represented by Rosmini and consists in his ability to elaborate a political theory capable of effectively interacting with the theoretical-metaphysical-speculative dimension and the practical-pragmatic one.[50]

The essay by P. Giroli, which turns on the osmosis between philosophical anthropology, supernatural anthropology, and Rosmini's theology, focuses with ample documentation on the genesis of Rosminian spirituality in reference to one of the central points of Catholic dogma, namely the justification made by the Savior. Here too we are faced with one of the most significant and evocative aspects of Rosmini's spirituality, in this sense indebted to Anselm of Aosta, in whose footsteps Rosmini elaborated the spiritual implications of the synthesism of the three forms of being: temporal-corporal charity (real being), intellectual charity (ideal being), and spiritual charity (moral being). In the light of what Giroli expounds, the easily instructed connection between Rosmini's spirituality, the anthropology of justification-justice, and his *Filosofia del diritto* (Philosophy of law) is spontaneous and illuminating. Were we to delve into this aspect, which reveals unquestionably immense depths even in these pages, we would certainly see the comparison that Rosmini made on these topics with the thought and work of Thomas Aquinas (as well, of course, with all the fundamental authors on the subject, not only of the ancient and medieval eras, but also of the modern period) emerges once again as fundamental.

Part 5 Rosmini's Suspended Middle (and the Comparable Social theory of Radical Orthodoxy's Suspended Middle): Possible Juridical Implications

Rosmini's *Suspended Middle* propitiates a real *social theory* with implications also and especially in the field of juridical science, explored in this fifth part.

The deontology of the foundation, a meaningful declination of the affective turning point of metaphysics, inscribed in the social theory derived from Rosmini's fundamental anthropology, gives rise to a specific legal

---

49. Malusa, *Teologia di Antonio Rosmini*.
50. See Rosmini, *Filosofia della politica* (The philosophy of politics).

aesthetic, in which the relationship between Vico and Rosmini on the topics in question is strongly emphasized.

This is the object of the last part of the volume, and it is accomplished by highlighting the interdisciplinary dimension of Rosmini's philosophy of law, which interacts with his philosophy of politics, with theology of law, and with ecclesiology. The performativity of the spiritual criterion in clarifying the connection between the juridical dimension of his social theory, and the Rosminian use of Vico's theory regarding the origin of law, is also highlighted. It also offers an original and interesting integrated theory of human dignity through which to reread human rights.

The contribution of P. Heritier provides a meaningful way to frame the possible development of the aesthetic dimension of legal anthropology and the affective turn of the juridical and humanistic sciences.[51] In particular, without neglecting, but rather integrating the neuroscientific question in a legal perspective, the concise historiographical reconstruction carried out by Heritier regarding fundamental aspects of Rosmini's contribution to the philosophical genetics of law, allows us to include his thought in the current debate on the topics in question—a debate having one of its possible fulcrums precisely on the Rosminian conception of reflection (and its orders, both in the pedagogical sense and in the juridical sense).[52] In introducing

---

51. On the theme of theological aesthetics developed by P. Sequeri and the presence of the same theme by A. Rosmini see the *lectio magistralis* by P. Sequeri, *Rosmini and Theological Aesthetics*, held in Modena on May 7, 2022, and available on YouTube— https://youtu.be/8MeHwSeyhT8. See the seminar on the book by Bergonzoni, *Artista dell'essere*, in Orthotes, Salerno, 2020, available on YouTube—https://youtube.com/playlist?list=PL4Px-XxaY4nomo5nnoWfsqe856D1thSUR.

52. Paul VI, *Ecclesiam Suam*, para. 43 (emphasis added): "A year before he died, at the general audience of July 22, 1977, Paul VI observed, 'Anyone who is content to build human morality in the purely natural measure, even if it is dilated as much as possible. But is this truly always possible? . . . And do we Christians . . . have a *religious* concept of human perfection, of justice in the full sense of the word, that we believe can only come through Christ, through our faith in a supernatural justice, that grants us the help, the grace to be truly good. We always remember the words of Saint Paul, 'the righteous will live by his faith.' We must draw from our faith the normative and operative principle for a just and good life (see Saint Paul's Letter to the Galatians 3, 11). From these words we can clearly see the 'religious concept' the spiritual foundation, the spiritual context of Pope Montini's humanity of charity. And he also spoke of the complex question of the consequences on the plane of the moral understanding and the moral life. However, this problem had already been considered by Paul VI some years before, during the general audience of September 20, 1972. He spoke of the operative human principle, the operativity, saying that the Christian welcomes human importance, above all modern, offered by operativity, but on the basis of different principles (we could say, the humanity of charity). 'We can say with the ancient Terenti *'homo sum: humani nihil to me alienum Puto,'* (nothing of that which is human is unfamiliar to me) . . . also for our own reasons, which give man's activities a decisive importance

this essay, the analysis of Rosmini's "five wounds of the Church," which Heritier "shifts" also into the wounds of civil society and institutions, deserves a mention.

Cioffi delves into one of Rosmini's most interesting and still largely unexplored topics: the relationship between his theology of law and his philosophy of law. It is again the ethics of education that illuminates the analysis of canon law, ecclesiastical law, international law, the law of nations, and, of course, the relationship between all these forms of law.[53] It is the formation of the orders of reflection, as genetics of law and rights, that interacts with them not only in a pedagogical perspective, but also, in the disciplinary context of law, the philosophical-theological ethics of the formulation of law and the rights of the person as subsisting law contains in itself criteria for (re)reading Rosmini's *Filosofia del diritto*, such that it is possible to reintroduce in a productive and profitable way his juridical perspective on the three societies (domestic-parental, civil, and ecclesial) within the contemporary theology of canon law, in resonance with *Delle cinque piaghe della Santa Chiesa* up to the current path of reform (also juridical) of the Catholic Church.[54]

The masterful contribution of Father Vito Nardin, superior general emeritus of the Isituto della Carità and recognized and respected expert in Rosminian spirituality, describes with breadth and abundance of investigation the ascetic and mystical profile of Rosmini. One of the most

---

in human perfection (see Blondel, *The Action*, Ollé Laprune, *The Value of Life*), and in our salvation: we shall be judged on our behavior in the balance for eternal life.' And he also said: 'Actions are the first value that qualifies life, even leaving in the shade the precedence of knowledge and the excellence of being, which, however, depends on us, whether we like it or not.' This was a Rosminian concept, expressed in not strictly Rosminian terms: the moral being is most important, but also part of the ideal being and the real being. In faith, therefore, the human being is called upon to do God's will: and God himself makes the human being capable of doing so, loving him, and granting him Grace, that in turn allows the human being to love God and his neighbor. Paul VI said, 'The will of God for man is this: that he love God and his neighbor.' And this is the central question, the utmost aim of will, the first principle of good behavior. . . . The whole life becomes Love. True love, pure love, strong love, happy love. And this is the first love, which is religious, as you can see, and cannot be otherwise, it is linked to the second, the love of one's neighbor, both as a ladder to climb to the love of God (see *1 Me*. 4, 20; S. Aug. *Tract. in I*., 17, 8), and as a reason for bending your actions to the service and benefit of your neighbor (see *Rom*. 13, 8–10; *1 Tim*. 1, 5). . . . Charity, this is the synthesis of our moral life.' And there also is the synthesis of the humanity of charity" (De Giorgi, *Scuola italiana di spiritualità*, 661–62).

53. See Dossi and Ghia, *Diritto e diritti*.

54. See the new Apostolic Constitution (Francis, *Praedicate Evangelium*), promulgated on Mar. 19, 2022, which entered into force on Sunday, June 5, 2022, and completely reforms the Roman Curia.

appreciable aspects of Nardin's text is to make evident with pertinent quotes the references that Rosmini, master of spirituality, made to Thomas Aquinas, throughout his life. The latter is an aspect still little explored by scholars, since, with reason, the reconstruction of the Italian school of spirituality that goes from Rosmini to Montini has so far highlighted the traits of Rosmini's spirituality attributable, among others, to the Franciscan-Capuchin references and to the spirituality of the Oratory of San Filippo Neri. On the other hand, this would not explain the fact that Pope Saint Paul VI found in A. Rosmini and J. Maritain two of the main references from which he elaborated his original spirituality, except for the fact that, once again, it is Thomas Aquinas who acts as a link of compatibility, also for Pope Saint Paul VI, and between Rosmini and Maritain. Nardin's contribution, therefore, inaugurates a wide-ranging and fecund field of study in consideration of the fundamental realization that goes beyond a certain neo-Thomism that (erroneously) supported an incompatibility, not only theoretical but *tout court* radical, between Thomas Aquinas and Antonio Rosmini. Indeed, if we return to the sources, the indisputable starting point from which to re-read Rosminian spirituality, it is precisely here that we find one of Rosmini's fundamental references, if not the main one—Thomas Aquinas—and the comparison between the spirituality of the Dominican school and that of the Rosminian school deserves further investigation. Moreover, following a non-superficial reading it is not surprising to find that the more one delves into the speculative rigor of Rosmini's theoresis, the more one is enthralled by his reasoning and the range of his original, notable and appreciable mystical stature.

In the essay by A. Andreini, attention is paid to the ecclesiological dimension of the community as a moral being in the synthesistic interaction between the three societies. In resonance with De Giorgi's contribution, in particular on the moral nature of education, Andreini offers a significant contribution to understanding the ecclesiological-spiritual dimension of Rosmini's conception of the moral form of triadic-Trinitarian being. Since Andreini is a member of the Comunità di San Leolino, who assisted the Cenacolo Rosminiano Emiliano-Romagnolo mainly in the content-based part of the conference, but also providing organizational assistance, it is no coincidence that the following quotation from the encyclical *Ecclesiam Suam* of Pope Paul VI was selected in the informative brochure of the conference:

> We are seized by the desire that the Church of God be as Christ wants it: one, holy, totally turned towards the perfection to which he has called and enabled it. Perfect in her *ideal* conception, in divine thought, the Church must strive for perfection

in her real expression, in her earthly existence. This is the great *moral* problem that dominates the life of the Church, the measure, stimulate it, accuse it, sustain it, fill it with groans and prayers, repentance and hopes, effort and trust, responsibility, and merit.[55]

It is precisely to Pope Paul VI that De Giorgi traces the final outcome of the Italian school of spirituality, which has its origin in Rosmini: "It seems clear that, at this point, Montini borrowed the Rosminian triniformity of being, applying it—in an original way—to the Church, distinguishing, in the one being of the Church, an ideal being, a real being and a moral being: an ideal Church, a real Church and a moral Church."[56]

Rosmini's triadic-Trinitarian ecclesiology, in synergy with his philosophical and theological anthropology, restores to us the fullness and globality of the moral form of being as a community that is both human and spiritual, source of the paths, processes, and dynamics of the juridical pedagogy of the human person as relationship and subsisting law.

In the last section of this volume there are contributions on spiritual theology, also from the perspective of philosophy of education and juridical pedagogy.[57] While it is true that Rosmini's beatification dates back to 2007, it is equally true that there are not yet many studies that deal comprehensively with the connection between Rosmini's spirituality and his theological-philosophical thought. Beyond the historical reasons for this, which can also and principally be seen in the "Rosminian question," this connection is scientifically achievable through the specific theological discipline that, after the Second Vatican Council, took the name of *spiritual theology* (an open debate is still underway on the definition and clarification of the epistemological status).

The affective turn of Rosmini's metaphysics, reinterpreted in terms of spiritual theology, can to all intents and purposes be identified and summarized under the figure of *desire*. It is precisely to the theme of desire in Rosminian spirituality that W. Abbruzzese dedicates the written form of his report to the conference on Rosmini. The author reviews the spiritual testament that Rosmini left as he died in the arms of his friend Alessandro Manzoni—be silent, enjoy, adore—providing for each of the three verbs insights into the writings and testimony of life of the Blessed Rosmini. What emerges, in the light of the fundamental interpretative criterion synthesizing Rosminian spirituality (that is, the first of the six maxims of Christian

---

55. De Giorgi, *Scuola italiana di spiritualità*, 663.
56. See Bellelli: *Percorsi storici* and *Teoria integrata*.
57. Rosmini, *Massime di perfezione cristiana*, 37.

perfection in which it is affirmed that it is necessary "to desire only and infinitely to please God, that is, to be just") is the intrinsic connection and intertwining of the deontology of the foundation of the justice of *agape*, as a configuration in which Rosmini's theoresis on the moral form of being culminates, the backbone of Rosmini's spiritual theology of asceticism and mysticism, also in a juridical and pedagogical perspective.

In his work Rosmini defines the human person not only as a right subsisting in law, but also subsisting relationship, in deontological isomorphism responding to the law of the *maior dissimilitudo* with the Persons of the Trinity, always defined by Rosmini as *subsisting relationships*. The triadic and Trinitarian synthesism of the three forms of being is effectively the fundamental theoretical device that allows us to fully grasp how and why Rosmini is a philosopher and theologian of the unity of science and holiness with Thomas Aquinas.

Bibliography

Barzaghi, Giuseppe. "Anagogia." In *Enciclopedia Filosofica*, 1:369–70. Milan: Bompiani, 2006.

———. *Anagogia. Il Cristianesimo sub specie aeternitatis*. Modena, It.: ETC, 2002.

———. *Il fondamento teoretico della sintesi tomista*. L'Exemplar. Bologna: ESD, 2015.

———. "Mistica anagogica." In *Nuovo Dizionario di Mistica*, edited by Luigi Borriello et al., 1452–56. Vatican City: Vaticana, 2016.

———. *Lo sguardo di Dio. Nuovi saggi di teologia anagogica*. Bologna: ESD, 2012.

———. *Lo sguardo di Dio. Saggi di teologia anagogica*. Siena: Cantagalli, 2003.

Barzaghi, Giuseppe, and Salvioli Marco, eds. *Che cos'è la storia? Un fatto o il fatto di vedere un fatto? Divus Thomas* 3 (2022).

Barzaghi, Giuseppe, et al. *Ai confini della contraddizione: Tommaso D'Aquino, Florenskij e Severino*. Savona, It.: Insedicesimo, 2021.

Bellelli, Fernando. "*Affezione* della *cognizione* nel metodo e nella metodica di Antonio Rosmini." *La metodica di Rosmini tra filosofia, teologia e pedagogia. Prospettive interdisciplinari*, edited by Fernando Bellelli, 89–105. Milan: Mimesis, 2022.

———. *Etica originaria e assoluto affettivo. La coscienza e il superamento della modernità nella teologia filosofica di Antonio Rosmini*. Milan: Vita e Pensiero, 2014.

———. "Genesi e ricezione della dimensione pedagogica della definizione rosminiana di persona." *Annali di Storia dell'educazione e delle istituzioni scolastiche* 29 (2022) 42–58. Proceedings of Centro Studi e Ricerche Antonio Rosmini of Università di Trento "Rosmini e la pedagogia" online conference, Oct. 15–16, 2020.

———. "L'importanza degli ordini di intellezione e degli ordini di riflessione nella pedagogia rosminiana: analisi storico-culturale di un vuoto della letteratura critica." *Rivista di Storia dell'Educazione* 1 (2020) 85–99.

———, ed. *La metodica di Rosmini tra filosofia, teologia e pedagogia. Prospettive interdisciplinary*. Milan: Mimesis. 2022.

———. *Percorsi storici della pedagogia giuridica. Vico, Rosmini e la dignitas hominis*. Rome: Aracne, 2020.

———. *Rosmini filosofo e teologo con Tommaso: unità di scienza e santità*. *Divus Thomas* 1 (2023).

———. *Teoria integrata della dignità umana*. *Affectio iuris* and Law and Humanities. Turin: Giappichelli, 2023.

Bergonzoni, Filippo. *L'artista dell'essere. Arte e bellezza nel pensiero di Antonio Rosmini*. Salerno, It.: Orthotes, 2020.

Bonafede, Giulio. *Rosmini e la scolastica. Prefazione e appendice critica di Giuseppe Muzio*. Quaderni di "Sodalitas Thomistica" 5. Rome: Salesiana, 1963.

Brancaforte, Antonio. *La laicità dell'idea di Dio. La performatività dell'argomento ontologico nell'Assoluto realismo*. Edited by Philip Cat. Milan: Mimesis, 2021.

———. *La portata metapolitica dell'Assoluto realismo. Vincenzo La Via essenzializza Rosmini*. Edited by Philip Cat. Vol. 1 of *Discussioni rosminiane e altri scritti*. Milan: Mimesis, 2020.

Campanini, Giorgio. *Antonio Rosmini fra politica ed ecclesiologia*. Bologna: EDB, 2006.

De Giorgi, Fulvio. "Antonio Rosmini e il Metodo italiano." *Sophia* 2 (2021) 275–88.

———. *Educare Caino. Per una pedagogia dell'eschaton*. Brescia, It.: La Scuola, 2004.

———. *La scuola italiana di spiritualità. Da Rosmini a Montini*. Brescia, It.: Morcelliana, 2020.

Dewhirst, Anthony J. *Our Light and Our Salvation: Blessed Antonio Rosmini's Supernatural Anthropology Edited and Explained*. N.p., UK: Rosminian Institute of Charity, 2010. Partial; originally published as *Antropologia soprannaturale*.

Donà, Massimo, et al. *Unità*. Edited by Massimo Marianelli and Emanuele Pili. Vol. 3 of *Dizionario dinamico di ontologia trinitaria*. Rome: Città Nuova, 2022.

Dossi, Michele, and Francesco Ghia. *Diritto e diritti nelle "tre società" di Rosmini*. Brescia, It.: Morcelliana, 2014.

Fornari, Pier L., et al. *Il pensiero virtuoso. Saggi su Edith Stein e Tommaso d'Aquino*. *Divus Thomas* 3 (2021).

Francis, Pope. *Praedicate Evangelium*: On the Roman Curia and Its Service to the Church in the World. Vatican, Mar. 19, 2022. https://www.vatican.va/content/francesco/en/apost_constitutions/documents/20220319-costituzione-ap-praedicate-evangelium.html.

Galvani, Martina. *Uno sguardo sull'umano. Antropologia e metafisica in Antonio Rosmini e Edith Stein*. Rome: Tab, 2020.

La Via, Vincenzo. *Coscienza e libertà. Rosmini e l'assoluto realismo*. Edited by Biagio G. Muscherà. Vol. 1 of *Saggi rosminiani e altri scritti*. Milan: Mimesis, 2020.

———. *L'idealismo attuale di Giovanni Gentile. Saggio di esposizione sistematica*. Edited by Biagio G. Muscherà. Milan: Mimesis, 2021.

Malusa, Luciano, ed. *La teologia di Antonio Rosmini sotto attacco: consensi e dissensi su una grande sintesi filosofico-teologica*. Milan: Franco Angeli, 2021.

Mantovani, Mauro et al., eds. *Oltre la crisi. Prospettive per un nuovo modello di sviluppo; Il contributo del pensiero realistico dinamico di Tommaso Demaria*. Rome: LAS 2011.

Milbank, John. *The Suspended Middle: Henri de Lubac and the Debate Concerning the Supernatural*. Grand Rapids: Eerdmans, 2005.

———. "Trinitarian Ontology and the Division of Being: A Rosminian Reflection." *Sophia* 8 (2021–22) 189–231.

Pagani, Giovan B. *The Life of Rosmini-Serbati*. London: Routledge and Sons, 1907.

Pagazzi, Giovanni C. *La singolarità di Gesù come criterio di unità e differenza nella Chiesa*. Milan: Glossa, 1997.

Paul VI, Pope. *Ecclesiam Suam*: Encyclical of Pope Paul VI on the Church. Vatican, Aug. 6, 1964. https://www.vatican.va/content/paul-vi/en/encyclicals/documents/hf_p-vi_enc_06081964_ecclesiam.html.

Rosmini, Antonio. *About the Author's Studies*. Vol. 1 of *Introduction to Philosphy*. Translated by Robert A. Murphy. Durham, UK: Rosmini, 2004. Originally published as *Introduzione alla filosofia*.

———. *Anthropology as an Aid to Moral Science*. Translated by Denis Cleary and Terence Watson. Durham, UK: Rosmini, 1992. Originally published as *Antropologia in servizio della scienza morale*.

———. *Certainty*. Translated by Denis Cleary and Terence Watson. Durham, UK: Rosmini, 1992. Extract; originally published as *Nuovo Saggio sull'origine delle idee*.

———. *A Commentary to the Introduction of the Gospel According to John*. Translated by Antonio Belsito, IC. Mansfield, UK: Rosmini, 2019. Originally published as *Introduzione al Vangelo secondo Giovanni*.

———. *Conscience*. Translated by Denis Cleary and Terence Watson. Durham, UK: Rosmini, 1989. Orginally published as *Trattato della coscienza morale*.

———. *The Constitution under Social Justice*. Translated by Alberto Mingardi. Lanham, MD: Lexington, 2007. Originally published as *La Costituzione secondo la giustizia sociale*.

———. "Del metodo filosofico." In *Scritti pedagogici*, edited by Fernando Bellelli, ENC 32, 393–437. Rome: Città Nuova, 2019.

———. *The Diaries of Blessed Antonio Rosmini*. Edited and translated by J. Anthony Dewhirst. Short Run, UK: UK, 2008.

———. *Edited Translation of Rosmini's Mathematics*. Translated by J. Anthony Dwhirst. Short Run, UK: UK, 2008.

———. *Filosofia della politica*. Edited by Fernando Bellelli, with editorial note by R. Cubeddu. Siena: Cantagalli, 2021.

———. "The Five Wounds of Holy Church." *Witness* 23 (2008) 245–65. Extract; originally published as *Delle cinque piaghe della Santa Chiesa*.

———. *The Five Wounds of the Church: A Study Dedicated to Catholic Clergy*. Translated by Denis Cleary. Leominster, UK: Fowler Wright, 1987. Originally published as *Delle cinque piaghe della santa Chiesa*.

———. "Frammenti." In *Scritti pedagogici*, edited by Fernando Bellelli, ENC 32, 491–506. Rome: Città Nuova, 2019.

———. *Fundamentals of Rosmini Epistemology*. Edited and translated by F. A. Dewhirst, IC. London, 1962. Extract; originally published as *Il Nuovo Saggio sull'origine delle idee*.

———. *Logica*. Edited by Vincenzo Sala. ENC 8. Rome: Città Nuova, 1984.

———. *Massime di perfezione cristiana*. Edited by Alfeo Valle. ENC 49. Rome: Città Nuova, 1976.

———. *Maxims of Christian Perfection*. Edited by Antonio Belsito. Ratcliffe-on-Wreake, UK: Rosmini Center, 2008. Originally published as *Massime di perfezione cristiana*.

———. *Meditations (Manuale dell'esercitatore)*. Unpublished manuscript.

———. *Nuovo Saggio sull'origine delle idee*. Edited by Gaetano Messina. 3 vols. ENC 3–5. Rome: Città Nuova, 2003–2004.

———. *On Christian Education*. Translated by J. Anthony Dewhirst. UK: Rosminian Institute of Charity, 2012. Originally published as *Dell'educazione cristiana*.

———. *The Origin of Thought by Antonio Rosmini: A New Essay on the Origin of Ideas*. Edited and translated by Terry Watson and Denis Cleary. Leominster, UK: Fowler Wright, 1987. Extract; originally published as *Nuovo Saggio sull'origine delle idee*.

———. *Our Life in Christ*. Translated by an English Rosminian Father. Stresa, It.: Centro Internazionale di Studi Rosminiani, 1983.

———. *A New Essay Concerning the Origin of Ideas*. 3 vols. Vol. 1 translated by Robert A. Murphy, vols. 2 and 3 translated by Denis Cleary and Terence Watson. Durham, UK: Rosmini, 2001. Originally published as *Il Nuovo Saggio sull'origine delle idee*.

———. *The Philosophy of Right*. Translated by Denis Cleary and Terence Watson. 6 vols. Durham, UK: Rosmini, 1993–1996. Originally published as *Filosofia del diritto*.

———. *Principi della scienza morale*. Edited by Umberto Muratore. ENC 23. Rome: Città Nuova, 1990.

———. *Principle of Ethics*. Translated by Terence Watson and Denis Cleary. Leominster, UK: Fowler Wright, 1988. Originally published as *Principi della scienza morale*.

———. *The Problem of Ontology: Being-as-One*. Vol. 1 of *Theosophy*. Translated by Denis Cleary and Terence Watson. Durham, UK: Rosmini, 1998. Originally published as *Teosofia*.

———. *Psicologia*. Edited by Vincenzo Sala. 4 vols. ENC 9, 9/A, 10, 10/A. Rome: Città Nuova, 1988–1989.

———. *Psychology*. Translated by Denis Cleary and Terence Watson. 4 vols. Durham, UK: Rosmini, 1999. Originally published as *Psicologia*.

———. *A Selection from Ascetical Letters of Antonio Rosmini*. Edited and translated by John Morris, IC. Loughborough, UK: Quorn Litho, 1995. Extract; originally published as *Epistolario ascetico*.

———. "Sistema filosofico." In *Introduzione alla filosofia*, edited by Pier P. Ottonello, ENC 2, 225–302. Rome: Città Nuova, 1979.

———. *Society and Its Purpose*. Vol. 2 of *The Philosophy of Politics*. Translated by Denis Cleary and Terence Watson. Durham, UK: Rosmini, 1994. Originally published as *La società e il suo fine*.

———. *The Summary Cause for the Stability or Downfall of Human Societies*. Vol. 1 of *The Philosophy of Politics*. Translated by Denis Cleary and Terence Watson. Durham, UK: Rosmini, 1994. Originally published as *Della sommaria cagione per la quale stanno o rovinano umane società*.

———. *Talks to Priests*. New York: New City, 1982. Extract; originally published as *Conferenze dei doveri ecclesiastici*.

———. *Teosofia*. Edited by Samuele F. Tadini. Milan: Bompiani, 2011.

———. *Theodicy: Essay on Divine Providence*. Translated by Terence Watson. Durham, UK: Rosmini, 1977. Originally published as *Teodicea*.

———. *Theological Language*. Translated by Denis Cleary. Durham, UK: Rosmini, 2004. Originally published as *Il linguaggio teologico*.

———. *Trattato della coscienza morale*. Edited by Umberto Muratore and Samuele F. Tadini. ENC 25. Rome: Città Nuova, 2012.

———. *Trine Being*. Vol. 2 of *Theosophy*. Translated by Terence Watson. Durham, UK: Rosmini, 2007. Originally published as *Teosofia*.

———. *Trine Being (contd.)*. Vol. 3 of *Theosophy*. Translated by Terence Watson. Durham, UK: Rosmini, 2011. Originally published as *Teosofia*.

Salvioli, Marco. "Beyond 'Philosophy' and 'Theology': A Radical Orthodox Reading of Bl. Antonio Rosmini." *Divus Thomas* 1(2021) 361–77.

———. "La misericordia invisibile del Padre nella compassione visibile di Gesù, il Figlio. Per una fenomenologia di Gesù in chiave anagogica." *Divus Thomas* 50 (2008) 22–110.

———. "Struttura della persona ed esperienza della grazia. A proposito di E. Stein." *Divus Thomas* 45 (2006) 162–85.

Sequeri, Pierangelo. *Iscrizione e rivelazione. Il canone testuale della parola di Dio.* Brescia, It.: Queriniana, 2022.

Staglianò, Antonio. *Ecce homo. La persona, l'idea di cultura e la «questione antropologica» in papa Wojtyla.* Siena: Cantagalli, 2008.

Tadini, Samuele F. *Il problema di Dio nella metafisica rosminiana.* Milan: Vita e Pensiero, 2015.

———. "Il Rosminianesimo in Gran Bretagna nel XIX secolo." In *Rosminianesimo filosofico. Anno I, 2017*, edited by Samuele F. Tadini, 27–59. Milan: Mimesis, 2017.

Part 1

Rosmini's Purification of the Scotist Aporias of Phenomenology (between Analogy and Paradox) and the Division of Being: Metaphysics and Ontology

I

Rosmini's Ontology

UMBERTO MURATORE

Ontology as an Exploration of the Essence of Being

ONTOLOGY,[1] AS THE WORD says, is the study of being in its totality, or, better yet, the search for the ultimate principles or reasons on which the principles of all other sciences rest.[2] As a young man Rosmini was stirred by

---

1. The Rosmini bibliography on metaphysics and ontology is increasingly vast. In this work I refer to Rosmini's main text, *Teosofia* (Theosophy). I have taken direct quotations from Rosmini from this volume. To facilitate comparison with other editions, I refer to numbered paragraphs, rather than page numbers. For further understanding Rosmini's work, I would suggest the following publications: Tadini, *Teosofia di Rosmini*; Tadini, *Problema di Dio*; Muratore, *Teosofia di Rosmini*.

2. Rosmini uses the traditional meaning of ontology, as well as the science that deals with the institution as an entity. Today to this general meaning of ontology, which is called *formal ontology*, are added, at least on the secular side, many ontologies called *materials*, depending on the aspects of the reality examined: ontology of physics, mathematics of common sense, etc. It could be said that material ontologies are analogous to those sciences that Rosmini calls *philosophies* (mathematics, politics, law, etc.) and which have as their end the first principles relating to that discipline. The real ontology for Rosmini comes before the principles of the other sciences, and founds them. Also on the difference between *ontology* and *metaphysics* today we detach ourselves from the Rosminian language: for Rosmini, there are no substantial differences, while for many, contemporary philosophy ontology is a kind of inventory and tells us what exists; while

the "speculative intemperance"[3] that had moved Kant, Fichte, and Hegel, believing that it was possible to directly penetrate the depths, and to climb to the heavens of being, to collect with the gaze of the mind the vision of the foundations and the ultimate reasons of all knowledge. But he soon realized that, before passing through the door of ontology, it was necessary to follow less ambitious paths and more precise visions. That is, it was necessary to cultivate *regressive philosophy*: to go in search of the origin of knowledge (ideology or gnoseology) in order to establish the correct way to proceed during exploration (logic), to collect as much as possible of the data offered by experience and contemplation on the various sciences (moral, political, legal, anthropological). This preliminary work would provide the *formal and material conditions* for advancing into theosophical thinking.

Only in the last nine years of his life (1846–Feb. 1855) did he finally feel ready to deal with this matter, and he did so by giving this new research the title of *Theosophy*, or *Wisdom of God*. He approached it boldly, but also with humility, aware that he could only "lift a few folds of the veil that covers such an immense body of truth."[4]

The treatise on theosophy was to include three sciences: *ontology, cosmology,* and *rational theology*. Ontology, in turn, was to be divided into six books, called respectively: *Categories, Being One, Being Triune, Idea, Dialectic, Reality*. Of these six books Rosmini was able to review and reorder the notes of only the first three. In the preface that Rosmini wrote for the whole of *Theosophy* (according to Paoli, writing in Aug. 1852), he combined the term *metaphysics* with that of *ontology*, specifying that the latter would deal with the entity in all its scope, finite entity and infinite entity, real entity and possible entity. Therefore, he established as fields of ontological research God, the world, and the self: rational theology, cosmology, and psychology. But, since the world becomes intelligible only through the human self, ontology deals with the two vast fields of psychology and rational theology. A few years earlier Rosmini had written *Psychology* and now, with *Theosophy*, he intended to focus on the study of "being." With the title *Theosophy* he wanted to indicate that this study, while always remaining on the terrain of philosophical method, led human reason to see in God the "supreme cause and culmination of all things."[5]

---

metaphysics tells us what is what and what exists. See Varzi, *Ontologia*, 7–8; Ferraris, *Storia dell'ontologia*, 822.

3. Rosmini, *T*, para. 8.
4. Rosmini, *T*, para. 32.
5. Rosmini, *T*, para. 3.

Precisely because these are exercises of reason, Rosmini's *Theosophy* would be not "supernatural" but "rational."[6] This meant that reasoning would develop by strictly observing the philosophical method. It would offer thinking reason the possibility of sharing in some way in the wisdom of God, because in theosophy the whole being is contemplated as the will and the intelligence of God have wanted and ordered it. This is the highest and most profound response that Rosmini could give to Pope Pius VIII's invitation to "lead men to religion by reason."[7]

Ontology, therefore, as a discourse of what is seen in the very nature of the whole entity in relation to its parts: finite and infinite, one and multiple, partial and total, relative and absolute, contingent and eternal, beginning and ending. A human attempt to "open the deep core of being,"[8] to contemplate "the eternal mirror of being,"[9] where all the other sciences find their ultimate foundation and their definitive place. In fact, theosophy is distinguished from other sciences by the fact that it examines the totality of being, while the other sciences carve out a portion of being. Moreover, the other sciences base their principles on some science that precedes them, while theosophy, finding nothing beyond the total entity, cannot base its principles on other sciences, but must find in itself a principle that justifies its existence. Finally, theosophical thinking is an *absolute thought*, that is, a thinking of every object in relation to "its ontological whole,"[10] reasoning that leads us to conclude that between the real entities and the absolute or creating cause there is an "ontological difference."[11]

In the present work, of course, I will only be able to give some faint trace of such an imposing opus and I will do so by mentioning some of the issues that, in my opinion, are relevant even today.

The Metaphysical Egg

Rosmini defines ontology as "the theory of being in all its possibility."[12] By *theory* he means the world of thought; by *being* he means that which originally appears to the mind of man in the form of an idea, the idea of being, the ideal being; by *possibility* he means all the ways in which being can be

6. Rosmini, *T*, para. 196.
7. See Rosmini, *IP*, para. 11.
8. Rosmini, *T*, para. 201.
9. Rosmini, *T*, para. 1924.
10. Rosmini, *T*, para. 2048.
11. Rosmini, *T*, para. 2049.
12. Rosmini, *T*, paras. 41, 23, 2917.

thought or known: finite, infinite, ideal, real, moral, imaginary, abstract, really existing or only thought and imagined, etc.

Man finds the notion or idea of being as the original presence in his mind. It is the primary idea, from which all other ideas originate. The being that presents itself to the mind in this idea appears indeterminate in its simplicity, empty of content. However, it is a "luminous essence,"[13] which manifests in itself the characteristics of objectivity, necessity, and intelligibility. This primary idea is the principle, the light that guarantees absolute knowledge to ontological science and will accompany us in the exploration of the self, of the world, and of God, because it is "the intelligibility of things."[14]

The light of being present in the idea first kindles the mind itself, making it intelligent. Thus, it accompanies the mind in the exploration of the self, the world, and God. This means that the mind becomes aware of the existence of itself and of the other entities it experiences only when it transforms everything it perceives into ideas or quintessence. But to take note of the existence of reality means to give realties existence, being. They therefore, at least for us, do not have being in themselves, they are not intelligible in themselves, until we confer it on them.

Hence, the philosopher is forced to transform into ideas everything that comes to him from the surrounding reality, and everything that he later elaborates in the form of contemplation. His is a world of knowledge, a theory, a dense network of ideas, a mental universe where everything is seen in the form of ideas. Therefore, even when we think of realities, we think of them as ideas. We deal with wisdom and moral acts as ideas and thus the ideal "being," the mother of all ideas, becomes "universal [dialectic, that is, mental] matter" of all things,[15] common ideal fabric, "form of forms."[16] This does not mean that real entities do not have an existence of their own, which Rosmini calls subjective. It just means that *for us* they exist only as the ideas we have of them. Even the existence in itself of the finite real entities, which comes to us through the feeling illuminated by the idea, is expressed as an *idea* of a force alien to us, a force that will require the existence of a creative act.

The mental universe, within which the mind of man moves as within a cone of intelligible light; Rosmini calls it "metaphysical egg," or "objective bark."[17] It is "egg" or "bark (as that of a tree)" because it encloses the ideal

13. Rosmini, *T*, para. 434.
14. Rosmini, *T*, para. 775.
15. Rosmini, *T*, para. 269.
16. Rosmini, *T*, para. 805.
17. Rosmini, *T*, para. 557.

world; it is "metaphysical," because the ideational "being" that contains the other ideas comes before other knowledge; it is "objective,"[18] because in the ideational "being" everything is objective and necessary. And, precisely because the mind thinks of things by transferring them to an objective world, it is said that it gives the objective form to things.[19]

It should be noted that when an entity, a feeling, an experience enters the world of knowledge or ideas, they acquire the characteristics of ideas. Ideas do not die, they are eternal; consequently, once any entity is known in the idea it is clothed with the eternity of ideas. The intellect therefore thinks of things in eternity, thinks the same time out of time, space out of space.[20] The real and finite entities, our experiences, the world as a whole flow and pass, but their idea, once printed in the mind, no longer passes, but lives in the mind outside of any space and time. This knowledge of things as in themselves and as in the metaphysical world offers human reason a glimmer of how things and the whole world exist in two ways: in God and in themselves, that is, outside of God. In God I am God himself, outside of God they are external terms of the creative act.[21]

Triadic and Trinitarian Ontology

One of the Rosminian positions that could arouse interest today is the solution that Rosmini gives us of being *one* in nature or essence and *triune* in forms. In fact, the vision of the ideal being, as it appears in the first *intùito*, is a simple vision of being in its totality: it appears without particular content, without determination of any kind. And this void of determination drives the mind that sees it to want to know more. Moreover, as the determinations appear, the mind notices the apparent antinomies or contradictions. For example, being "is one and is also more, it is necessary and it is also contingent, it is infinite and it is also finite, it is immutable and changeable, it is eternal and temporary, it is simple and composed, it is maximum

---

18. We remind you that Rosmini uses the term *objective*, in the traditional sense, not to indicate a real object, but an entity *ideal*, present to the mind as an object to the subject. Alessandra Saccon writes: "Up to the threshold of the modern age . . . what exists *subiective* is that which is endowed with a certain autonomy and subsists outside our mental universe, while *obiectum and objective* always indicate the relationship to a mental faculty (Ferraris, *Storia dell'ontologia*, 71n).

19. Rosmini, *T*, para. 867. Rosmini also writes: "Do not confuse objectifying with inobjectivation; objectifying is the dressing of an entity as an object; inobjectivation is a transportation of oneself to another" (para. 857n).

20. Rosmini, *T*, para. 663.

21. Rosmini, *T*, paras. 1332, 1389, 1664.

and minimum."[22] Hence the main problem of ontology: *How is it possible to reconcile the unity of the entity with its multiplicity of entities, one with the many?* It is an age-old problem. In order to resolve the apparent contradictions between the unity of being and the plurality of entities, between one and many, mankind sets his mind in motion (dialectical thinking) and faces it as a navigation in the open sea.[23]

The solution given by Rosmini to the question of the one and the many is that being presents itself to the mind essentially in "three acts, which are objectivity, subjectivity and morality."[24] They are the three original forms of being (ideal, real, moral), the three ways that will encompass all the other ways in which being can be thought of, the ultimate classes of all varieties of being without breaking its unity. Thus, "being [is] necessarily identical in three forms."[25] We find these three forms both in God, infinite entity or subject, and in the finite entity (man, animal, real things): with the difference that, in God the three forms are identified with being, and are the divine Persons, while the finite entity is not being but only *has* being.[26]

There is, therefore, a real multiplicity also in God, and it is that of the divine Persons: Father, Son, Holy Spirit. The Father is conceived by us as an intelligent subject, an act that produces all of itself in the form of an object. This production is the act of generation, from which is born both the fatherhood that we attribute to the Father, and the name of Son that we give to the second Person. The divine essence received by the Son as an object is also lovable, and this act of common love is the Person of the Holy Spirit. So, the intellectual act of the divine essence is one as a principle but with two expressions, whose relations with the principle form a trinity. Unity lies in the common divine essence, the Trinity in the relationships of Father to Son and vice versa, of lovable and loved by Father and Son through the Holy Spirit and vice versa.

The intellectual and volitional act of God, which gives rise to the Trinity, is the same that gives rise to the world, and being "identical in all three persons,"[27] the world is the external effect of the whole Trinity. In this act, moreover, if it is considered *internal* to the Trinity, the Father is called the *principle*, because he transfuses all of himself into the Son; if it is considered external, he is called the *cause*, because he produces an entity different from

22. Rosmini, *T*, para. 62.
23. Rosmini, *T*, para. 1997.
24. Rosmini, *T*, para. 103.
25. Rosmini, *T*, para. 135.
26. Rosmini, *T*, para. 732.
27. Rosmini, *T*, para. 1284.

himself.[28] (n. 1284). The cause is also said to be *efficient* in that the Father *makes* the world, *exemplary* in that he *creates* the world by extracting it from the exemplar that is in his Word.

Arguing that the first, the ideal and objective form, belongs to the nature of being, Rosmini tells us that being as an idea exists. So, when we talk about the *existence* of being it is not enough to think only of reality, for which Rosmini uses the term *subsistence*, but we must also include its ideal way of existing, existence in the mind. The ideal being has an existence of its own and cannot be an abstraction produced by man: neither abstraction on the finite entity, as the sensists would have it, nor abstraction on the real infinite, as the ontotheists state.

It follows that universals or abstract ideas are neither real, as the realists affirm; nor simple names, as the nominalists avow. Perhaps the misunderstandings arose from the fact that as ideas, universals must, by the law of synthesism, be held in a mind. This statement makes a positive contribution to the solution of the age-old problem of universals. They are ideal essences that have an existence of their own, distinct from reality.

Characteristic of the forms of being is that each of them includes, in its own way, the other two, so that it can be the being in its totality in any form you want to attribute to it. For example: the ideal being (first form) contains in its own way the real being (finite and infinite) and the moral being. The same can be said of the real and the moral. It is the theory of *synthesism* of being or *ontological synthesism*, through which reason comes to know that "both unity and multiplicity coexisting in it without discord is essential to being."[29] This theory has considerable value in Rosmini's work and leads to the *reciprocal circuminsession* of the forms themselves, that is, to the need "that these forms must interpenetrate, without confusion, and mutual inexistence."[30] In this sense there is also a circuminsession of the three divine Persons, because they "exist in each other without being confused, indeed distinguishing themselves."[31]

Rosmini confesses that what helped him find the solution of being one and triune was the revelation of the mystery of the Trinity. He does not use this mystery to reach the solution, which as we have said remains philosophical, but it has served as a suggestion, an external indication of the path to be taken in the exploration of being; as if the mystery had suggested to him: *try this way and see if it works!* Once the solution was reached, then

---

28. Rosmini, *T*, para. 1284.
29. Rosmini, *T*, para. 199.
30. Rosmini, *T*, para. 992.
31. Rosmini, *T*, para. 1141.

the problem of the existence of the Trinity and of God, one in its essence and triune in the divine Persons became clearer to man.

Creative Act

Rosmini discusses another stimulating topic, that of the *creative act*, following the analysis of the finite real entity. This entity, unlike the infinite real entity, is not one's own being, because it is not intelligible for itself, but it really exists (Rosmini would say *subjectively*). For it to exist, there must have been an act that made it exist without making it a participant in the being.

This act transpires as the creative act, common to the whole Trinity. But man cannot see this act. Why not? Because, Rosmini replies, this act has a principle and an expression. The principle of the act remains in God, because every act of God in God is God; the finite real entity is instead the expression of the creative act, its extremity, the external effect to the act itself.[32] And the human mind can see only the expression.

Not being able to see the creative act, because it remains in God, means not seeing the act through which God creates the world. For the human mind this means not being able to see "the connection, the communication, the bridge, the *trait union* between the creative God and that created."[33] Finite things and the universe, for human reason, remain "an arcanum, a mystery, an enigma to which we lack the key."[34] To human reason this inability to enter into the nature of the finite real being may seem an unbearable limit, an ignorance that does not accept and attempts to subjugate by incorrect means. Another exaggeration, at the opposite pole, is to react with a nihilistic position. Recognizing this limit is a sign of healthy philosophical humility.

The Ontological Chain

Rosmini, as we have said, left us only a few notes on cosmology or real entity. However, thanks to the fact that each form somehow also contains the other forms, and by virtue of the solid circle used by the philosopher, it gives us broad insight into the world and its Creator. When he contemplates the whole real entity, whether finite or infinite, he sees it as a living, dynamic and organic relationship between the entities, which together constitute an "ontological chain" or chain of being. There is a dynamism or continuity of

32. Rosmini, *T*, para. 1424.
33. Rosmini, *T*, para. 1281.
34. Rosmini, *T*, para. 1706.

action that flows eternally in God: it comes from God as an effect in the world and from the world it goes back to God as "sublimation of the caused."[35]

There are twelve links in this chain. Six belong to the cause (God), six to the caused (the world). They are: "1. beginning, 2. Verb, 3. Holy Spirit, 4. final cause, 5. exemplary cause, 6. efficient cause, 7. finite reality, 8. intelligible form, 9. final appetite, 10. operation of the Holy Spirit through which he is incarnated, 11. the Word that reveals 12. the Father."[36] Rosmini described the order and the links in this chain—which contemplate the procession of people, the creation of the universe, the *exitus* of the finite real entity by God and its *reditus* to God—almost as if it were a pleasant tale, in which each link is coupled to the next.

The first three links illustrate the eternal constitution and dynamism within the infinite entity: the Father (*Beginning*) gives rise to the Son (*Word*), Father and Son breathe the *Holy Spirit*. The other three links summarize the eternal constitution and dynamism of the cause. Since God is love without boundaries, he wanted to extend his love also to the finite entity outside of himself, that is, to make the finite entity an end unto itself, *the final cause*. To achieve this, he conceived the finite entity in the model of the world, which he provided in the Son, or *exemplary cause*. Then with the creative energy of the eternal resolve he produced its realization (*efficient cause*).

The six links relating to the cause are followed by three links that concern the constitution of the world, or caused reality, or finite entity. The effect of the efficient cause, the sixth link in the chain, is the *finite real* (seventh link), in particular the intelligent creature, which senses an *intelligible form* (ideal being, eighth link) and possesses a will that tends to good (*final appetite*). But the goodness to which the intelligent creature aspires, if that is what God himself is, can rationally be known only in a negative way. In order for man to attain this goodness, which is the aim of creation, God came to meet man through a supernatural communication of himself. Then the last three links: by the power of the *Holy Spirit* (tenth link) the *Word* (eleventh link) is incarnated, which in turn reveals to us the *Father* (twelfth and last link).

The ontological chain tells us of the supernatural order grafted into creation, an order through which "creation is accomplished according to the eternal established design."[37]

It should be noted that the narration of what we might call the divine plan *of a story of love*, as man would conceive it, is a logical process of

---

35. Rosmini, *T*, para. 1403.
36. Rosmini, *T*, para. 1403.
37. Rosmini, *T*, para. 1403.

successive acts only due to the limitations of the human mind. In reality, it was just one act. Let us also remember that while attributing to the Father the efficient cause, to the Son the exemplary cause, and to the Holy Spirit the final cause, in reality the creative act belongs to the whole Trinity. Finally, it should be noted that the central term of each triad of links is always the same: the Word, the exemplar, the intelligible form, the incarnate verb. The Person of Christ is found everywhere "as *an immutable mediator.*"[38]

The Ontological Proof of the Existence of God

Among the numerous proofs of the existence of God that Rosmini presents, the most original is the ontological proof, where he proposes once again, with appropriate modifications, that of Anselm of Canterbury. He looks for many ways to present this demonstration, ways that essentially say the same thing. One of these ways is the following:

> The virtual and initial being, that is, the being intuited by nature of which contemplation discovered the relationships of virtuality and inceptuality, is necessary as we have seen, because being cannot but be. However, He is not an entity, He is therefore some part of an entity. But this entity of which that being is part, cannot be a contingent entity, because the contingent is the opposite of the necessary. Therefore, the *being intuited* by man must necessarily be something of a *necessary* and *eternal* entity, the creative, determining and final cause of all contingent entities, and this is God.[39]

Explained in our own words, this proposition tells us that the ideal being perceived by man presents itself to his mind with the character of necessity. Elsewhere Rosmini adds other characteristics to the ideal being, such as objectivity, eternity, etc. The ideal being, as such, can exist only in a mind; the human mind examining the qualities of the being presented to it, understands that it cannot have produced this being, because it (the human mind) does not possess these qualities. From here we come, through contemplation, to seek the cause of the ideal being in a mind that has the characteristics of this being. The mind that we are looking for can be none other than that of God.

The reasoning is called *ontological*, because it is derived from the observation of the very nature of being. And it is a priori, because it is based

---

38. Rosmini, *T*, para. 1403.
39. Rosmini, *T*, para. 298.

on something (ideal being), that man is given before experience. Experience and contemplation will serve only as conditions for revealing the connection between the ideal being and God, not for founding it.

The a priori demonstration of the existence of God leaves open another problem: "Whether it is known *per se* that God exists,"[40] that is, whether the human mind can directly intuit God. And it is here that Rosmini, like Thomas, separates himself from both the medieval Anselm and his contemporary Gioberti. In fact, in the proposition *God exists*, to the human mind the subject God remains unknown, "since man has no other knowledge of the divine essence in the natural order than negative."[41] The ideal being present to the human mind, in fact, cannot be God, because God is real and is also a Person, while the ideal being is only an idea that needs a real mind to exist. Indeed, by reasoning man comes to understand that this mind is necessary for the ideal being, but he does not see it, he can only demand it by negative means, that is, excluding that it can be the human mind.

Rosmini is very clear about this. Yet it seems strange that in the last years of his life some of his contemporaries were keen to call him an *ontologist* (direct vision of God) and a *pantheist*. Even stranger is the fact that it took more than a century to clarify that he was neither an ontologist nor a pantheist.

The First Cause of the World Is an Intellect

There has always been discussion, especially in our time, about the origin of the universe, and whether it is the work of chance or of an intelligent mind.

Rosmini in this regard is clear: *the first efficient cause in the world is an intellect*. He repeats this many times: "God is not an infinite blind power, but an infinite intelligence," "creative intelligence," "creative power," "an eternal intelligence in permanent action," a "reality intelligible for itself."[42] And since "emotion is contained in the concept of an intelligent subject that understands itself," God, too, "lives to himself and is essentially emotion."[43]

In describing the logical process of creation, as a limited human mind can conceive it, Rosmini explained that God, after having abstracted the exemplar of the world from the Word, through his imagination, had thought of the real entities of the universe, and by thinking them had given them an existence of their own. So finite real entities exist in the mind of God by eminence, outside of God, on their own.

40. Rosmini, *T*, para. 299.
41. Rosmini, *T*, para. 299.
42. Rosmini, *T*, paras. 2202, 361, 348, 744, 1643.
43. Rosmini, *T*, para. 748.

Although the world originated from a first intelligence, to which a first will is always united, it does not continue blindly, it contains in its bosom laws, an intrinsic order, a culmination towards which it tends.[44]

From the fact that a divine intellect is the first cause of the world come many consequences. One is that if entities have been thought of by an intelligence, then every being and every entity is intelligible, it can be thought of within the objective form of being. And this means that "an intellectual element necessarily enters into the constitution of the real entity."[45] If, moreover, the divine mind produces everything that thinks, then everything that is thinkable becomes possible, as long as it does not involve contradiction.

We also know that in the divine mind all the essences of things correspond to their reality, because the divine intellect contains all things "totally in itself as intelligible and intended essences."[46] If man "could see these essences, as they are in God, he would know the world fully," and with this he would reach "the culmination of Wisdom to which the mind tends ceaselessly."[47] But, unfortunately, we are obliged to gather the knowledge of the world through our own experience, imperfectly. When we have known them, we can only "preach" their existence, while the divine mind "produces" the existence of the real. However, knowing that a perfect intelligence presides over their existence encourages us to continue to discover and understand, because all things have meaning in God's ordained plan. In a sense man has an unconscious perception of the fact that the world has been made and is governed by an intelligence, so he is intelligible. In fact, he continues to ask himself the *reason* for things, and does not stop until he encounters an ultimate cause.

Even the desire for contemplation and the value that philosophers attribute to it is a sign that the search for the intelligibility of things presupposes in the human mind the hope of being able to better understand the world, oneself, the Creator.

However, we must avoid assuming that the human intellect can, by its research, attain the knowledge of the divine intellect. As we have said, the essence of things is revealed to us imperfectly, limitedly, and outside of God, because of the creative act, we know only the term, while the principle

---

44. We must recall that the concept of *culmination* is different from that of *end*: "Every natural and spontaneous movement has a *culmination* to which it tends, but not an *end*, which is only in the mind of the creator and the artist," that is, in the mind of an intelligent person (para. 1382).

45. Rosmini, *T*, para. 1348.

46. Rosmini, *T*, para. 1350.

47. Rosmini, *T*, para. 1350.

which is in God remains hidden from us. The human intellect knows things, it does not produce them, and knows them only by degrees.

Finally, if a divine intelligence presides over the creation of the world, then the universe is *ordered*. The divine intellect, in fact, by its nature, operates in an orderly way, because it is the same being and "being is in itself ordered." "If, therefore, all the things of the universe are the effect of the first intellect, they must be ordered." And God, in addition to being "the effective cause of all things," is also "the ordering cause." When with experience and contemplation we succeed in attaining this truth, then "even where we cannot verify an order *a posteriori*, either because it is a matter of entities beyond our experience, or because our power of understanding is limited, (perfect) order must necessarily exist."[48]

The Bodily Principles[49]

Rosmini had already discussed the presence of bodily principles in the constitution of the human body, the fact that they must be distinguished from the body and that they have an "arcane nature" in *A New Essay Concerning the Origin of Ideas (Nuovo Saggio sull'origine delle idee)*.[50] But it was in *Psychology (Psicologia)* that he fully developed the concept. In *Theosophy (Teosofia)* he returned to it, but left the question open.

For Rosmini the true nature of finite (bodily) reality is conceived as feeling, and feeling is composed of beginning and end. As for man, in the perception or feeling of his own body whoever feels the body has a principled nature, and is called the sentient principle, or sensitive soul; the body, on the other hand, has the nature of a felt termination. When man senses other bodies, he experiences his own bodily feeling as a force spread in extension, a force foreign to him. This force cannot come to him from the matter of other bodies, matter which in itself is inert. It can come to him only from a sentient principle of these bodies foreign to him, a principle that Rosmini calls *corporeal*.

Every real entity has a sensory principle, that is, an activity of its own. Man feels only his own sensory principle. He hears only the culmination, the matter, of the other bodies which is the effect of their bodily principle. Instead, the acting principle of other bodies remains "unknown" to him,[51]

---

48. Rosmini, *T*, para. 1356.

49. For this paragraph I referred to the articles by Gray, "Rosmini, la realtà pura," and Brunello, "Principi corporei."

50. Rosmini, *NE*, paras. 855, 856, 869, 1014n, 1216, 1217n.

51. Rosmini, *PY* 2, para. 820.

because it is "an agent that escapes our experience."[52] We can form only a negative concept of it, as of a reality prior to feeling. And when one's own sensory principle feels in itself the force of other bodies, which is almost a form of violence, then it can be said that the communication of substances occurs, in the sense that one's own body becomes the end of both principles (that of one's own body and that of the body of others) and allows them to come into contact.

The proper principle is the soul, the foreign one is the principle of bodies not ours, "the living principle of bodily matter."[53] And sometimes in the same soul we witness the "struggle between several principles."[54]

It should be noted that matter exists only if it is combined with the principle, which is equivalent to reducing the subsistence of matter to that of spirit, that is, to affirm that reality cannot exist without synthesizing with the ideal. Matter is the way bodily principles appear to each other in the world. Pure reality is conceived in fact as the transcendent place of spirits, so there is a spiritual world underlying that of matter, which is conceived according to spirits.

In this view the whole of matter is considered to be a combination of animate atoms, whereby "life, the sensory soul can be found united to matter even when it does not appear with extra-subjective external phenomena."[55] Here Rosmini recovers, though modifying it, the hypothesis of the general animation of matter, a hypothesis that meanders through the history of philosophy, "although such a concept has been filled with a thousand errors."[56]

Animate atoms, depending on their arrangement and organization, give rise to the passage from a latent life to a feeling, respectively, of extended continuity (matter), of occasional excitation, of harmonic excitation (animal), of the sentient principle the idea (man).[57] These principles all derive from an original, simple and unlimited principle, which constitutes the soul of the world, "a primitive principle . . . which could be called . . . the *common soul*, or rather the common principle of sensitive souls (of bodily feeling)."[58] The consequence is that all real entities are rooted and have in common a reality prior to them. The bodily principle remains the principle

---

52. Rosmini, *T*, para. 1416.
53. Rosmini, *T*, para. 656.
54. Rosmini, *T*, para. 1437.
55. Rosmini, *PY* 2, para. 500.
56. Rosmini, *PY* 2, para. 508.
57. Rosmini, *PY* 2, paras. 533–41.
58. Rosmini, *PY* 2, paras. 554–58.

and center of spontaneous motion in nature, a dark force that modifies our own feeling through our body.

One might wonder if there was any identification between bodily principles and angels. Rosmini does not give a definitive answer, because he reserved the right to deal with the question of angels at another time. From the notes on reality, we know that for him angels have no matter, they are therefore separate intelligences, and to identify them is the creative act.[59] To be separated from each other they must have a feeling of their own, even if incorporeal.[60] As pure spirits, to be perceived by mortal men, they should present themselves with a bodily garment.[61] In a note concerning cosmology he mentions that he would deal with angels when he spoke of the "organs of the universe," that is, of the "intelligences active with respect to matter."[62] From what he left us, however, it would seem that, although he found similarities, he did not want to identify bodily principles with angels.

Agape Ontology

I would like to end my considerations with an overall judgment on Rosmini's ontology or metaphysics. It presents itself essentially as a metaphysics of charity, as an *agape ontology*, that is, open to the vision of a God who is essentially love, "loving intelligence,"[63] "lives to himself and is essentially feeling."[64] The creation of man and the world is seen as the external effect of God's free love. There is no *need* for the world to exist. At most there is a *moral congruity*, in the sense that the will of God, although not forced by anyone, freely decides to want even the finite good in addition to the infinite good that is himself. God therefore wants the creature to share in his own love. Therefore, the reason for the existence of the world must be sought "in the depths of the moral being."[65]

If we pass from the universe in general to the intelligent creature in particular, we notice that man comes out of the creative act of God, which is an act of love, he travels his short or long existential path always sustained by the love of God, he has before him the freedom to return to the God from whom he started, and thus participate in the eternal beatitude of God. The

59. Rosmini, *T*, para. 2134.
60. Rosmini, *T*, para. 2390.
61. Rosmini, *T*, para. 2146.
62. Rosmini, *T*, para. 2936.
63. Rosmini, *T*, para. 466.
64. Rosmini, *T*, para. 748.
65. Rosmini, *T*, para. 2029.

creation and government of the world thus unfold in a series of free and conscious acts suggested by the love of God, which is "the love of Himself, who is also loved in the creatures."[66]

Man is endowed with a natural light, the intelligible being, which is a free gift of God's love. This intelligible being, by the qualities it carries within itself, is the divine in nature, more similar to God than to creatures.[67] Therefore, each individual is the bearer of a permanent gift, the light of reason, which recalls within itself the need to bring oneself into God. In fact, thanks to this gift, he can kindle the will that is fundamentally the desire for good, and guide his reason towards the ultimate goal of every human person, union with God. Hence one of the most stimulating Rosminian definitions of man. "Man is a power, the last act of which is to join the limitless Being by loving knowledge."[68] *Loving knowledge* means that human reason freely comes to understand both the gift received and the need to complete the truth he has theoretically seen in a practical act of love, an act that by essence is unitive.

The logical process of the ontological chain of being, within the Trinitarian process begins with God the Father, beginning and cause, continues in the Son who is the substantial object, closes with the Holy Spirit who is love, union and culmination of the love of the Father and the Son, God-Trinity "is the same loving subject (Father), understood for Himself and thus all science (Word), and then loved for Himself, all perfect love (Holy Spirit)."[69] (n. 1032 note). In the likeness of this process, creation was realized, with its three forms: real (corresponding to the Father), ideal (corresponding to the Word), moral (corresponding to the Holy Spirit). It should be noted that both the process within the Trinity and the effect of the creative act culminate in the moral form which is the joining of the other two forms. And the moral form is nothing but love.

God created the universe by contemplating it in the Word and abstracting from it the contemplated specimen, which Rosmini calls *an exemplar of the world*.[70] Man does not have the vision of the exemplar of the world, because this original model remains in God. He can only get an imperfect idea of it by gathering with experience and contemplation what he can. The

66. Rosmini, *T*, para. 51.

67. In commenting on the definition of created man *in the image and similitude of God*, Rosmini explains that the mind in and of itself is a subject contingent. But as it is designed, nonexistent in the ideal being, which is the image and similitude of God, it therefore participates in the image of God (*T*, paras. 2620–21).

68. Rosmini, *T*, para. 35.

69. Rosmini, *T*, para. 1032n.

70. Rosmini, *T*, paras. 369, 438, 465.

more he comes to know of reality, the more he comes to know new pieces of that ordered and beautiful mosaic that is in the mind of God. And the more he knows about the world and its order, the more he participates in some way in the wisdom of God, helping himself with a deontological reasoning, which from what we experience finds something else that must be there, even though hidden from us but implicit, it passes from being to having to be. Here ontology takes an immense step: from the knowledge of finite entities, it passes to an "ideological first," evident in itself, and then rises to the recognition of a "theosophical first."[71] To recognize things as they are in the exemplar of the world, that is, in the mind of God, means to affirm reality in analogy to what God did in creating it: "man pronounces what God has previously pronounced."[72]

But the wisdom that man with his natural forces can acquire always remains a limited wisdom, due to the natural limitations of his mind. He cannot always respond to what he knows by returning love, because there is in man a radical evil that is the original sin. So, the wisdom that can be acquired by human strength is not sufficient to save the creature. It is still a wisdom that leads to the threshold of salvation, but to cross this threshold reason understands that something else is needed. At this point the goodness of God intervenes once again, and with the incarnation of the Word brings man the gift of justification, that is, opens the doors to salvation.

Then, human wisdom is enriched by supernatural wisdom, and the human creature is given back the freedom to pass,[73] if he wants and with the help of grace, from the journey of the mind *towards Christ*, to the itinerary of life *in Christ*, which is carried out through the *imitation* of Christ. Here the *light of truth* is completed as *a fire of charity*;[74] and "in this *charity* exercised in *truth*[75] genuinely consists the work of *Christian wisdom*."[76] Christian wisdom thus becomes an *anthropology of charity*, and charity takes the two forms of *fraternity* (charity among believers) and humanity or "Christian philanthropy" (charity towards all).[77]

Rosmini also wondered how a person eager to put Christian wisdom into practice could live. He began to try for himself. He soon found himself

---

71. Rosmini, *T*, paras. 1177–78.

72. Rosmini, *T*, paras. 2662, 2763.

73. Rosmini warns us that freedom "is in the *can* do, not in the *doing*" (*T*, para. 2225).

74. Rosmini, *IP*, para. 198.

75. See Eph 4:15.

76. Rosmini, *IP*, 183, para. 104.

77. Rosmini, *IP*, para. 106.

next to people eager to share his experience. Thus, the Istituto-Società della Carità was born, to which the Sisters of Providence later also adhered. The constitutions that he wrote for this institute of his follow the agape vision of his ontology. In fact, Charity, from which the society he founded takes its name, is the God-Charity of the apostle John. Since God is essentially being, the love that comes from him takes the three forms of being, forms that transposed into the field of charity become, respectively, *temporal charity, intellectual charity, spiritual charity*. In these three forms of charity lies "the ontological origin of all good."[78] The Rosminian who is part of the Society of Charity, while continuing to do the best possible in the specific field of charity entrusted to him, must within his heart always remain open to all forms of charity. To the point of being able to pass from one degree to another, from one form to another, if God's will so orders him.

Bibliography

Brunello, Bruno. "I 'principi corporei' secondo Rosmini." *Rivista Rosminiana* 4 (1971) 265–69.

Ferraris, Maurizio, ed. *Storia dell'ontologia*. Milan: Bompiani, 2009.

Gray, Carlo. "Rosmini, la realtà pura e i principi corporei." *Rivista Rosminiana* 4 (1936) 197–208; 1 (1937) 22–30; 2 (1937) 124–230; 1 (1938) 20–29; 4 (1938) 260–68.

Muratore, Umberto. *La Teosofia di Rosmini. Sunto organico elementare con brevi commenti*. Stresa, It.: Rosminiane, 2015.

Rosmini, Antonio. *Introduzione alla filosofia*. Edited by Pier P. Ottonello. ENC 2. Rome: Città Nuova, 1979.

———. *Nuovo Saggio sull'origine delle idee*. Edited by Gaetano Messina. 3 vols. ENC 3–5. Rome: Città Nuova, 2003–2005.

———. *Psicologia*. Edited by Vincenzo Sala. 4 vols. ENC, 9, 9/A, 10, 10/A. Rome: Città Nuova, 1988–1989.

———. *Teosofia*. Edited by Samuele F. Tadini. Milan: Bompiani, 2011.

Tadini, Samuele F. *Il problema di Dio nella metafisica rosminiana*. Milan: Vita e Pensiero, 2015.

———. *La teosofia di Rosmini. Invito alla lettura*. Stresa, It.: Rosminiane, 2012.

Varzi, Achille C. *Ontologia*. Bari, It.: Laterza, 2008.

---

78. Rosmini, *T*, para. 1034.

2

Identity "as" Difference

"A-dialectical" Denial in the Rosminian God

MASSIMO DONÀ

It is necessary "to identify in Rosmini and to separate the speculative content from the contingent form with which that content was clothed in order to conform and adapt to the moral character of the time."
—Giovanni Gentile

Rosmini notes in his indeterminate being of some certainties that are simply relations of the mind with the end of his intuition, subsequent to the act of intuition, which, however, grasping the entity, grasps it as purely indeterminate . . . Spaventa understood him very well, when he observed that the Rosminian entity is not the result of judgment, but prior to any judgment, because every judgment presupposes it.
—Giovanni Gentile

ROSMINI RIGHTLY POINTS OUT that the entity, although always and in any case *one* (each entity, being what it is, is always also *an* entity: precisely, what it is), "it is not always simple: in fact, there are many compound entities."[1] But how is it possible (Rosmini rightly asks) that "every entity is one, yet

---

1. Rosmini, *Theos*, 1:564.

not every entity is simple?"[2]—provided that it is agreed that the One is, as such, "simple."

Here, according to Rosmini, it is only a certain type of simplicity that "can never be lacking in any entity . . . and which is therefore indivisible from the quality of *one*, essential to the entity";[3] and which therefore must also be appropriate to those entities that are not simple, even though they are, each individually, one.

But then he also notes that "when it is said that an entity is multiple, it is not said that this entity is more than one entity";[4] but only "that in the very unity of the entity falls a multiplicity not of entities, but of something else, that is, of elements that make up the entity."[5]

In short, when unity and multiplicity are preached of the same entity, Rosmini specifies that "these two qualities of the same entity are not preached under the same aspect, but under a different aspect."[6] That is to say that unity is preached of the entity—Rosmini again specifies—while "the multiplicity and composition are not preached of the entity, but of its components."[7]

And then, he further specifies that the concept of compound makes known a *dianoetic essence*; such that "the act of the mind is involved in forming it."[8] Which is what, always in his opinion, must also be said of the "real" compound (and not only of the objective or dialectical one); a concept that "imports a *relationship* of the components with the one that results from it, and every relationship can have its foundation in the subsistence, but the complete nature of the relationship cannot receive it elsewhere than in the mind, which alone embraces the two extremes of the relationship."[9]

This last clarification is very important; here, Rosmini makes us aware of the fact that only the mind can establish "relationships," or rather, thought. In short, where there is multiplicity, thought must also be at work. It is the latter, in fact, that connects and relates (*logon, legein*); so as to allow us to deal with something like a "multiple."

---

2. Rosmini, *Theos*, 1:564.
3. Rosmini, *Theos*, 1:564.
4. Rosmini, *Theos*, 1:565.
5. Rosmini, *Theos*, 1:565.
6. Rosmini, *Theos*, 1:565.
7. Rosmini, *Theos*, 1:565.
8. Rosmini, *Theos*, 1:565.
9. Rosmini, *Theos*, 1:566.

IDENTITY "AS" DIFFERENCE

It being understood that, to be thought, it is in any case a multiplicity held together (insofar as it is relational) by thought. Because, perhaps, to the latter, it is always and, in any case, "a" multiplicity.

In fact, it is "in" the relationship and "only in" the relationship that the many *are one*. It is precisely the latter that unifies them. Or rather, to design the unity (an existence) in relation to which, only the elements that are preached from time to time are recognized. Therefore, "a mental element *always* enters"[10] in compounds.

In any case, one thing is certain, continues Rosmini a few pages later; that the human mind comes to make a comparison "between this multiplicity and subjective variability and the object that in itself does not really suffer it ... and he says *precisely* that the object is identical to itself."[11] Because the latter is "immune from the differences found in the acts of the subject."[12]

And, it is already clear for this reason, in the eyes of Rosmini, that "the word *identity* always implies *also* some relationship with a *diversity* and without this one would never think of that which expresses nothing else (*therefore*) if not the *denial of diversity*."[13] Hence, the inevitable question: "Is identity therefore something negative, and not even positive?"[14]

Of course, because it is also only by noting that he does not suffer from any diversity related to thinking, that the latter "connects" the object in some way—albeit in a sort of inalienable identity with itself—to the multiplicity he denied.

Then, Rosmini asks, will it also have to be said of identity that it is constituted only in the act by virtue of which it "denies" multiplicity? Is identity a purely *negative* concept?

This is difficult to admit, he continues, because, if diversity always has to do with something defective and missing, how could we not attribute to its opposite (that is, identity) an eminently positive nature?

In any case, even in book 3 of *Ontology (Ontologia)* Rosmini reiterates and explains, with even greater abundance of details, that the pure being "is not threefold in itself, but it has a triple relationship of identity to the three forms under which finite and determined entities are conceived ... in short, the mind does not make that distinction for itself, but takes it away from the determined entities, and applies it to the pure and indeterminate being."[15]

---

10. Rosmini, *Theos*, 1:566.
11. Rosmini, *Theos*, 1:594.
12. Rosmini, *Theos*, 1:594.
13. Rosmini, *Theos*, 1:594.
14. Rosmini, *Theos*, 1:594.
15. Rosmini, *Theos*, 2:54.

In his view, *it is always the mind that becomes responsible for the triplicity of being*; that is, for the fact that an identity can, on the model of finite and determined entities, be "thought" and made multiple. "Although then the mind thus implements distinctions that are not there."[16]

Looking at the determined entities, then, the mind creates distinctions that are not its own (that is, of being); or rather of its perfect unity. In fact, for Rosmini being is not thought; however, "being is also thought."[17] Of course, it (being) has an "essential relationship with thought"[18]—to the point that he notes, "If all 'mind' (thought) were taken away, there would no longer be any being."[19]

A very strange relationship is thus determined between "being" and "thought"; an *essential* relationship, certainly, which in any case, does not distract us from their *distinction* (so that we can say that "there is a distinction between what is contained in the concept of being, and what is contained in the concept of thought").[20] A paradoxical relationship, undoubtedly; which forces us to recognize how, in any case—without prejudice to their distinction (without prejudice to the distinction between being and thought)—if we dared to eliminate the mind (thought) *in its entirety*, there would be no longer any being left!

An affirmation that seems rather to imply the perfect overlap of one with the other.

For Rosmini, there remains an unbridgeable gap between one and the other; this does not prevent him from pointing out how "these essential relationships between being and mind, far from counterfeiting or falsifying being, are those that at the same time constitute it and make it known."[21]

Rosmini, to be brief, knows very well that "if it were not the object of our mind, being pure and indeterminate," it would be absolutely unpronounceable, unthinkable, and incommunicable. "It would be impossible to think about it."[22]

Yet, a few lines later, he also reiterates that "this (pure and indeterminate) being is not intuited by the mind itself, because the mind that senses it is subsistent and determined, and it, instead, is an indeterminate, as we

---

16. Rosmini, *Theos*, 2:54–55.
17. Rosmini, *Theos*, 2:56.
18. Rosmini, *Theos*, 2:56.
19. Rosmini, *Theos*, 2:56.
20. Rosmini, *Theos*, 2:56.
21. Rosmini, *Theos*, 2:56.
22. Rosmini, *Theos*, 2:57.

IDENTITY "AS" DIFFERENCE

said; and, as such, cannot exist."[23] The mind, although it knows how to think, also knows, continues Rosmini, "that it is not the indeterminate and impersonal being; it knows that it is a determined entity and a person who senses another."[24]

In short, it is the determination of the mind that constitutes itself as the reason for the certainties that the being definitely cannot present where it is conceived in terms of pure *indeterminacy*—or of pure *unity*. The mind, therefore, grasps the specificities of the world with which it always has to deal and, as determined, finds them in the form of a multiplicity as the very essence of being; like the essence of being that, again for Rosmini, "remains the essential form of intelligence."[25]

On the other hand, it is precisely for this reason that "the pure being intuited by intelligence is the intelligibility of things and this is the essence of being, so that the essence of being cannot stand without being intelligible."[26] In a word, "the essence of being is the essential form of intelligence."[27]

Interesting, in this regard, is Rosmini's radical overturning of a very long tradition that, from Heraclitus to Gentile, has always seen the absolute indeterminacy delivered to the subject (or thought, or mind) and therefore even "the power of the negative" (think of Hegel's logic of essence). For Rosmini, in fact, as we have just seen, it is not so much the reflection, the subject or the thought that becomes indeterminate (condemned to say no), but rather what thought is allowed to be conceive (and it is connected to thought by an essential relationship), but it is not, as such, "thought." Rather, *pure positivity*; pure being, however indeterminate, and therefore coinciding with that identity which, if on the one hand it denies the multiplicity given to it by thought, on the other hand it offers itself to thought as the being that the latter absolutely cannot help but posit, even just to be the thought it is.

To sum up, the Rosminian subject has very little to do with the impalpable indeterminacy characterizing the modern subject in an increasingly clear way; that is, with the elusive ghost perfectly embodied by Iago—who, not surprisingly, said, "I am not what I am." Or with the crumbling mask tragically staged by Pirandello. It is rather the world that, in the eyes of Rosmini, appears as a real reflection of the original chaos; or as a determination that it is always and only for thought to return to the radical indeterminacy

23. Rosmini, *Theos*, 2:57.
24. Rosmini, *Theos*, 2:57.
25. Rosmini, *Theos*, 2:58.
26. Rosmini, *Theos*, 2:58–59.
27. Rosmini, *Theos*, 2:58.

of pure being—of which it serves precisely as an original predicate. Thus, returning it to its original "negation" (*negation of diversity*, Rosmini called it in the second book of *Ontologia*, dedicated to being one—in particular, I refer to article 1 of the eighth chapter of the second book, the one entitled *Teoria dell'identità*); *negation* of that same multiplicity or diversity that thought knows and experiences as it itself, first and foremost, *de-termined*.

Of course, it should also be pointed out at this point that Rosmini's *being* does not reject differences at all, although it is, in itself, perfectly indeterminate and simple; it understands them, albeit "denying" them. It does not reject them by itself, but understands them *in the very act in which it denies them*—reaffirming, just like that, and *ad libitum*, its own perfect *indeterminacy*. Which relates precisely to establishment of the "objective" form of being, as a real principle of the "relationship." It being understood that the relationship is placed and known at the same time by the subjected mind "with the act of positing itself as an object."[28]

In any case, the mind places itself first as an object to itself; it sees itself as *objectum*; and, in so doing, it inscribes the being thought of by itself, even in this first and original form of relationality. The mind thinks of being as *something else*; what the object must always also indicate, while constituting itself as an effect of a relationality entirely connected to the thinking mind. Like the *other* to be thought of, that is, but at the same time as radically unthinkable, if it were not for the simple awareness of the fact that this "denial of thought" must in any case be thought of; while allowing itself to be thought only as that which, to thought, always and only gives itself in the articulation of a "relationship."

The mind, in fact, does not see *absolutely* what the indeterminate being is; here is the unthinkableness of being conceived in its absoluteness; "the mind instead sees that being absolutely is, and to see this it is enough to have in mind the indeterminate being as that which contains the essence of being."[29] The mind sees that being absolutely is, of course; "but it does not see that it is an absolutely indeterminate being."[30] That is, it does not see what it is in its absoluteness. It only sees that it "absolutely is."[31]

In a word, it only sees that being absolutely is. *A later search* would allow it to know "whether that being that absolutely is, is determined or indeterminate."[32]

28. Rosmini, *Theos*, 2:220.
29. Rosmini, *Theos*, 2:133.
30. Rosmini, *Theos*, 2:133.
31. Rosmini, *Theos*, 2:133.
32. Rosmini, *Theos*, 2:133.

The mind sees the absolute being as what *there must be*; but it seems to be capable of sensibly saying nothing about it, while recognizing it precisely on the basis of the illumination it produces; that is, produced by the same principle from which this same argument receives its strength.

"That same indeterminate being [is] the object of intuition that contains the pure essence of being," by virtue of which the mind sees what is convenient or inconvenient for the being and therefore also judges whether certain certainties and terms are lacking in the face of intuition.[33]

The mind knows that it "is," but it does not know "what it is." *It does not see what it absolutely is.* It sees only that this indeterminate being, while denying them, "does not exclude certainties or terminations."[34] It sees only "that it does not show them to intuition and does not exclude them."[35]

And it knows that being so pure (separate from its certainties) it manifests the essence of being in such a way that the mind can know "what being is, although it does not know where it ends."[36]

It sees above all (in this sense *it knows what being is*, despite its *unknowability*) that "being would not be, if it were not in itself and only appeared to a mind."[37]

In short, being cannot be resolved in its appearance to a mind; much less to the mind that knows it. It must always also be *"in itself"*; and therefore, it cannot allow itself to be resolved in what the mind knows of the matter.

This is an interesting way of conceiving the unknowability and knowability of a pure being, also valid as a principle of everything; a being that "does not" exclude the many, despite being multiple precisely because it is thought (posited) as an object by a subject. On the other hand, without a mind (without a subject), we would not even know of the absoluteness of a being that is in no way relativized by this, its always constituting itself also as an object for a subject (that is, as *relativum*), which is not relativized simply because this relationship remains precisely the "original negation," far beyond any abstractly "defective" sense of purity or simplicity.

By now, Rosmini has decided to inscribe in the divine reality the perfect unity and the relationship (multiplicity) without denying either one or the other. Without making unity manifold or transforming the composite of multiplicity into simplicity. Without preventing either form from "being

---

33. Rosmini, *Theos*, 2:133.
34. Rosmini, *Theos*, 2:134.
35. Rosmini, *Theos*, 2:134.
36. Rosmini, *Theos*, 2:134.
37. Rosmini, *Theos*, 2:134.

what it is"; one is perfect unity and the other is real and no less absolute multiplicity. And he does so by precisely distinguishing the *absolute* from *absoluteness*; that is, the notion of absolute from what would be, more properly, absolute. That is, distinguishing the "positing" *of what is absolute* from the "absolute being" of *what is posited precisely as absolute.*

There is a "relationship" that requires the very simple to constitute itself as its *negation*; as a negation of a relationship that, alone, moreover, could have posited it as so existing—as a *negation of the relationship that posits it.*

The absolute, then, is not such (that is, absolute) only insofar as it *is posited and recognized* as such; but at the same time nothing can ever be in a certain way except when it is *posited and recognized as such*. Therefore, there is certainly an original inseparability of "being" and "thinking" (Parmenides!!!); that, Rosmini understands and recognizes perfectly. But at the same time, this does not prevent him from recognizing that what is constituted by virtue of this same "relationship" is something anything but relational.

Although, even this *non-relational* recognition has an essential relationship with the relationality it has denied.

In short, the indeterminate being is one, but it does not exclude multiplicity; the same applies to multiplicity, which must always be one—even if only in order to be able to resolve itself in that particular multiplicity that it claims to be. In that (*one*) multiplicity.

Therefore, according to Rosmini, "what is one subsists in multiplicity, and multiplicity is in what is one."[38] Which, however, is what can only happen "in the Supreme Being, where . . . *while* the completed essence is perfectly one and does not admit plurality, *it is also true that* it subsists in an identical manner in the three persons who are three subsistent relatives."[39] Three Persons who, for Rosmini in fact, are never more or less than each other, "because each is the whole absolute being identical."[40]

In short, in being absolute, there is an intimate union of absolute and relative to be given; although, "we can neither conceive the *absolute* without the *relative*, nor the relative without the absolute, except by way of abstraction";[41] in such a way that the thought stops either of them "neglecting the other."[42]

---

38. Rosmini, *Theos*, 2:231.
39. Rosmini, *Theos*, 2:231.
40. Rosmini, *Theos*, 2:231.
41. Rosmini, *Theos*, 2:231.
42. Rosmini, *Theos*, 2:231.

IDENTITY "AS" DIFFERENCE

For this reason, Rosmini suggests that the thing signified should be distinguished from the way it is signified.

It is in fact the way to make multiple what, as a signified thing, remains perfectly simple and "immune to all plurality."[43] As far as it is meant *in this or that way*; and hence destined to involve "a relationship, since the word and the concept of absolute, is a word and a concept relative to the relative that excludes."[44]

Let us also say that the *way* of expressing the simplicity of the pure and indeterminate being is necessarily *relational*; that is, we say that the essence of the original unity appears understandable only because it is multiplied, and therefore betrayed, by the "logos." That is, from the thought that it posits; which says and, in saying, precisely distinguishes (at least the said from saying). Logos, Son; what the Father says to express the one God who is neither Father nor Son, without excluding either one or the other. Being everything, identical and perfectly indeterminate, in each of the two. Becoming *ab origine* distinct, and therefore Person; so that even the relationship is always and only as a Person. Not limiting himself to relating the Father and the Son; this last relationship (that of Father and Son) is in fact the very "way" in which the one God expresses himself; precisely as the Son—that is, as the Son of a Father. And therefore, as a relationship that leaves unexpressed what is said about it; also because the relationship itself, far from constituting itself as transparency capable of revealing the true face of divine unity, itself becomes a Person, that is, Spirit. Therefore, the Subject determines the various entities; "we do not know it either intuitively, neither for an analysis of the object of intuition, nor for an analysis of the entities perceived by us, the nature of this determining subject, and therefore we can only have a negative cognition of it."[45] In short, the "reason for the diversity of finite real entities . . . remains hidden from us."[46] And therefore, the determining being that remains pure act one and identical remains hidden."[47]

That which makes the Father, the Son, and the Spirit, the same God remains hidden. That is, their sameness, that despite their diversity always and in any case manifests in the form of three Persons. To the point where the religion devoted to them is defined, without any approximation, *monotheism*.

---

43. Rosmini, *Theos*, 2:232.
44. Rosmini, *Theos*, 2:232.
45. Rosmini, *Theos*, 1:379.
46. Rosmini, *Theos*, 1:378.
47. Rosmini, *Theos*, 1:378.

In a word, Rosmini tries to account for the irreplaceable role of the Son as *Logos*, or "relationship." And he tries to account for the originality of this relationship (*in the beginning was the Son*), without diminishing the absoluteness of an identity that, in the relationship itself, constitutes precisely what, for it, always and only said (regardless of the way, always relational, in which the subject and the object of saying are expressed); that which, in the relational *way*, which is moreover inevitable (insofar as it is original) its own, is always said and meant as the same God—what the subject posits by positing himself as an object to himself. Which he posits as a "thing in itself"—of which the subject will only be able to know the objective declination—and which we could define as the objective way of its being more proper. And therefore, its very intrinsic and absolute *unknowability*. If it is true that "identity with oneself makes the 'being' of the formula *being is being a decidedly incommunicable property*."[48] It being understood that, as an "object" of the mind, this pure and indeterminate being ("which appears to thought as antecedent to its forms")[49] hides not only its absolute unity, but also the multiple forms ("he, as an entity thought of by man, is a being that does not show, but closely hides the forms"),[50] those that "while not excluding or denying, which indeed contain all three virtually."[51]

That is why, according to Rosmini, this pure being has two fundamental characteristics: "the infinite extension and the lack of understanding: infinite extension, since if it had limits it would no longer be a pure being and the news of these limits could be acquired from those who knew first the being and who received them, so that the limits are logically subsequent to being; understanding nothing, for it could not comprehend except its limitations, or reality. But those and this are posterior, and such, that by sensing the pure being can be known by successive acts."[52]

To come to the point, for Rosmini, intuiting the pure being, its perfect identity, its unbreakable simplicity, does not mean "knowing it." And therefore, what the subject has before him, in his positing (in positing as *logos*), is the same *unknowable* to which the terms of the subject-object "relationship" refer; mentioning it for the simple fact that they show themselves *denied* "in" and "by" the relationship cannot avoid becoming (*third*) Person. The one in relation to which, once again, the pure identity of being will be denied—given that, to be neither Father nor Son, means necessarily being

---

48. Rosmini, *Theos*, 1:304.
49. Rosmini, *Theos*, 2:261.
50. Rosmini, *Theos*, 2:261.
51. Rosmini, *Theos*, 2:261.
52. Rosmini, *Theos*, 2:31.

something else: that is, the Spirit. If only for the fact that everyone is made to distinguish the relationship of subject and object from the ones that, in this same relationship, always constitute themselves, one as a subject and the other as an object.

In short, the indeterminate being (the perfect unity of being), intuited but not known, indicates for Rosmini something that lives only in People (no abstract "excess" is in fact conceived in these pages), in relation to a mind (logos) intended to distinguish the subject from the object (Father from the Son), but that, in doing so, and doing it originally (in the beginning it was the Logos)—if it is true that there would be no indeterminate existence without a mind capable of conceiving and placing it as such (as the content of a knowing that always happens in the way of an objectification)—, it makes a third Person able to show, even more precisely (if ever it were needed), that, in relating to the Father and of the Son (of the subject and of the object), the identity is not indicated as a third party, left to appear by the indeterminacy connected to the purely negative form of the relationship (which would sanction precisely the "knowability" of the indeterminate being to).

Also, because the pure being itself is indeterminate, like the relationship between Father and Son, it lives only in this relationship.

Rather a third party is indicated who is not, even it, "the indeterminate being," but only the determinacy that always and only belongs to the manifestation of that indeterminacy; which, if it appears, properly, is determined. And so, it is denied.

In short, it is always in the denial of some determination that the identical, the one God, manifests himself, showing himself with the face of a Person. Because "*being* is presented to our spirit with a limitation that is not its own, but proceeding from that of our thought."[53]

It is understood that, for Rosmini, there are still two real multiplicities: the first in God, "and this is the one that does not constitute plurality of entities, but of persons, the other that draws its origin from the first, that is, from the divine trinity, is in the world, which is plurality of relative entities."[54]

Even in God, however, we conceive of a twofold multiplicity: one that is not in him, but only in our concepts, and one that is in him truly "independently of our concepts, whose multiplicity is the trinity of *divine*

---

53. Rosmini, *Theos*, 2:33.
54. Rosmini, *Theos*, 3:100.

persons."⁵⁵ And, in relation to this multiplicity, Rosmini specifies, God "is Father, Son and Holy Spirit; and none other than this."⁵⁶

No excess will therefore mar this perfect *multiplicity*; for no abyss, in fact, wounds it. For this reason, it is already in naming God the Father that we should "conceive of him as an infinite *act* of intelligence which, being the very first and absolute, is at the same time *suffered*."⁵⁷

Here is that which must be conceived as a "pure being." Intelligence and being are in fact separated only "for us"; while "when they apply themselves to God, they express only one essence,"⁵⁸ the one that we are never given to see in its ultimate act, but only in its virtuality (the one "intuited by nature, by us").

It is we, in fact, who have a concept of being imperfect. In conceiving God the Father (in relation to the what, and not to the how he is conceived by us), we conceive an infinite "pure, intellectual" act that is not distinguished from his own being. An absolute intellectual act "which is at the same time suffered, having as its object itself to be absolute."⁵⁹ And therefore produces its object, precisely as "absolute"; and produces it, ultimately producing itself (because "being is one without anything remaining outside of it");⁶⁰ that is, generating itself. This is what alludes to his true "fatherhood"; the same that "in God it is absolutely different from the way it is in the finite entities, which have only an analogy with what is in God."⁶¹

But, again for Rosmini, this principle does not resolve his act in the object generated as a Person; but "he produces it as infinitely lovable and loved and loving, because such is the absolute being communicating";⁶² and not only as *intelligible*. For a dynamic that remains that of being pure; which, despite everything, Rosmini continues to define *real essence* as that "we do not see."⁶³ "That *unique essence* in which the said abstract essences are realized and which remains unknown to us, as we said, unless we know we have to be there."⁶⁴ What "cannot" be there, as *something other* from

---

55. Rosmini, *Theos*, 3:101.
56. Rosmini, *Theos*, 3:101.
57. Rosmini, *Theos*, 3:101.
58. Rosmini, *Theos*, 3:102.
59. Rosmini, *Theos*, 3:102.
60. Rosmini, *Theos*, 3:102.
61. Rosmini, *Theos*, 3:103.
62. Rosmini, *Theos*, 3:103.
63. Rosmini, *Theos*, 3:105.
64. Rosmini, *Theos*, 3:105.

IDENTITY "AS" DIFFERENCE

the three Persons, and yet *must* be there, precisely, as their perfect identity. Although not "beyond" the same.

Rather like the absolute opposites (absolute good and evil, absolute being and nothing) that Captain Ahab would like to decide by harpooning once and for all the white Leviathan. The *monstruum* that Melville evokes as an emblem of the fusion that absoluteness makes is in any case phenomenally unexperienceable, nonetheless, making it possible to experience the widespread greyness that the entire color wheel produces, making us believe that there really is, in this world, a high and a low, a good and a bad, etc.

Yes, because absolute identity can reverberate and manifest itself only in the drawing of a truly absolute opposition. That which is never given, if it is true that in this world everything (every reality, every existence) is always good and bad, existing and nonexistent, true and false at the same time.

That which is never given, because the absolute being in which the nature of God consists could never present itself as simply *opposite* to nothing. It is never given except in the absolute relationship that says, for example, that the Father is perfectly distinct from the Son; in a way that is not simply relative, as happens in the horizon drawn by this world. But as perfectly distinct from something else; indeed, so distinct—so radically distinct from the absolutely other—that it no longer implies things, or finite existences, but expresses the only and very simple identity: precisely that of being pure and absolute. What can never be given if not in the inaccessible whiteness that obscures at the highest level the opposition of which the same always remains, despite everything, perfect (and precisely in its *impossibility*) manifestation.

Therefore, Rosmini can affirm that "the Father is the same absolute being, the first act, subject in itself essentially producing, or production, in such a way that all these denominations no longer indicate things, but a single very simple one, on which all agree."[65]

Precisely because this productive act which is the absolute being, the first act, or the essentially productive subego, "it is necessary that it has an object, and can have no other object than itself";[66] therefore, it is in the viscera of being itself—always according to Rosmini—that "a duality is primarily manifested."[67]

Yes, because, only by producing himself could the Father have found himself coming to terms with an *absolute duality*. And therefore, with another in which to find himself mirrored, precisely because he is valid as

---

65. Rosmini, *Theos*, 3:117.
66. Rosmini, *Theos*, 3:117.
67. Rosmini, *Theos*, 3:117.

absolutely *different from himself*. That is, as "absolute" like the Father; and *therefore identical* to the same.

That is, valid as the *other* that the Father himself would have produced, even if not as a simple *effect* of his original productive act.

For Rosmini, in fact, the divine Persons "of the Son and of the Holy Spirit must not be conceived as *effects*, because when the three persons have the whole being identical numerically, and the only way in which the whole being is identical, it is different."[68] Here, in fact, there is no difference between being identical and being different; if it is true that "the only way in which all the identical being is, is different."[69] The Son was begotten, and the Spirit was loved, always according to Rosmini. And the Father was "the *beginning* and not the *cause* of the Trinity."[70] A principle that gives reason for a *distinction* independently from which the Logos certainly could not have been *in the beginning*.

This is the brilliant Rosminian solution to one of the crosses on which thought would be constantly crucified, and that only the Trinitarian dogma could transform into a surprising explanation of the possibility of being, on the part of identity and difference, "perfectly identical" *precisely in constituting themselves as perfectly distinct*. Indeed, as *absolute opposites*.

So as to make the same three Persons irreducible; who, in their distinction, nevertheless show themselves capable of expressing the same God, that is, the same (identical) absoluteness—without any residue—precisely in their "perfect" difference. Consigning their multiplicity, therefore, to a "thinking-relating" function operating in fact already in the heart of divine unity (in the figure of the Son), before being relativized or made dependent on the limited possibilities available to the human.

The relational *logos* is in fact what the perfect unity of God denies, but at the same time recognizes as a condition of a miraculous "excess" that is anything but residual or in some way *determined*. An excess, therefore, capable of becoming a miraculous testimony of a *negativity* certainly unknown to the *logos* in any case decisive articulated by the human intellect, but, always by the same, also experienced . . . at least in terms of unconditional, loving passion.

A feeling whose power cannot and must not be experienced as abstractly extraneous to the rigor of knowing, because, in fact, incessantly operating right in the heart of a cognitive exercise capable of experiencing this unprecedented form of "denial" even if only starting from the fact that,

68. Rosmini, *Theos*, 3:118.
69. Rosmini, *Theos*, 3:118.
70. Rosmini, *Theos*, 3:119.

of the same, it can always be said that it exists . . . even if it is known only by virtue of a how that, in any case, far from translating it into a positive "method," will be experienced only by virtue of that absolute loving passion that always knows how to make everything irrefutable and indestructible creative power.

Bibliography

Rosmini, Antonio. *Teosofia*. Edited by Maria A. Raschini and Pier P. Ottonello. 6 vols. ENC 12–17. Rome: Città Nuova 1998–2002.

3

Laicity of Rosminian Theoresis

SAMUELE FRANCESCO TADINI

A Proposal for Escaping Marginality

THE CONCEPT OF *THEORESIS*, as I have already pointed out elsewhere,[1] is the expression of the logic of the thinking thought of the concrete subject. We could say that it is the dynamic through which the subject, the concrete I, thinks according to truth in their utmost freedom, that is, free from any form of conditioning. Theoretical thought, if it is such, is amplifying and dynamic, that is, *theoresis*, thinking thought; which is to say speculation of the intelligence of the concrete subject in action in the process and procedurality in which *logic* and *ethics* contribute to explain the ontoprismatic aspects that the investigated object presents.

In the context of Rosminian thought we are faced with a *theoresis* that finally becomes theory, that is, thinking thought as set out in his works; and it is precisely with regard to this explication that interpretations can be advanced that elsewhere[2] I have found to be *legitimate* and *illegitimate* in the light of what I have defined as a "chrono-theoretical" mode of reading of the Rosminian text: taking into account the when, the how, and the why

---

1. See Tadini, "Interpretazione 'crono-teoretica,'" 13.
2. See Tadini, "Necessario chiarimento metodologico," 29–30.

a given text was exposed, in fact, it is possible to adequately consider the objective data that can be traced in the very context in which a given theory was put forward; so that "this mode of interpretation attempts to answer the following questions: *when* did a certain theory arise? (chronological element); *how* did a certain theory arise? (logical-procedural element); *why* did a certain theory arise? (motivational element)."[3]

It should also be noted that Rosmini, like every thinker, possesses a *theoretical device*, that is, a fundamental nucleus of his *theoresis*, which can be understood as the "essence of the theory." Depending on how this device is interpreted, we can derive different consequences and make the Rosminian theoresis more or less performative. If we consider what historiographically and theoretically, beyond the most varied interpretations, is considered as the fundamental theoretical nucleus of Rosminian metaphysical thought, we realize that it is essentially made up of two elements: the *idea of being* and the *fundamental bodily feeling*. This essential nucleus, however, has been variously understood and where the problematicity has been identified in *innatism* or *a-priorism* (either to create, especially in the Catholic context, the Rosmini/Tommaso contrast; or to foster the interpretation of the "Italian Rosmini Kant"), without construing an alternative way of seeing *how* that particular *type* of Rosminian innatism has been configured, a triple "evaluative prejudice" has survived—in an almost decisive way—that has compromised for a long time the possibility of a revival of the Rosminian theoresis in the context of the contemporary metaphysical debate (at least from the Seventies of the twentieth century onwards), which, it must be remembered, moves in a secular environment, not necessarily secularist, but which certainly rejects—*right or wrong*—any form of conditioning of a theological-confessional nature.

This "evaluative bias" is configured in this threefold way:

1. The *innatism* of which Rosmini has been accused countless times refers to a Platonic tradition, whose metaphysical presuppositions of transcendence are rejected in the contemporary context. The only form of "accepted" Platonism, beyond the historiographical and reconstructive aspect of the "history" of Platonism, is the mathematical one of Bernays, Cantor, Frege, Russell, and Gödel, which is configured as a sort of realistic conception of mathematical and logical entities. In the current context, in fact, no one speaks of "meta-Platonism" and very few have adequately understood what this "meta-Platonism" can be after the gentilian season.

---

3. See Tadini, "Interpretazione 'crono-teoretica,'" 17.

2. The conception of *metaphysics* expressed by Rosmini in *Theosophy (Teosofia)* is as follows: "discipline that surrounds the entity considered in its entirety,"⁴ while in the current context the term *metaphysics* means "many things."

3. Rosmini was also a theologian and moreover Catholic, so his Christian philosophy, in Heideggerian terms, would have been oxymoronic, but perfectly suited to being "theologized." Now, theologization is a possible operation, but one that leads to self-exclusion of the theoretical scope of an assertion, as considered, by the current metaphysical debate, as conditioned by dogmatic elements; so, what remains of Rosmini in the contemporary international metaphysical debate is only the recognition of having been a great metaphysicist in the context of the "*history* of metaphysics,"⁵ that is—to put it bluntly—a museum piece that has served its purpose. So, it is not surprising that in the international philosophical field Rosminian ontology and metaphysics are almost absent today, since they are not attributable (whether we like to admit it or not) to the dictates provided for by the current dominant lines; and where, in the recent past, a critical, "ideal," and constructive dialogue could also have become possible, as I have shown elsewhere,⁶ proposals published have been lacking until today that would make available the texts of the Rosminian tradition of "critical metaphysics"⁷ not bound to the dominant paradigm,⁸

---

4. Rosmini, "Prefazione," para. 2.

5. On this point, however, there are discordances. If we leave aside specific monographs and dwell on the most recent manuals published in Italy on the subject in question, it is easy to note that Rosmini's ontology and metaphysics are adequately treated by Mondin (see *Storia della metafisica*, 3:423–66) and by Krienke (see "Metafisica di Rosmini"), while they do not find space either within the *Storia dell'ontologia* edited by Maurizio Ferraris, nor in the most recent volume edited by Fausto Fraisopi entitled *Ontologie*.

6. See Tadini: "Rosmini e nuova metafisica"; "Teosofia rosminiana e ontologie"; "Teologia naturale rosminiana"; "Metafisica rosminiana."

7. I mean that theoretical tradition which combines the need for semantic rigorization of the Rosminian text of Giuseppe Buroni with the essentialization of the Rosminian theoretical nucleus of Vincenzo La Via.

8. The dominant paradigm in the Rosminian context, in fact, is not theoretically able to overcome the problematic nature of the aforementioned three prejudices. Although legitimate and historically relevant, it now seems to be fluidifying too much in at least two questionable directions. The first is that of the Rosminian "scholastic"—something that Rosmini himself did not wish to happen; the second is that of the "theo-politics," represented by the attempt to oust metaphysics in order to constitute the possibility of a correlation between a certain type of theology (deaf to the theme of justice and that of affectivity, but open to the instances of some well-known a-metaphysical philosophies)

so as to be transposable in the context of those same methodologies used today. The Rosmini Institute is trying to accomplish this feat, having chosen to maintain its secularism as a distinctive feature of its theoretical vocation in the context of what I would call "metapolitical Rosminianism." By reconstructing historiographically and theoretically the history of philosophical Rosminianism—an activity that sees me personally engaged[9]—the Rosmini Institute is developing an editorial logic designed to highlight the texts of a theoretically relevant Rosminianism,[10] which is considered as such even by its opponents, capable of overcoming those aforementioned evaluative prejudices.

Allow me simply to point out a significant aspect of the interpretation put forward by the strand of absolute realism in relation to the first evaluative prejudice concerning *innatism*. When, a few years ago, I dealt with the essentiality of Rosminian Platonism,[11] I briefly focused also on that aspect that I called "meta-Platonic," that is, of overcoming Platonism starting from Platonism, but I did not focus on the heart of this problem, since I was aware that this theme would occupy the space of another monograph. Yet I warned, historiographically, that many criticisms of Rosmini in theory concerned precisely this aspect; so that, in the course of my studies on the history of Platonic metaphysics, I wondered if Rosminian innatism could be understood *differently* from the way it was often presented and understood, since Rosmini himself had realized in the New Essay Concerning the Origin of Ideas *(Nuovo Saggio sull'origine delle idee)* that a possible solution need not necessarily be configured by bending towards the excesses of Aristotelianism, or, on the contrary, towards those of Platonism.

---

and a certain *type* of leftist, socialist political vision excluding—of course—everything Rosmini said against such a position (see Rosmini, "Comunismo ed il socialismo"). As for the origins of the dominant paradigm, consider that, historically—as I have shown elsewhere (see Tadini, "Rosminianesimo filosofico in Italia. Dopo Rosmini: dal 1878 al 1879")—one of the fundamental reasons that inspired him arose from the need to *demonstrate* one consonance of Rosmini's thinking with that of Thomas, rather than *show* what Rosmini intended; an evident sign of a theoretically inadmissible conditioning, but very possible in the context of the time (i.e., 1878–1879).

9. See Tadini: "Rosminianesimo in Gran Bretagna"; "Rosminianesimo negli Stati Uniti"; "Rosminianesimo filosofico in Italia. 'Gli anni di Rosmini'"; "Rosminianesimo filosofico in Italia. 'Dopo Rosmini: dal 2 luglio 1855 al 1877'"; "Rosminianesimo filosofico in Italia. 'Dopo Rosmini: dal 1878 al 1879.'"

10. See Brancaforte, *Portata metapolitica dell'assoluto realismo*; La Via, *Coscienza e libertà*.

11. See Tadini, *Platone di Rosmini*.

When Rosmini affirms that the idea of being "is not contained by other previous ones, because it is the first and most universal,"[12] he undeniably means that the knowledge that the concrete subject can have of being in universal precedes all other knowledge, but, in order to be able to affirm this, the concrete subject must first of all exist, therefore, as Brancaforte rightly observed, it follows "that it must be innate, in the sense of 'anterior' and 'conditioning,' in addition to the idea of being, which as indeterminate still has to develop the fundamental feeling or the feeling of the ego, which is what allows and makes possible this growth."[13]

The concept of innate, or innatism, or a priori re-thought outside the semantic framework that Rosmini had already in effect overcome, that is, that of the typically modern antithesis of subjectivism and objectivism, could be understood as Brancaforte interprets it. He does not hesitate to say that

> the true meaning of "innate" must be such that one can univocally preach experience as a first and fundamental act which although within experience, does not derive from it because it makes possible the objectification of its data, causing the experience to shift from sensation to become intellectual perception of the world and self-consciousness. In other words, "innate" must be known as knowledge as it is an experience necessary to increase and determine the idea of being, but insufficient to give itself the value of objectivity; and inasmuch as it is an idea of being necessary to give the value of objectivity to all the primitive elements derived from experience, but insufficient to cause within itself and without its exercise in experience the unfolding of its infinite virtuality to itself. So, finally, "innate" must be able to call itself consciousness as it is a unity of experience and idea, of reality and possibility; unity, however, that is not something "done" and "accomplished," but something that is still "to be accomplished" and "in the process of being completed.[14]

This reading is confirmed in a passage of *Psychology (Psicologia)* where Rosmini affirms that "everything that man knows or can know is divided into two parts, first in what is given to man by nature: and, second, in what man draws and deduces with reason from what is given to him by nature."[15] This means that "innate" takes the meaning of "given to man by nature" as a real and current constituent, in the sense that the essence of being "by

---

12. Rosmini, *NE* 1, para. 233.
13. Brancaforte, "Rosminianesimo," 140.
14. Brancaforte, "Rosminianesimo," 141.
15. Rosmini, *PY* 1, para. 14.

making itself known to the spirit informs it in such a way as to make it intelligent, that is, it produces the *faculty of understanding*, because every act of understanding always has the entity as its object."[16] Now, I cannot linger here any further, entering into the heart of the interpretative question of the absolute realism of the Rosminian theoretical device, since the theme I have set myself is that of the secularity of the Rosminian theoresis, but I think this very brief mention is enough to make us understand the epochal importance that a reading of this type could arouse, especially if the critical comparison takes place on a terrain, like the contemporary one, typically "secular."

Secularism as Logic

The concept of *secularity*[17] should not be confused with that of *secularism*, which is not only a misleading exaggeration, but is also a term that expresses an attitude which has nothing to do with Rosminianism.

It should be noted, however, that in recent times there has been a tendency to identify the term *secular* with the term *secularist*: but this has happened because—as I have shown elsewhere with regard to other terms[18]—we find ourselves immersed in a cultural, social, and media context in which there is a tendency to impose a vague and misleading terminology, with the consequent modification of the meanings of the terms and with the natural consequence of widespread explanatory and interpretative confusion, as happened with the term *vaccine* in relation to the COVID health emergency.[19]

---

16. Rosmini, "Sistema filosofico" (Philosophycal system), para. 36.

17. The term *secularity* comes from the term *làicos* (λαϊκός), which in Greek meant "of the people" (λαός) or "profane," later defined in medieval Latin as *laicus*, one who did not belong to the ecclesiastical *status*, in the sense of not holding any rank in the ecclesiastical hierarchy; so that the term *laicus* came to be used, in a distinctive sense with respect to that of *clericus*: the layman could certainly be a baptized person and therefore in all respects a member of the Church, but his *status* distinguished him from those who were part of the hierarchy of the Church (monks and nuns, deacons, priests, bishops and cardinals), who, in addition to recognizing the pope as the vicar of Christ on earth, which was common to the Catholic and the lay believer, were subject to particular rules deriving from their *status*, from which—burdens and honors—derived duties and privileges.

18. See Tadini, "Democrazia in questione."

19. On Feb. 11, 2020, as you will remember, the World Health Organization had announced the official name of the new virus COVID-19 (co = corona; vi = virus; d = disease; 19 = year of identification of the virus), whose spread has affected many people and continues to cause casualties. There was then talk of "vaccines" to counteract the advancement of the pandemic, while what was administered is a sort of "immunostimulator," which is certainly a drug, but *is not* a vaccine, as it is mistakenly called.

The term *secular*, from which the term *secularism* is derived, does not identify those who declare themselves "agnostic," "atheist," or "anticlerical," as some mistakenly believe. This is a semantically incorrect and ideologically biased use of the original term in the secularist direction; so much so that one can speak, without any problem of oxymoronic nature, of "a secular Christian," as I have already demonstrated elsewhere,[20] and it can also be argued on the basis of Rosminian thought and as Philip Cat observed, that, properly speaking, even the idea of God presupposes "secularity," because "the secularity of the idea of God consists in the impersonal foundation of the freedom of the ego (ontological freedom) that allows us to 'fill' the void of experience of the kenotic certainty of the idea of God; yes, because the idea of God founds the same freedom, in practice it founds the instrument to 'fill' one's own certainty with real experience."[21]

Yet the attempt to exacerbate has occurred, above all, in the political sphere, ensuring that an incorrect conception of "freedom"—understood in an abstract and "socialistic" sense—has come to overlap semantically with the correct declination of "freedom," which, of course, does not concern the abstract "society" and the indifferent opinion, but the concrete person, each existing individual who can express himself by saying "I," because he discovers "in the depths of the Ego a *feeling* prior to *awareness*, which properly constitutes the pure substance of the soul";[22] so that to say person *is* to say awareness, that is, freedom; for this reason the very appurtenances of the person, such as the *property* and *dignity of life*, are included in the context of authentic freedom.

What was once a simple distinction of *status* between those who were *secular* and those who were *clerics*, but which did not determine an opposition (secular = anti-clerical), has gradually turned into a clear separation between "clerical" and "secularists" (not laymen!), where authentic secularism is properly expressed in the use of a logic that rejects alogical and immoral impositions. If, at the level of example, we want to remain in the political field, we could say that the secularist rejects any imposition that damages the three fundamental freedoms—of Lockian memory—that are proper to each concrete individual: the right to *life*, the right to *property*, and that of *opposing* to anyone who tries to threaten the first and the second. This means that authentic secularity is not opposed to the church, but to every form of dogmatic statolatry (cult of the State with a capital letter *s*) that would like to deny, in addition to the three fundamental freedoms of

---

20. See Tadini, "Laico cristiano."
21. Cat, "Introduzione," 33.
22. Rosmini, *PY* 1, para. 81.

the concrete individual, also those connatural rights of the church of which Rosmini spoke in *Philosophy of Law (Filosofia del diritto)*, namely: "1. Right to exist, 2. Right of recognition, 3. Right to freedom, 4. Right of propagation, 5. Right to property."[23] For this reason, the term *secularity* precedes *confessionality* (even the pope before becoming a cleric was a layman!) and could be taken as a synonym for that *logic* through which every critical conscience ethically needs to express itself.

Elsewhere I have stated frankly that

> philosophical thought is by its nature theoretical thought (there is no philosophy where there is no theoresis), that is, thought of the ethics of thought expressed by a thinking subject, in the sense that, in his reasoning with the utmost logic, the thought produced can only be *ethical*: the ethics of thought is manifested in the coherence with which the reflective dynamism develops according to a *logic* whose individual steps are perfectly linked. If theoretical thinking did not proceed according to this logic, which is its own ethics (that is, its own procedural modality, its structural *ethos*, its norm of "essential life" as thought), it would end up disavowing that perfect correlation existing between *logic and ethics* which is, ontologically speaking, the very essence of thinking thought in its maximum freedom of truthful research.[24]

A Performative Proposal

If we understand the concept of "secularity" as a synonym of "logicality" it becomes possible to attempt a more adequate critical positioning of Rosminianism in the context of contemporary metaphysics. Today's metaphysics, from this point of view, pursue a remarkably articulated formal "logicality" aiming at the essentiality of the assertions, at a radical minimalism (brief metaphysics), but, above all, they arise in a secular context (that of logic), not necessarily secularist, and while they often end up not leaving the scope of an ontology of the finished, although they elaborate very refined logical arguments, they seem well disposed to a precise critical comparison, since they are free—at least so it appears—from the demands of school of thought and from academic or political subjections of any kind. This means that the logic to which they refer is not intended either to deny that the concrete ego, that is, the investigating subject, exists, nor to deny

---

23. Rosmini, *Filosofia del diritto* (Philosophy of law) 3, para. 766.
24. Tadini, "Interpretazione 'crono-teoretica,'" 12.

that the truth exists; otherwise, one might ask, why deal with these issues even in such a context?

It is interesting to note that contemporary metaphysics deal with *being, essence, existence, truth, ego, God, power, act, relations*, etc., an unequivocal sign of the importance of the thinking thought that investigates, and it is equally interesting to note that, among all the so-called proofs of the existence of God, the most studied today is precisely the ontological one,[25] in all its possible declinations. Now, Rosmini has certainly dealt with all this, but in the contemporary context it has not yet—if I dare to say so—been rediscovered in its most performative theoretical scope, because there is a lack of a correct knowledge of the "chronicity,"[26] of the Rosminian texts that should be read and understood, an *examination* of the rigorization introduced by Buroni[27] and an *understanding* of the essentialization carried out by La Via.[28] These theoretical-editorial gaps—I do not intend here to show the reasons—need to be filled in the light of the value of the inquiring thought, trying to maintain an intellectual honesty that should be—at least that—guaranteed.

Nowadays no one would question the inescapable fact of thinking (if one did not think, one could not know, examine and understand) and although I am convinced—as Brancaforte stated—that *thinking* is "the most concrete and indisputable testimony of the existence of God";[29] I am equally certain that, although produced by a theoretical reasoning, this statement could, today more than ever, find fierce opponents, who could question the veracity of what is expressed in at least two ways: (1) denying thought its ability to affirm that content: "Thinking *is not* the most concrete and indisputable testimony of the existence of God"; (2) denying that the existence of God can be witnessed through thought: "Thinking is the most concrete and indisputable testimony of the *nonexistence* of God." In both cases it remains undeniable that the ego exists and that thought is the product of a concrete thinking ego, regardless of the type of assertion (I do not want to go into the possible preventive question: "Who established that ego that affirms or denies, since it has not given itself?"). It could be said that the scope of the content passes through logic, that is, secularity, with which an assertion, in relation to that content, is produced. In order to demonstrate the validity of

---

25. See Dombrowski, *Rethinking the Ontological Argument*, and Oppy, *Ontological Arguments*.

26. Tadini, "Interpretazione 'crono-teoretica,'" 17.

27. See Buroni: *Dell'essere e del conoscere; Nozioni di Ontologia; Trinità e la Creazione*.

28. See La Via, *Coscienza e libertà*.

29. Brancaforte, *Portata metapolitica dell'Assoluto realismo*, 153.

my assertion I am obliged to logically explain the passages and be willing to face an inevitable dialectical conflict in the field of metaphysical multifaceted and contemporary ontologies, where it is clear that the testimony of an institution, however prestigious, or the argumentative typology of the *ipse dixit*, do not contribute to proving the veracity of what is to be proven.

We now come, in conclusion, to identify the two reasons that lead me to consider appropriate the possibility of a proposal that I have defined as "secular" in relation to the Rosminian theoresis and aimed at bringing it out of marginality, appropriately, to try to introduce it into the broader context of the contemporary metaphysical debate.

The first is a motive *intrinsic* to the personal and concrete experience of the author. It should be remembered that Rosmini was asked, by Pope Pius VIII, to take men "with reason, and by means of that to lead them to religion."[30] Clearly, he was not being asked to lead men to religion by coercive means or by virtue of fanciful fairy-tale speculations, nor to make compromises of all kinds to achieve the goal. Now, reason,[31] however limited, is the tool that man has at his disposal to argue and demonstrate, on the basis of theoretical rigor, the veracity or otherwise of an assertion. In this sense, theoretical reason aims at a *logical* truth, but also at an *ontological* truth, for this reason Rosmini clarifies in *Il Reale*—the most important and least known book of *Teosofia* in my opinion—that "logical truth is the truth of propositions. It is customary to speak of this when it is said that truth and falsehood belong to the judgments which are expressed in propositions; that is, when it is said that truth and falsehood belong to that way of knowing that is called to know by way of preaching,"[32] while "ontological truth is therefore the entity by essence: everything as it is entity has this truth and has it all the more it has of the entity."[33]

The second is a motive *intrinsic* to the very elaboration of Rosminian metaphysics. The theoretical device of Rosminian metaphysics, in fact, exists logically in itself, that is, rationally, logically, or "secularly," if one accepts what has been stated here so far. Rosminian metaphysics—understood as the highest expression of Rosmini's theoretical thought—contributes to "reestablishing a system of Philosophy ... true and healthy and sufficiently accomplished" and to ensuring that this system, that is, the "system of

---

30. Rosmini, "Degli studi dell'Autore" (On the author's studies), para. 11.

31. Reason, like faith, is also for the believer—at least for me—a gift from God. But we cannot start from this assertion to dialogue critically with those who do not recognize this.

32. Rosmini, *Teosofia*, para. 2535.

33. Rosmini, *Teosofia*, para. 2548.

truth," "can be received by theological science as its auxiliary,"[34] because the logic, rationality, "secularity" of the *theoresis* does not constitute either the attempt to propose a sort of "theological rationalism" (a position criticized by Rosmini himself), nor of advancing a form of "anti-theology" (if anything, it could be said that it differs from theological elaborations in that they can only be *analogical*), but rather than avoiding what I call "genitive theologies"[35] they produce questionable results on the basis of opinions free from an ethics of thought, just as in the philosophical field as many "metaphysics in the genitive"[36] of a problematic nature have been presented: a rather evident sign, I would say, of the shattering of Knowledge. Hence I believe that only a convincing theoresis, in its secularity (logicality), would allow theology itself to develop a greater performativity,[37] that is, a more

---

34. Rosmini, "Degli studi dell'Autore," para. 18.

35. Theologies of this type can be found in the context of Christianity and concern both Catholicism and other confessions. Consider, to cite a few examples, the following: the theology of culture (see Tillich, *Theology of Culture*), the theology of secularisation (see Gogarten, *Destino e speranza*), the theology of ecumenism (see Congar, *Chrétiens désunis*), the theology of preaching (see Jungmann, *Frohbotschaft und unsere Glaubensverkündigung*), the theology of the anthropological-transcendental method (see Rahner, *Corso fondamentale sulla fede*), the theology of history (see Cullmann, *Mistero*), the theology of hope (see Moltmann, *Teologia della speranza*), the theology of politics (see Metz, *Sulla teologia del mondo*), the theology of experience (see Schillebeeckx, *Esperienza umana e fede*), liberation theology (see Gutiérrez, *Teologia della liberazione*), the theology of African Americans (see Washington, *Black Religion*), the theology of feminism (Cady Stanton, *Original Attack on Bible*), the theology of the Third World (see Torres and Fabella, *Emergent Gospel*), the theology of ecology (see McFague, *Body of God*), the theology of religions (see Knitter, *Introduzione alle teologie*), and the theology of postmodernity (see Lakeland, *Postmodernity*).

36. We must take into consideration the following titles to get an idea: Evola, *Metafisica del sesso*; Sombart, *Metafisica del capitalismo*; Evola, *Metafisica della guerra*; Casalino, *Nome segreto di Roma*; Melendo Granados, *Metafisica del concreto*; Giannini, *Metafisica del conflitto*; Callini, *Arcani al lavoro*; Corradetti, *Elementi di simbolismo matematico*; Incampo, *Metafisica del processo*; Zangwill, *Metafisica della bellezza*; Givone, *Metafisica della peste*; Renik, *Vedo cambiare il tempo*; Heim, *Metafisica della realtà virtuale*; Nothomb, *Metafisica dei tubi*; Bachelard, *Metafisica della matematica*; Mina di Sospiro, *Metafisica del ping-pong*; Coccia, *Vita delle piante*; Simmel, *Metafisica della morte*; Scansani, *Metafisica del tortello*; Lenti, *Metafisica di Harry Potter*; Abécassis, *Piccola metafisica dell'omicidio*; De Sutter, *Metafisica della puttana*; Carulli, *Metafisica delle mestruazioni*; Rinaldi, *Metafisica dello sterco*.

37. Personally, I think a performative theology is possible; to be such, it should not be "theology *of* something," but, in its most lively and experiential dynamism, concrete affectivity expressed according to justice in the light of that same Truth that makes us free. It goes without saying that if the theological elaboration allows itself to be conditioned by the sociological anthropologies and political ideologies in circulation, it ceases to "deal with God as he is supernaturally known by man," where the *Logos* shows itself as *Love*, but ends up becoming "theology *of* something" at the service *of* someone,

fruitful ability to be decisive in what should be its purpose: to deal "with God insofar as he is known supernaturally, and this is strictly called theology."[38] If we focus on some aspects of the progressive elaboration of Rosminianism, in the light of the proposal offered by absolute realism the very value of theoreticism (that is, of theoresis in its secularism, logicality), would make it possible, as Rosmini foresaw, that philosophical thinking and theological thinking, would be understood as "two branches of knowledge reunited in that unity to which they were born, and in which they mutually benefit, both flourishing for the benefit of mankind."[39] Such reunion, of course, cannot be adopted as a theoretical presupposition, because it would be rejected in the current context, while a rational demonstration of the truth of this assertion could not be rejected.

Bibliography

Abécassis, Éliette. *Piccola metafisica dell'omicidio*. Genoa: Il Nuovo Melangolo, 2004.

Bachelard, Gaston. *Metafisica della matematica*. Rome: Castelvecchi, 2016.

Brancaforte, Antonio. *La portata metapolitica dell'assoluto realismo. Vincenzo La Via essenzializza Rosmini*. Edited by Philip Cat. Vol. 1 of *Discussioni rosminiane e altri scritti*. Milan: Mimesis, 2020.

———. "Il Rosminianesimo come superamento dell'antitesi moderna di soggettivismo e oggettivismo." In *La portata metapolitica dell'Assoluto realismo. Vincenzo La Via essenzializza Rosmini*, edited by Philip Cat, vol. 1 of *Discussioni rosminiane e altri scritti*, 139–53. Milan: Mimesis, 2020.

Buroni, Giuseppe. *Dell'essere e del conoscere. Studii su Parmenide, Platone e Rosmini*. Turin: Paravia e Comp., 1877.

———. *Nozioni di Ontologia per introduzione allo studio della Teologia. Confronti fra la Teosofia di Rosmini e le Somme di San Tommaso. Edizione Seconda accresciuta di una lettera sulla Teorica del Progresso Infinito*. Turin: Paravia e Comp., 1878.

———. *La Trinità e la Creazione. Nuovi confronti tra Rosmini e S. Tommaso dedicati alla Civiltà Cattolica con un cenno alla risposta seconda al P. Cornoldi e un'appendice sulla necessità di liberar la Chiesa dalla calunnia, ed. II accresciuta di molte aggiunte e della Disamina di due Proposizioni teologiche della Civiltà Cattolica*. Turin: Paravia e Comp., 1879.

Cady Stanton, Elizabeth. *The Original Attack on the Bible*. New York: Arno, 1974.

Callini, Daniele. *Arcani al lavoro. Metafisica della vita organizzativa*. Milan: Franco Angeli, 2008.

Carulli, Antonio. *Metafisica delle mestruazioni*. Genoa: Il Nuovo Melangolo, 2017.

Casalino, Giandomenico. *Il nome segreto di Roma. Metafisica della romanità*. Rome: Mediterranee, 2003.

---

who, of course, is not God, but rather—if I may say so—a theologically-politically-roped party that could reveal very different purposes.

38. Rosmini, *SA*, 1:54–55.

39. Rosmini, "Degli studi dell'Autore," para. 11.

Cat, Philip. "Introduzione. Minimal metaphysics. L'*idea dell'essere* come dispositivo." In *La laicità dell'ida di Dio. La performatività dell'argomento ontologico nell'Assoluto realismo*, by Antonio Brancafote, edited by Philip Cat, 13–50. Milan: Mimesis, 2021.

Coccia, Emanuele. *La vita delle piante. Metafisica della mescolanza*. Bologna: Mulino, 2018.

Congar, Yves M. J. *Chrétiens désunis. Principes d'un "oecuménisme" catholique*. Paris: Cerf, 1937.

Corradetti, Daniele. *Elementi di simbolismo matematico*. Vol. 1 of *Metafisica del numero*. Messina, It.: Pavone, 2008.

Cullmann, Oscar. *Il mistero della redenzione nella storia*. Translated by Aldo Prini. Bologna: Mulino, 1966.

De Sutter, Laurent. *Metafisica della puttana*. Macerata, It.: Giometti & Antonello, 2017.

Dombrowski, Daniel A. *Rethinking the Ontological Argument: A Neoclassical Theistic Response*. Cambridge: Cambridge University Press, 2006.

Evola, Julius. *Metafisica della guerra*. Padova: AR, 2001.

———. *Metafisica del sesso*. Rome: Mediterranee, 1993.

Ferraris, Maurizio, ed. *Storia dell'ontologia*. Milan: Bompiani, 2010.

Fraisopi, Fausto. *Ontologie. Storia e prospettive della domanda sull'ente*. Milan: Mimesis, 2014.

Giannini, Gianluca. *Metafisica del conflitto*. Genoa: Nuovo Melangolo, 2007.

Givone, Sergio. *Metafisica della peste. Colpa e destino*. Turin: Einaudi, 2012.

Gogarten, Friedrich. *Destino e speranza dell'epoca moderna. La secolarizzazione come problema teologico*. Translated by F. Coppellotti. Brescia, It.: Morcelliana, 1972.

Gutiérrez, Gustavo. *Teologia della liberazione*. Translated by L. Bianchi and E. Demarchi. Brescia, It.: Queriniana, 1972.

Heim, Michael R. *Metafisica della realtà virtuale*. Translated by D. Rossi. Naples: Guida, 2015.

Incampo, Antonio. *Metafisica del processo. Idee per una critica della ragione giuridica*. Bari, It.: Cacucci, 2010.

Jungmann, Josef A. *Die Frohbotschaft und unsere Glaubensverkündigung*. Regensburg, Germ.: Pustet, 1936.

Knitter, Paul F. *Introduzione alle teologie delle religioni*. Brescia, It.: Queriniana, 2005.

Krienke, Markus. "La metafisica di Rosmini." In *Storia della metafisica*, edited by Enrico Berti, 279–303. Rome: Carocci, 2021.

Lakeland, Paul. *Postmodernity: Christian Identity in a Fragmented Age*. Minneapolis: Fortress, 1997.

La Via, Vincenzo. *Coscienza e libertà. Rosmini e l'assoluto realismo*. Edited by Biagio G. Muscherà. Vol. 1 of *Saggi rosminiani e altri scritti*. Milan: Mimesis, 2020.

Lenti, Marina. *La metafisica di Harry Potter*. Monselice, It.: Camelozampa, 2012.

McFague, Sallie. *The Body of God: An Ecological Theology*. Minneapolis: Fortress, 1993.

Melendo Granados, Tomás I. *Metafisica del concreto. I rapporti tra filosofia e vita*. Rome: Leonardo da Vinci, 2005.

Metz, Johann B. *Sulla teologia del mondo*. Brescia, It.: Queriniana, 1969.

Mina di Sospiro, Guido. *Metafisica del ping-pong. Un'introduzione alla filosofia perenne*. Milan: Ponte alle Grazie, 2016.

Moltmann, Jürgen. *Teologia della speranza. Ricerche sui fondamenti e sulle implicazioni di una escatologia cristiana*. Translated by A. Comba. Brescia, It.: Queriniana, 1970.

Mondin, Battista. *Storia della metafisica*. 3 vols. Bologna: Studio Domenicano, 1998.

Nothomb, Amélie. *Metafisica dei tubi*. Rome: Voland, 2016.

Oppy, Graham, ed. *Ontological Arguments*. Cambridge: Cambridge University Press, 2018.

Rahner, Karl. *Corso fondamentale sulla fede*. Translated by C. Danna. Rome: Paoline, 1977.

Renik, Salomon. *Vedo cambiare il tempo. Metafisica del macchinismo e le passioni dell'anima*. Milan: Mimesis, 2015.

Rinaldi, Raffaele. *La metafisica dello sterco*. Ferrara: Pluriversum, 2017.

Rosmini, Antonio. *Antropologia soprannaturale*. Edited by Umberto Muratore. 2 vols. ENC 39–40. Rome: Città Nuova, 1983.

———. "Il comunismo ed il socialismo. Ragionamento." In *Opuscoli politici*, edited by Gianfreda Marconi, ENC 37, 81–116. Rome: Città Nuova, 1978.

———. "Degli studi dell'Autore." In *Introduzione alla filosofia*, edited by Pier P. Ottonello, ENC 2, 13–194. Rome: Città Nuova, 1979.

———. *Filosofia del diritto*. Edited by Michele Nicoletti and Francesco Ghia. 4 vols. ENC 28, 28/A, 29, 29/A. Rome: Città Nuova, 2014.

———. *Nuovo Saggio sull'origine delle idee*. Edited by Gaetano G. Messina. 3 vols. ENC 3–5. Rome: Città Nuova, 2003.

———. "Prefazione." In *Teosofia*, edited by Samuele F. Tadini, 245–65. Milan: Bompiani, 2011.

———. *Psicologia*. Edited by Vincenzo Sala. 4 vols. ENC 9, 9/A, 10, 10/A. Rome: Città Nuova, 1988–1989.

———. "Sistema filosofico." In *Introduzione alla filosofia*, edited by Pier Paolo Ottonello, ENC 2, 225–302. Rome: Città Nuova, 1979.

———. *Teosofia*. Edited by Samuele F. Tadini. Milan: Bompiani, 2011.

Scansani, Stefano. *Metafisica del tortello. Storia, filosofia, ricette della pasta ripiena*. Mantua, It.: Tre Lune, 2007.

Schillebeeckx, Edward. *Esperienza umana e fede in Gesù Cristo*. Translated by D. Pezzetta. Brescia, It.: Queriniana, 1975.

Simmel, Georg. *Metafisica della morte e altri scritti*. Translated by L. Perucchi. Milan: SEI, 2018.

Sombart, Werner. *Metafisica del capitalismo*. Padova: AR, 1994.

Tadini, Sameule F. "Democrazia in questione. Una riflessione metapolitica sulle ragioni dell'antidemocraticismo." *Rivista Rosminiana* 3-4 (2019) 253–85.

———. "Il laico cristiano." In *Chiamati alla santità. La scuola rosminiana della santità oggi*, edited by Gianno Picenardi, 175–85. Stresa, It.: Rosminiane, 2015.

———. "Metafisica rosminiana e 'metafisiche' contemporanee." In *La Filosofia dopo le "filosofie." La sfida rosminiana alla contemporaneità*, edited by Samuele F. Tadini, 99–129. Milan: Mimesis, 2019.

———. "Un necessario chiarimento metodologico." *The Rosmini Society-Rosminianesimo Filosofico International Journal* 1-2 (2020) 25–33.

———. *Il Platone di Rosmini. L'essenzialità del platonismo rosminiano*. Soveria Mannelli, It.: Rubbettino, 2010.

———. "Il Rosminianesimo filosofico in Italia. 'Dopo Rosmini: dal 1878 al 1879.'" *The Rosmini Society-Rosminianesimo Filosofico International Journal* 1–2 (2021) 35–150.

———. "Il Rosminianesimo filosofico in Italia. 'Dopo Rosmini: dal 2 luglio 1855 al 1877.'" *The Rosmini Society-Rosminianesimo Filosofico International Journal* 1–2 (2020) 35–150.

———. "Il Rosminianesimo filosofico in Italia. 'Gli anni di Rosmini.'" In *Rosminianesimo filosofico*, edited by Samuele F. Tadini, 33–90. Milan: Mimesis, 2019.

———. "Il Rosminianesimo in Gran Bretagna nel XIX secolo." In *Rosminianesimo filosofico*, edited by Samuele F. Tadini, 27–59. Milan: Mimesis, 2017.

———. "Il Rosminianesimo negli Stati Uniti d'America nel XIX secolo." In *Rosminianesimo filosofico*, edited by Samuele F. Tadini, 33–65. Milan: Mimesis, 2018.

———. "Rosmini e la nuova metafisica ontoprismatica: un dialogo possibile con l'ontologia analitica." In *Ontologia, fenomenologia e nuovo umanesimo. Rosmini ri-generativo*, edited by Fernando Bellelli and Emanuele Pili, 59–75. Rome: Città Nuova, 2016.

———. "Teologia naturale rosminiana ed epistemologia riformata: le premesse per un possibile "dialogo ideale." In *Il divino nell'uomo e l'umano nella rivelazione*, edited by Fernando Bellelli, Rosminianesimo teologico, 65–107. Milan: Mimesis, 2017.

———. "Teosofia rosminiana e ontologie dominanti. Per un pluralismo costruttivo." In *I semi del Verbo nel pluralismo religioso, teologico e filosofico. Nel 50° anniversario del Centro Internazionale di Studi Rosminiani*, edited by Gianni Picenardi, 141–61. Stresa, It.: Rosminiane, 2017.

———. "Valore e significato dell'interpretazione 'crono-teoretica.'" *The Rosmini Society-Rosminianesimo Filosofico International Journal* 1–2 (2021) 9–27.

Tillich, Paul. *Theology of Culture*. New York: Oxford University Press, 1959.

Torres, Sergio, and Virginia Fabella, eds. *The Emergent Gospel. Theology from the Underside of History*. New York: Orbis, 1978.

Washington, Joseph R. *Black Religion. The Negro and Christianity in the United States*. Boston: Beacon, 1964.

Zangwill, Nick. *La metafisica della bellezza*. Milan: Marinotti, 2011.

4

In Search of a Metaphysical Rooting of Phenomenology

Rosminian Perspectives on Purifying Hermeneutical Reductionism

ALBERTO PERATONER

IN THE CONTEMPORARY SCENARIO of philosophical thought, and particularly in the field of relations between the philosophical and theological sciences, it seems urgent to evaluate, at least in some respects, the terms and conditions of a possible fusing and re-proposal of a reason for continuity of the disciplinary areas of metaphysics—understood in its classical-scholastic, but also, in some ways, early-modern expression—and phenomenological investigation.

This perspective appears today, in the most widespread understanding of the philosophical sciences, undermined by the deep-rooted prejudice that the phenomenological and hermeneutic approach of philosophical reflection should supplant that proper to metaphysics, which would be considered outdated.

This prejudice, all the more ineradicable as it is uncritically conveyed as an assumption that is no longer even worth demonstrating or at least arguing, being established and widely—although, it must be said, not universally—shared, derives from a triple misunderstanding.

First, on the nature of metaphysics and its confusion with the ontology generally considered.

Second, on its alleged failure, all too easily and hastily decreed, in the face of its inadequate representation.

And finally, on the consequent preferability of the "weak" forms of philosophical reflection, apparently more "free" and undoubtedly more plastic and malleable to a nuanced, evocative and symbolic use in language, up to a poetic leavening of philosophical discourse and its transformation into a "narrative" of being and experience, often a pretext for disengagement from the onto-practical responsibility of argumentative rigor and a "truth" discourse.

From Phenomenology to the Phenomenological: Scalarity of Three Levels of Understanding

According to a now rather common understanding, the philosophy most useful and "pleasing" to theology itself should now be conducted on the lines of development of phenomenology and hermeneutics, but—and this is the point from which we dissociate—as an *alternative* and not as a profitable and also necessary *complementary integration* to ontological-metaphysical reflection. The hermeneutic-phenomenological perspective would thus not flank and articulate with, but surrogate the metaphysical enquiry, on the basis of the simple assumption of the irreconcilability of the two methodological registers and of the respective disciplinary fields, considering the latter now impracticable and outdated. With the paradox that, while this perspective of substitution presents itself with the benevolent face of a "softer" and more friendly, more tolerant and, so to speak, "democratic" philosophical attitude—metaphysics, at least of a classic-scholastic mold, in its claim to articulate a truthful discourse, in its categories of universality and objectivity, it would in fact be perceived as an illiberal form, a "strong" and therefore "violent" knowledge aimed at imposing pretended "truths" on others.[1] It does not tally then that while metaphysics *has always* admitted alongside and in relation to itself a hermeneutical and phenomenological space of investigation, the hermeneutic-phenomenological approach, at least in the contemporary version, should not categorically allow any space to metaphysical ontology. In other words, the question arises: Between a metaphysics that by its very configuration not only allows for

---

1. See, with regard to these prejudicial collimations, the still actual Vigna: "Debole, forte, violento"; then *Frammento e l'intero*, 2:35-45. On the relationship between metaphysics and hermeneutics and their compossibility, with interesting evaluations on the historical-philosophical genesis of the modern and especially contemporary alienation of hermeneutics (and phenomenology) from metaphysics, see Vigna, "Sulla verità dell'ermeneutica." 1:111-129.

a sort of benevolent concession of tolerance, but recognizes the need for a hermeneutic-phenomenological register of the philosophical discourse and a phenomenology that not only does not contemplate, but excludes—and not rarely categorically—a space for ontological-metaphysical knowledge, which is the perspective with the broadest and most comprehensive horizon? Which is the most "open" and "tolerant"? What, in reality, is the most "open-minded" theoretical framework?[2]

For our part, we therefore believe that this illogical "logic of exclusion" must be overcome for a philosophical thought of greater breadth and speculative courage.

With this objective, we will establish, in our discourse, three meanings or, we could say, three levels of understanding, of the term *phenomenology*, with regard to the complexity and polyvocity it assumes in the intersection between the speculative and historical-philosophical layers.

In a first and more precise meaning, *phenomenology* designates the discipline inaugurated by Edmund Husserl and the method that supports and innervates it intimately, to the point of making it a whole, as a unit of method and development of intentional investigation that, starting from the description of phenomena, seeks the profound and authentic meaning of the objects and structures of experience.

In a second sense, we can consider *phenomenology* the broad philosophical panorama of what seems to be derived from the Husserlian conception—the "school" or the so-called phenomenological "movement"—and has retained some of its essential traits or characteristics, such as, primarily, the theory of intentionality, while modulating them with significant variations, to the point of departing from the original Husserlian theoretical framework.

A wide panorama, because from the original theoretical structure of the thought of the "school" of immediate derivation, the philosophy of Max Scheler differs significantly, on the one hand, with the shift of the axis on the

2. Some will object that an assertive and categorical philosophy such as that of metaphysical investigation, by the very fact of posing itself in terms of knowledge with a claim to truth, is not in principle admissible in the philosophical agora, just as in the political arena within a democratic system there is no room for neo-fascist and neo-Nazi positions since they stand in denial of that same democratic space and of the right to freedom of thought and political pluralism, to which we will reply that the one thus outlined corresponds to an inadequate and caricatured representation of metaphysics and has no real historical and textual confirmation—and a simple reading of some classical *loci* of the great metaphysics tradition would be enough to dissolve such prejudices—, and that the clear attestation of this discrepancy is already internal to the fact that, as mentioned above, metaphysics, rightly understood, admits, not only next to, but in relation to itself, and therefore in synergy with its own argumentative articulation, the register proper to hermeneutic-phenomenological investigation.

Selbstgegebenheit (self-dating) of the phenomenon, and, on the other, the thought of Martin Heidegger, with the transcending of the phenomenology itself in the ontology of the existential presentiality of *Dasein*, or even the theoretical structure of Merleau-Ponty, which tends to almost exhaust the task of the investigation apparatus of Western thought on the phenomenological front, but where the Husserlian construct can hardly be recognized.

In a third and broader sense we can finally consider *phenomenology*—with the tendency, we would say, to allow the adjective *phenomenological*, which best lends itself to the semantic extension of this further level, prevail—every path of investigation on the structure of experience that moves from *phenomena* as they are offered to the conscience in its relationship with the real, where we can envisage some prevalence of the inductive component, which allows us to grasp those constants of experience functional to the deciphering of its structure and of what it, in its relationship, comes to express and represent.

In this sense we can recognize in the course of Western thought a long and articulated modulation of phenomenological reflections and investigations, which emerges decisively in Hegel's *Phenomenology of Spirit*, "science of the experience of consciousness," in its advancing in knowledge through historical becoming and the assumption of the figures that embody it. These same phenomenological elements are discernible in classical thought itself in its highest expressions. In fact, we dare to consider, more remotely, phenomenological the same Aristotelian ethics, its psychology, and large tracts of philosophical investigation paths of many ancient, medieval, and modern authors, from Augustine—how much "phenomenology" nourishes the *Confessions* in the movements of the interioristic exploration of the spirit?—to Thomas Aquinas, up to Nicholas of Cusa, from Pascal to Rousseau (we can refer, for example, to the acute introspection of some splendid pages of the *Reveries du promeneur solitaire*), from Maine de Biran (just consider his *Journal*), along the fruitful and rich vein of French spiritualism, to Bergson and, for the nineteenth century, Rosmini and Newman.

With the distinction between these three meanings we do not intend to equivocate, passing, when it would be useful, from one to the other, to lead treating as phenomenology—and phenomenological—the various levels or extensions in the same way, but to consider them analogically, in full awareness, therefore, of the central focality of the Husserlian proposal, which backlights the true meaning and the real scope of the questioning on the experience that allows us to consider much of all-time philosophy as *phenomenological* under various aspects.

We could also in some way recognize in the first (to which we can associate the second) and in the third of the levels described, what we can consider as the *empirical layer*—the phenomenology *stricto sensu* in its historical determination, as it was formulated and inaugurated by Husserl and developed by his philosophical descent, with a theoretical horizon and a defined method—and the *transcendental layer* of philosophizing—phenomenology as a perspective inherent in philosophical reflection in itself, practically found throughout its entire historical development and regardless of the historical connotation of the philosophical school that codified it—since the latter would respond, much more than a historical turning point and a school of thought, to a specific all-times need, to which the school that took his name imparted a development of unprecedented breadth and systematicity, causing it to lose its functional position in the organic corpus of philosophical sciences.[3]

An Exploration Downstream of Husserlian Phenomenology: Edith Stein

A central figure to the practicable approaches to the third of the levels described is undoubtedly that of Edith Stein, of whom Angela Ales Bello writes: "Her investigation can be gathered under a unitary title that is, precisely, that of a philosophical anthropology with a phenomenological approach that subsequently seeks completions and supports in the ancient and medieval metaphysical tradition."[4]

Stein's is, in fact, a personalist anthropology that, through the analysis of enteropathy and the configuration of lived experiences, achieves the definition of the contours of subjectivity as consciousness, and the identification of a *nucleus* of the personality in which, according to the German thinker herself, "that immutable consistency of its being which is not the result of development, but which, on the contrary, imposes a certain course to development."[5] Phenomenological analysis does not, therefore, consign the

3. In the spirit of grasping this level of understanding of the phenomenological perspective, two recently published instruments are noteworthy: the collective volume of Manganaro and Marchetto, *Maestri perché testimoni*, and the monograph by Galvani, *Sguardo sull'umano*. For a more specific focus on the phenomenological in Rosmini, see the collective volume of Bellelli and Pili, *Ontologia, fenomenologia* (and in particular the second section, "Rosmini e la fenomenologia," 99–185), and Nobile, *Rosmini e la fenomenologia*.

4. Ales Bello, "Persona in Edith Stein," 116.

5. Stein, *Psicologia e scienze*, 123–24. As a useful illustration of the text, Ales Bello in *Persona in Edith Stein*, 124, comments: "The nucleus is the unitary moment of the human being. Edith Stein writes that the spiritual life of an individual is determined by the singularity of this nucleus; however, the nucleus is something new compared to spiritual life itself, and not even a complete knowledge of the spiritual or psychic life would be sufficient to grasp it in its entirety."

investigation of the being-person to an endless referral of meanings which, being inexhaustible, would impede to transcend the variability of the finite determinations of experiential factuality with which they would not be able to form stable ties, but rather tend to curve it towards the person "center" as their "original interior place," a task entrusted to the considerations of *Potency and Act*, in which Stein takes up and further explores the constitution of the "nucleus" as the person "formative principle," whose constitution is considered in the tripolarity of *soul*, *spirit*, and *body*, but whose "individuality is impressed in a wholly pure way, devoid of any admixture, only in the soul."[6]

Edith Stein's path of philosophical reflection, moving from the phenomenological horizon through a history of successive implementations—the research path through which, under the impulse and guidance of Erich Przywara, she approached the thought of Thomas, applying herself in particular to the *Quaestiones disputatae de veritate*, is well known—then leads to a substantialist anthropology of a classical-scholastic mold, without the significance of phenomenological investigation as such, with the value of its method and its acquisitions, being lost or liquidated.

But the task of bonding phenomenology and metaphysics in Stein seems to remain unfinished, also because of the problematic character of the phenomenological *epochē*. This, in fact, seems to be the theoretical element most in contrast with metaphysical investigation, which assumes as its object the real being.

It is a downstream exploration of Husserlian phenomenology, that by Stein, and makes it interesting to verify the convergence (and peculiarity) of the exploration traveled upstream of it: that by Antonio Rosmini.

An Upstream Exploration of Husserlian Phenomenology: Antonio Rosmini

The grandiose design of Rosmini's metaphysical ontology, in its structural constitution around the idea of being, where the original is synthetical, presents at its very core an evident coessentiality of the phenomenological moment in the setting of the investigation starting from the idea of being recognized as the luminous background of consciousness—the *light of the intellect*—where there is a gnoseological *primum* that does not compromise the ontological primality of the real being, but where the originary source of knowledge is, as we said, synthetical, because the solidary circularity between the forms of being and the living experience that the subject has of

---

6. Stein, *Potenza e Atto*, 172.

it and to which it applies in its investigation is originary too. For Rosmini "observation of the fact shows us that the evidence of the essence of the entity is given to our spirit before any other knowledge; and if we meditate on its nature, we find that it cannot be otherwise, that such evidence cannot be acquired and formed in any other way, and finally that it is knowable for itself."[7] Therefore, by its very movements, introspection attests the originary presentiality of the idea of being to the conscience, which at every step must presuppose it: the gnoseological moment, cadenced by a broadly phenomenological course, is supported by an originary ontological primality, since, Rosmini continues,

> the fact truly tells us that man does not begin to use the faculties of his spirit, except on the occasion of external sensations, and that man's thought begins to realize that there are bodies, that he himself exists, that there is something real. Now, this first thought is nothing more, as we have said, than an assertion, it is to affirm an entity; which presupposes that the essence of the entity is known first. Therefore, the essence of the entity is known to man before all the acts of his thought.[8]

The originary source of knowledge is therefore the synthesis of the unity of experience, which relies on the synthesism of the forms of being, where the same experience unity, when analyzed, is recognized to be marked by the ontological horizon of the concrete real and, at the same time, already inhabited by the synthesism of the forms of being in which it is enveloped too, and from which it cannot withdraw. Neither can it abstract from experience the model of the circuminsession of the forms of being, so that phenomenology comes to merge into one with ontology—and, naturally, metaphysical ontology; it warms itself, so to speak, on the flame of vivid experience, that which, for the Western tradition, before it knew the grafting of Christian knowledge, remained inert, and we refer to that categorial setting of the classic tradition which, without the qualitative leavening offered by the suggestions and research inspired by the biblical revelation, it would end up being not even consequent to itself. See for example, Rosmini's masterly critique of Aristotelian philosophical theology, and the specific remark that only in the perspective of the Triune God offered by Christian revelation is the aporetic character of the conception of God as νόεσις νοήσεως (*Metaphysics* XII) solved.[9] And the analysis of this

---

7. Rosmini, "Sistema filosofico" (Philosophical system), 234.

8. Rosmini, "Sistema filosofico," 234.

9. See Rosmini, *Theos* 1, bk. 3, sect. 4, ch. 3, 1301; and above all bk. 3, sect. 5, ch. 12, §4, para. 1245, 2°.

structure is—with reference to the third level of comprehension previously set out—authentic phenomenology.

In the work *Renewal of Philosophy in Italy (Il rinnovamento della filosofia in Italia)*, Rosmini writes, looking retrospectively at the form of his methodological approach in relation to the method mainly followed in the elaboration *milieu* of speculative theology of his time, "The theological school started from the meditation of God, I simply started from the meditation of man."[10] *Simply*, that is to say, in support of the simple and incontestable evidence of experience, observed in the folds of interiority, which is precisely the first place of properly phenomenological exploration,[11] and which is the distinctive feature of Rosmini's approach to philosophical investigation in its phenomenological-inductive attitude, and does not for this reason renounce being a solid metaphysical ontology. An authentic phenomenology that is an authentic metaphysical ontology. And this seems to be precisely the normative indication of Rosmini's theoretical proposal: the truth of metaphysics—and more than ever in the Rosmini "system"—is in the truth of phenomenology. It is already so in its structural arrangement and in its articulation and proceeding and in what it achieves in the results of its own investigation.

As pointed out by Angela Ales Bello, it is with regard to the polarization of the subject that the convergence of Rosmini[12] and Husserl is most felt, since, to express ourselves in the synthetic restitution of these collimations offered to us by F. Bellelli and C. Vecchiet, "Rosmini's sensory perception coincides with Husserl's perception as an intentional living, and what in Rosmini is the *ego* as an active principle coincides with what in Husserl it is the functional center of all intentional livings."[13] Here, we again find the discourse of the *nucleus* of the person that in Edith Stein actually seems to constitute the ideal bridge of conjunction between Husserlian phenomenology and a substantialist metaphysics of classical-scholastic inspiration as

10. Rosmini, *Rinnovamento della filosofia* (Renewal of philosophy), 2:468.

11. Galvani, in *Sguardo sull'umano*, 325, writes, comparing the phenomenological perspectives of Rosmini and Edith Stein, that "in the considerations of both authors we can see the conviction according to which the human subject, in his philosophical research, can only start from his own interiority, revealing the constant and habitual presence of himself to himself, which distinguishes it as an intelligent entity."

12. See Ales Bello, "Complessità e stratificazione," 114–15.

13. Bellelli and Vecchiet, "Fenomenologia e metafisica," 103. Ales Bello writes in this regard: "Certainly the analyses of the two philosophers are different in results, but similar in affirming that the constitutive elements of all human knowledge must be traced back to what the human being lives in himself: feeling himself and intuiting being for Rosmini, the experiences of which we are aware for Husserl" (*Complessità e stratificazione*, 115).

we can observe in Rosmini, where onto-phenomenological anthropology translates and pours its results into an authentic metaphysics of the person.

As a philosophy of the presence of being, the phenomenological moment that in Rosmini himself gives as an incisive description of the processes of experience in relation to the world in its sense rooted in subjective intuitions and in their intersubjective foundation—the person as a "substantial relationship"[14]—necessarily leads back to the proper sense of being to which it thus testifies and of which the ultimate custodian is metaphysical ontology in its capacity to grasp the universal—*scientia de universalibus*, the Scholastics affirmed—and thereby restore those stable links of meaning that hermeneutic-phenomenological work can travel in the pluriform actuality of experience, recording its constants as circumstantial elements that come back to confirm it, to illustrate human condition in its rich and varied existential articulation.

Metaphysics and Phenomenology: Conditions for a Regained Compossibility

We initially posed the problematic character of the overdetermination of the hermeneutic-phenomenological plexus in its claim to replace metaphysical investigation, whose impracticability is hastily decreed. A claim, as has been mentioned, that meets the late-modern inclination to weaken the epistemic form of knowledge, even in its practical implications, thus dismissing any truthful scope of philosophical discourse. The course of historical thought, in consideration of the horizon precisely at the phenomenological component as being always connatural to philosophical reflection, shows, on the contrary, the supportive relationship of the two forms as necessarily complementary.

Of the compossibility, indeed, even more, of the metaphysical destiny of an authentic phenomenology, we have interesting attestation in the critical observation moved in *Voice and Phenomenon* by Jacques Derrida, according to whom "the resurgence of phenomenological criticism is the metaphysical project itself in its historical fulfillment and in the only restored purity of its origin."[15] Thus, with the intention of deconstructing

14. Rosmini, *AAMS*, 460.

15. Derrida, *Voce e il fenomeno*, 33–34. Again, if for Derrida "on the one hand phenomenology is the reduction of naïve ontology, the return to an active constitution of sense and value, to the activity of a life that produces truth and value in general through its signs," on the other, "at the same time, without simply juxtaposing itself to this movement, another necessity also confirms the classical metaphysics of presence and marks the belonging of phenomenology to classical ontology" (Derrida, *Voce e il fenomeno*, 56–57).

the phenomenological method, and wanting to reveal what he considers the re-proposal of a theoretical system that would remain governed by a poorly concealed metaphysical texture—the need for phenomenology, the aspiration to restore with it a maximum epistemological rigor, would, in other words, conceal a metaphysical presupposition—Derrida discovers in reality that the true destiny of the phenomenological dimension is in its integration into a broad metaphysical-phenomenological, or hermeneutic-phenomenological-metaphysical perspective.

The conditions of such integration must therefore respect the statute of the individual disciplines, in order to guarantee their mutual, complete, and noncompetitive arrangement, where the clear warning of knowledge of finiteness, multiple and becoming, assumed as its object by the rich and vast field of hermeneutic-phenomenological investigation, incapable by itself to generate a description of the sense of the entire, can do nothing than admit an indispensable graft onto the trunk of epistemic knowledge that, despite the (quantitative) limitation of the acquisition of knowledge, in content—and therefore in the apparent scarce existential significance of the gained acquisitions—as knowledge of the *foundation* is the only guarantee of the structural stability of the contents that the same phenomenological recognition fruitfully brings.

The greatness proper to the precious phenomenological investigation can thus be envisaged on condition of the execution of the necessary and in fact still fully practicable—as demonstrated by the theoretical structure of Rosmini's thought—purification of itself from its reductionist compression to the merely *doxic* level of the description of the meaning of the entire (which, moreover, would not even be such anymore) and of experience, a layer limiting to which, denied the very possibility of recognizing *stable* links of meaning, it would condemn itself to an insignificance from which only the reference to the noncontradictory structure of the constants of experience as expressive of the constants of being, of which it is ultimately guarantor knowledge of the foundation guarded by metaphysical ontology.

Bibliography

Ales Bello, Angela. "Complessità e stratificazione dell'essere umano: a proposito di antropologia e psicologia. Un confronto tra Antonio Rosmini e Edith Stein." In *Ontologia, fenomenologia e nuovo umanesimo. Rosmini rigenerativo*, edited by Fernando Bellelli and Emanuele Pili, 111–25. Rome: Città Nuova, 2016.

———. "La persona in Edith Stein." In *Maestri perché testimoni. Pensare il futuro con John Henry Newman e Edith Stein*, edited by Patrizia Manganaro and Michele Marchetto, 115–36. Rome: Lateran University Press, 2017. Proceedings of *Maestri perché testimoni* conference, Istituto Universitario Salesiano, Venice, Jan. 19–20, 2017.

Bellelli, Fernando, and Cristian Vecchiet. "Fenomenologia e metafisica. Questioni introduttive." In *Ontologia, fenomenologia e nuovo umanesimo. Rosmini rigenerativo*, edited by Fernando Bellelli and Emanuele Pili, 99–109. Rome: Città Nuova, 2016.

Bellelli, Fernando, and Emanuele Pili, eds. *Ontologia, fenomenologia e nuovo umanesimo. Rosmini rigenerativo*. Rome: Città Nuova, 2016.

Derrida, Jacques. *La voce e il fenomeno*. Edited and translated by Gianfranco Dalmasso. Milan: Jaca, 1984.

Galvani, Martina. *Uno sguardo sull'umano. Antropologia e metafisica in Antonio Rosmini e Edith Stein*. Rome: Tab, 2020.

Manganaro, Patrizia, and Michele Marchetto, eds. *Maestri perché testimoni. Pensare il futuro con John Henry Newman e Edith Stein*. Rome: Lateran University Press, 2017. Proceedings of *Maestri perché testimoni* conference, Istituto Universitario Salesiano, Venice, Jan. 19–20, 2017.

Nobile, Mauro. *Rosmini e la fenomenologia*. Trento: University of Trento Press, 2020.

Rosmini, Antonio. *Antropologia in servizio della scienza morale*. Edited by François Evain. ENC 24. Rome: Città Nuova, 1984.

———. *Il rinnovamento della filosofia in Italia*. Edited by Gaetano Messina. ENC 6. Rome: Città Nuova, 2007.

———. "Sistema filosofico." In *Introduzione alla filosofia*, edited by Pier Paolo Ottonello, ENC 2, 225–302. Rome: Città Nuova, 1979.

———. *Teosofia*. Edited by Maria A. Raschini and Pier P. Ottonello. 6 vols. ENC 12–17. Rome: Città Nuova 1998–2002.

Stein, Edith. *Potenza e Atto. Studi per una filosofia dell'essere*. Rome: Città Nuova, 2003.

———. *Psicologia e scienze dello spirito. Contributi per una fondazione filosofica*. Rome: Città Nuova, 1999.

Vigna, Carmelo. "Debole, forte, violento. A proposito di alcuni discorsi di filosofia." *Bollettino della Società filosofica italiana* 128 (1986) 20–32.

———. *Il frammento e l'intero. Indagini sul senso dell'essere e sulla stabilità del sapere*. 2 vols. Naples: Orthotes, 2015.

———. "Sulla verità dell'ermeneutica." In *Il frammento e l'intero. Indagini sul senso dell'essere e sulla stabilità del sapere*, 1:111–29. Naples: Orthotes, 2015.

Part 2

Rosmini's Trinitarian Ontology and His *Suspended Middle*: The Primality of the Moral Form of Being in the Synthesism with the Real and Ideal Forms

5

Knowledge and Justice of Pro-Affection

PIERANGELO SEQUERI

The Phenomenological Irreducibility of Loving

THE AFFECTION THAT ALLOWS itself to be resolved entirely in the desire for the good, or interpreted as the enumeration of the good, may be led to distance itself from the poor, from the sick, from the unhappy, from the sinner. Loving, on the other hand, in the experience of millions of men and women, is not measured only by this correspondence with the most lovable aspect.

An enigmatic experience, without doubt. Yet, profoundly human. An experience of extraordinary lightness, but also of unimaginable tenacity. Not to mention the fact that this is how the Christian believer has learned about his God. And loving. "When we were still enemies and sinners." Loving, in fact, does not simply coincide with the desire for good: it reaches the point of affection for that which is defective, wrong, deprived. And it tries to do some good there too. It is not a question of loving evil, on the contrary: it is a question of digging out some good feelings even from the rubble, of igniting some spark even in the cinders. A formidable and contagious experience of the strength of affection. Of course, loving is rich in very different forms and forces, which must be enacted with careful and creative discernment. To give another example, taken from the paradoxical language of Jesus; the commandment to "love" even your enemy does not simply translate into the command to "fall in love" with him, affections have their own justice, which must be carefully identified. At the same time, none of these differences can prevent you from loving. The basic form of loving inscribes all the affections and does not allow itself to be deducted from any of them. It is no coincidence that Jesus peremptorily affirms: "No one is good but God alone" (Mark 10:18). Not simply the "supreme good," therefore, but the absolute "loving."

The fundamental concept of loving allows a dimension of human sensitivity to emerge: not simply a corporeal, not simply intelligible. The effectiveness of loving is *the elementary experience of freedom*: it is, so to speak, the zero degree of its constitution and its evidence. This dimension does not tolerate reduction to the ontology of the entity, nor to the metaphysics of being.

Loving without freedom is simply inconceivable. In its simplest forms, loving is defined precisely by the overcoming of compulsion, calculation, imposition, utility. When we perceive that we are loved for a calculation, for an interest, for an outburst of desire or for the possession as of an object, we immediately feel that the loving vanishes, giving way to something else. Although it is not easy to precisely define this "residue" of loving, which "resists" compulsion and takes the form of freedom, this difference is perceived by everyone. To be "loved" must make you feel the fragrance of affective freedom: which cannot be reduced to attraction, or even dedication. The genuine quality of loving is not only based on freedom: loving is its most basic form. Loving is the primary experience of freedom. When I accept or decide to love I take myself beyond the deduction of a reasoning and a calculation: but I also go beyond the force of a drive and a desire. A truly free human relationship becomes evident in the form of deliberate affection: in short, through a declination of loving. Freedom in the form of affection, or affection in the form of freedom, brings to light the profound relationship that is established, precisely in the experience of loving, between freedom and bond. Affection is precisely that figure of freedom that expresses a bond: freedom, here, is not emancipation from compulsion, it is a promise of attachment. In activating a feeling of bond that leaves the other the freedom to inhabit it, the affection realizes the synthesis of the love-wanting that is proper to it.

The ethics of affection is an inseparable ethics of freedom and bond. Hence the importance of the experience of affection for the very discovery of the form of freedom, in its properly human sense. Freedom is not only a matter of the absence of compulsion; it is also a question of unprejudiced bonds. Freedom unfettered by any bond is an anaffective freedom: abstract, sterile, dangerous. Are bonds hostile to the freedom of love? Do affections disorient knowledge? A widespread conventional sense thinks so: and it preserves the separation between justice and love, reason and affections.[1]

In the contemporary world, love has regained its share in philosophical cogitation. The cogitation, however, emblematically frequents above all its symbolic condensation, exciting and enigmatic, in the erotic feeling represented in the sexual union of the couple (real or imaginary). Love, resolved in the mystique of fusional falling in love and in the metaphor of sexual enjoyment that is, symbolically identified with the erotic understanding of the couple of lovers—appears as the exciting irruption of a *folie à deux* that enhances the affective power of nature and spirit, and transcends the utilitarian reason of conveniences and calculations.[2] The focus on this model of love, assumed as the archetype of its radical ontological meaning, is an obvious legacy of romantic love. In fact, romantic *eros* replaces the effectiveness of human love with the emotion of ecstatic falling in love: idealization of a feeling of fusional attraction (virtually mystical) that aspires to live by self-realization (tendentially narcissistic). Such a contraction of the love is destined to remain substantially unprepared in the face of *the beauty and drama of the fundamentals* of the ethical sensitivity of meaning: birth, death, work, community. Faced with this exciting concentration of love in the erotic phenomenon, any other differentiation of affectivity, not defined by erotic understanding, appears to be *a weak and secondary form of love*. Or, it appears necessary to look always and only in that direction: that is, in the direction of the erotic phenomenon and sexual intimacy.

    1. The impulse for the renewed discussion of the basis of the relationship between reason and affections, which must open the way to the recomposition of freedom and bonds, in which the quality of the human is decided, we can draw it from the courageous openness of the phenomenologist Max Scheler (1874–1928). See Scheler, *Amore e conoscenza*. In theology, the modern reopening of the theme, in the face of the intellectualistic and rationalistic drift of the idea of faith, must be mentioned Pierre Rousselot (1878–1915). See Rousselot, *Gli occhi della fede*. Scheler's philosophical revival, of exceptional hermeneutic and constructive importance, can be read in Cusinato, *Periagoge* (2017) and *Biosemiotica e psicopatologia*. For the revival of Rousselot's theology, in my view, the systematic reworking of H. U. von Balthasar remains unsurpassed, *Percezione della forma*.

    2. The theorization of free erotic dissipation as a principle of anti-capitalist criticism, formulated explicitly by G. Bataille, in the wake of Nietzsche, was later taken up by the "political masters" of sexual liberation of '68 (for example, E. Fromm). Subsequent events then showed the clamorous fallacy of this association: capitalist accumulation coexists very well with erotic consumerism, while profiting from it; and the community, instead of the circulation of new affective energies, accumulates the effects of disintegration, depression, and conflict. Authors not akin to theological thought also bear witness to this: Perniola, *Sex-appeal dell'inorganico*, and Badiou, *Elogio dell'amore*.

PART 2

The Metaphysical Enigma of Loving

The ontology of loving is an orthogonal addition to the logic of being and entity, power and act. Effect without cause and process without substance. Only a god can justify it, reveal it, and make it intelligible. We need to fix it imaginatively in the action of a subject and in the definiteness of an object; we would not know how to govern it otherwise, for practical use.

When the early school spoke of the charitable compulsion as a supernatural, elusive dimension, specifically different from any other human motivation, it alluded to this. The idea of having to hinder the creaturely possibility of pure love, to be reserved exclusively for God, had this meaning. However, the enormity of the paradoxical implications of this reserve were not realized: binding it, on the one hand, to the radicality of a wounded love in need of compensation that obtains redemption thanks to the incarnation and sacrifice of its own Son; and on the other hand, to the lack of debt or need for the divine substance, saturated with self-love and indifferent to any added or missed affection. Without mediation—either ontic or adjective—being really possible. If this is pure love, its exercise is terrible; and its imitation, far from being impossible, must be avoided. In other words, the clarification of the ontological essence of loving—in terms that are not purely substantial and not purely relational—which God alone is able to honor in absolute terms—there are many benefits, but God alone is good—imposes the preparation of a metaphysics that, until now, the Christian-Western culture has lacked. Pro-affection is settled in the place of having to be, as much as it is in that *of being-giving*. *An addition, with respect to the substance and the constitutive* relationship of the subject and the object. Because its plasticity has the generosity of the *chōra*—affective *chōra*, metaphysical *chōra*, semiotic *chōra*. In the luminous shadow of the Spirit of pro-affection, the difference between the material and the immaterial, between the past and the future, between the intelligible and the ineffable, is not decisive. Yet, separated from the *chōra* of pro-affection, nothing in the world—and of God himself—would be amenable to meaning.[3] Loving

---

3. In the *Nuovo Saggio* (New essay) by Rosmini, the antecedent spiritual sensitivity is clearly indicated. While the impression concerns the materiality of the human body that is modified by the external agent, the sensation is an "inner feeling of the soul," therefore it consists of a completely spiritual passivity, although it arises from an impression. Sensation therefore does not exist without a sentient subject, while impression has no relation to the subjective body, against which the external body acts, although it offers itself to sight and touch. Only in this way can it be ascertained. However, seeing and touching that impression is already "sensation" (*NE* 2, para. 86): "The sensation that accompanies that impression (a blow that injures the arm) is not visible, not tangible: it is only sensitive for an inner feeling of the soul (man looks at and

leads to being and pro-affection is the key to its justice. Practicing justice, which gives generative content to the freedom of loving and honoring God, who testifies to the edifying character of his injunction, overlap. The justice of pro-affection is not accomplished without the love of justice: the self-referentiality and anarchy of the act of love are not its perfection, they are its perversion. And the love of justice is empty rhetoric, when it decides not to take into account the need to examine its link with pro-affection.

The fundamental beauty of morality lies here, in *the justitia per se servata* as Anselm says, that is, in the love for justice that inspires the search for the justice of loving as the power of the truth that makes-be. The search for justice is the search for *how* the act and the object of our affections *must be*—knowledge and will, understanding and action, generation and relationship, the city and the world—if they are to be truly redeemed and fulfilled. That is, to be *as they* should.[4]

In our culture, however, both in the civil and religious spheres, the social horizon of the category of justice has slipped below the normative ideality of the true and the good referred to the meaning of life: of its culture and its history, of its meaning and its destination. It essentially concerns the economic-legal sphere of rights-duties related to biological-civil life and to the social-political regulation of benefits, property, and contracts.

---

touches the dimple, but does not see and does not touch the consequent sensation he feels)." See also NS 2, para. 696: the perception of the continuity of the sentient body, of its permanence, is a fundamental and innate feeling, which is not seen and not touched, and which philosophers neglect. The sensitive experience is a unity of sentient and felt, not opposition to be overcome with which to come to terms. For this crucial step see: Soliani, "Esperienza e metafisica."

4. In that exact point, in my opinion, it is possible to place the innovative potential of the epistemological and ontological rigorization of the profile of affective intentionality, elaborated by Antonio Rosmini (1797–1855). Burgeoning studies that are brilliantly increasing these potentials, showing at the same time the fecundity of the classical roots and the audacity of modern confrontation that inspires the synthesism of being (ideal, real, moral) where the primacy of the original ethics of theological anthropology is justified; for the pro-affection of the spirit, persuasively identified in the irreducibility of human sensitivity to sensitive perception, see Bellelli, *Etica originaria*. At this stage, I am convinced that an in-depth comparison of Rosmini's thinking and that of Max Scheler could represent a turning point for the definitive phenomenological and ontological settlement of the rehabilitation—theoretical and practical—of the link between the foundation of ethics (society, politics, law) and the transcendence of the ontological. The history of every identity is in the contradiction between the injunction (ethics) and the liberal exchange (justice) of what is in the other waiting for me and what is in me waiting for the other for whom it is destined. The right of life is this, the justice of love is this: this is how history moves according to creation and the hope of its fulfillment (the kingdom of God); thus the particular and the universal of divine pro-affection, the singularity, and the commonality of human pro-affection are reconciled.

Mind you, it would be completely unacceptable to denounce this social *specialization* of the category of justice as a *degradation* of its value. It is not about that at all, of course. Rather, it is a question of restoring affective reasoning to human justice, the choreographer of the concept of social justice. This integration, in effect, appears irrelevant in many respects: often rich in pathos, but very poor in logos. Enlightenment reasoning, trusted in the natural sciences as a factor of civil hope, showing its ability to host, without offering adequate resistance, *affective catastrophes* that were by then judged anachronistic: ethnic racism, planned genocides, totalitarian law, genetic manipulation, ecological devastation, economic selection, religious wars. The denunciation initially came, with great fanfare, precisely from within the critical-social thought, certainly not religiously inspired.[5] The emblematic place of this schism, destined to produce the degradation of democratic reason itself,[6] is the transformation of the society of free equals into a society of the individual mass: with the obvious expulsion of the category of "fraternity" which, at the beginning of the modern revolution, had intoned the form of social bond to affective sociality.[7] "Freedom" and "equality" are principles that can also be declined individualistically and anaffectually; "fraternity" cannot. The first form of the modern scission is precisely that which is consumed between love, as a sentimental aspiration of private life, and justice, as a rational interest of the public sphere. This separation has profoundly shaped the theory of our legal, political and economic culture. A paradoxical drift, if we think about it, if we consider the fact that (1) all these areas of social anthropology were born from a rational elaboration of fundamental affections (mutual respect, sanctioned by the *jus*; shared friendship, pillar of *the civitas*; the fiducial disposition, a prerequisite of *negotium*); (2) finally, the impoverishment of a public culture of the justice of affections also wears out the love for justice: the space left empty by humanistic anthropology is quickly occupied by its scientific reduction. The most interesting human qualities are becoming those that robots will be able to simulate (*machine learning*) and enhance (*human enhancement*); the others will tend to be considered illusory and devoid of scientific basis.

In fact, for all these reasons and for others, expressions such as "justice of affections," or "justice of love," resonate today, if not just as oxymorons, as rather enigmatic syntheses to decipher.[8] Despite the fact that literary nar-

5. See Adorno and Horkheimer, *Dialettica dell'Illuminismo*.
6. See Argenio, *Alexis de Tocqueville e Hannah Arendt*.
7. See Baggio, *Il principio dimenticato*.
8. See Archer, *Essere umani*; Prandini and Cavazza, *Potere dell'amore*; Nussbaum, *Emozioni politiche*; Donati, *Scoprire i beni relazionali*; and Sequeri, *Deontologia del fondamento*.

ration and common language normally speak of "mistaken loves," in the postmodern conception (unlike the same romantic conception, to which it is partly inspired) love is "always right," by definition.

The Law That Regains Its Social Meaning

Should we therefore resign ourselves to the idea that a "commandment of love" is an oxymoron? And are we to conclude that, in the final analysis, justice does not draw any real knowledge from love? There is, in truth, a passage that allows us to reopen the door to the justice of love, introducing us into the ethical-ontological bond of its anthropological dynamism. And not without arousing the need for a profound rethinking of the philosophy of law.

We find this passage (now hidden and forgotten) right at the heart of the reduction of justice to the recognition of law: which in modernity has ended up solving the very idea of justice. The formula of reduction, as is well known, is the one we owe to the Roman politician and jurist Domitius Ulpianus (170–228): justice is "to give to each his own" (*suum unicuique tribuere*). Justice therefore has a dynamic character: it is a matter of assigning/ granting to each one what is "his," that is, what "by right" belongs to him. It is therefore not sufficient that he is casually the holder of a good, if he is in possession of something to which he is not entitled, that object is not his. In any case, if "his" is to be "attributed" to him, it also means that he does not have it yet: either in the sense that he does not yet possess it materially, or in the sense that he lacks the recognition of the justice of his ownership. The right to have something as one's own implies the duty of others to recognize that right. This means that the "own" is not yet where it must be; therefore, it is with others, it is elsewhere, and it is a matter of getting it where it should be, that is, in the actual ownership of the person entitled. The recognition of the other and the mediation of the third, moreover, in the rule of law, are considered essential components of its completion: because they express the dignity and human quality of the act of justice in which "one's own" is attributed and received.[9]

Let's think of our "beginning," of our pure and simple coming into the world. Our conception, our gestation, our birth and its continuation in the initiation into life, are events radically directed to the delivery of a *proprium* that allows me to be me—and no one else. This *proprium* is originally taken

---

9. See Vimercati and Bearzot, *Giustizia dei Greci*; Eusebi, *Giustizia riparativa*; Forti, *Cura delle norme*; Cartabia and Violante, *Giustizia e mito*; Paglia and Cantone, *Coscienza e la legge*; and Cacciari and Irti, *Elogio del diritto*.

from an *alienum* that is predisposed for its transformation into *something other than itself*: indeed, *into others by itself*, identical to me.[10]

In this sense, the *new* human subject is always also a causeless effect, whose mystery has its roots in God's creative pro-affection: the only one who can dispose of this totally virgin space-time and available for a new and irreproducible human singularity. Let's take one more step. In this event, it is very clear that the justice that "gives to each his own" has nothing to do simply with the recognition of property, but also with the disposition to donate. Yet the donation, here, lives, from the beginning, precisely in the form of mutual exchange. The exchange—being with, living with—is guided by the gift and its destination, and awaits its relational and affective recognition, through which I finish being born and seal my personal, irreducible, unrepeatable singularity. In this justice of the delivery and reception of my own, initially hosted by the other as his, *the intention* to get him to his destination and *the way* in which he is sent to his destination is very important. By love or by force, by chance and by will, by inertia or by tenderness, by calculation or by grace? In a word, pro-affection, that is, the love that restores us to the human mode of our mutual dependence (we are always, at the origin, parts entrusted to others, destined for us, which become part of us) makes the quality of justice. The effectiveness (material and legal) of the service does not become irrelevant for this: on the contrary. Haggling or violating this process is the mother of all possible violations.

Let's try to imagine the nightmare and the degradation of a "performative" society of the justice of the affections of the generation (of law and governance, of the clinic, of the economy) that "rationally" removes the interest in the affective quality and the human modality of its recognition and its exercise in gift and exchange. Where my human beginning is lost, no continuity can remain intact.

Every human singularity is generated in the transmission of the human: parts of the human destined for us, so that they may become our *proprium*, are originally with the other as *munus alienum* waiting for recognition and destination.[11] The destination is fundamentally anonymous, that is, intrapersonal and suprapersonal circulation of a *bonum diffusivum* that draws on the shared human. However, this transmission is destined to a nominal singularity: that is, it does not act *as it should* without passing through *personal donation*: intentional, deliberate, enjoyed as sensitivity and justice of

10. "All human life on our planet is born of a woman. The only unifying, incontrovertible experience, shared by all, men and women, is the period spent forming ourselves in the womb of a woman. . . . Throughout life and even in death we keep the imprint of this experience" (Rich, *Nato di donna*, 7)

11. See Cusinato, *Periagoge* (2019).

self-sacrifice that recognizes the enchantment of its unexpected *fruitfulness*. Social justice exists only in this relational circularity: that which is mine is always with someone else, and I myself am the depositary of one of that destined for others. Developing the affection of this justice means revisiting the contents of ethics in this anthropological key. In this process we can see the concrete, non-nebulous and non-sentimental, non-indeterminate meaning of the concept of "awareness of the justice of affections" would appear definitively clear. Individuals and peoples live—and die—of their most sacred and dearest affections. From them they draw the impulses of their highest choices and their best intelligence; it would be really strange if the affections were impervious to the *logos* of reason and to the *nomos* of justice.[12] Anaffective reason is an internal *limitation* to reason itself; it condemns one to separation from the life of the spirit and from the sensitivity to meaning that are proper to the human singularity. The injunction of affective justice is—and must remain—the very spirit of the law: not the hermeneutics of its sentimental complement or enfeeblement, but the theory of the constitution of the law as a social and therefore humanistic bond.[13]

An impossible task without cultivating the fundamental understanding of the meaning by which loving founds the human world and refunds it, faces its dramatics and bears witness to its blessing. It is the mystery of pro-affection: as a sublime antecedent and necessary addition: without which being is never as it should be (even God) and justice would not even have the concept (let alone the practice).

Bibliography

Adorno, Theodor W., and Max Horkheimer, eds. *Dialettica dell'Illuminismo*. Turin: Einaudi, 2010.
Angelini, Giuseppe. "Diritto e teologia. Una mediazione dimenticata: la morale." *Hermeneutica* (1998) 81–108.
Archer, Margareth S. *Essere umani. Il problema dell'agire*. Translated by P. Zanna. Turin: Marietti, 2007.
Argenio, Antonella. *Alexis de Tocqueville e Hannah Arendt. Un dialogo a distanza*. Naples: Editoriale Scientifica, 2005.
Badiou, Alain. *Elogio dell'amore*. Milan: Neri Pozza, 2019.

12. See Bollnow, *Tonalità emotive*, and Giammusso, *Forma Aperta*.

13. See D'Agostino, *Diritto come problema teologico*; Angelini, "Diritto e teologia" (that entire issue of *Hermeneutica* is dedicated to the clarification of the theme "law and theology"); Ricoeur, *Amore e Giustizia*; De Luise, *Civiltà nell'anima*; Supiot, *Homo juridicus*; Lentiampa Shenge, *Paul Ricoeur*; Wolterstorff, *Justice in Love*; Heritier, *Estetica giuridica*; Sequeri, "Diritto e teologia"; Sala, *Italo Mancini*; and Sequeri, "Lettera e lo spirito."

PART 2

Baggio, Alberto. *Il principio dimenticato. La fraternità nella riflessione politologica contemporanea*. Rome: Città Nuova, 2007.

Balthasar, Hans Urs von. *La percezione della forma*. Vol. 1 of *Gloria. Un'estetica teologica*. Translated by Giuseppe Ruggieri. Milan: Jaca, 2012.

Bellelli, Fernando. *Etica originaria e assoluto affettivo. La coscienza e il superamento della modernità nella teologia filosofica di Antonio Rosmini*. Milan: Vita e Pensiero, 2014.

Bollnow, Otto F. *Le tonalità emotive*. Edited and translated by Daniele Bruzzone. Milan: Vita e Pensiero, 2009.

Cacciari, Massimo, and Natalino Irti. *Elogio del diritto*. Milan: Nave di Teseo, 2019.

Cartabia, Marta, and Luciano Violante, eds. *Giustizia e mito. Con Edipo, Antigone e Creonte*. Bologna: Mulino, 2018.

Cusinato, Guido. *Biosemiotica e psicopatologia dell'ordo amoris. In dialogo con Max Scheler*. Milan: Franco Angeli, 2019.

———. *Periagoge. Teoria della singolarità e filosofia come cura del desiderio*. Verona: QuiEdit, 2019.

———. *Periagoge. Teoria della singolarità e filosofia come esercizio di trasformazione*. Verona: QuiEdit, 2017.

D'Agostino, Francesco. *Il diritto come problema teologico*. Turin: Giappichelli, 1997.

De Luise, Fulvia. *La civiltà nell'anima. Note sulla questione della giustizia in Platone*. Milan: Franco Angeli, 2003.

Donati, Pierpaolo. *Scoprire i beni relazionali. Per generare una nuova socialità*. Soverìa Mannelli, It.: Rubbettino, 2019.

Eusebi, Luciano, ed. *Una giustizia riparativa*. Milan: Vita e Pensiero, 2016.

Forti, Gabrio. *La cura delle norme. Oltre la corruzione delle regole e dei saperi*. Milan: Vita e Pensiero, 2018.

Giammusso, Salvatore. *La Forma Aperta. L'ermeneutica della vita nell'opera di O. F. Bollnow*. Milan: Franco Angeli, 2008.

Heritier, Paolo. *Estetica giuridica*. 2 vols. Turin: Giappichelli, 2012.

Lentiampa Shenge, Adrien. *Paul Ricoeur. La justice selon l'ésperance*. Brussels: Lessius, 2009.

Nussbaum, Martha. *Emozioni politiche. Perché l'amore conta per la giustizia*. Translated by R. Falcioni. Bologna: Mulino, 2014.

Paglia, Vincenzo, and Raffaele Cantone. *La coscienza e la legge*. Milan: Rizzoli, 2019.

Perniola, Mario. *Il sex-appeal dell'inorganico*. Turin: Einaudi, 2004.

Prandini, Riccardo, and Gianpietro Cavazza, eds. *Il potere dell'amore nell'epoca della globalizzazione*. Genoa: Melangolo, 2011.

Rich, Adrienne. *Nato di donna. Cosa significa per gli uomini essere nati da un corpo di donna*. Milan: Garzanti, 1977.

Ricoeur, Paul. *Amore e Giustizia*. Translated by I. Bertoletti. Brescia, It.: Morcelliana, 2000.

Rosmini, Antonio. *Nuovo Saggio sull'origine delle idee*. Edited by Gaetano Messina. ENC 3–5. Rome: Città Nuova, 2003–2004.

Rousselot, Pierre. *Gli occhi della fede*. Milan: Jaca, 1983.

Sala, Vincenzo. *Italo Mancini, filosofo del diritto*. Turin: Giappichelli, 2014.

Scheler, Max. *Amore e conoscenza*. Brescia, It.: Morcelliana, 2009.

Sequeri, Pierangelo. *Deontologia del fondamento*. Turin: Giappichelli, 2020.

———. "Diritto e teologia: congetture e ritrattazioni." *Jus. Rivista di Scienze Giuridiche* 60 (2013) 183–99.

———. "La lettera e lo spirito della legge, oggi. Prospettiva teologica." *Iustitia* 3 (2018) 345–56.

Soliani, Gianpietro. "Esperienza e metafisica. Rosmini e Bontadini oltre Kant." In *Pedagogia del sapere di Dio. Una prospettiva storico-culturale*, edited by Fernando Bellelli, Rosminianesimo teologico, 215–47. Milan: Mimesis, 2019.

Supiot, Alain. Homo juridicus. *Saggio sulla funzione antropologica del diritto*. Milan: Bruno Mondadori, 2006.

Vimercati, Emanuele, and Cinzia Bearzot, eds. *La giustizia dei Greci tra riflessione filosofica e prassi giudiziaria*. Milan: Vita e Pensiero, 2013.

Wolterstorff, Nicholas. *Justice in Love*. Cambridge, UK: Eerdmans, 2011.

6

Beyond Extrinsecism between Philosophy and Theology, in a Solid Circle in Rosmini Theology
Twenty Years after the Doctrinal Note

ANTONIO STAGLIANÒ

Therefore, the doctrine of the Trinity, that is, the doctrine of being one and triune profoundly, entirely dissolves that problem from the human spirit always proposed as an enigma to itself, never conquered: it communicates to man the doctrine of being in all its forms.
—Antonio Rosmini

Knowing how to penetrate that mystery with philosophical reflection, and make it speak to all men, believers or nonbelievers, can be the task and ambition of a philosophy that knows how to learn from religious experience without claiming to translate it into philosophical terms and without enslaving itself by speaking its own language and maintaining its rigorous autonomy.
—Luigi Pareyson

Introduction

WHEN ANTONIO ROSMINI STUDIED theology at the Faculty of Theology at the University of Padova, there were very few students. In the early nineteenth century, the condition of theology was "pitiful," in the opinion of the great Rosmini. In the work *The Five Wounds of the Holy Church (Delle cinque piaghe della Santa Chiesa)*, dealing with the wound on the right hand (*Dell'insufficiente istruzione del clero* [On the insufficient education of the clergy]), he denounced the "bloodless" "abstract" nature, "with manuals lacking in spirit, in principles, in eloquence, in method" that had abandoned "everything that belonged to the heart and to the other human faculties, only caring about the mind."[1] Today, in theology there is quite a different question. The Vatican Council II has acquired the historical character of the revelation and the anthropological dimension of the faith: the revelation is the self-communication of God in human events, and not only a set of doctrinal propositions to be adhered to with intellectual assent. The faith—which welcomes this revelation—is a wholly human act, involving conscience, heart, mind, sentiment, emotion, affections, imagination, aspirations for the future, intelligence, and certainly critical reasoning. Theology is the critical form of that which we come to know believing in Jesus Christ, the truth of God in person. The historical-critical method is the way to elaborate dogmatic theology: the inseparably "positive" way (in relation to the revelation, which communicates itself and acts in history, advancing in the tradition of the faith) and "speculative" (referred to the need to critically explain to the "reason" of Christian hope in changing and often adverse cultural contexts).

The Intrinsic Reason for Faith

Apart from the other, more typically historical and economic issues, Rosmini's accusation in *Forty Propositions (Quaranta proposizioni)* was matured in an ecclesiastic-theological cultural context dominated by a certain theoretical intransigence in the philosophical field: with the neoscholastic version of Thomistic philosophy it was presumed that the "exclusive" way of defending the faith against attacks of fideism, rationalism, ontologism and pantheism had been found. The revealed truth thus seemed so closely linked, thanks to its orthodox mediation, to a particular interpretation of the thinking of Saint Thomas, practiced by the neoscholastic movement of the time, which was authoritatively (but perhaps inappropriately) recognized and legitimized by the *Aeterni Patris* of Pope Leo XIII. "This

---

1. Rosmini, *FW*, para. 39.

Thomism" did not seem capable of harmonizing with the philosophical sea change in the Rosminian system of Truth, as the Nota also clearly emphasizes: Rosmini's thinking "was different with regard to the language and the conceptual structure of Saint Thomas Aquinas's philosophical and theological elaboration."[2] The problem of the orthodoxy of the faith, therefore, was effectively traced back to the general question of the "philosophical instrument" to be used to mediate the doctrinal truth.

From this point of view, we must recognize the considerable thrust towards renewal produced by the Vatican Council II. Thanks to this council, contemporary theological epistemology, with increasing awareness, stated that it would not be to a particular philosophy (neither Thomistic, neoscholastic, nor Rosminian) that the task of founding (or justifying) and conveying the truth of the content of the faith in the culture of the time would be entrusted, but rather the theological reason intrinsic to the faith itself, in its typically catholic quality of *fides quaerens intellectum*, that is faith capable of expressing itself through rational thought, also philosophical, that is born directly from it, as an expression of the redemption-donate to the human reason of faith and as manifestation, when the credibility of the faith, in the universal opening-destination of the *depositum fidei*.

On the one hand, therefore, it is possible to emphasize the doctrinal validity of the *Post Obitum* as a condemnation of pantheist, ontologist, and rationalist propositions. On the other hand, it is not possible to ignore its hermeneutic weakness inasmuch as it proscribes these propositions *in proprio auctoris sensu*.

With this statement, the document of the magisterium intends a priori to avoid the tendency (which had already emerged at the time of the Jansenist controversy) to discredit the pronouncement, because the proven propositions did not express the authentic meaning of Rosmini's thought. It is however worth mentioning, from the hermeneutic standpoint, that many of the condemned propositions were taken from works published posthumously, whose authentic interpretation could only emerge from the personal defense of Rosmini himself, and not simply from the thinking of Rosminian followers.

Now, Rosmini had died some years earlier, while the paladins of his defense do not seem to have grasped the originality of his thinking, precisely on a central point, decisive for the controversy and for the subsequent sentence: the problem of the choice of the philosophical instrument that more than anything else (and excluding all the others) could have saved the believers from the error, preserving the authentic orthodoxy of the faith.

2. Congregazione per la Dottrina della Fede, "Nota sul valore," para. 4.

At that time, not only the neoscholastic Thomists, but also the "Rosminists" shared the idea that the philosophy should (and could) guarantee the faith its scientific mediation: theology consisted, in fact, of the application of philosophy to the revealed dogma.

Unfortunately, however, this vision was practiced in the ideological perspective established with Descartes, and typified modernity, according to which philosophy was conceived as separate (extrinsic) to faith and an expression of neutral and pure reason.

For Rosmini's accusers, the philosophy best suited to defending the orthodoxy of the faith was the Thomistic neoscholastic (not Rosminianism, which appeared in their eyes, to be a betrayal, because it was excessively compromised by the modern idealistic-subjectivistic system). But the rigidity of the relationship that had been instituted between dogma and its Thomistic philosophical mediation, although it seemed to guarantee the faith a rigorous conceptual protection, in fact led to neoscholastic philosophy being attributed the authority of the dogma itself, conferring on it a sort of canonization.

The Unforgettable Distinction between Faith and Theology

It is also wise to distinguish between (but obviously not to separate) faith and theology, in order to avoid giving faith the inevitable hypothetical nature of theology as a scientific application, and to theology the dogmatic nature of faith. Apart from faith, in fact, every attempt at theological mediation can be judged "good" or "insufficient," "impossible" or "successful." But theology itself, when it remains at its own level, is not faith, nor is it simply a theory. This distinction, which could have served to soothe the bitter tones of the theological polemic, does not seem to have been much practiced in the context of the argument that led to the condemnation of Rosmini; perhaps it was not felt, presumably because the doctrinal truth and its theological mediation appeared to be rigidly all one, univocally. This rigidity unfortunately also involved philosophy, in the quality of scientific instrument of the theological explanation of the faith.

It is, after all, a common mentality, shared also by Rosmini. The continual and impassioned appeal to the uniqueness of his "system of truth" effectively seems at first glance to curb any philosophical pluralism: it was as if he had arrived at the elaboration of an "absolute philosophy," capable of expressing human rationality in the best and most complete way. The enthusiasm, with which from time to time he showed how "suited" this philosophy was to the dogma, manifested this awareness.

For Rosmini, however, theology was strongly characterized by its historical nature. In the work *The Theological Language (Il linguaggio teologico)*—written with the intention of clarifying some points of his theological writings and, thus, with a single text, meeting the requests of the theological commission that issued the *Dimittantur*—faith refers to the deposit, theology as a critical measure of faith "it penetrates the truth of the faith with understanding" and illustrates it with words and writings. The resulting theological study can produce a genuine dogmatic development, which, nevertheless, is not sufficient to determine an increase or a change in the "deposited" truth. The deposit of faith "because it is a divine thing, cannot be either diminished nor increased, nor in any slight way altered," and therefore, "how can these truths still be and must they be meditated on, lived and illustrated?"[3]

The reference to the fathers is an exemplary model: proceeding by different and individual ways, "adorned with various riches and various styles" they maintained unity in the variations, contributing to the dogmatic progress.[4] The important aspect is that "this progress does not detract from the faith, but only helps it."[5] Theology "serves" the faith and never leaves it. From here derives the principle of coherence of the revelation, as the great rule to follow "both to laudably amplify the good doctrine, and to judge where the mind strays and misunderstands it."[6] The theologian is thus bound to the church. In this bond, he finds the guarantee of the authenticity of his progress: in the church, with the church, for the church, because the church is one with the Spirit of Christ, which "guides the ecclesiastic doctor, so that he teaches the listener to understand well."[7] It is clear why, according to Rosmini, the work of the theologian is not homogeneous in the strict sense of the "judgment of censorship." Only the magisterium of the church can judge the orthodoxy of an ecclesiastic author. The intervention of the theologian, on this matter, can only be given as an opinion. Indeed, not all theologians are "good theologians," because not all theologians know how to be good philosophers or "ideologists."

---

3. Rosmini, *TL*, 49.
4. Rosmini, *TL*, 50.
5. Rosmini, *TL*, 51.
6. Therefore: "Does this outcome proceed by necessary inference from this truth revealed and defined by the Church? Accept it without hesitation and it will not be an advance. Does it not rather proceed and derive from the opposite? Judge it, for it is an erroneous doctrine and one to be avoided. Thus, the principle of coherence with what is revealed unlocks a great source for increasing and developing sacred doctrine." (Rosmini, *TL*, 54).
7. Rosmini, *TL*, 68.

A Good Theologian Must Not Ignore the Nature of the Mind

Like Saint Augustine, one who cannot arrive at a true conception of the nature of the human mind and intelligence must declare himself inept in theology. In this impotence, in fact, Rosmini sees the never-ending source of daring heretical statements about God and the Trinity.[8] In this sense, the bond between "ignorance of the mind" and "ignorance of God" is very close, because it is structural and the link between philosophy (to which the ideological task is entrusted) and theology (the science of God). On the level of method, the ideal being (a typical and genuine expression of a philosophical system that has attained the intelligence of the mind) is fundamentally led to theology, inasmuch as the mind's knowledge begins with "good philosophy," "that philosophy which can soon be usefully applied to divine things."[9] It is not, therefore, a matter of just any philosophy, but of Christian philosophy established in its truth of the discovery of the "light of our intelligence in which lies the origin of a time of our ideas, and the certainty of our judgments."[10]

It remains to ask Rosmini how and to what extent this adventure of the discovery of the human mind, so necessary and fundamental for faith and theology, can and must find completion "independently" or "in dependence" from faith itself. His answer is clear: there is no extrinsecism between the truth of faith and the truth of reason, for which the former become the content of a supernatural instruction, believed precisely because it transcends human rationality, and the latter are the content of a natural order, that can only be pursued through the "pure" exercise of thought, in a philosophy that is elaborated neutrally with respect to faith. In Rosmini there is a distinction, but never a dualistic separation between theological faith and philosophical reason. Rather, his research aims to establish, on the basis of the distinction, their profound unity, for a "reciprocal benefit." The "Rosminian question"—in epistemological terms—does not so much lie in noting how authentic philosophy benefits theology (which appears evident), but vice versa, how theological faith benefits philosophy and its independence (something that is difficult to consider even nowadays).[11]

This "dualism," on the other hand, seems to be typical of Rosmini's critics, of his "neo-Thomist judges." Rosmini would wholly agree with a

---

8. Rosmini, *TL*, 38.
9. Rosmini, *TL*, 39.
10. Rosmini, *TL*, 40.
11. For a clarification in this direction see Stagliano, "Autonomia della ragione."

passage from an illuminating conference by Cardinal J. Ratzinger, which is—I believe—expressively brief in Rosmini's apologetic intention:

> I consider that neoscholastic rationalism has failed in its attempt to reconstruct the *Preambula Fidei* with a reason quite independent from faith, with a purely rational certainty; all other attempts, which follow this same path, will attain the same results. On this point, Karl Barth was right in refusing philosophy as a foundation of faith, independently from the latter: our faith would then be based, after all, on changing philosophical theories. But Barth was mistaken in defining faith as a simple paradox, which can only subsist against reason or in total independence from it. One of the functions of faith, and not one of the least important, is that of offering a rehabilitation of reason as reason, not to harm it, not to be extraneous to it, but to lead it back to itself. The historical instrument of faith can once again free reason as such, so that it can—once set on the good road of faith—see itself. We must make every effort to attain a similar new dialogue between faith and philosophy, because they need each other. Reason cannot heal itself without faith, but faith without reason cannot become human.[12]

Rosmini, noting that heresies were born of Platonism and Aristotelianism and having noted the "influence of philosophical errors in religion itself," stated "moved mainly by this consideration I have proposed in *Nuovo Saggio sull'origine delle idee* . . . that ideological system that being true, also seems to me the only one that can perfectly agree with Christian dogma."[13]

The evident intention of his philosophical research expresses *forma mentis* profoundly rooted in the Catholic dogma that does not philosophize for its own sake, but philosophizes to serve the faith and the church.

Rosmini is above all a theologian, also when he writes of philosophy. His life and his thought are attracted by and tend towards a single purpose: the glory of the triune God, manifested in Christ, the eternal Son in human flesh, who is the absolute Savior of history, recapitulatory of the beginning, the beatific future of mankind. His Christocentric beliefs are to be found in all the themes of human knowledge, seeking unity, synthesis, and system.

---

12. Ratzinger, "Conference during the Meeting." Conference held by Cardinal J. Ratzinger during the meeting between the Congregation for the Doctrine of the Faith and the presidents of the Doctrinal Commissions of Latin America (Guadalajara/Messico, May 1996).

13. Rosmini, SA, 1:234. It is sufficient to read the preface to *Nuovo saggio* to understand the rhetorical nature of this discussion and, inversely, Rosmini's profound awareness of having reached the elaboration of the "system of truth," the only one truly practical for Catholic dogma. (See Rosmini, "Prefazione.")

Thus, not only theological problems, but also philosophical and political ones would find in Christian truth a constant reference point for their development and their solution.

All Rosmini's works (none excluded) are a precise testimony of this. For example, all the Rosminian philosophical system is based on the discovery of the ideal being (for the regressive phase) and on that of synthesism of the three forms of being (for the progressive or theosophical phase); both these pillars have a constitutive relationship (in the sense that they are founded and fulfilled) one with the divine Word and the other with the Trinity of the divine Persons.

Once again, Rosminian philosophy, although remaining independently such, does not hide (rather it boasts) an inwardly religious inspiration, a profound theological intentionality, an explicitly apologetic-missionary character. The Rosminian *forma mentis* assumes the primacy of faith, of grace, of the church as an existential and speculative criterion. Thus, Rosmini knows of the greatness of human reason, of the freedom of man and the possible civil progress of society, because he believes in the redemptive and transforming capacity of faith, of grace, of the church. In every passage of his writings, we can note his "radical theocentric bias" that leads him to recognize the true existence of the real inasmuch as it is related (founded) by God.

Rosmini distinguishes, but does not separate. The Christocentric orientation of his thought is manifested above all in this: no man is God and no God is man, but in Christ and for Christ, safeguarded by the difference in human nature and divine nature, it is necessary to love, to contemplate the real unity of man and God. In Jesus, truly the eternal Son is human flesh: God, in the Person of the Son, is truly present in history: man finds himself essentially in the condition of a "real contact" with God. How can we think critically of all this? How could he express its character of saving and not mythological truth? How could he communicate it to the people of the nineteenth century, settled on the diametrically opposite and conflictual poles of enlightenment and tradition, but united by the same dislike of speculative reason? What categories should be used for a possible dialogue, necessary and not superficial? Where to start so that the intelligent mediation of Christian dogma was not rejected from the start?

Rosmini had great plans, he intended to pursue the restore the mind to its rationality, he decided on a Christian encyclopedia based on a first truth, present in every man, expressed in all its implications and conceived as a manifestation of the divine Verb, its twilight, a natural sketch of Christianity. So, he held back the theological production and dedicated his efforts above all to philosophy and politics. On July 5, 1849, he wrote: "The major works, that is *Teosofia* and *Antropologia soprannaturale* I do not intend to publish for now, since I see that unfortunately the times are not yet ready to receive them, still needing milk and not capable of eating solid food."[14]

We can understand, therefore, how widely his thinking ranged: the reason and the revelation. Rosmini's solution can be simplified as follows: reason carries with itself an innate capability, the ideal being, as an indeterminate horizon of concrete human intelligibility and creatural element in which the supernatural and personal self-communication of God, which in turn not only elevates, but heals it. From here, generally, his program of "believing thought": seeking the necessity and the reason of that which is believed. "Of that which is believed," I repeat, and as such it is welcomed by the faith of the church: it seems to me that I have rigorously shown in my scientific research on Rosmini's "theology" the eminently traditional nature of his theological method, which, while it intending to clarify the belonging of some truths of the faith to the ecclesiastic tradition, has no intention of critical verification or genetic derivation in their regard. His speculative task was rather that of making these truths less repugnant by using his own philosophical intuitions, of which the "convenience" with respect to Christian doctrine was constantly evident.[15]

The Trinitarian Revelation of God and the Ontology of the Three Forms of Being

The close relationship between the synthesism of the three forms of being and the Trinitarian revelation of God is unexceptionable. Also in this field, Rosmini's methodical perspective receives an illumination that confirms his precise *forma mentis*. The movement of "discovery" is not such as to deduce the Trinity of divine Persons from the triadicity of the forms of being, but vice versa it is precisely the Christian doctrine that opens the horizon of Trinitarian ontology to reason. Here is the Rosminian prescription from *Supernatural Anthropology (Antropologia soprannaturale)*:

> To find the most complete vestige of the Trinity in the universe, or rather to find a formula that fully expresses the Holy Trinity, which impressed itself in things when creating them, seemed to me to have followed this method. In the first place, I observed

14. Rosmini, *Epistolario completo*, 10:667.

15. This is a deliberately traditional theology that concentrates on self-information or rediscovering that which was revealed (dogma) and is Christian doctrine: it is based on the *auctoritates* and by authority proceeds, asking philosophical reason (that is a particular system of philosophy) to illustrate and defend the truths of the faith ascertained as such by recourse to the traditional sources: Councils, Holy Scripture, church fathers, and Saint Thomas Aquainas. See Staglianò, "Rosmini tra tradizione e modernità."

the created being in all its possible forms and ways. I then began to classify these forms and these ways and by reducing them from class to class, I subsumed them into real original genres, irreducible to each other, nor having any other generic essence above them, but only the universal essence, the being. Now, this operation led me to find three primitive and original forms that could not be mistaken one for the other, which I recognized as the three forms of which the universe was informed, that is, the three forms of the created being. These three forms or modes of being are: 1. the real being; 2. the ideal being; 3. the moral being.[16]

The following pages, dedicated to "the traces of the Trinity scattered throughout the created being are not sufficient to find the Trinity of the divine persons, without the revelation,"[17] clarify the extent to which Rosmini's thinking avoids the rationalistic risk of deriving the Trinity from the forms as its cause is deduced from the effect. In fact: "The divine Trinity is something entirely different from that triune way in which the created being subsists."[18]

Of very similar tenor are the important statements found in *Theosophy (Teosofia)*. Here they assume a systematic and speculative value *in actu exercito*. The emanationism of the ancient and modern unitary systems (Plotinus and Hegel) is a philosophical error of considerable scope because it does not provide a solution to the problem par excellence that concerns the first being: "how the perfect unity of the first being is reconciled with that sort of multiplicity which is necessary for it to be full, active and the cause of things."[19] This problem presents an opposition "that has confused philosophy ... throughout the centuries, which Christ has satisfied, but only by revealing the mystery."[20] In this sense it is not surprising that the Trinity of divine Persons is "at the basis of theosophy as the mysterious foundation."[21]

---

16. Rosmini, *SA*, 1:141.

17. Rosmini, *SA*, 1:46–48.

18. Rosmini, *SA*, 1:46. In the movement of thought one can descend from the Trinity to the forms of being, but it is not possible to ascend from the forms to the Trinity. Therefore, "I agree that where the mystery of the Christian Trinity is not admitted, nothing is explained and the whole universe is an impenetrable enigma. So, has reason alone found the solution to this enigma? Certainly not, because in order to have recourse to the mystery of the Most Holy Trinity, if one wishes merely as a hypothesis, in order to sufficiently explain the existence of the world it would be necessary to be able to conceive this mystery, because no-one ever has recourse to a hypothesis, if it has not already been conceived. Now, reason could not and still cannot conceive the mystery of the Holy Trinity; and faith alone prompts us to believe" (Rosmini, *SA*, 1:47).

19. Rosmini, *Theos*, 1:14.

20. Rosmini, *Theos*, 1:119.

21. Rosmini, *Theos*, 1:140.

Thus, the Trinitarian mystery revealed enters philosophy: "This sublime mystery is therefore the profound and unchanging foundation on which it is possible to raise the edifice not only of the supernatural doctrine, but also of the rational theosophy . . . this will have this important consequence, that to the divine revelation philosophy itself will owe its perfection, its unshakeable base and its unattainable splendor."[22]

If on this front, the Trinitarian revelation is "seminal" for philosophical reasoning, since the work *Theosophy* remains a structurally rational elaboration, but historically possible because the fact of Christianity has shown the triune face of God: "It would therefore be impossible to continue with the research, that remains to be done around the nature of being . . . if we do not take as given two postulates: . . . 1. That the absolute Being, which we call God, exists; 2. That the absolute Being exists identical in three distinct persons, each absolute and infinite."[23]

This impossibility of proceeding in a philosophically rigorous manner, clear testimony of Rosmini's believing *forma mentis*, is by identity, the essential content of the rational demonstration of the existence of the Trinity for which, among other things, he was condemned.[24]

To accredit an orthodox sense of this Rosminian position, I have again proposed the schematic vision of his reasoning, without prejudice to the needs of an interpretation that respects both the immediate and the remote context of the author: (1) For Rosmini, the Triune nature of God is a revealed mystery that can be attained only through the Christian faith; (2) Dogma has a certain analogy with the three forms of being: ideal, real and moral, but it is "an infinitely different thing"; (3) Following the gratuitous revelation, the Trinitarian face of God shed its truthful light also in the sphere of philosophy, helping reason to resolve ontological and theosophical problems that, historically, had never been unraveled; 4) The acquisitions reached by

---

22. Rosmini, *Theos*, 1:145. In *Introduzione alla filosofia* (Introduction to philosophy) he reiterates it even beyond any possible misunderstanding: "The doctrine therefore of the Trinity, that is, the doctrine of being one and triune profoundly, entirely dissolves the problem that the human spirit has always proposed to itself as yet another enigma, never understood: it communicates to man the doctrine of being in all its forms. The doctrine therefore of the most august of the mysteries descends from heaven like a golden dome that is placed on the edifice of natural knowledge, which otherwise would remain uncovered and exposed to the rains and winds, and man, even the philosopher, would be condemned to live badly satisfied with himself, as he who continually seeks what he never finds. Here is the *supernatural of science* as necessary as the *supernatural of life*" (161). Not for reasoning, but by reasoning, but in "by virtue of faith" man knows the Triune God, and so he is "suddenly transported to that infinitely distant point, to which he implicitly wanted to go" (160).

23. Rosmini, *Theos*, 1:144.

24. See Congregazione del Sant'Uffizio, "Post Obitum," proposition 25.

philosophy are rational and therefore incontrovertible; to deny them would entail a philosophical shortcoming and deficiency, or a relapse into contradictions; (5) Since reason has historically reached these conclusions thanks to the communication of the Trinitarian mystery, this constitutes an indirect demonstration of the truth of the revelation or, as Rosmini calls it, "a de-ontological demonstration," "because it demonstrates not that the thing is, but that it must be so; and this too, if it is in compliance with an undeniable certainty."[25] Treating the Trinitarian truth as a scientific proposition, like any other, does not deprive the dogma of its mystery and its transcendence (faith is faith and remains so). We are moving here towards the recognition of the extent to which faith can help reason to be itself rationally, and not merely on the level of rationalizing the mystery.[26]

We are, therefore, fully in line with the entire Catholic tradition, which has always spoken of a healing and elevating exercise of faith with respect to human reason as such. Rosmini's methodological perspective, after having adequately distinguished between reason and faith, is that of uniting, enacting the fruitfulness of the "salvific" union of faith with reason, which helps reason and does not impoverish faith, but rather justifies it and gives it credibility.

Those who started from the theoretical assumption of the separation between faith and reason could not understand this "project of union." The model of separation, in fact, was dominant in the neo-scholasticism of the time. But, whoever separates, if he then wants to unite, can do so only by extrinsically juxtaposing. This is not so in Rosmini's work, since he sought the inner unity between faith and reason and, therefore, was hopelessly misunderstood and accused by his critical interlocutors of both rationalism and fideism.

With the synthesis of Bruno Forte who reflects on the Trinitarian ontology in Rosmini: "Only the Trinitarian scandal radically introduces the multiple into the One, without mixing or confusion, without division or separation, inasmuch as he sees the One as Triune: only he is capable of

25. Rosmini, *Theos*, 1:144.

26. Tugged by one side and the other, Rosmini was accused of fideism and rationalism at the same time, while instead he was trying to elaborate "an ontological theory that was promising for a rational explanation of the Trinitarian mystery," as Piero Coda was trying to thematize his programme on *Ontologia trinitaria* (a perspective assumed by K. Hemmerle). In my *Trattato sulla teologia trinitaria*, I specified: "The Rosminian perspective of a personalist Trinitarian ontology would also allow us to "think" of the otherness of God as Agàpe, avoiding the failing of a certain methodological agnosticism, which due to a lack of adequate ontological conceptual infrastructures, does not "backtrack" from the economy of the incarnation to the immanent theology of the God Trinity" (Staglianò, *Mistero del Dio vivente*, 359).

founding the consistency of the world as other than God, and yet not separated or opposed to God."²⁷

The Modern-Day Extrinsecist Cultural Climate

The extrinsecism between reason and faith, between philosophy and theology, could be traced back to the extrinsecism between natural and supernatural, typical of those who had made neoscholastic Thomism an essential paradigmatic point of reference for appreciating the "service of philosophy" for theology. Even on June 21, 1965, the historian of medieval thought Étienne Gilson wrote to Henri de Lubac, expressing surprise at the Jesuit's appreciation for the work of Maurice Blondel and Teilhard de Chardin. These authors, in his opinion, confused nature and the supernatural, philosophy and theology. Unlike Rosmini, who as a theologian wrote about philosophy, Gilson accused Blondel of having succumbed to the temptation to philosophize on matters of theology, as a philosopher pretending to be a theologian.²⁸ Not separating, he confused, creating an ideal continuity between the two orders and originating a dependence of the supernatural over the natural, with an intrinsecism that made it impossible to recognize the distinction between the two planes, typical of the Thomistic lesson. The misunderstanding is particularly evident in *L'Action*: "Blondel speaks of philosophy, while the problem that he intends to resolve by means of philosophy concerns the supernatural, a field that by definition belongs to theology. Blondel wanted to sustain by philosophical means that mankind aspires to a supernatural end: he wanted therefore to reach a theological conclusion through philosophy."²⁹ This unappealable judgment was not alone. The Thomistic school teemed with renowned thinkers who shared this "prejudice." One stands out above all, Cornelio Fabro, critic of Rosmini in the sixties who in his *Rosmini postumo*—in contrast with the conciliar climate—still incited the Jesuits to resume, without fear, the battle against Rosmini and the Rosminists. Fabro, like Gilson, condemned the intrinsecism of *L'Action*: "Blondel refuses to apply the Leibnizian principle for the relationship between the natural and supernatural order, but the entire Leibnizian conception of the structure of the finite is in solidarity

---

27. Forte, *Bibbia dei filosofi*, 57.

28. He wrote: "I cannot share his admiration for the thinking of Blondel and for that of Teilhard de Chardin," and referring to Blondel he confesses to De Lubac, "When I was young, he led me to believe that Scholasticism was an enterprise of "extrinsic monomorphism" (Gilson, *Dialogo fecondo*, 61).

29. Gilson, *Problemi d'oggi*, 68.

with the continuity of the passage between the two orders." In the distinction between finite and infinite and between human thought and divine thought, adherence to Thomism is compromised and the way is opened for the *théologie nouvelle*.[30]

In the sixties—in this extrinsecist cultural climate—it was possible to consider "unreformable" Rosmini's judgment of heterodoxy, while at the same time admitting his saintly life and the possibility of proceeding with the beatification, whatever his thinking. Rosmini, on the other hand, had theorized *L'idea di Sapienza* (Idea of wisdom) as a profound unit, in a solid circle, of "science and virtue," of "science and sanctity," stating that "a drop of moral life is worth more than a sea of science": and therefore the true theology is that which interiorly unites critical reasoning, spirituality and the mystic, the experience of the revelation of God, or better, to use Rosmini's words, the perception of God, through which man is deiformed, Christoformed, spiritiform, triniform. The experience of the faith redeems and transfigures human reason, restoring it, authentic, true, and upright. Unfortunately, the hermeneutics of an idealistic nature, dominant in the twentieth century, was able to purge Rosmini's philosophy from his religious faith and his theology. The whole Rosminian project aimed at maintaining the two branches of the sole knowledge in inner and intrinsic unity was fragmented in the name of the exaltation of the "purity" of the philosophical thought of the "Italian Kant." And everyone agreed. It is a sharing that functions—not only out of inertia—even today, it is possible to find (acritical) supporters also in the world of Rosminian philosophy. After all, the separation between faith and reason creates *hortus conclusus*, avoiding the embarrassing question of contamination of knowledges and leaves everyone contentedly digging in perfect autonomy in their own specific field.

Nonetheless, for nonnegligent Catholicism, that is to say of *Fides quaerens intellectum* Anselmian memory (or also of *Fides nisi cogitator nulla est*), the extrinsecism between faith and religion, between philosophy and theology is not obvious, it must be theologically denied to the benefit of philosophy itself, according to Rosmini's authentic position. The resumption of Rosmini's (apologetic) program must therefore be carried out within the coordinates set out in the author's "On the Author's Studies" *(Degli studi dell'Autore)*, where he dwells on clarifying the means to achieve the objectives of his thought, in particular the freedom to philosophize. This lengthy declaration of intent, with a dissertation committed to thinking about what is said about the intrinsic character of reason in faith and of faith in reason, represents an insuperable lesson from Rosmini that cannot be passed over

---

30. See Fabro, *Dall'essere all'esistente*, 472.

in silence, forgotten, or even purposely omitted for fear of no longer being able to account for Rosmini's philosophical purity, due to its being confused with his theology.

My personal proposal to think of the relationship between philosophy and theology in terms of "epistemological inclusion of philosophizing believing in theology" could again bring into play Rosmini's contribution to the quarrels of the 1930s about Christian philosophy. At the same time, it might convince even the modern-day Catholic philosophers to resume the solid circle of Christian theology in order to philosophize better, escaping the inferiority complex imposed by Heideggerian hermeneutics, according to which to philosophize it was necessary to ask, and to ask it was essential not to believe, because faith is already the answer to all questions. This Heideggerian prejudice—described with unheard of clarity in *Introduzione alla metafisica*—considers believing philosophizing to be impossible, urging the *epochē* on one's faith to think intensively. For Martin Heidegger the Christian philosopher is a "wooden iron" (*hölzernes Eisen*), it is a "misunderstanding" (*Missverständnis*).[31] There is a radical opposition between the adherence to faith and the free disposition of existing. In fact, it is necessary to say with Rosmini that the Christian revelation, welcomed by the faith, offers the answer to all man's possible questions and, by acting as the "surplus answer" to all questioning, it demands that reason always asks, that it asks well, and that it asks more, that it asks without repose, without stopping and in an authentic way, critical and without limits. Rosmini would suggest to the Catholic philosophers that they do not dwell too long on considering theology a sort of "conceptually equipped predication," thus reaching Heidegger's position in phenomenology and theology, in which theology is possibly recognized as an ontic, but not an ontological science. For a simple reason: the "atheoretical prejudice" thrust on theology by eventual Catholic philosophers, for the essential direct reference to the theological reason of the Christian revelation, would turn like a boomerang on these Catholic philosophers, who would not be able to practice the *epochē* of their Christian faith, thus seeing their philosophical reason not recognized by their self-styled lay colleagues, because they were not Catholics and were presumably atheists.

31. Rather than "wooden iron" (literal translation) translators have generally used the expression "square circle." It is possible that they were inspired by another text (*Der europäische Nihilismus*) in which Heidegger ironically describes the philosophy of theologians with that metaphor. This is: "such only in name, because a Christian philosophy is even more absurd than a square circle. Indeed, the circle and the square agree at least in being geometric figures, while Christian faith and philosophy remain abysmally different." For Heidegger, that which includes a contradiction is null and a "round square" is a contradiction and therefore null. (See Capelle-Dumont, *Filosofia e Teologia*, 43.)

Conclusion: The Rosminian Synthesism beyond the Divisive Extrinsecism and the Confused Intrinsecism

Here, the way of presenting Rosmini's thinking offers an encouraging lesson to recuperate and return to the "solid circle," for the service that theology can offer to philosophy and all other knowledges and, vice versa, for the service that philosophy and all other knowledges can offer theology. It is the solid circle of a "reciprocal benefit" for that adventure of transdisciplinarity of knowledge that Pope Francesco's *Veritatis Gaudium* invited, also quoting Rosmini and his four pillars, a reform of Christian education: "the uniqueness of science, the communication of holiness, the habit of life, the mutuality of love."[32] It is worth remembering the words of Pope Benedict XVI at the Angelus of November 18, 2007: "May the example of Antonio Rosmini assist the church, especially the Italian ecclesiastical communities, to grow in the awareness that the light of human reason and of Grace, when they walk together, may they become a source of blessing for mankind and for society."[33]

The *sinodare* (walking together) of human reason and faith "full of grace," in the perspective of the relationship between philosophy and theology, was illustrated by Benedict XVI in the allocution of his expected visit to the Università della Sapienza: "Theology and philosophy must be interrelated 'without confusion and without separation.'"[34] The reference is to Chalcedon, but expressly also to Saint Thomas Aquinas: let each retain its own identity, because philosophy cannot be attracted fideistically, almost absorbed by faith, maintaining its own freedom and responsibility; however, philosophy "does not start again from zero with every thinking subject in total isolation, but takes its place within the great dialogue of historical wisdom, which it continually accepts and develops in a manner both critical and docile."[35] This historical wisdom—which we must interpret—is not extraneous to the

---

32. Francis, *VG*, para. 4.

33. Lorizio wrote: "All of this is possible from the perspective of a Christian, or rather a Catholic, faith that is truly a friend of reason," consistent with the Rosminian approach and assumption, succinctly asserting: "If Christ plays the role of liberating man, one does not see why his function should not also be liberating for reason and its paths." And one must also allow for the stressing of an "important condition," "so that the search for the foundation is authentic and the formula of 'Christian philosophy' is not understood in a triumphalist sense: fidelity to the Crucified One and to his radical kenosis, to which Rosmini dedicated pages of notable speculative and spiritual significance" (Lorizio, "Filosofia cristiana e teologia," 392). The entire text is a precious contribution that corroborates the perspective examined here, to be found in the Rosminian sources available, and contextualized in critical dialogue with the positions of the philosophies of Schelling, Heidegger, and others.

34. Benedict XVI, "Lecture," para. 10.

35. Benedict XVI, "Lecture," para. 11.

contribution made by mankind to the religions and, in particular, by Christianity, whose message "on the basis of its origin . . . should always be an encouragement towards truth, and thus a force against the pressure exerted by power and interests."[36] It is necessary to be more direct and concrete and to question the specific ways that the Christian faith can "serve" philosophical knowledge and help itself (almost as a handmaid of philosophy, to invert the ancient metaphor). The response of Benedict XVI is clear and coherent with everything he wrote and pondered and which is also to be found in the *Fides et Ratio* of Saint John Paul II: "The message of the Christian faith is never solely a 'comprehensive religious doctrine' in Rawls' sense, but is a purifying force for reason, helping it to be more fully itself."[37]

Within these premises, I would like to repropose the hermeneutic hypothesis of the epistemological inclusion of believing philosophizing in theology in order to fully understand the relationship between philosophy and theology not just "saying" it, but "thinking" it.[38] In order to think, in fact, it will always be necessary to profoundly understand that this "purifying force for reason" itself, as Benedict XVI said, consists of, or also the ways in which it happens for that philosophy, that "redemption" or even that "transfiguration" as others have said, and finally, why and how the Trinitarian revelation of God can constitute "the basis and the enactment" of the theosophic (philosophical) doctrines, as Rosmini says, speaking even of "mysterious foundation."[39]

36. Benedict XVI, "Lecture," para. 11.

37. Benedict XVI, "Lecture," para. 11. Saint Thomas clearly set out the autonomy of philosophy: "And with it the right and responsibility proper to reason which questions itself on the basis of its strengths" and this was by "differentiating itself from Neo-Platonist philosophies, in which religion and philosophy were inseparably intertwined." Therefore, "theology and philosophy thus form a peculiar pair of twins, which cannot be totally detached from each other and must yet each retain its own task and its own identity" (Ratzinger/Benedetto XVI, "Allocuzione," 706–7).

38. This is the conclusion of the doctoral work at the Università Gregoriana, on the relationship between faith and reason in Rosmini, in which I took the dogma of Chalcedon as a reference paradigm for understanding and thinking about that relationship. The epistemological inclusion of believing philosophizing in theology brings into play not only the essential expressions "without confusion and without separation" but also and above all, the union of the divine Person of the Son in the incarnation, which is not "approximation," but true "grafting." The christological dogma must therefore be taken to its radical aftermath, thinking of the interweaving, the co-implication of faith, reason, philosophy, and theology starting from the real union of the Word in the flesh: it is, in fact, the way the christological controversies of the first centuries have matured with all the difficulties represented by heresies—by virtue of the union that the human and divine natures are mutually not confused and not separate. Therefore, "without confusion and without separation" must always be understood to refer to the hypostatic union. See Staglianò, *Teologia secondo Antonio Rosmini*, 384–87.

39. Benedict XVI, "Lecture," para. 11; Rosmini, *Theos*, para. 190.

In an attempt to think "the thing" (*die Sache*), the transcendental method of Bernard Lonergan did not indulge any desire for acritical actualism that did not take into account the epochal distances between the two thinkers, a criticism that has been levelled at me. It was rather the need to find a contemporary language for "thinking" the entanglement of philosophy and theology, of reason and faith *in actu exercitu*, in the act itself of seeking the truth and the comprehension of all reality. It is an interesting way to verify the Rosminian theory of synthesism which—as far as we can see—appears to be the only one capable of overcoming both the divisive extrinsecism of faith and reason, of philosophy and theology, and the confused intrinsecism: it is in Rosminian synthesism that we can imagine the possibility of a "being-in" of each of the forms of being in the other, remaining resolutely oneself, without confusion and without separation, but "within," intimately grafted.[40] Thus, speculation and contemplation are synthesized in the form of life that is Christianity. The Christian faith is not simply a doctrine, but a way of being in the world, it is a way of life;[41] knowledge therefore of "science and holiness" synthesize. It is no wonder then if Rosmini confessed that many developments in his speculative thinking occurred to him more during periods of prayer and meditation in church, than during his studies in his room. It is an experience of reason when it discovers its origin in another.

Bibliography

Benedict XVI. "Lecture by the Holy Father Benedict XVI at the University of Rome 'La Sapienza.'" Vatican, Jan. 17, 2008. https://www.vatican.va/content/benedict-xvi/en/speeches/2008/january/documents/hf_ben-xvi_spe_20080117_la-sapienza.html.
Capelle-Dumont, Philippe. *Filosofia e Teologia nel pensiero di Martin Heidegger*. Edited by Giovanni Ferretti. Translated by Lorenzo Gianfelici. Brescia, It.: Queriniana, 2011.
Catuogno, Lorena. "Antonio Rosmini e Bernard Lonergan: un'indagine preliminare." In *Pedagogia del sapere di Dio. Una prospettiva storico-culturale*, edited by Fernando Bellelli, Rosminianesimo teologico, 153–79. Milan: Mimesis, 2019.

---

40. See Stagliano, *Teologia secondo Antonio Rosmini*, 373–79. I note with great pleasure that, in the world of Rosminian studies, we are beginning to reflect more precisely on "Rosmini and Lonergan": "Rosmini's metaphysical-epistemological itinerary is aroused and developed on two different conceptual levels which, as will be demonstrated in the present research, also in Lonergan, albeit in different eras and in different ways, are continuously joined: the first concerns the integration of scientific rationality with philosophical rationality and questions gnoseology, epistemology and anthropology; the second concerns the integration between natural reason and the experience of the faith, between philosophy, understood in a broad sense as knowledge of reality and questioning conscience and theology" (Catuogno, "Antonio Rosmini e Bernard Lonergan," 153).

41. Theobald, *Stile della vita cristiana*.

Congregazione del Sant'Uffizio. "Post Obitum." In *La Civiltà Cattolica* 39 (Mar. 30, 1888) 63–78.

Congregazione per la Dottrina della Fede (Congregation for the doctrine of the faith). "Nota sul valore dei decreti dottrinali concernenti il pensiero e le opere del Reverendo Sacerdote Antonio Rosmini-Serbati" [On the force of the doctrinal decrees concerning the thought and work of Father Antonio Rosmini-Serbati]. Vatican, July 1, 2001. https://www.vatican.va/roman_curia/congregations/cfaith/documents/rc_con_cfaith_doc_20010701_rosmini_it.html.

Fabro, Cornelio. *Dall'essere all'esistente*. Brescia, It.: Morcelliana, 1965.

Forte, Bruno. *La Bibbia dei filosofi. Il Grande Codice e il pensiero dell'Occidente*. Brescia, It.: Morcelliana, 2019.

Francis, Pope. *Veritatis Gaudium*: On Ecclesiastical Universities and Faculties. Vatican, Dec. 27, 2017. https://www.vatican.va/content/francesco/en/apost_constitutions/documents/papa-francesco_costituzione-ap_20171208_veritatis-gaudium.html.

Gilson, Étienne. *Un dialogo fecondo. Lettere di Étienne Gilson a Henri de Lubac*. Translated by Armido Rizzi. Genoa: Marietti, 1990.

———. *Problemi d'oggi*. Turin: Borla, 1967.

Lorizio, Giuseppe. "Filosofia cristiana e teologia. La lezione di Antonio Rosmini." *Lateranum* 55 (1989) 369–92.

Ratzinger, Joseph. "Conference during the Meeting between the Congregazione per la Dottrina della Fede and the Presidents of the Commissioni per la Dottrina della Fede delle Conferenze Episcopali dell'America Latina (Guadalajara/Messico, May 1996)." *L'Osservatore Romano*, Oct. 27, 1996.

Ratzinger, Joseph/Benedetto XVI, Pope. "Allocuzione per la visita all'Università 'La Sapienza.'" In *Fede, ragione, Verità e amore. La teologia di Joseph Ratzinger*, 699–710. Turin: Lindau, 2009.

Rosmini, Antonio. *Antropologia soprannaturale*. Edited by Umberto Muratore. 2 vols. ENC 39–40. Rome: Città Nuova, 1983.

———. *Epistolario completo*. 13 vols. Casale Monferrato, It.: Pane, 1887–1894.

———. *Introduzione alla filosofia*. Edited by Pier P. Ottonello. ENC 2. Rome: Città Nuova, 1979.

———. *Il linguaggio teologico*. Edited by Antonio Quacquarelli. ENC 38. Rome: Città Nuova, 1975.

———. "Prefazione." In *Nuovo Saggio sull'origine delle idee*, edited by Francesco Orestano, 1:35–60. Rome: Cedam, 1934.

———. *Teosofia*. Edited by Maria A. Raschini and Pier P. Ottonello. 6 vols. ENC 12–17. Rome: Città Nuova, 1998–2002.

Staglianò, Antonio. "L'autonomia della ragione nel pensare teologico-filosofico di A. Rosmini." *La Scuola cattolica* 125 (1997) 633–60.

———. *Il mistero del Dio vivente. Per una teologia dell'Assoluto trinitario*. Bologna: EDB, 1996.

———. "Rosmini tra tradizione e modernità." *Teologia* 13 (1988) 250–56.

———. *La teologia secondo Antonio Rosmini. Sistematica critica e interpretazione del rapporto fede e ragione*. Brescia, It.: Morcelliana 1998.

Theobald, Christoph. *Lo stile della vita cristiana*. Translated by Valerio Lanzarini. Bose, It.: Qiqajon, 2015.

7

Antonio Rosmini in *Veritatis Gaudium*

Unity of Knowledge and Trinitarian Ontology

PIERO CODA

THE THEOLOGICAL PREFACE OF the Apostolic Constitution *Veritatis Gaudium*, promulgated in 2018 by Pope Francis with regard to ecclesiastical universities and faculties, and containing a revision of the norms governing their statutes and purpose, is certainly of particular relevance in the context of the current ecclesial season, because when we speak of the church we speak of her specific mission in history, at the service of the human family: a season of "discernment, purification and reform," as we read in *Evangelii Gaudium*.[1] The "change of epoch" and not the mere "epoch of change"—as Pope Francis often emphasizes—to which we bear witness, being called upon to become creative and responsible actors, in fact requires—we read in the first section of this document—"thoughtful and prophetic determination the renewal of ecclesiastical studies at every level, as part of the new phase of the Church's mission."[2]

---

1. Francis, *EG*, para. 3. On this topic, see two of my papers: "Il Proemio della *Veritatis Gaudium*: una prospettiva programmatica di rinnovamento," 45–55; "La missione della teologia nella cosmopoli. In dialogo con gli impulsi della *Veritatis Gaudium*," 117–32.

2. Francis, *VG*, para. 1.

Pope Francis himself offers, in para. 2, some essential clarifications regarding the *statement* that constitutes the foundation and *focus* of the proposal formulated from there. On the one hand, it is a question of seriously addressing and understanding the overall anthropological and socio-environmental crisis in which we find more and more symptoms of a breaking point every day, in order to highlight the underlying causes and prepare trenchant avenues of solution; which also imposes "a broad and generous effort at a radical paradigm shift, or rather . . . at 'a bold cultural revolution'" and at the same time, it is a question of recognizing with sincerity and courage that, in the face of this formidable challenge, "the problem is that we still lack the culture necessary to confront this crisis. We lack leadership capable of striking out on new paths."[3]

Given this reading of the situation, in *Veritatis Gaudium* Pope Francis commits himself to promoting the "strategic role" of ecclesiastical studies, inviting "an adequate renewal." In fact, they constitute "a sort of providential cultural laboratory in which the Church carries out the performative interpretation of the reality brought about by the Christ event and nourished by the gifts of wisdom and knowledge by which the Holy Spirit enriches the People of God in manifold ways—from the *sensus fidei fidelium* to the magisterium of the bishops, and from the charism of the prophets to that of the doctors and theologians."[4]

The critical risk imposes, first of all on theology, but in concert, on all the other disciplines provided for in the *curricula* of ecclesiastical studies, starting from philosophy, a decisive and ongoing assumption of the form and the practice of Christian existence and witness proposed by Vatican II and the protracted process it triggered. *Veritatis Gaudium* follows this trajectory with conviction and new impetus: because one of the main contributions of the council, writes Pope Francis, is "precisely seeking a way to overcome this divorce between theology and pastoral care, between faith and life. I dare say that the Council has revolutionized to some extent the status of theology—the believer's way of doing and thinking."[5] The meaning and scope of this affirmation—"revolution of the statute of theology, of the believer's way of doing and thinking"—should not be underestimated: it is only on the basis of the indispensable instance of this overall paradigm shift that we can fully understand the new strategies proposed by the decree *Optatam Totius* of Vatican II with regard to the training for the priesthood, reproposed and accomplished by the Apostolic Constitution *Sapientia*

---

3. Francis, *VG*, para. 3.
4. Francis, *VG*, para. 3.
5. Francis, *VG*, para. 2.

Christiana of John Paul II dated 1979, which punctually takes up the innovative magisterium of Paul VI in this regard, inspired by the council.

Determinedly undertaking this journey, Pope Francis—indicating the threshold that must be crossed today—, energetically points out, "The time has now come for it to be consolidated and to impart to ecclesiastical studies that wise and courageous renewal demanded by the missionary transformation of a church that 'goes forth.' The primary need today is for the whole People of God to be ready to embark upon a new stage of 'Spirit-filled' evangelization. This calls for 'a resolute process of discernment, purification and reform.'"[6] And he describes the task that awaits us in these terms: "Today it is becoming increasingly evident that "there is need of a *true evangelical hermeneutic* for better understanding life, the world and humanity, *not of a synthesis but of a spiritual atmosphere of research and certainty based on the truths of reason and of faith*. . . . The good theologian and philosopher has an open, that is, an incomplete, thought, always open to the *maius* of God and of the truth, always in development."[7]

In this broad and stimulating horizon of commitment, *Veritatis Gaudium* presents four basic criteria for a renewal and revival of the contribution of ecclesiastical studies to a church that is setting out on a missionary journey.[8] It should be noted, in the first instance, that a distinction must be made between the first three criteria, of a more specifically epistemological character, and the last, of a more functional nature. This distinction is indicated, in the *proemium*, by the fact that, at the end of the illustration of the third criterion, reference is made to two prophetic testimonies of the renewal necessary today because it is now mature: that of John Henry Newman and above all, more widely and in detail, that of Antonio Rosmini, whose specific testimony, precisely because of its collocation and its depth, deserves adequate study. Moreover, the very lemma *criteria* used to express the guidelines of the proposed reform clearly indicates that it is a question of vigorously and rigorously implementing a radical, articulated, and comprehensive discernment capable of propitiating the effective process of the desired renewal. Before recalling the meaning and implications of the reference to Rosmini's thinking, it is therefore necessary to spend a few words at least on the criteria that are enunciated.

(1) The first to be presented is the criterion of *concentration* and *wholeness*. It is a question of the commitment to the existentially and intellectually appreciable proposition of the radiating center of the Christian *kerygma*

---

6. Francis, *VG*, para. 3.
7. Francis, *VG*, para. 3.
8. See Francis, *VG*, para. 4.

that shows itself as a principle in itself integral to the original and determining dimensions of personal and social being in the light of the phenomenon of Jesus Christ.

Thus, the first task that the *proemio* concretely sets is to promote universities and higher institutes of ecclesiastical studies as places and paths of formation, study and research profitably and serenely habitable by the new generations since they are marked by two inseparable objectives: on the one hand, existential and intellectual immersion in the heart of the Christian experience (therefore: "to experience," to live and share the faith, also in its cultural significance, in the field, inhabiting the existential peripheries and courageously frequenting the frontiers of today); and on the other, the acquisition of the skills necessary to weave meaningful social relations at all levels, moving from the conviction that God, in Christ, does not want only the good of the individual but also of social relations in their dynamic and complex articulation in the context of the "common home."[9]

Four specific notes supplement these indications:

d. The fact that the Gospel of Jesus is intended not only on the basis of its original and normative attestation, but also, historically and culturally, in its becoming flesh "ever more and ever better" in the life and doctrine of the church, in the journey and in the culture(s) of humanity

e. The centering on the Christian message as the mysticism of "us" that becomes the leaven of universal fraternity

f. The reference to "the least of these" as essential to the very occurrence of the ecclesial mission in the following of Christ

g. The suggestion to read the cultural change taking place through the prism of relationality in a Trinitarian key (an indication already at the center of Benedict XVI's *Caritas in Veritate*)

(2) The second criterion proposed is the *dialogical* one, which is clearly presented, to avoid misunderstandings and inappropriate reductionism and preconceived resistance, as "an intrinsic requirement to experience the joy of truth in community and to deepen its meaning and practical implications."[10]

This orientation, in harmony with the spirit of Vatican II, takes up the program outlined by Paul VI with *Ecclesiam Suam* in determining the form and style of *experientia* and *intelligentia fidei* today and is connected, from the theoretical point of view, to Benedict XVI's affirmation that, in

---

9. See Francis, *EG*, para. 178; *VG*, para. 4a.
10. Francis, *VG*, para. 4b.

itself, "truth is *logos* that creates '*dia-logos*' and therefore communication and communion."[11]

The step forward that the *Proemio* invites is demanding and concrete, to "review in this perspective and in this spirit the architectural and methodical dynamics of the *curricula* proposed by the system of ecclesiastical studies, in their theological origin, in their inspiring principles and in their different levels of disciplinary, pedagogical and didactic articulation." It is in the perspective of this new stage that the church is called upon to live and the "cultural workshop" of ecclesiastical studies is therefore invited, with a decisive assumption of responsibility, to offer an evangelically pertinent and historically incisive contribution to the realization of a "*culture of encounter between authentic and vital cultures*" that works from within, with evident *chiaroscuro*, today's conjuncture. If this criterion is not taken into account, it is illusory, in fact, to presume to "arrive where the new stories and paradigms are formed."[12]

(3) The third criterion is the epistemologically and academically most demanding. On the foundation of the long and consolidated intellectual tradition that has characterized the historical effectiveness of the culture of Christian inspiration in its decisive reference to the event of Jesus Christ, the *Proemio* begins with an observation: "That which qualifies the academic, formative and research proposal of the system of ecclesiastical studies, on the level of both content and method, is the vital and intellectual principle of the *unity of knowledge* in distinction and respect for its multiple, correlated and converging expressions."[13]

This principle, Pope Francis remarks, on the one hand, "makes explicit the intrinsic truthful meaning of the system of ecclesiastical studies," on the other "it also highlights, especially today, its effective cultural and humanizing relevance," in the face of the "fragmented and often disintegrated panorama of university studies today and the uncertain, conflictual or relativistic pluralism of cultural convictions and options."[14]

In reality, the question that is thus introduced and the commitment that is entrusted to the different expressions of ecclesiastical studies are foundational and strategic. At a time of crisis in the epistemological awareness of modernity and with the consequent temptation to yield either to the (often far from tolerant) post-truth or to the resistance (also violent, because ultimately desperate) of fundamentalism, it is necessary to reiterate

---

11. Benedict XVI, *Caritas in Veritate*, para. 4; see Francis, *VG*, para. 4b.
12. Francis, *VG*, para. 4b.
13. Francis, *VG*, para. 4c.
14. Francis, *VG*, para. 4c.

the possibility—which John Paul II already indicated in *Fides et Ratio*—indeed, the vital need to "arrive at a unitary and organic vision of knowledge. This is one of the tasks that Christian thinking will have to take on in the course of the next [now present] Christian millennium."[15]

The task is certainly more than substantial, but not renounceable and epochally decisive. To avoid it would mean not only not honoring the precious and pressing heritage of revelation, but, in fact, making the *performance* of the system of ecclesiastical studies less relevant. The solitary, but stimulating and guiding indication that the *Proemio* contemplates is the one that directs the interpretation and management of the principle of interdisciplinarity not to its "*weak* form of simple multidisciplinarity": but rather to its "*strong* form of transdisciplinarity, as a collocation and fermentation of all knowledge within the space of Light and Life offered by the Wisdom that emanates from the Revelation of God," open and founded in becoming present in God's transcendence of human history through Christ in the breath of the Holy Spirit.[16]

Significant in this regard—but only evoked, and as such delivered to a precise allusion to the difficulty of the concept—is the reference a little later to the "form of knowledge and interpretation of reality" exercised "in the light of the 'thinking of Christ' (the νοῦς Χριστοῦ of 1 *Cor* 2:16)."[17] In what sense and according to what modalities of expression of the exercise, indeed of the essential vocation of human thought *qua talis*? Dialogue and research on the subject are ongoing.

(4) The fourth and final criterion, which—as I said—is placed more on the functional and organizational level, "concerns the urgent need for 'networking' between those institutions worldwide that cultivate and promote ecclesiastical studies, in order to set up suitable channels of cooperation also with academic institutions in the different countries and with those inspired by different cultural and religious traditions."[18]

It should be noted that this indication, at first glance mainly pragmatic, in the intention of Pope Francis has above all a properly theological meaning. In fact, he explains, it is necessary today to become aware that, in correlation with the tendency to conceive the planet as a homeland and humanity as a people who inhabit a common home[19]—which "obliges us

---

15. John Paul II, *Fides et Ratio*, para. 85.
16. Francis, *VG*, para. 4c.
17. Francis, *VG*, para. 4d.
18. Francis, *VG*, para. 4d.
19. See Francis, *Laudato Si'*, para. 164; *VG*, para. 4d.

to think of *one world with a common plan*"[20]—the Church is called upon to experience and promote in practice the *catholicity* "that makes her a leaven of unity in diversity and communion in freedom."[21]

This must be thought of and implemented—as *Evangelii Gaudium* illustrates—according to the model of the "the polyhedron, which reflects the convergence of all its parts, each of which preserves its distinctiveness,"[22] also taking charge of historical conflicts in the commitment to an effective, and not simply arbitrational "resolution [of them] which takes place on a higher plane and preserves what is valid and useful on both sides."[23]

In this precise context, the reference to the Blessed J. H. Newman, now canonized, and to the Blessed Antonio Rosmini, whose canonization we sincerely hope will soon be reached, is important. We refer to Newman's work, now classical but circumscribed in objective and context, *The Idea of a University*, of 1852;[24] while by Rosmini, we would mention some dense and luminous passages from the well-known and for some time controversial essay *Delle cinque piaghe della Santa Chiesa* (The five wounds of the holy church) (which, given the brevity of the *Proemio*, just six sections, is even more important). This work was written between 1832 and 1833, being published in 1848, prior to Newman's aforementioned opus: it is not my intention to obscure the contemporaneity of the polished performance of these two distinguished thinkers, who are first of all men of God, together with "prophets and doctors," according to *Veritatis Gaudium* with regard to the "gifts of the Spirit" that enrich the church's journey "into all the truth."[25]

What is the relevance and—as far as it is possible to give a plausible and incisive interpretation—what is the meaning and scope of this robust and indicative reference to Rosmini's thinking with regard to the renewal of ecclesiastical studies? A few years ago, with documented rigor and positive interpretative inspiration, Fulvio De Giorgi answered in a persuasive and reasoned way the question: *What regeneration of the church is to be found in the Rosminianism of Pope Francis?* coming to the conclusion that: "The Rosmini of Pope Francis is above all—at least in what he has said so far—the spiritual and pastoral Rosmini, the Rosmini of *The Five Wounds*, the Rosmini of the reform of the church and that is, precisely, of the regeneration of the church, with the creative breath of the Spirit: ecclesial regeneration as

---

20. Francis, *VG*, para. 4d.
21. Francis, *VG*, para. 4d.
22. See Francis, *EG*, para. 236; see *VG*, para. 4d.
23. Francis, *VG*, para. 4d.
24. See, among others, Pillay, *Idea di università*.
25. Francis, *VG*, para. 3 (see John 16:13).

pneumatic critical creativity. This is Rosmini's Bergoglian reading: a reading accompanied by evident consensus, indeed by an admired recognition of an exemplary witness."[26]

The extensive and articulated quotation in *Veritatis Gaudium*—a couple of years after De Giorgi's masterful intervention—of some excerpts from *The Five Wounds* confirms this interpretation, offering material for further study. In my opinion, there are at least three aspects that make appreciable subjects for careful investigation and organic development—at a theoretical and practical level—the authoritative and I would say almost paradigmatic resumption of the Rosminian proposal made by *Veritatis Gaudium* in relation to the renewal of the contribution offered by theology and thinking of Christian inspiration to the sociocultural transition today in gestation: (1) its specific role in the overall reform of the church; (2) its springing from the decisive and concrete reevaluation of the fact that all knowledge has to "receive unity from the unity of the principle," as Rosmini wrote;[27] (3) its concrete establishment and articulation—writes Pope Francis, summarizing Rosmini's thinking—"on the four pillars on which it firmly rested during the first centuries of the Christian era."[28] A few words about each of these aspects.

(1) The first: *the ecclesial and ecclesiological context* of Rosmini's proposal and the reference that *Veritatis Gaudium* makes to it. The strategic value of integral, existential, and intellectual formation, and of the commitment to research and dialogue that must be produced by that "cultural workshop"—the academic institutions of Christian origin, is clear, in the reforming intentionality of the ecclesial discernment promoted by Pope Francis—as I have emphasized from the beginning, since they are a key agent of the reform of the church with regard to the truly incisive insertion of the gospel of Christ in the abundant sowing of a new culture and a civilization of the covenant between cultures.

Now, this is precisely the most strategic aspect of the program for reform of training, first of all for the clergy, but not only (as I will say later) advocated by Rosmini. At a practical level, it triggers and constantly accompanies the process for the *ab imis* regeneration, in the Spirit, of the church. In the architectural construction of *The Five Wounds*, it is easy to see the fundamental affront of the second "wound" (that of the "right hand") which comes after that of the "left hand," *the division of the people from the clergy during public worship*, unmasking the cause and tracing the lines of a

26. De Giorgi, "Quale ri-generazione," 210.
27. Rosmini, *FW*, para. 45.
28. Francis, *VG*, para. 4c.

healing that while healing the second "wound" (the insufficient education of the clergy) also heals the first and shows itself to be a condition of possibility, not only theological and anthropological, but effectual and historical, of healing the third "wound," *the disunity of the bishops*, which, ultimately, is a division of the church within itself. The third "wound," being that of the "side" touches the core of the *ecclesiae form* and then expresses itself, consequently and concretely, in the healing of the fourth "wound," that of the "right foot," *the appointment of Bbshops who are devoted to lay power*, and of the fifth, that of the "left foot," *the servitude of ecclesiastical resources*.

In a sort of ascending journey, that is, moving from the historical phenomenology of being a church which risks losing its *proprium*: that—Vatican II will teach—of being the people of God who all enjoy the same dignity as children of God in a plurality of ministries, charisms and skills, by setting aside (at least in principle) the deadly degeneration of clericalism (to which Pope Francis, unsurprisingly, frequently refers), we thus rise to that summit which is the *re-inventio* of integral formation of the identity of the people of God that flourishes in and from *ut unum sint*, in Christ and in the Trinity, of the shepherds and of all the disciples (see John 17:21): making the church rediscover awareness and practical experience of its original status in the freedom of the *koinonia* of the children of God and in the poverty of their universal *diakonia*, starting with the poorest, in body and spirit.

From this emerges undoubtedly the observation—which profoundly unites the reform pursued by Pope Francis and the reasoned Rosminian inspiration—that the Holy Spirit drives towards a renewed figure of the church (not an "other" church, but a "different" one, says Pope Francis, taking up Yves Congar in *Vraie et fausse réforme dans l'Église* [True and false reform in the church]),[29] that can be regenerated and nourished only by a profound reform of the living, believing and thinking, called to draw upon—enriched by the development of the *traditio vivens ecclesiae*[30]—the very source of the gospel: indeed, to that "being in-Christ"—wrote Rosmini—which is the "briefest formula" of Christian existence.[31]

(2) And this is the second fact that can be deduced from the reference to Rosmini so central to the architecture of *Veritatis Gaudium*. Central to the tenor of what is expressed and reiterated there, also for the simple fact that it is placed intentionally as a synthesis and seal of the first three criteria outlined by the document those that, as already mentioned, exhibit a robust

---

29. Francis, *Address of His Holiness* (2021).
30. See Paul VI, *Dei Verbum*, para. 8.
31. See Rosmini, *Theos*, para. 899.

and correlated epistemological caliber, and before the fourth criterion, of a more functional and pragmatic character.

The *focus* of Pope Francis's references to the Rosminian proposal is enunciated with these words. It is essential, Rosmini argued "to restore the unity of content, perspective and aim of the science being taught, on the basis of the Word of God and its culmination in Christ Jesus, the Word of God made flesh. Without this living center, science has 'neither root nor coherence.'"[32]

Even just rereading the pages dedicated to this aspect in the second chapter of *The Five Wounds* (but it would be necessary and extremely profitable to broaden one's gaze to the overall design of the magnificent and multifaceted Rosminian opus)[33] one can realize the centrality of this assumption. In fact, for Rosmini, it is a question of recovering with the vital and desiring impulse of freedom and the performing and responsible creativity of thought, the specific quality of that wisdom of Christian stamp that marked the golden age of the church, the one delivered by the apostolic and the New Testament attestation of the event of Jesus Christ to the Fathers of the first centuries: that is, receiving this "*unity* from the unity of the beginning," that is, "the single object proposed to truly Christian studies."[34] The decisive reference to the "beginning" and the "single object" enunciated here refers—in the pondered Rosminian ontological lexicon of Trinitarian imprint, explored in depth, in *Theosophy*—to that Word of God made flesh which, through the Eucharist, propitiates the "inobjectivation" of the human creature in the very interiority of the life of the Triune God.[35]

From the point of view of formation in effective and affective participation, of mind and heart, in the feeling and thinking that flows from *the sequela Christi*, inasmuch as in the Word made flesh "are hidden all the treasures of wisdom and knowledge" (Col 2:3);[36] according to Rosmini, it is a question of propitiating the dynamics capable of making Christ's disciples appear "interiorly possessed, dominated by the sentiment of the Word . . . which, absorbing the whole soul, takes it away from the transitory world, makes it live in the eternal, and from the eternal mansions precisely teaches it to kidnap a fire that is the capable of scorching the world itself."[37] These

---

32. Francis, *VG*, para. 4c.
33. See Catuogno, "Restaurare l'unità del sapere."
34. Rosmini, *FW*, para. 45.
35. See Rosmini, *Theos*, para. 899; see also Pili, *Se l'uno è l'altro*.
36. See Francis, *VG*, para. 4c.
37. Rosmini, *FW*, para. 34.

are "mystagogical" dynamics: Rosmini speaks of "science of the arcane,"[38] an expression that recalls the "discipline from the arcane" of which Dietrich Bonhoeffer wrote in the letters from prison, collected and published in *Widerstand und Ergebung* (Letters and papers from prison).

Here, therefore, in the foreground is the unitary and synthetic reference to the principle (the ἀρχή referred to in the Prologue of the Gospel of John, in the *incipit* of the book of Genesis, in the Gospel of Mark, in the First Letter of John) of the Christian and academic formation advocated by Rosmini, who, without this being misunderstood in a nostalgic, integralist or fundamentalist sense, since rather it must be read in a perspective and innovative sense, bypassing centuries-old fractures and separations, thus hoped for the return, obviously "updated" in form and tools, to that figure of thinking in which "all the sciences spontaneously subordinate themselves to the Word of God, receiving unity from it, lending service and homage to Christ, and disposing souls and minds to better feel the beauty and preciousness of Gospel wisdom. Therefore, there were not two educations, one pagan and the other Christian, one of the profane sciences and with profane spirit, and the other of the ecclesiastical sciences, one opposite and inimical to the other . . . but rather a single end, as one doctrine, that of Christ."[39]

That this essential primacy of the Word of God, both written and transmitted (as *Dei Verbum* would say, para. 9), should not be confused with a misunderstood biblicism, but points straight to the vital need for immediate contact at the spiritual and intellectual level with the event of Jesus Christ made contemporary at all times and in every place by the Holy Spirit, is evident from the two comments with which Rosmini enriches and clarifies the declaration of this "unity of principle," to which Christian and human formation is called upon to conform.

The first emphasizes that—especially on the basis of a certain declination of medieval Scholasticism and its decay in the centuries of modernity—"Christian doctrine was curtailed . . . abandoning entirely all that belonged to the heart and to the other human faculties, trying to satisfy only the mind"[40]: so that that "element of rationalism" was subtly introduced which, in the end, led to "leaving the Church and revelation itself."[41] Very perceptive historical hermeneutics—so succinctly enunciated by Rosmini—aimed at tracing the ultimate root, at least *ex parte ecclesiae et theologiae*, of the separation between revelation and reason that constitutes the drama of modernity.

38. Rosmini, *FW*, para. 42n41.
39. Rosmini, *FW*, para. 44.
40. Rosmini, *FW*, para. 39.
41. Rosmini, *FW*, para. 35.

The second clarification concerns the fact that, with the advent of modernity, in singular contradiction with the rationalistic germ surreptitiously propagated by a certain theology poor in spirit and devoid of nerve, Christian formation was "lacking the leaven of Christian philosophy" (a lemma to which the meaning that would become usual in the well-known controversy of the twentieth century should not be attached): so that "the importance of the great, intrinsic reasons for the doctrine of the faith, contemplated by the Scholastics,[42] were no longer seen." An invitation—as all Rosmini's work attests with extraordinary speculative vigor—to exercise thought in its properly ontological intentionality within the horizon of truth, indeed "from the viscera" of the very truth of Revelation.

(3) But let us come to the third point offered by *Veritatis Gaudium* on our topic. Pope Francis emphasizes that Rosmini's reforming project in relation to Christian formation invites the reestablishment of "the four pillars on which it firmly rested in the first centuries of the Christian era: "communion in learning, holy intercourse, habit of life, interchange of affection." Only in this way is it possible to overcome the "fatal separation of theory and practice," because in the unity between knowledge and holiness "we find the true spirit of that doctrine which is destined to save the world," whose teaching "in ancient times, 'did not end with the brief daily lesson; it was continued in the constant intercourse of the disciple with his master.'"[43]

While "the unity of the beginning," previously mentioned for its founding and architectural centrality, looks at the epistemic status and the decline of believing thinking in the various disciplinary expressions, each with its own peculiarity and specific formality, the reference to the "four pillars" makes explicit its method. Meaning by μέθοδος, in the original etymological sense, the journey together (σύν-οδος) in the way that is truth offered and accepted and life lived in the joy of surprise and excess—and thus shared in the practice of solidarity and justice.

This methodology, intrinsic to the supporting pillar that governs it, "the uniqueness of science" which is that *of* Christ—in the objective but at the same time the subjective sense of the term: the science that learns Christ and learns from Christ himself, the one Master because the Word made flesh describes, as Rosmini explains,

> the first principle and the whole foundation of the method used in the first centuries: knowledge and holiness were closely united, one arising from the other. Indeed, it can be said that knowledge was born of holiness; because knowledge was desired for

---

42. Rosmini, *FW*, para. 40.
43. Francis, *VG*, para. 4c.

the very love that it brought, because holiness was intrinsic to it and thus everything was unified: and in this unity lies the genuine nature of the doctrine destined to save the world; it is not pure, ideal doctrine, but practical and real truth and therefore, having removed holiness from it, will we believe that there remains that the wisdom taught by Christ? It would deceive us to believe it: we would consider ourselves to be wise, and we would be foolish; we would take for the doctrine of Christ a vain and dead effigy of it, empty of vigor and of all life.[44]

Suffice it to highlight three characteristics of this global and integral method, capable—Pope Francis would say—of involving mind, heart and hands: "educate to think well, not only to learn concepts; educate to feel good; educate to do well. So that these three languages are interconnected: that you think what you feel and do, you feel what you think and do, you do what you feel and think, in unity."[45]

a. The first, very modern, characteristic is that of *performativity*, as perceptively suggested by Pope Francis in the introduction to the *Global Compact of Education*. Rosmini speaks of "pure love of effective truth (which is the proper character of the doctrine of Christ)," that is, of a truth that is made in charity (see Eph 4:15) of a truth that sets us free (see John 8:32), of an operative truth of justice and peace. Because, ultimately, it expresses the growth together, for and in the gift, until the full maturity of Christ (Eph 4:7–13): fulfilling of his recapitulating pleroma that liberates and unifies the distinct identities of each one.

b. The second characteristic is *the intrinsic correlation between preaching and the liturgy* as "the two great schools of the Christian people." "They were not voices that were understood by the mind alone, or symbols that had no other power than the senses; but both by the way of the mind and by the way of the senses, both anointed the heart, and instilled in the Christian a feeling above all creation, mysterious and divine; whose sentiment was operative, as omnipotent as the grace that constituted it."[46]

c. Hence—the third characteristic—*the joyfully pursued practice of the "custom of life" and of the "exchangeability of love" between teachers and learners*. A decisive approach to methodology like the previous ones. And not only because—as Rosmini frequently reiterates—"only great

44. Rosmini, *FW*, para. 41.
45. Francis, *Address of His Holiness* (2018).
46. Rosmini, *FW*, para. 24.

men can form other great men,"[47] as happened in the apostolic era, when Irenaeus of Lyons recognized that he had learned the doctrine of Christ from Polycarp of Smyrna, and Polycarp from John the Evangelist, a witness in the first person of the teaching of the Word of life (see John 1:1): being that only through this vital and personal *traditio* in which—Newman liked to say—*cor ad cor loquitur*, "the teaching derived not from books but from the living voice, to which only the most sublime mysteries were entrusted: and this they desired more, and the disciples found it more beneficial. This is one of the merits of the method used by the great of that time to form the great."[48] Not just for that reason, but also because, at root, it is precisely in the locus described by mutual love for all, open, true, transparent and free—as described by Saint Augustine in book 5 of *De Trinitate*[49]—that certain substantial knowledge and fruition of the *Deus Trinitas in Christo*, which is a realistic anticipation of the ultimate destiny of living and thinking, becomes possible and tangible in *statu viae*.

I will begin my conclusion by noting a fact which, of course, at the time of the publication of *Veritatis Gaudium* was not yet emphasized, but which can now come to full light. The program of reform proposed by Pope Francis, in truth, invests not only ecclesiastical studies but the whole of that great "school of life" and thinking which is the church as a community, embarked on the journey of the disciples of the Word of life made flesh and alive, crucified and risen, in the midst of her followers, listening to the Holy Spirit and to the heart of the world. Today, thanks to the inauguration of the great synodal process convened by Pope Francis, we can become even more concretely aware of its truth and effectiveness.

Pope Francis has called a synod that does not focus on a particular topic: but challenges the conscience of the church to rediscover her synodal vocation. Not, therefore, to respond to a crisis (which exists) but to welcome a divine grace that highlights the evangelical crisis that is a permanent invitation to conversion: spiritual, pastoral, cultural. Vatican II was the providential start (long nurtured and springing from the very viscera of the gospel and of the Christian *traditio* down the centuries) of the process that today leads to the start of this synodal process.

I would go so far as to say that what we are called upon to live is the most important—and also strategically more decisive—church event since Vatican II. Because the ecclesiology of Vatican II is the most genuine

47. Rosmini, *FW*, para. 27.
48. Rosmini, *FW*, para. 42.
49. See Coda, "Fraterna dilectio."

expression, and today the most fitting and challenging. The central word in the initiation and execution of the synodal process is the third question between communion and mission highlighted by the council: *participation*. It is a matter of making concrete and practiced that gift and that experience of *communion* by which the church lives and which the church is called to communicate and express throughout her mission. And participation means *taking part*. Not to take *a part*, only a portion of the inheritance of which Christ has made us co-heirs—the superabundant love of the Father, of the Son, of the Holy Spirit—but to take part in it all, *in full*. Each according to their own charism, their own ministry, their own vocation, their own specific competence. In synergy always with others. At the service of their brothers and sisters. This is the duty of the church that is asked of us.

To achieve all this it is necessary, like the bread that nourishes us, to have the intelligent and responsible experience that Pope Francis invites of "walking together in synodal style, as the people of God. And this is the solid and indispensable basis of everything: *the school of the people of God*."[50] It is striking that Rosmini, from the beginning of his treatment of the "second 'wound,'" speaks of "the school of the Christian people,"[51] then explains how, in the beginning, it was "divine Scripture, and with it the whole immense canvas of the religion of Christ," that served "together as a school for the people and the clergy,"[52] from which "came—he explains in the 'third wound'—that often wanting the vote of the people in disciplinary things, so that it can be said that he was at that time the faithful counsellor of the governors of the church; and that account that the Bishop gave to the people themselves for all that he did in the government of the Diocese; and that yielding and condescending to the will of the people in all that could be done."[53]

And this is because—remarks Rosmini—"the perfect agreement of sentiments and affections is almost a condition of the worship that Christians render to Christ, so that it may be acceptable to him, and He is in the

---

50. Francis, *Address of His Holiness* (2018).

51. Rosmini, *FW*, para. 24. As Alfeo Valle noted, "The first and fundamental merit of Rosmini lies in having defined the ecclesiological context in which the idea of 'Christian people' can and must be inserted" so that "precisely the conscious use of the idea of Christian people in a specific substantially new ecclesiological context, allows Rosmini on the ecclesiastical level, deeper innovative audacities" (Valle, "Introduzione," 20). F. De Giorgi underlines in fact that the reform of the Church proposed by Rosmini "*ad intra* meant an appreciation of the synodal and conciliar dimension of the Church" (De Giorgi, "Quale ri-generazione," 212; with reference to De Giorgi, "Rosmini e i rosminiani").

52. Rosmini, *FW*, para. 35n22.

53. Rosmini, *FW*, para. 54.

midst of them. . . . Christ is so solicitous of the unity of his followers, unity not of bodies, but of mind and heart, for which unity the Christian populace of every condition, gathered at the foot of the altars of the Saviour, form no more than one person."[54] This is ultimately what in Rosmini's performative and reforming Trinitarian ontology, is the church as a living Body, historical and pilgrim pleroma of the crucified and risen Christ who, raised from the earth, draws everyone to himself (see John 12:32).

Yes, "the time has now," writes Pope Francis in *Veritatis Gaudium*.[55] Because—Rosmini prophetically echoes him in *The Five Wounds*—"*today everything shows that a new Epoch is being prepared for the Church.*"[56] To which we are ready and happy—with amazement, gratitude, humility, in the patience and perseverance of Christ—to offer our hearts, minds and hands.

Bibliography

Benedict XVI, Pope. *Caritas in Veritate*: On Integral Human Development in Charity and Truth. Vatican, June 29, 2009. https://www.vatican.va/content/benedict-xvi/en/encyclicals/documents/hf_ben-xvi_enc_20090629_caritas-in-veritate.html.

Bonhoeffer, Dietrich. *Letters and Papers from Prison*. London: SCM, 1980.

Catuogno, Lorena. "Restaurare l'unità del sapere. L'istanza transdisciplinare negli scritti di Antonio Rosmini." PhD diss., Sophia University Institute, 2017.

Coda, Piero. "'Fraterna dilectio non solum ex Deo sed etiam Deus est.' L'ontologia trinitaria nel Libro VIII del 'De Trinitate' di Agostino." In *Trinità in relazione. Percorsi di ontologia trinitaria dai Padri della Chiesa all'Idealismo tedesco*, edited by Claudio Moreschini, 105–42. Panzano in Chianti, It.: Feeria, 2015.

———. "La missione della teologia nella cosmopoli. In dialogo con gli impulsi della *Veritatis Gaudium*." *Ho Theológos* 1 (2020) 117–32.

———. "Il Proemio della *Veritatis Gaudium*: una prospettiva programmatica di rinnovamento." *Educatio catholica* 2 (2018) 45–55.

Congar, Yves. *Vraie et fausse réforme dans l'église*. Paris: Cerf, 1968.

---

54. Rosmini, *FW*, para. 15. Rosmini's statement is clearer than that of Thomas Aquinas's, which speaks of *quasi una mystica persona*. This assertion is based on and justified by the Trinitarian ontology that Rosmini illustrates in *Theosophy*. So in *Theos*, para. 899: "Christian wisdom adds that the Word of God, the Object person subsisting assumed humanity, and as a man is called Jesus Christ, and that men who come to Christ united with very powerful and mysterious sacramental bonds, like members who are joined to the head: that therefore and can and owe to these intimate conjunctions, effect of the Sacraments, to unite also that of a voluntary inobjectivation in Christ. And inobjectivizing oneself in Christ as man, of the same kind as they are, they find themselves reached to the Word, Christ being Christ as a most holy man, indivisibly and personally united to God as the second person, who reveals the Father in himself, and the Holy Spirit breathes with the Father."

55. Francis, *VG*, para. 3.

56. Rosmini, *FW*, para. 69.

De Giorgi, Fulvio. "Quale ri-generazione della Chiesa nel rosminianesimo di Papa Francesco?" In *Ontologia, fenomenologia e nuovo umanesimo, Rosmini ri-generativo*, edited by Fernando Bellelli and Emanuele Pili, 205–91. Rome: Città Nuova, 2016.

———. "Rosmini e i rosminiani. Gli ordini religiosi e l'educazione tra riforma ecclesiale e rivoluzione nazionale." In *Chiesa, educazione e società nella Lombardia del primo Ottocento*, edited by Roberto Sani, 329–58. Milan: Centro Ambrosiano, 1996.

Francis, Pope. *Address of His Holiness*. Vatican, May 10, 2018. https://www.vatican.va/content/francesco/en/speeches/2018/may/documents/papa-francesco_20180510_visita-loppiano-focolari.html.

———. *Address of His Holiness Pope Francis for the Opening of the Synod*. Vatican, Oct. 9, 2021. https://www.vatican.va/content/francesco/en/speeches/2021/october/documents/20211009-apertura-camminosinodale.html.

———. *Evangelii Gaudium*: On the Proclamation of the Gospel in Today's World. Vatican, Nov. 24, 2013. https://www.vatican.va/content/francesco/en/apost_exhortations/documents/papa-francesco_esortazione-ap_20131124_evangelii-gaudium.html.

———. *Laudato Si'*: On Care for Our Common Home. Vatican, May 24, 2015. https://www.vatican.va/content/francesco/en/encyclicals/documents/papa-francesco_20150524_enciclica-laudato-si.html.

———. *Veritatis Gaudium*: On Ecclesiastical Universities and Faculties. Vatican, Dec. 27, 2017. https://www.vatican.va/content/francesco/en/apost_constitutions/documents/papa-francesco_costituzione-ap_20171208_veritatis-gaudium.html.

John Paul II, Pope. *Fides et Ratio*: On the Relationship between Faith and Reason. Vatican, Sept. 14, 1998. https://www.vatican.va/content/john-paul-ii/en/encyclicals/documents/hf_jp-ii_enc_14091998_fides-et-ratio.html.

———. *Sapientia Christiana*: On Ecclesiastical Universities and Faculties. Vatican, Apr. 15, 1979. https://www.vatican.va/content/john-paul-ii/en/apost_constitutions/documents/hf_jp-ii_apc_15041979_sapientia-christiana.html.

Newman, John H. *The Idea of a University*. Providence, RI: Cluny, 2016.

Paul VI, Pope. *Dei Verbum*: Dogmatic Constitution on Divine Revelation. Vatican, Nov. 18, 1965. https://www.vatican.va/archive/hist_councils/ii_vatican_council/documents/vat-ii_const_19651118_dei-verbum_en.html.

———. *Optatam Totius*: Decree on Priestly Training. Vatican, Oct. 28, 1965. https://www.vatican.va/archive/hist_councils/ii_vatican_council/documents/vat-ii_decree_19651028_optatam-totius_en.html.

Pili, Emanuele. *Se l'uno è l'altro. Ontologia e intersoggettività in Antonio Rosmini*. Bari, It.: Pagina, 2020.

Pillay, Gerald J. *L'idea di università in J. H. Newman*. Rome: Città Nuova, 2013.

Rosmini, Antonio. *Delle cinque piaghe della Santa Chiesa*. Edited by Alfeo Valle. ENC 56. Rome: Città Nuova, 1988.

———. *Teosofia*. Edited by Maria A. Raschini and Pier P. Ottonello. 6 vols. ENC 12–17. Rome: Città Nuova 1998–2002.

Valle, Alfeo. "Introduzione." In *Delle cinque piaghe della Santa Chiesa*, by Antonio Rosmini, edited by Alfeo Valle, ENC 56, 11–39. Rome: Città Nuova, 1988.

8

Between "Theosophy" and "Philosophy of Law"

Intersubjectivity as a Way to the "Other" in Rosmini

EMANUELE PILI

Introduction: The Terms and the Route Taken

THE SUBTITLE ADOPTED FOR the present essay recalls and shares the idea—made plain, for example, by Michele Dossi—according to which "the dialogical philosophy of the twentieth century has in Rosmini a great, though often ignored, precursor."[1] At the same time, it does not intend to evade the contexts (fundamental in a historical-philosophical work) regarding the thinking, such as that of Rosmini, which has matured in a precise *Sitz im Leben*, and which therefore requires great meticulousness in the application of categories and terminologies frequented with greater consuetude only later.

Among the words used, the lemma *intersubjectivity*, absent in Rosmini, certainly stands out, although this does not imply that he does not discuss the themes usually involved in it in various ways. Perhaps, in this case, it would be more correct to speak of *interpersonality*? In some respects, the latter would undoubtedly be a more precise term, yet here we

---

1. Dossi, *Il santo proibito*, 72.

use both phrases (*intersubjectivity* and *interpersonality*) without generating significant oscillations of meaning, drawing—on the other hand—from the Rosminian distinction between *subject* and *person*. In fact, Rosmini specifies that the difference between the two nouns is "the one that runs between the genus and the species. . . . So, the person is but one class of subjects, the noblest."[2] In this sense, speaking of *intersubjectivity* has a more general value, whereas *interpersonality* expresses a peculiar, more specific quality of relationality. The second part of the subtitle, "as a way to the Other," intends instead to express the idea that intersubjectivity, in Rosminian thinking, can be considered a *way*, in the etymological sense of *methodos*, of access to the inexhaustible mystery of Being that is God, that is, to the perennial newness of the event that is the encounter with him. *Other*, in this direction, certainly means *God*, although the term may appear less personal than the second. Its use, however, is suggested by Rosmini himself, who coined in the wake of Dante the verb *inaltrarsi*,[3] that is, the transport and living in o/Other (literally, *inothering*), as a figure of the encounter between the subjects and between the human and the divine.

Having clarified the meaning of the subtitling, it is now a question of explaining the path proposed here as a whole. It can be divided into three moments, which take the Rosminian works into account transversely and, while revealing a particular interest—as the title says—for *Theosophy (Teosofia)* (1846–1855, incomplete and published posthumously) and, above all, on the last aspect, for *Filosofia del diritto (Philosophy of Law)* (1841–1845).

(1) First of all, it must be considered that the experience of the encounter with the Other invites us to place at the center of attention the dimension of morality and, more specifically, of the so-called third form of being: the *moral being*. In this direction, it is of primary interest to find, in Rosmini's ontology, some decisive and paradigmatic definitions of morality, in order to open up its *interpersonal* meaning. (2) Second, it is necessary to return to the anthropology of the person, and in particular to the distinction between person and ego, as well as to the understanding of the moment in which the person meets others, inaugurating the dynamic of recognition. (3) Finally, it is necessary to concentrate on one of the places where the rhythm of mutual recognition opens up to the encounter of the human with God and of God with human history, individual and communal, with particular reference to the pages of *Philosophy of Law* concerning the theme of spousal and sexual union.

---

2. Rosmini, *AAMS*, para. 833.
3. See Rosmini, *Theos*, para. 869.

PART 2

Morality and Interpersonality

Although it is not possible to dwell on every definition of the moral being, as has happened elsewhere,[4] it is very important to identify those moments that most directly show how a precise study of the notion of *being moral* requires taking into account the interpersonal dimension. To this end, at least two passages of the aforementioned *Theosophy* are particularly significant. In book 1 on "Categories," in fact, after specifying that reflecting on subjectivity implies reflecting on intelligence and will, Rosmini writes:

> Assuming that the essence of being requires that there is also a feeling (a real and intelligent subject) a consequence is that the subjective being, feeling (affection) and intelligence, can love the real being (itself or other) in so far as it is known or perceived in the ideal or objective being; and this is the moral act: the moral relationship is therefore essential to the entity.[5]

This is one of the first definitions of morality contained in *Theosophy*, and what is to be noted, in particular, concerns the direction that love that flowing from the subject can take. Rosmini is very clear: the subject can love himself or other than himself, but only in that the latter is known in the object. The bond of morality, therefore, is not constituted *only* as a relationship of subject and object, but as a relationship of subjects (of the subject with himself or with other than himself), mediated by the object.[6] If morality were *only* the bond between the real and the ideal, we would have had to witness a different interpretation of the question: hence, Rosmini specifies that morality is the bond between reality and . . . reality mediated by the ideal.

A second definition that deserves to be taken into serious consideration refers to the end of section 5 of book 3 ("Of the Ontological Order of Abstract Concepts" [*Dell'ordine ontologico dei concetti astratti*]). Here, in chapter 12, Rosmini returns to the moral form of being, since this is a

---

4. See Pili, *Se l'uno è l'altro*, 59–102.

5. Rosmini, *Theos*, para. 174.

6. In "Sistema filosofico" (Philosophical system, 1845), Rosmini affirms this in the two paragraphs in which ontological research on morality is defined: "But the sentient principle, that is the subject, may have for its term a thing that is not itself, such as the extension and the body, and this term is not an object, nor is it even a subject, and it is outside the subject, hence it is called 'extra-subject.' But this extra-subject, as such, has an existence only in relation to the subject of which it is the term. Therefore, there are two forms of real entity, the subjective and the extra-subjective. Inasmuch as the entity is moral, it has the property of being the act that brings the subject into harmony with the object, of being a perfecting virtue, fulfillment of the subject through union and adaptation to the object, the blissfulness of the entity" (282).

"terminative essence,"[7] that is, a predicable entity, albeit predicable of the complete entity only (God) or the intelligent entity (the human being) since morality imperatively requires the intervention of freedom. Well, in God the moral being coincides with the *koinonia* of the Father and the Son, that is, with the Holy Spirit. In the human being, on the other hand, things are different, because—Rosmini specifies—the object present to the mind is not immediately God: "In God this accomplished Being recognized and loved, is himself a fulfilled subject, that is, a person, but in man, the initial Being by divine abstraction, devoid of subject, this object being is *impersonal.*"[8]

The attribute of impersonality, referring to the object present in the mind of the finite intelligent being, is an element on which it is not possible to reflect extensively in this paper, even though this may leave room for some misunderstanding, especially when it is encountered in the movement of inobjectivation.[9] For now, it is sufficient to point out that impersonality indicates the mere ideality of the object present to the mind, which is not a person, but precisely indeterminate and possible ideality: dark in itself, but luminous in making visible that which can be visible. Shadow *in itself*, light *for other*: objectivity, originally, is present with such characteristics to the human mind, which only "subsequently acquires the knowledge of the existence of people, that is, of itself and of other finite intelligent entities."[10] From here in any case, a decisive step follows:

> In man, therefore, the terminative essence of morality appears divided into two series: the first *embraces impersonal moral essences*, and such are the objects in that they manifest a moral requirement, a moral amiability, which when formulated take the name of *moral laws*, and applied to the subject of *duties*; the second embraces *personal moral essences*, and these are all those *acts* and *habits*, for which the subject man obeys the moral requirements of the objectors, that is, he conforms to the laws, he fulfils his duties, whose acts or habits morally perfect the subject man, who becomes *moral* by participation, and adhesion to another.[11]

7. Rosmini, *Theos*, para. 1251.
8. Rosmini, *Theos*, para. 1252.
9. See what is argued in Pili, *Se l'uno è l'altro*, 203–15.
10. Rosmini, *Theos*, para. 1252.
11. Rosmini, *Theos*, para. 1252. Shortly thenceforth, a similar reflection occurs: "Returning therefore to the moral essence that refers to man, we said, that it is twofold because it is either a *pure objective and impersonal moral essence*, or a *sub-reflective form that perfects the subject man*: the former receives the name of *moral law* and those propositions that express moral obligations or duties are preached: the latter are the moral virtues and virtuous acts, and are preached of the subject man, in whom morality subsists as an accident of perfection" (*Theos*, para. 1254). The expression "accident

The sense in which the *moral being* should be understood is further revealed. Of course, it appears as the link between subject and object, inasmuch as reality conforms to the law of the ideal being. However, it is a first dimension of morality, which cannot neglect the second: the law is, in fact, impersonal, and requires to be *the way* for a current encounter with a personal subject (the same ego, the other than self and God). The moral being cannot be reduced to the first dimension (real-ideal), but must consider itself up to this interpersonal (real-real) fulfillment, because it must involve another.[12]

These few elements, to which many could be added,[13] are already sufficient to understand in what respects the moral being refers to the dynamics of intersubjectivity.

1. In the first place, on the theological level, it must be observed that morality expresses the same interpersonal *koinonía*—which is in turn a Person, the Holy Spirit—of the Father with the Son and the Son with the Father.

2. Second, on the ontological level, Rosmini describes the moral form as the bond of real and ideal, that is, as the expression of the perpetual communication of one form with another. Thus placed, the third form does not seem to involve the movement of one subjectivity towards another. However, in the same contexts, Rosmini argues that the moral being is the union of a reality with itself or with another, mediated by the ideal. In this second option, the moral form describes the circularity and relationship of subjectivity to itself, and signals an *intrapersonal* event; but, when it expresses a relationship with the other, then it becomes an *interpersonal* event, in the sense that subjectivity leaves itself to meet another, contemplated in the ideal object. It should be noted, however, that, in this declination of morality, the event is interpersonal, but it is not yet expressed in a *reciprocity*, since nothing is said about the return movement of the other subject.[14] However, that

---

of perfection" is used to distinguish the essential morality present in God from the nonessential but shared morality present in man.

12. In "Del principio," Rosmini is very explicit: "Now it should be noted: when I spoke of love that has ideality as its object, I was not speaking of a love that excluded reality. If this love excluded reality, it would be an incipient love that is more solid than formed: it is Platonic love, and which does not take place in children or even in the people: but only in natural philosophers who come to ideas, but cannot penetrate them, that is, achieve them" (para. 240).

13. See at least Rosmini, *Theos*, paras. 739, 906, 1297, 1944; and Rosmini, *Filosofia del diritto* (Philosophy of law) 1, para. 99.

14. On closer inspection, it is possible to argue that Rosmini reflects and articulates

this last statement is not always tenable. In fact, when the moral bond between the two realities relates to God and man, then Rosmini does not hesitate to show how man's encounter with God responds to man's encounter with man. In this sense, therefore, a form of interpersonal reciprocity is once again unfolded, which involves the real man and the real God, projecting man into the depths of God and God into the depths of man, in a relationship of mutual indwelling.

3. Finally, Rosmini announces a further realization of the moral bond, when it is established *for* and *in* interpersonal reciprocity, mediated by the ideal thirdness (or by God himself, when the moral bond is perfect, that is, lived in Christ), between two or more subjects who consciously unite their freedoms in the same end.[15] Although it does not seem that such an operation can be found explicitly in the pages of *Theosophy*, some of his passages in this regard are enlightening, since they reveal that the original finding in the being of the one and of the many concerns all things, considered not only individually, but also in their mutual relationship:

> All the natures of things are connected, and linked together, one calls the other, continuing and mutually supporting each other: hence the admirable unity of the whole without any confusion of the parts, hence the harmony and consonance of these that

---

a form of reciprocity that does not contemplate the response of the other, but rather concerns the subjectivity that inhabits this other. In his opinion, therefore, there is a form of reciprocity in the person, even in the absence of the response of the other (see *Theos*, para. 867). This form of reciprocity, inhabiting its internal movement, perhaps invites us to go deeper into the understanding of the interpersonality. In fact, even when the other—for whom the subject gives himself—does not recognize the gesture, this does not mean that reciprocity is interrupted, in absolute terms. The subject who has given himself can still reciprocate with the absence of the other, or, even better, with the presence of the absence of the other, who remains a merely objective, indeterminate figure, that is, not active—impersonal—towards him. Therefore, when the other does not respond positively, one is still in reciprocity with the negative of the other, that is, with its lack. With this, the person experiences a reciprocity that, in Rosmini's language, allows him to develop *impartiality*, that is to say, *gratuitousness*, because he loves authentically, without the certainty of receiving something in return (see *Theos*, para. 882). On all this, see Pili, *Se l'uno è l'altro*, 216–18.

15. See Rosmini, *AAMS*, para. 894: "All intelligent beings, who are the beings who have the purpose, and in which and among whom the moral good is born, are ordered to esteem each other for what they are mutually and to love each other, and with cognition and love to communicate themselves to others mutually: and in this communication of intelligences among themselves, and in this universal love lies being happy; which is nothing more than a pleasure in all the fullness of being, fullness that has its seat and consummation in the first intelligence, in the infinite intelligence, in God."

from the same intimate viscera of being comes out and resonates: the very high base of which necessary attachments and essential relationships of the entities lies in the original synthesis of the three categorical forms, in which being one, is equally still triune.[16]

Person and Recognition

Entering now in the second moment, of a more markedly anthropological slant, it is necessary to understand what Rosmini means by *person*, and to articulate when and how that person can meet with others. In the panorama of essences, the person is a being who, by virtue of freedom, can realize in the most complete and perfect form the participation in the uni-triadicity of being. The definitions that Rosmini offers are different from, but complementary to each other. He says, that first of all, a person is—as emphasized in Anthropology as an Aid to Moral Science (*Antropologia in servizio della scienza morale*)—"a substantially intelligent individual, insofar as it contains an active, supreme, and incommunicable principle."[17] This formula—sometimes summarized simply in "the person can be defined as an intelligent subject"[18]—proves to be indebted to the Boethian tradition (according to which the person is *naturae rationalis individua substantia*) and the Scotist definition (for incommunicability), but at the same time expands on them. In fact, to the extent that the subjective principle (intellectual will or freedom) operates only in relation to the objective being that underlies it, then "the noun person does not mean either merely a *substance*, nor merely a *relationship*, but a *substantial relationship*."[19]

As is fully stated in *Theosophy*, this "subsisting relationship"[20] of objectivity and subjectivity thus expresses the identity of the person. Rosmini consequently expands the classical links to Boethius, such as Thomas Aquinas, because this meaning of person is not reserved only for Trinitarian Persons (and therefore for the theological sphere), but is inherent in the concept as such, entering into an exquisitely onto- and anthropological context. Nevertheless, the existing relationship of which Rosmini speaks

---

16. Rosmini, *Theos*, para. 2188. The ontological and essential reciprocal relation between things is also a foundation of the unit of knowledge; see Catuogno, "Restaurare l'unità del sapere."

17. Rosmini, *AAMS*, para. 832.

18. Rosmini, *AAMS*, para. 832.

19. Rosmini, *AAMS*, para. 832n50.

20. Rosmini, *Theos*, para. 903.

must not be understood (at least immediately) in *an interpersonal* sense, as if the person were expended in his historical-cultural, political and social dimension. Rather, he understands objectivity first and foremost as ideality; for this reason, the first term of the relationship, for the subject, is that infinite horizon of being (impersonal, we said) *for* and *in* which, as a relational *medium*, it is then possible to meet any otherness.

There is a further Rosminian definition contained in *Philosophy of Law*, according to which the person is the "right subsisting in law."[21] With this expression, the philosopher specifies that, being primarily an opening to infinity, the person has his own individual intimacy, or infinite dignity, irreducible to the relationship with others, who—precisely because of this— have "the corresponding moral duty not to harm it, not even to consider or attempt to offend or subdue it."[22] The person is therefore the beginning and the end of the law and, in this sense, only improperly *has* rights, since if anything he coincides with the law itself. The person is therefore a peculiar species of the subject genus, that is, he is the relational subject being immediately open in the horizon of being, and therefore immediately unbalanced[23] towards everything that is: himself, others, the world, the Other. Thus, although the person exists even if he were deprived of the actual relationship with others, without such experience he could not initiate any volitional-intellectual motion and, remaining simply immobile, would live a life that—as is stated peremptorily in *A New Essay Concerning the Origin of Ideas* (*Nuovo Saggio sull'origine delle idee*)—would be "similar to nonexistence."[24]

In this direction and debating with Fichtean idealism,[25] Rosmini believed that the notion of ego (which he understood as self-awareness and self-consciousness) must be carefully distinguished from that of person, since the former is always the result of reflective activity and, therefore, is always subsequent to the manifestation of the latter.[26] However, the reflective capacity develops only in the relationship with the world and in interpersonality.[27] Thus, the ego is traversed from top to bottom by what

---

21. Rosmini, *PL* 2, para. 52.
22. Rosmini, *PL* 2, para. 52.
23. See Sciacca, *Uomo questo squilibrato*.
24. Rosmini, *NE*, para. 514.
25. See Pili, "Altro nell'Io."
26. See Rosmini, *Saggio storico critico*, 201–4.
27. See, in particular, with regard to the complex dynamics of language: Brugiatelli, *Problema filosofico del linguaggio*.

Rosmini called, in *Teodicea*, the "wound"[28] of the othernesses that gradually supports the ego and its possibility of knowing itself as such. Whenever the person pronounces the monosyllable "I," therefore, he mirrors an encounter with other than himself. Even more: the other is in the ego precisely because he has proposed the same reflection by which the ego affirms itself. An important consequence follows, well noted by Giuseppe Beschin in the wake of the personalism of Luigi Stefanini: "The more I descend into myself, the more I find others and the more I open myself to others, the more I delve into myself."[29] The truth of the person is thus revealed in the "sliding" into the wound of the other. Descending into oneself means in fact opening up the dimension of the other that constitutes the "I," as an expression of a single and irreducible person. That is why an authentic knowledge of oneself cannot be separated from re-knowing the otherness inhabiting the ego, esteeming it for who it is. The recognition of oneself and the recognition of the other are reciprocal other and, therefore, the inexhaustible commitment to self-discovery is always accompanied by the discovery of the other. More precisely, being a person, manifests itself in fullness the more it realizes the aforementioned ability to move forward, that is, to live in something else, since only in this way, on closer inspection, can one truly live also in oneself.

"Inaltrarsi" and Reciprocity

The dynamism propitiated by the *inaltrarsi* finds its fulfillment in interpersonal reciprocity, where it is shown—as Michele Federico Sciacca pointed out—the fact that "the less I am and the more I am him, the more I am I and he is him,"[30] since *each is himself*—paradoxically—*being the other*: to speak of the person also means knowing how to articulate these coherent paradoxes that, in a certain sense, preserve and animate its *mystery*.[31] Now, if we wanted to look for a Rosminian place in which the movement of the gift of self is unfolded organically in interpersonality, then we should certainly meditate on the pages of *Philosophy of Law* dedicated to conjugal and sexual union. Indeed, it is precisely that one of those *loci* can be found in which Rosmini tries to penetrate, as far as possible, the mystery of interpersonal reciprocity punctuated by love that involves body and soul.[32]

28. Rosmini, *Th*, para. 91.
29. Beschin, *Comunicazione delle persone*, 9–10.
30. Sciacca, *Atto ed essere*, 120.
31. See Pili, "'In questa gran parola."
32. Among the most recent studies, see Bellelli, *Nuzialità trinitaria*. On the centrality of the affective, see Bellelli, *Etica originaria*.

He formulates his examination of spousal and sexual union in book 3 of the *Philosophy of Law*, dedicated to social law. Here, the second part of "Social-Special Law" *(Diritto sociale-speciale)* studies the law of domestic society *(Diritto della società domestica)*, the first chapter of which is entitled *Natura della società coniugale* (The nature of the conjugal society). It is from article 4 onwards that we find the most significant Rosminian arguments on the subjects encountered so far. First of all, Rosmini believes that, in order to understand what conjugal union really is, it is necessary to first examine and classify "every other possible union between human persons"[33] since conceiving the dignity of the conjugal union means "contemplating the union between two persons of different sexes as far as the mind can go."[34] Thanks to these meaningful words, Rosmini confides, on the one hand, that he is facing a "challenge"[35] and, on the other, precisely because of this, he forewarns that he will exploit every resource of his intellectuality to make the mystery contained in marriage shine forth.

He explains, in the first place, that the exercise of morality implies an ever-fuller union with others, which is implemented in that feeling of mutual esteem that binds in a "very strong union"[36] in this love, "one loves all that is in the other."[37] From here, the various shades of love evolve further and the tension of unity inherent in the human unfurls, also reflecting on the entry of God into his events (and soon we will see the terms in which we talk about it). Subsequently, Rosmini begins to enumerate the multiple diversities that can emerge within the couple. Among them, those due to defectiveness that do not make the relationship easily liveable, but which can nevertheless be reinvigorated and saved when the *love of love* is cared for, that is, that tension for which

> the person who loves can love the defective person in spite of their defects, can love them with the love of compassion, benevolence, charity; and, I say, for their very faults; because this love finds the opportunity to exercise itself in the defects to which it pities, and desires to remedy.[38]

Diversity, however, is not an obstacle *in itself*. Indeed, in line with the setting of the Rosminian ontology, it is required as a condition of possibility

---

33. Rosmini, *PL* 4, para. 998.
34. Rosmini, *PL* 4, para. 999.
35. Rosmini, *PL* 4, para. 999.
36. Rosmini, *PL* 4, para. 1008.
37. Rosmini, *PL* 4, para. 1008.
38. Rosmini, *PL* 4, para. 1032.

of the encounter. Sometimes, the author points out, diversities harmonize and support each other in complementarity,[39] but on many occasions the Rosminian pages, more profoundly, invite us to keep away from the temptation of uniformity, which ultimately coincides with the death of the relationship: only the *con-venientia* of differences, in fact, makes unity possible.[40] It is only in diversity that unity is possible; it is mere illusion to think that difference impedes the vitality of the union.[41]

At the same time, Rosmini is committed to presenting the affective development of the person. The references to homosexual orientation are surprising from a certain point of view. Considered by Rosmini "genuine" in its original form of ideal-platonic love, but "detestable and vile" as soon as it is corrupted in the form of incontinence,[42] and therefore in the form of effectively exercised sexuality, on closer inspection, this is, in fact, a very modern position. At the same time, the physical attraction between different sexes is also described, not without dwelling on the reality of the kiss, understood as one of those human gestures that contain deep mysteries,[43] up to the reality of sexual union, which Rosmini defines as "an act of the soul, which operates in bodies, and through bodies; nor already through the parties, to the exclusion of the others; which concurs with the whole soul."[44] For the author, nothing of the human is excluded in the sexual act, which instead reflects—in the words of Tadini—"an ontological reality."[45] The *coming together* in the desire to give reciprocal pleasure opens up to that reality that Rosmini defines as a "social person,"[46] that is, to a third dimension inherent in the relationship "between" the two people who wish to give themselves to each other: "This bond is formed by more than one person collaborating in an objective, and having the awareness and willingness to collaborate jointly in the said objective. The people with wills thus disposed are associated together."[47] In sexual union, however, it also happens that the reciprocal uniting of the act of will coincides with the reciprocal uniting of bodies:

39. See Rosmini, *PL* 4, para. 1035.

40. See Rosmini, *PL* 4, para. 1038. On the notion of *con-venientia*, see Marianelli, *Ontologia della relazione*.

41. See Rosmini, *PL* 4, para. 1036.

42. See Rosmini, *PL* 4, para. 1046.

43. See Rosmini, *PL* 4, para. 1051: "What mystery then, what communication of life is enclosed in the kiss . . ."

44. See Rosmini, *PL* 4, para. 1058.

45. Tadini, "*Eros e Agápe*," 327.

46. Rosmini, *PL* 3, para. 34.

47. Rosmini, *PL* 3, para. 34.

> Of these approaches of the bodies the most intimate is certainly that of sexual coupling; in which it seems that for a moment from two fundamental sentiments of individuals only one is formed, that the feeling of one is the feeling of the other mutually [that is: that the subjectivity of one is the subjectivity of the other reciprocally]; which cannot be expressed more effectively than by the words of divine Scripture, which define marriage by saying: "... and the two will become one flesh." (Matt 19:5)[48]

The one and the other discover themselves as each is returned to himself *in* and *by the other*. They are perfectly one, each being himself in giving and giving to each other. Perfect unity, therefore, but in the most perfect distinction:

> Only one thing remains distinct in them, the *person*. Of two natures the spouses come to form one; but they cannot form one person. Therefore, at the same time, that God, defining the conjugal union, said, that the spouses must be one flesh, He also said that in that one flesh they will be two: *erunt duo in carne una*. It is true that such a total personal communication intervenes between the lovers, and therefore between the spouses, as one enjoys the same personality as the other, but this kind of transfusion of persons does not blend them, nor does it take away their proper and inalienable being.[49]

Rosmini, however, does not interrupt his analysis without gradually signifying the role that God can play in this reciprocity. Therefore, at first he recalls that he is the *real being* in a strong and primary sense and when real beings naturally tend to unite they yearn—at least implicitly—for the real par excellence that is him. The problem, Rosmini continues, is that will and intelligence are not able to communicate immediately with God (given that man can only grasp something of his being and action): consequently, if God does not take the initiative, then he remains inaccessible to the human being. If, on the other hand, it were he himself who revealed himself, the human, says the author, could "really adhere to the infinite Being."[50] In other words, if the infinite is revealed in the finite, then the finite can participate, even within its intrinsic limits, in life and contemplation *in* and *of* the infinite, which—by virtue of such a revelation—does not intend

---

48. Rosmini, *PL* 4, para. 1060. It is significant that the perfect mutual union is reported in the horizon of the *moment*, which in Rosmini has a clear Platonic derivation: see Martino, *D'improvviso*.

49. Rosmini, *PL* 4, paras. 1065–66.

50. Rosmini, *PL* 4, para. 1009.

to continue to reaffirm an unbridgeable distance from the human: this is why Rosmini says, with courageous consistency, "to really adhere" (which clearly implies the help of grace).

Starting from here, however, it is necessary to consider that in marriage the relational bond is consecrated, so that God no longer divinizes the individual, but the relationship of reciprocity and, *in* it, the two who live it. And the divinization, pay close attention, does not simply say that God emanates some of his love from above, without getting too involved. Rather, and much more radically, Rosmini asserts that "God himself enters [as] third in the . . . [marital] society; becoming God, the common good of God, and of the spouses."[51] Here then is a thirdness, since, in this reciprocity, God himself assumes the role of a third party, welcoming into his bosom not only one person, but two, by virtue of the relational bond. Evidently, it is not a question of a third to be read, Hegelianly, as a synthesis of the two; rather, the figure of the Rosminian thirdness is that delivered in the reality of the kiss (another figure of the *moral being*),[52] where the *contact* expresses the "between" of a perfect union in the distinction.

Rosmini, however, goes even further. In fact, at the moment in which God enters into the relationship, since he is that same relationship of love,[53] he no longer intervenes only on the basis of the initiative of the individual person entrusted to him, rather, Rosmini affirms, "God becomes a fully and social good," so that he also informs the relationships of which history is woven. Moreover, the use of the adverb *fully* is not a small moment: as long as God dwells in the individual, in fact, his presence in the events is mediated only by the action of that individual, where this action cannot already be *fully common and social*, since it is not involved in intersubjective reciprocity. If, on the other hand, God transfigures or, better yet, transubstantiates the social relationship itself, it is precisely because it is precisely in this way—since relationality is shaped by him—that he also becomes *fully social*:

> If [God] himself descends to man, and becomes perceptible to him, then man can truly adhere to the infinite Being; God becomes a fully common and social good; in whose enjoyment the men who possess it are unified. This is the religious bond,

---

51. Rosmini, *PL* 4, para. 1009. In addition to the conjugal union, it is possible to see a dynamic similar to the so-called theocratic society (the church); see Baggio, *Incivilimento e storia filosofica*, 333–61.

52. See Rosmini, "Storia comparativa e critica," 188, since here the being morality is defined as "mystical kiss."

53. In this regard, the words of the *De Trinitate* of Agostino d'Ippona: *Fraterna dilectio non solum ex Deo, sed etiam Deum est* (8:12). On the relationship between Agostino and Rosmini, see Pili, "Interpersonalità."

fulfilment of the previous ones, which develop the two human creatures destined to live united in all the possible unions that can be formed between them, which ultimately merge into one that is said to be conjugal. Supernatural religion therefore sublimates marriage beyond nature, tightening the spouses of the maximum bond that is charity, and divinizes their union. Aware that God himself enters for as a third in their society; becoming God the common good of God, and of spouses. . . . Being, the moral law and God made perceptible to men, are goods of infinite price. Men who love them in common find themselves united with souls more than just accidents; whose souls yes with respect to their intellectual part, as with respect to their volitional part, dwell in a common center, in the true place of intelligences.[54]

The significance of the verb *to dwell*, used to express the *locus* that has opened up thanks to an intersubjectivity crossed by a love consumed "to the end" (John 13:1), is not intended to distort human reality with its corporeality. On the contrary, as clearly emerges in the case of sexual union, this dimension of the *sarx*—exercised oblatively—is a *conditio sine qua non* of that dwelling: therefore, one can live *in the true place of intelligences*, that is, *in sinu Patris*, only because one lives *in carne Verbi*. The contradictions, fragilities and wounds of the flesh are not only not erased or forgotten, but are indeed the properly human way of the encounter with the Other *in statu viae*.[55] Dwelling in him in the *already and not yet* of human history, these contradictions, fragility and wounds remain, they do not fail (even the Risen One does not cease to be the Crucified One): they, therefore, in him can still be looked at, felt, touched and named. What changes is that they now enjoy an anticipation—as far as allowed in a time not last, but penultimate—of their *transfiguration*, that is, of the elevation to their most intimate truth, since in the light of an unprecedented and surprising gaze.

Bibliography

Baggio, Alberto. *Incivilimento e storia filosofica nel pensiero di Antonio Rosmini*. Trento: Università degli Studi di Trento, 2016.

---

54. Rosmini, *PL* 4, para. 1009.

55. In the Rosminian verb *dwell* we hear the echo of New Testament Greek ἐσκήνωσεν (John 1:14), which translates the Hebrew verb that indicates precisely the precarious and fragile *dwell under a tent*, thus expressing the form through which God dwells in the midst of men, in the experience of the exodus of the desert.

Bellelli, Fernando, ed. *Nuzialità trinitaria: relazione e identità. Rosmini e il fondamento simbolico dell'umano*. Florence: Feeria, 2017.

———. *Etica originaria e assoluto affettivo. La coscienza e il superamento della modernità nella teologia filosofica di Antonio Rosmini*. Milan: Vita e Pensiero, 2014.

Beschin, Giuseppe. *La comunicazione delle persone nella filosofia di A. Rosmini*. Milan: Marzorati, 1964.

Brugiatelli, Vereno. *Il problema filosofico del linguaggio in Antonio Rosmini*. Bologna: EDB, 2000.

Catuogno, Lorena. "Restaurare l'unità del sapere: Antonio Rosmini verso l'istanza transdisciplinare." *Rosmini Studies* 5 (2018) 79–89.

Dossi, Michele. *Il santo proibito. La vita e il pensiero di Antonio Rosmini*. Trento: Margine, 2007.

Marianelli, Massimiliano. *Ontologia della relazione. La "convenientia" in figure e momenti del pensiero filosofico*. Rome: Città Nuova, 2008.

Martino, Marco. *D'improvviso. La via del "non," a partire da Platone*. Rome: Città Nuova, 2020.

Pili, Emanuele. "L'altro nell'Io. Fichte fonte di Rosmini." *Philosophia* 1 (2018) 75–100.

———. "'In questa gran parola sta ogni cosa.' La negazione nella mistica di Antonio Rosmini." In *Pedagogia del sapere di Dio. Una prospettiva storico-culturale*, edited by Fernando Bellelli, 35–60. Milan: Mimesis, 2019.

———. "L'interpersonalità come 'vero luogo delle intelligenze'. Agostino in Rosmini, passando per Leibniz." In *Agostino e la sua eredità. Teologia, filosofia e letteratura*, edited by Vito Limone and Giulio Maspero, 191–98. Brescia, It.: Morcelliana, 2021.

———. *Se l'uno è l'altro. Ontologia e intersoggettività in Antonio Rosmini*. Bari, It.: Pagina, 2020.

Rosmini, Antonio. *Antropologia in servizio della scienza morale*. Edited by Evain F. ENC 24. Rome: Città Nuova, 1981.

———. "Del principio supremo della Metodica" [The ruling principle of method applied to education]. In *Scritti pedagogici*, edited by Fernando Bellelli, ENC 32, 37–364. Rome: Città Nuova, 2019.

———. *Filosofia del diritto*. Edited by Michele Nicoletti and Francesco Ghia. 4 vols. ENC 27, 27A, 28, 28A. Rome: Città Nuova, 2013.

———. *Nuovo Saggio sull'origine delle idee*. Edited by Gaetano Messina. 3 vols. ENC 3–5. Rome: Città Nuova, 2003–2004.

———. *Saggio storico critico sulle Categorie*. Edited by Pier P. Ottonello. ENC 19. Rome: Città Nuova, 1997.

———. "Sistema filosofico." In *Introduzione alla filosofia*, edited by Pier P. Ottonello, ENC 2, 225–302. Rome: Città Nuova, 1979.

———. "Storia comparativa e critica de' sistemi intorno al principio della morale." In *Principi della scienza morale*, edited by Umberto Muratore, ENC 23, 161–459. Rome: Città Nuova, 1990.

———. *Teodicea*. Edited by Umberto Muratore. ENC 22. Rome: Città Nuova, 1977.

———. *Teosofia*. Edited by Maria A. Raschini and Pier P. Ottonello. 6 vols. ENC 12–17. Rome: Città Nuova, 1998–2002.

Sciacca, Michele F. *Atto ed essere*. Milan: Marzorati, 1963.

———. *L'uomo questo squilibrato*. Palermo: Epos, 2000.

Tadini, Samuele F. "*Eros* e *Agápe* nella metafisica ontoprismatica di Rosmini." In *Nuzialità trinitaria: relazione e identità. Rosmini e il fondamento simbolico dell'umano*, edited by Fernando Bellelli, 309–32. Panzano in Chianti, It.: Feeria-Comunità di San Leolino 2017.

9

Thinking about Faith in Time of Its "Foaming" Relevance

Notes from *Supernatural Anthropology*

GIAMMARIA CANU

Introduction: What Is the Use of Studying Theology?

"ANTONIO ROSMINI: UNITY OF Science and Holiness." The title of the Rosminian conference held at the Certosa of Florence appears appropriate to describe the fruitful parable of Antonio Rosmini which seems to me to echo Rahner's luminous and provocative definition of dogmatic theology: "Dogmatics is an effort of intelligence and a science that must serve its time, as it grows from it . . . because it must serve salvation and not theoretical curiosity."[1]

For the theologian from Freiburg the dual essential and existential vocation of theology has always been clear and we would not be mistaken if we applied that same definition to the encyclopedic work of Antonio Rosmini. Identifying the insufficient education of the clergy as a second scourge of the church, he speaks of science and holiness:

---

1. Rahner, "Saggio di uno Schema," 53–54. This is the well-known article by Rahner that inaugurates the great theological project of the *Mysterium Salutis*.

> This was the first principle and the whole foundation of the method used in the first centuries: science and holiness united very closely.... In this unity consists properly the genuine disposition of the doctrine destined to save the world: it is not pure ideal doctrine, but practical and real truth.[2]

Rosmini puts into action that theoretical, sapiential, and evangelical device for which it is necessary that every discipline (and not only the theological one) converges in its recapitulation (Pauline *anakephalaìosis*) both christological and soteriological. Referring once again to Rahner, it is possible to read in Rosmini's encyclopedism a passionate search for an "anonymous soteriology" that underlies the pages and thoughts of every scientific gesture, humanizing by vocation. Taking a critical look at the current theological act, it seems that theology has not yet succeeded in responding with sufficient reason in the scientific agora of this soteriological vocation common to every research. And on this epistemological feebleness I also base the fundamental question of this essay.

The Silent but Karstic Relevance of the Sloterdijk Case: A Foaming Faith

I come to the theme by exploiting a phenomenon that has peeped into the intellectual history of Europe in the new millennium but without touching, if not marginally, the theological debate, at least as far as I know of the Mediterranean area. This is the powerful irruption of the *Sphären* trilogy (1998–2004) by Peter Sloterdijk. For this eclectic, encyclopedic, and hyperbolic German thinker, the history of human thought acquires a plasticity and a representation of its many "wheres" in the image of the sphere and in its historical declinations of bubbles, globes, and foams.

This is one of the many definitions of *sphere* present in the first volume of the trilogy:

> The search for our where is more sensible than ever, since it questions the place that men produce in order to have what they can appear in what they are. This place bears here, in memory of a respectable tradition, the name of sphere. The sphere is the roundness endowed with a further, used and shared, that men inhabit to the extent that they come to be men. Since living always means building spheres, small as in large, men are the creatures who bring into being circular worlds and look outwards,

---

2. Rosmini, *FW*, 170.

towards the horizon. Living in spheres means producing the dimension in which men can be contained. The spheres are creations of spaces endowed with an immune-systemic effect for ecstatic creatures on which the exterior works.[3]

Every human life is born built and circumscribed in a sphere and the spherical figure pursues it throughout its existence. One does not give existential identity outside the spheres, that is, one is not what one is without a topical relationship, a residential qualification and a spatial quantification that clearly differentiates what is internal from what is external.

In particular, Sloterdijk accompanies the reader in the parallel journey of the history of humanity and the history of each person from microspherology to macrospherology, from bubbles to globes and foams.

From the first volume of *Sfere* (Spheres), *Bolle* (Bubbles), comes the following reflection: the primordial sphere that has all the characterizations of the bubble, that original and originating microsphere that is the maternal uterus, defines man as "inhabitant of the interior." The anthropological structure of every man is a continuous replication of the uterine sphere. Up to the technological neurosis that represents the maximum expression of human powers: the history of technology is the history of "uterotechnics," or the continuous reproduction throughout life of intrauterine conditions.

In the second volume, where the sphere assumes the figure of "globe," the ever-living temptation is represented to try to crystallize, build, objectify (the Rosminists would gasp in recognizing the "inobjectification" of the subject in the object!), give shape and concreteness to the whole world of what in the bubbles was a "non-object" (that world deriving from fetal bubbles in which one lives in the indistinction between object and subject and has a pre-subjective and mixed pre-consciousness informedly with each object). The globes are the spaces in which the subject is one with the world object, but at the same time begins to explore an alienating otherness: the great geographical and philosophical explorations (those globes that then passed through Nietzsche's court which sentenced God to death, of Heidegger in the critique of onto-theology and of Lyotard in the end of the great narratives) would be nothing but the efforts to give consistency to the non-object through an immunological device that tries to protect from the restlessness of the non-object, attributing to the unique and all-embracing macrospheres (Jaspers) that powerful uterine capacity to free man from the contingent and give him the global background of a hospitable house

---

3. Sloterdijk, *Bolle*, 82.

(effective image of Noah's ark) built with technique and blessed by God (who is on board that ark and destined for shipwreck together with the globes).

Everything falls apart (third volume) when macrospheres competing with the Greek-Christian immune system appear: the cosmic and immune totality, solid and holistic, enveloping and inclusive, collapses and is reduced to the image, always spherical, of a gelatinous foam, a lumpy mass of interconnected micro-individualities. There is no longer that shared immunological space, but "we share loneliness" (oxymoron *tremendum et fascinans*) defining every attempt of *Weltanschauung* as criminal and violent, but at the same time surrendering to a threatening exogenous world: "From each point of the foam you have only regional visions in the neighboring area, but you do not have an overall vision. There is no exit to the whole."[4] In this sense, every microsphere of this foam remains orphaned of its interiority since the gaze is perpetually turned to the neighboring world and the space of attention towards the invisible, the imperceptible, the hidden is occupied by the discoveries of atomic energy, the immune system, the deciphering of the genome and the analysis of the brain: "The infinitely small has won. The way of the atomic bomb is philosophical," said Canetti, quoted by Sloterdijk.[5] On the other hand, after the immunological era of the metaphysical globe in which "only the divinity can know how to think simultaneously the salvation (or immunization) of all things (in god) and the real being together of things (in the world, theatre of mutual consumption),"[6] we swim floundering in the egosphere, whose embryonic phase Sloterdijk identifies precisely in a visit by Le Corbusier, the famous Swiss architect naturalized French, to the Certosa of Florence in 1907. Precisely the charterhouse that hosted the Rosminian conference during which this paper was delivered: the fascination exerted on Le Corbusier by monastic buildings was well motivated—in fact, in the cells of the monks of the early Middle Ages lies the germ of the form of modern subjectivity. In these containers for self-recollection was realized the original accumulation of that attention from which modern individualism in Western style would later develop—after the reversal of the fundamental setting of transcendence over immanence.[7]

Precisely the place par excellence of the inner experience of transcendence lent its womb for the birth of the unwanted child: the intramundane hedonistic individualism that aims at the "coupling of the individual with

---

4. Sloterdijk, *Schiume*, 53.
5. Sloterdijk, *Schiume*, 215.
6. Sloterdijk, *Schiume*, 220.
7. Sloterdijk, *Schiume*, 559.

himself . . . that is, the manifest individual remains perpetually on the trail of the *individuum absconditus*"⁸ which is always immanent.

Thus, at the center of Sloterdijk's investigation lies precisely the reading of a humanism collapsed into anthropocentrism and sabotaging not only every figure of transcendence, but also every attempt to "look interiorly" on the world. The anthropo-technology closely allies man to his artifact, mechanical yesterday and digital today, just as the *berît* of the Old Testament linked *Eloìm* to his creature and just as the blood of the Crucified One spilt on Calvary to renew the covenant: "He entered once for all into the sanctuary, not with the blood of goats and calves but with his own blood, thus obtaining eternal redemption" (Heb 9:12). According to the same paradigm of alliance, today in the new sanctuaries, abolished sacrifices and rites,⁹ branded as uncivilized, archaic, and even apotropaic, and indifference to every "objective interiority" is declared;¹⁰ the new technocratic civilization born with digital conversion is celebrated, in French *conversion numérique*¹¹ and visibly gathered in liturgical assembly in the department stores of the marketing giants, those digital and commercial "non-places"¹² of which the Apple Park in Cupertino, the most expensive private structure in the world, is merely an epigone, "digitally visited" in the keynote period by billions of virtual followers of the people of the bitten apple.

To draw conclusions. Sloterdijk's thesis from which we want to derive our question to interrogate Rosmini is to be found in the middle of the third volume of the *Spheres*: "The twilight of the gods brings with it the twilight of mortals. The common destiny of all that is invisible is to become irrelevant."¹³ And so, the capital question for our time: how can humanism be removed from the anthropo-technical-centric neurosis that drags down, in one fell swoop, the question about man and the question about God? That is: in this time in which every *lògos*, including therefore that on faith, has become foamy, is it possible to rethink the question of God in such an effective way as to drag up, in a single stroke, even the question of man?

We are all capable of hurling accusations, but we do not have the tools to even sketch a solution and therefore we turn aside. But it can be fruitful

---

8. Sloterdijk, *Schiume*, 568–69.

9. See Byung-chul Han, *Scomparsa dei riti*. The denunciation is aimed at the postmodern "noise" that stifles rituals in their intent to "objectify the world."

10. See Sciacca, *Interiortà oggettiva*.

11. I have deliberately mentioned the French expression *conversion numérique*, which in English sounds like "numerical conversion," to highlight the "care for the number" that replaced the "care for the name" (see Lacan, *Dei Nomi-del-Padre*).

12. See Augé, *Non-lieux*.

13. Sloterdijk, *Schiume*, 435.

to *nourish the question*[14] with three exercises of thought that I personally acquired from Rosmini, especially by reading with care and passion his incomplete *Supernatural Anthropology (Antropologia soprannaturale)*. I therefore propose a path of intellectual charity that can be shared (synodality!).

First Quick Exercise of Thought: Rethinking the Interiority of Faith

In *Supernatural Anthropology*, Rosmini often questions the place of faith that can only be in the interior experience of grace. Faith is in fact precisely the ever new and continually reaffirmed recognition of "that real action which God himself works in the spirit of man."[15]

For Rosmini, the hermeneutic key to every act of faith is that the gospel really, substantially, existentially "produces a feeling, a new soul full of virtue and strength to work"[16] or better still "in us is by grace something divine that did not exist before, joined and incorporated with the essence of our soul"[17] and creates in us of a new power, a new principle of action. The human soul is reached and enriched—"accelerated"—Rosmini says several times—with a new feeling:[18] next to the fundamental bodily sentiment (that of animality) and the fundamental intellectual sentiment (that of humanity) a feeling essentially different from others dwells in man, "a new principle of action which is what is called the *instinct of the Holy Spirit*,"[19] "that real action which God does in the essence of the soul to magnify its fundamental feeling."[20] The inner man and his fundamental feeling are therefore the *Rosminian locus theologicus* to speak of grace, faith, and salvation. It is an open and welcoming space, "elastic"[21] and metaphysically true, anthropologically synthetic, and theologically frequentable.

---

14. In the precious pages of Vattimo, *Che cosa significa pensare*, Heidegger suggested the need to handle the questions by bringing them to the most important problematic. Thus, the question remains open and increasingly capable of delving into the mystery that it conveys, rather than resolving its provocation and settling for a mediocre absolution from the problem.

15. Rosmini, *SA*, 1:78.

16. Rosmini, *SA*, 1:96.

17. Rosmini, *SA*, 1:107.

18. I refer the reader to my work (Canu, *Pensare la fede*) where I analyze faith as the inner birth of a new "fundamental believing sentiment."

19. Rosmini, *SA*, 1:110.

20. Rosmini, *SA*, 1:112.

21. "We ourselves are finally but a feeling and therefore the WE is magnified by enlarging the feeling" (Rosmini, *SA*, 1:111).

PART 2

Second Exercise of Thought: Rethinking the "Reality" of Faith

The theological theme is therefore that of the realism of grace.

In the *Introduction to Philosophy (Introduzione alla filosofia)*, Rosmini firmly states:

> Man is a *real* subject: therefore, he cannot stop at the idea, he aspires to join with reality. The real given to man in nature is finite, and the idea leads man to know and love this finite real, but at the same time it shows him finite, and being infinite the idea shows him the possibility, the need for another infinite real, which is not given to man. Man to what he knows, also extends his desire.[22]

And in the first lines of *Supernatural Anthropology*, almost at the head of everything, he can see: "Everyone, who pays attention to what happens in himself, can feel the difference that runs between a thing, which he thinks as *possible*, and a real thing."[23]

It was therefore a radical, serious, and intelligent reading of the human that led Rosmini on the path towards the real being of faith starting from the intuited ideal being. And it is in the *chiaroscuro* contrast between the "cold" negative ideal being of God with the positive real inner perception (in other Rosminian pages defined more effectively as "affirmative") that the figure of the biblical God of the Covenant emerges in the form of a "verbalized feeling," fully "new."[24] It is only this "new feeling" that moves life always towards a light that human forces alone could not even know how to desire, because they know only a negative intuition incapable of moving the subject and accompanying him in the field of the third form of being, the moral one, that loving form of being for which the subject "adheres to being with his will and with his whole self."[25] The mysterious dimension of faith is clear in this "revealing realism" that plays so much on the Johannine, Pauline and Augustinian metaphor of the light-darkness dynamism (blindness-vision). But it is equally clear that revealed theology is the new great investment in reason, the theology revealed in *interiore homine*, which

---

22. Rosmini, *IP*, 156–57.

23. Rosmini, *SA*, 1:1.

24. New in the sense of "different, modified, accelerated, accomplished, realized while remaining the same" (*kainòs*), not in the sense of "totally other" (*neòs*). Rather along the lines of the "new covenant" (*Kaine dithèke* of Jer 31:31, mentioned several times in Heb 8): "Do not think that I have come to abolish the law or the prophets. I have come not to abolish but to fulfill" (Matt 5:17).

25. Rosmini, *T*, para. 879.

the Pontifical Lateran University's manual of fundamental theology ascribes to the cosmic-anthropological dimension of revelation.[26]

Therefore, the theology of mystery underlies the "reality" of the "fundamental believing sentiment." A mystery to be brought to light fragment after fragment, without any claim of uncovering the totality of the mystery, but rather by submitting our life to the law of digging deeper (*abyssus abyssum invocat*: Ps 42). It is the mystery that creates discomfort, Bonhoeffer suggests, loading the theological and anthropological category of mystery with realism and truth.

> We are not at home in his presence, because it speaks of a "being at home" that is different from the meaning we attribute to this phrase. . . . To live without mystery means seeing no decisive facts of life or even denying them. We do not want to know that the roots of the tree lie in the darkness of the earth, that everything that lives in the light comes from the darkness and mystery of the womb, that all our thoughts, our whole spiritual life, also come from the mystery of a hidden darkness, as does our life and all life. . . . It is not the farthest man who is the greatest mystery for us, but the closest one. And his mystery does not diminish in our eyes because we continually learn something about him, on the contrary his closeness makes him more and more mysterious. There is the greatest depth of every mystery when two people come to be so close to each other that they love each other. When two people know everything about each other, the mystery of life becomes infinitely great between them.[27]

These three Bonhoefferian concepts could be said to synthesize the concreteness ("reality") of the inner revelation proposed by Rosmini: first, in the new fundamental feeling one truly feels at home with oneself, but also "a parishioner" (etymologically: neighbor) of being,[28] and roommate, if not a guest/host of God; second, the roots of everything real, that is, the foundations, the meaning and the end sink into the hidden abyss of the "truest"[29] that grants flashes of brightness very sparingly; and third, closeness, "intimacy," as Augustine would say, operates, contrary to physical phenomena, an ever greater sinking of the mystery as we unveil its fragments, since every abyss has an intrinsic vocation to draw down those who lean over it.

---

26. See Lorizio, *Teologia fondamentale*.
27. Bonhoeffer, *Gli scritti*, 400–401.
28. See Heidegger, *Lettera sull' "umanismo,"* 74.
29. See the poem of Rebora, "Pioppo." Rilke echoes in *Wladimir, il pittore di nuvole*.

PART 2

Third Exercise of Thought: Rethinking Faith in the Horizon of Salvation[30]

Let us quote once again the position of Sloterdijk: "The twilight of the gods brings with it the twilight of mortals. The common destiny of all that is invisible is to become irrelevant."[31] It is a question of taking a stand on the terrible question of twilight. Whether it is *twilight of the gods* (a funeral march by Wagner), *twilight of idols* (a caustic essay by Nietzsche), or *twilight of mortals* (Sloterdijk), the reference to physical phenomenon offers the metaphor for doubting the twilight position: it is the dusk that follows the sunset and leads us into darkness, or the gleam that precedes the dawn of a new day, how did women happen on Easter morning in that auroral dynamism which is the heart and *arché* of the Christian *kérygma*? Better yet: it is a post-theism (with tremendous lucidity Sloterdijk seals his spherological trilogy with his *Nach Gott* [After God],[32] dated 2017, a decade after Taylor's *A Secular Age*) or yet another pre-theism (see Dominique Collin's acrobatics both theological and theoretic in the text *Le christianisme n'existe pas encore*).

Those who frequent Rosmini have in mind the image of twilight referring to philosophy:

> Therefore, the *principle* of Christianity, the TRUTH, is unique; and the TRUTH is also the *beginning* of philosophy. Hence, Philosophy, even though it wants to be true, must always be a *propaedeutic* to the true Religion: for man will be better prepared for adoration and faith if he has turned away from error and occupied himself with recognizing and loving even that framework, so to speak, of natural Christianity, which is in man the natural truth, a glimpse, I would call it, of the divine Word.[33]

In this regard, Professor Lorizio has in his repertoire numerous pages on the image of *semina Verbi*[34] abundantly disseminated in the *cooperatores veritatis*, that is, the many philosophers who, as "anonymous theologians" or

---

30. With these words I refer to my doctoral effort for those who had the curiosity to peek at what other thought exercises can derive from Rosmini's theology: Canu, *Pensare la fede*.

31. Sloterdijk, *Schiume*, 435. Sloterdijk continues: "He looks back at all this as a dead man who left no will, a procedure that, for better or worse, leaves no legacy—uncharged batteries that no longer fascinate us enough to bring us to splendor, coming to meet us from above."

32. See Sloterdijk, *Dopo Dio*.

33. Rosmini, *NE* 1, para. 13.

34. Please refer to his last great work: Lorizio, *Semi del Verbo*.

"sentinels of theology," "carefully emphasize the sapiential and metaphysical dimension of philosophy":[35] "Watchman, how much longer the night?" (Isa 21:11), which is equivalent to the Pharisees's question to Jesus "when the kingdom of God would come."[36] And regarding this last Lucanian quote. To that question about the delay of the kingdom, Jesus replies: "The coming of the kingdom of God cannot be observed, and no one will announce, 'Look, here it is,' or, 'There it is.' For behold, the kingdom of God is among you" (*in interiore homine*) (Luke 17:20–21). Rosmini has no doubts in seeking the kingdom of God not "in our midst," as if it were a widespread presence in the community (all translations, including the Vulgate, thus translate the adverb of luogo *entòs*), but first of all the kingdom of God is "within us."[37]

Confirmation can be found in the image, once again very dear to the Rosmini who wrote *Supernatural Anthropology*, of the midwife who draws from the darkness of the viscera of Christianity, a "healthy and true philosophy,"[38]

> this [Christian] philosophy that lies hidden in the viscera of Christian theology and which we have proposed to help to bring to light, almost giving us too (if we are allowed to use quote Socrates out of context) the role of midwife.[39]

Having completed this first "role of midwife," theology does not change its profession, but continues its maieutic art by investigating the visceral night of its interiority, discovering its "fundamental feeling of existence"[40] and slowly discovering it to change touched by grace.

In a possible *analysis fidei* drawn from *Supernatural Anthropology*, the following elements referring to Rosmini's triadic and dynamic ontology could therefore be noted: the primordial supernatural grafting is obtained with the intuition of the idea of being that corresponds to an "incipient perception of God" in the form of a negative idea; it follows the confirmation of an immediate positive perception, the one that touches the sphere of objective interiority, "objectifying," "realizing," and "substantiating" that idea;[41] to define and complete oneself with the third faculty, that of the will

---

35. Francis, *VG*, para. 64a.
36. See Luke 17:20.
37. Rosmini, *SA*, 1:74.
38. Rosmini, *Epistolario completo* (Complete epistolary), 4:609.
39. Rosmini, *SA*, 3:235.
40. See Evain, *Être et personne*, 297–313.
41. See Rosmini, *SA*, 1:131.

that moves man with love in the same direction from which absolute love comes to him:

> This perception (in receiving which we are entirely passive as in receiving all direct knowledge) is lucid, beautiful, gentle, all convenient and adapted to our nature: then the feeling of affection towards these known and perceived things arises in us provided with "those" sweet persuasions of which Saint Augustine spoke, which incline our soul to lend full adherence and faith even to what is perceived in things only virtually and obscurely understood.[42]

This is faith, that is, "the assent that is given to what that supernatural feeling has perceived of God."[43] And once again the doctrine of fundamental sentiment is the host:

> God works with a real and occult action in the essence of the soul: thus, everything is born without our intervention. This action produces, creates in our essence, without us being aware of it, a new element, a new fundamental feeling.[44]

And therefore, faith is a continuous maieutic of the mystery that uses a vocabulary comprehensible only to the believer's interiority, the humus where the gracious action of God is realized as he, "giving and uniting himself with man" brings about salvation.[45]

It is the vocabulary of soteriology that dictates the rules of the game. But here I stop. I think, however, my personal apprehension with regard to the soteriological soul or the properly soteriological ministry of theology, of which I spoke in the epigraph to this paper, has been perceived.

Humble Conclusions Leaving the Viscous Foam

This dash around the gymnasium set up by Sloterdijk has simply tried to show the fruitfulness and abundance of the *semina Verbi* hidden and guarded in the exercise of thought, when this is provoked by the frothy (ir)relevance of faith. The still winning weapon in the face of any reduction of relevance continues to be the *intellectus fidei*. In this sense, Christianity is structurally "agonic," not only in the tragic sense of Unamuno's *Agony of*

---

42. Rosmini, SA, 1:131.
43. Rosmini, SA, 1:128.
44. Rosmini, SA, 1:127–28.
45. Rosmini, SA, 1:132n131.

Christianity, but in that of Mounier's passionate agony, which was already the meaning given by Pascal: "Jesus will be in agony until the end of the world; we must not sleep during that time."[46]

Combining the image of Sloterdijk's anthropocentric and foaming society with Günther Anders's whiplashes, we can say: despite the fact that man has once again become "antiquated" and despite his "Promethean shame" in seeing artificial intelligence paradoxically more intelligent than the intelligence of *homo sapiens*;[47] despite the turbo-capitalistic risk that the subject sinks into the condition of becoming the object of his own objects, there is still an infinite space to train thought in the many passages from uterine bubbles to foamy twilights, or in the many "Passovers" of existence and being! Gymnasiums of intellectual charity are needed for philosophy and theology, for science as for poetry, so that one becomes ever more familiar with the experience of the ever-new twilight. It is necessary to train every *lògos* to live with serenity the paradoxical half lights of being, both those that introduce the dawns of new horizons, and those that ferry us towards the dark nights of the abyss.

For his part, Rosmini gave a precious example of well-trained intellectual charity. His great revolution of the "system of truth" gives us a humble and open love for the truth in all its symphonic expressions (Balthasar), which is always complex (Morin) and contradictory—in the sense of the "polar opposition" of Guardini's "living concrete" rather than in that of the purely speculative Hegelian dialectic. Among other things, in the lexeme itself "intellectual charity" is already included and implicit the profound experience of a mild research, of a humble metaphysics (Berti) and even agapeic (Lorizio) which, purged of every dross of pride, arrogance or "metaphysical violence" (Adorno, Derrida, Vattimo[48]) is indeed invested with the

---

46. Pascal, *Pensieri*, 496. See De Unamuno, *Agonia del cristianesimo*, and Mounier, *Agonia del cristianesimo?*

47. See Anders, *Uomo è antiquato*.

48. To the latter I respond with the authority of Pareyson's "revelatory thought": "Truth carries men, exalting them, making even the humble capable of great things; ideas take possession of men, subject them to the realization of their program, reduce them to mere instruments, whether it is the cosmic-historical hero or the depersonalized mass. No slavery is comparable to that of man with respect to the ideas which he himself has produced. . . . But if obedience to reason deprived of truth is the most intolerable of tyrannies, there is nothing servile in man's obedience to the truth. In this case obedience coincides with freedom, because truth inspires, it does not dominate, it stimulates, it does not rule, it supports, it does not subjugate, it is an appeal that asks for response and testimony not an imposition that oppresses or constrains, it is a call that demands man face his responsibilities and urges him to freely perform the act with which he affirms himself by reaffirming his being, recovering his origin, indissolubly tightening the bond of person and truth" (Pareyson, *Verità e interpretazione*, 31).

humble attitude of reason (Repole[49]) that in a state of perennial Advent, awaits with the patience of a sentinel and industriousness of a gymnast the revelation of the truth-being-God.

We have also indicated the place where intellectual charity welcomes the maximum expression of its potential: faith, especially in its interior dimension, but always permitted to external revelation, as this passage from *Logic (Logica)* testifies:

> Wherefore although the truths of the faith are attested by innumerable testimonies, agree with each other and throughout the centuries, although the prophecies and miracles and the authority of very learned men, the constancy of the martyrs, its portentous propagation and other internal and rational arguments accumulated in every way confirm the truth so as to produce the maximum normal and practical and even apodictic certainty; however, the truth of this religion is not based only on demonstration, but more on the evidence of the inner light, which God by grace communicates, giving to those who believe a perception of themselves and an immediate criterion of truth. This is in conformity with divine attributes, also for this reason that depending on faith the health of all men, if it were based purely on a rational demonstration, it would be for a few; because for few it is the demonstrative truth, and God would not have achieved his end.[50]

By virtue of the convergence between interior and exterior revelation, it is therefore decisive that reason should appear more and more and ever better as that "humble thinking" described by Pascal: "The last proceeding of reason is to recognize that there is an infinity of things which are beyond it. Only a weak reason fails to recognize it. And if natural things surpass it, what shall we say about supernatural ones?"[51]

And to conclude on the figure of faith in time of its foamy relevance.

In the postmodern context of theology it might be effective to understand "marginally relevant faith" as a pedagogy of life: it is a very effective training ground for thought that, while dwelling in the open sea, on the edge of shipwreck and in the bath of mystery, offers us the opportunity to take seriously and inhabit the paradoxical, contradictory and humble complexity of what Saint Augustine recognized as the tenant of his *intus* and

---

49. See Repole, *Pensiero umile*.
50. Rosmini, *Logica* (Logic), para. 895.
51. Pascal, *Pensieri*, 71.

that Rosmini caressed with the care of a man of faith and with theoretical delicacy as a "sentiment of God":

> Christian doctrine teaches us that man through gracious communication also receives the sentiment of God, with which he is raised to the supernatural order. The science that deals with this deiform perception is called *Supernatural Anthropology*: it goes beyond the boundaries of simple philosophy.[52]

Bibliography

Anders, Günther. *L'uomo è antiquato*. Vol. 1 translated by Laura Dallapiccola; vol. 2 translated by Maria A. Mori. 2 vols. Turin: Bollati Boringhieri, 2007.

Augé, Marc. *Non-lieux*. Paris: Seuil, 1992.

Bonhoeffer, Dietrich. *Gli scritti*. Translated by Maria C. Laurenzi. Brescia, It.: Queriniana, 1979.

Byung-chul Han. *La scomparsa dei riti. Una topologia del presente*. Translated by Simone Aglan-Buttazzi. Milan: Nottetempo, 2021.

Canu, Giammaria. *Pensare la fede nell'orizzonte della salvezza. Una teologia fondamentale ispirata ad Antonio Rosmini*. Rome: Città Nuova, 2020.

Evain, François. *Être et personne chez Antonio Rosmini*. Paris: Beauchesne, 1981.

Heidegger, Martin. *Che cosa significa pensare*. Translated by Gianni Vattimo. Carago, It.: Surgarco, 1971.

———. *Lettera sull' "umanismo."* Edited by Franco Volpi. Milan: Adelphi, 1995.

Lacan, Jacques. *Dei Nomi-del-Padre*. Edited and translated by Antonio Di Ciacca. Turin: Einaudi, 2006.

Lorizio, Giuseppe, ed. *Semi del Verbo. Segni dei tempi*. Rome: San Paolo, 2021.

———. *Teologia fondamentale*. 4 vols. Rome: Città Nuova, 2004–2005.

Mounier, Emmanuel. *Agonia del cristianesimo?* Edited by Albert Béguin. Translated by Laura Fossetti. Vicenza: Locusta, 1960.

Pareyson, Luigi. *Verità e interpretazione*. Milan: Mursia, 1972.

Pascal, Blaise. *Pensieri*. Edited by Philippe Sellier. Translated by Benedetta Papasogli. Rome: Città Nuova, 2003.

Rahner, Karl. "Saggio di uno Schema di dogmatica." In *Saggi teologici*, translated by Alfredo Marranzini, 51–111. Rome: Paoline, 1965.

Rebora, Clemente. "Il pioppo." In *Canti dell'Infermità*, 32. Milan: Scheiwiller, 1957.

Repole, Roberto. *Il pensiero umile. In ascolto della Rivelazione*. Rome: Città Nuova 2007.

Rilke, M. Rainer. *Wladimir, il pittore di nuvole*. Edited by Giorgio Cusatelli. Translated by Maria Teresa Ferrari. Rome: Studio Tesi, 1995.

Rosmini, Antonio. *Antropologia soprannaturale*. Edited by Umberto Muratore. 2 vols. ENC 39–40. Rome: Città Nuova, 1983.

———. *Delle cinque piaghe della Santa Chiesa*. Edited by Nunzio Galantino. Cinisello Balsamo, It.: San Paolo, 1997.

———. *Epistolario completo*. 13 vols. Casale Monferrato, It.: Pane, 1889.

---

52. Rosmini, *IP*, 269.

———. *Introduzione alla filosofia*. Edited by Pier P. Ottonello. ENC 2. Rome: Città Nuova, 1979.

———. *Logica*. Edited by Vincenzo Sala. ENC 8. Rome: Città Nuova, 1984.

———. *Nuovo Saggio sull'origine delle idee*. Edited by Gaetano Messina. 3 vols. ENC 3–5. Rome: Rome 2003–2004.

———. *Teosofia*. Edited by Samuele F. Tadini. Milan: Bompiani, 2011.

Sciacca, Michele Federico. *L'interiortà oggettiva*. Edited by Alessandra Modugno. Venice: Marsilio, 2019.

Sloterdijk, Peter. *Bolle*. Translated by Gianluca Bonaiuti. Vol. 1 of *Sfere*. Rome: Meltemi, 2009.

———. *Dopo Dio*. Translated by Gianluca Bonaiuti. Milan: Raffaello Cortina, 2017.

———. *Schiume*. Translated by Gianluca Bonaiuti. Vol. 3 of *Sfere*. Milan: Raffaello Cortina, 2015.

Unamuno, Miguel de. *Agonia del cristianesimo*. Edited by Enrico Rubetti. Milan: Bompiani, 2012.

Part 3

Rosmini's *Suspended Middle* (and the Comparable Social Theory of Radical Orthodoxy's *Suspended Middle*): Possible Pedagogical Implications

10

Notes on the Rosminian Pedagogical Method

FULVIO DE GIORGI

REFERRING TO AN UNDATED note, but by the mature Rosmini (perhaps from 1845 or 1848–49), we can establish a structure that was, in different ways, implicit in Rosmini's thinking with regard to the educational field: although the explicit formulation is certainly attributable to the 1840s.

In this brief note—perhaps a draft of a letter to Giovanni Antonio Rayneri and Domenico Berti on a pedagogical newspaper project—Rosmini indicated what were, in his opinion, elements of the "pedagogical," that is, of pedagogy as a science that refers to the art of education.

Purpose of Education

Means of Education

Methods

The *purpose* of education includes all the aspects that improve the human being, with the ultimate aim of making him capable of using them "for the true benefit of himself and of others; thus making him the author of his own good and especially of his own virtue and happiness."[1]

1. Rosmini, "Progetto di Giornale Pedagogico" (Project of pedagogical journal), 343. See Lanfranchi, *Genesi degli scritti pedagogici*.

The *means* of education are all those sciences (moral, economic, political, sciences) and special arts that education itself uses to make the human being sound.

The *methods* indicate the ways in which the *means* can be used with art and not haphazardly. The present contribution aims to explore some relative aspects of the last question: the *educational method*.

Rosminian philosophy reached its maturity in the thirties and so both the prospect of an "Italian method" (as a method of observation of the facts) and the question of the method of education were set out. It was in this mature season of Rosmini's thinking that he began to write "The Ruling Principle of Method Applied to Education" (*Del principio supremo della Metodica*). He started the project 1839 and, as we know, it remained unfinished.

Rosmini had probably been collecting ideas on those issues for some years. In 1832, in Florence, Tommaseo had written a letter to a friend giving him suggestions on the education of his new-born daughter (also inspired by the first chapter of Rousseau's *Émile ou De l'éducation*) observing that: "Here we have a beautiful and great ideological study to begin with, on the order in which children perceive ideas, grasp the meaning of words: note how much the formation of abstract ideas, of relationship ideas costs them."[2] With clear reference to these statements, Rosmini wrote to Tommaseo, from Trento, on August 14, 1833: "The subsequent and graduated formation of the abstracts in the child, on which you touch, is a beautiful subject, and I propose to describe it diligently in another work, God willing. However, He is where I would wish to see your wits at work: and therefore, I specifically abstain from lecturing you on this, also I could not do so for lack of time."[3]

In "The Ruling Principle of Method Applied to Education," Rosmini restored the "expositive method" of teaching. But pedagogy, as a "science that contains the documents of the great art of educating youth," researches, orders and rigorizes and distinctly organizes the fixed and very useful principles"[4] that regulate the art of education, that is, the application of the method itself. There is therefore a difference between the logical-theoretical level and the applicative-didactic plan: on the first, there is the clarification of the method that logically characterizes pedagogy; on the second there is the rigorous articulation of the methodologies used in Pedagogy, that is, the "scientific" identification of the principles of the art of education.

2. Tommaseo, "Di quella educazione," 48.
3. Rosmini, *Epistolario completo*, 4:658.
4. Rosmini, RPMAE, 40.

Rosmini's writing addressed this second area, wanting to raise pedagogy—precisely as a methodological rigorization—to the level of a science, with an initial application of the method of observation, of the Italian method:

> The diversity of opinions and attempts, the different ways in which each educator acts, and the disputes between them openly show that the art of method of which we speak, a firm base admitted by all and such that, where it is understood., no one can deny it is lacking.... Hence we believe that our research is mainly directed at finding the *supreme principle* from which the whole method of exposition descends; but we do not know that this has been done so far by anyone. Thus, the discussion is reduced to the state and condition of science: since in no discussion there can be scientific accuracy and true system, if the most special cognitions are not ranked under the most general, and the general under the very general, which is the leader of both and a fecund mother.[5]

It should be noted that, however, Rosmini did not speak of an "educational system," but rather of a "method": evidently, in harmony with Tommaseo's warning against pedagogical systems and their rigidities. He did not want to propose a practical systematicity, but a rigorous methodology (suited to the art and therefore to the abilities of the educator) designed to order the action, without caging it in predefined and abstract schemes. That is, it was a question of improving the quality of teaching: in 1840 Rosmini said he wanted to reform the methods followed in the schools held by the clerics of the Istituto della Carità (and for this purpose he considered Francesco Paoli suitable). After all, the system already existed: it was the system of truth (connected to the system of charity), that is, the three forms of being.

Rosmini was, moreover, convinced that his was only the beginning of broader research that would engage many scholars for many years. Hence the "provisional" form—explicitly, we would say, *in progress*—of his statements, with repeated precautionary expressions, which are not found in any other Rosminian work: "The first observation is, that what I assumed ... it is not an assumption made by me without evidence, but thanks to effective experience with children";[6] "Let us therefore remain a little longer attentive observers of what the childish mind usually does";[7] "I have long been

---

5. Rosmini, RPMAE, 41 and 43.
6. Rosmini, RPMAE, 60.
7. Rosmini, RPMAE, 64.

doubtful how to resolve this question: but finally I have been persuaded";[8] "I tend to believe not . . . and I conjecture . . . It is possible . . .";[9] "Hence, if we admit this conjecture, it would mean that . . .";[10] "It would be difficult to state whether . . . It seems moreover . . .";[11] "I have already mentioned, that I suspect that I have . . . This would be a fact worthy of being better verified with more accurate observations. In the meantime, it is permissible for me to say more, always in the form of conjectures . . .";[12] "it seems . . . in a way that is to be believed . . .";[13] "I think it is likely that . . .";[14] "do not confuse with the conjecture I made above";[15] "I believe that more causes contribute to producing it, and it is perhaps difficult to know them all";[16] "We try to point out some of the main causes that we believe influence to produce it, without however making sure that we detect them all. It seems likely to me that . . .";[17] "this rule shall not apply to determining time except by approximation."[18]

This conjectural trend of thought was linked to the interpretation of the observations on children that either Rosmini had made directly or that he drew from the work *L'Éducation progressive* by Albertine-Adrienne Necker de Saussure, a cousin of Madame de Staël.

Rosmini clearly argued that it was necessary—through observation—to methodologically adapt the educational action to the various evolutionary phases of the child. But he was aware of moving, pioneeringly, in a land then almost virgin (in fact, only the book by Necker de Saussure stood out):

> In a word, what are the boundaries [of education] in the individual ages [of the child]? This is what we can determine, by multiplying the experiences and observations, which, thank heaven, have already started (and it is still time that we take away from applying the art of observing and experimenting to pedagogy). Meanwhile, we are content to point out the way (because more than this we naively confess not to know); we will

8. Rosmini, RPMAE, 84.
9. Rosmini, RPMAE, 93.
10. Rosmini, RPMAE, 94.
11. Rosmini, RPMAE, 95.
12. Rosmini, RPMAE, 96.
13. Rosmini, RPMAE, 100.
14. Rosmini, RPMAE, 140.
15. Rosmini, RPMAE, 163.
16. Rosmini, RPMAE, 177.
17. Rosmini, RPMAE, 178.
18. Rosmini, RPMAE, 192.

put forward a principle that is self-evident, and on this we will then conduct the reasoning.[19]

It would therefore be impossible to determine in a treatise of the Method, at precisely what time each age of the child begins and ends. Yet it is not useless, indeed we consider it very advantageous, to determine these periods by approximation.

This remains a difficult task, and we can only try it out on that little experience that we have gained of young people. We hope, however, that the experience of others will in time correct and perfect our attempts, perhaps the first of its kind.[20]

Therefore, the taxonomy of the developmental age that Rosmini established[21] has a considerable historical importance, but—as Rosmini himself predicted and hoped—it was followed by observations and studies that made it, in its specific articulation, outdated. Moreover, the increasing complexity required by the analysis of the orders of understanding (and, even before that, of the observations necessary for this analysis), as the child grew, is perhaps the reason that led Rosmini to discontinue the work (which in fact remained unfinished, halted in 1840, and not resumed in the following fifteen years of his life).

On the basis, however, of this taxonomy, Rosmini observed that it was necessary to ensure that the child "is led, in stages always proportionate to his strength, from what he knows to what he does not yet know and that he wants to be taught"[22]: that is, paying attention to the "natural scale" by which the human mind ascends,[23] therefore to the necessary and immutable series of orders of intellect,[24] to the natural path of development of human understanding.[25] Hence, from this gradual development, the fixed point or "supreme principle":

---

19. Rosmini, RPMAE, 158.
20. Rosmini, RPMAE, 191.
21. He, therefore, imagined the first age corresponding to the first six weeks of life (until the baby begins to smile); a second one reached the age of the first year (when the child began to speak); the third ended at the age of the second year (until the child reached the ability to read); the fourth age, which included the third year of life, saw precisely the possibility of learning to read (Rosmini, RPMAE, 191). Of course, Rosmini observed that "not all children make these intellectual passages at the same times" (Rosmini, RPMAE, 190).
22. Rosmini, RPMAE, 47.
23. Rosmini, RPMAE, 49.
24. See Rosmini, RPMAE, 73.
25. See Rosmini, RPMAE, 69.

> Having thus discovered the immutable order of human intellects, we have also discovered in them the solid foundation on which we can erect the *method of teaching*. . . . This method is precise and very clear: it is unique: because all the good methods invented so far are encompassed by it, they are only partial views of it or means to be implemented, and all the methods that oppose ours are bad.
>
> The formula that expresses the teaching method in general and that forms the supreme principle of the method is therefore the following: "Let the mind of the child (and one can say in general of man) be represented primarily by the objects that belong to the first order of intellects; then the objects that belong to the second order of intellects; then those of the third and so on."[26]

It was therefore a question of following "the graduation that holds the human mind," that is, better, of following "in general the law of its graduated course."[27]

While this supreme principle did not accept Rousseau's negative pedagogy, because it referred to a positive education, nevertheless it was structurally critical of any pedagogical authoritarianism and postulated a pedagogy of natural freedom.[28] See, in fact, the four fundamental educational errors identified by Rosmini:

> 1° sometimes the intellectual activity of the child appears boring and annoying [to the educator], and yet we want to compress it with authority, denying it sufficient pasture.
> 2° Sometimes the material *memory* of the child is aggravated by forcing the *intelligence* to fast: this is very harmful and very serious for that little intelligent being who aspires to nothing else than to understand: it is a cruel and inhuman thing to do.
> 3° Sometimes intelligence is given a pasture not suited to it, that is, it is asked to make insights of a higher order than that which has been reached; in which case it is absolutely impossible for it to understand anything except words. Sometimes the insights that are invoked are accessible, but cannot be elaborated due to lack of stimulus of the intellectual attention.
> 4° Finally, even if all the insights that are required of it are proposed to a well-disposed young intelligence by degrees, and the stimuli are not lacking, one still errs, passing from one thing to another without having first verified whether that first thing

---

26. Rosmini, RPMAE, 74.
27. Rosmini, RPMAE, 64.
28. Rosmini, RPMAE, 156.

has been understood, whether the intelligence of the child really followed the steps of instruction, in a word, without leaving the child the time necessary to penetrate the thing, to absorb it, to recover from that so much dismay, which every new idea brings.[29]

In short, Rosmini considered it appropriate "not to touch the child, when he found himself quiet and content in his state" and "to make him converse more with things than with people."[30] This natural freedom derived from an evaluation of great importance in the history of education: although it did not have a positive anthropology like Rousseau and, indeed, explicitly recognizing—even in this work—original sin[31] and corruption inherent in human nature (so much so as to be accused of Jansenism, by his detractors, especially Jesuits), Rosmini underlined with clear and unequivocal statements (and with reference to the Jesus of the Gospels), the innocence of the childish heart and its benevolent inclination,[32] which were to make us reflect on the appropriate forms of the education of his moral being[33] and, in any case, to bring the educator to a wise patience:

> What patience and what wisdom this demands of the educator! . . . This is the gift that is lacking in the majority of the educators: so they reluctantly agree to be involved in the children's activities and experiences; and even often disturb the innocent child in his work of placidly observing and experimenting. . . . In this matter, I have often pondered and wondered why the divine Master never scolded the children and rather, so to speak, praised everything, when to the severity of the human sages that early age seems so full of thoughtlessness and lacking in serious occupations. It does not seem that Jesus Christ judged it to be so. Rather, he seems to view these childish activities as anything but a waste of time, a procrastination: but rather as an important activity for their understanding, eager, wishing to know, to grasp the truth, an eagerness of which "the simple soul that knows nothing" and that even so is made to know, throwing itself on a sensitive world, draws knowledge and understanding by incessantly observing and in a thousand ways experimenting these and those objects, whenever they are presented to their senses. We had better, therefore, with utmost patience accompany the

---

29. Rosmini, RPMAE, 144.
30. Rosmini, RPMAE, 156.
31. Rosmini, RPMAE, 113.
32. Rosmini, RPMAE, 177.
33. Rosmini, RPMAE, 162.

child in this very solemn and continual study according to his age; helping him and *guiding* him through it.[34]

Therefore, the mind of the child who enthusiastically threw himself into learning "any and all cognitions and new things," then came to enjoy a triumphal explosion of joy in the awareness of these new concepts: "Every new idea in the child is a joy: for with every opening that appears before him, his intelligence rushes in. As the first act of knowing melts the lips of the child to laughter, so the pleasure of understanding the maternal language is manifested in him with many acts of exultation. . . . The instituter must benefit from this innate and most noble inclination; they must not rebuke him, for it would be an insult to the divine light that shines in the human soul; they must wisely occupy and direct it. What is more, this is a very difficult art."[35]

Rosmini's perspective, neither rigid nor severe, could only be misunderstood by an authoritarian educational orientation and pedagogical tyranny (moreover still widespread in traditional Catholic circles, but also more generally). It was, however, a perspective that leaned towards loving-kindness.

In a broader and more general vision, using a scheme similar to that of the *A New Essay Concerning the Origin of Ideas* (*Nuovo Saggio sull'origine delle idee*), we could historically place Rosminian pedagogy as the "middle ground" between the two main pedagogical currents of its time, namely Herbartism and Froebelism, currents that had a vast and long-term influence, certainly reaching up to the first half of the twentieth century and, in some cases, even later.

If, therefore, to put it in the words of the *New Essay*, Herbartism sinned by insufficiency, while Froebelism sinned by excess, then pedagogical Rosminianism aimed to be more balanced. In Herbart's realism we can see a pedagogy oriented towards the real being, in Froebel's idealism a pedagogy oriented towards the ideal being. Rosmini, we could say, synthesizes, in his vision, Herbartian realism and Froebelian idealism and can do so, in the triniformity of being, because he assigns primality to the moral being.

In Herbart the centrality, in the educational process, belongs methodologically to the teacher who "governs" the student, completely shaping his will and leading him to the instructive education. In Froebel, on the other hand, in continuity with Rousseau's pedocentrism, but reread in a romantic perspective in which Schelling's contribution is decisive, the centrality is of the child, who learns through play on the one hand (nature becomes

---

34. Rosmini, RPMAE, 113.
35. Rosmini, RPMAE, 143.

spirit) on the other expresses himself (spirit becomes nature) and so, spontaneously and freely, flourishes like a bud in the garden of childhood, and gardener-teachers play only an extrinsic and external care role.

In Rosmini there is no unicentric scheme: nor a master-centric or student-centric one. This would still be an asymmetrical dualism: either unbalanced on the master's plane or unbalanced on the student's level. Rosminian pedagogy is triniform: there is the teacher, if we consider the ideal essence of education; there is the pupil, if we consider the real essence of education; but there is also the community—or, as Rosmini said, community friendship—if we consider the moral essence of education. And this community is not only the communion between teacher and student: it understands it but is not reduced to it (as it would have been in Gentile). It is not only the class-group, the educational collective: includes it but is not reduced to it (as it would have been in Makarenko).

The community, as a figure of the moral essence of education, includes both the set of human personal relationships that have formed (or are forming: at an early age) the moral conscience of the student and the set of human personal relationships that have formed the moral conscience of the teacher and precisely for this reason it also includes the current relationship between teacher and student and the current and friendly personal relationships between students (and between collective of students and master), as well as the student's relationships with the educational environment structured by the teacher. Seen in this way, the educating community is historical and social: two dimensions that cannot be forgotten in pedagogy. This also implies the consideration of intersubjective processes, not excluding those of a juridical, political and religious nature, which are not internally homogeneous, indistinct and formless, but see personal influences of different scope, starting from the context of the home environment.

In the ideal essence of education, that of teaching, there is an active asymmetry, which is configured as dependence, that is, it postulates an authority (the teacher): an authority that is not enslaving, but liberating, that is, functional to the "liberation" of the student, whatever the teaching method (which can also be predominantly indirect). In the real essence of education, that of learning, there is a passive asymmetry, progressively deactivated, which is configured as independence and gradual autonomy of the student. In the moral essence of education, that of the educating community, there are multiple symmetries, which configure a cooperative interdependence.

In the tripolar pedagogical dynamic, then, the relationship of the teacher with the student and with the community is *intellectual charity* (morality in-existing in the ideal being). The student's relationship with the teacher and with the community is perfection (or self-perfection) in view of happiness, that is, *emancipation* (morality absent in the ideal essence). The relationship of the community with the teacher and with the student is the pedagogical action, the being and doing of education, the *educational praxis as a moral life*, and therefore effective education in freedom (ideality and reality of morality). Teaching, learning, and the moral life, therefore, to use a Rosminian term, synthesize.

And by synthesizing they bring graduality as an exponent. In a Herbartian perspective, a gradation experienced by apperceptions can be foreseen in the teaching methodology. In a Froebelian perspective it is the opposite ideals that, in learning, make development possible (as seen in the progression of gifts). Rosmini does not have opposites in the real teaching, but rather the distinction of gradations, more Herbartian than Froebelian, to which is added the gradual "logical" demonstration: from the known to the unknown, also here in harmony with Herbart. But in addition to the gradation there is also the gradualness of the intellectual growth of the child, the various ages of his evolution, more on the Froebelian side, that is, the development of the different orders of intellect that determine the gradualness of learning. The moral form, that is, the pedagogical action in its unfolding in action, methodologically synthesizes the gradation of the real form and the gradualness of the ideal form. It is in this that we could better understand what, as we have seen, Rosmini called the supreme principle of the method.

In this context, the attention to childhood and its degrees of intellectual development reminds us of the connection that existed between Rosmini and Ferrante Aporti, the great Italian apostle of kindergartens (and Rosmini greeted with convinced appreciation the "beautiful invention of kindergartens").[36] Not to mention the developments and renewals of Aporti's ideas, such as the one attempted by Giuseppe Sacchi with the "experimental method."

Of the broad reasoning developed in "The Ruling Principle of Method Applied to Education" I would now like, in particular, to underline three aspects that seem to me particularly significant in reference to the long-term history of the Italian method: the perspective of grading; the preventive dimension; the primary importance of language teaching.

The perspective of the grading is certainly, among the three, the aspect discussed with greater breadth and with greater analytical depth. In fact, Rosmini himself observed how the "admirable connection" of meaning and

---

36. Rosmini, RPMAE, 145.

understanding was difficult to understand[37]: that is, to understand "the mutual influence of sensual and intellectual operations"[38] without confusing the order of meaning with the order of intelligence.

In his opinion, the force with which the spirit knows is "attention"[39]: attention is drawn to accidental sensations, that is, to new stimuli that change the sensitive state of the spirit. Accidental sensations are—in the Rosminian vision—real modifications of the fundamental bodily feeling. But they are not intellections: "When man moves to apply his intellectual virtue to what he feels, then it is the moment in which his development, as an intelligent being, begins."[40] Education is therefore the art of appropriately directing the attention of the spirit of the students.

And if the age of sensory development begins with birth, the age of intellectual development begins with the child's first laugh.[41] The stimulus that excites the intellectual attention of the human being from the beginning is need.[42] Intellectual activity, as an understanding, first of all perceives: "the first intellects, which man makes, want to be the perceptions of external bodies."[43] But perceptions receive a "graduated perfection"[44]: that is, the spirit carries out a repeated and improving work on intellectual perception,[45] to achieve a gradual improvement.[46]

On this basis, derived with scientific method from observation, Rosmini founded a consequent educational perspective, structured on the grading of perceptions. Beyond, therefore, the specific Rosminian construction of the overall series of sequences of orders of intellection—a largely conjectural construction, or rather of first approximation, but which

37. Rosmini, RPMAE, 87.
38. Rosmini, RPMAE, 100.
39. Rosmini, RPMAE, 80.
40. Rosmini, RPMAE, 81.
41. Rosmini, RPMAE, 94.
42. Rosmini observed: "It therefore seems that the sensations, which first excite human activity, are those that contain a feeling of need and that consequently give movement to instincts and spontaneity. Hence intellectual activity is not excited at all; but sets itself in motion when man needs it: man calls it to his rescue, as he calls to his rescue all the other powers when he wants to either avoid harassment, or to procure a need" (Rosmini, RPMAE, 82).
43. Rosmini, RPMAE, 85.
44. Rosmini, RPMAE, 86.
45. Rosmini, RPMAE, 89.
46. Rosmini, RPMAE, 5–88.

can now be considered outdated—this methodological indication proves to be of great importance.[47]

This perspective of gradation, as attention to sensory development, but in its connections with intellectual activity, seems to me historically significant, reaching outcomes adjacent to what would become Montessorism.

The second aspect that seems to me to be relevant on the historical level—that of the preventive dimension—it is less developed than the former, limiting itself to a few hints.

Rosmini maintained that: "It is certain that the nature of the child has a beneficial influence which should be respected by the educator, and it is important to avoid interrupting or disturbing it."[48] However, he also added: "All those who do not want to flatter human nature, recognize it as partly defective: it very soon manifests malignant dispositions. . . . There is no doubt that art must rush to amend the defects of nature and will: to prevent them: to ward off temptations: to bring closer the opportunities for virtue. Divine providence, by giving birth to man in the bosom of society, gives him over to his fellows so that they may help him in his weakness, direct him in his ignorance and correct his defective tendencies."[49] That is, Rosmini—albeit in an "amending" responsibility from social pedagogy—recommended prevention rather than correction: meaning prevention as a positive work of education that distances the temptations of evil and brings opportunities for good closer.

Considering then how the "seeds of falsehood in understanding and of misdirection in the heart" could in fact appear in the human being, he concluded: "As therefore it is appropriate sometimes to prevent, sometimes to resist passion; so, it is useful to correct the false concepts of the child."[50] In other words, the corrective action was directed above all to erroneous cognitions, to the intellect, while the preventive action addressed evil passions in the heart.

On the question of passions, impatience and anger, "which have their cradle in animality," can attract the assent of the will and then pass "promptly into the order of understanding." This is why, then, Rosmini, considering the educational field, concluded: "Now these accidents are to be prevented with diligence in children, because they can hardly sustain the gravity of temptation, nor do they have weapons to defend themselves from it."[51]

47. Rosmini, RPMAE, 111–12.
48. Rosmini, RPMAE, 156.
49. Rosmini, RPMAE, 157.
50. Rosmini, RPMAE, 175.
51. Rosmini, RPMAE, 176–77.

The preventive aspect of education, therefore, emerged quite clearly in the Rosminian vision, although it was not very well developed analytically. As is well known, the preventive dimension would acquire a central role in Don Bosco's thought and work in the educational field.

In conclusion, there was, in Rosmini's work, a third and final aspect that seems relevant to me on the historical educational level, and that is the importance assigned to language and, therefore, to language education (or pedagogy of the word).

In an original way, Rosmini started from "sympathy" (in a consideration contiguous to subsequent phenomenological studies on "empathy"). He specified: "*Sympathy* means feeling together, feeling things themselves."[52] That is, it was the "admirable faculty of participating in the feeling and understanding of others"[53] which he believed to be generated by the instinct towards animate things,[54] conjecturing that "in bringing together two human persons, beyond *material impressions*, and *animal sensations*, a hidden way of communication between spirits intervenes, whose means, however, is sensation."[55] It was, therefore, at the level of animality, therefore as a communication between sensitive souls, which was implemented, according to Rosmini, together with the communication of intellectual souls.[56] And he believed that "not only the *intelligent subject* together with the sensations that he receives from a person, experience a feeling that is the immediate effect of the intelligent soul operating in the sensations caused, but that such communication also takes place between merely sensitive souls."[57]

In human beings, the mutual communication between sensitive souls, that is, in the order of animality but at the same time in the order of intelligence, caused "the animistic feelings." The "animistic sensations naturally produce in the child physical *affection*, and therefore *sympathy*."[58] That is to say, Rosmini explained, "a soul feels its companion in a given state, for example in that of joy: *sympathy* arises from natural benevolence, that is, the composition of the same feelings: from sympathy comes *the instinct of imitation*. Sympathy in this case is the passive operation, *imitation* its corresponding active one."[59] Sympathy and instinct of imitation were consid-

52. Rosmini, RPMAE, 98.
53. Rosmini, RPMAE, 306.
54. Rosmini, RPMAE, 99.
55. Rosmini, RPMAE, 94.
56. Rosmini, RPMAE, 97–98.
57. Rosmini, RPMAE, 96.
58. Rosmini, RPMAE, 101.
59. Rosmini, RPMAE, 98.

ered, by Rosmini, among the natural predispositions for language[60] (as well as having importance in the transmission of the sense of the sacred from mother to child.)[61]

Here then is the analytical context in which Rosmini placed the development of language.[62] But in addition to natural predispositions, social influence is necessary for the development of language in the child, that is, "the language that he hears, and is communicated to him by society."[63]

On these foundations, Rosmini assigned, in education, a primary role to the teaching of the language, from childhood onwards: "It is clear that the first subject of education at this age must be language."[64] But in a perspective of "permanent education": "By its very nature language expresses the intellections of all orders, and therefore it is an instrument very suitable for the development of the intellect in all the ages of human life." To the child, therefore, "it is better to teach him to name all things well, and first those that are around him, later the most distant; wherefore he will acquire great wealth of language, and for this very reason great ease and correctness in speaking, which is what to say in thinking, and in its time also in writing."[65]

But also, "the education of young people must rely entirely on language"[66]: the preeminence of language in education derives from its fungibility both for cognitive progress, but also for providing the tools for a critical sense, so that the educated subject could not be confused and deceived by anyone due to linguistic ignorance. The property of language, which was to be aimed at in education, therefore did not have an esthetic purpose, but a moral and a practical one.

Here, therefore, began a perspective that would be taken up, a century later, by Don Milani.

The Rosminian perspective of the educational method—which flourished in the historical context of nineteenth-century European pedagogy and of the Italian Risorgimento—therefore had, in obviously complex ways and according to various lines of continuity, long-term outcomes in the work of Giovanni Bosco, Maria Montessori, and Lorenzo Milani.

---

60. Rosmini, RPMAE, 120–21.
61. Rosmini, RPMAE, 306–7.
62. Rosmini, RPMAE, 171.
63. Rosmini, RPMAE, 121.
64. Rosmini, RPMAE, 145.
65. Rosmini, RPMAE, 149.
66. Rosmini, RPMAE, 376–78.

Bibliography

Lanfranchi, Rachele. *Genesi degli scritti pedagogici di Antonio Rosmini*. Rome: Città Nuova, 1983.

Rosmini, Antonio. *Epistolario completo*. 13 vols. Casale Monferrato, It.: Pane, 1889.

———. "Del principio supremo della Metodica." In *Scritti pedagogici*, edited by Fernando Bellelli, ENC 32, 37–364. Rome: Città Nuova, 2019.

———. "Progetto di Giornale Pedagogico." In *Della educazione cristiana. Sull'unità dell'educazione*, edited by Lino Prenna, ENC 31, 342–44. Rome: Città Nuova, 1994.

Tommaseo, Nicolò. "Di quella educazione che incomincia con la vita. Lettera al professore Emilio Tipaldo." In *Dell'educazione. Scritti vari*, 22–50. Lugano, Switz.: Ruggia, 1834.

11

Pedagogical Parallels between Saint Augustine and Rosmini

JACOB BUGANZA

Introduction

AMONG ITS MANY MERITS, Rosmini's philosophy has taught us that the apex of reality is nothing more than the single being in its triple dimension, that is real, ideal, and moral. These three forms of being reciprocally vindicate themselves and constitute the utmost categories, to use an Aristotelian term, of all that which is. Alongside this fundamental theory, there is another constant in the framework of Rosminian speculation that was present throughout his life, and consists in the classification of the sciences. One of the most complete classifications is to be found in the work *Philosophical System (Sistema filosofico)*, a true compendium of his philosophy. Without entering into the detail of the classification he sets out in this work, it is sufficient to note that the sciences are called "ideological," "metaphysical" and "deontological," and that they deal with the perfection of being and that this doctrine is divided into three parts, that is relative to the purpose, to the actions and to the means. "Human deontology" therefore implies a "teletic," an ethic and doctrine of the media, where we find ascetics, pedagogy, economy, politics, and cosmopolitics. Rosmini was interested in pedagogy as the doctrine of methods applied to others, since it tries to lead others towards human perfection; thus, *"pedagogy* and *asceticism* do not differ in their purpose, which they pursue together, but in the nature and setting of the application of the methods, since *asceticism* is an individual pedagogy, and *pedagogy* is a social ascetic."[1] This is why, rightly, we speak of "very personal Rosminian pedagogy," which is based on the close bond between education and morals.[2]

But there is yet another teaching of Rosmini's that should be recovered and appreciated. Just as it acts against the subjectivism, phenomenalism (sensism) and idealism of his time, the Rosminian philosopher of the present reacts to the attacks of postmodernity and a certain declination of constructivism that leads to the dissolution of the truth. The lesson that Rosmini teaches is that the way to deal with these movements is to contrast them with a specific configuration, also genuinely subjective, of conceiving objectivity. In fact, the object is other, since being objective is nothing more than the radically other, so that man, seen as the subject is morally and educationally open to other, to otherness which, as we said, is the fundamental meaning of "object" for Rosmini. Now, the aim of this work is more modest than the titanic task of recovering all the premises of Rosminian pedagogy for modern-day education: it consists rather in highlighting, in a Thomistic perspective, some pedagogical parallels between the *De catechizandis rudibus* of Saint Augustine and the *Catechism of Christian Doctrine Arranged According to the Order of Ideas (Catechismo disposto secondo l'ordine delle idee)* by Rosmini,[3] to gather the definitive meaning of the pedagogical indications between the Thomistic interpretation of Augustine's works and that of the philosopher from Rovereto.[4] To carry out this task it is necessary to consider that both

1. Prenna, *Dall'essere all'uomo*, 91. Rosmini's mainly pedagogical works are collected in vols. 31–32 of the Edizione Nazionale e Critica delle Opere di Antonio Rosmini, published by Città Nuova, respectively edited by L. Prenna and F. Bellelli. There is a further pedagogical text, *Della libertà d'insegnamento*, contained in vol. 37 of the National and Critical Edition edited by Gianfreda Marconi.

2. Indellicato, *Personalismo pedagogico*, 83–115.

3. "Del modo di catechizzare gl'idioti di Santo Aurelio Agostino, vescovo d'Ipona, volgarizzato" was published for the first time in Venice (Giuseppe Battagia, 86 pp); it was later published, in his lifetime, by Rosmini, in Milan, at the Tipografia Pogliani nel 1839, subsequently in Naples, at the Tipografia Batelli, in 1843. With regard to both, see Raschini, "Agostino e Rosmini"; Ottonello, "Rosmini e Agostino."

4. See Silvestrini, *Educazione come processo interiore*. Among the most significant reference contributions on the pedagogical-educational topic in Saint Thomas that have been offered by the journal *Divus Thomas*, also with reference to Rosmini, in the wake of which the present contribution also intends to place itself, we note: De Giorgi, "Per un'archeologia culturale"; Sapienza, "Questione educativa"; Echeverria, "Educatión como generación"; Panero, "Eccellenze virtuose"; Porcarelli, "Educability as a Prerogative"; and the recent Benetollo, *Sancto Thoma Magistro*.

offer manifestations of the same philosophy, which Rosmini, making constant reference to Saint Thomas's thinking, coherently called a "system of truth" and which can be translated, in the pedagogical field, into the idea that philosophy is the guide and the master of the human spirit.[5]

Philosophy as Pedagogy of the Human Spirit

The philosophy that Rosmini elaborates has an initial reforming vocation (based on the notions of unity and totality, as expressly stated in the *Philosophical Booklets [Opuscoli filosofici]*), but at the same time it assumes the task of indicating, pedagogically, where the gaze of the individual who is perfecting himself should be directed. From the standpoint of the philosophy, a central passage in which, in our opinion, the Rosminian position is set out very clearly, that is where he states that philosophy has an eminently pedagogical vocation, is in the conclusive lines of the monumental *Philosophical System*, when he says:

> If the purpose of philosophy is to find quiet and rest from the curiosity of the mind, its most precious fruit is to assure the human soul of the possibility that it will attain all its desires, to remove all uncertainty and to point out the certain path, by which it can reach the peak it aspires to. This path him leads to God, to whom the consummate philosopher is allowed to teach as a disciple and to perfect as a creature. This is the aim of the philosopher, this his fruit. But if, instead of considering the science, we consider the school of philosophy, in that case it becomes the true pedagogy of the human spirit, of the mind that leads to the most complete science, and of the soul to whose affections it reveals beforehand the most complete good. Under which aspect Plato conceived a pedagogy of humanity.[6]

There are a number of interesting aspects in this quotation. The last, apparently, but the first in terms of doctrine, is the reference to Plato, who conceived philosophy as pedagogy of the human spirit. Plato's influence is considerable and has been reflected from ancient times in the movement

---

5. Piero Sapienza opportunely emphasized that the crisis of contemporary education also implies an anthropological crisis. Here are his words: "Who is man? If you do not answer this question correctly, you cannot talk about education. As happens in our liquid society, where the anthropological crisis and ethical relativism are investing the setting of the pedagogical question" (Sapienza, "Questione educativa," 171.

6. Rosmini, "Sistema filosofico," 262–63.

that carries his name, above all in the rich developments of Middle Platonism and Neoplatonism, where it is possible to see that the human spirit is educated when it turns to moral ascetism. We can still hear the echo of the words of Plotinus in *Enneads*, when he said, in a mystic tone, that it is necessary to be faithful to the being, faithful to the model, since this is what allows us to reach the objective of the pilgrimage, because through virtue we can accede to the Intelligence and from this to the Wisdom, and finally to the One. "And this life of gods and men, divine and blissful, liberation from other things, life without pleasure from things, flight alone towards only" (καὶ οὗτος θεῶν καὶ ἀνθρώπων θείων καὶ εὐδαιμόνων βίος, ἀπαλλαγὴ τῶν ἄλλων τῶν τῇδε, βίος ἀνήδονος τῶν τῇδε, φυγὴ μόνου πρὸς μόνον).[7]

This same thesis, but now comprised in the field of Christianity, is taken up above all by Saint Augustine in whose doctrine we can see a Christian Neoplatonism. Indeed, the imprint of Plato is, above all, of Plotinus (and Porphyry), it is evident in the Augustinian *lex aeterna* thesis, which as explained in *De libero arbitrio*, consists of subjugating the inferior to the superior, the temporal to the eternal, in metaphysical terms, which can be translated in the case of the problem of evil from an anthropological standpoint, as subjugating passions to reason. The Augustinianism emphasizes that the origin of evil is not metaphysical, but originates in the *voluntas*. It is in every will that the individual follows and acts out this subjection which he indicates as the *lex aeterna*. While this law states that the temporal must be subject to the eternal, evil is nothing more than despising the eternal goods (*quam neglectis rebus aeternis*).[8] When the will superimposes temporal good over eternal good, when it subjugates the superior to the inferior, then it does evil: and since the will is individual, it is evident that the individual is the origin of evil. Evil is nothing other than a mistakenly

---

7. Plotinus, *Enéadas*, 6:9, 11, *in fine*. For this reason, he asserts, following the authority of Plato, that "it is not possible to live happily in society. Plato rightly judges that 'the wise man' must take his good from above, and that he turns his gaze to it; and to that conforms to live the one who wants to be wise and happy (Οὐκ ἔστιν οὖν ἐν τῷ κοινῷ εὐδαιμόνως ζῆν. Ὀρθῶς γὰρ καὶ Πλάτων ἐκεῖθεν ἄνωθεν τὸ ἀγαθὸν ἀξιοῖ λαμβάνειν καὶ πρὸς ἐκεῖνο βλέπειν τὸν μέλλοντα σοφὸν καὶ εὐδαίμονα ἔσεσθαι καὶ ἐκείνῳ ὁμοιοῦσθαι καὶ κατ' ἐκεῖνο ζῆν)" (1:4, 16, 9–12). On Plotinus, see Buganza, *En busca*. The considerable differences between the metaphysics of Plotinus and that of Rosmini must not be overlooked. The latter criticizes the Neoplatonist on several points, although he emphasizes that he realizes the difference between *the ideal* being and the *real being*. However, Plotinus's error, according to Rosmini, would consist in considering the One as superior to being (because, in this way, multiplicity would be required); see Tadini, "Metafisica antica e medievale," in particular 14–19.

8. Agostino, "De libero arbitrio," bk. 1, dialogue 16, para. 34.

distributed love, because although what the will itself does is to love,[9] often it loves without giving priority to that which by right demands it.

The fulfillment of Saint Augustine's *lex aeterna* is that which allows the human creature to attain the summit to which it is called, and this vocation is realized through charity, since, as Saint Augustine himself says in *De catechizandis rudibus*, "the purpose of the precept and the fullness of the law is charity" (*finis praecepti et plenitudo legis caritas est*);[10] the accomplishment concerns the attainment of *fulfillment*. From a Christian standpoint, that good which manages to satiate all appetites, the waiting, the tendencies of mankind, is the infinite good. And it could not be otherwise, since, as Rosminian anthropology states, man is constituted and through memory (as we can see in his juvenile *Essay on the Unity of Education (Saggio sull'Unità dell' Educazione)*, where it is possible to note an Augustine imprint) the intelligence and will, which are infinite abilities; and are infinite abilities because they are informed by the idea of good-being. Altogether, the infinite ability of the intellect and the will can be filled only by the infinite Being, who is God, who from an intellectual standpoint assumes the form of truth and from the standpoint of the will assumes the form of goodness. God, then, is the only one who can guarantee the mind rest. Philosophy, from a pedagogical standpoint, is the genuine guide of the mind, from the human spirit that, advancing and climbing the peaks of knowledge and science, shows that the end of the journey is nothing more than finding God, as Middle Platonism, Neoplatonism, and Christianity have maintained since antiquity, "since God is the ultimate and full reason for all the things that exist in the universe or can fall into minds."[11] This pedagogy of the spirit is nothing other than the formation of man, and this formation means "perfection," above all of the will, because when man reaches the aforementioned summit, we say that he has really reached perfection.[12]

In addition to the theory of the three forms of being and the classification of the sciences, Rosminian philosophy also insistently indicates that, in the case of intelligent creatures, the search for the unity to which they aspire

9. See Arendt, *Concepto de amor*.

10. Agostino, "Del modo di catechizzare gl'idioti," 57.

11. Rosmini, "Degli studi dell'Autore" (On the author's studies), para. 9. From the Christian point of view, Rosmini's educational project is linked to religion; see Indellicato, *Personalismo pedagogico*, 65, 80, 106, 140.

12. It is important that *Sull'unità dell'Educazione* says: "The spirit of ancient education tended to the unity of objects, because everything was reduced, as to a single end and principle, to God: the spirit of modern education on the contrary tends to the multiplicity of objects, because considering natural and sensible things without referring them to their primitive cause, they disintegrate and scatter among themselves; And being disordered is what multiplies them" (Indellicato, *Personalismo pedagogico*, 27–28).

has its nucleus in the moral being (a unit in which the various educative agencies converge, such as self-education, domestic education, the training of teachers, civil education, ecclesiastic education) and that moral good lies in the "perfection" realized through the practical recognition of the entity, of the will, a faculty considered the peak by the theologian from Rovereto. This was the foundation for writing that "the education of the human individual must have perfect unity, and it is a serious error to believe that physical, intellectual and moral education are three separate and independent things," the nucleus of this education being moral good.[13] It is the will that crystalizes the unity of the human individual, and the perfection to which they aspire, consequently, it is destined to the will. It is not by chance that at the start of his appreciated philosophical production he published, the year in which *A New Essay Concerning the Origin of Ideas (Nuovo Saggio sull'origine delle idee)* (1830) was published, *Maxims of Christian Perfection (Massime di perfezione Cristiana)*, in which the title makes explicit reference to the "perfection" to which the Christian aspires. And this is completed considering that pedagogy defines it, as we already said, and as emphasized in the "Preface to the Works of Moral Philosophy" *(Prefazio alle opere di filosofia morale)*, as the art of leading or educating other men to perfection.[14]

We must not confuse, as Rosmini asks, between science, which belongs to the order of ideas, and the *"goodness of life,"* "which belongs to the order of actions and real things, which is certainly bordering on science, but extends a long way beyond it."[15] The reason the practical ambit extends beyond mere speculative knowledge is that the will, to be practical, requires knowledge, but adds consent.[16] This is why Rosmini considers that: "If we

13. Rosmini, "Sistema filosofico," para. 246. Education is "the form in which the free man, the person, governs his whole being, his inferior principles of action, subordinating them to the decisions of freedom and integrating them with it; and freedom is subordinated and integrated with truth" (Indellicato, *Personalismo pedagogico*, 65). On the importance of the concept of freedom, from a metaphysical point of view, in Saint Augustine and Rosmini, see Bennardo, "Libertà dell'uomo."

14. Rosmini, "Prefacio a los trabajos."

15. Rosmini, "Degli studi dell'Autore," para. 57.

16. "News is therefore necessary and essential to the constitution of the will, or it is the objective form of the will itself. Since as the activity of the subject, abstracted from all news, is no longer, I would almost say, the constitutive matter of the will, so when that activity is informed by the news of the good, then it has become will; it is no longer a simple material rudiment of the will, it is the fully formed will; it is not the will that is still on the way to being, in which state it is called nonentity in an ancient manner of the Italian school, but it is the will that has reached its complete being. This is therefore the intrinsic order, in which the will is nature: first there is the objective news in the intellect, then the subjective activity is joined to it, by assent: the subjective activity thus joined to the object has become a active principle, which is called will: this joint,

seek that which is perfect in mankind, and that can properly be called wisdom, we should not stop at the first element, that is science, or more generally cognition, but we must add the second, which is real action, in which the moral goodness is considerable."[17] In fact, according to Saint Augustine, the virtue, which is realized in the exercise of the *via moralis*, and which is part of the wisdom of the Rosminian perspective (which is perfected in religion) opens the way to truth."[18] This is why Rosmini concludes with this thesis, very much in line with the best Western wisdom:

> To sum up, therefore, we said that in the knowledge of the Truth, of which science is only a reflected form, lies the first element of Wisdom; but this same cognition does not begin to be an element of Wisdom until it is purely speculative, and not yet assent, and loved until mankind has added its own to it, until cognition becomes free action; that the same vision of truth is twofold, one necessary, the other voluntary and loving, to which the latter more properly belongs becomes the name first of contemplation, then of practical cognition. Therefore, there is a knowledge and a science psychologically prior to that point where Wisdom begins.[19]

The Pedagogy of *De catechizandis rudibus* and *Catechism of Christian Doctrine Arranged According to the Order of Ideas*

As is known, one of the long-term intellectual tasks undertaken by Rosmini is the translation of the work *De catichizandis rudibus* by Saint Augustine, to which Rosmini gave the title *Del modo di catechizzare gl'idioti*. In this

---

this power of will is the principle of human operations: and it has a degree of strength proportionate to the degree of its adhesion to the intellectual object: whereby it can be said that the news of the intellect becomes operative for the adhesion to it of the subject and therefore that it operates for the will of which it has become the formal part, and it can also be said, that the will operates for the news that is its form." (Rosmini, "Degli studi dell'Autore," para. 59).

17. Rosmini, "Degli studi dell'Autore," para. 62. Thomas Aquinas also confirms this *via moralis*, as Sapienza explains: "In fact, parents cannot exhaust their task by giving their children only '*esse et nutrimentum*,' but they also have the duty to guide them through discipline, whose purpose consists in leading the human subject '*usque ad perfectum statum hominis inquantum homo est, qui est status virtutis*'" (Tommaso D'Aquino, *S. Th.*, *Supplementum*, q. 41, a. 1). Therefore, for Thomas, pedagogical action must accompany man to the full realization of his humanity, through the attainment of moral virtues." (Sapienza, "Questione educativa," 180–81).

18. See Rosmini, "Degli studi dell'Autore," 3, para. 75.

19. See Rosmini, "Degli studi dell'Autore," 3, para. 79.

work, Augustine substantially deals with the topic of how the catechist, who in this case personifies the educator, must proceed to present the truths if they want to be considered Christian. Bearing in mind his theory of the signs and of the *verbum mentis*, Saint Augustine recovers his experience of preacher, shepherd and, in the widest sense, educator, which consists in swiftly understanding a topic, but the transmission of what we have understood through the words is a slow and difficult task. The words, which are signs of the intelligible, not only the knowledge itself (a theory reiterated by Saint Augustine in various works); knowledge is impressed on the mind as "traces" (*vestiges*) and is not Hebrew, Greek or Latin, but is formed in the *mens* (the mind).[20] Here, in our opinion, the aforementioned *lex aeterna* can again be applied, since there is the priority of the concepts over words (similarly of the soul over the body); in the same way, there is priority of the affections of the heart over the mere verbal expression.[21] From a pedagogical standpoint, the concepts take precedence over words, over the way of expressing oneself, over rhetoric, and so on. Briefly, the educator has a duty to linger on the concepts, so that these can allow the pupil to understand the doctrine, which in this case is the dogma.

Similarly, Rosmini built his *Catechism of Christian Doctrine Arranged According to the Order of Ideas* following the theory that ideas have a natural order or succession, and it is this order that establishes and prescribes the steps through which the mind must proceed to understand a doctrine. This is quite evident in the title itself: Rosmini is interested, pedagogically, in clarifying the central concepts in their natural development with the aim that the pupil, the catechized, understands above all the doctrine in its natural movement. The natural order of ideas, as we said, prescribes, so that intelligence does not move of its own accord: in other words, the unfolding of the ideas themselves indicates the order in which the concepts must be taught; "the nature itself has established a series of steps, and this series should be respected, none of the steps should be passed over in any way; but from one truth, we must only pass to the next, and from that also to the next, and so on, proceeding through the chain of truths, without any link in the chain being conceded, omitted or passed over."[22] The order that establishes the passage from one concept to another, from one truth to another, emphasizes that for Rosmini, concepts are more important than words, and that among them there is a natural grading dictated from within. This law of being generates a law for the human mind and for its objects, which does

20. Agostino, "Del modo di catechizzare gl'idioti," 51.
21. Agostino, "Del modo di catechizzare gl'idioti," 71.
22. Rosmini, "Catechismo," 196.

not belong only to children or to adults, but to all created minds. And if it is a universal law for the created mind, it is clear that there is a law for every instruction or education, so that it is governed by the need to guide the minds of the students for the subsequent passages from one truth to another. This means that the created mind begins from an evident truth and, from that, following the order of ideas, gradually understands the concepts that follow, less obvious, but equally true. In order to understand this theory, here are the words of Rosmini:

> But, by education I mean the way of communicating knowledge to men, education not being that which entrust to the memory of sounds subjects, vocabulary and locutions not fully understood, which they have learned by repetition. And here an illusion is soon born in many, who believe they have admirably taught a child or an adult, when they have managed to make them speak a discourse, which undoubtedly expresses many fine sentiments to all those who hear it spoken, because they understand it; this is not so for the one who recites it, because he does not understand it.[23]

The heart of education is to be found, therefore, in the comprehension of the concepts and not in merely reciting them, and the didactic method is nothing more than passing from one truth to another following the natural order of truth, of ideas. And although Rosmini knows that until the nineteenth century no express mention was made of this kind of didactics; he insists that this method was practiced from ancient times. In this context, Rosmini admits that he was inspired by *De catechizandis rudibus*, "the best compendium of catechesis that I ever found to present to our catechists."[24] The work by Saint Augustine, in fact, clearly indicates that, in order to catechize, to teach, it is necessary to start from the person who wants to educate, and to fine in him his innate tendency towards happiness. For this reason, Augustine repeatedly exhorts us to question the condition of the student, their intentions and their objectives, which is no more than questioning the condition of the catechumen himself, of the individual person. Similarly, in his catechism, Rosmini begins from the question on the person, precisely on what he is, and the answer is "a man." It is from the realization that the pupil, the catechist, is a man, that the aim is to lead him to God: for the ignorant it is necessary to start from what they best know; which is nothing more than themselves, that they are men, in order to reach the more complex ideas. For this reason, Rosmini sets out his didactic principle in

23. Rosmini, "Catechismo," 196..
24. Rosmini, "Catechismo," 197.

these terms: "The truths should be set out in an ordered series, so that those which come first do not need those that follow in order to be understood."[25] This principle is not limited to catechism, but extends to any type of education or instruction, as we already said. It is a principle, since it is based on the evidence that all education starts from some known truth or one which can be easily understood, that is that it is sufficient to know the meaning of the terms that express this truth.

Now, Saint Augustine takes into account of the two actors in the educational relationship, that is the educator on the one hand and the pupil on the other, assumed to be catechist or catechized. In both cases it is necessary to respect the law which, as we have seen, is *lex aeterna*, in our opinion, set out in the work *De libero arbitrio*. The catechist or educator, in order to respect the law, must direct his actions towards the pursuance of charity, because the law is fully respected when it is understood that its purpose is charitable, so that, bearing in mind, "Therefore, with this love for you as a purposed end, with which you relate all that you say, whatever you say, say it in such a way that he to whom you speak may believe by hearing, may hope by believing, may love by hoping" (*Hac ergo dilectione tibi tamquam fine proposito, quo referas omnia quae dicis, quidquid narras ita narra, ut ille cui loqueris audiendo credat, credendo speret, sperando amet*).[26]

The pupil must also have certain aptitudes, above all to want to learn, which in the case of the catechist means wanting to become a Christian, because, as Saint Augustine said, "faith is not a matter of saluting the body, but of the believing soul" (*Fides enim non res est salutantis corporis, sed credentis animi*).[27] It is not possible to definitely know whether someone is determined to learn (or to convert), because this remains within his innermost self, and the root is nothing other than the decision. The act of deciding is totally interior and corresponds, once again, to the will. Another important element is the condition of the pupil, since it is not the same thing to teach erudite men and uneducated men, since for the former it is necessary to review the doctrinal nucleus, rather than teach it adequately, illustrating this or that truth. Rosmini would agree with this observation by the golden author, but, in the spirit of his thinking, he would add that the student must start from the most evident truths and, subsequently, reach the more complex; he could not respond, for example, what the Christian doctrine is, if he had not first known that the Word of God became flesh and lived among us, and so on: "It is then wise to begin catechistic instruction with other,

---

25. Rosmini, "Catechismo," 201.
26. Agostino, "Del modo di catechizzare gl'idioti," 61.
27. Agostino, "Del modo di catechizzare gl'idioti," 61.

more simple, questions, so that they are fully understood by those learning them: by questions, that are clear to the pupil even before he learns the rest of the catechism."[28]

In relation to the content, Saint Augustine proposes to start from the creation, and this has, from the Christian perspective, the character of producing good things, up to the present times of the church. For the saint from Hippo, it is necessary to select the events from the history of the faith to understand the dogma: history and dogma must explain and complete each other. Rosmini seeks a similar objective: the catechism includes both the historical and the dogmatic part, since the dogma have their basis in the history of the church, which is the history of salvation, because, he said, "It does not seem too appropriate to compile catechisms that are exclusively dogmatic, others exclusively historical; but, as St. Augustine does, the narration of history should rather be mixed and woven with dogma."[29] For Rosmini, in fact, the history of the church gradually reveals the new truths and ideas that follow, so that man is educated about that which is fundamental for him, salvation. This does not mean that starting from the question, for example, "What is Christian doctrine?" is wrong, but rather that it is more complex because it contains all that which must be taught in synthesis from the scientific standpoint, but which, from a didactic standpoint must begin with the simplest.[30] And this Rosmini tries to corroborate turning to God as a model of Master: he, indeed, has educated mankind starting with the simplest truths, to arrive at the most complex.

Saint Augustine adds that it is important to highlight the causes or the reasons for the historical events in the church, emphasizing the ultimate reason for everything, which is love.[31] Saint Augustine also recommends insisting on the topic of the resurrection, of the last judgment, the punishments for the unjust and the hope for the good. And here the Augustinian note is very clear and helps to link it to the Rosminian system. Saint

28. Rosmini, "Catechismo," 202.

29. Rosmini, "Catechismo," 197.

30. This is analogous to the procedure of Thomas Aquinas as Piero Sapienza explains: "For Aquinas the pedagogical-didactic work of the teacher is articulated in the following way: in the first place, the teacher must offer the student aid, so that his intellect can be facilitated to acquire science. Such aids may consist, for example, in the presentation of less universal propositions, which the pupil can discern with the notions already possessed. Moreover, the teacher, respecting the sensitive-intellectual structure of the learner, following the ancient Aristotelian-scholastic axiom according to which *nihil in intellectu quod prius non fuerit in sensu*, will take care to propose and illustrate *sensible examples*, so that the disciple is guided almost by the hand (*manuducitur*) to the knowledge of the still unknown truth" (Sapienza, "Questione educativa," 180).

31. See Agostino, "Del modo di catechizzare gl'idioti," 63–64.

Augustine, in fact, teaches that hope should not be placed in mankind, but in God:

> For it is not easy for a man to judge which man is righteous, and if it were easy, examples of the righteous should not be set before us, that we might be justified by them, but that, imitating them, we might know that we too are justified by their justifier. For from this it will be done that which is most commendable, that when he who hears us, indeed hears God through us, he begins to advance in manners and knowledge, and to enter the way of Christ with zeal, and dare not assign it to us or to himself; but both himself and us and whomsoever he loves as friends, in him and for his sake, let him who loved him an enemy, so that he who justifies him may make a friend.[32]

As we can see, the final progressive transformation that the saint from Hippo indicates as a catechetic, and pedagogical, objective refers to the moral life, to its progressive refinement that reaches its apex in the love of self, of others and, above all, of God.

The theory is then repeated in metaphysical-moral terms, since those who want to place their treasure, their will in ephemeral and fleeting things will never attain definitive rest and safety. Therefore, those who want to attain happiness, must do so by perfecting themselves as a creature, as Rosmini says in *Philosophical System*, which translates into placing trust not in corruptible things, but in those that are constant: thus the morally perfect man will see that "that the fruits of justice are sweeter than those of iniquity, and that it is more true and pleasant for a man to rejoice in a good conscience"[33] In this way, those who perfect themselves through the will, that is morally, will become inflamed, as the final exhortation of *De catechizandis rudibus* says, in the love of, and the longing for eternal life in the saints,[34] since, philosophically and theologically speaking, anyone who places God above all that which exists, lives in and for him and not for

---

32. Agostino, "Del modo di catechizzare gl'idioti," 67. The Latin text: *Quia neque facile ab homine iudicari potest quis homo sit iustus, et si facile posset, non ideo nobis proponi exempla iustorum, ut ab eis iustificemur, sed ut eos imitantes ab eorum iustificatore nos quoque iustificari sciamus. Hinc enim fiet quod maxime commendandum est, ut cum ille qui nos audit, immo per nos audit Deum, moribus et scientia proficere coeperit et viam Christi alacriter ingredi, nec nobis id audeat assignare nec sibi; sed et seipsum et nos et quoscumque alios diligit amicos, in illo et propter illum, diligat qui eum dilexit inimicum, ut iustificans faceret amicum.*

33. Agostino, "Del modo di catechizzare gl'idioti," 95.

34. See Agostino, "Del modo di catechizzare gl'idioti," 123.

himself, so that, at the end of time he adheres to the extreme good and, as Rosmini would say, is *satisfied*.

Conclusion

Rosmini is convinced that there is only one true system. All the systems linked to the truth start from the same principle; and they can be different inasmuch as they highlight a new aspect of the truth, or they illuminate it, because the truth is manifested in various ways. Still, in the end, all these systems are actually the same system, and he calls it the "system of truth." This is what he says in *Introduction to Philosophy* (*Introduzione alla filosofia*). "The wise man who is animated by the spirit of conciliation will find under many different expressions, within plentiful thoughts, the beautiful unity of truth, multiplied without measure in its appearances, but always in agreement and consent with himself."[35] For Rosmini, wisdom consists of the mingling of knowledge and virtue, the latter requiring the use of human freedom; and we should add that if we live according to knowledge of the truth, it is "more luminous and more developed."

Bibliography

Agostino. "De libero arbitrio." In Agostino, *Obras completas*, edited by Victorino Capánaga, 189–410. Madrid: BAC, 1963.

———. "Del modo di catechizzare gl'idioti, libro di Santo Aurelio Agostino, vescovo d'Ippona volgarizzato." In *Catechetica*, by Antonio Rosmini, edited by Eduino Menestrina, ENC 46, 39–135. Rome: Città Nuova, 2018.

Arendt, Hanna. *El concepto de amor en san Agustín*: Translated by Agustín Serrano de Haro. Madrid: Encuentro, 2009.

Benetollo, Ottorino V., ed. *Sancto Thoma Magistro. Educare alla felicità*. Divus Thomas 2 (2022).

Bennardo, Michele. "La libertà dell'uomo in Agostino, Tommaso e Rosmini." *Rivista Rosminiana* 4 (2008) 357–65; 1 (2009) 45–72; 4 (2009) 321–44.

Buganza, Jacob. *En busca de la unidad perdida. La ética de Plotino*. Mexico City: Torres, 2021.

D'Aquino, Tommaso. *Summa Theologica*. 4 vols. Turin: Marietti, 1950.

De Giorgi, Fulvio. "Per un'archeologia culturale del rosminianesimo." In *Tommaso e Rosmini: il sapere dell'uomo e di Dio fra due epoche*, edited by Fernando Bellelli. *Divus Thomas* 1 (2011) 42–90.

Echeverria, Mauricio. "La educatión como generación de la persona en cuanto persona." *Divus Thomas* 3 (2018) 189–97.

Indellicato, Rosa. *Il personalismo pedagogico di Antonio Rosmini*. Brescia, It.: Morcelliana, 2019.

---

35. Rosmini, "Degli studi dell'Autore," para. 53.

Ottonello, Pier P. "Rosmini e Agostino." *Rivista Rosminiana* 4 (2005) 399–407.

Panero, Marco. "Le eccellenze virtuose come regola morale e scopo dell'educazione morale." *Divus Thomas* 2 (2021) 209–34.

Plotinus. *Enéadas*. Edited by Jesús Igal. 3 vols. Madrid: Gredos, 2015.

Porcarelli, Andrea. "Educability as a Prerogative of the Human Being: The Influence of Thomas Aquinas' Thought in Pedagogical Personalism of the Twentieth Century." *Divus Thomas* 3 (2018) 256–67.

Prenna, Lino. *Dall'essere all'uomo*. Rome: Città Nuova e Centro Internazionale di Studi Rosminiani, 1979.

Raschini, Maria A. "Agostino e Rosmini, maestri comuni." *Studi sciacchiani* 1 (1988) 83–85.

Rosmini, Antonio. "Catechismo disposto secondo l'ordine delle idee." In *Catechetica*, edited by Eduino Menestrina, ENC 46, 187–325. Rome: Città Nuova, 2018.

———. "Degli studi dell'Autore." In *Introduzione alla filosofia*, edited by Pier P. Ottonello, ENC 2, 13–194. Rome: Città Nuova, 1979.

———. "Della libertà d'insegnamento." In *Opuscoli politici*, edited by Gianfreda Marconi, ENC 37, 183–239. Rome: Città Nuova, 1978.

———. *Dell'educazione cristiana*. Edited by Lino Prenna. ENC 31. Rome: Città Nuova 1994.

———. "Prefacio a los trabajos de filosofía moral." In *El carácter de la filosofía rosminiana*, edited by Jacob Buganza, 347–36. Xalapa, Mex.: Universidad Veracruzana, 2021.

———. *Scritti pedagogici*. Edited by Fernando Bellelli. ENC 32. Rome: Città Nuova, 2019.

———. "Sistema filosofico." In *Introduzione alla filosofia*, edited by Pier P. Ottonello, ENC 2, 225–302. Rome: Città Nuova, 1979.

Sapienza, Piero. "La questione educativa in Tommaso D'Aquino e in Rosmini." In *Tommaso e Rosmini: il sapere dell'uomo e di Dio fra due epoche*, edited by Fernando Bellelli. *Divus Thomas* 1 (2011) 170–209.

Silvestrini, Emilio. *L'educazione come processo interiore. S. Agostino e S. Tommaso. Confronti con la pedagogia moderno-contemporanea*. Rome: Borla, 2000.

Tadini, Samuele F. "Metafisica antica e medievale nella Teosofia di Rosmini." In *Rosmini e la Teosofia*, edited by Gianni Picenardi, 7–27. Stresa, It.: Rosminiane Sodalitas, 2013.

12

Philosophical Anthropology of Antonio Rosmini Compared to the One of Viktor Emil Frankl

DOMENICO CRAVERO

Introduction

CONTEMPORARY SCIENCES, BOTH HUMANISTIC and empirical, mostly adopt complex reference models and self-organized, nonlinear systems responding to their sociocultural environments, in a continuous relationship with people and things. The end of mechanism and biologism appears to have been decreed.

However, in the West, also for complex historical-cultural reasons that it is not possible to set out here, the context of the cure has been fragmented into various disciplines, with an emphasis on experimental logic and hard sciences and difficulty in understanding that the metaphysical perspective is not alternative or opposed to them, but, through an adequate epistemology, complementary and integrative. The dominant medical paradigm, on the other hand, continues to consider the parts and not the whole whereas everything is connected and the connection must always be kept in mind even when focusing on the detail. Today it is even more evident that care interventions obey certain assumptions that define the quality of the therapeutic relationship, influence the maps and strategies used and guide the techniques. These assumptions determine the climate of the therapeutic setting. Explicit or not, the founding commencements of a therapeutic practice always concern the essence of the human condition and the nature of interpersonal relationships. These perceptions constitute the paradigms that inspire clinical practice. These views, mostly unstated, determine the general climate in which therapies involving patient and therapist take place. Whatever the founding commencements of the therapist, they imply (or deny) a philosophical-spiritual basis for clinical practice. The founding commencements are the most critical and highly influencing aspects of any clinical practice. They guide general orientation, strategy maps, clinical orientation, ways in which they see patients and how they interpret symptoms.

The comparison between the thinking of A. Rosmini[1] and V. E. Frankl[2] regarding the epistemology of the human sciences, in the perspective of the relationship between the whole and the parts, in a perspective of harmonious interaction, is very stimulating.

This juxtaposition is possible because of the anthropological position of both authors, who, albeit with different tools and horizons, converge in attention to anthropological datum and its dimension of transcendence.

The person, capable of producing symbols and generating meanings, infers that something greater than pure materiality is contained in empirical reality, something that projects, exceeds, *transcends* in emotion and thought what the sensation captures here and now (*immanence*). *Immanence* and *transcendence* occur simultaneously in every daily behavior.

The uni-duality[3] of immanence-transcendence[4] can be investigated by knowledge in a complete way mainly through philosophical reflection. The philosophical perspective, in fact, brings to light the ontological discriminant between philosophy and the other sciences, an ontological discriminant at the service of the organic nature of knowledge and not of its fragmentation and fragmentation.

It is precisely the possibility of self-transcendence that makes possible a comparison that is illuminating and fruitful with the brilliant intuitions of A. Rosmini and V. E. Frankl.

I have dealt this topic as a psychotherapist active for years principally in the social practice of contrasting discomfort and marginality, with

1. Antonio Rosmini (Rovereto, 1797–Stresa, 1855).

2. Viktor Emil Frankl (Vienna, 1905–1997).

3. See Morin: *Sette saperi necessari*; Morin, *Testa ben fatta*; Morin, *Sfida della complessità*.

4. The Christian faith explicitly themes it in one of its central dogmas: the incarnation. On the incarnation see Canullo and Gilbert, *Emmanuel Falque*.

particular attention to neuroscience and the mind that inside and beyond nature constitutes, in the language of G. Bateson, a "sacred unity."[5]

The thesis I would like to show is that openness to transcendence is not against the empirical dimension of the sciences, but rather is propitious to it, and implies an original and rigorous epistemological perspective.

Some Epistemological Aspects of Antonio Rosmini's Philosophical Anthropology

The Rosminian approach is an important and decisive contribution in undertaking a dialogue with the human sciences that guarantees the anthropological quality of research, in the era of post-humanism and neuroscience.

In the circular unity of immanence-transcendence, Rosmini decides to start from man to arrive at God. He thus proposes an investigation into the person, an alternative to the prevailing sensism in Italy and France, to German idealism and subjectivism. His discourse is never abstract or disembodied, it always remains oriented towards the human and its depth, the dominant motif of his writings. Always present is the awareness that philosophy must present a whole truth, composing modernity and tradition, overcoming the controversy artificially created by the Enlightenment. Rosminian thought is a complex of well-ordered truths, constantly evolving, yet always in continuity and coherence, in the original perspective of the triple circularity of being. In fact, *being*, is recognized in his theoretical analysis as triadic and Trinitarian: the discovery of the synthesism of the three forms of being is the fulcrum of the entire open system of truth elaborated by Rosmini. The three forms of being are: the ideal form (or ideal being, concerning the idea of being), the real form (or real being, concerning the fundamental feeling), the moral form (or moral being, concerning reflected morality as a speculative judgment of a practical judgment at least of the second order of reflection).[6]

With regard to the ideal being, human knowledge proceeds through the formation of ideas. The *ideal* being (which for Rosmini is condensed in the idea of being, about which in this contribution his characterizations in conclusions of intellection, cognition and reflection are highlighted) is truth as it shows itself to the mind, an objective form that is expressed through

---

5. See Bateson, *Verso un'ecologia della mente* [Steps to an ecology of mind].

6. The investigation of the three forms of being is the cornerstone and recurring theme of Rosmini's production. To learn more, see Sciacca, *Ontologia triadica e trinitaria*, and Bergamaschi, *Essere morale*. For an overview of Rosminian thinking see Bergamaschi, *Grande dizionario antologico*.

the commencement of cognition, among the characteristics of which there are indeterminacy, possibility, universality.[7] The idea is also the possible being, present to the human spirit as endowed with the capacity for intellection and intuition: the idea of being is being intuited by the mind. The idea of being shows itself to the intelligent soul resulting from its synthesistic composition with the real being as affection, which is aroused by the extra-subjective real being in the subjective fundamental feeling. Thus, a modification of the subject takes place through cognitive reflection on empirical experience: this subjective power is the intellectual *sense* (which is obtained when intellectual affection becomes an *affective intellection*). The adjective "intellectual" refers to the fundamental and primordial capacity and attitude of the person: understanding, which already originally had a moral characterization. The idea of being for Rosmini is intuited by the person and needs nothing more than to be recognized, since it is the first commencement of all knowledge, and enjoys an innate ontological status. Being, the starting point of human knowledge, known for itself, cannot be defined. The person is an animal subject endowed with the intuition of the ideal-indeterminateness being.[8]

With regard to the real being, we feel sensations, we perceive reality. The real *form* of being is "what is felt," the real as feeling, which presents a double subjective and extra-subjective aspect. Before knowing rationally, one must have experience, the condition of all reasoning. Experience therefore plays an irreplaceable role. Feeling (awareness), in its broadest sense, constitutes the matter of human cognition. It is the *fundamental* bodily feeling, the commencement of any feeling, that is, the irrepressible and constant perception of one's own body, of one's own existence and of external reality, which continually intervenes to solicit the feeling, supplying material for thought.

The natural and immediate awareness of being is therefore accompanied by the further co-original given that is feeling, which receives even accidental modifications. Every sensation is felt as a modification of oneself, of one's sensory state. The sensation also makes the existence of one's own body evident. The act of "feeling" is the awakening that external things exert on the person. You meet things and you "feel" your person. In sensation, therefore, two different kinds of bodies are perceived: the self-body and external realities. Sensation is an immediate fact of consciousness. It is therefore not possible to deceive oneself about its passivity, which thus becomes

---

7. On the order of knowledge, see Rosmini, *IP*, para. 85.

8. See Rosmini, *AAMS*, 33; para. 43. More generally, the definitions of person/man and their characteristics treated in this paragraph are taken from this work by Rosmini.

a guarantee of the veracity of an experience of which the person is not the origin. External stimuli could not, however, by themselves turn into sensations if the spirit did not give it feeling. Underlying sensory perception there is therefore a primitive feeling, not originating from any external reality, but which identifies with oneself. This fact makes it possible to recognize both the relevance of the fundamental feeling and the presence of something transcendent in the constitution of the rational subject.

The fundamental feeling is what the spirit has of itself. Rosmini calls the perception of things *extra subjective*, because it must refer to something different from the subject, but always in relation to him. The subjective *perception* is what the person makes of himself as a subject. The first aspect of this subjective perception is the affection of *sensation*. It reveals the coexistence of two facts: the modification of the fundamental feeling in the affected sensory organ and the sensory perception of the external body. The act of sensation is both *subjective* and *extra subjective*. The external body is in a relationship of dependence with respect to the proper body (subjective). The modifications of feeling are felt by the soul immediately. Sensations would not be experienced as a modification of oneself if there were no feeling of oneself, even before feeling the modification. The sensation could in no way communicate the feeling of one's existence: the feeling is given originally. In its first state, feeling is a uniform object, it has no differences or multiplicity, it does not attract intellectual attention and has no self-awareness. The essence of the person consists in the feeling of life, indefinite and endless. It is necessary to distinguish between body and feeling. The *sensiferous* commencement makes us feel and is the cause of extra subjective phenomena. The extra-subjective feeling contains in itself an intelligibility of its own, which, from human intelligibility is incipiently understood through the idea of being, which is intuition of truth, which informs reason and gives it the evidence and knowledge of what is. The sensiferous commencement (body) and the sentient commencement (soul), when they are united in the moral form of being, constitute the human subject. The person is sentiment and intelligence, inseparable in what by uniting them takes on a thirdness having an ontological consistency of its own, morality. This is what synthesism consists of: that each of the three forms of being can never stand without the other two, since it would be a pure abstraction to want to separate absolutely each of the three forms from the other two. The person always hears and understands. The spirit brings the feeling back to being, making it known to a mind. This shows the intimate relational structure of the person, who already in measuring up to himself and to the reality outside himself places himself in a receptive relationship, towards an ontologically connoted reality that performs an active function.

In the metaphysical structure of the person, the ideal form of being and the real form or feeling are taken as the starting point of all reasoning, which is fully such to the extent and at the moment in which it is carried out through the loving form of knowledge proper to the moral being. The idea of being and feeling are original data.

The person is an animal subject endowed with the perception of his own fundamental bodily feeling, and operating according to animality and intelligence. Recognizing the spiritual commencement within corporeity, the intellectual perception of feeling consequently appears as the animal and spiritual uni-totality of the human being. The fundamental bodily feeling is one with the intellectual, constituting the sentient, intelligent and moral subject.

Intellectual perception is objective, that is, thinking of anything as it is in itself, whether or not it is perceived by the senses. Things other than oneself are not in themselves objects of the mind, but can and must become so, not by virtue of the sensation produced in feeling, but of something that must be an object for itself, intuited by the mind as something that is in itself. If the person were not both a sentient and intelligent commencement, he could not know the sensation intellectually and say what it is. The subject who feels, intuits the ideal being, in order to objectify the sensation. The person is a living synthesis of intelligence and feeling, he always *feels* and *understands* (without being immediately aware of this), with the aim of acting correctly by doing and loving his own good and that of others.

An entity is such by virtue of synthesism, the real being, the ideal being and the moral being. In the analysis of perception three distinct faculties cooperate:

1. The faculty of feeling that which can be sensed, or bodily sensitivity

2. The faculty that possesses the idea of being, inasmuch as it intuits being (the predicate of judgment), commonly called *intellect*

3. The faculty that unites the predicate to the subject and thus forms judgment itself, the morality of reason

The sentient commencement and the intelligent commencement, despite the diversity of their actions, constitute a single moral subject. In the person, the feeling is unique, animal and spiritual, and the animal feeling is not pure animality, but always refers to spirituality, since in it is the spirit that addresses the sensiferous. The fulcrum of this reality is, in particular, affection, transversal to the real, ideal, and moral being, through what has been identified and called "synthesism within synthesism of affection, intellection, volition, cognition and reflection."[9]

What is felt (through the real being) is known (through the ideal being) and willed (through the moral being). The unveiling of the final and original human at the same time, therefore, takes place through the completion of the relational circle, or in the retrieval and explication of the third form of being, where the felt-known is also *loved* for its intrinsic and ontological connotation of being: love, in other words, is the absolute transcendental of being. The synthesism of the real with the ideal takes place in the moral (just as the synthesis of the ideal with the moral takes place in the real and that of the real with the moral takes place in the ideal), which structures the other two modalities, and highlights and gives the form of an absolute goodness that is the justice of *agape*. The moral *form* of being constitutes, in synthesism that considers the other two forms of being, starting from the moral being, the point of origin and arrival of all speculation, because it is the intimate conjunction of the first two. From it derives the loving dimension of the whole being. The apex of the human is morality, a moment of anthropological unveiling of relationship and freedom.

The ontological syntheticism (or "nesting") of the three forms represents the keystone of the whole Rosminian metaphysical and theological edifice: the entity cannot exist under one of the three forms if it does not also exist under the other two. The anthropological place where the synthesis of the three forms of being takes place is the rational soul, in the ontological horizon of a man integrally understood, substantially composed of the inseparable dual unity of rational soul and sentient body.

In this solid triadic-Trinitarian ontological synthetical basis is contained the metaphysical foundation of Rosminian anthropological doctrine. The person is an animal, intellectual and volitional subject. Defining the person as an animal, intellectual and volitional subject, indicates the perspective in which both the passive part (animality and intellect) of human nature and the active part (will) emerges.

Rosmini fixes in the doctrines of the real and ideal Being/being the feeling-intellect as a place of insistence of the subjective-objective relations of the person with the Being/being. In the inseparable unity of body-intellect-spirit, the composition of these complementary relationships is found in the doctrine of the moral being, in which the ontological dimension of reflection is detectable starting from the connection between the affection

---

9. See Bellelli, *Etica originaria*, 113–31. The lemma has been extensively argued by the same author also in Bellelli, *Percorsi storici*.

of feeling that synthesizes with intellection, which in turn synthesizes with volition, producing cognition first and reflection-judgment later.

The wording is precise: the person is first and foremost a subject. To this subject are added the three conditions of animality, intelligence, and will. Thus, the qualities listed reveal the same relationship with the "subject," without one being privileged over the other.

This space of synthesis is properly identified in *human action*. An intellectual and volitional subject means that he is endowed with the intuition of the ideal-indeterminate being and the perception of the fundamental bodily feeling, and acts morally in accordance with the animality and intelligence he possesses.

The transcendent immanence (the immanent transcendence) of the human is constituted by animality and spirituality, in a perfect synthesis, which, in turn, embraces intellectual and volitional power. The human is grasped in its entirety. In the metaphysical-anthropological discourse, the ontological commencement insists on unity, the condition of human existence. Everything is connected in the person; everything tends to a single end. So, the science of the person is one, even in the multiplicity of knowledge. It is possible to avoid reductionism, provided that we accept the incompleteness of the individual parts and the need for integration and connection with the whole. The excessively sectoral nature of knowledge, the closure of the human sciences to metaphysics, the difficulties of dialogue between the sciences and philosophy (and theology) damage the development of knowledge, but also human development.

The metaphysical perspective provides the basis and structure of the mystery of the human, of which no science can define its essence, its beginning and its end, its origin, and its conclusion. By studying a part of the human one cannot possess (or worse manipulate) the human: soul (*form* of the human) and body are united in the person. "Form" means that an entity is what it is, rather than something else. It is the being human of the human.

In its metaphysical structure, the human is made up of several faculties: drives, sensoriality, the original power of the intellect, the derived power of reason, the will and freedom. Each of them is a first act and is power in relation to the second acts: the fundamental bodily feeling is an act with respect to one's own body, power in relation to particular sensations; the *intellect* intuits the idea of being and is power in relation to indeterminate ideal entities. *Reason* applies the idea to reality in intellectual perception. *Will* is the supreme commencement that guides all others. Although essential to the understanding of the human, philosophy is nevertheless not sufficient for its perfection. Truth belongs to intelligence but virtue belongs to will. Philosophy is love (*philia*) of wisdom. The human is bodily sentiment and intelligence of truth, united by the vigor of rationality and morality, which, in freedom being the summit of morality, is the highest point, at which human forces and faculties converge.

The fundamental doctrine of Rosminian metaphysics is that of the commencement and the conclusion. In relation to bodily feeling, the commencement is sentient, the conclusion is felt (affection); intelligence is the commencement, and the ideal being is the conclusion (together they constitute the intellectual feeling—intellection and intellectual affection). The will is the commencement; the conclusion is the moral law (volition, cognition, and reflection).

The commencement is the first act of an entity from which proceeds an activity that tends towards an end. The conclusion is that which is present in the beginning, that in which the commencement ends as actuality. Intellectual and bodily feeling have different conclusions: sentient commencement and felt conclusion, intelligent commencement and intellectually understood conclusion, willing commencement, and beloved conclusion (each faculty is a first act that produces second acts). The soul is first active and then passive, and the body first passive and then active. They are, however, in morality, and all this is comprehensible in an original way through the moral form of being, a single reality. As action produces passion, so passion produces action in that virtuous circle, in that circular integration, which is human existence.[10]

A fundamental characteristic of the body is extension: having parts outside of parts. If the sentient commencement were also extended, each part would be felt separately. Body and soul therefore have different natures: the former is extended, the latter simple and immaterial. Without the conclusion extended-understood, the human soul could not be called act and therefore substance. The feeling is their relationship. The extended is always felt by an un-extended. The *sentient* commencement is necessarily immaterial. The fact of consciousness is indubitable: there is a body that one can call one's own. One must consider the body as it is given by experience and internal observation: as a co-subject of one's feeling.

In *Psychology (Psicologia)*, consciousness indicates the reflected life of oneself as a thinking subject and the awareness of one's own acts. The ego expresses self-consciousness in the identity of the percipient self and the perceived self. It is self-conscious self-affirmation. The soul is not consciousness. The soul as substance is an essence that contains the intellectual and sensory commencements. Rosmini reserves the term *conscience* for the rational act of reflection. The term *I* indicates the subject who feels, knows,

---

10. See Bellelli, "Rosmini and Blondel."

and exists. The primitive and stable feeling of the substantial soul makes one experience the permanence of the ego, the feeling of subjectivity (sentient and intelligent commencement) that is ontologically prior to consciousness.

The act is the adaptation of the ego to the objective truth of things, to their being lovable, an intellectual act of love. In anthropology, the onto-ethical nexus of universal love is implemented.

Hence a precise path from intelligence to love, in which the person is "a vital feeling that leads to being." Intelligence corresponds to the will, which is the subject who moves behind the objects of his mind, operates according to the reasons he contemplates.

The act, that for which an essence is, constitutes the place of composition of every bond of participation in being, the onto-epiphanic moment of the relationship.

The primitive and fundamental perception of all the felt (beginning and conclusion) is the thalamus, so to speak, where the real (animal-spiritual feeling) and the essence that is intuited in the idea form a thing; And this only thing is the person.

The human then is a circularity of relationships. The synthesism between beauty as the form of ideal being, the real being as a good being and the good as the form of the moral being constitutes the aesthetic profile of the relationship, in all its realities, the subjective and objective experience of affection, in the "synthesism within synthesism" of affection, intellection, volition, cognition and reflection. The human is the thalamus[11] that welcomes and brings about this nuptial relationship, in the substantial realization of that characteristic of the moral being that realizes the three forms of being. From such a union arises a single supreme commencement, the will, substance of the rational soul, form to the body and first commencement that identifies the ego as being-knowing-agent. The nuptial dynamic pervades creation, ordering it to the wonderful synthesis that takes place in the human.

Some Epistemological Aspects of the Philosophical Anthropology of Viktor Emil Frankl

In the works of Viktor Frankl,[12] we find the criteria for a respectful and epistemologically correct dialogue between philosophy, which focuses on the

11. See Grandis, "Rosmini e la nuzialità," and Mastracchio, "Talamo dell'essere."
12. Please see the bibliography at the end of this essay for a basic listing of V. E. Frankl's work. Of the works on Frankl and logotherapy see: Bruzzone, *Autotrascendenza e formazione* and *Ricerca di senso*; Giovetti, *Viktor Frankl*; Fizzotti, *Logoterapia*

person as a totality of incarnate spirit and psychotherapy as attention to the uniqueness of the subject, caught in his mystery, and his search for meaning.

While Freudian psychoanalysis and its subsequent specifications have highlighted the conditioning of defence mechanisms and sexual determinants, as limiting the individual's ability to choose, in Viktor Frankl the conditions that allow patients to decide according to the founding values of their life project become explicit.

The founder of logotherapy adhered at first to the Adlerian doctrine, of which he preserved and incorporated in an original way some intuitions while rejecting and surpassing others.

On individual psychology, he assumed the concept of compromise. To get rid of guilt, the neurotic develops the symptom. In this way he relieves his responsibility and justifies himself towards himself and the community. The therapy aims to bring the patient back to his responsibility, the only way to free him from his guilt and his symptoms. Adlerian psychology recognizes the need for therapy as "upward movement," the meaning of life.[13] The true purpose of life is, ultimately, to overcome concern for oneself and develop a sincere and deep interest in others, social feeling. Logotherapy welcomes this solicitation and develops it in a broader sense and in an original and fruitful way.

Of Freudian psychoanalysis, Frankl recognizes the merit of reflexively developing the dynamics of the unconscious, in particular through the mechanism of removal and the function of transference. The fundamental task of the defense mechanism is to reduce the distressing id/ego dialectic. Frankl, however, recognizes the limitations of depth psychology that would like to cancel the threat of the id, making the contents of the unconscious reappropriate by the awareness of the ego, thus increasing its power. Even more reductive, Frankl considers the commencement of *transference* that psychoanalysis interprets in a functional way as mere regression.

Viktor Frankl abandoned psychoanalysis and individual psychology because he considered them both reductive in the interpretation of human experience and therefore in the treatment of nervous symptoms. One insists only on the id-consciousness, the other only on the id-responsibility. To be human, on the other hand, means at the same time to become aware and responsible.

According to Viktor Frankl this reductive vision of the human is the result of a theoretical prejudicial constraint, rather than a real and historical

---

per tutti and *Il senso come terapia*; Lukas, *Dare un senso alla vita*; *Prevenire le crisi*, and *Dare un senso alla sofferenza*.

13. Adler, *Senso della vita*.

consideration, of man. Decisive in the theory of the founder of logotherapy was his experience as an internee (deported in September 1942 to Auschwitz, he escaped death, but lost his loved ones).[14]

According to Frankl, Adlerian individual psychology rightly insists on the need for the patient to take responsibility for the meaning of his own life, but forgets the existence of the values that underpin the meanings that are attributed to life.

Of individual psychology he adopted the purposive principle, that is, the fact that man always tends towards an end and that he structures his person according to the goal that he has set himself. It is possible to stimulate a compensating force that helps man to remedy his intimate insecurity (sense of inferiority), elevating his "feeling of personality." To the causality of psychic life and from the Adlerian finalistic commencement (will to power) Frankl contrasted what he called "will to meaning," to indicate that the person makes himself responsible for the meaning that he freely attributes to life.[15] The person can become mentally ill not only as a result of the feeling of "organic inferiority" and, therefore, of "feeling of inferiority," but also, and even more so, as a consequence of the feeling of meaninglessness. So, he suffers not so much from the feeling of his low value, but rather from the feeling that his existence has no meaning.

"Depth psychology" is oriented towards the liberation of *libido*, while "height psychology" is oriented towards meanings, that is, towards spirituality, an essential human dimension that psychotherapy never deals with, as Frankl emphasizes.

The real human, in fact, must be grasped in the totality of its dimensions: physical, psychic, spiritual.[16] The latter turns towards the realization

14. He verified "in the field" the theoretical assumptions of logotherapy starting precisely from this experience, systematizing them by narrating his personal tragedy in the bestseller *Uomo in cerca*.

15. Frankl wrote: "The profound and radical need inherent in the living person is not the will to power, nor the will to please, but the will to meaning. On the basis of his desire for meaning, man is oriented to the search for and realization of meanings, but also to the encounter with another human being as a 'you', loving 'him'" (Frankl, *Come ridare senso*, 18).

16. Frankl also spoke of dimensional ontology: "The unity of man—a unity despite the multiplicity of body and psyche—cannot be found in the biological or psychological dimension, but must be sought in that noetic dimension, starting from which man is projected in the first place. . . . The closed system of physiological reflexes and psychological reactions is not, however, at odds with the humanity of man. . . . If we talk about higher dimension (the noetic one Editor's note) opposed to smaller dimensions does not imply in any sense a value judgment. Rather, a higher dimension indicates that we are dealing with a more comprehensive dimension" (Frankl, *Senso e valori*, 40–41).

of values, to intentionality and invests its freedom. They are the values that give consistency and meaning to life. In order to make sense of the void, which produces existential frustration (which Frankl calls "noogenic" neurosis), it is necessary to take care not only of the biological and psychological sphere of the patients, but also of their spiritual experience.

The psychologism of psychotherapy is overcome by logotherapy, which recognizes the psychic-spiritual unity of the person and respects the autonomy of each science, thus recognizing the threshold of the different interventions.

In psychotherapy as a fully human experience, *transfer* is experienced as an interpersonal encounter. The founder of logotherapy doesn't tire of repeating that only an ego that understands a "you" can integrate its own id.

The Oedipal complex and inferiority complex created empty psychotherapy. It can be supplemented with spiritual psychotherapy.

The *logos* is a word those questions, conscience that insists, awareness that changes the lifestyle. Logotherapy, which starts from the *logos* (the spirit), aims to make people aware of their fundamental responsibilities. Therapeutic accompaniment does not primarily seek pleasure, the power of the ego or even self-realization, where the person does not access any transcendence. Speech therapy proposes existential fulfillment, the analysis of becoming fully responsible. The patient finds himself having to realize meanings to give meaning to life. In achieving this goal, Frankl insisted, the patient must be able to rely on guides who are not mere comforters (peacemakers) but courageous witnesses of the meaning that life can assume.

There is a biological destiny (organic inferiority) or there is a historical condition (inferiority complex), to which one can react, train oneself to the decision with creative choices. There is an anti-fatalistic attitude to be integrated into everyday life.

Authentic diagnosis involves "knowing through" (dia-gnosis): going through *pathos* (pain) to grasp the *logos*. There is a biological disposition and there is a social conditioning, to be faced through responsible freedom. Suffering can lead to human development. Logotherapy, in fact, leads the *patiens* to become *agens*, in the unrepeatability and singularity of every personal story. Life questions: it is not enough to analyze oneself; it is necessary to act, according to one's duty. Work, for example, which is a human activity and not pure economic performance, ennobles and cares because it activates the specificity of man who, with his work, relates to the world.

Logotherapy, which starts from the spirit, does not deal only with the pathological but tends towards an existential analysis of spiritual suffering, one that concerns the meanings of living. Existential analysis can lead the individual to "know" that he suffers,[17] while psychological analysis promises only to make him "capable" of enjoying or rejoicing. The value of living (not the length of life but its height, its quality) is derived from how one faces death and from the meaning that is attributed to it. The limit set by death questions every existential act and empowers to make the best use of the time available. It poses the decisive question that guides the freedom of every choice: What's the point? Consciousness is an organ of meaning that orients every act (conscious and reasonable) to the dimension of what is properly human.

Meanings and values are not invented (mentally constructed) but discovered experientially, freely and responsibly.[18] The factor of human freedom to transcend towards values, which impose themselves and, at the same time, are found and appreciated as fundamental, is deeply involved. Values make it possible to relate to and to go beyond libido, sexual and instinctive strength, and the feeling of inferiority itself.

The spiritual act that survives time is only love. Death may eliminate the physical existence of the person, but it finds the road blocked by love. The uniqueness of the person, made such by love, remains beyond death.

In love, the person reveals himself as unrepeatable in his historical life and unique for what he is. Frankl's criticism of Freud basically lies in his having reduced love to a product of sublimation, that is, of unfulfilled aspirations, in a sort of irreconcilable antinomy between libido, understood as the force of sexual drives, and what the Judeo-Christian tradition calls agape (which Freud nevertheless appreciated). Only on the basis of an original and primary existential capacity to love, that is, of a fundamental orientation of man towards love, is sublimation, that is, the integration of sexual experience into the whole person, understandable. In love the individual is grasped as a "whole" (Hegel), as a you, capable of entering into intimacy with another I: in an encounter that can only be described as grace, enchantment and miracle.

---

17. Frankl affirmed: "Those who cannot forge their destiny with the values of creation can subdue and dominate it in another way, through the realization of values of attitude, taking a right attitude in the face of a destiny marked by authentic suffering. This presupposes a prior acquisition of the capacity to suffer. Such an inner overcoming, with the renunciation of an external conformation, turns out to be, ultimately, a configuration: indeed, a self-configuration. In fact, the conquest of the capacity to suffer is an act of self-configuration" (Frankl, *Homo Patiens*, 77–8).

18. "Certainly, man is free to answer the questions that life poses to him. But this freedom must not be confused with arbitrariness. Rather, it must be interpreted in conclusions of responsibility. Man is responsible for giving the *just* answer to a question, in finding the *right* meaning of a situation. Meaning to be found and not assigned, to be discovered and not invented" (Frankl, *Senso e valori*, 76).

A concise characteristic of love is its eternity. One cannot, in fact, propose to love "for a certain time." Love, however, is expressed in many forms, at different levels: sexual drive, erotic desire, passion in love, commitment, and a project for married life. Different experiences become love in a spiritual relationship. Moreover, love always has a social vocation, it presupposes a community life, not in the mode of gregariousness but according to the metaphor of the tile that makes up the mosaic. Social life—Frankl consistently maintained—is not a function nor does it obey for reasons of pure utility but is based on the value of fraternity, because the person can only be fulfilled in the community.

People's sexual development, according to Frankl, must deal with the inevitable neurotic disorders when erotic desire fails: resentment, resignation, inactivity. Neurotic symptoms can expand to four levels of the human: organic, psychic, social, and existential. The methodology of therapeutic care, in particular pathological states related to the sexual area, uses two peculiar techniques: *paradoxical intention* (which induces a condition of self-distancing) and *dysreflexion* (which is expressed at the highest level in self-transcendence, but also acts through humor).[19] The therapeutic treatment creates a saying and listening in a reciprocity that goes beyond the regressive manipulation of *transfer* to achieve an existent encounter that seeks a direct confrontation with the *logos*, that is, a "meaning," especially when affective frustration turns into noogenic pathologies that trigger feelings of death. The symptoms, in fact, are symbols, always allude to vital meanings for the person.

The Franklian therapeutic setting is centered on the practice of empathy with the patient in the free search for responsibility towards himself and others. In contrast to Freudian psychodynamics, *logotherapy* develops a "nondynamic" dynamism: tension between existence and the essence of the human, between the values and meaning attributed to life.

Human social attitude, communal feeling, vital tasks such as love, friendship, and work, are Adlerian concepts that Frankl used in an original way, assuming them in a global human vision in which subjectivity and freedom are intertwined with spirituality and transcendence.

---

19. "Spontaneity and activity are hindered if they are given excessive attention. Think of the centipede, the story goes that when an enemy asked in what order he moved his feet, he was no longer able to move, because he was paying close attention to his feet. It is said that he died of starvation. Are we to say that he died from a fatal hyper-reflection? In logotherapy, hyper-reflection is neutralized by dereflection. . . . Paradoxical intention means that the patient is encouraged to do or wish for exactly what he is afraid of to happen" (Frankl, *Senso e valori*, 111–12).

In the thought of Viktor E. Frankl, human freedom is considered with absolute respect and appreciation. The "will to meaning" challenges freedom towards a movement of transcendence, a state of "plus," of upward change.

The existential analysis of V. E. Frankl is close to, although it never identifies with, the humanist psychology of Abraham H. Maslow, where the values of subjectivity, freedom, and self-realization enter the global vision of the human, which is the apical objective of the "pyramid of needs," characterized by the needs of growth. Frankl, however, considered self-realization more precisely as man's ability to transcend himself for what is other than himself. Frankl, in fact, criticized the vision of humanist psychology when it does not know how to overcome the immanent dimension of the human, neglecting the authentic motives of transcendence. The essence of existence according to Frankl is in fact self-transcendence. Frankl's philosophical reference can be found in M. Scheler's reflection. The person cannot ignore his being considered both immanent and transcendent, just as the body is both *Körper*, an outwardly perceived reality, and *Leib*, lived in personal experience, as a sensible reality expressive of the spirituality of the soul. Another fundamental anthropological presupposition of Scheler is the reflection on love as *ordo amoris*, the fundamental nucleus of values, the original source of every authentic ethical experience, the dynamic center of the person.[20]

For Frankl the life that challenged the human and guided him to the threshold of the absolute. From Frankl's overall approach we can deduce, therefore, the possibility of full and definitive self-transcendence of the subject, in the openness to the religious phenomenon, which psychology cannot fail to deal with its own tools. Psychotherapy can remain open to transcendence, even within the limits of one's disciplinary competences. *Logotherapy*, as a "care of the soul," can free the person from conditioning to leave him free to enter into metaphysical horizons, in which to seek "the ultimate meaning."

It is on the phenomenological terrain that one can fruitfully encounter the thought of Rosmini and Frankl on the themes of sentiment and transcendence. It is undoubtedly necessary to continue in the line of studies already started in this direction, focusing on the dimensions of the relationship between philosophy, human sciences[21] and neurosciences with regard to the theme of sensitivity.

20. See Cusinato, *Biosemiotica e psicopatologia*.

21. It is a pertinent observation also in sociology, as in N. Luhmann's consideration of religion. The world, the horizon of totality, which is continually "presented" (a conclusion borrowed from Husserl), which is always referred to in asking questions of meaning, remains unrepresentable in Luhmann, since the reality of the world is complex. Religion would have the (functional) task of representing, that is, of specifying,

The human sciences are knowledge of the threshold, and, in the context under examination, they are placed at the meeting point between psycho-neurology/psychotherapy and the speculative theoresis of philosophical knowledge.

It is precisely the possibility of self-transcendence starting from feeling-affection that makes possible a comparison that is illuminating and fruitful of the thought of V. E. Frankl with the brilliant intuitions of Antonio Rosmini. The philosophical perspective brings to light the ontological factor of philosophy as a solid basis for the other sciences, to the development of which the other sciences also contribute according to their epistemological statutes.

Relevance and Interest in Undertaking a Fruitful Integrated Comparison of the Philosophical Anthropology of Rosmini and Frankl

The relevance of immanence and transcendence collected in the theoresis of A. Rosmini and in Franklian psychotherapeutic practice can be compared with today's development of neuroscience, including cognitive neuroscience. According to the most accredited idea by neuroscience, in fact, the mind can be defined as an emergent, complex and self-organized, embodied and relational process that regulates the flow of energy and information. Energy consists of electric charges circulating in the nervous system, while information concerns meanings and symbols.

The main convergence between Rosminian philosophical anthropology and Franklian philosophical anthropology can be found in the analogy

---

of making "determinable the undeterminable," of symbolically signifying the unrepresentable. In advanced societies, according to the German sociologist, religion preserves intact and irreplaceable the vital function of "representing the presented"; see Luhmann, *Funzione della religione*, 36. "In every experience lived and acting endowed with meaning, more is continually 'presented' than can be represented" (Luhmann, *Funzione della religion*, 32). The constitutive element of religious experience is therefore the discovery, made within the daily dimension of life, that what is at stake is greater than what is given to experience immediately. The religious question may no longer be recognized, religious practice may become extinct to the point of insignificance. In these cases, Luhmann suggests, "functional equivalents" can act provisionally, such as *idolatry* (or ideology) and *drugs*. While religious experience contains the simultaneity of *immanence* and *transcendence*, sensitive form and mental content, *idolatry* brings everything back to immanence, the *drugs*. They resolve everything in "transcendence" (from corporeity). Idolatry deifies the world; drugs produce, on the contrary, the escape from the world. The immanence-transcendence unity (which the Christian faith explicitly thematizes in one of its central dogmas) can be investigated only by philosophical reflection.

and isomorphism between the Rosminian synthesism of the three forms of being (ideal, real, and moral) and the three dimensions characterizing the Franklian conception of the person (structured according to the physical, psychic, and spiritual dimensions). The common reference of both has its roots in the origin of the Augustinian anthropological conception (*esse, nosse, velle*). Not only for Rosmini but also for Frankl, in this sense, the structure of being, knowing and wanting has both an ontological-metaphysical value and an epistemological-gnoseological value. The merit emerging from Rosminian anthropology compared to Franklian anthropology, on the one hand, is the highlighting that the triadic (and Trinitarian) characteristics of finite being and eternal being, are not only intra-subjective, but inter-subjective, while in Franklian philosophical anthropology it would appear that the intra-subjective consideration of these characteristics is practically almost exclusive. The emerging merit of Franklian anthropology compared to Rosminian anthropology, on the other hand, is that it is placed, from a phenomenological point of view, at the origins of the scientific-experimental developments that led to the contemporary acquisitions of neuroscience. In this sense, therefore, the interaction between Rosminian anthropology and Franklian anthropology can have its main nucleus of validity and relevance in allowing us to appreciate the essential elements of Rosminian philosophical anthropology in the current debate and in particular in the importance that there is a good argument and for this effective epistemological interaction between the philosophical-juridical-humanistic sciences and the bio-engineering-experimental-digital sciences and medical-neuroscientific.

The brain (which is not enclosed in the skull but is widespread in the body) is characterized by its neuroplasticity: the production of protein synthesis at the origin of synapses and new neurons, myelin that covers axons and enhances the speed of electrical stimuli and also of epigenetic alterations. The brain is then shaped how it will act in response to experiences. So, the brain, itself incomplete, is formed from the outside. The phenomenon is particularly evident in early childhood brain development. Intense maternal communication develops brain mass and shapes the mind (psychological attachment). The highest immaterial good (affection) generates the most material basis of the human. It is not the physical vibrations of the arms that support, the visual stimulations of the face, the physical warmth of the maternal body. It is the pro-affection that passes through the feelings and gestures of the body. It is the enjoyment of the mother's face that gives flavor to her milk. Without that enjoyment, in fact, the child rejects the milk. This process, in obviously different ways, lasts a lifetime. It is the interiority that makes the fibers of the brain grow, the beauty (of art, of music . . .) that animates the nerve cells, the contemplative life and the practice of justice (and their education) that give vitality to the brain. It is in immanence that transcendence is discovered.

It is still the most accredited discoveries of neuroscience to explain how mental distress emerges in an altered mental integration. The healthy mind takes care of integration, the binding of differentiated parts into a complex. Neural and relational integration, argues clinical neurobiology, are mutually reinforcing.[22]

In the natural environment that one learns to recognize, in the habitat that one becomes capable of living, one obtains the immediate perception of something that guides one to decipher a way of feeling the things of the world, a widespread affectivity, a gift received and transmitted to the generations to come. Things communicate with personal intelligence through a sensitive experience that cannot be reduced to mere sensoriality. This is testified by the story of those who immersed themselves in the life of nature: "Today I lived a beautiful experience, the contact with nature and the company of animals have communicated something to me, they have produced in me a deep pleasure. I felt a sense never so felt before—amazement. It happened as a meeting of grace." Human sensitivity is the receptor organ of nature's vitality. It enables us to receive a sense of wonder from things. Through the senses one receives a trace of intelligence, a transcendent input of meaning. This intelligence is very refined: sensitivity unfailingly perceives the infinite modulations of the language of nature and the reverberation in emotional interiority. This sensitivity finds within things some contact of one's own interiority, which allows one to understand and decipher the environment, which teaches to be with people, to grasp desires and intentions, to discover the pleasure of inhabiting the world.

The normal sensorimotor stimuli of agricultural operations incorporate intelligence and sensitivity until they become true forms of thought, without which some parts of the spirit would not become self-aware.[23] The

22. See Siegel, *Mente relazionale*. The uni-duality immanence-transcendence thus builds bridges between science and spirituality. Around this secret—says Bateson—one can also develop "great art and great religion" (*Verso un'ecologia della mente*, 68). That is, the "structure that connects" the encounter between scientific intelligence and religious intelligence of the world can be activated, making our troubled planet a *unicum* in which we place our dwelling, continue the process that confers unity on the totality of life and evolution. "Religion"—it is always the thought of Bateson—can be recognized is no longer as a synonym of stupidity, but an integral dimension of the experience of the world to which to give the attribute of *sacred*: uniqueness of the set of connections and feeling of being part. Destructiveness is always in disconnection. Dupuy writes: "Men do not destroy nature because they hate it. They destroy it because, hating each other, they do not care about the third parties that their blows bump in the way. And nature is in the first rank of these excluded third parties" (*Marque du sacré*, 38).

23. With Fernando Bellelli, Francesco Preziosi, and Giovanna Gabbi we engaged

transcendent immanence of nature regenerates and heals, in a perspective of integral human ecology, to be put in the field in all respects, even in the face of the bio-onto-ethical challenges that, in particular, the climate emergency and the need for a world order of peace pose to humanity in a way that can no longer be postponable.

Bibliography

Adler, Alfred. *Il senso della vita*. Translated by Francesco Parenti. Novara, It.: De Agostini, 1990.
Bateson, Gregory. *Verso un'ecologia della mente* [Steps to an ecology of mind]. Translated by G. Longo and G. Trautteur. Milan: Adelphi, 1977.
Bellelli, Fernando. *Etica originaria e assoluto affettivo. La coscienza e il superamento della modernità nella teologia filosofica di Antonio Rosmini*. Milan: Vita e Pensiero, 2014.
———. *Percorsi storici della pedagogia giuridica. Vico, Rosmini e la dignitas hominis*. Rome: Aracne, 2020.
———. "Rosmini and Blondel: Interpreters of Aristotle." *Rosmini Studies* 5 (2018) 141–58.
Bergamaschi, Cirillo, ed. *L'essere morale nel pensiero filosofico di Antonio Rosmini*. Genoa: Quercia, 1982.
———. *Grande dizionario antologico del pensiero di Antonio Rosmini*. 4 vols. Rome: Città Nuova, 2001.
Bruzzone, Daniele. *Autotrascendenza e formazione. Esperienza esistenziale, prospettive pedagogiche e sollecitazioni educative nel pensiero di Viktor E. Frankl*. Milan: Vita e Pensiero, 2001.
———. *Ricerca di senso e cura dell'esistenza. Il contributo di Viktor E. Frankl a una pedagogia fenomenologico-esistenziale*. Gardolo, It.: Erickson, 2007.
Canullo, Carla, and Paul Gilbert, eds. *Emmanuel Falque. Tra fenomenologia della finitezza e teologia dell'incarnazione*. Florence: Lettere, 2014.
Cravero, Domenico. *La terra che genera, cura, guarisce*. Rome: Ecra, 2020.
———. *Terra, cibo, vita. Teoria e metodologia dell'agricura**. Milan: Mimemis, 2018.
———. *Terra, lavoro, autismo*. Rome: Ecra, 2020.
Cusinato, Guido. *Biosemiotica e psicopatologia dell'ordo amoris. In dialogo con Max Scheler*. Milan: Franco Angeli, 2019.
Dupuy, Jean-Pierre. *The marque du sacré*. Paris: Flammarion, 2008.
Fizzotti, Eugenio. *Logoterapia per tutti. Guida teorico-pratica per chi cerca il senso della vita*. Soveria Mannelli, It.: Rubbettino, 2002.
———, ed. *Il senso come terapia. Fondamenti teorico-clinici della logoterapia di Viktor E. Frankl*. Milan: Franco Angeli, 2007.
Frankl, Viktor E. *Alla ricerca di un significato della vita*. Translated by Eugenio Fizzotti. Milan: Mursia, 1986.

---

in therapeutic practice through contact with the land: agricura*. The curative value of agriculture is developed precisely through the development of the sensibility through which we experience what things have to communicate to us. On this topic, see Cravero: *Terra, cibo, vita*; *Terra che genera, cura*; and *Terra, lavoro, autismo*.

———. *Come ridare senso alla vita*. Translated by G. Garbelli and E. Schreil. Milan: San Paolo, 2007.
———. *Dio nell'inconscio. Psicoterapia e religione*. Translated by Eugenio Fizzotti. Brescia, It.: Morcelliana, 1990.
———. *Fondamenti e applicazioni della logoterapia*. Translated by Chiaffitelli Vincenzo. Turin: SEI, 1977.
———. *Homo Patiens. Soffrire con dignità*. Translated by Eugenio Fizzotti. Brescia, It.: Queriniana, 2001.
———. *Lettere di un sopravvissuto. Ciò che mi ha salvato dal* lager. Translated by R. Pentangelo. Soveria Mannelli, It.: Rubbettino, 2008.
———. *Logoterapia e analisi esistenziale*. Translated by Eugenio Fizzotti. Brescia, It.: Morcelliana, 2001.
———. *Logoterapia. Medicina dell'anima*. Translated by Eugenio Fizzotti et al. Milan: Gribaudi, 2001.
———. *Psicoterapia nella pratica medica*. Translated by Bruno Frick. Florence: Giunti-Barbèra, 1952.
———. *Le radici della logoterapia. Scritti giovanili 1923–1942*. Translated by Eugenio Fizzotti. Rome: LAS, 2000.
———. *Senso e valori per l'esistenza. La risposta della Logoterapia*. Translated by Vincenzo Chiaffitelli. Rome: Città Nuova, 1998.
———. *La sfida del significato. Analisi esistenziale e ricerca di* senso. Translated by Nicoletta Schmitz Sipos and Matteo Franco. Trento: Erickson, 2005.
———. *La sofferenza di una vita senza senso*. Translated by Eugenio Fizzotti. Turin: LDC Leumann, 1978.
———. *L'uomo in cerca di senso. Uno psicologo nei lager e altri scritti inediti*. Milan: Franco Angeli, 2017.
———. *La vita come compito. Appunti autobiografici*. Translated by F. Terranova. Turin: SEI, 1997.
Giovetti, Paola. *Viktor Frankl. Vita e opere del fondatore della logoterapia*. Rome: Mediterranee, 2001.
Grandis, Giancarlo. "Rosmini e la nuzialità: la teoresi dell'amore." In *Nuzialità trinitaria: relazione e identità. Rosmini e il fondamento simbolico dell'umano*, edited by Fernando Bellelli, 257–76. Panzano in Chianti, It.: Feeria-Comunità di San Leolino, 2017.
Luhmann, Niklas. *La funzione della religione*. Translated by Sergio Belardinelli. Brescia, It.: Morcelliana, 1991.
Lukas, Elisabeth. *Dare un senso alla sofferenza*. Translated by G. Lupi. Assisi: Cittadella, 1995.
———. *Dare un senso alla vita*. Translated by G. Lupi. Assisi: Cittadella, 1991.
———. *Prevenire le crisi*. Translated by F. Terranova. Assisi: Cittadella, 1991.
Mastracchio, Francesca. "Il talamo dell'essere: indagini sul carattere nuziale dell'antropologia rosminiana." *Rosmini Studies* 5 (2018) 91–106.
Morin, Edgar. *I sette saperi necessari all'educazione del futuro*. Translated by S. Lazzari. Milan: Raffaello Cortina, 2001.
———. *La sfida della complessità*. Translated by G. Bocchi and M. M. Rocci. Milan: Feltrinelli, 1985.
———. *La testa ben fatta. Riforma dell'insegnamento e riforma del pensiero*. Translated by S. Lazzari. Milan: Raffaello Cortina, 2000.

Rosmini, Antonio. *Antropologia in servizio della scienza morale*. Edited by François Evain. ENC 24. Rome: Città Nuova, 1981.

———. *Introduzione alla filosofia*. Edited by Pier P. Ottonello. ENC 2. Rome: Città Nuova, 1979.

———. *Psicologia*. Edited by Vincenzo Sala. 4 vols. ENC 9, 9/A, 10, 10/A. Rome: Città Nuova, 1988–1989.

Sciacca, Michele F. *Ontologia triadica e trinitaria. Discorso metafisico teologico*. Palermo: Epos, 1990.

Siegel, Daniel J. *La mente relazionale. Neurobiologia dell'esperienza interpersonale*. Translated by L. Madeddu. Milan: Raffaello Cortina, 2013.

13

Affection and Intersubjectivity in the Thought of Antonio Rosmini and Edith Stein

MARTINA GALVANI

Bodily Affection and Pneumatic Affection According to Rosmini

ROSMINI EXPLORES THE THEME of affections with reference to various contexts: both from the pedagogical point of view in the description of the moral development of the child, which is at the center of the work entitled "The Ruling Principle of Method Applied to Education" (*Del principio supremo della Metodica*), but also from a strictly anthropological point of view, in particular in *Anthropology as an Aid to Moral Science* (*Antropologia in servizio della morale*) (1838) and in *Psychology (Psicologia)* (1846–1848).

In these last works Rosmini refers to the affection that is inherent in the sensory capacity of the human being. He writes: "From the association of several feelings in the unity of the soul, certain general modifications redundant in these, which we call *affections*, which are almost feelings between singular *feelings* and passions."[1] It is, therefore, the affection linked

---

1. Rosmini, *PY*, 2:269, para. 1071.

to the power of sensitivity. The powers (or activities) of the soul, Rosmini affirms, are manifold and are defined by the ends, which "are acting entities in the soul: the search for how they diversify from each other is a . . . matter that concerns the intrinsic order of being"[2] and therefore its triadicity. The real and ideal being, as ends of the soul, arouse in it the sensitive and intelligible power; these "joined together in the unity of the soul give rise first to a third power, that is, to *reason*, and then to moral power."[3] The powers, distinguished according to the ends that inform the soul, are initially receptive and only later will they be active.[4] Thus, sensitivity and intelligence will have an active faculty and a passive faculty, unlike moral power, which is only active.[5]

Following the scheme of the beginning-end, Rosmini states that when the reason of the soul is itself, it will essentially be felt as a beginning and therefore we speak of psychic sensitivity.[6] The soul, in this case, is both beginning and end: "The beginning and the end are identified, which means, that the feeling soul itself is felt in its end, so that the beginning, being felt in the end also becomes felt, which is what to say that it is identified."[7] It is the soul's ability to feel itself, closely connected with another ability, namely that of feeling its living body, called special bodily sensitivity. The latter, like all special sensitivities (bodily, pneumatic, ideological and theoretical), implies an otherness, in that the soul feels something different from itself, however, in this case, diversity manifests itself as passivity: "At the encounter in *passivity*, the entity that acts in the soul, takes something from the nature and activity of the patient, that is, of the soul itself, which contributes to giving

2. Rosmini, *PY*, 2:223, para. 951.

3. Rosmini, *PY*, 2:224, para. 953. Here Rosmini goes on to specify that reason, joining ideal and real, sees one in the light of the other and therefore sees the order of being to which the soul can adhere or not. In fact, it does not possess moral power from the beginning, but only virtually.

4. Rosmini, *PY*, 2:221, para. 946: "In the second acts the observation shows that passivity precedes activity in the soul, not only in the logical order, but also in the chronological order; since first the soul feels and receives, and then it moves and works. But this is not possible with respect to the first act, which is the one for which the soul exists, since before existing it cannot be passive; hence at the first act the liability and the activity are contemporary."

5. See Rosmini, *PY*, 2:225, para. 958: "As for the moral power, having no end in actuality, but only in virtue, that is, this end having to be produced by the acts of the other two powers, or to put it better, of the rational soul itself that directs them; it cannot have passivity, and therefore remains purely active power; since the passivity that refers to it is none other than that of the powers that produce it." See the synoptic table concerning the powers of the human soul: Rosmini, *PY*, 2:228.

6. Rosmini, *PY*, 2:230, para. 970.

7. Rosmini, *PY*, 2:227, para. 967.

that entity its being. Thus, the *extended feeling* receives from the soul the extension."[8] The objective of body sensitivity is the extension with all its movements and modifications. The sentient is struck by the extended feeling and the affections generate the sensations that, says Rosmini, the subject feels as separate, that is, localized in different parts of the body, despite this, the sentient principle is unique and simple. In fact, individual sensations are easier to perceive than the fundamental feeling, even if they depend on it,[9] as they arise from the change that occurs in that feeling on the occasion of an external agent.

The soul, therefore, is able not only to feel itself, but also to perceive its own extended body thanks to the fundamental feeling, which "does not go beyond the boundaries of its extended" and it is precisely from the excitement of this feeling that sensations are born. Rosmini then wonders how it is possible to distinguish the surface of one's own body from the surface of another's body and responds by stating that "if I am touched by a foreign body I have only one sense, but if I touch myself, I have two senses, which I refer to the same place: from which I conclude that I am not only the touched, but also the one touching."[10] In this description that dwells on "how we feel our sensory body,"[11] he uses a language that seems to anticipate the phenomenological one. This is how he describes the double perception that the subject has of his own body:

> In the first place I observe, that our body . . . is perceived in two ways: first like any other external body, that is, with looks, with touching, with the five senses in a nutshell. When I perceive this sensory body of mine as an *agent* through my five organs, I then perceive it as a participant of sensitivity itself . . . , but yes like any other external body. . . . In that case one organ of my body perceives another. . . . second, for that *fundamental* and universal feeling for which we feel life to be in us . . . , and for the modifications that the feeling itself suffers.[12]

In the first way, the extra-subjective one, one's own body is perceived like any other bodily object, therefore from the outside; while perceiving it subjectively, thanks to the feeling, we feel it as "consentient" or "consubject." It is a unity with the individual spirit and becomes part of the sentient subject. This dual mode of perception, however, needs further clarification, in

---

8. Rosmini, *PY*, 2: 230, para. 974.
9. Rosmini, *AAMS*, 103, para. 138.
10. Rosmini, *AAMS*, 233–34, para. 980.
11. Rosmini, *NE*, 2:240., para. 700.
12. Rosmini, *NE*, 2:240–41, para. 701.

fact we subjectively perceive the sensitive parts of our body both with the fundamental feeling and with the modifications that this feeling undergoes at the hands of impressions, which act on the nervous system producing different sensations.[13] Feeling extends throughout the sensory body and the subjective extension is not separated from it, but is its matter.[14] Sensations are precisely modifications of this feeling,[15] by the action of a physical body on ours, since the fundamental feeling occupies all the sensory parts of the body, that is, it extends completely into it: "The extension of one's own body is therefore a *fundamental way* of feeling."[16] In *Anthropology as an Aid to Moral Science (Antropologia in servizio della scienza morale)*, Rosmini takes up this concept by stating that the soul is scattered throughout the body and therefore affection is also present in it: "Now these nervous movements primarily produce a widespread feeling, which I call *affection*, or even *universal* affection; because the activity of the soul is scattered, as we saw, throughout the body, and therefore more or less this affection spreads."[17] This is not to say that feeling has a material extension, but rather he speaks of a "fundamental or internal or subjective extension," difficult to define, felt in a "constant, necessary and uniform" way.[18]

The theme of fundamental feeling is therefore closely connected to that of corporeity and to that of special bodily sensitivity. The human body can be described by the characteristics of extension, solidity, mobility,

13. See Rosmini, *NE*, 2:241, para. 702.

14. See Rosmini, *NE*, 2:262–63, para. 729–31.

15. Rosmini highlights the difference between feeling and bodily sensations also in *Anthropology as an Aid to Moral Science*, where he describes in depth the particular extent of this feeling: "Now, I believe it to be an unquestionable thing, that the extension is felt in the fundamental feeling, as I have already said, that same extension that is felt with external sensations, but devoid of those phenomenal and not all true and legitimate qualities of which the external sensations make us believe it to be endowed, and the extension so felt I call it *fundamental* or *internal extension*. I confess that it is difficult to form a correct concept of this extension, since the community of men does not know how to conceive of a real extension except through figure, colors, limits. . . . however, he will see that by removing these things from the extension, he will not remove the extension itself; but he will be left with something (however indefinable) that was the foundation and almost the subject of those limits, of those colors, which he took away" (Rosmini, *AAMS*, 107, para. 149).

16. Rosmini, NE, 2:265, para. 735.

17. Rosmini, *AAMS*, para. 470, 283.

18. Rosmini, *NE*, 2:266, para. 737: "And these four differences are sufficient to see clearly, how the fundamental feeling is not capable of shaking us and making us observe it. It is connatural to us, and thus one with our nature, which forms part of it; therefore, it gives us neither wonder nor curiosity that makes us intent on it, it being to us as ourselves."

visibility, and all those properties that characterize material things. In this sense, it is subordinated to physical, mechanical and chemical laws; however, as Rosmini notes, it is mainly subject.[19] In fact, through the body we feel the sensations of pleasure, pain, we perceive colors, flavors, sounds, etc.; such sensations come from external bodies acting on us, but this relationship is not regulated by physical-mechanical causal laws. On the contrary, the understanding of the relationship between ourselves and external bodies passes through the sensory principle that, in joining our living body, produces the fundamental bodily feeling. As we said, it is the latter that makes possible the affection of the various sensory parts, thus generating "modifications to which various species of external sensations respond in us, and in them, the perception of bodies external to ours."[20] Thus, in each sensation, one can distinguish the sensory perception of the external body and the mutations of the sensory bodily organ, felt thanks to the modifications undergone by the fundamental feeling. For example, in the act of touching a rough surface we distinguish: the surface, as a "sensory perception" of the external body, and the hand, as a "modification of feeling."[21] It is clear that the external and inner perception of my own body are both present in the sensation.

Moreover, the human being perceives through a further special sensitivity, also of a passive nature, that is the pneumatic sensitivity, which allows us to move from the plane of exclusively bodily affection, described up to now, to a spiritual affection. In fact, Rosmini defines pneumatic sensitivity as follows: "By this we mean the faculty of feeling the spirits of others or of receiving a feeling from them, which represent them to us."[22] The philosopher states that it is a new and little-studied faculty, but he believes that it is evident to observation. The human being is a "mixed being," that is, corporeal-spiritual, therefore his soul cannot have as an end a pure spirit, however he writes: "I believe that a soul feels the soul of others or other spirit with the interlude of the body and in the body."[23] In fact, an animated living body communicates to the other sensations different from those communicated by an inanimate body; in some communications between individuals, the philosopher affirms, there is "something living and spiritual," which cannot be attributed to matter alone. He also writes: "In love and friendship it seems that in the affection and union of bodies, the two souls themselves

---

19. Rosmini, *NE*, 2:233–34, paras. 692–94.
20. Rosmini, *NE*, 2:238, para. 696.
21. See Rosmini, *NE*, 2:242, para. 704.
22. Rosmini, *PY*, 2:237, para. 991.
23. Rosmini, *PY*, 2:237, para. 992.

feel and communicate."²⁴ This mode of affection no longer concerns only the bodily perception of oneself, of the other or of the external world, but it is a so-called "pneumatic" affection; a spiritual communication that according to Rosmini would even imply the possibility that angelic creatures made themselves sensitive to men, operating in their bodies.

What Is Affection for Stein?

Let us now see in what sense it is possible to speak of affection even within Stein's thought. To deal with this topic in Steinian philosophy, it is necessary first of all to refer to the research on the *Einfühlung*.²⁵ As is known, enteropathy is an *Erlebnis* that concerns the relationship with the other and therefore the human capacity to perceive other human beings as similar to us, that is, endowed with the same transcendental structure. In addition, important information on the theme of perception—of oneself, of others and of the outside world—can be found in the 1922 text, published in the fifth volume of the *Jahrbuch für Philosophie und phänomenologische Forschung*,²⁶ the first part of which is entirely dedicated to the study of the human body-psychic and spiritual dimension. The theme of affection is also particularly present in *Einführung in die Philosophie*,²⁷ a text written in the early twenties, but reworked later.

In her doctoral thesis, the philosopher tries to grasp the essence of empathic acts, through the sapient application of the phenomenological method and dwells on the psychophysical constitution of the subject, through the analysis of the body and the relationship with the "other," finally reaching its spiritual dimension. First, she examines the human perception of one's own body, since this is given to the subject in a very specific manner, that is, through an external perception, like any other material object, but also through an internal perception, which has nothing to do with the senses. We are faced with the well-known phenomenological distinction between *Körper*, that is, physical body occupying a given space, and *Leib*, that is, living body, or own body felt from within. Stein writes:

> Even if we close our eyes and stretch out our hands before us so that no limb touches another limb, so that we can neither grasp nor see our own body, even in this case we cannot be rid of it,

---

24. Rosmini, *PY*, 2:237, para. 992.
25. See Stein, *Sul problema dell'empatia* (On the problem of empathy).
26. See Stein, *Psicologia e scienze* (Philosophy of psychology and the humanities).
27. See Stein, *Introduzione alla filosofia* (Introduction to philosophy).

since even then it is inevitably present in its full "corporality of its own," and we find ourselves inextricably linked to it.[28]

Therefore, even trying to eliminate any type of external stimulus, the body is still felt by the subject, in fact the inner perception does not depend on the external perception of oneself. However, internal and external perception are closely linked, through sensations (*Empfindungen*). Just as Rosmini had described the soul capable of perceiving itself as sentient and as felt, Stein also examined the body just as the medium of external sensations, therefore as sentient, and at the same time as what is felt inwardly. The own body is defined by the phenomenologist as the place of the manifestation of sensations, such as pressure, pain, cold, heat, etc., which can be located in a "where" that is configured as "something" that fills a space. Therefore, the phenomenologist writes: "All these 'somethings', in which my sensations are manifested, are gathered together in a unity, the unity of my own body";[29] and she continues: "The own body is given (also) as a sentient body and the sensations are given on the own body."[30] According to Stein, the different body parts are "constituted" in me by virtue of sensations and can be considered more or less close to my ego; in this sense, the sensations are localized on my body. The torso is closer to me than the limbs, while the heart seems to coincide with my ego; the head also represents a central point of reference, in particular for sensations that do not have a corporal location.[31]

This peculiarity is evident not only in the state of stillness, but also during the movement, of the "sentient own body." In fact, it is "perceived" by the subject through sensations: "Now, as a completely new fact, moving in space presents the experience "I move," that is, the apperception of one's own movement built on multiple sensations, and this movement is completely different from the movement of the body perceived externally."[32] The movement that I see or perceive externally to me and the apperception of my movement, however, are also in a close dependence, in fact I intentionally grasp the movement of an external object that comes to meet me but, at the same time, this perception of the space world depends on the parts of my body suitable for this perceptual function. The "movement of the own body" is therefore configured as an apperception of the corporal own movement, but also as external perception, from the visual and tactile point of view. For example, if I raise an arm in front of my face, I feel my own

28. Stein, *Sul problema dell'empatia*, 126.
29. Stein, *Sul problema dell'empatia*, 126.
30. Stein, *Sul problema dell'empatia*, 129.
31. See Stein, *Introduzione alla filosofia*, 241, and *Sul problema dell'empatia*, 127.
32. Stein, *Sul problema dell'empatia*, 131.

movement and at the same time I see this member of my body in motion, rising before me.

The particular reality of the own body also implies the relationship with the outside, that is, with other bodies that, as we have said, produce stimuli in the subject. The reception of such stimuli is initially passive, as the individual is "affected" by the other material body, however the sensations received are subsequently felt and stimulate a reaction, which can be mechanical, but also voluntary and therefore conscious. This is the dimension that Edmund Husserl had defined as *hyletic* or sensitive. In this regard, in *Introduction to Philosophy*, Stein writes: The human body "possesses a quality that, as such, occupies all its extension, but which is not found in any simple spatial thing: sensitivity [*die Empfindsamkeit*], the ability to be a carrier of current sensations or—rather, distinguishing them from sensations not localized in a corporeal way such as sight and hearing data—of *physical sensations* [*Empfindnisse*]."[33] Like the fundamental feeling described by Rosmini, sensitivity also occupies the entire bodily extension of the subject and physical sensations are perceived as localized by the human being, who is able to "record them internally." This means that these sensations are real parts of consciousness and, although the subject lives them primarily in a "deaf and passive" way, at a later time they generate the perception (*Wahrnehmung*) of the external world, which instead is conscious and intentional.[34] After a first affection, that is, the reception by the living body of the stimulus of the thing with its qualities, consciousness recognizes the sensations and localizes them—for example the feeling warmth in a certain part of the body—and in this way distinguishes them from what has affected the sensory organs. This is possible because consciousness (*Bewusstsein*) is able to *take note* that something external has affected the sensory organs and this lived experience is so to speak "recorded" and restrained.[35] Therefore, the phenomenologist speaks of a flow of experiences (*Erlebnisstrom*) that characterizes the life of consciousness of the subject, that is, his inner life. Sensations are considered as immanent data inseparable from this flow;[36]

33. Stein, *Introduzione alla filosofia*, 162.

34. See Stein, *Introduzione alla filosofia*, 104: "In perception as in all acts in which something is grasped, the ego is directed towards a separate object (we indicate this moment as the intentionality of the lived experience); there is no intentionality of this type in the sensation, the subject is 'implicated' in a particularly unvoiced and passive way."

35. See Ghigi, *Etica fenomenologica*, 18–19: "This consciousness is therefore the diversifying element between the two types of extended body: unlike the merely physical and inanimate body, a living body is able to locate sensations, inasmuch as it previously possesses a consciousness, that is, an ability to recognize and retain the stimuli that stimulate its sensory organs and locate them in a specific part."

36. See Stein, *Introduzione alla filosofia*, 105: "If we mean by immanent everything

they make possible the perception in general,[37] therefore also that of the own body. In this sense, the impossibility of taking the sensation in isolation with respect to the perception of the sentient body is evident; in fact, Stein says: "What makes the link between sensation and perception of the own body particularly close lies in the fact that the own body is given as sentient and the sensations are given on the own body."[38]

This consideration of sensation from the side that concerns one's own body is particularly interesting also in relation to the Rosminian analysis of sensations, understood as modifications of the fundamental feeling.[39] In fact, the philosopher from Rovereto, as we have seen, affirms that all our sensations are extra subjective and subjective at the same time. Sensation concerns the sensory perception of an external body, but at the same time the perception of our body organ, which is possible as it is a modification of the body-fundamental feeling.

According to Stein, moreover, the specific reality of the living body is for the subject the "zero point of corporality," while the other bodies are located at a certain distance from it.[40] This pole consists of the corporeal, psychic and spiritual ego. From the analysis of the sensations inherent in the sensitive sphere, it is therefore necessary to move on to that of causality, which characterizes the human psychic dimension. This dimension includes the set of "vital states" (*Lebenzustand*), different and changeable, which follow one another in every real self: fatigue, vitality, visual sensation, tactile, etc.[41] We are faced with affections that, subsequently, are felt at the level of consciousness, that is, in the "vital feelings" (*Lebensgefühl*). However, there is not always correspondence between states and feelings, for example I can be tired, but experience a feeling of vitality and energy; in this case I will deceive myself about the content of the experience, because my feeling of freshness does not correspond to a real vital state of that kind. Or I may feel cold, even if there is not actually an external cold condition; this

---

that belongs inseparably to the life of consciousness, then we must consider the contents of sensation as immanent data."

37. See Stein, *Introduzione alla filosofia*, para. 4, "L'essenza delle sensazioni ed il loro significato per la percezione; la costituzione della cosa" [The essence of sensations and their meaning for perception; the constitution of the thing], esp. 104–7.

38. Stein, *Sul problema dell'empatia*, 129.

39. See Rosmini, *NS* 2, paras. 696 and 237.

40. See Stein, *Sul problema dell'empatia*, 127: "If I speak of distance with respect to 'me,' saying this is an inaccurate way of expressing myself: in fact it is not possible for me to ascertain that there is a distance from the ego due to the fact that the ego is devoid of space, it is not locatable; but I relate to the parts of my body, as well as all to the spatiality that lies outside of it, to a 'zero point of orientation' that my own body surrounds."

41. See Stein, *Psicologia e scienze*, 50–55.

means that I experience the sensation of cold, of which I am certainly aware, although the cold is not objectively present. These feelings, of an egological type the former and non-egological the latter, depend on what Stein calls the "life force" (*Lebenskraft*), that is, a persistent quality that is shown in vital feelings.[42] This force, which feeds the psychic life of the individual and is at the origin of changes and transformations,[43] approaches the Rosminian notion of "vital instinct," defined as that which produces the first and immediate feeling of self. This is what Rosmini writes: "The vital instinct tends to bring into being the greatest possible fundamental feeling";[44] it extends throughout the body and is linked to every bodily change that depends on the action of the soul.

According to Stein, it is not the experiences, of which I have immediate consciousness, that are subject to causality, but the vital states characterizing the psyche, which are transcendent with respect to conscious living. Causality concerns only psychic qualities, but it must also be specified that it is not a question of physical causality, since the life force is not a measurable datum, but is rather a quality.[45] Finally, according to Stein, the perceptual capacity that characterizes the human being in his relationship with the outside, also implies a conscious and voluntary reaction. The ego—says the philosopher— can open its spiritual gaze[46] to the outside and grasp its meaning. Therefore, from passive reception we move on to a different involvement of the ego, that is, to the taking of a position towards what has solicited its attention and, above all, to the choice of a certain reaction. This form of causality is not of a psychic type, since it is not an instinctive reaction, but we are faced with a spiritual and free attitude, guided by motivation.[47]

42. See Stein, *Psicologia e scienze*, 57: "The current state of my ego is presented in the vital feeling, its vital state and in the change of states a persistent quality is shown: the *life force*."

43. See Stein, *Psicologia e scienze*, 59: "The fact that the energies are supplied or taken away from the life force is the 'cause' of the psychic process; the effect consists in the change of the other psychic qualities."

44. Rosmini, *PY*, 4:12, para. 1785.

45. Ales Bello writes: "Causality, linked to the life force, is very different from the causality of which the physical sciences speak, because here the relationships are not predictable and are not measurable; in fact, it is not foreseeable what impulse may arise, therefore, it is a relationship of cause and effect to be understood in a qualitative and not quantitative sense" (*Assonanze e dissonanze*, 118).

46. Stein, *Psicologia e scienze*, 72.

47. See Ghigi, *Etica fenomenologica*, 30–31: "Thus if psychic reactivity presented an inevitable causality for the ego, from which the ego could not escape (one reacts to the stimulus of thirst by drinking, etc.), now the causal 'stance' is in the hands of the ego which, alone, has the possibility of moving and implementing a behavior. This form of causation is certainly not psychic, but spiritual. Its engine is not directly the world of things, but the motivation that they provoke, stimulating the ego to act."

PART 3

Affection and Intersubjectivity

Even in the intersubjective dimension, analyzed by Stein, these same passages can be distinguished, namely: affection, reaction and subsequent conscious awareness. The ego, in fact, is at first affected by the other, that is, it passively receives the sensations that arise from the encounter and, only later, welcomes them in a conscious way. Thanks to empathy, however, the relationship takes on a further meaning, as the subject is given the opportunity to "realize" the experience of others; the individual feels that the relationship with another human being is different from any other relationship. The ability to grasp, in a more or less conscious way, this particular proximity is the prerequisite of any encounter between individuals and relationality as a "lived experience" is described by the author in technical-phenomenological terms as "an act that is original as lived present, while it is unoriginal for its content."[48] This means that it is not possible to prove exactly what the other (content) feels, but only to understand its meaning (structure).

The encounter entails a first form of *Einfühlung* that is a sort of "proto-empathy"—as Nicoletta Ghigi defines it—as the affection of the other is the protagonist; subsequently it is possible to freely choose to grasp the experience of others in the originality in which it is offered, putting aside one's own representation.[49] Here the affection is an indispensable moment, even if not exclusive, in the process that leads to the understanding of the other. The transition from the passive to the active, conscious and free moment is equally fundamental since the interpersonal relationship is of a spiritual nature and therefore implies free choice.

In the description of intersubjectivity, proposed by Stein, the initial and immediate perceptual moment is highlighted which, as already mentioned, is constituted thanks to the physical sensations received of which the ego becomes aware. The "perception of the other," however, has a higher complexity than other types of perception in fact, in addition to the perception of the physical body, it implies the perception of a set of movements, which come from internal impulses; through this internal impulse "the physical body appears as an *animate* body, which possesses an active *vital center*."[50] From the outside it is not possible to feel or see the internal impulse of the other living being but, Stein writes: "I can intuit this vital

---

48. Stein, *Sul problema dell'empatia*, 77.
49. See Ghigi, *Etica fenomenologica*, 48.
50. Stein, *Introduzione alla filosofia*, 198.

process grasped in an empty way, even if with a *presenting consciousness*. We call this presenting consciousness . . . empathy [*Einfühlung*]."[51]

In these analyses highlight the complexity of the empathic act, which cannot be reduced to an external perception. The experience of empathy makes it possible to perceive the moods of the other, even if it is not an intellectual intuition but a sensitive intuition that needs the moment of affection. In fact, like anything external, the other also presents himself to me through affection; however, the impression he creates in me is different, because thanks to empathy I can grasp in an original way the structure of his experiences and perceive its content, which however remains unoriginal for me. As in the pneumatic sensitivity, described by Rosmini, we are faced with the faculty of feeling the other as a spiritual person and of receiving his feelings.

According to Stein, they are "the forms of the living body" that make it possible to grasp intuitively from the outside the living being as a spiritual person, endowed with an inner nucleus or center (*Kern*) and capable of free acts; she writes:

> When I look at a person in the eyes, then I immediately see his being an I, from the direction of the gaze is expressed the being regulated by the spirit, the turning to an object. . . . I also see the degree of his being awake or his tension, in the continuity of his gaze I see the continuity of his being spiritually regulated and in the restless wandering of the gaze the agitated wandering from one object to another. In addition, I see the whole scale of feelings, anger, joy and sadness, I see pride, goodness and nobility of soul, and I also see the "totally personal" way, in which this person is good, affectionate or unreliable. The vitality with which all this spiritual life invades me cannot be compared at all to the way in which sensitive data comes to me.[52]

It is not enough to be affected or passively touched by the other for us to speak of a real encounter, but this moment is necessary, since "the look, the expression, the facial features 'signify' what they 'express' and lead the gaze to their 'meaning.'"[53] There is therefore a deep connection between affection and intuition of the meaning that the expressive forms of the other

---

51. Stein, *Introduzione alla filosofia*, 199. A little further on, Stein explores the difference between original and presented experiences and, as regards *Einfühlung*, writes: "Now the *empathy*, as a presentification, it is an original experience, a present reality. What it presents, however, is not one's own past or future 'impression,' but a present and original vital movement that is not found in some continuous relationship with one's life and cannot be made to coincide with it" (200).

52. Stein, *Introduzione alla filosofia*, 207–8.

53. Stein, *Introduzione alla filosofia*, 208.

contain.[54] This does not exclude the possibility of deception into which, as Stein clearly points out, the subject who empathizes can fall,[55] yet the sensitive intuition of the other is an indispensable step, followed by the deliberate choice to look at the authentic emotional feeling of others in all its peculiarity and uniqueness. This choice is conscious and free, it springs from a reflection and can lead to an emotional involvement up to feelings of affection, friendship, love, etc. In this sense, Stein highlights the spiritual character of the will that guides the formation of relationships aimed at the realization of good. The encounter, made possible by mutual openness, leads the subjects in relation to wanting the good of the other. Reciprocal action, aimed at building good for oneself and for the other, or for others, is guided, according to the phenomenologist, by the ability to intuitively perceive the hierarchy of values thanks to *emotional intuition*.[56] In fact, the various feelings are inextricably linked to the hierarchical order of values and the ability to grasp the latter concerns the spiritual dimension of the subject. Every person is potentially able to perceive the axiological order and to recognize love at the top of it, however that doesn't mean that he will choose by his own action to respect this order.

The importance of the passive-affective moment in the intersubjective dimension is also underlined by Rosmini. In particular, he attributes the human possibility of grasping otherness in its bodily, psychic and spiritual dimensions to that particular capacity that he calls "inobjectivation" and of which he speaks in particular in *Theosophy*. An exhaustive analysis of this important issue would take us far from the path taken so far.[57] However, it is interesting to remember that Rosmini believes that thanks to subjective inobjectivation the human being is able to intuit that "the principle of the person is common and unique in all"[58]—that is, it is universal (although in each individual it remains incommunicable and personal)—and he continues: "If I see a man who suffers, or who enjoys, although I can deceive myself in imagining the degree or precise quality of his sufferings or his pleasures,

---

54. See Stein, *Introduzione alla filosofia*, 209: "The individuality of what is expressed in the soul is brought to light in the individuality of mimic expression."

55. See Stein, *Sul problema dell'empatia*, 189.

56. Stein takes up the theme of the hierarchy of values from Max Scheler's thought and refers explicitly to him, citing in particular *Formalism in Ethics and Non-Formal Ethics of Values*; see Stein, *Sul problema dell'empatia*, 208.

57. For further information on the subject, see, among others: Beschin, "Inoggettivazione in Antonio Rosmini"; Giannini, "Comunicazione come 'inoggettivazione'"; Pili, *Se l'uno è l'altro*.

58. Rosmini, *T*, 939, para. 872.

but I am not deceived to think that he suffers and that he enjoys."[59] As has already been noted,[60] this intuition is very close to some considerations that Stein explored in her doctoral thesis, where it is precisely the example of the pain of others that introduces the theme of the *Einfühlung*. The identification of the *Erlebnisse* that result from the reduction to the essence applied to the ego remains a specific novelty of phenomenology; however the particular act of enteropathy refers to the duplicity of the body, which, as we have seen, is also emphasized by Rosmini when he highlights the difference between the perception of pain from the outside and the inner sensation of those who are experiencing it.[61] This duplicity is evident in the perception of oneself, but also in the encounter with the other; in the case of the suffering of others—for example—I see from the outside the signs of his pain, but I intuit that it is not only the external perception of pain that allows me to realize it.

Sensations, which have as an effect physical affection, according to Rosmini, also have an important role in moral development up to the exercise of the will. In the pedagogical text "The Ruling Principle of Method Applied to Education," he dwells on affective volitions, characteristic of the first year of life, described as a first moment in the development of morality. They, he writes, derive instinctively (and not freely) from perception and, therefore, from what is sensitively pleasant or unpleasant. Through these volitions, in fact, the child wants the object he perceives without being able to judge it as good, but he wants it only because he sees it as pleasant.[62] With affective volition alone, it is possible to express the will, but it is still instinctual, since, according to the philosopher, without abstraction there is no judgment. In this first phase, there are sympathy and instinct of imitation, which we could define as "primitive affections," as the child wants without giving reason for what he wants and imitates without knowing that he is imitating. For example, writes Rosmini in his moral anthropology, to judge that a loaf of bread is good, and not simply to want to eat it, I must express a judgment, that is, I must have the specific idea of nutrition and know that that bread

---

59. Rosmini, *T*, 942, para. 874.

60. See also: Ales Bello, "Complessità e stratificazione"; Ales Bello, "Intersubjectivity"; Galvani, *Sguardo sull'umano*; Losacco, "Rosmini e Stein."

61. See Rosmini, *AAMS*, 50, para. 58.

62. Rosmini, RPMAE, para. 132: "The first movement of the will consists in those volitions, which we have called *affective* (*Antropologia morale*, paras. 612–16), in which the sensitive and volitional subject wants the perceived object without having judged it good, but only for having felt it pleasant: mysterious volitions and as difficult to understand as is intellectual perception."

is edible and nutritious.[63] Judgment is necessarily preceded by abstraction, which has its possibility in the intuition of the indeterminate ideal being. However, according to Rosmini, this intuition, constitutive of the human essence, becomes manifest in the individual gradually, together with his moral growth, giving rise to the capacity for judgment. Until the child develops language and capacity for introversion, he cannot access this "law," that is, the ideal plane, but his knowledge remains linked to the feeling, therefore to the sensitive reality and he will exercise only affective volitions.

The gradual moral development of the child goes hand in hand with that of the ability to know through abstraction,[64] so much so that the child in what Rosmini calls "third age," that is, from the first to the third year of life, begins to grasp in a semi-abstract way some concepts, such as beautiful, ugly, good, evil, etc. and appreciative volitions arise in him. In this phase of his growth the "norms behind which the child directs his affections take another form," and Rosmini continues: "This semi-abstract idea of beauty and goodness is the closest of ideas after the imaginals to objects: it is with a rule so close that it does not have to take a step to reach the object."[65] It is a question of a gradual approach to the objective order, which must then be recognized by the will. This passage takes place in a full way when the child has developed the appreciative volitions, which imply a judgment and therefore can be called moral.[66]

> That an intelligent being first perceiving and knowing another intelligent being rejoices and acts on the esteem and benevolence towards this being; this is certainly a moral thing. That an equally intelligent being, in whom this affection and this esteem was born should bow and bend to conform to the feelings, thoughts, and will of another intelligent being, as soon as he comes to know them, this too is entirely moral: because every act, which makes an intellectual will towards a being of equal intelligence is moral.[67]

Therefore, affective volitions, even if instinctual, are important for the development of relational capacity, since the sensitive perception of the

---

63. See Rosmini, *AAMS*, 314, para. 544.

64. See Rosmini, *AAMS*, 315, para. 546: "This appreciative volition takes on new forms as abstraction increases."

65. Rosmini, RPMAE, para. 209.

66. Having reached the fifth order of intellection, the child is able to act morally in fact, writes Rosmini: "This is the period in which his spirit passes from concrete moral principles to abstract moral principles or ideals" (Rosmini, RPMAE, para. 395).

67. Rosmini, RPMAE, para. 395.

good represents the initial and irreplaceable moment of voluntary motion. However, the full development of morality, which is exercised in relationships, requires the passage from the real to the ideal, or rather, the realization of the real through the ideal. This development can first be seen in the exercise of appreciative volitions and above all in those appreciative volitions, which make possible a voluntary and free choice, that is, a moral choice. Love, which according to Rosmini is the basis of morality,[68] is fully exercised only when the desired reality is loved by virtue of the ideal law, discovered by abstraction and in this case "the love of the real is not lacking, but regulated by the idea is always love of the realized idea; and yet he remains free, not locked up, not blind, not exclusive."[69]

We come, therefore, to what Rosmini calls rational affection, that is, that affection that is related to the intellectual and volitional principle. In fact, as already mentioned, the morality that is exercised in action and relationship cannot be conceived outside the relationship between real (feeling) and ideal (object). The first cause of human action—Rosmini notes—are internal affections, some of which belong to animal nature (anger, lust and all passions), others instead concern rationality.[70] The latter are based on the intuition of the value of objects: "Consider, therefore, that *love* and other rational affections always depend on our *estimate* of the value of objects, and that those affections are reasonable or unreasonable, according to whether the estimate that precedes them is true or false, is in conformity with their value, or is even different."[71]

Rosminian analysis of intersubjectivity, in its ethical-pedagogical implications, shows that the encounter between individuals consists of a first affective moment, or psychic as Stein would say, that is, the instinctive recognition of the other and the affection towards them, and a subsequent development of affection in an intellectual sense, which makes moral action. The moral order, which is gradually revealed to the child, consists in the awareness that what he has judged as good for himself is good for all human beings, by virtue of the objective order of beings. Therefore, the individual will be in the moral order when he is able to "evaluate all things *objectively*, to estimate them for what they are, and not for what they are relative to himself."[72] However, this moral necessity, which has the character

---

68. See Rosmini, RPMAE, para. 285: "So, in being intelligent, in the depths of nature, there is a such a primitive need to give esteem and love to any intelligent being known. This is the great fact, on which, as a very solid basis, all morality is founded."

69. Rosmini, RPMAE, 185, para. 243.

70. See Rosmini, *PMS*, 170–71.

71. Rosmini, *PMS*, 172.

72. See Rosmini, *AAMS*, 319, para. 561.

of *a natural law* and springs from the ideal being intuited, is not always realized in action, because the human being is capable of *free choice*.[73] As we have already seen, Stein also describes an objective order underlying the structure of reality, that is, a hierarchy of values that the human being intuits and that can guide his moral action. In fact, although this order is not necessarily consonant with the feelings to it gives rise to, since the human being is free to exercise his freedom even in an "irrational" way,[74] Stein speaks of an ideal correlation between intuition of values, related feelings, and moral action:

> Here essential relationships are revealed between the hierarchy of values, the in-depth ordering of axiological feelings and the stratifications of the person that are revealed in them. So, *every step forward in the realm of values is simultaneously an achievement in the realm of one's personality*. This correlation makes possible a rational legality of feelings, their anchoring in the ego and a decision in this area on what is "right" or "wrong."[75]

Bibliography

Ales Bello, Angela. *Assonanze e dissonanze. Dal diario di Edith Stein*. Milan: Mimesis, 2021.

———. "Complessità e stratificazione dell'essere umano: a proposito di antropologia e psicologia. Un confronto fra Antonio Rosmini e Edith Stein." In *Ontologia, fenomenologia e nuovo umanesimo*, edited by Fernando Bellelli and Emanuele Pili, 111–26. Rome: Città Nuova, 2016.

———. "Intersubjectivity in Husserl, Stein and Rosmini: Community and Society." *Rosmini Studies* 5 (2018) 251–64.

Beschin, Giuseppe. "L'inoggettivazione in Antonio Rosmini." *Rivista Rosminiana* 69 (1975) 43–75.

Galvani, Martina. *Uno sguardo sull'umano. Antropologia e metafisica in Antonio Rosmini e Edith Stein*. Rome: Tab, 2020.

Ghigi, Nicoletta. *L'etica fenomenologica di Edith Stein*. Rome: Fattore Umano, 2021.

---

73. This free act, writes Rosmini, "falls only into those appreciative volitions in which there are several objects before our souls, to each of which we give a certain value. Then, since we cannot have them all, let us choose one of them" (Rosmini, *AAMS*, 328, para. 580).

74. For example, writes Stein, "one who, for the loss of his own patrimony, is 'overwhelmed,' that is to say, one who is affected in the most intimate part of his ego, feels in an 'irrational' way and overturns the hierarchy of values, that is, he generally lacks the *emotional intuition* with regard to higher values and lacks correlative personal strata" (Stein, *Sul problema dell'empatia*, 208).

75. Stein, *Sul problema dell'empatia*, 208.

Giannini, Giorgio. "La comunicazione come 'inoggettivazione' in Rosmini." *Rivista Rosminiana* 78 (1984) 209–24.
Losacco, Luigi. "Rosmini e Stein: '*Einfühlung*' e '*inoggettivazione*.'" *Rivista Rosminiana* 84 (1990) 353–67.
Pili, Emanuele. *Se l'uno è l'altro. Ontologia e intersoggettività in Antonio Rosmini*. Bari, It.: Pagina, 2020.
Rosmini, Antonio. *Antropologia in servizio della scienza morale*. Edited by François Evain. ENC 24. Rome: Città Nuova, 1981.
———. "Del principio supremo della Metodica." In *Scritti pedagogici*, edited by Fernando Bellelli, ENC 32, 37–364. Rome: Città Nuova, 2019.
———. *Nuovo Saggio sull'origine delle idee*. Edited by Gaetano Messina. 3 vols. ENC 3–5. Rome: Città Nuova, 2003–2004.
———. *Principi della scienza morale*. Edited by Umberto Muratore. ENC 23. Rome: Città Nuova, 1999.
———. *Psicologia*. Edited by Vincenzo Sala. 4 vols. ENC 9, 9/A, 10, 10/A. Rome: Città Nuova, 1988–1989.
———. *Teosofia*. Edited by Samuele F. Tadini. Milan: Bompiani, 2011.
Stein, Edith. *Introduzione alla filosofia* [Introduction to philosophy]. Translated by Anna Maria Pezzella. Rome: Città Nuova, 2001.
———. *Psicologia e scienze dello spirito* [Philosophy of psychology and the humanities]. Translated by Anna Maria Pezzella. Rome: Città Nuova, 1999.
———. *Sul problema dell'empatia* [On the problem of empathy]. Translated by Elio Costantini and Erika Schulze Costantini. Rome: Studium, 2014.

14

Affection of *Cognition* in the Method and Methodology of Antonio Rosmini

FERNANDO BELLELLI

Introduction

IN THIS CONTRIBUTION I will delve into the topic I intend to address, recognizing that it can be an opportunity to present a synthesis of the current state of my research, and on this synthesis to graft a specific development through the increase of a focal aspect: (1) in a specific theoretical sense of philosophy of education and general (and social) pedagogy, a real vital nucleus, in which, with Rosmini and starting from Rosmini, the elaboration of the pertinent *juridical* pedagogy is placed;[1] (2) in a special, experimental and clinical pedagogical sense (in a special and nonspecific sense),[2] a possible perspective of dialogue with multiple approaches of pedagogy, also practiced, in which the epistemological criteria focused on the aforementioned vital nucleus can be applied and applied.

---

1. On this subject, see Bellelli, *Percorsi storici*.
2. For the foundation of clinical pedagogy as specific pedagogy see Sola, *Introduzione alla Pedagogia clinica*.

In the first part of this contribution I offer, therefore, a reasoned and articulated perspective on the connections of the definitions that Rosmini gives of the concepts of method and methodology, *affection* and *cognition*[3]—not only in pedagogical terms, but also in philosophical, theological, juridical, and political terms[4]—and, in the second part, I emphasize what is the approach on the basis of which I would consider that it can be fruitful today—not only "inside" the context of the "Rosminian question,"[5] but also outside of it[6]—to propose Rosmini's pedagogy in the circles of scientific research, specifically in the educational sciences, with significant usefulness and relevance.

Philosophical Ethics and Moral Philosophy's "Heart" of Method and Methodology: Moral Logic and Pedagogy

The versatility of Rosminian thought is such that, in his genius, he was able, not only to treat with scientific correctness and competence more than one discipline of knowledge—philosophy, pedagogy, theology, law, and politics, as well as, to varying degrees, the mathematical[7] and experimental[8] sciences—but also, and in a certain sense *litteram*,[9] to determine and elaborate—with all the limits due to the contextualization in the degrees of advances and scientific discoveries of his time[10]—epistemological and theoretical devices to all effects inter-multi-trans-disciplinary.

    3. I first dealt with the subject in Bellelli, "Rosmini, il trascendentale."

    4. On these disciplines and their interaction mainly from the pedagogical point of view see Bellelli, *Pedagogia del sapere*.

    5. On this subject I refer to De Giorgi, *Scuola italiana di spiritualità*, and Bellelli: "Quattro fasi"; "Genesi e ricezione"; *Rosmini e l'educazione*.

    6. See Bellelli, "Ricezione statunitense di Rosmini." One of the most significant "frontier" contexts between what is internal to the "Rosminian question" and what is external to it is, with its own pedagogical focus, the one elaborated by Vincenzo La Via; see La Via, *Coscienza e libertà*. See also the very significant monographic journal issue *Metafisica e pedagogia*.

    7. See Rosmini, *Equazione dell'appagamento*.

    8. One of the admirers and popularizers of Rosmini's thought was Antonio Stoppani, who also applied it in particular to the empirical sciences; on the subject see: Zanoni, *Scienza, patria, religione*; Galluzzi, *Galileo Rosmini Darwin*; Galati, *Galileo and Rosmini*; Bellelli, "Rosmini e l'epistemologia"; Bellelli, "Teodicea rosminiana del verum/factum e teoria." Rosmini's expertise in medical sciences is well known; for example, see Pangallo: *Antonio Rosmini* and *Rosmini e il fallimento*.

    9. See Bellelli and Gabbi, *Profezia e attualità*.

    10. Consider, for example, of the fact that Rosmini lives and before S. Freud elaborated (and spread) the cornerstones of the theory and practice of experimental

In this paragraph I intend to focus on the description of Rosmini's pedagogical epistemology, keeping in the background and indicating the mutual connections of pedagogy with the other knowledge he dealt with. This operation is not to be considered misleading, imprecise, vague, inappropriate or generic, as not only in Rosmini "everything is valid," but to better understand some specific aspects, in this case pedagogical, it is also necessary to keep in mind how they are connected by Rosmini with other knowledge, even more so when the epistemological question is dealt with. As mentioned in the introductory paragraph, Rosmini's pedagogy can be "framed": (1) in the current scientific and academic context, as a philosophy of education (within which *specific* pedagogies are concretized, such as, for example, legal pedagogy), also defined as general (and social) pedagogy; (2) in the current scientific and academic context, since in Rosmini's work, in differentiated mode and measure, almost all of what are now called "special pedagogies" are embryonically present, in particular experimental pedagogy.

The articulation of the relationship between Rosmini's pedagogy as a philosophy of education and as experimental pedagogy has its fulcrum in the relationship between the method (philosophical) and the methodology (in this case the pedagogical one, both general and experimental). The intrinsic ethical-moral constitutiveness in Rosmini of the fulcrum that connects the method (philosophical) and the methodology (in this case the pedagogical one, both general and experimental) is undoubtedly attributable to the synthesism of the three forms of being (ideal, real and moral) and to the primality between them (which is not primacy) of the moral form.[11]

In fact, when Rosmini has to define the method, he makes a premise and refers the method to the question of logic and moral good. In fact, he affirms:

> When, therefore, in a given state or act of man there will be moral good? And on the contrary, when will there be evil? What rules will we see in making a right judgment on this? In the former there is a general rule that all others understand and that is like the principle of moral *logic*: it is the following: *The moral good results from the union of three elements, will, norm, relationship. If only one of these elements is missing, the moral order cannot be fulfilled; there can be neither good nor evil.* Therefore:

---

psychology and psychoanalysis, and before C. Darwin elaborated (and spread) the cornerstones of the theory of evolution.

11. See Bellelli, *Etica originaria*.

it must be judged to be the moral order, when it will be ascertained that all three elements are found in the fact: then it must be judged to be the moral good, when the relationship between the will and the law is of *conformity: then one must judge there to be moral evil, when the relationship between the will and the law is of nonconformity.*[12]

The ethical-moral question for Rosmini is traced back to the question of logic. In the synthesism of the three forms of being one can and must grasp that and how the objectivity of ethics and morality, which is found in the ideal form of being, can and must be understood in and by the subjectivity of ethics and morals, which can be found in the moral form of being: affection, as I illustrate in the following paragraphs, probing the synthesism of the three forms of being starting from the real being, It becomes cognition (preparatory to reflection and judgment) after becoming intellectual affection and volition (appreciative and appreziative), after which, therefore, the real form of being has entered into synthesism with the ideal form first and then the moral form. Continuing to question Rosmini about the method we are enlightened as follows:

> By the word Method we mean the order that is given to the various operations of the mind necessary for the intent of similar reasoning to achieve it. From which definition we gather: 1. that not every intent of the man who reasons is the purpose of the Method but that which is proper to reasoning itself which always has truth as its purpose; 2. that the intent of reasoning can be considered in a more general or more special way and yet if we want to classify the methods according to the intentions, they are many, how many intentions proper to the reasoning there may be, and more or less general methods according to the more or less general intentions.[13]

The definition of methodology that Rosmini gives is a specification of what is expressed above:

> The formula that expresses the teaching method in general and that forms the supreme principle of the methodology is therefore the following: "Let us present to the mind of the child (and it can be said in general of man) first the objects that belong to the first order of intellections, then the objects that belong to the second order of intellections, then those of the third and so on, so that it never happens that one wants to lead the child to

12. Rosmini, *Compendio di etica* (Compendium of ethics), para. 160.
13. Rosmini, *Logica* (Logic), para. 750.

make an intellection of the second order without first having ascertained, that his mind made the intellections to the respective ones, of the first order, and the same is observed with the intellections of the third, the fourth, and the other higher orders."[14]

In a certain sense, therefore, it is true that we can understand method and methodology as synonyms: method and methodology *are* synonymous, but it is also true that, when Rosmini defines the methodology, we can say that the difference between method and methodology is experienced in the relationship that exists between logic and morality. Precisely because the methodology comes to give epistemological specification to pedagogy as a science.

Here we encounter the controversy, in which the cultural history of the reception of Rosminianism, also in a pedagogical sense, has strongly debated (and continues to debate) whether pedagogy is as such a philosophy or whether it has, even in Rosmini, an epistemological status of its own.[15] To all intents and purposes, it can be said that, in Rosmini's work, pedagogy is constituted as a method having its specificity precisely in in the definition that he offers, the way he understands the methodology, with regard to which definition it is necessary to focus on the theme of intelligence, where Rosmini states: "The objects that belong to the orders of intellection are represented to the mind of the child."[16] This operation and activity of representing to the child's mind—and the act of representing as such—is closely connected with the dimension, reality, and dynamics of the imagination.[17]

---

14. Rosmini, RPMAE, para. 80, which is preceded by para. 79: "Having thus discovered the immutable order of human intellections, we have also discovered in them the solid foundation on which we can erect the *Teaching method*. This method becomes natural and invariable as natural and invariable is the foundation on which it rests, that is, the law indicated constitutive of human intelligence. This method is precise and very clear: he is unique: because all the good methods invented so far are reduced to him, they are only partial views of him. or means to implement it, and all the methods that oppose ours are bad."

15. In particular, it is the Gentilian interpretation and neo-idealism-Neo-actualism who would argue that pedagogy, even in Rosmini, would be exclusively attributable to his philosophy. There is, on the other hand, a history of the reception of Rosminianism, which reaches up to Fulvio De Giorgi, who maintains that it is also possible to find in Rosmini the coexistence of a perspective at least complementary to and/or integrative of the Gentilian one; see Bellelli, "Vlijanie Rozmini."

16. Rosmini, RPMAE, para. 80. Rosmini uses precisely the verb *represent*, which, as I indicate in the last paragraph, constitutes a solid and valid point of contact between the Rosminian pedagogical perspective and the epistemological approach of the cognitive-behavioral psycho-pedagogical sciences.

17. On the subject of imagination, I would like to refer to Bellelli, "Rosmini e l'immaginazione divina."

Imagination, in fact, and, in it, representation, are characteristics proper to the moral form of being, and, from the pedagogical point of view, belong unequivocally to methodology as a practical and experimental dimension of pedagogy: imagination and representation, therefore, attest eminently that pedagogy, as such, is not totally attributable to philosophy understood as pure theoretical speculation.[18]

As the title of this paragraph states, from what has been explained it is clear that the epistemological structure of Rosminian pedagogy, both as a philosophy of education and as an experimental pedagogy, is configured through the connection between the Rosminian methodology and the (philosophical-theological) method: it is the ethical-moral method (in turn in connection with the juridical-political method) of Rosminian theoresis that acts as a frontier and epistemological ridge without which the epistemological status of Rosminian pedagogy is not comprehensible.

The Trans-Disciplinary Epistemology of "Synthesism within Synthesism" of Affection, Intellection, Volition, and the Specificity of Cognition Expressed by Affection in Reflection

In this paragraph we focus on the description of the terms indicated in the title of this contribution, to explain how the direction of highlighting the autonomy of pedagogy in Rosmini can be considered interesting and viable, not for a conflict with philosophy and with the other knowledge that Rosmini deals with, but to propitiate just the opposite.[19] When we enter into the Rosminian definition of methodology, in fact, understanding methodology as a science distinct from method, which *iuxta propria principia* is also a disciplinary specification of the method, to which is added the *art* of imagining and representing, Rosmini places us before the need to understand in depth what *intellections* are.

To understand what Rosmini means by the term *intellection*, necessarily addressing his works in a comparative way, it is necessary to grasp what *synthesism* within *synthesism* is.[20] It must be understood that it is possible to identify an isomorphism, that is, a similarity of forms, between the forms of being that Rosmini identified and elaborated in his theoresis—ideal,

---

18. Addressing the question of the nature of philosophy and the debate on the relationship between theoretical philosophy and practical philosophy transcends the scope of this contribution.

19. See on these aspects my PhD thesis in humanities at the University of Modena and Reggio Emilia, "Filosofia e pedagogia."

20. See Bellelli, "Importanza degli ordini."

real, and moral—and, correspondingly, the intellections, affections, and volitions. That is, to the *ideal* being correspond the *intellections*, to the real being correspond the *affections*, to the *moral being* correspond the *volitions*. *Affections*, *intellections* and *volitions*, in other words—compared to the *real*, *ideal* and *moral* being—are forms, to use an image, like Russian matryoshkas: nesting one "inside" the other. The *affection*, therefore, is "inside" the real being (just as the *intellection* is "inside" the *ideal* being and the *volition* is "inside" the *moral* being) and at the same time it is its emergence, that is, the point of manifestation, that through which the *real* form of being is expressed precisely in its propitiating the in-existence, that is, the insession, the synthesism of a form of being, in this case the real being, with the other two. The "synthesism within synthesism" of affection, intellection and volition, implies two other realities, which are precisely cognition and reflection. Proceeding with order, some definitions are offered that have been selected with a view to propitiating an overall overview (which, among other things, can also act as a potential connector between the various disciplinary areas of the conference in which this contribution was presented).

We start from affection because, to understand what intellections (which are mentioned in the definition of methodology) are, it is important to understand how for Rosmini in the conscientiousness of the human person the intellection cannot be formed without first being solicited by an affection. Affection is what belongs to the essence of reality and, to the essence of anthropological reality, to the fundamental feeling: the fundamental feeling in synthesism with the intuition of the idea of being, in other words, what is inherent in the reality of being and that in the formative, educational and didactic dynamics activates the ability of the intellect to learn things, therefore to determine apprehensions and to elaborate abstracts.

Two definitions of affections have been selected:

> The legitimate affections that bind men together are classified comfortably into two series: some are native, or spontaneous, others aroused. The former are calm and constant, the latter vehement and subject to mutation; of those, man has almost no conscience, but they suddenly arise at times, let us say when the dear object of his habitual affections is endangered. It is then that he begins to feel that he loves; the thought of the contrary, the fear of loss, draws its reflection on itself, and makes him vividly aware of what he has, with the comparison of what he may no longer have. Spontaneous affections are therefore the foundation and root of the aroused ones. That if the affections aroused are not founded spontaneously, if they are not a development and a greater implementation of these; they succeed

like a flash in the pan, or they are bastards, hypocrites, spurious children of selfishness, not of the great faculty of loving which is the demure mother of all true affections.[21]

In the second definition Rosmini expresses himself as follows:

> 33. We call *affection* the way in which the will unites itself with its subjects, that is, with known entities. Wherefore, the good of the will and its acts consists in distributing its affection to the various known entities in proportion and according to the order of their entity. 34. And since the good of the will is called honest good, therefore the honest good consists in this, that the order of the affection of the will corresponds to the order of being, the object proper to that power and its acts.[22]

From these two definitions it can be deduced that: (1) the dynamics of affection implies the need for specific training, education and instruction for its retrieval and for its effective and incremental development; (2) the dynamics of affection is not only from being real to being moral passing through being ideal, but also, synthesistically, from being moral to being real passing through being ideal (as well as, in the hypothesis that is not considered here but only indicated, from being moral to being ideal passing through being real, and vice versa).

The cruciality of intellection in these dynamics implies that it is necessary to focus on the definition of intellection given by Rosmini: "I call *intellection* every act of the mind, whether it has completed an idea, either alone, or with another joint thing, or one of its modes."[23] The completion of that act of the mind which is *the intellection* can therefore be both an *affection* and a *volition* (or, as I indicate below, a *cognition* and a *reflection*). Let us verify how Rosmini describes the fact that the intellection of an affection becomes a volition, providing below one of the main definitions that he offers of volition:

> There are therefore three kinds of acts of reflection: there is a kind of reflection, which is nothing but an immobile contemplation on things already known; this neither produces new cognition, nor is it a volition: there is a kind of reflection that analyses, unites, and integrates the things cognited; this produces new cognition, but it is not a volition: there finally is a kind of reflection, which in the time that it looks at a cognitive object,

---

21. Rosmini, *Filosofia del diritto* (Philosophy of law) 2, para. 1000.
22. Rosmini, *Compendio di etica*, paras. 33–34.
23. Rosmini, *NE* 2, para. 505.

willingly draws pleasure from it, enjoys it, enjoys that delight that redundant in being intelligent, when it *fully recognizes* the good of cognitive things, not putting obstacles, indeed promoting in itself this delight, and abandoning oneself to it or lending oneself to that pleasant action, which everything well liked in the mind causes; snd this is a *volition*.²⁴

In this quotation given regarding volition, described as a result of reflection, since, in any case, synthesistically, reflection is also a result of volition, the other two words of which it is necessary to give a definition also resound: cognition and reflection. As has already been illustrated and argued, there can be no intellection in action if there is no affection (in action), so there can be no volition (in action) if there is no intellection (in action). There are many types of volition—Rosmini, among other things, distinguishes between appreciative and *appreziative*—in any case, it is found that volition is a reality that then produces cognition and reflection.

We read Rosmini, and we are faced with a crucial passage of the synthetic restitution of these very significant aspects of his thought, as can be clearly seen from the previous quote, precisely distinguishes volition from cognition. For Rosmini, in fact, cognition and the principle of cognition are the architrave, the fulcrum of his entire open system of truth and his thought. When Rosmini must define what cognition is, he defines it in *Theosophy (Teosofia)*:

> The act that is aroused in the principle of the ideal term is the cognitive, the effect of which is a disposition or habit of the subject called cognition. Nothing would prevent cognition from being counted among the feelings, but since it is totally different from all the feelings that have space as their basis, it is not customary to use such a name, lest it appear that it has something in common with them, is a kind of them. The idea is essentially an object, the cognitive act and the resulting cognition belongs to the subject. Therefore, the source of the error of subjectivism, which does not distinguish cognition from idea, and due to this confusion of two such distinct entities, attributes to the idea the subjective character of cognition and of the cognitive act and however considers it as a production of the subject.²⁵

This definition, combining and composing the historical-cultural reading with the chrono-theoretical²⁶ one of Rosmini's thought, is to be

24. Rosmini, *PMS*, 121.
25. Rosmini, *T*, para. 2378.
26. See Tadini, "Interpretazione 'crono-teoretica.'"

considered very interesting, since, in this perspective of analysis, it is clearly grasped that Rosmini is not an a priori enemy of sensism and does not reject the question of sensitivity as something that authorizes abstractionism and legitimizes idealism, rather, Rosmini is able to offer a perspective of theoretical and pedagogical balance also pertinent in the contemporary debate on the subject.[27]

Rosmini defines the principle of cognition thus: "The principle of cognition means that intelligence conceives in everything only the being or an act of being, and therefore that a thing can be thought of as much it has to be"[28] and "an antecedent principle, which I call the *principle of cognition* and I express in this proposition: 'The object of thought is being or the entity.'"[29]

This is the point of the argument that is put forward to introduce the Rosminian definition of reflection. For Rosmini, reflection is defined as follows: "The faculty of applying the idea of being to our cognitions and their objects."[30]

> There are therefore three kinds of acts of reflection: namely, there is a kind of reflection, which is nothing but an immovable contemplation of things already known; this neither produces new cognition, nor is it a volition: there has a kind of reflection that analyses, unites, and integrates the things known. This produces new cognition, but it is not a volition: there finally has a kind of reflection, which in the time that looks at a cognitive object, willingly draws pleasure from it, enjoys it, enjoys that delight that redundant in being intelligent, when *it fully recognizes the good of things understood.*[31]

It is therefore necessary to distinguish between *intellection* and reflection, and it is *cognition* that allows us to grasp how an account is the idea, which we can bring back to understanding, but one thing is reflection (which, moreover, allows us to move from one order of reflection to another). For Rosmini, in fact, the conscience of man is formed when there is a speculative judgment of a practical judgment at least of the second order of reflection. Reflection, therefore, is able to recompose cognition in such a way that the correspondence between the being of the subject and the being of reality is well understood. "A distinction should therefore be made

27. See Sequeri, *Sensibile e l'inatteso*.
28. Rosmini, *Logica*, para. 340.
29. Rosmini, *NE*, para. 565.
30. Rosmini, *PY* 2, para. 1182.
31. Rosmini, *PMS*, 121.

between the order of cognitions, and the order of the real. In our minds real objects are not, if it is not their cognition. The order, therefore, of cognitions and ideas precedes the order of real objects. It is therefore advisable to move from the problem of the validity of cognitions, before reasoning on any real object, even if it is the same absolute."[32]

At the end of the paragraph, it is useful to resume the definition and analysis of affection, precisely because it allows us to grasp and underline why we have chosen to focus in this contribution on the topic of the affection of cognition. Affection of cognition means that synthesism must not be considered only in the direction that goes from affection to reflection through intelligence, volition, and cognition, but must also be considered in the other sense, that is, in the direction that goes from reflection to cognition, volition, intellection and affection. This is precisely because the amative knowledge of which Rosmini speaks, which is the main and specific object of pedagogy, is such that cognition is able to distribute in an orderly way, through affections to each entity of reality, the affection that belongs to it.

When one has represented—through the exercise of imagination as a triadic and Trinitarian expression of the moral form of being—to the mind of the child the intellection of the corresponding order of intellection which the child is able to perform corresponding to the level of formation of his mind, it is possible to do this not only because one has derived intellection from affection, but also because the effect of reflection, which has produced a cognition such as to generate a volition (which synthesizes from the moral being towards the ideal being and from the ideal being towards the real being), through the intellection, distributes-recognizes to the affection of reality (both intra-subjective and extrasubjective) the order and the degree of being that corresponds to the interiority of the person and to the reality of things (animate or inanimate) that the person knows and with which he relates (possibly also in terms of unobjectification).[33]

This is why I believe that to all intents and purposes we can speak of an affective turning point not only of metaphysics but also of the humanities in Rosmini, because he emphasizes the capacity of the amative dimension as an essential cognitive coefficient for formation, for education, to allow the person to know, to understand, to be formed and to be educated. The *affection* of cognition, therefore, within the dynamics of synthesism within the *synthesism* of the natural order and the supernatural order of being and knowing (and of the orders of reflection), should be understood not only in

---

32. Rosmini, *NE* 3, para. 1408.
33. See Pili, "Vivacissima quiete."

the sense of the objective genitive, that is, in the sense that affection (intellectual and volitional) is the object of *cognition*, but also and above all in the sense of the subjective genitive, that is, in the sense that the affection (reflected) is a subject capable of structuring cognition precisely in connotative as well as denotative terms of cognition itself, so that from the reflected affection volitional and intellectual cognitions are generated capable of joining in love the conscious being of the person with the being in all its forms of existence/act of being and essence.

Focus on the Possible Fruitful Interactions between Rosminian Pedagogy in the Perspective of the Affection of Cognition and Contemporary Orientations in the Educational Sciences

The contemporary scientific debate in the field of humanities, and educational sciences in particular, is very articulated, differentiated and complex, which is why, given the limited nature of this contribution, I limit myself to expressing three examples of possible concrete applications of the interactions that can be developed between Rosminian pedagogy and the contemporary orientations of these disciplines. The entry point in this regard, from the Rosminian side, is constituted by the real being, perspective of approach to the synthesistic consideration of affection (which, in the Rosminian opus is real, ideal, and moral *affection*, both in being triadic and in being Trinitarian): it is the real form of being, in fact, to act as a connector that allows, on the one hand, to effectively access the understanding of the thought of Rosmini, and, on the other hand, to indicate in an objective and open way what in all respects can be a fertile and fruitful meeting ground and epistemological dialogue between pedagogical perspectives, which, at times, are exposed to the temptation to transform differences into conflictually irreconcilable, which, rather than divergences, are differences (in most cases even complementary).[34] On the contemporary side, therefore, I

---

34. This perspective, in particular, is very compatible with the phenomenological orientation: see for example in the continuation of this paragraph, in fact, how Edith Stein deals with the theme of affections in a phenomenological-metaphysical way compatible with the way in which Rosmini treats it, in addition to the fact that there is convergence in the intervention of Martina Galvani and related report to the conference, which is published in this volume. On Rosmini and phenomenology, see Bellelli and Pili, *Ontologia, fenomenologia*. This perspective of analysis of Rosmini's thought in terms of the relationship between *affection* and *cognition* is also very fruitful; see for example how these topics are dealt with embryonically always in this paragraph, even with the dimension of cognitivism-behaviorism and structuralism.

focus on three of the main orientations among those developed in the field of educational theories: the cognitive-behavioral, the phenomenological, and the structuralist. In addition to these three areas, in a transversal way, I address, in both an emblematic and exemplary way, the theme of language and the theme of education (*Bildung*).[35]

With regard to the point of view of the *affection* of cognition in Rosmini and the presence of this theme in the cognitive-behavioral line,[36] we can identify convergences that can be argued and verified, and that would really propitiate, for example, also the comparison between Rosmini's perspective and organismic models in the pedagogy of *cognition*. It is the representation, by way of example, that allows us to explain the synthesistic passage from affection to cognition, highlighting that *cognition* is a *cognitive affection* capable of representation: it is *representation*, in fact, one of the cardinal points and one of the theoretical foundations at the base of cognitive sciences. As already pointed out in the preceding paragraphs, representation—in the broadest and most complex and articulated channel of *imagination*—is also one of the main elements of the theoretical structure and application of the Rosminian supreme principle of the Method. Rereading Rosmini's pedagogy in the light of cognitive science concepts such as cognition and *consciousness*[37] is an interesting and significant research horizon, which has its characteristic of novelty precisely in finding the affective dimension intrinsic to cognition: the fact that *cognition* is such because it is capable of *affection*—and all this not only in a passive-receptive sense but also and especially in an active-applicative sense—seems to all intents and purposes to be an interesting and significant scientific element of the learning and development process of the mind not only in progress recently identified by cognitive sciences (also in a bio-neuro-scientific perspective), but also within Rosminian pedagogy, and in the process of first effective enhancement by the critical literature concerning Rosmini's thought and the "Rosminian question."

Rosmini's perspective on the affection of *cognition* is also able to interact with the phenomenological line, with even terminological correspondences precisely on the word affection, as can be found in the following quote from Nicoletta Ghigi, an expert scholar of Edith Stein:

---

35. On the subject of *Bildung* see Gennari, *Dalla paideia classica*; Gennari, *Eidos del mondo*; Gennari, *Interpretare l'educazione*; Gennari, *L'educazione estetica*; Gennari and Sola, *Logica, linguaggio e metodo*; Sola, *Formazione originaria*.

36. Stella, *Cognizione e coscienza*.

37. On the theme of consciousness in Rosmini and in the context of postmodernity see Bellelli, *Etica originaria*.

Precisely in his reaction with a "realization," a new possibility is offered for the Ego: he can understand what happens in the other. *That* is, it can glimpse something of the other's world, and thus pass from a proto-empathy in which affection is the protagonist, to the *choice* to look at the experience of others in the original nature in which it is offered, leaving aside its own representation, simply putting it in brackets. *From becoming merely spontaneous (reactively almost exclusively psychic), it is therefore possible to reach an awareness of the object of what one realizes* (the *life* of the other and thus establish a genuinely empathic bond with the other.[38]

The leading role of affection in the thought of E. Stein undoubtedly deserves some deepening, in turn to be compared with those in place regarding the presence of the theme of affection in Rosmini. From this simple example it can be deduced that the commonality of the meeting ground between Rosmini's thought and phenomenology,[39] in particular that of Stein, is motivated by the metaphysical tension present in both these authors, metaphysical tension with which the first anticipated, in a certain sense and in its own way, the modern phenomenology inaugurated by E. Husserl, and the second entered it.

In the structuralist psycho-pedagogical field,[40] the integration of developmental models can foresee a significant comparison between Heinz Werner's theory of orthogenesis and development, with Henri Wallon's theory of act to thought and with Jean Piaget's theory of intelligence and adaptation. In this context, the *affection* of *cognition* can constitute a pertinent and significant criterion, since it makes it possible to contribute to the elaboration of an epistemological paradigm of the relationship between the psychological sciences and the pedagogical sciences, such that the importance of sensible experience on the one hand and that of the mental structures of knowledge and data processing on the other hand can find a fruitful articulation with the theories of which above, by virtue of the fact that, in Rosmini's approach, the more one enters pragmatically into the concreteness of reality, the more one experiences a rigorous and harmonious, non-extrinsic, openness to a transcendence that does not dehumanize and alienate the human person, but gives him the sense of the excess of fulfillment.

38. Ghigi, *Etica fenomenologica*, 48.

39. The common reference of both Rosmini and Stein is Thomas Aquinas. A comparison between Rosmini and phenomenology is possible not only through Edith Stein; see Vecchiet, *Dall'essere alla persona*.

40. See Rizzardi, *Modelli organismici in pedagogia*.

Rosmini's philosophical-pedagogical elaboration is also able to interact with the themes and issues that concern language,[41] especially in contemporary debate. Language, for Rosmini, is born, in fact, when the sound of the word, that is, of the vocal expression, associates a sound emission as affection with an operation of the mind as an intellection (which for Rosmini we have seen consist in the conjunction of an act of the mind with another entity, in this case the sound emission): language is the return of the sound affection received through a further sound emission that has transformed the sound in the expression of an abstract mental concept: that is, from reflection a cognition is formed which, through a deliberative volition, gives the supersensible intellection of the concept a sensitive affection constituted precisely by the word (sound is an affection that expresses an intellection). This dynamic of language would be further deepened, in any case the question is undoubtedly posed in a pertinent way and capable of arousing interest and relevance for scientific study.[42]

Deepening the European and American perspective of *Bildung* and *Neobildung*[43] in the perspective of the ethics of education present in Rosminian philosophy of education and pedagogy, the aesthetic theme serves as an emerging unifying and synthetic perspective.[44] The aesthetic dimension of the affection of cognition, which includes representation as an expression of the imagination proper to the moral form of being, is the decisive coefficient of the ethics of Rosminian formation, which, to all intents and purposes, allows us to grasp the ethical-moral value of the epistemology of Rosminian philosophy of education and the pedagogical-juridical value of Rosminian political philosophy and theor-ethical-moral, in addition to the value of full and legitimate distinction and disciplinary autonomy of this knowledge.

Bibliography

Bellelli, Fernando. "Ecopedagogy e responsabilità estetica nelle trasformazioni socio-antropologiche della religiosità." In *La responsabilità della pedagogia nelle trasformazioni dei rapporti sociali Storia, linee di ricerca e prospettive*; Proceedings

---

41. See Chomsky, *Linguaggio e problemi*.
42. See Muscherà, *Manzoni filosofo*.
43. See Di Bari, *Neo-Bildung negli USA*.
44. I have already had the opportunity to trace the scientific references for the relevant instruction of this possible debate and research area and its scientific assumptions in the following contributions; see Bellelli: "Ecopedagogy e responsabilità estetica" and "Estetica relazionale e trinitaria."

of the SIPED 2021 Conference, edited by Simonetta Polenghi et al., 171–78. Lecce-Brescia, It.: Pensa MultiMedia, 2021. Ebook.

———. "L'estetica relazionale e trinitaria di Antonio Rosmini." *Sophia* 2 (2021) 343–55.

———. *Etica originaria e assoluto affettivo. La coscienza e il superamento della modernità nella teologia filosofica di Antonio Rosmini*. Milan: Vita e Pensiero, 2014.

———. "Filosofia e pedagogia della dignità umana. Il contributo di Giambattista Vico e Antonio Rosmini." PhD diss., University of Modena and Reggio Emilia, 2020.

———. "Genesi e ricezione della dimensione pedagogica della definizione rosminiana di persona." *Annali di Storia dell'educazione e delle istituzioni scolastiche* 29 (2022) 42–58. Proceedings of Centro Studi e Ricerche Antonio Rosmini of Università di Trento "Rosmini e la pedagogia" online conference, Oct. 15–16, 2020.

———. "L'importanza degli ordini di intellezione e degli ordini di riflessione nella pedagogia rosminiana: analisi storico-culturale di un vuoto della letteratura critica." *Rivista di Storia dell'Educazione* 1 (2020) 85–99.

———. "Le quattro fasi della questione rosminiana e la pedagogia." *Nuova Secondaria* 9 (2020) 25–35.

———. "La ricezione statunitense di Rosmini tramite *Del principio supremo della Metodica*." Nuova Secondaria 3 (2019) 26–29.

———. *Percorsi storici della pedagogia giuridica. Vico, Rosmini e la* dignitas hominis. Rome: Aracne, 2020.

———, ed. *Pedagogia del sapere di Dio. Una prospettiva storico-culturale*. Rosminianesimo teologico. Milan: Mimesis, 2019.

———. *Rosmini e l'educazione nella quarta fase. La questione antropologica e l'epistemologia tra scienze dell'educazione, filosofia e teologia*. Rosmini Institute, Nov. 17, 2011. https://www.rosminiinstitute.it/la-rosminiana/rosminianesimo-filosofico/rosmini-e-leducazione-nella-quarta-fase/.

———. "Rosmini e l'epistemologia delle scienze sperimentali e umane. Rileggere Stoppani con Tanzella-Nitti." In *Rosminianesimo filosofico*, edited by Samuele F. Tadini, 311–66. Milan: Mimesis, 2017.

———. "Rosmini e l'immaginazione divina, l'antropologia religiosa della coscienza e la fenomenologia di Gesù. Dal corpo di Cristo al corpo della Parola di Dio: contributo teologico per l'analitica dell'*affective turn* dell'epistemologia contemporanea delle scienze, specificatamente umanistiche." In *Il divino nell'uomo e l'umano nella rivelazione*, edited by Fernando Bellelli, Rosminianesimo teologico, 19–63. Milan: Mimesis, 2017.

———. "Rosmini, il trascendentale e l'affezione tra l'essere e il soggetto." In *Tommaso e Rosmini: il sapere dell'uomo e di Dio fra due epoche*, edited by Fernando Bellelli. *Divus Thomas* 1 (2011) 389–410.

———. "Teodicea rosminiana del *verum/factum* e teoria dell'evoluzione in Teilhard de Chardin." *The Rosmini Society Rosminianism Philosophical International Journal* 1/2 (2020) 451–71.

———. "Vlijanie Rozmini na ital'janskuju pedagogiku XX veka" [The influence of Rosmini in Italian pedagogy in the twentieth century]. In *Religioznoe Obrazovanie v Rossii i v Evrope v XX veke: istoritcheskij opyt i peredathca zennostej*, edited by E. Tokareva et al., 133–50. Moscow: Indrik, 2020. Proceedings of "Religious Education in Europe in the Twentieth Century: Historical Experience and Transition of Values" conference, University of Latvia, Riga, Aug. 23–25, 2015.

Bellelli, Fernando, and Giovanna Gabbi, eds. *Profezia e attualità di Antonio Rosmini.* Stresa, It.: Rosminiane Sodalitas, 2016.

Bellelli, Fernando, and Emanuele Pili, eds. *Ontologia, fenomenologia e nuovo umanesimo. Rosmini ri-generativo.* Rome: Città Nuova, 2016. Proceedings of "Rosmini per la nostra epoca: elementi di ri-generazione" conference, Modena, It., Nov. 13–14, 2014. Video of conference at www.rosminiinstitute.it.

Chomsky, Noam. *Linguaggio e problemi della conoscenza.* Translated by C. Donati. Bologna: Mulino, 2021.

De Giorgi, Fulvio. *La scuola italiana di spiritualità. Da Rosmini a Montini.* Brescia, It.: Morcelliana, 2020.

Di Bari, Cosimo. *La neo-Bildung negli USA. Autori e modelli di pedagogia critica.* Rome: Anicia, 2018.

Galati, Domenico. *Galileo and Rosmini: Manifesto for a New Civilization.* Rome: Kairos Edimedia, 1996.

Galluzzi, Paola. *Galileo Rosmini Darwin. Triumviri del cattolicesimo riformatore (1870–1918).* Pisa: Normale, 2022.

Gennari, Mario. *Dalla* paideia *classica alla* Bildung *divina.* Florence: Giunti, 2017.

———. *Interpretare l'educazione. Pedagogia, semiotica ermeneutica.* Brescia, It.: Scuola, 2003.

———. *L'educazione estetica.* Milan: RCS, 20076.

———. *L'eidos del mondo.* Milan: Bompiani-RCS, 2012.

Gennari, Mario, and Giancarla Sola. *Logica, linguaggio e metodo in pedagogia.* Genoa: Melangolo, 20162.

Ghigi, Nicoletta. *L'etica fenomenologica di Edith Stein. Dalla vita emotiva all'individuo comunitario.* Rome: Fattore Umano, 2021.

La Via, Vincenzo. *Coscienza e libertà. Rosmini e l'assoluto realismo.* Edited by Biagio G. Muscherà. Vol. 1 of *Saggi rosminiani e altri scritti.* Milan: Mimesis, 2020.

Metafisica e pedagogia. Monographic issue of *Rivista Formazione Lavoro Persona* 23 (2018). https://www.diocesimolfetta.it/wp-content/uploads/2020/04/AA.-VV.-Metafisica-e-Persona-in-%C2%ABRivista-Formazione-Lavoro-Persona%C2%BB-VIII-23-2018._compressed.pdf.

Muscherà, Biagio G. *Manzoni filosofo. L'invenzione della parola. In dialogo con Antonio Rosmini.* Milan: Jaca, 2019.

Pangallo, Mario. *Antonio Rosmini e il Collegio medico di San Raffaele. Errore di valutazione o progetto illusorio?* Verona: Fede & Cultura, 2007.

———. *Rosmini e il fallimento della facoltà di medicina di S. Raffaele. Diffidenza della Curia romana o incompetenza giuridica rosminiana?* Verona: Fede & Cultura, 2007.

Pili, Emanuele. "'Vivacissima quiete.' Rosmini e il brivido dell'inaltrarsi: un'ipotesi sul negativo." In *Il divino nell'uomo e l'umano nella rivelazione*, edited by Fernando Bellelli, Rosminianesimo teologico, 147–64. Milan: Mimesis, 2017.

Rizzardi, Mario. *Modelli organismici in pedagogia della cognizione.* Bologna: Pendragon, 2012.

Rosmini, Antonio. *Compendio di etica.* Edited by Maria Manganelli. ENC 29. Rome: Città Nuova, 1998.

———. "Del principio supremo della Metodica." In *Scritti pedagogici*, edited by Fernando Bellelli, ENC 32, 37–364. Rome: Città Nuova, 2019.

———. *L'equazione dell'appagamento. Manoscritti inediti di scienze matematiche.* Edited by Paola Tessaroli and Santo Tessaroli. Milan: Mimesis, 2021.
———. *Filosofia del diritto.* Edited by Michele Nicoletti and Francesco Ghia. 4 vols. ENC 27, 27/A, 28, 28/A. Rome: Città Nuova, 2014.
———. *Logica.* Edited by Vincenzo Sala. ENC 8. Rome: Città Nuova, 1984.
———. *Nuovo Saggio sull'origine delle idee.* Edited by Gaetano Messina. 3 vols. ENC 3–5. Rome: Città Nuova, 2004.
———. *Principi della scienza morale.* Edited by Umberto Muratore. ENC 23. Rome: Città Nuova, 1990.
———. *Psicologia.* Edited by Vincenzo Sala. 4 vols. ENC 9, 9/A, 10, 10/A. Rome: Città Nuova, 1989.
———. *Teosofia.* Edited by Samuele F. Tadini. Milan: Bompiani, 2011.
Sequeri, Pierangelo. *Il sensibile e l'inatteso. Lezioni di estetica teologica.* Brescia, It.: Queriniana, 2016.
Sola, Giancarla. *La formazione originaria.* Paideia, humanitas, perfectio, dignitas hominis, Bildung. Milan: Bompiani/Rizzoli, 2016.
———. *Introduzione alla Pedagogia clinica.* Genoa: Melangolo, 2008.
Stella, Aldo. *Cognizione e coscienza. Precisazioni su alcuni concetti di scienza cognitiva.* Milan: Angelo Guerini e Associati, 2004.
Tadini, Samuele F. "Valore e significato dell'interpretazione 'crono-teoretica.'" *The Rosmini Society Rosminianism Philosophical International Journal* 1/2 (2021) 9–27.
Vecchiet, Cristian. *Dall'essere alla persona. Contributo ad un'interpretazione fenomenologico-realista dell'ontologia personalista di Antonio Rosmini.* Monographic issue of *Divus Thomas* 2 (2011).
Zanoni, Elena. *Scienza, patria, religione. Antonio Stoppani e la cultura italiana dell'Ottocento.* Milan: Franco Angeli, 2014.

Part 4

Rosmini's *Suspended Middle* (and the Comparable Social Theory of Radical Orthodoxy's *Suspended Middle*): Possible Political Implications

15

Philosophy of Politics and Philosophy of Right and Law in Rosmini

MARTA FERRONATO

Before getting into the matter, it is necessary to clarify and explain some literary choices made.

In fact, *filosofia del diritto* can be either "philosophy of law" or "philosophy of right."[1]

In this contribution, I have chosen to stick to the latter, since I believe it is more in keeping with Rosmini's system and logic as developed in one of his masterpieces, *Filosofia del diritto*. It is also in line with the wording used by Denis Cleary and Terence Watson in their English translation of Rosmini's *Filosofia del diritto* (The Philosophy of Right).

It is beyond the scope of this research to reflect in depth around the most appropriate lexical choices.

After all, the Italian tradition—in which Rosmini is embedded—is that typical of a "closed" legal system and cannot be assimilated to the typically "open" tradition of the Anglo-Saxon world. For instance, we Italians distinguish natural right from natural law. I would add that Rosmini defines the essence of law as a *podestà di godere* (power to enjoy) or *autorità di*

---

1. By the editor's and the publisher's choice, all translations from Italian to English, including those from Rosmini's works, are my responsibility, although the books I discuss have already been translated into English—as I will say below.

operare (authority to act) that manifests itself in a moral horizon within which right is generated by duty, which is expressed in law, that is, a moral law rather than a legal one.

I analyzed the Rosminian conception of the essence of right and its relations to law, duty and politics in both *La fondazione del diritto naturale in Rosmini* (*The Foundation of Natural Right in Rosmini*) and *Politica e passività. Percorsi nel pensiero di Antonio Rosmini* (*Politics and Passivity. Paths in Rosmini's Thought*), to which I refer for further considerations of these relevant topics.[2]

It is beyond the scope of this paper to reflect in depth around the most appropriate lexical choices.

Some Previous Considerations

Politics and law (or right) are two of the many areas of life on which thinkers of all times offered and offer reflections, arguments, and theories. Philosophy of politics and philosophy of right constitute, as everyone knows, two distinct disciplines at an academic level. At the same time, (if written in italics) they express the titles of two of the most famous works of Antonio Rosmini's practical philosophy, translated in English. The title of this paper intends to emphasize the twofold significance involving two different levels of reading and investigation.

The topic in question has a much greater scope than can be approached in an essay. The space of an extensive monograph would be needed to analytically compare the two treatises or to find the connections between the two disciplines, in synchronic or diachronic dimensions.

I will deal with only some of the profiles useful for grasping the quality of the relations between the two works and the two matters, and develop some considerations, based on objective data. Then I will analyze the definitions of the subjects proposed by Rosmini, and finally I will try to highlight the meaning of the "relations" intertwining them.

A brief methodological remark is needed. One of the privileged keys to understanding Rosmini is to lean on his "passivity principle." This principle is relevant not only in the domain of asceticism, but also in the domain of gnoseology, from which it spreads the other areas of knowledge. Giuseppe Capograssi also made the principle of passivity his own and wrote to his beloved Giulia that it "perhaps contains in itself all the possible virtues of

---

2. Ferronato: *Fondazione del diritto naturale in Rosmini*, 66–84; and *Politica e passività*.

the Christian."³ We can grasp the meaning of Rosmini's "passivity principle" by reading the following lines:

> Judging . . . with rectitude, *simplicity* is only necessary, which, free from prejudice, abandons itself to the truth that, as it were, comes to meet man. To judge wrongly, it is necessary for us to go against nature, to invent *cunning*, to commit violence. To be good, we have almost nothing to do but be passive to the truth and follow nature. To be bad, we are better off deploying an unhappy activity, and go against the truth, which is also in us and motionless, and in itself unconquerable.⁴

This is an excerpt from the introduction of *Philosophy of Right*, and that's significant. Inspired by that rule, I will try to establish a comparison between the two works and the two disciplines, following, as far as possible, the letter of the Rosminian texts. To this end, I shall focus on the "Prefazione alle opere politiche" in *Filosofia della politica* (Philosophy of politics), and on the introduction to *Filosofia del diritto* (Philosophy of right)—of course, without precluding incursions into other parts of the Rosminian works, where necessary.

A Comparison between the Two Treatises

In Rosmini's intellectual biography, *Filosofia della politica* certainly occupies a prominent place. In 1848, he himself recalled the gestation of his political writings in the very first pages of a work posthumously published in 1887, thanks to Francesco Paoli: *Della naturale costituzione della società civile*.⁵ Rosmini says he conceived the project very early in his life, when he was still young and unaware of the limitation of his strengths, guided only by the immense desire to know and to contribute to every men's knowledge.⁶

The intentions and aspirations of the young Rosmini—then barely twenty-four years old—would in time be scaled down. He returned to deal with politics in his full maturity, when he had developed his own original philosophical perspective.⁷ He considered of "lesser use . . . a work that

---

3. Capograssi, *Pensieri a Giulia*, 666.

4. Rosmini, *Filosofia del diritto*, 1:127. The national and critical edition of Rosmini's *Filosofia del diritto* has been printed in four volumes.

5. See Rosmini, *Della naturale costituzione*, 73–74. I refer to Gadaleta's introduction for the reconstruction of the genesis, and the presentation of the content, of this book (7–22).

6. Rosmini, *Della naturale costituzione*, 73.

7. Regarding the link between political reflection and exploration of philosophical

by its excessive bulk would have alienated a large number of readers from himself."[8]

For this reason, he published two distinct texts, two years apart, as pamphlets, which would later become the two parts of *Filosofia della politica*: in 1837, *Della sommaria cagione per la quale stanno o rovinano le umane società* (The main cause of the stability or downfall of human societies), and in 1839, *La società e il suo fine* (Society and its purpose). The "Prefazione alle opere politiche" was published along with the first issue and is the articulated foreword to what, in the author's plans, should have formed only the first of the two volumes of the great work he had planned.[9]

The second volume, only provisionally drafted and never published by Rosmini, has recently appeared in an extensive and rich critical edition, while in the twentieth century it was only printed as an appendix to the edition of the *Filosofia della politica* edited by Sergio Cotta in 1985, which was limited to the fragment composed in 1848.[10]

Filosofia della politica itself had known few editions, indeed, after the printing of the two pamphlets in 1837 and 1839: it was reproduced in 1842 in Naples (without Rosmini being informed[11]) and again in 1858. It would have been necessary to wait over a hundred and ten years for the printing of the next edition, at the initiative of Mario d'Addio.[12] Thirteen years later, in 1985, the one edited by Sergio Cotta was published. In 1994, an English translation of the treatise was prompted by Denis Cleary and Terence Watson.[13] Finally, on the bicentenary of Rosmini's birth, in 1997, the critical edition came out, edited by Mario d'Addio himself. I would add that, in 2021, a large selection of pages from *Filosofia della politica* was published in current Italian, edited by Fernando Bellelli.[14]

---

questions in Rosmini, Sergio Cotta in his "Introduzione," 12, observes: "As Solari acutely stated, the political considerations stimulated [Rosmini's] interest in philosophy."

8. Rosmini, *Della naturale costituzione*, 73.

9. See also D'Addio, "Introduzione," 11–3.

10. Rosmini, "Della naturale costituzione."

11. D'Addio, "Introduzione," 36.

12. D'Addio himself reports that, until then, only a few extracts had been published (see D'Addio, "Introduzione," 37).

13. "This translation of Rosmini's *Philosophy of Politics* was prompted in part by the need of an English edition of works frequently quoted by the author in his *Philosophy of Right*" (Denis Cleary and Terence Watson, in Rosmini, *Philosophy of Politics*, 1:vii). This is a very interesting remark in order to understand the relations between the two important treatises.

14. The initiative was promoted because Rosmini, "although commonly counted among the most important works of Catholic reflection on Italian politics and political thought . . . has had many admirers, not a few critics, but few readers" (Cubeddu, "Nota Editoriale," 5). The "Prefazione alle opere politiche" was not included in the selection.

A strange destiny, for this book, both with regard to the intellectual and biographical events of its author and on a more general level. The travail that Rosmini himself encountered throughout his life in elaborating and publishing it, departing from the projects he had carefully prepared, was then accompanied by over a century of "hiddenness"—followed by three distinct editions over twenty-five years. Investigating its reception in the last fifty years is beyond the scope of this paper, but I am convinced that attention will have to be paid to this delayed "flowering," in order to fully understand its deepest reasons.[15]

Filosofia del diritto did not suffer the same strenuous labor. Its critical edition was published in four volumes between 2013 and 2015; its editors report that Rosmini would have started working on it in 1826-27.[16] Anyway, the first volume was printed in 1841 by Tipografia e Libreria Boniardi-Pogliani and the second (only) two years later: and the work was so finished. Rosmini himself wrote, at the end of the second volume: "end of the second and last volume"[17]—an unequivocal sign that the project had been completed. Not so, as far as is known, for the whole project concerning a treatise about philosophy of politics, which engaged Rosmini at least from 1821 to 1848: a good twenty-seven years, and without having reached the point of writing the word *end*.

Other editions of *Filosofia del diritto* appeared in the years 1856 (with the same Neapolitan publisher who printed *Filosofia della politica*) and in 1865-66. Since then, the complete work has not been published again; only some more or less extensive parts have been published[18] until it was printed in six volumes as part of the National Edition of Antonio Rosmini-Serbati's published and unpublished works, directed by Enrico Castelli and edited by Rinaldo Orecchia, one hundred years after the previous one. The latter was followed by the more recent critical edition edited by Michele Nicoletti and Francesco Ghia between 2013 and 2015. The above-mentioned English translation was published in six volumes, in the years 1993-96.

The extension and framework of both *Filosofia della politica* and *Filosofia del diritto* present considerable external differences. First, comparing the respective volumes in the critical edition—excluding introductions and

---

15. In this regard, I refer to Armellini, *Rosmini politico*, and the extensive bibliography on political Rosmini included therein (258–75).

16. See Nicoletti and Ghia, "Introduzione," 15 and 40. It should be noted that, otherwise, we read that (also) this text "was first published in instalments between 1841 and 1845" ("Introduzione," 40). The national and critical edition of *Filosofia del diritto* is printed in four volumes.

17. Rosmini, *Filosofia del diritto*, 4:645.

18. Orecchia, "Introduzione," 1:x–xi.

indexes—one observes that the former is packed into less than five hundred pages in a single tome. The size of the second, on the other hand, required it to be printed in four volumes, which together count more than 1900 pages: almost four times those of the book dealing with politics.

Again. As already seen, *Filosofia della politica* results from the juxtaposition of three distinct "pamphlets," each with an autonomous structure, although intimately connected: the *prefazione*, which has no internal partitions and includes, in its thirteen pages, the brief "Prospectus of the Philosophy of Politics" (*Tavola della filosofia della politica*)—the outline that the entire work should have taken on in the author's intentions—; *La sommaria cagione*, which consists of seventeen chapters, covering about sixty pages; finally, *La società e il suo fine*, which unfolds in over three hundred pages, divided into four books (respectively of seventeen, fifteen, twenty, and thirty-seven chapters) that follow a short introductory part.

The architecture of *Filosofia del diritto* appears much more elaborate and complex. The two most important parts of the work together form what Rosmini calls "derived rational right" (*diritto razionale derivato*), divided into "individual right" (*diritto razionale*) and "social right" (*diritto sociale*). The approach to these macroscopic partitions would not be possible if they were not preceded by an exhaustive introductory section, which lays down and explains their fundamentals. To guide the reader, Rosmini goes through, in order, defining the discipline, distinguishing it from related sciences, dwelling on the history of natural law and natural rights, and then moving on to define the purpose of rational law. Having done so, he goes on to illustrate his moral system (to which he devotes three sections), without which it would not be possible to fruitfully access the substantive questions concerning the essence of right (of which he offers four definitions) and its relation to duty. After establishing the principle of the derivation of rights, he begins to investigate individual right—connatural (or inherent) and acquired rights, their transmission and alteration. The most extensive and substantial part of the work is reserved for *diritto sociale*, which in turn provides for an analytical reflection on the right of the three societies necessary for the right organization of mankind, subsequent to the investigation of universal social right: the right of the theocratic society and that of the domestic society (society whose origin is natural), and, finally, the right of civil society—the nature of which is artificial. The latter, divided into two sections—"Theory of Civil Society" (*Teoria della società civile*) and "Right (or law) of the Civil Society Already Established" (*Diritto della società civile già costituita*)—each further subdivided internally (four parts the first, two the second), is followed by an appendix that deals with the best construction of civil society (*Della costruzione migliore della società civile*).

Despite the external differences highlighted, a significant analogy between the two works must be emphasized. *In exergo* to the "Prefazione alle opere politiche" and to "Introduzione alla filosofia del diritto," Rosmini appends two distinct quotations from Plato. In the first, he recalls some lines taken from the fifth book of *Republic*: *In idem civilis potentia et philosophia concurrant; neque, quod nunc fit, a diversis duo haec tractentur ingeniis* (Civil power and philosophy should act in harmony for the same end, they should not be dealt with, as they are now, by people of different talents).[19] In the second, he quotes, in Italian, a passage from the fourth book of *Laws*: "He is too frivolous to seek brevity or length in writing laws, because it is not the very short ones, in my opinion, that should be chosen, nor the very long ones, but the excellent ones."[20] On the other hand, while the critical edition of *Filosofia della politica*[21] bears an epigraph, in Greek, taken from the fourth book of Aristotle's *Politics* and written in Greek characters, nothing appears on the frontispiece of *Filosofia del diritto*.

Philosophy of Politics and *Filosofia della politica*

Rosmini, in approaching every new subject, believed it was necessary to define it accurately, specify its nature, limits, method, status, relations with other branches of knowledge, and place it in its precise position in the system of sciences. In addition to that, he critically takes into consideration the outcomes of other thinkers' reflections with respect to the same field of knowledge.[22] With this methodological approach he manifested extreme care in offering the reader the nature, object, and purpose of both the philosophy of politics and philosophy of right. We find its outlines in the "Prefazione alle opere politiche" and in the first two paragraphs of the introduction to *Filosofia del diritto*, entitled, respectively, "Importanza della filosofia del diritto" (Importance of philosophy of right or law) and "Distinzione della filosofia del diritto dalle scienze affini" (Distinction of philosophy of law from related sciences).[23]

19. Rosmini, "Prefazione alle opere politiche," 41.
20. Rosmini, *Filosofia del diritto*, 1:51.
21. Previous editions do not have this epigraph.
22. Rosmini, *Filosofia del diritto*, 1:77. See also Ferronato, *Fondazione del diritto naturale*, 6–20, where I discussed these profiles of Rosmini's method, and the bibliographical references indicated therein.
23. The other paragraphs deal with: "History of the Science of Natural Right," "Extension of Rational Right," "Partition of Natural Right," and "Aids to the Study of Philosophy of Right."

In the political treatise, the *prefazione* occupies fourteen pages, while the first two paragraphs of *Filosofia del diritto* cover twenty-six pages. The difference in scope is also accompanied by a different approach to the issues raised and, for that matter, as is well known, while the *prefazione* was intended to introduce what Rosmini himself called "fragments,"[24] the *introduzione* was aimed at presenting and analyzing a set of notions essential for accessing an eight-hundred-page book (in the 1841 edition), in which the author also offers the entire treatment of *diritto individuale*.

The entry into the subject matter—defining the discipline—takes place, in the two works, in styles that do not present external similarities.

The *prefazione* immediately enters *in medias res*: in the first lines, Rosmini enunciates a definition of philosophy as a "science of the ultimate reasons"—according to what he himself had explained in his *Introduzione alla filosofia*—and shortly afterwords points out that he believes "it is necessary to preface a few words, aimed at clarifying the concept and the assumption of philosophy of politics."[25] Thus, the purpose of the booklet has already been effectively outlined and, after pointing out that each government has the task of leading society to the end for which it was established, the author writes that politics is "the greatest of the arts." He specifies its "office," which is divided into five distinct aspects: first, "to determine the nature of civil society and its proper purpose; next, to derive from it the concept of civil government, and to determine the means that are in its possession and at its mercy, no less than the most suitable way of using them."[26] Obviously, politics as a science and philosophy of politics, are related to each other, but diverge in nature and purpose. In a few words, Rosmini focuses on the methods a government uses to direct society to its end and, a few pages later, he can already present what he means by the expression *philosophy of politics*, which "must be that science, which seeks the ultimate reason or reasons, so that political means can achieve their effects."[27]

This definition is further clarified by the author as follows: philosophy of politics "is the science of ultimate reasons, is also *political wisdom*, that, placed at the highest point, guides all political means straight to the end that men proposed to themselves, when together they formed civil communities."[28]

---

24. See Rosmini, "Società e il suo fine," 123.
25. Rosmini, "Prefazione alle opere politiche," 41.
26. Rosmini, "Prefazione alle opere politiche," 41.
27. Rosmini, "Prefazione alle opere politiche," 44.
28. Rosmini, "Prefazione alle opere politiche," 45.

It should be noted that Rosmini takes care to distinguish, in the discipline, the *office*, the *essence*, and the *disposition*. If the essence of philosophy of politics lies in investigating the ultimate reasons for the art of government, if its task consists in teaching the best way to use political means, its nature is such that it "leads the governors of nations to the hearts of individuals, and reveals their secrets,"[29] instructing them so that they may perceive the fallacy of some of their reasoning to avoid errors in directing their own actions to the purpose of society, which is in the true human good.

Regarding his conception of the discipline, Rosmini does not make comparisons with other thinkers. I will briefly compare him to Norberto Bobbio who, in his famous aptitude for expressing himself and classifying with particular clarity, distinguished four different profiles or tasks inherent to political philosophy. The first one is searching for the best form of government; the second one, investigating the foundation of the state and, consequently, that of political obligation; third, searching for the nature of politics, distinguishing it from morality; finally, constituting the methodology of political science by analyzing political language.[30] If we wanted to compare it, albeit *ad oculos*, with this classification, it is quite clear that Rosmini's definition would be in a cramped cage. Of course, for him too, philosophy of politics is concerned with government and its forms and with the most appropriate or best form of it.[31] But, as we know, politics and morality are inseparable, so much so that the true human good is the "remote" purpose of every society—including civil society, therefore. Nor does he think that the state is the place within which man necessarily and completely deploys his social and political relations. The last meaning, then, linked to the development of political studies in the twentieth century, is completely far from Rosmini's understanding of politics as the greatest of the arts.

Rosmini recognizes that philosophy has the vocation of contemplating reality in defining the nature of a particular philosophy. He brings into it the whole experience of man, albeit foreshortened and analyzed from a peculiar point of view: it is always the whole man, the whole nature and human person, in his extraordinary richness and dignity, who is summoned to the presence of even the analysis of the narrowest and most limited spheres of his acting and being.

---

29. Rosmini, "Prefazione alle opere politiche," 47.

30. See Bobbio, "Considerazioni sulla filosofia politica."

31. After explaining that he intends to illustrate the concept and assumption of the discipline, Rosmini immediately introduces the government.

Philosophy of politics looks at man, at men, in order to explore what are the reasons why they live together, in societies in which someone—the ruler—must take care of others—the ruled—in order to achieve the end of association, undoubtedly establishing a hierarchical relationship between the former and the latter. The question of political obligation, of obedience to political power, cannot be examined if one does not first know the human heart, if one does not know the what for which society exists, if one does not know how to distinguish substance from accident.

Philosophy of Right and *Filosofia del diritto*

I now turn my attention to *Filosofia del diritto*. Its introduction begins with some considerations regarding the request addressed to governments for legislation to be "certain, unique, universal"[32]: they are certainly highly estimable and shared ideals that began to find implementation through the process of codification, widely promoted in Europe and inaugurated by the *Code Napoléon* in 1804. However, Rosmini is somewhat perplexed and wonders why the demand that laws be just does not resonate in the same way.

Immediately he sets up a dialogue with some (unknown) interlocutors. The dialogue that seems to resume the content of the motto in the epigraph and continue the one in which Plato, in his *Laws*, hopes that the "excellent" laws should be chosen, not the short nor the long ones. Rosmini becomes a new Socrates—indeed, to be fair, a new Athenian: in fact, in *Laws*, the mask of Aristotle's master corresponds to the elderly Athenian, with Clinia and Megillus on a pilgrimage to Knossos. And it is precisely the Athenian who pronounces the quoted words, with which Rosmini stands in continuity. In the manner of Socrates, he adopts a certain ironic tone in his interjections and tries to practise the maieutic art.

Rosmini's objective is very clear: to bring out the absurdity of certain high-sounding and celebrated principles when they are detached from their foundation. This happens because those "egregious men, and full of doctrine and humanity" consider "it is not necessary to express what is so common and vulgar" and feel "ashamed to say what seems too old, or what is commonly known to all, they are only vague to put out doctrines that are always rare and hidden," so much so that he himself feels "resigned to receive in return the title of simple and impervious man." In accordance with the classical tradition, Rosmini indicates justice as the first and necessary attribute of laws, recalling Plato himself, Cicero, Seneca, Clement of Alexandria, Saint Augustine, Saint Thomas Aquinas, Francisco Suarez: justice is

---

32. Rosmini, *Filosofia del diritto*, 1:51.

"the essence of all laws: no does any authority exist except as a minister of justice: justice is also the essence of authority itself."[33]

I have not yet introduced any consideration about nature and purpose and importance of philosophy of right, that is the subject of the paragraph under examination. As I mentioned above, in this treatise Rosmini does not immediately face such question. First, he explains that justice is "the most simple, vulgar idea, and therefore above all other most noble ideas,"[34] from which all solid reasoning around laws must start, only on the seventh page of the treatise does he mention "philosophy of right" for the first time, recognizing its purpose in "seeing in this idea of justice the facts, ... seeing in the general the particulars."[35] He mentions it a second time a few lines below and arrives at a first definition only nine pages later. Philosophy of right, "considered as the science of justice, is that which lays the unquestionable foundation of all human authority, no less than of all legislation proceeding from it."[36]

A little further on, right at the beginning of the second paragraph, he adds that it is "the life of *positive* laws and of the *art* of jurisprudence."[37] He then specifies its contours, by appreciating it as "the doctrine of the *first reasons in the work of juridical justice*. I say it is *juridical* that justice that lies in the rights."[38]

It should be remembered that, in this introductory part of the treatise, Rosmini himself deals with other ways of conceiving the subject and criticizes them. This is why I avoid making comparisons about philosophy of politics, as I did in relation to Bobbio.

An analytical discussion of the statements expressing the identity of the disciplines is beyond the scope of this paper. I left out any historical contextualization and any comparisons Rosmini engaged in with coeval or earlier thinkers, because I wanted to highlight only some of the most significant profiles. Therefore, I finally come to the "relations."

---

33. Rosmini, *Filosofia del diritto*, 1:59–60.
34. Rosmini, *Filosofia del diritto*, 1:56.
35. Rosmini, *Filosofia del diritto*, 1:57.
36. Rosmini, *Filosofia del diritto*, 1:66.
37. Rosmini, *Filosofia del diritto*, 1:68.
38. Rosmini, *Filosofia del diritto*, 1:69.

PART 4

The Relationships between Philosophy of Politics and Philosophy of Rights

It is Rosmini himself who explicitly asks the question: "What is the relationship of philosophy of right with philosophy of politics?"[39]

Moreover, the question was inescapable, since he was dealing precisely with distinguishing philosophy of right from related sciences, in agreement with those recent philosophers who "separate ... the science of right from all the others."[40]

He himself, therefore, suggests a way. First, he briefly recalls some of the contents of his political treatise: since society is a collection of rights and duties, of conventions, it is necessary to recognize that "justice comes first and foremost in the construction of every human society."[41] He then alludes to another argument developed in *La società e il suo fine*, which moves from a well-known Platonic thesis made even more famous by Saint Augustine: no human association can exist without (a minimum of) justice. It follows that those who govern and must favour the preservation of society, (should) perform a work of justice.

Now, in the domain of philosophy of right, Rosmini separated a profile that concerns the science of social justice from another that deals in detail with what he calls *diritto individuale* and is traditionally known as private law (or right). In both branches, given the primacy of justice, the relationship between philosophy of politics and philosophy of right is shaped as a relationship of medium with respect to the end.

The argument for explaining this thesis revolves around the intertwining of moral good and eudemonological good, which are at issue here. This is a problematic question of primary relevance, as well highlighted by Giuseppe Capograssi,[42] namely, the conception of right as a medium science between eudemonology and ethics. Politics concerns what is useful, so it is related to the first side, which is eudemonology.

A few lines later, we read: "Who does not see that Politics cannot exist, except on the condition of having first of all almost before its eyes described the rights all of individuals, whose rights thus form its purpose?"[43]

A slippage of plane is evident here: from philosophy of politics to politics. However, I observe that the philosophical disciplines (of politics and of

---

39. Rosmini, *Filosofia del diritto*, 1:74.
40. Rosmini, *Filosofia del diritto*, 1:92.
41. Rosmini, *Filosofia del diritto*, 1:92.
42. Capograssi, "Recensione a G. Gonella," 99.
43. Rosmini, *Filosofia del diritto*, 1:75.

right) under consideration are united by the same theoretical method, but are directed towards different objects: thus, the "slipping" is only apparent. While politics is an art, the major one, the right is a "power to be enjoyed,"[44] indeed: its essence coincides with that of the person who is "the subsisting human right."[45] It is also for this reason, in my opinion, that politics—and, consequently, philosophy that deals with it—plays the role of a means: because it deals with the means and because the person, the subsistent right, is the end and constitutes the ontological and axiological core of civil society. Politics is nourished by philosophy because it has the task of "teaching the best way to use political means"[46] so that they are not only good from a moral point of view, but also effective with respect to the end—otherwise civil government would be useless.

Rosmini's analysis of the definition of philosophy of politics appears less rigorous and detailed in relation to the rigor, breadth, and the examination of the more minute aspects that characterize the same research on philosophy of right.

I would like to suggest the following hypothesis: it is not Rosmini who put forth a different committment, who put forth a different effort, his genius is not "deficient" or lacking in penetration toward this object, but it is the object itself that lends itself with greater resistance to systematization.

In other words: although both disciplines have a contemplative character, their nature and purpose necessitate different methods and reflections of dissimilar extents, precisely because of their epistemological status and their nature. It is also the difference between politics and right (and law), in short, that explains why Rosmini knows what I have called greater travail in elaborating the text of *Filosofia della politica*, compared to the greater linearity, even in the vastness of its internal articulation, of the *Filosofia del diritto*. Moreover, the arguments inherent to method, systematicity and order in which truth is structured—one of man's greatest goods, together with virtue and happiness—are carried out, not by chance, in *Filosofia del diritto*.

Nevertheless, the contiguity and permeability between the two disciplines is evident, on a practical level, in the arrangement of the themes in *Filosofia del diritto*, as well as in writing and theoresis. Not only that, Rosmini is convinced that many errors in history were caused by their improper and insipient separation—the explicit reference goes to Machiavelli. Moreover, philosophy of politics can be usefully taught only to those who

---

44. Rosmini, *Filosofia del diritto*, 1:191.
45. Rosmini, *Filosofia del diritto* 2:25, para. 49.
46. Rosmini, "Prefazione alle opere politiche," 63.

have first learned philosophy of right and law. He adds that, in the collection of his works, he gives "moral and juridical works precedence over politics."[47]

Such considerations might perhaps come as a surprise to the reader, who has followed the young priest from Rovereto philosophically grappling with the most pressing political and social issues of his time as early as 1821, and then returning to them almost cyclically throughout his life, until his (politically and humanly) failing mission to Rome. Whereas, as we have already seen, he was able to devote himself to philosophy of right in a more circumscribed period but, undoubtedly, after he had already composed and published the *Filosofia della politica*. In this regard, one could observe that the collection of works follows a systematic criterion and that this scientific approach does not detract from the fact that different trajectories can be followed in the study. Another remark: Rosmini mentions teaching, emphasizing the order in which the subjects must be taught. Therefore, this is most probably a didactic and pedagogical concern, which does not necessarily interfere with the philosopher's research itineraries.

Conclusion

In the appendix to the *Filosofia del diritto* (titled "The Best Construction of Civil Society") we read a reflection that allows us to illuminate further the issues on which I question Rosmini: "The ... vast and most noble science of civil society must be bipartite, since the town cannot be excellently ordered except by means of two supreme virtues, *justice*, and *prudence*. Justice is the object of Right (and law), and *prudence* of Politics."[48]

Two observations. The first: without thematizing, I wish to point out that, curiously enough, he reverses the classical relationship between justice and law: not *ius obiectum iustitiae*, according to the magisterium of Saint Thomas,[49] but *vice versa*. This would certainly deserve careful consideration.

The second: thanks to the virtue of prudence—relating, as we know, to the choice of means—the man of government makes decisions with respect to what must be determined and led towards its end. Since a society can be just in many ways, it is up to politics and governments to identify the way in which a just—"regular" with Rosmini's words—order can be achieved, choosing that which "protects it from disturbances, and most facilitates the progress of human happiness."[50] Thus, Rosmini explains that

47. See Rosmini, *Filosofia del diritto*, 1:74.
48. Rosmini, *Filosofia del diritto*, 4:606, para. 2578 (emphasis added).
49. Saint Thomas Aquinas, *Sum* II–IIAE, q. 57, a. 1c.
50. Rosmini, *Filosofia del diritto*, 4:607, para. 2580.

since prudence, if it does not follow justice, would no longer be a virtue, but "would become cunning and villainy," necessarily philosophy of politics "is the discipline that begins precisely there, where philosophy of right ends: it is therefore the second part of civil social science, the first part of which is law."[51]

Now, another problem would open up. Strictly speaking, what does Rosmini mean by prudence? In these lines, he seems to allude not only, or not so much, to that conception of prudence as a dianoetic virtue that, according to Aristotle, in *Nicomachean Ethics*, is the indispensable "key" to be able to choose the right means, which distinguishes as such every ethical virtue; otherwise, he would not have mentioned cunning and wickedness. It must be assumed, therefore, that he has in mind (at least) two distinct meanings of prudence.

However, here, it is necessary to stop, to give the last word to Rosmini:

> Philosophy of right . . .ends here for us. But we cannot let the thread of sciences fall from our hands, which, although divided, by reason of method, are in our eyes truly no many, but are a *single science*, just one, almost diffused over a wide space, light of mind, one wisdom. Of which, though imperfectly, the most beautiful image remains outlined in our soul, which we cannot reproduce in our many and too narrow writings, nor can we faithfully deliver to the late and broken signs of words.[52]

Bibliography

Armellini, Paolo. *Rosmini politico e la storiografia del Novecento*. Rome: Aracne, 2008.

Bobbio, Norberto. "Considerazioni sulla filosofia politica." *Rivista Italiana di Scienza Politica* 2 (1971) 367–79.

Capograssi, Giuseppe. *Pensieri a Giulia. 1918-1924*. Edited by Giuseppe Lombardi. 2 vols. Milan: Giuffrè, 1979.

———. "Recensione a G. Gonella. La Filosofia del diritto secondo Antonio Rosmini." *Rivista Internazionale di Filosofia del Diritto* (1936) 98–99.

Cotta, Sergio. "Introduzione." In *Filosofia della politica*, by Antonio Rosmini, edited by Sergio Cotta, 11–12. Milan: Rusconi, 1985.

Cubeddu, Raimondo. "Nota Editoriale alla Filosofia della politica di Antonio Rosmini." In *Filosofia della politica*, by Antonio Rosmini, edited by Fernando Bellelli, 5–18. Siena: Cantagalli, 2021.

D'Addio, Mario. "Introduzione." In *Filosofia della politica*, by Antonio Rosmini, edited by Mario D'Addio, ENC 33, 11–37. Rome: Città Nuova, 1997.

Ferronato, Marta. *La fondazione del diritto naturale in Rosmini*. Padua: CEDAM, 1998.

---

51. Rosmini, *Filosofia del diritto*, 4:606, para. 2578.
52. Rosmini, *Filosofia del diritto*, 4:2577, para. 2577 (emphasis added).

———. *Politica e passività. Percorsi nel pensiero di Antonio Rosmini*. Milanofiori Assago, It.: Wolters Kluwer–CEDAM, 2022.

Nicoletti, Michele, and Francesco Ghia. "Introduzione." In *Filosofia del diritto*, by Antonio Rosmini, edited by Michele Nicoletti and Francesco Ghia, ENC 27, 7–44. Rome: Città Nuova, 2013.

Orecchia, Rinaldo. "Introduzione." In *Filosofia del diritto*, by Antonio Rosmini, edited by Rinaldo Orecchia, 1:i–xvii. Padua: CEDAM, 1967.

Rosmini, Antonio. "Della naturale costituzione della società civile." In *Filosofia della politica*, edited by Sergio Cotta, 661–96. Milan: Rusconi, 1985.

———. *Della naturale costituzione della società civile* [The natural constitution of civil society]. Edited by Ludovico A. Gadaleta. ENC 34. Rome: Città Nuova, 2017.

———. "Della sommaria cagione per la quale stanno o rovinano le umane società" [The main cause of the stability or downfall of human societies]. In *Filosofia della politica*, edited by Mario D'Addio, ENC 33, 57–117. Rome: Città Nuova, 1997.

———. *Filosofia del diritto*. Edited by Michele Nicoletti and Francesco Ghia. 4 vols. ENC 27, 27/A, 28, 28/A. Rome: Città Nuova, 2013–2015.

———. *Filosofia della politica*. Milan: Ditta Boniardi-Pogliani, 1858.

———. *Filosofia della politica*. Edited by Fernando Bellelli. Siena: Cantagalli, 2021.

———. *Filosofia della politica*. Edited by Sergio Cotta. Milan: Rusconi, 1985.

———. *Filosofia della politica*. Edited by Mario D'Addio. Milan: Marzorati, 1972.

———. *Introduzione alla filosofia*. Edited by Pier P. Ottonello. ENC 2. Rome: Città Nuova, 1979.

———. *Philosophy of Politics*. Vol. 1: *The Summary Case for the Stability or Downfall of Human Societies*. Vol. 2: *Society and Its Purpose*. Translated by Denis Cleary and Terence Watson. Glasgow: Bell & Bain Limited, 2010.

———. *The Philosophy of Right*. Translated by Denis Cleary and Terence Watson. 6 vols. Durham, UK: Rosmini, 1993–1996.

———. "Prefazione alle opere politiche." In *Filosofia della politica*, edited by Mario D'Addio, ENC 33, 41–54. Rome: Città Nuova, 1997.

———. "La società e il suo fine" [Society and its purpose]. In *Filosofia della politica*, edited by Mario D'Addio, ENC 33, 121–514. Rome: Città Nuova, 1997.

16

Ethics and Society in the Political Thought of Antonio Rosmini

CHRISTIANE LIERMANN

IN THE SECTION "JURIDICAL and Political Implications of Rosmini's Thought" of the seminar entitled "Unity of Science and Holiness" I will attempt to develop the topic entrusted to me, that is "ethics and society in Rosmini's thought," with recourse to the conversation developed by Rosmini in his essays with pagan and Christian Roman authors on public-social dynamics. I would like to address my theme by focusing on the "case of Rome" and how it was read and interpreted by the thinker from Rovereto. In short, this is the *question* of what forces had pushed forward and conditioned the historical path of Rome. My goal is to shed light on the relationship between *ethics and society* in Rosmini starting from his analysis of Roman history.

His political reflections on this subject are part of the centuries-old European debate concerning the end of the Roman Empire. Through the centuries, the "case" of Rome has represented for intellectuals in Europe the paradigm par excellence of the rise and decline of a political community, but at the same time it has been considered in its singularity and extraordinary character, reputedly according to the British historian Edward Gibbon in his *History of the Decline and Fall of the Roman Empire*: "The greatest perhaps and most awful scene in the history of mankind." Since late antiquity the collapse of Rome has been referred to as the deepest crisis in the world, the greatest disaster that ever occurred. Numerous works of art represented the sack of Rome in 410 as a catastrophe of civil coexistence: once the walls of the city were destroyed, barbarism reigned supreme.[1]

The meditations around this dramatic "end of a world" naturally led to the question of the reasons and trajectory of the fall. Had it happened *ex abrupto*? Or was it rather a gradual process? From there arose the further great questions of the European conversation with the case of Rome before our eyes: Was it possible for states, nations, or peoples to die, disappearing completely? Could empires and republics vanish from the face of the earth, perish definitively, or was some *translatio* that would guarantee their continuation conceivable? In this case it was necessary to investigate factors and tools to ensure the survival in other forms of a civil consortium. Were there suitable means to make a political community eternal or at least lasting? The "case" of Rome meant precisely the fall of Rome, a perennial intellectual stimulus for entire generations of thinkers from all European cultures.

But what is the relationship between this order of questions and the theme of this article on "ethics and society in Rosmini"? My thesis would be that Rosmini used the parable of Rome to highlight a series of links between cause and effect called "laws," which he believed determined the trend of civil societies in general. Clearly, he knew all the Christian and non-Christian authors, who had reflected on the exceptionality and/or paradigmaticity of Rome. And he was convinced that lessons could also be learned from such an extraordinary and singular historical case by studying in depth its reasons and dynamics. For Rosmini there was no doubt about the twofold meaning, exceptional (and at the same time) demonstrative-instructive on the level of philosophy and political teaching, of Roman history.

In his eyes, the path of Rome—foundation, rise, flourishing, decline, annihilation—should be read as proof of the role of collective ethos and the morality of the individual in the stability or instability of civil society and the state. Studying the history of Rome and evaluating the immense number of previous interpretations, Rosmini found important points of reference for his own political theory and philosophy in the reflections of classical authors with respect to the questions considered the factors that made Rome great, and its greatest weaknesses. Based on the study of the fate of the Romans, Rosmini concluded that external enemies represented an existential threat to the civil consortium only if the internal architecture was already in a phase of collapse.

---

1. See Demandt, *Fall Roms*, 1776.

To the great question "Why Rome in particular?," a key question that has accompanied the entire span of European cultural history, Rosmini tried to give systematic answers in his essay "The Main Cause for the Stability or Downfall of Human Societies" (*Della sommaria cagione per la quale stanno o rovinano le umane società*), the first part of *Philosphy of Politics* (*Filosofia della politica*), trying to identify the reasons for an unprecedented rise and an unprecedented decline, convinced of the appropriateness of examining first the vehicles of Rome's fortune, and then of its misfortune, as indicated by ancient authors. Rosmini, on principle, as in all his works, did not exclude any reason offered by other thinkers. In this perspective he pondered the thesis of those who had attributed the success of the Romans to the grace of the gods of their pantheon; he confronted those who had considered Roman loyalty to the *mores maiorum* the distinctive feature of their superiority in the first centuries, or even their self-esteem due to confidence in their *virtutes*.

In the essay "The Main Cause" the general context of Rosmini's study of the case of Rome was represented by reflections on the conditions of stability or ruin of society as such, in the abstract, but at the same time also of societies in the plural, as concrete historical organisms. First of all, it is worth noting that the author started from the assumption of the scientific cognitive possibility of identifying causes for social developments. The main methodical instrument of such identification consisted, in his opinion, in the examination of an infinity of historical cases. Reconstructing the genesis and biographies of cultures and peoples on a global scale, Rosmini came to the conclusion that stability represented an overriding political-social good whose existence depended on the ethos of the community in question. The examination of the many cases showed him that this law of *ethos-society* interdependence was universally valid, despite the plurality of associative forms found in human history, from the *polis* to modern states. Conversely, the realization of the greater good of stability in very heterogeneous political-social configurations made the variety of civil consortia perfectly legitimate, since they are products of the imagination of men and the results of their ability to adapt to the widely varying conditions of life (geocultural, climatic conditions, etc.). The result was the singularity of the biographies of peoples, if one looked, for example, at the unmistakable traits of their migratory behavior or of constituting themselves in more or less compact groups.

For Rosmini, the history of humankind was split into two parts: there was one history without Christianity and another, very different, under Christianity. Without knowledge of the gospel of Christ, social biography depended on the rules that determined the life of the individual marked by birth, adolescence, mature age, old age, and death. Under Christianity, on the other hand, the immortality of the social body was guaranteed, like that of the soul of every single human being.

Two aspects of Rosmini's elaboration in this regard seem to me worthy of remarking: the first concerns the fact that the thesis of the radical diversity of history "under" Christianity compared to that without the Christian religion certainly corresponded to a dictate of faith. However, in the context of political ethics, it was not religious logic that interested Rosmini but rather the historical evidence he identified. In the field of political thought, the argument had to be carried out through historical-empirical methodologies.

The second aspect, on the other hand, consists in the Rosminian hypothesis that in both existential conditions of humanity, without and under Christianity, the individual-society analogy was in force as regards the vital path and the law of interdependence between the ethos of the individual person and the political community also applied, from the point of view of its stability/instability.

Rosmini offered a series of answers, at various levels, to the fundamental question regarding which interventions or tools had allowed Christianity to radically change human history, transforming it from circular and cyclical to linear, tendentially ascending to spiral. According to Rosmini, theological-eschatological and philosophical-ontological explanations were certainly possible. But in the field of politics he was interested, as I mentioned, in a methodical approach that I would call a "historically-based psychology of collective behavior" or even a "historical-psychological sociology." Considering the question of the means available to Christianity to revolutionize history, Rosmini positioned himself in opposition to Machiavelli. The Florentine politician, in Rosmini's reading, had affirmed the irreconcilability between the virtues and moral objectives of Christians on the one hand and the needs of a republic and the attitudes required of *cives-miles* on the other, because the state, in the eyes of Christians, did not represent the ultimate objective of their aspirations. The philosopher from Rovereto, on the contrary, supported the idea of the maximum usefulness of Christian virtues and moral objectives in the service of the state precisely because the latter was not identified with the supreme goal of the ethical commitment of the citizen. The Christian relativization of the state, according to Rosmini, had proved to be its most solid foundation, and this was historically demonstrable.

In Rosminian political thought, the mechanism activated by the Christian religion, worked thanks to the personalization of the gospel message. In this way, the structural rift between the elites and the masses, typical of pagan societies, was overcome. The Christian religion provided a third point of reference, outside and above the republic. The Christian relativization of the political dimension was the guarantor of the perception of the instrumental character of the body politic, no longer an end in itself, not sacred, but profane and negotiable. Consequently, the state under Christianity could be considered an instrument, certainly precious and useful, in the service of individuals and society. It became malleable, a work to be structured with the help of a constitution built by the members/citizens.

The laws of the movement of political bodies identified by Rosmini along the lines of the history of Rome concerned the conditions of stability and led him to investigate also the possibilities of progress of collective bodies. Wondering about the impulses capable of advancing or regressing civil societies, the philosopher participated in what could be called the conversation of European intellectuals around the phenomenon of "civilization." It was not only a matter of the era in which Rosmini lived, but following the French Revolution, the causes of the transition from a state of nature, wild and primitive to civilization and from this to decadence and collapse were discussed with particular fervor. It is legitimate to remember the fascination exerted by this theme also on contemporary painters of Rosmini. The *Course of the Empire* was the title of a cycle of paintings by the artist Thomas Cole (1801–1848), which began with *The Savage State*, moving on to *The Consummation* of the *Empire*, and ending with the catastrophe imagined as the end of civilization and the known world. The clash between a primitive age and a society weakened by too much refinement offered painters rich material for staging the violence of the horrendous barbarians, but was to some extent justified by the decadence of the Romans. The *Sack of Rome* by Évariste-Vital Luminais of 1890 or the painting of the same title by Joseph-Noël Sylvestre (also dated 1890) was echoed by representations of a Thomas Couture (1815–1879) of *The Romans of Decadence* and a John William Waterhouse *The Favourites of Emperor Honorius*. These were historical-pictorial stories animated by the *clash of civilizations* that Rosmini, a critical reader of Roman-Latin and Christian authors and their interpretations of the drama of the year 410, had placed at the center of his reconstruction of the passage from the pagan world to the Christian world. Clearly Rosmini knew and cited the great writers, Saint Jerome and Saint Augustine *in primis*. According to them, the invasion of the barbarians culminating precisely in the sack of Rome had given an idea of the apocalypse. The devastation of the *urbs* in their eyes corresponded to a divine judgment and had been programmed by divine providence of which the invading peoples represented the instruments. Rome fell as the proud Troy fell; Saint Jerome had noted with reference to Virgil's *Aeneid*. The city that had conquered the world had been conquered. In an apologetic sense, the fathers of the church had rejected the attribution of blame for the Roman ruin to Christians, reversing the scheme of responsibility (attribution resumed, as is known, by the Enlightenment which in turn is refuted by Rosmini): it was the corrupt Romans who were the cause of their own fate. But although he had drawn inspiration from Christian apology, Rosmini did not search for culprits, rather looking to sociohistorical laws. In the latter, the moral factor represented a powerful thrust. Thanks to the examination of history and the great historians, Rosmini came to the conclusion that the morality of the many always acted as the engine of history, for better or for worse. He found in the classics narrative (and moral) models that taught him and confirmed, from Tacitus, to Procopius to Sismondi (quoted extensively, for example, in the third book of *Society and Its Purpose (La società e il suo fine)*). Following in their footsteps, with the help of the study of ancient history, Rosmini elaborated the thesis that peoples were devastated and dispersed when as a result of their self-weakening they had become defenseless. In these reflections he partly followed the interpretation of Saint Augustine about the instrumentality of peoples in the service of divine providence. Let us recall in this context the famous passage in *The Five Wounds of the Holy Church (Delle cinque piaghe della Santa Chiesa)* about the angel sent by God to wipe out the people of Rome. But Rosmini also went beyond apology in the search for the reasons for the ruin of the Empire. Meanwhile, the explanation that indicated the particular physical strength of the Romans as the cause of their superiority appeared to him possible but superficial. The real motive instead had to be sought in the ethos of the community that worked or no longer worked. If eschatological criteria were applied, the fall of Rome was to be read as a punishment in the perspective of salvation history; in this perspective, the collective groups suffered the lessons of Providence. But in the historical-political sphere the laws of the movement were in force, identifiable even outside the theological context. These were universal laws that Rosmini saw confirmed by authoritative voices such as Procopio, author of *De bello vandalico*, and Simonde de Sismondi with the essay on "Les colonies des anciens comparées à celles des modernes sous le rapport de leur influence sur le bonheur du genre humain" (1837). In addition, according to Rosmini, it was possible to identify some characteristic traits and recurring moments in these historical processes that in all times followed the same path. One, particularly dear to Rosmini, was that there was no autarky. Universal history, on the other hand, was a perpetual chain of actions, a continuous merging of peoples. In relations between communities there was the "law of compensation," again readable, in an eschatological key, as a perennial distribution, by providence, of benefits and penalties, while from the historical-political point of view that law expressed the greater or lesser capacity of the communities to adapt to the conditions in which they found themselves living and which they were able to build around themselves. Their continuous interaction, however, pushed that great process that attracted the attention of Rosmini and many of his peers: the process of "civilization." It was precisely the study of the civil progress of peoples that provided Rosmini with the rich material that again proved the fundamental difference of pagan history from Christian history. To the civilization of pagan societies, he dedicated the aforementioned book 3 of the *Philosophy of Politics*, insisting on the inexorable law that determined the natural course of those consortia: that is, the automatism of the parable first ascending and then descending, from birth through a phase of flourishing and a descent towards ruin. The historical-sociological approach (which Rosmini himself defined precisely his philosophy of politics) demonstrated the dependence of this natural, inevitable process towards decline, on the gradual loss of the original *primitive ethos* of every non-Christian community that had been the initial cause of the foundation of the consortium, considered as organized coexistence the supreme common good.

The mechanism that according to Rosmini directed the subsequent destiny of every community without Christian enlightenment was due to the nature of things, in other words, to the "time" factor that acted as an automatic social destroyer. The mere passage of time distanced the community from the founding ideals of the *res publica*. As a result, the community was no longer identified with the greater common good, while in the orientations of the members the weight of individual interests grew to the detriment of social ones. Thus, the inevitable decline of the single society as a component of the universal cyclical movement would begin. Here, it seems to me, we touch the core of the relationship between ethics and society in Rosmini. Philosophy of politics, in his work, meant examining the social consequences of the moral habits of citizens, and vice versa conceiving public and constitutional structures capable of directing collective attitudes towards the common good, rather than towards a dispersal in selfishness.

The Rosminian philosophy of politics resorted to more authors of antiquity than of the Christian era, perhaps because Rosmini perceived in the ancients a greater sensitivity to this link between ethics and society, the basis of his reflections on the stability or instability of the civil consortium. The list of classics is long and includes Thucydides, Xenophon, Plato, Aristotle, Cicero, Sallust, Varro, Livy, Seneca, Tacitus, Plutarch, and Macrobius, cited as witnesses with respect to the theme of social decadence, who all describe how there is a moral weakening before becoming a public, institutional, military destabilization, etc.

Retracing their doctrines, Rosmini implicitly proposed political recommendations from the perspective of modern society. The Greek and Latin classics had told of the original concentration of the republic on a few cults, as opposed to their typical multiplication of the late age. While at the beginning obedience and respect to only a few authorities was due, the decline was characterized by the inflation of laws. The initial identification of the whole community with the common good or the community itself had led to the participation of all in public affairs; at that time there was no exclusivity of rites and liturgies. Every war was to be justified as *bellum justum*, not to satisfy conquering ambitions for greater power and wealth. Rosmini followed its authors in their reflections on the dilemma of the expansion of state power, both within society and externally. Was there the beginning of the end? The extent of Roman power *extra muros*, in the tales of the classics, highlighted a potential underlying conflict concerning the ability of each community to deal with and manage the heterogeneity of members.

However, Rosmini's appreciation for ancient authors did not lead him to share their nostalgia for the good times of the past (Rosmini's rejection of the idea of revitalizing past times, notoriously, finds an echo in his critique of postrevolutionary restorative policies). He did not make his own the identification of the archaic ages with glorious phases of youth and heroism, in the romantic sense, but consistently aimed at a greater understanding of the laws of social course. The writers whose stories illustrated to him the functioning of civil consortia led him to suppose the impotence of all the means invented by men and imposed on societies, to repair and stabilize the political community. Rosmini was convinced of the inefficiency of the tools produced by human imagination to oppose the natural decline of social constructions. Among these instruments, was the legislation that particularly attracted his interest. Increasingly numerous and severe laws, the increase of control and various restrictions characterized the phases of decline, but also the multiplication of new philosophies and new moral prescriptions all to be considered bankrupt with respect to their goal of stopping the downward social curve.

According to Rosmini, only the supernatural point of reference of the Gospel message was able to put an end to this natural-human trend, without however guaranteeing an infinite continuous ascent. Even enlightened by Christianity, societies suffered moments of regression, but they had instruments of salvation capable of rebuilding, reforming, reestablishing the community, precisely because of the spiral shape indicated as an icon of history "under Christianity."

Summarizing the points that I consider decisive regarding the relationship between ethics and politics in Rosmini, I would emphasize his double reading of the catastrophe of the fall of Rome: analyzed in an eschatological key it does not represent the end of high pagan culture because of barbaric Christianity, enemy of civilization (according to the Enlightenment interpretation, as it was masterfully elaborated in Edward Gibbon), but a necessary step in the history of redemption. Read instead in a historical sense, with political and constitutional implications, the collapse of the Roman Empire constitutes proof of Rosmini's thesis on the dependence of the stability and flowering of civil coexistence on the collective ethos which, in the Christian era, has a supernatural foothold capable of directing the morality of individual members towards the common good and renewing it when it is weakening. To introduce this external and superior instance, according to Rosmini, it was necessary the complete destruction of the political world hitherto dominant, namely the Roman-imperial one. Therefore, in the eyes of the philosopher from Rovereto, the narration of the gradual transition to the Christian era is wrong.

One can ask, in conclusion, whether a stable post-Christian civil society would have been conceivable for Rosmini. I do not think so. His hypothesis would perhaps have included the probability of the long duration of such a society thanks to the cultural heritage of Christianity, but once faith in the afterlife collapsed, the natural exclusive concentration on earthly goods would have triggered the dynamics of cyclical law.

Bibliography

Demandt, Alexander. *Der Fall Roms. Die Auflösung des römischen Reiches im Urteil der Nachwelt*. Munich: Beck, 1984.

Gibbon, Edwar. *The History of the Decline and Fall of the Roman Empire*. London: Strahan & Cadell, 1776–1789.

Rosmini, Antonio. "Della sommaria cagione per la quale stanno o rovinano le umane società." In Rosmini, *Filosofia della politica*, edited by Mario D'Addio, ENC 33, 57–117. Rome: Città Nuova 1997.

Sismondi, Jean Charles Léonard Simonde de. *Les colonies des anciens comparées à celles des modernes sous le rapport de leur influence sur le bonheur du genre humain*. Genoa: 1837.

17

Can Rosminian Thinking Have Meaning within the *Italian Theory*?

LUCIANO MALUSA

Rosminian Philosophy as a Speculative Synthesis Useful for the Formation of National Knowledge and the Harmonious Cohesion between the Christian Religion and Philosophy

THIS INTERVENTION IS TO be included in the reports of November 5 and 6 of the conference. I directed the work in the afternoon of November 5 in Reggio Emilia, dedicated to the topic *Dal metodo alla metodica: prospettive interdisciplinari sulla pedagogia di Rosmini* (From method to method: Interdisciplinary perspectives on the pedagogy of Rosmini). On November 6, 2021, I attended the session dedicated to the topic *Cultura e spiritualità nel pensiero di Rosmini* (Culture and spirituality in the thinking of Rosmini), which was held in Modena. I think I can make my contribution regarding the two sessions, which were interesting because they addressed the various aspects of Rosmini's thinking and pedagogical and cultural commitment, producing a specific intervention that can be said to be "both adjustment and polemic" towards those who have, in the present time, set aside the thinking of the philosopher from Rovereto, excluding him from the ranks of major Italian philosophers. The discussion, underway for some centuries, on the Italian philosophical tradition has today reached the affirmation by some exponents of our philosophical culture (headed by Roberto Esposito) of a strong characteristic of our thinking, first manifested in the Renaissance, and today almost universally recognized, that is its ethical-practical-political (or bio-political) value, with the emphasis on the concrete, the sensible, the immediate.[1]

An intervention of this kind is not really a report, but it falls within the intentions of this conference, which, I repeat, deals with the figure and thinking of Rosmini as *Unità di scienza e santità (*Unity of science and holiness). The conference intended to proclaim the timeliness of Rosmini's testimony, which manifested itself at different times and with different outcomes, from the moment of the affirmation of his thought (with the Roman edition of *A New Essay Concerning the Origin of Ideas* [*Nuovo Saggio sull'origine delle idee*] in 1829–1830) to the moment of the condemnation, by the Catholic Church, of some propositions extrapolated from his works (that is, with the decree *Post Obitum* of 1887) and then in the period of the slow revaluation of orthodoxy and the relevance of the thinker, to arrive at the *Nota* of the Congregation for the Doctrine of the Faith of 2001.[2] During the nineteenth century Rosmini's thinking became well-known, with a considerable following among Christians, spiritual consensus, but it was also attacked by powerful opponents convinced that it concealed reasons of heterodoxy regarding the Christian faith. No one ignored the greatness of his philosophical-theological synthesis, neither opponents nor followers. What divided the critics from the people who had chosen to follow the

---

1. Roberto Esposito set out his vision of Italian thought in the work *Pensiero vivente*. The merit for the formulation and dissemination of the interpretation of the *Italian Theory* (or *Italian Thought*) is all his. There are several works dedicated to the topic; see a list of them in the bibliography of C. Claverini, *Tradizione filosofica italiana*, 189–213.

2. The bibliography is vast. I limit myself to indicating Malusa, "Antonio Rosmini-Serbati." On the sentences that have been "imposed" for various reasons on Rosmini's work, see Malusa, "Rosmini, Antonio." I remember that Rosminian works were published in national editions at two different times. In the first instance, starting in 1934, the Edizione nazionale delle opere edite e inedite di Antonio Rosmini (henceforth EN), promoted by the Società Filosofica Italiana and directed by E. Castelli, Anonima Romana Editoriale, Rome (1934–77), forty-nine volumes. Subsequent publications, thanks to the impulse given by Michele Federico Sciacca and the Centro Internazionale di Studi Rosminiani in Stresa, include, after 1975, Opere edite ed inedite di Antonio Rosmini, Edizione Nazionale, promoted by Enrico Castelli. The critical edition promoted by Michele Federico Sciacca is edited by Istituto di Studi Filosofici, Rome; Centro Internazionale di Studi Rosminiani, Stresa; Città Nuova, Rome 1975*ff* (henceforth ENC). The edition is completed as far as the works are concerned. The publication of the *Lettere* is for the moment limited to two volumes.

Rosminian philosophy for its systematicity and for its closeness to the unity of Christian knowledge and belief was the fact that precisely the greatness of thinking concealed the danger of doctrinal deviations. It was asserted that freedom in the use of language that was precise, but at the same time different from that of the scholastic tradition, could induce Christian followers to support interpretations of dogmas not perfectly in line with the teachings of the church. It was an unfounded, unjust, improbable statement. But it was believed. Starting from 1841, writings denigrating the fame of Rosmini's thinking and doctrinal coherence were published: accusations were made and then books were written in defense of the overall orthodoxy of the Rosminian system. A chapter of Rosmini's life and his fate not always adequately studied until now, in part due to the vast quantity of writings that were published for and against, and which constituted the "Rosminian question." It has divided Christians and not all the relative texts and documents have been made known and examined.[3]

3. I will limit myself to giving some brief indications. The "Rosminian question" began with the first accusations of heterodoxy formulated anonymously in 1841 (but attributable to members of the Compagnia di Gesù). There were in life and later after the death of Rosmini condemnations of his works and doctrines by the Church authorities and other accusations and evaluations were made against the figure of our thinker. The "first phase" of the Rosminian question was the one after 1841, which ended with the imposition by Pope Gregory XVI of "silence" regarding the controversy (1843); the "second phase" was that of 1848–49 when the works *The Five Wounds of the Holy Church (Delle cinque piaghe della Santa Chiesa)* and *The Constitution under Social Justice (La Costituzione secondo la giustizia sociale)* were condemned by the Congregation of the Index; the "third phase" lasted between 1851 and 1854 when all the Rosminian works were examined by the Congregation of the Index, and it concluded with a decree of "dismissal" of the Rosminian writings because they manifestly lack reprehensible doctrines (*Dimittantur opera*, 1854). To understand these three phases the work of S. Zanardi, *Filosofia di Antonio Rosmini*, is useful. The "fourth phase" took place after the death of Rosmini and consisted of controversy especially on the contents of his posthumous works, ending with the condemnation by the Congregation of the Index with the decree *Post Obitum* (1887), which criticized as *haud consonae catholicae veritati* forty propositions taken from different works. It was the culmination of a real persecution of the memory of Rosmini and the vitality of the Istituto della Carità (Rosminiani) that he founded. See on this phase the publication of the acts of the decree 1887: Malusa et al., *Antonio Rosmini e Congregazione*. One could consider the "fifth phase" of the Rosminian question the whole debate on Rosmini's orthodoxy from 1887 until, with the *Note* of the Congregation for the Doctrine of the Faith dated July 1, 2001 (Congregazione per la Dottrina della Fede, "Sul valore"), the merely precautionary nature of the so-called "condemnation" of 1887 was not specified, and Rosmini was relieved of any accusation of heterodoxy. One of the reasons for this conference is precisely the memory of this *Note* twenty years after its emanation (2001–2021). The most recent developments on the "Rosminian question" were formulated by a group of scholars from Genoa (University and Faculty of Theology) in the following works: the aforementioned work of Zanardi (Italy); and Malusa, *Teologia di Antonio Rosmini*.

It must be admitted that, for several years, despite the contrasts, both for better and for worse, in Italian philosophy a system similar to the Rosminian one was considered to be of the first magnitude, on a par with other great metaphysical systems of the time. Moreover, it was exalted because it proposed a unitary vision of philosophy and Christian religion. During the period of the *Risorgimento*, a consensus was reached on the recognition of the importance of the doctrines and method of Rosminian philosophy, although it was evaluated differently by the secular-neo-idealist culture and the Catholic Christian culture, but was always considered of a high theoretic level, important in the development of the Italian landscape, and also in the development of European thinking. It should be borne in mind that the interpretations of a secular nature, by people like Bertrando Spaventa and Donato Jaja, who considered Rosmini, despite his position as a philosopher of transcendence, a philosopher of transcendental creativity, were formulated after Rosmini's death. Rosmini's followers did not accept them, but neither did they strongly object, to these interpretations that reversed the evaluation of the ideal being in its objectivity to the evaluation of the idea as a category, a form of knowing. The opponents of Rosminian philosophy, on the other hand, insinuated that Rosminian treatises on the idea of being and its objectivity could present compromising forms of language. The period of a shared positive evaluation of the Rosminian system ended when, the fervor of the *Risorgimento* having dissolved, the theoretic climate changed and negative interpretations of his theoresis crept in, the accusations against his ethical and theological vision increased.

The truth in my opinion is that the interpretation that made Rosmini the "Italian Kant" was unfounded because the idea of "being" could be considered the utmost of the categories of the mind as an "ideal object" and not a pure transcendental form. Instead, Spaventa's school insisted on considering Rosmini very close to Kant's categoricality, and Gioberti very close with his "ideal formula" to Hegelian idealism. The interpretation had some success and was accepted and redefined by Giovanni Gentile. The majority of Rosmini's followers rejected the neo-idealistic interpretation, but it remained in the field taking advantage of the fact that the destiny of nineteenth-century Italian philosophy was indicated in the ability to reappropriate Kantianism and Hegelianism. Nonetheless, Rosminian philosophy was considered a fundamental link for the passage of Italian culture to ideal forms of responsibility in the context of philosophy as a whole.[4]

---

4. On the positive evaluation of Rosminian thought by the Hegelian exponents of Italy, present above all in the University of Naples in the late nineteenth century, led by Bertrando Spaventa, until the resumption of Hegelism in actualism by Giovanni Gentile, see De Lucia, *Istanza metempirica del filosofare*.

In the nineteenth century Rosmini was known throughout Europe for the events in which he was involved and for his "misfortune" in the life of the Catholic Church. The antipathy between the powerful Jesuit order and the small Istituto della Carità, considered by the Jesuits dangerous for a sort of competition on the apostolic, spiritual, and cultural level, was considered the result of a misunderstanding: the Rosminian system increased the richness of Christian thinking, and did not misrepresent it at all. In this sense Rosmini was well known, and many were inclined to believe that the accusations spread by the Jesuits were false. However, the difficulty of certain doctrines and the abstruse language in which some works were written contributed to diverting Catholic culture from his work. This created that mixture of distrust and indifference that prevented Rosmini's overall system from being clearly disclosed and above all from being appreciated as a "system of truth."[5] Hence, after a period of development of the knowledge of his doctrines during the 1930s, in the '40s he became unpopular and this did not favor the far-reaching circulation of his thinking. His political doctrines were disseminated above all, that is, he was recognized as a strong exponent of the Catholic-liberal current, with the consequence, however, that in 1849 two of his works more of ecclesiastical politics were condemned. Later it became clear that his philosophical system represented a considerable contribution to the defense of Christian doctrine, the ideals of education and civil ideals. It became clear that he could give the Italian nation the stimulus to promote the spiritual life of the citizen of the new Italy, thanks to his ideas and the methodology of his research. But at the same time the opponents of the process of unification of our country, and the church-institution and the majority of its leaders, rejected that spiritual methodology and sought increasingly refined pretexts to make its doctrines lose credibility. So it was that even in Italy Rosminian thinking was confined to the margins, and despite the constant consensus that accompanied his thinking both on the part of Christian religious thinking and immanentist thinking of idealistic matrix, his voice was rarely heard in the universities and in particular in the faculties of theology.[6] I would like to point out, however, that the reasons for the poor following in Italy of the Rosminian system after 1887 were not

---

5. Also on the debate on these issues, there is a remarkable bibliography. In this case, I quote the bibliography prepared at the end of the recent edition of ENC 1/A, a fundamental Rosminian work: Rosmini, "Bibliograpfia."

6. We refer to the writings *The Five Wounds of the Holy Church* and *The Constitution under Social Justice*, both published in 1848 and then condemned by the Congregation of Index. We refer to the edition of the acts of that sentence, which took place on May 30, 1849: Malusa, *Antonio Rosmini e Congregazione*. Also for this episode of the struggle against Rosmini and against his Catholic-liberal vision see Malusa's bibliography, 566–70.

due to the fact that the fundamental characteristic of Italian thinking had become practical tension, the search for a happiness based on the sense of the concrete. The Italian philosophy that developed in the so-called age of positivism was not only characterized by the practical element, as the same theoretical perspectives prevailed, but curved on scientific knowledge and "positive" thinking.

Therefore, the doctrines of Rosmini were scarcely disseminated abroad; problematic circulation of Rosmini's works within Italy, especially after the decree of the Holy Office *Post Obitum* (1887), was the reason why, with the advent of positivism in Europe, there was a sharp decrease in interest in his work. There was no longer any harmony between that philosophy and the new positions based on materialistic or atheistic or agnostic doctrines. The same fate befell the philosopher who in life had been an opponent of Rosmini's thinking, namely Vincenzo Gioberti. Despite having been less coherent than Rosmini in his life and in his political choices, despite having embraced a view of the renewal of the Italian nation that now took for granted the hegemony of the kingdom of Sardinia in guiding the future of Italy, Gioberti had been similar in many conceptions to his ancient rival. It was Rosmini who firmly believed that the Piemontese thinker had fallen into an erroneous perspective with the ontologism, and that Being as a creative Idea was proposed with pantheistic accents.[7] In reality, an overall evaluation of the metaphysical conceptions of Rosmini and Gioberti shows that the two thinkers did not understand the consistency and orthodoxy of the fundamental doctrinal points of each other's thinking. They exchanged prodigious accusations, but they can be dismantled overall and brought back to the fear, especially in Rosmini, of being condemned for adherence to certain doctrines of his rival. The two thinkers were certainly quite distant in certain positions, but they can never be considered to have taken opposing positions regarding the Christian faith. The censure of Gioberti's works on January 14, 1852, for prevalently political reasons, worried Rosmini, but in the end it was never accompanied by a precise theological note.

---

7. Let's not forget that in 1846, Rosmini published an anonymous response to the Giobertian accusations contained in the work *Degli errori filosofici di Antonio Rosmini* in the journal *Il Filocattolico* of Florence. In 1847, the work was republished, in a corrected version entitled *Vincenzo Gioberti and Pantheism (Vincenzo Gioberti e il panteismo*; Milan: Boniardi-Pogliani). It was then published with additions, in 1853, by Lucca Giusti. Then, while the writing remained formally anonymous, Rosmini made it known that it was his work. The paper was published in EN 41, edited by R. Orecchia (Padua: Cedam, 1970); and in ENC 21, edited by P. P. Ottonello (Rome: Città Nuova, 2005).

The fact remains that the church, as it did for Rosmini, tried to halt the success of the most restless and combative exponent of liberal Catholicism.[8]

The Thinking of Rosmini and Gioberti, Reevaluated at the Beginning of the Twentieth Century and Almost Ignored in Our Times

The restoration of idealistic thinking in Italy because of the resourceful cultural efforts of Benedetto Croce and Giovanni Gentile also meant the resumption of knowledge of the various doctrines of Rosmini and his rival, Gioberti, who held similar views on the Catholic-liberal creed; leading to a privileged placement of these two thinkers in the overall judgment given for them in the rise of Italian thinking in Europe.[9] With a notable surge of self-esteem it was Croce and Gentile who attributed to Italian philosophy a useful development in the spiritual guidance of Europe also thanks to these two Catholic thinkers. The study of the history of Italian philosophy in the first half of the twentieth century then regained momentum and it can be said that it played a decisive role over the centuries. Until about the second half of the twentieth century Rosmini and Gioberti were read, cited, and above all considered relevant: they established themselves in Italy and were educators of several generations of Italian thinkers and men of culture who referred to them and made their spiritual methodology their model; for example, Augusto Guzzo, Felice Battaglia, Armando Carlini, Luigi Stefanini, and Michele Federico Sciacca. The doctrines and methodologies of Rosmini and Gioberti can therefore be considered the ideal support of different thinkers who developed spiritualistic doctrines gradually freed from the idealistic thinking of the Gentile mold and instead able to inspire a dynamic personalistic vision. But when idealism declined, currents of Marxist, immanentist thinking and epistemological philosophy, taken up by the neopositivism of Central Europe and the English-speaking countries, prevailed over the personalistic perspective. The clash between spiritualism of idealistic derivation, even if it referred to a transcendent idealism, and materialism and immanentism, mixed with the so-called "analytical" philosophy, gradually produced the end of spiritualistic hegemony. Consequently, the

---

8. The acts of the judgment on Giobert's works were published as Malusa and De Lucia, *Vincenzo Gioberti e Congregazioni*.

9. See Malusa, "Rosmini and Gioberti." For some considerations on the "parallel" luck of the thinking of Gioberti during the idealistic hegemony in Italy see Malusa, "Dove vanno oggi gli."

noble fathers of spiritualism, precisely Rosmini and Gioberti, lost their appeal and were increasingly neglected.[10]

This process did not mean, however, that Italian thinking was internationally considered a speculative manifestation of little value, and that it was surpassed and almost cancelled by other currents of thinking of other stronger and more appealing nations. There is no doubt that the recognition of a hegemony of the philosophy of the English-speaking countries, manifested towards the end of the twentieth century, called into question other hegemonic claims, including that of Italian thinking, which, together with French and German thinking, had to suffer the fact that English was the language in which philosophical knowledge was now spreading in the world. But it should not be forgotten that, thanks to the diffusion of the works of our philosophers, starting with those of the Renaissance, an interesting evaluation of their writings was manifested among educated people all over the world. Italian thinking, however, continued to be spoken of above all for certain thinkers, whose ability to attract consensus on the practical level proved to be important. Esposito therefore considers relevant and explains the reasons with complicated arguments: Dante (for the sufferings of the *Inferno*), Leonardo (for the sketches of the painting of the Battle of Anghiari), Machiavelli, Bruno, Campanella, Vico, Beccaria, Cuoco, Leopardi, De Sanctis, Croce, Gentile, Gramsci, and Pasolini. At the end of the presentation of the most significant thinkers Esposito presents authors who bring further elements of growth of the indeterminacy of its thinking to Italian thinking: Tronti, Del Noce, Vattimo. The evaluation of these exponents of thought in Italy leads us to consider the existence of thinkers who have interpreted the essence of Italian thought in terms of breaking the patterns and dissolving the real-metaphysical line. Esposito neglects the contributions of metaphysical and ethical-systematic works to the benefit of writings that can move readers to better understand the practical orientations, the tensions towards happiness and the expansion of ethical freedom, the materialistic tensions. Therefore, considering the importance of Italian thought in the key of bio-politics leads Esposito to practically dissolve the possible line of an Italian philosophical tradition, understood in an educational sense and clarification of the duties and aspirations of Italians when they consider themselves a nation. Italian thinkers are presented, studied, quoted, discussed, according to that which is attractive from the point of view of liberation from the shackles of hypocrisy and spiritual inertia.[11]

10. For an overall vision of post-idealistic Italian philosophy, see Ferrari, *Mezzo secolo*.

11. See Gentili, *Italian Theory*; Gentili, "*Italian Theory* nella crisi"; Gentili and Smerilli, *Differenze italiane*.

The recent works of Esposito and companions have given a significant impulse in the spread of Italian thinking abroad and above all have outlined a sort of Italian "style" to be explored.[12] Faced with the exaltation of *Italian Thought*, it is clear that only a part of what has been expressed in the history of our thinking is accepted and considered as authentically "made in Italy," and that above all the fruition of particular authors offers an impressive picture of our own quality as Italians. In other words: Italians have become important in their cultural choices over the centuries as they have established a "style" of their thinking that has also taken on a more than national, decidedly civil value. Philosophy has been a factor in the growth not so much of Italian nationality, but of original aspects of the Italian character. Mind you: "speculative originality" does not in itself mean that in thinking some Italians were the first in terms of inventiveness and ability to rise to the top; it simply means that the Italians when they expressed that particular "philosophical form" proved to be original, new, able to stand out. Neither traditional nor intellectual systems win consensus. For Esposito and his companions only some of the philosophers who worked in Italy stood out because they expressed ethical-political needs of their own, which also met the interest of many exponents of foreign cultures.

The time has come to ask ourselves what our philosophical tradition may have been in its history of several centuries. Currently it is a fact that Italian thought is appreciated, although it is not declared the best of the expressions of the various national situations. In its history there have been philosophical works that are universally accepted, which have given rise to consensus and debate and which have provoked interest. Esposito and his companions express their often questionable criteria to affirm that sections of our thinking, individual thinkers or particular works, have met with favour and interest, while other thinkers and their writings, other currents, have not expressed any significant contribution, due to being stuck in inflexible syntheses and above all for having lost all contact with reality. But these are criteria that I believe to be arbitrary. A series of criticisms of the methodology of Esposito and Agamben was formulated in the context of meetings and debates promoted by a group of scholars of Rosminian matrix, headed by the Rosmini Institute, who examined the issues of bio-politics formulating a series of observations in my opinion relevant and decisive. They criticized, in the light of Rosminian anthropology, the theories on the body and the person of these Italian scholars. From the close criticism of the exaggerations of bio-politics, therefore, there is also the possibility of

---

12. We also remember the contributions of Agamben: *Homo Sacer* and *Categorie italiane*.

considering that the most significant Italian philosophical tradition is not at all the one arising from Foucaultian theories or biologism.[13]

What Does Italian Philosophical Tradition Mean?

The thesis that had been presented by many parties since the beginnings of the *Risorgimento*, was this: some fundamental elements had characterized the development of philosophical thinking in Italy since the people of our peninsula had identified themselves as such, thanks to a language and a series of cultural centers in which this language was spoken, and to the cultural fruits that this language had presented, fruits of various kinds, literary, poetic, rhetorical, political, and then also philosophical. The people who supported the unity of the Italians, people of the same nation, and who therefore hoped for a political unity of the people of Italy, also argued that in their thinking the Italians had tried their hand at research, philosophical and theological schools, then scientific, and then also political schools. These researches had given rise to a body of doctrines and attitudes of thinking that had characterized "Italianness." The existence of a philosophy that could properly be called "Italian" was therefore sustainable. It was a philosophy built from the end of the Middle Ages, variously articulated in different schools, sometimes in agreement with each other, sometimes in bitter conflict, sometimes in parallel development of motives. But it could be said that Italy had its own philosophy.

Giovanni Gentile and Eugenio Garin above all argued in their writings that from the end of the Middle Ages a patrimony of thought had been built, the result of different schools.[14] Italian philosophy started from the Middle Ages, from the birth of the Italian language itself, although Latin was the language of philosophy in the West. Garin posed the problem of the nature of Italian philosophy considering that it was only with humanism that philosophical practice was born in the various Italian cultural centers,

---

13. The analysis of the theories of Esposito and Agamben is found in Krienke, *Oltre il corpo* (proceedings of the Ninth Cenacolo Rosminiano, 2014, with the participation of Luca Ferrara, Markus Krienke, Biagio Muscherà, Vincenzo Parisi, Gian Luca Sanna and Luca Vettorello).

14. The first of these two great historians of philosophy had received around 1904 from the publisher Vallardi the task of writing a history of the literary genre *philosophy* in Italy. He accepted, but then failed to complete it, having to limit himself to tracing the history of Italian thought up to Lorenzo Valla. See Gentile, *Storia della filosofia italiana*. See Ferrari, *Mezzo secolo*, 169–71. The publisher realized that Gentile would not complete his research, and decided to entrust the task to a valid young Florentine academic, Eugenio Garin, who in 1937 had published a work on Giovanni Pico of Mirandola, *Giovanni Pico della Mirandola*. So, we have: Garin, *Filosofia*.

which had become increasingly important, expanding the knowledge of the ancients and achieving a superb conquest of the philosophy of life and of the city, but also of ontological thinking and of nature.

I have summarized the thesis that Esposito does not consider possible, that is, that a spiritual unity of our nation has been configured since humanism thanks also to the fruits of a complex culture, among which the thought, doctrines, and philosophical theories themselves have had the most relevant space next to the works of literature and poetry. Esposito does not actually recognize the creation of a real Italian nation despite the fact that a philosophical production of Italians manifested itself, in Italian, with some contributions in Latin at the beginning of the Middle Ages and the Renaissance, a vast and rich production, in the fray of world philosophy. He does not deny that philosophical literature in the Italian language has had and still has its weight today. However, according to Esposito, the complex of this Italian production of philosophy cannot be given a precise characterization: it is placed in very particular relationships with the practical horizon. We cannot identify in the vastness of our history of philosophy master lines, hegemonic thought, alienated or even striking characteristics. In other words: we cannot ask ourselves what the "nature of Italian philosophy" is.

Esposito knows that he is presenting a questionable interpretation of our history of philosophy. In the nineteenth century, in fact, historians of philosophy even wondered in which speculative elements our nation had played a decisive role among other nations. Our authors of the nineteenth century spoke of a "primacy" of our thinking over the thinking expressed by other countries, by other nations, by other orientations of the spirit of countries similar to each other. For Esposito, Gioberti's work, which speaks of a moral and civil primacy of Catholic Italy, linked to the philosophy of creation, does not make sense: it is the expression of a misunderstanding. Does it make sense that in the nineteenth century we speak of a primacy of the Italian people in philosophy and in the arts and culture in general? I would say yes: the doctrines of Gioberti[15] and others such as Terenzio Mamiani,[16] are the result of both historical studies (their conclusions are certainly exaggerated, but they are documented) and of cultural tensions aimed at supporting the claim of an Italian political unity, which was considered possible. But, on the other hand, for scholars like Esposito the development of Italian philosophy was not so linear.

15. See Gioberti, *Del Primato morale*.

16. Mamiani's interpretation of the history of Italian thought has been published in the volume *Renewal of Philosophy in Italy* (*Del rinnovamento dell'antica filosofia italiana*). See an analysis of this work in Malusa, "Storiografia filosofica in Italia." The work is now also available in an English translation: *Models of the History of Philosophy*.

We are therefore faced with the denial of the entire interpretation of our philosophy in the modern and in the contemporary age. A refutation of Esposito's theses is possible, however. The majority of twentieth-century scholars have asserted the existence of an Italian philosophy in development over the centuries. They also asserted that at a certain moment thanks to philosophy, Italian culture began to support the value of a national conscience and therefore also the sense of claiming the political unity of our country. Two questions are fundamental for us: is our national tradition and recognized?

Esposito leans towards the following answer: yes, it exists, but not as Rosmini and Gioberti think of it (Esposito cited them only in relation to Gentile's consideration of their work).[17] The analysis of the "Italian tradition" proposed in Esposito's writings, however, is not based on a critical-historiographical work, but on impressions and misrepresentations. We reiterate that the Italian tradition is for Esposito and followers a complex of actions and reactions in the face of life and the concrete, which develop not so much in a context of "nation" as in a context of "territory," and therefore free to compare themselves with other territories and other contexts, without the need to constitute an organic reality, spiritually structured and logically definable. The way in which Italian thinking exists, which does not make effective a national autonomy originates in the context of the humanistic movement, therefore it manifests itself mainly in the sixteenth century, and comes to be the explanation of something that goes beyond theory, systematicity and even social and political organization as derived from pure reasoning. Esposito considers Niccolò Machiavelli the first exponent of this thinking of protest and resistance. I find his interpretation of Machiavelli interesting, but I often can't square his reasoning.[18] Gradually other thinkers appear, who Italian by birth, engage in the struggle for existence and in the defense of contested positions. Italian thought does not present systematic theories; on the contrary, it defends positions in which the freedom of philosophizing is expressed as freedom from binding structures. This explains the presence of men like Giordano Bruno, Tommaso Campanella, Giulio Cesare Vanini, and even Galileo Galilei. Esposito, in my opinion, isolates certain characteristics of the late Renaissance era, the age of the Counter-Reformation, and discovers a sequence of positions that overlap and reconcile, understood as heterodoxy, rebellion, claim to absolute freedom. This philosophy is not national, but on the contrary abandons respect for the rules of the Italian states, and does not seek an abstract political unification.

17. See Esposito, *Pensiero vivente*, 173–75.
18. See Esposito, *Pensiero vivente*, 47–66.

The rhythms of the history of renewed Italian thinking, for Esposito, are alien to both the rhythm of conservation and that of explication; he denies that there can be close harmony between the characteristics of the nascent Italian nation in the consciousness of Italian intellectuals and intellectual achievements. Neither conservation nor dialectic in living and resistant Italian thinking, according to Esposito. Here is one of his considerations:

> It is precisely the absence of a profound national vocation and, until the mid-nineteenth century, of the unitary State itself, that gives Italian philosophy something more, or at least different, than other philosophical traditions which have experienced a more direct identification between territory and nation. Not being located within the perimeter of the national form, pointing rather to its external margins, from the beginning Italian thinking has travelled a different path from that of other European philosophies. For this reason, at a time when the time of the nation seems, if not exhausted, at least questioned in its assumptions and ends, it can face the future with a greater innovative charge.[19]

This text has several contradictions. The alleged absence of a national vocation is all to be proven, and I believe we can affirm the opposite. Especially during the nineteenth century, one of the main characteristics of the idea of the Italian nation was the philosophical vocation of many of its representatives. The existence of a philosophical background in the nature of Italians is affirmed with great vigor. Rosmini himself believed that the philosophy that had appeared in Italy since the Renaissance was significant for the education of Italians. Gioberti founded the reasons for a resumption of the movement of political and spiritual unification on the primacy of Italian philosophy over the other philosophies that arose in different times, supported by different languages and different cultural contexts. Both of these thinkers of ours were approved and followed in their positions.

Nationality and Territory

The testimony of Giovanni Gentile is significant for me. Gentile was the Italian philosopher who gave Esposito the most radical version of political philosophy, in his latest writing *Genesis and Structure of Society*.[20] Gentile,

---

19. Esposito, *Pensiero vivente*, 22–23.

20. Esposito, *Pensiero vivente*, 177. Gentile's work is "the extreme, paroxysmal, complement of a political theology that holds in a mortal grip, the entire thought of Gentile. It does not lie so much in the sovereign identification of politics and the State

in the Roman lecture of 1918, pronounced words that brought together the pages of Gioberti with those of Rosmini in the significant evaluation of the tradition of Italian philosophy that revived the spirit of the nation. Gentile, in truth, assigned to Gioberti (and not to Rosmini) the role of a recovery of the mission of Italian philosophy, not only that of "primacy," but also that which Spaventa had exalted, that is, the philosophy of creation. He asserted that Rosmini "is still tied to the past: his philosophy wants to be, and is not, this living consciousness of the divine that dwells in the human spirit." Rosmini does not have the courage to make the divine completely immanent. "He envelops and recreates the spirit within bands over and over again bent by subtle distinctions between the purely human subject, even if illustrated by the divine light, and God, the absolute real being who bears within himself the secret of our happiness." Instead Gioberti "broke the bonds; and not wishing to overthrow Catholicism, to which he saw the Italian spirits cling, he did not believe it capable of surviving without reforming; and reform in the triumph of the absolute freedom of the spirit, having become fully aware of its infinite nature and power." In any case, the episode of the closeness of the two thinkers, who then differ in the passage from transcendence to immanence, makes clear the value of philosophy for national redemption. In philosophy, says Gentile, the rays converge and depart—

> all the rays of the moral life of a people. It is time to resume the great Giobertian tradition; and that the experiments of thinking of which the first half century of this new Italy abounded, reap the fruit, establishing in philosophy, and with it and for it in all our spiritual activity, that fullness, which makes thinking a burning forge, not of simple speculative systems, but of systems of life.[21]

The philosophy of the spiritualists of the Risorgimento should return, according to Gentile, in its ability to give our intellect and our social forces the strength to guide the nation with authentic "systems of life." Therefore, it is not the metaphysical and ontological visions of Rosmini and Gioberti which for Gentile give the national spirit its effectiveness, but the idealistic recovery that they themselves advocate as fidelity to the creativity of the spirit. It is interesting that Gentile considers Gioberti the leader of this development of Italian thinking and that thanks to him, philosopher of the "supremacy" certainly, but above all philosopher of the great system of life

---

and not even, only, in the absorption in this of the whole social sphere, public and private, of existence, but in the immediate transcription of religious monotheism into ethical-political monism."

21. Gentile, *Carattere storico*, 46.

that is that of the idea and of the ideal creation. Gentile recovered the greatness of the metaphysical syntheses of Rosmini and Gioberti and inserted them into the idealistic rebirth. Which means that these two thinkers, in life rivals, but in the reality of the Italian spirit much closer than it seemed, represent the philosophical and therefore spiritual basis of the nation.

It could be said that language, literary culture, and philosophy are, for our intellectuals and politicians who brought about Italian unity, the pillars of unification. Since a highly committed philosophical culture with varied directions was widespread throughout the territory where Italian was spoken, this phenomenon indicated the unity of thought that existed among the men of the different regions, and also allowed the different regional states to communicate with each other and to propose unifying elements within a federal perspective. Rosmini based his hopes of realizing the Italian Confederation, which supported the effort of the Italian states most sensitive to the fate of national dignity, on the living and industrious philosophical spirit.[22] Esposito does not demonstrate with historical data the nonexistence of a national vocation, which, on the contrary, seems to have been nourished precisely by philosophical knowledge, in its intertwining with civil life. If Esposito's thesis on the nature of the estrangement and contestation of Italian thinking is valid, even now, it can be explained as an awareness that certain Italian intellectuals have of the contestative role that philosophy plays with regard to spiritual inertia, the despotism of certain sovereigns and certain social classes. But such a contestation raises the national conscience, it does not replace it. Italian philosophy in its various exponents and in the various currents believes that its main task is to free civil life from conformism, from closure to the values of freedom, from religious fanaticism, from corruption and from bad government. Since the mid-eighteenth century the critical thinking of the Enlightenment has challenged bad governance and despotism to hope for a moral rigor and a spirit of ethical and juridical reform that enhances the national spirit.

I believe therefore that, while it is true that a part of our philosophical thinking assumed between the late eighteenth and nineteenth centuries the characteristics of criticism and contestation, taking up what had been thought and written since humanism, these attitudes enhanced the demand for national cohesion. If Esposito also sees in the current exponents of philosophical thinking the resumption of a role of struggle and distancing from the systematic and dogmatic spirit, this does not mean that what can be found today means the abandonment of national cohesion, disintegration.

22. See my works "Nazione e nazionalità"; "Antonio Rosmini ed suo 'credo'"; "Spunti di un personalismo."

It is true that the idea of nation is now under revision, but in the sense that it is being replaced by the idea of super-nation, that is, of an expansion of national characteristics and a fusion of them in the dialogue between the different cultural situations. The notion of "globalization" also appears in philosophical historiography in the sense that philosophical production, thanks also to the growth in the use of the English language, is less and less characterized by the national linguistic note and is increasingly assimilated to the way of thinking that now prevails at the international level. So: not so much a thought of the "made in Italy" type, aimed at giving weight to individual life and disengagement, to bio-politics, but a thought that collects the synthesis of different styles, trying to assimilate them all. Which would mean that the Italian thought that foreign intellectuals like so much is such precisely because it is Italian and has its own characteristics. They like the way it is written in Italian and practiced by Italians who in the past have struggled significantly to make certain values prevail. In other words: it pleases because it has not been assimilated into globalization.

The Italian national tradition existed before the phenomenon of globalization and will exist, perhaps participating more closely in the spread of other traditions, seen as competitors and not as divisive. Scholars will be able to extol the primacy of certain philosophical ideas over the centuries, and their outcome today, over other minority or even counterproductive ideas. They will be able to uphold, in order to judge the different primacies that have occurred, the method of exhaustion and conservation or the dialectical method; they will be able to argue that the method of contestation and distancing has been able to highlight philosophical contributions over the centuries of the past that are today fruitful of suggestions. All these interpretations, however, accept the existence of a tradition to be exploited and exalted. If they deviate from certain judgments, if they refuse to see that certain traditions can be internalized and valued, they nevertheless accept that they can dispose themselves against others more capable of constituting the national spirit. Nation is different from pure territoriality, we agree; however, a pure spreading of events over contiguous territories and this passage of phenomena of thought from one place to another cannot exist in the life of a people as a whole (this term must certainly be kept. For Italians, the nation has not only existed, it has also manifested itself since the Middle Ages.

Precisely the different movements existing in the late Renaissance testify that Italians tended to be open to discussion, always within the great mass phenomena and cultural innovations such as the Counter-Reformation (in Italy the Reformation was marginal) and the Baroque. The seventeenth century was not the century of the cultural decadence of the Italians, as has been written. It was certainly the century of political oppression, of civil insignificance. But it was also the century of great European movements which Italy did not ignore. It is true that Vico's genius manifested itself in isolation, contesting the prevailing ideas and launching some fundamental ideas about history and civilization. But it also true that the kingdom of Naples was very active in the reformist culture during the eighteenth century, while Vico was ignored, or only partially understood. The nineteenth century was the century in which the greatness of Vico was recognized; but this did not mean that the Enlightenment of the eighteenth century in our country was an instrument of levelling and oppression. We must not forget that Genovesi and Filangieri were intellectuals of great weight and contributed considerably to uniting the national conscience, while also contesting the existing status quo. Moreover, let us not forget that they were also influenced by Vico's ideas, albeit in their own way.

With these clarifications I think I have shown that some of Esposito's theses are unfounded. The criticisms that Esposito's work has received do not mean that it is not to be discussed and evaluated as a serious contribution to the study of our national tradition. Piero Di Giovanni launched the series of Italian Philosophy and made it a cultural instrument.[23] The message that comes from an initiative like that of Di Giovanni is: we must not reject the various tendencies and that have occurred in Italian culture nor the idea that perhaps even in antiquity there was a series of philosophical schools that made their influence felt until the Renaissance and beyond; nor the idea that in the Middle Ages there were also philosophical schools of an ontological nature that then determined movements capable of increasing our philosophical culture; nor the idea that Italian philosophy was born only with the Renaissance from the destruction of medieval dogmatism and the myth of ancient wisdom. The acceptance of all these interpretations and the methods that have led us to support them represents the richness of our historiography. The Italian nation has not been hegemonic in Europe and today it is not hegemonic in the world: however, it has made a contribution that cannot be ignored.

To those scholars who have launched the idea that what distinguishes Italian thought in its originality is civil and social commitment, the break

---

23. The series born at the publishing house Franco Angeli, among the most interesting and comprehensive dedicated to the dissemination of philosophical culture and the publication of specialized monographs on the history of philosophy (as well as being the publishing house that has been publishing for years the precious *Rivista di Storia della filosofia* founded by Mario Dal Pra), is co-directed by Piero Di Giovanni and Caterina Genna. This series, and its premises, were the subject of a conference held in Genoa on Oct. 22, 2021, at the Department of Antiquity, Philosophy, History (DAFIST) with the participation of P. De Lucia, P. Di Giovanni, L. Malusa, S. Langella, and S. Zanardi.

from traditions, the contestation of every crystallization up to a movement of breaking even the traditional partitions of philosophy, we ask therefore not to neglect that alongside these centrifugal tendencies, very clear at certain times, there are sometimes moderate needs of a metaphysical foundation, almost wanting connect certain speculations to the purpose of critical thought, which is not only intellectual. In the nineteenth century Rosminian philosophy responded to the needs of our people and many adhered to it, even if it was difficult to understand, and if its systematicity prevented easy syntheses. Contesting from the point of view of intellectual reasoning both sensism and extreme rationalism Rosmini, in his first phase of thought, wanted to open the way to the search for an integral truth that would allow the exercise of intellectual charity as an orientation of man to the effusive truth of itself.

There was a circulation of Rosminian systematicity, and many thinkers and professors of philosophy were happy to feed on such a rich and well-structured knowledge, combining holiness and knowledge, civil commitment and religion, speculation and practical operation. It should be remembered that after the *New Essay* Rosmini undertook to trace the entire philosophical system by contesting the errors of his time. In this he first outlined the principles of moral science, placing a complicated appendix of comparative and critical history on the principle of morality, and fighting utilitarianism and hedonism; then he traced the lines of anthropology, having understood that the vision of the integral man required to spread the doctrine of the person as an intellectual, moral, juridical subject. The completion of the moral doctrine then required addressing the most crucial themes of the vision of man and of human society, the themes that confronted the Christian revelation of original sin, the doctrine of sin and guilt, and the doctrine of freedom. After the publication of the *Trattato della Coscienza Morale* (Treatise on moral conscience) Rosmini encountered the first misunderstandings of his work. Here, in the history of Italian thought, criticisms of Rosmini appeared regarding his orthodoxy as a Christian, probably due to the ethical rigorism that was believed to spring from the vision of the absolute necessity of divine grace for the salvation of man wounded by sin and dragged into lust. In this vision one can insinuate an assertion of ethical necessity, of inability to earn salvation by one's own strength. It was 1841, and Rosmini had so far known consensus and a considerable following among Italian intellectuals. From this year on contrasts and controversies would begin, which would make it difficult for Rosmini even to develop his educational and ascetic projects. This presence of the Rosminian system in the development of Italian philosophy, at the moment of the great unitary intellectual and political momentum, confirms that it is not always the ethical contestative thinking that expresses the best of philosophy in Italy.

Nationally, Rosminian philosophy was important, and did not deserve to be set aside. Other doctrines followed in Italy: Rosmini's philosophy of the forms of being and Gioberti's vision of the "ideal formula"; above all idealism, as we have already stated, guided the development of our culture. The decline of idealism, however, did not mean in Italy the decline of every primacy of theoresis and metaphysics, but certainly other tendencies were affirmed and perhaps the supporters of *Italian Thought* were right to consider openness to practical life prevalent for the fate of our thought. Rosmini was no longer a respected and successful philosopher; but neither is he a thinker whose value should not be acclaimed. His theoresis, his correlation to holiness and ethical and educational seriousness, are also practiced today and no one who has read his work thinks he stands outside the line of Italian thought. It can be concluded then that the followers of Rosmini's ontological thinking have no reason to separate themselves from Italian exponents of other tendencies, who perhaps exercise with more clamor the vocation of being Italian. It is not a question of raising the voice or exploring certain topics rather than certain others; it is not a question of adopting methods of reflection that are contestative to the classical vision of philosophizing. At stake are the destinies of our country, which thrives on a tradition, which sets out on different paths in order to continue to dialogue with other nations and thus conquer increasingly adequate roles where authentic thought is in jeopardy.

Bibliography

Agamben, Giorgio. *Categorie italiane. Studi di poetica e di letteratura*. Rome: Laterza, 2010.

———. *Homo Sacer*. 9 vols. Macerata, It.: Quodlibet, 2018.

———. *Homo Sacer. Il potere sovrano e la nuda vita*. Turin: Einaudi, 1995.

Claverini, Corrado. *La tradizione filosofica italiana. Quattro paradigmi interpretativi*. Macerata, It.: Quodlibet, 2021.

Congregazione per la Dottrina della Fede (Congregation for the doctrine of the faith). "Sul valore dei decreti dottrinali concernenti il pensiero e le opere del Reverendo Sacerdote Antonio Rosmini-Serbati." Vatican, June 30, 2001. https://press.vatican.va/content/salastampa/it/bollettino/pubblico/2001/06/30/0385/01124.html.

De Lucia, Paolo. *L'istanza metempirica del filosofare. Metafisica e religione nel pensiero degli hegeliani d'Italia*. Genoa: Accademia Ligure di Scienze e Lettere, 2005.

Esposito, Roberto. *Living Thought: The Origins and Actuality of Italian Philosophy*. Stanford, CA: Stanford University Press, 2012.

———. *Pensiero vivente. Origine e attualità della filosofia italiana*. Turin: Einaudi, 2010.

Ferrari, Massimo. *Mezzo secolo di filosofia italiana*. Bologna: Mulino, 2016.

———. *Mezzo secolo di filosofia italiana. Dal secondo dopoguerra al nuovo millennio.* Bologna: Mulino, 2016.
Garin, Eugenio. *Giovanni Pico della Mirandola. Vita e dottrine.* Florence: Monnier, 1937.
———. *Giovanni Pico della Mirandola. Vita e dottrine.* Rome: Edizioni di Storia e Letteratura-Istituto Nazionali di Studi sul Rinascimento, 2011.
———. *La filosofia.* 2 vols. Milan: Vallardi, 1947.
———. *Storia della filosofia italiana.* 3 vols. Turin: Einaudi, 1966, 1978.
———. *Storia della filosofia italiana.* 3 vols. 2nd ed. Turin: Einaudi, 1978.
Gentile, Giovanni. *Il carattere storico della filosofia italiana.* Bari, It.: Laterza, 1918.
———. *Storia della filosofia italiana fino a Lorenzo Valla.* Edited by Vito A. Bellezza. Florence: Sansoni, 1962.
———. *Storia della filosofia italiana fino a Lorenzo Valla.* Florence: Lettere, 2003.
Gentili, Dario. *Italian Theory. Dall'operaismo alla biopolitica.* Bologna: Mulino, 2012.
———. "L'*Italian Theory* nella crisi della globalizzazione." In *Made in Italy e cultura. Indagine sull'identità italiana contemporanea,* edited by Daniele Baricco, 243–47. Palermo: Palumbo, 2016.
Gentili, Dario, and Elettra Smerilli, eds. *Differenze italiane. Politica e filosofia: mappe e sconfinamenti.* Rome: Derive Approdi, 2015.
Gioberti, Vincenzo. *Del Primato morale e civile degli italiani.* Edited by Gustavo Balsamo-Crivelli. Turin: Unione tipografico-editrice torinese, 1925.
Krienke, Markus, ed. *Oltre il corpo. Metafisica e biopolitica.* Milan: Mimesis, 2016.
Malusa, Luciano. "Antonio Rosmini ed il suo 'credo' cattolico-liberale tra fedeltà al Papato e critica del 'dispotismo statalistico.'" In *Filosofia Italiana* 1 (2016) 1–32. http://www.filosofiaitaliana.net/announdicesimo-uno/.
———, ed. *Antonio Rosmini e la Congregazione dell'Indice. Il decreto del 30 maggio 1849. La sua genesi ed i suoi echi.* Stresa, It.: Rosminiane, 1998.
———. "Antonio Rosmini-Serbati in Antonio Rosmini-Serbati." In *Enciclopedia italiana di scienze, lettere ed arti. Il contributo italiano alla storia del pensiero,* 8:415–22. Rome: Istituto della Enciclopedia Italiana, 2012.
———. "Dove vanno oggi gli studi sul pensiero di Vincenzo Gioberti?" *Rivista di Filosofia Neo-Scolastica* 110 (2018) 323–50.
———. *The Hegelian Age.* Edited by Gregorio Piaia et al. Vol. 4 of *Models of the History of Philosophy.* Cham, Switz.: Springer, 2022.
———. "Nazione e nazionalità nelle riflessioni e iniziative di Rosmini dell'anno 1848." In *Nazione, Stato e società civile. La filosofia e l'Unità d'Italia,* edited by Francesco Totaro, 48–84. Lecce, It.: Pensa Multimedia, 2013.
———. "Rosmini and Gioberti." In *Croce and Gentile. La cultura italiana e l'Europa,* edited by Luciano Malusa et al., 24–31. Rome: Istituto della Enciclopedia Italiana, 2016.
———. "Rosmini, Antonio." In *Dizionario storico dell'Inquisizion,* edited by A. Prosperi et al., 3:1341–47. Pisa: Normale, 2010.
———. "Spunti di un personalismo nelle argomentazioni rosminiane sui mezzi e sui fini per realizzare l'unità d'Italia." In *Alla fontana di Silöe. Studi in onore di Carlo Vinti,* edited by Antonio Allegra et al., 289–306. Naples: Orthotes, 2019.
———. "La storiografia fiosofica in Italia nella prima metà dell'Ottocento." In *Storia delle storie generali della filosofia,* edited by Giovanni Santinello and Gregorio Piaia, 4/2:203–386. Rome: Antenore, 2004.

———, ed. *La teologia di Antonio Rosmini sotto attacco. Consensi e dissensi su una grande sintesi filosofico-teologica.* Milan: Franco Angeli, 2021.

Malusa, Luciano, and Paolo De Lucia, eds. *Vincenzo Gioberti e le Congregazioni romane. I giudizi, le procedure e l condanna nei documenti inediti dell'Indice e del Santo Uffizio.* Rome: Fabrizio Serra, 2011.

Malusa, Luciano, et al., eds. *Antonio Rosmini e la Congregazione del Santo Uffizio. Atti e documenti della condanna del 1887.* Milan: Franco Angeli, 2008.

Rosmini, Antonio. "Bibliografia." In *Della missione a Roma di Antonio Rosmini-Serbati*, edited by Luciano Malusa and Stefania Zanardi, ENC 1/A, 563–80. Rome: Città Nuova, 2020.

———. *Nuovo Saggio sull'origine delle idee.* Edited by Gaetano Messina. 3 vols. ENC 3–5. Rome: Città Nuova, 2003–2004.

———. *Rinnovamento della filosofia in Italia.* Paris: Pilan-Delaforest, 1834.

———. *Vincenzo Gioberti e il panteismo.* Edited by Pier P. Ottonello. ENC 21. Rome: Città Nuova, 2005.

Zanardi, Stefania. *La filosofia di Antonio Rosmini davanti alla Congregazione dell'Indice. 1850–1854.* Milan: Franco Angeli, 2018.

18

Antonio Rosmini: Spirituality of Justice and Anthropological Conception

PIERLUIGI GIROLI

Introduction

THIS IS WHAT ROSMINI wrote in the *Directorium Spiritus*, an unpublished collection of mainly patristical texts that he composed in view of the foundation of the Istituto della Carità:

> Love for justice, when it is considered in its practical implementation, is transformed into love for God. In God alone, in fact, everything else can be loved. Hence the need for purification of other affections other than love for God. The older one is, the more one must strive for edification and perfection. May he never cease to progress, and set no limit to the acquisition of this perfection, hearing him say: "Act with the end in mind" and again: "do not wait until death to fulfill them" (Sir 18:22); and again: "Wisdom is praised in the end." The more we progress, the more we humble ourselves, because the humbler we are, the more we will progress. Now, let no elder believe that he is so learned as to think that obedience does not suit him, since God also submitted to it. In fact, humility and obedience are still a

necessity in the young, while in the elderly they are an ornament. Good progress is made by those who perform each action well and those who act day by day as if they were always in their infancy. That is why Scripture says that the increase in merit is an incentive to progress. As for those who, while ignoring the first negligences, increasingly incur others, so it is written: "A stubborn heart will have many a hurt; adding sin to sin is madness" (Sir 3:27). As for progress, then, it is said: "He who is holier, he will sanctify himself even more" (Holste, Appendix, *Second Discourse of Faustus of Lérins to the monks*).[1]

The passage cites three times the works *Sapienziali*, for which Rosmini in his love for sacred Scripture, had a particular sympathy, as evidenced by Antonio Quacquarelli in his work *La lezione patristica di Antonio Rosmini*:

> Rosmini deduced from the patristic conception that the Old is in the New Testament and points to Christ. We can see this in the advice to Maria Geltrude Cerutti, mother superior at the nunnery of Arona. It is necessary to read the New Testament and "have recourse to some books of the Old Testament, and especially to the Psalms, the Book of Wisdom, Tobit, Judith, Esther, Job and Deuteronomy, trying to steer these books towards Jesus Christ and his love: because they all truly refer to Christ."[2]

Man and Person in Rosmini: Education to the Order of Values

The study and consideration of man in all his interiority is a topic dear to Rosmini, who wants it at the foundation and on the horizon not only of those who deal with the study of sciences such as pedagogy, psychology or medicine (think of the statutes of the Collegio di San Raffaele elaborated by Rosmini himself), but also of the studies and actions of those who deal with economics and politics (Rosmini goes so far as to say that there are no true politics where there is no authentic formative purpose of the person).

The Person: How Can We Synthesize This Concept?

A work to which we can refer in particular is *Anthropology as an Aid to Moral Science* (*L'Antropologia in servizio della scienza morale*), and I will

---

1. Rosmini, *Directorium Spiritus*, 1:13.
2. Rosmini, "Lettera a Madre Maria" 3:143–46, para. 850, quoted in Quacquarelli, *Lezione patristica*, 47.

refer to it with the mediation of a conference held by Father Giuseppe Bozzetti on the subject.

Rosmini often recalls the importance of a concise overall vision of human nature, criticizing various contemporary philosophies of abstractionism, because they cease to consider man, absolutizing a dimension that in reality is only partial, at the service of immediate interests of a different nature than a sincere anthropological investigation. For example, he reproaches Gioia for a *sensistic* vision of the person and Romagnosi for an *intellectualistic* vision of the same, aimed only at social life.

Rosmini clearly declares that man's *social and intellectual* development, however important, cannot exhaust his *moral development*, which alone can be called properly personal.

Beginning to see man in his two dimensions, *physical-sensistic* and *intellectual*: their complementarity in human nature implies that *the one identifies man, defining his individuality and therefore his limit*; the other *opens him to the relationship with the other from himself and therefore with the infinite*, making him at the same time aware of his finitude. It is in this impulse that man finds in himself the capacity and vocation to *love the whole being, as far as he can*, and it is in this that man recognizes *his greatest good*. In him it therefore takes place as a *continuous confrontation*, or better *a dialogue*, between the tendency to withdraw defensively into oneself and the *irrepressible need to open oneself to the other*. And in this confrontation, all his faculties unfold, to use the words of Bozzetti: "talking, laughing, crying, walking, studying, working material and art, etc."[3]

These are faculties in which man expresses himself, either by enjoying their positivity and perfection within himself, or by continually expanding through them his range of action around himself. In the *balance* between the two tendencies of *closure in oneself* and *openness to the other*, man's *natural freedom*, a characteristic of his human nature, is expressed and realized.

Demands and Challenges for a Just Society

Returning to the fundamental value that Rosmini attributes to justice, and to society as a place where the necessary help to cultivate it is given and received, we can then say that the educator, who on the one hand must respect and wisely accompany the individual spontaneity of the subject by educating, on the other, must lead them: (1) to learn and be able to evaluate the essential goods as supreme, and above all the capacity to enter into communion with God the Creator; (2) to learn to confer dignity and value

---

3. See Bozzetti, "Natura umana," 3:3379.

of personal goods on all other goods, using them as a means of preserving and increasing one's personal value. Rosmini, speaks of bringing the person to *effectively recognize being within his own order.*

Father Bozzetti then schematizes, as deriving from this principle, some duties, positive and negative, of the subjects who undertake the path of growth in justice. Four negatives:

> 1. Do not disturb the order of your natural faculties inasmuch as they serve the good of the person, and therefore keep subordinate the inferior (sensitive) powers to the superior (rational-moral); 2. Do not offend human nature in the use of will and freedom by introducing into you vicious habits that prevent or weaken the consciousness of the essential goods of the person; 3. Do not offend human nature in intelligence, with culpable errors, which diminish the person's adherence to the truth; 4. Do not damage or allow the bodily sensory life to be destroyed without just cause, inasmuch as it is the ordinary means for the individual to carry out the rational moral life, and therefore for the elevation of the person.[4]

Three positives:

> 1. Promote in yourself adherence to the moral good by voluntary and free acts, because in this lies the actual value of the person; 2. Serve your intellectual development for the same purpose; 3. It cares for the health and strength of the body, as it makes you more apt to fulfil your duties and to carry out personal good.[5]

And from this he concludes: "Education in the exercise of the person's freedom is practiced precisely [in helping him] to become freely aware of the ever deeper inner convictions of these maxims of conduct."[6]

The Justice of Christ and the Christian: Complementarity between Thought and Asceticism in Christian Perfection

Fulvio De Giorgi, in his book *Rosmini e il suo tempo*, quotes the great jurist and scholar of Rosmini's work, Giuseppe Capograssi:

> [Rosmini's] is a vision of life as an affectionate tendency, according to Rosmini's own words, of being towards being, whose

---

4. Bozzetti, "Natura umana," 3:382–83.
5. Bozzetti, "Natura umana," 3:383.
6. Bozzetti, "Natura umana," 3:383.

> salient characteristic is to have trust, peace, lack of effort, trusting expectation: in the face of the holiness of creation and the infinite affectionate tendency of being, there is nothing but letting oneself live, There is only to recognize, that is, to love, the inexhaustible and unique richness that makes up the concrete. conception of life as secret rest, as secret enjoyment, which is so far from the harsh and cruel modern idea of expecting nothing from reality but of incessantly creating reality, that we contemporary readers cannot really understand it.[7]

In this dynamic, De Giorgi also strongly emphasizes the indispensable unity that is found in Rosmini between clarity of thought, education of mind and heart and personal asceticism, aimed at giving substance to what has been learned through free and coherent choices. And about the role of Grace in the achievement of justice, De Giorgi cites a letter from Rosmini to Count Giulio Padulli, responding to a request for advice regarding the education of the Count's two grandchildren:

> It would be better to make them feel more deeply the importance of a strong labor: and to instill in their souls a strong will. . . . Grace comes to the rescue: it makes us feel what is insensitive to a secret sense of man: the things of the spirit, then that grace infuses them, acquire, I will say a spiritual body for us, and our soul sees them, gropes them, flirts with them and mingles with them.[8]

Grace and Justice

These last lines introduce us to a more specific discourse about the search for justice by the man who desires perfection. Rosmini speaks of justice in various parts of the *The Constitutions of the Institute of Charity (Costituzioni dell'Istituto della Carità)*, but in particular he dedicates an entire chapter to it, the third, in part 6, entitled *Fondamento di tutta la società*. The *Istituto della Cartià* is founded on four pillars, which correspond to the chapters of the sections: (1) *La Provvidenza del Padre Celeste*; (2) *La Grazia del nostro*

---

7. Capograssi, *Il diritto secondo Rosmini*, 326, quoted by De Giorgi, *Rosmini e suo tempo*, 409.

8. Rosmini, "Lettera al Conte Giulio Padulli," 1:315–16, quoted by De Giorgi, *Rosmini e suo tempo*, 409–10.

Salvatore Gesù Cristo; 3. *La giustizia*; 4. *L'amore di Dio*.[9] The discourse on justice starts precisely from what has just been said about the gift of grace:[10]

> Just as . . . he who is without eyes cannot see, so man can do nothing in what concerns eternal life if the grace of the Lord and Savior our Jesus Christ, which, being gratuitous (otherwise it would not be grace), must be received with the infinite love of gratitude, and at the same time with fear and trepidation of losing it after receiving it.[11]

The gift of grace, however, implies a possibility of correspondence that is left to the freedom of man, and that is realized, according to Rosmini, in the constant commitment to purify the spirit from everything that can prevent its work, as far as the person himself is capable:

> And in order for the grace that God has granted to us can gradually increase sanctification in us and in our neighbor, we must strive with unceasing diligence to amend our spirit with continual purification. Indeed, the infinite goodness of God comes to the man in whom there is no obstacle of sin. And it is not enough to avoid in part the filth of sin and in part to preserve it, "For whoever keeps the whole law, but falls short in one particular, has become guilty in respect to all of it." (Jas 2:10). And it is no use closing something evil in the depths of one's heart as an occult thing, for "No creature is concealed from him, but everything is naked and exposed to the eyes of him to whom we must render an account." (Heb 4:13). And the practices of religion and piety do not give the right to sin and not to repent of it, nor do they make less rigorous the judgment of the Lord, who warns us: "Not everyone who says to me, 'Lord, Lord,' will enter the kingdom of heaven . . ." (Matt 7:21).[12]

This commitment to purification must have no limits in the Christian, and constitutes the index of authenticity of his desire for perfection, as well as the necessary assent to God's action in his heart. For this reason, Rosmini recommends:

> Therefore, let each proceed with perfection before God and truly desire to become free from every stain, for, as Scripture

---

9. Rosmini, *Costituzioni dell'Istituto della Carità* (The constitutions of the Institute of Charity), paras. 462–83.

10. See Rosmini, *Directorium Spiritus*, 1:45–47. In the context of quotations from *Costituzioni dell'Istituto della Carità*.

11. Rosmini, *Costituzioni dell'Istituto della Carità*, para. 473.

12. Rosmini, *Costituzioni dell'Istituto della Carità*, para. 474.

says, "The appointed time is near.... The righteous must still do right, and the holy still be holy." (Rev 1:3; 22:11). Indeed, there must be no limit to purification. The opening of conscience is an effective instrument, which each one will undertake with the utmost candour and sincerity to his superior and father, in the full conviction that, if he does it in the best way, he will soon become pure by the grace of God our Lord. In fact, Christ came into the world to make everything manifest and to subject everything to a judgment that no one can avoid. But God is merciful to those who manifest themselves for the sake of justice.[13]

Trinitarian Life: Archetype of All Justice

The basic approach proposed by Rosmini in this discourse is that the justice of Christ has its roots in the intimacy of the Holy Trinity, in the full communion of the Father and the Son and the Holy Spirit. In this harmony, the Word, living, personal and eternal contemplation of the Father, is also the pattern in which everything is created. The Word, in becoming flesh and entering as a man into human history reveals to man the way to rediscover this full harmony, lost through sin. This is the way of obedience as an intelligent and loving adherence to the truth, as life in truth, which is God himself. And it is precisely because victory over disorder and corruption introduced into the world by the disobedience of sin that Christ's obedience arouses hatred and persecution of the enemies of goodness and truth. Man's way to return to the Father in Christ is therefore union with Christ himself, the just man who *justifies*, the *Son who makes man a sharer in his communion with the Father*. The man who seeks justice therefore passes gradually, by the gift of grace and in the free exercise of his will in corresponding to it, from a simple *imitatio Christi* to an ever more intimate communion with the Son, and in the Son with the Father. In this dynamic man increasingly discovers and intensifies the reality of Christ the Way, the Truth, and the Life. Way because it indicates the path to follow concretely, in asceticism: the first step on the path of perfection, which is abstinence from sins. Truth because revelation of the reality of God, according to the Rosminian motto of *justice* as recognition *of Being in its order*. Life because participation and real communion with the Father and in this full realization of God's plan for man and creation.

13. Rosmini, *Costituzioni dell'Istituto della Carità*, para. 475.

According to Rosmini,[14] the justice of Christ is the splendor of the glory of the Father, which the Father himself contemplates in the Son, and in which the universe, and in particular mankind, is created in the image and likeness of God. And this is the only image of God granted in the Old Testament, before God himself became man. But when God became man, in the humanity of Christ the Word showed himself fully as the model and plan of creation. First, he did so by showing in the traits of the Man-God the beauty of the human creature. Then showing in the evolution of his life the beauty of the full realization of God's plan, of which a part is entrusted to man (justice), with indispensable help, indeed in response to the gift of grace.[15]

Thus, the way in which Christ brings back to the world the perfection of the Father's plan is to "fulfil all righteousness in himself" (Matt 3:15). That is, to respond fully as a man to the will of the Father. In Christ, in his prayer, in his sentiments, in his affections and in his works, the Creator's plan grows in creation:

> The exemplar in which God saw *ab aeterno* the world created in time and in which he did his work, and . . . gloried in it, is the divine Word. And yet when the Redeemer prayed with these words: "Now glorify me, Father, with you, with the glory that I had with you before the world began" [John 17:5], he then recalled that glory which he had and had as the divine Word. . . . Wherefore he asked . . . , that that glory . . . , be realized in time, . . . and of the humanity of the Word communicated. For the Word . . . , that glory never failed . . . ; but it remained that she would realize herself and thus communicate herself in time to the same Word inasmuch as he was made man . . . . This is what Christ asked. And he asked for it, because this fulfilment in time had to be done by virtue of his prayers, by way of imploration . . . : and he had to do it also by way of merit, by preaching, and by heroic virtues, and by the magnanimous offering of his life that Christ made. . . . In order for the realization of the glory, which Christ was to receive as a risen man, it was conditioned to the operation of Christ himself; and yet he tells the Father that he has already done what he had been joined to himself. . . . In order to accomplish all righteousness with the most holy life, the Father alone was left to accomplish and realize the other part that it was up to him to do. . . . And Christ said that he had consumed the work . . . , for the fullest and most perfect offering

---

14. Part of the speech that follows is taken from Lorizio, "Il Cristocentrismo."
15. See Colombo, *Bilancio della teologia*, 3:36–62.

... made of himself, and for the unbloody sacrifice celebrated at the supper, which was equivalent to the reality of death, to the *consummatum est* that he pronounced on the cross.[16]

Thus, in the face of his life, if on the one hand evil and imperfection in all their repugnance appear ever more evident, on the other, precisely in the struggle and victory of good over evil and justice over sin, the nobility and strength of man appear ever more evident as he, responding to the gift of grace, can aspire to be good and therefore happy.[17] According to Rosmini, when he asks the Father to be glorified, Jesus is speaking precisely of the manifestation of this greatness of man in God. Jesus asks the Father that the glory he received before creation may be realized in time and thus communicated to humanity (John 17:5):[18] "If, therefore, in the eternal model we see the glory of the Word communicated to humanity, this must be realized in time and this is what Christ asked."[19] Part of the plan of creation is therefore that the glory that the Son received from the Father should be fully grasped by man through the righteousness of the Son of God made man. Although it is true that man can come to the knowledge of God also through the natural light and the investigation of created reality. When God himself wished to reveal himself fully and definitively to man in Christ, faith in him was the fullest way: (1) to know ever more deeply and authentically creation and creatures; (2) to know ever more deeply the mystery of the eternal wisdom of the Father, which is manifested in the Word made man.

Sin and Redemption: The "Debt of Justice"

Man, who originally lived in union with God, has separated from him by sinning, thus obscuring in himself the light of reason, which is the heritage of the heavenly light, and he has found himself led astray by an imagination now incapable of guiding him to the truth. But God has not abandoned him. In the history of salvation, God has patiently guided man to bring him back to himself, first of all, by showing through his own errors, how foolish human wisdom is before him[20] and then by showing him how impossible it is for man alone to be able to rekindle in himself the light of joy without

---

16. Rosmini, *Th*, 396–97.
17. See Rosmini, *Th*, 162–63.
18. Rosmini, *Th*, 396.
19. See Rosmini, *Th*, 397.
20. See Acts 17:30; 1 Cor 3:19–20; Isa 29:14; 33:18.

the oil of justice.[21] Deprived of the light of good, man found himself a prisoner of chaos, lost in a labyrinth that seemed to continue to spread around him in his wanderings, and from which God alone could lead him.[22] And God did. This work of redemption appears in the Gospels, for example, in miracles or signs, in which Christ opens the eyes of the blind and frees man from various forms of slavery, ultimately death.[23]

The monstrous extension of the labyrinth of sin only increases what Rosmini calls with a Pauline expression "a debt of justice." The distances increase, the paths become complicated, the price of redemption increases, the energies are less, hope fades:

> Man ... would have been irreparably lost if these effective evils of sin had not been repaired ... he had to avoid the vengeance of the Almighty; and He had to draw him back again. But this could not have been if the order of justice had not first been "reestablished"; order which is necessary, and God who is essentially justice cannot will anything other than Himself. But Saint Augustine wrote: ... since *no one* overcomes the *laws* of the *almighty Creator*, it is *not* permitted for the *soul not to repay its debt*. ... But it was impossible for humanity to restore the order of justice. ... For to reestablish said order, it was fitting that man not only give God all the honor that the divine nature deserves for itself; but beyond that also a cult of honor more than that ... which was worthwhile to compensate her for the honor previously stolen from her by thus paying her that credit, which she had acquired from the man. ... For in giving man to God wholly of himself he still gave him nothing of that which was equal to the divine majesty and worthy of it; and was excused from giving more only because he had nothing more to give; which reason for not having ... meant that just giving all of oneself was not imputed to injustice. Through sin ... he had also once stolen himself from God, and therefore whatever was done [since after the sin] it could no longer happen [not even] that he honored his Creator with all of himself. ... Human nature was therefore, as it was said, irreparably lost, because it no longer had itself in order to reestablish the order of eternal justice which it had disturbed.[24]

---

21. See Matt 25:1–8.
22. See Prov 8:4–7.
23. See Isa 42:6.
24. Rosmini, SA, 1:51–52.

It would take little to convert the vicious circle of perdition into the virtuous circle of righteousness: it would be sufficient to recover that capacity for deep and trusting listening to the voice of the Father (the ability to hear—*ob-audire*), which God gave mankind as an intelligent and free creature. But man has lost the way of this return to the Father, also because with sin he deliberately burned its bridges. And then it is God himself who becomes obedient, who makes himself an obedient Son to the Father, and obedient to the highest degree, to the point of giving his life. Then his gift rises physically on the cross, above the dark walls of man's labyrinths, illuminates the tunnels and breaks through the false walls, fills the ditches, and rebuilds the bridges, until they are transformed into the straight path that from the deserts of exile leads back to the land of the fathers:

> [After the sin] 1. God could no longer be appeased . . . 2. nor could God approach man . . . and man could neither 1. recompose the disintegrated harmony of his powers . . . 2. nor could he regain communication with the supernatural order. . . . The principle therefore of man's restoration was not in human nature . . . he does not even have us in God, because he is far from man, and . . . moved by his justice to punish him: therefore, the remedy for everything is lacking. . . . Pure human nature was saved . . . because the incarnate Word had the power to fully satisfy the debt contracted by man, even superabundantly. On the other hand, man was able to give God greater worship than was due to him in justice. Because justice wanted Christ to be the most innocent and most holy, to be completely blessed and to have no pain. But now he was abandoned by the Father to pain until death . . . and he obediently submitted to this cruel decree . . . renouncing his own right to the love of God the Father. Then two questions were found to be open. On the one hand, man owed an infinite debt to God; on the other, there was among man, one who had infinite credit with God . . . who held the chirograph of their debt, and he tore it up, affixing it to the cross. . . . Once this order of justice was reestablished . . . nothing prevented God from approaching man once again, returning him, through the communication of grace to the order of supernatural perfection, and therefore he healed and reformed all man's perverted nature.[25]

Calvary is therefore the mountain on which God's justice triumphs in the crucified Son. It is a small mountain, it is not Sinai, it is not Mount Zion, Carmel, or Horeb. It is a place unknown to most and ignored by ancient prophets. But it is precisely this place that God chose to fully reveal his

---

25. Rosmini, *SA*, 1:52–55.

justice in order to confuse the scholars of this world. After all, on Calvary, the failure of human justice, which condemns the just to an infamous death and mocks their apparent impotence, becomes the means of fully revealing God's justice, which he justifies in the gift of life. From the cross reigns the "King of the Jews," according to David's prophecy,[26] from the new Zion,[27] the new temple, and the new royal palace.[28] This is what Rosmini says, in a passage of great transport, as he exhorts the brothers on the day of their religious profession, in the Shrine of the Most Holy Crucifix at the Sacred Mount Calvary of Domodossola:

> Oh Calvary, oh mountain of blood, ignoble mountain in the eyes of men, not celebrated by the canticle of ancient prophets, almost obliterated in the Scriptures of the old covenant, where evildoers leave their evil life and their opprobrious bones, you were beloved *ab eterno* by him who would to confuse all human wisdom, and the only divine glorify; you were preferred to the splendid Zion of regal magnificence and superb with sumptuous edifices; to you, more than every other mountain, are God's wishes for Jeremiah fitting: "Thus says the Lord of hosts, the God of Israel: When I restore their fortunes in the land of Judah and in its cities ... At this I awoke and opened my eyes; my sleep was satisfying."[29]

The image of the king is compared to that of the bridegroom, who in love feels as if he were awakening, and sees the world with new eyes. As when the eyes of the person you truly love transfigure even the most ordinary reality and make it feel in its providential nature a place of encounter with the greatest good of life. Mountain, temple, palace, all this is the rocky and barren sketch of Golgotha because it is there that the Son, after a long journey, throws himself fully into the arms of the Father. It is the power of love that illuminates with its deepest meaning the apparent drama of the passion:

> But it is also strong, O brothers, the charity of Christ as well as death itself, *fortis est ut mors dilectio*.[30] True love is love of

26. See Ps 2: 6–8.
27. See Ps 50: 2–6.
28. See Ps 65: 2.

29. Rosmini, "Spirito dell'istituto della carità," 31; see Jer 31:23–6; we can mention here Rosmini's words in *Storia dell'amore* (History of charity) with regard to the mountain on which the bridegroom slept at midday; see Song 1:7.

30. Song 8:6, with regard to the same passage from the Scriptures in *Storia dell'amore*. See also ch. 2, para. 4.1.

blood. Love and sacrifice are inseparable.... We have here all day before our eyes the divine Master of love, the sole legislator of our society bloodied, torn, hanging from a cross. He hangs there resolutely, pierced in his chest, hands, and feet, not so much by the spear and the nails, but more by those loving bolts of lightning that really killed him. He is the immense example that every Christian and every member of the Istituto di Carità, of which he is also the first member, the head, the great founder, must emulate. Justice led him directly to charity, charity sacrificed him.[31]

The sacrifice of charity, however, is not for death, but for life. Through the cross Christ comes to new life with the resurrection, a destiny with which he associates every baptized person and to which he calls every man.[32] It is in this supernatural life of love that the full union of the Son with the Father, eternal in the Trinity, is also realized in history. And in this union the Christian also enters, through the mystical door of justice, to give thanks to the Lord.[33] The justice of Christ is therefore essentially charity, and the charity of Christ is the intra-Trinitarian love that is manifested in the world on the cross and in the resurrection. Here Christ, completely exposed, entrusts everything to the Father to do his will, and here everything is reborn to new life in union with him. Calvary thus becomes the new Jerusalem, the place of rest of peoples, the place of sleep in which the old man dies and the new is born,[34] in which Christ no longer lives and reigns from Zion, no longer even from Calvary, but from the right hand of the Father, in his arms.

Moral Perfection and Intimate Union with God: The Mystical Dimension of the Spiritual Life

While the *Imitatio Christi* is an important aspect of Rosminian ascetics, it is not the goal of the Christian's efforts. It is not a moral perfectionism that makes man perfect, but union with the Father in Christ. This union passes through the unique relationship that the Christian is called on to cultivate with the Word of God. With regard to the unique relationship that is established between the Christian and Christ, it is useful to remember that Rosmini identifies and emphasizes it in a particular way as a relationship

31. Rosmini, "Spirito dell'istituto della carità," 23.
32. Rosmini, "Spirito dell'istituto della carità," 23.
33. Ps 118:19–20: "Open the gates of righteousness; I will enter and thank the Lord. This is the Lord's own gate, through it the righteous enter."
34. See Rom 6:6; Eph 4:22; Col 3:9.

with man as a living and intelligent being. In Scripture, the image of God is properly the Word,[35] but it also says man is made in the image of God. Rosmini notes that the Scriptures[36] speak of man as a being constituted both in the natural order, with the communication of the ideal being, and in the supernatural order, with the communication of the real being. Man created in the image and likeness of God therefore has within himself the three forms of being in an analogical way, as subjective, objective and moral being. If, as we have said, it is in union with God that man finds his fullness of life, and if this union must take place in all these components, man needs a mediation that leads him to reach a union with God that surpasses and transcends him.

In the *A Commentary on the Introduction to the Gospel of John* (*Introduzione al Vangelo secondo Giovanni*) Rosmini starts from the assumption that the Word of God is the divine essence manifest to himself, and that therefore the invisible God is known through the Word, light that is seen and in which everything is seen:[37] form, character, figure, model.[38] These attributes already present in the Old Testament refer to divine Wisdom,[39] manifestation of the "face of God":

> Whenever in the divine scriptures the countenance or face of God is named, these metaphors express the knowability of God; for by their countenance, or face, men are known; and therefore, these expressions name the object God, the knowable God, whom we know to be the Word: so many priests excellently interpret those ways of saying of the divine Word, which is light or shining life for itself. Man was therefore instituted in the image of God, that is, with the perception of the divine Word . . . , and therefore he was placed in a supernatural state, endowed with divine grace.[40]

The full manifestation of this wisdom in man is then realized in the justice of Christ, in which that providential law is fully fulfilled which

35. See 2 Cor 4:4; Col 1:15.

36. See Gen 2:7.

37. See Eph 5:13.

38. See Rom 8:28; which according to Rosmini provides an interesting explanation of what form is; Heb 1:3.

39. See Wis 7:25–6, where it is said: "For she is a breath of the might of God and a pure emanation of the glory of the Almighty; therefore nothing defiled can enter into her. For she is the reflection of eternal light, the spotless mirror of the power of God, the image of his goodness."

40. Rosmini, *Introduzione al Vangelo* (A Commentary on the Introduction to the Gospel of John), 184.

requires the greatest possible good to be manifested in an individual in the greatest measure, and which, in *Teodicea*, Rosmini calls the law of the "accumulation of good." Because in Christ every good is accomplished, it is in union with him that all creation is reconciled with the Father, and therefore it is in union with him that man and creation rediscover true justice, overcoming their own limitations:

> If the accumulation of good is required by the law of wisdom, then it must necessarily be the utmost, given that an infinite wisdom presides over the government of the universe. So, all the good and all the gifts and graces that God intended to communicate to man, were to unite and accumulate in one single man (because this is the utmost accumulation that can be conceived), and could only be communicated from him to the very poor and miserable. And so he was; this man is Jesus Christ. This is the very simple point on which the entire universe depends; true good is found only here and only those who know Him possess it. Since "He is the image of the invisible God, the firstborn of all creation. For in him were created all things in heaven and on earth, the visible and the invisible, whether thrones or dominions or principalities or powers; all things were created through him and for him. He is before all things, and in him all things hold together. He is the head of the body, the church. He is the beginning, the firstborn from the dead, that in all things he himself might be preeminent. For in him all the fullness was pleased to dwell, and through him to reconcile all things for him, making peace by the blood of his cross [through him], whether those on earth or those in heaven."[41] But the law of accumulation was fulfilled in Christ and the same law is fulfilled, as far as possible, also with respect to other men, to whom Christ communicates its fullness.[42]

The perfect justice of Christ thus spreads through the saints who, united with him, also realize in their humanity the greatest possible good:

> What Christ has with all fullness, he shares among his own, except the incommunicable hypostatic union, and what properly adheres to it. Because grace was given to Christ, says Saint Thomas, "as a universal principle in the kind of beings having grace."[43] Hence the humanity of Christ draws not only from the divinity to which all grace is joined *per se*, but also all that

---

41. See Col 1:15–20.
42. See Rosmini, *Th*, 539–40.
43. See Saint Thomas Aquinas, *Sum* III, q. 7, a. 9.

immense mass which he was destined to share among men; wherefore he says, "And I consecrate myself for them, so that they also may be consecrated in truth;"[44] almost meaning: "I deduce first from the source of my divinity this grace into my humanity, which I intend then to transfer from the fullness of my humanity into the humanity of other men." Thus, the habitual grace of Christ is divided, so to speak, and is renewed in the saints in every possible way; so that the assembly of all the saints doubles in a certain way the realization of the archetype of humanity, except that in Christ the union of all graces and the inexhaustible source of divinity, which is his own person, makes his grace even greater without measure, and makes it thus his own, that he is the lord of graces, and in this consists the *specific eminence* of Christ.[45]

It is then the saints who, having received, welcomed, and cultivated the gift of justice from Christ, in turn communicate this good, the fruit of holiness of life in union with him, to all those whom they meet and who are willing to receive it. In this way a progressive spread of goodness is achieved, and God's justice shines ever more brightly in history. A testimony of this intuition is found, for example, in the Old Testament in Ps 89, which Rosmini quotes in a passage of *Theodicy (Teodicea)*.[46] Still speaking of the Psalms, Rosmini recalls that they reaffirm several times that only one is the Just One, and refer prophetically to Christ. Upstream of this spread of justice and goodness there is therefore the only justice and the only good, which are in God and which are given to the world in Christ. Every other justice and every other good comes from participation in his justice and good.[47]

Christ the just is the guide of those who seek justice: "The God of Jacob is Jesus Christ: those who seek his face are the spiritual generation of Christ who is saved with Christ from the impulses of the seas and rivers in the mountain of righteousness."[48]

---

44. See John 17:19.
45. Rosmini, *Th*, 551–52.
46. See Rosmini, *Th*, 550–53.
47. See Rosmini, "Maniera di recitare utilmente," 127.
48. Rosmini, "Maniera di recitare utilmente," 150n58.

The Circle Closes (or Opens?): The Life of Grace

Justice is the rediscovered gift of divine life, of perfect union with the Father, who alone constitutes for man the fullness of life, the life for which he is made. Man, however, cannot give himself this divine life: he needs to receive it, and he receives it with the gift of grace, which places him in a supernatural state. This gift is not linked to human nature, which in itself does not possess grace, nor is the perception of the Word proper to human nature in itself, since it in itself has only the intuition of the ideal being. The gift of grace is a gratuitous gift, which fits perfectly into the dynamic of love with which God created man, inasmuch as the Word who is the light of men is also life, and it is only with the gift of grace that the effect (redeemed man) responds fully to the cause (the divine Word):

> And although on the side of man there was no right to this supernatural state, neither grace constitutes an element of his nature, nor even an intelligent element of his nature was such a conjunction of him with the Word, not belonging to the constitution of nature human if not the intuition of the ideal being, without which he could not be intelligent, and therefore neither a man; however, on God's side it was very fitting, and of a moral necessity, that man coming out of the divine hands should be sublimated to such heights, since the Word was the light of men; and by giving them this light, life was also given to them, because "in the Word there was life, and life was the light of men": the effect thus fully corresponded to the condition of the cause.[49]

Grace is a gift of Christ and it is in him that man receives it. True justice therefore comes to man from intimate union with Christ in grace. In this regard, Rosmini recalls that it is from the idea of this physical, intellectual, and moral union of man with Christ that formulas of Scripture derive such as: "to be in Christ"[50] like the branches in the vine, to participate in some way in Christ's progress from the Father, and to "generate in Christ,"[51] that is, to give birth to the new creature, the new man.[52] It is therefore in participation in Christ's justice that the renewal of all creation is founded, in which the realities that live in it are in Christ as means that follow the

---

49. Rosmini, *Introduzione al Vangelo*, 184–85.
50. See 1 Cor 1:30.
51. See 1 Cor 4:15.
52. See Rom 6:6–11.

end.[53] In the harmonious adherence of all creation to the justice of Christ, the ancient prophecies are fulfilled,[54] so that everything may be established in him.[55] Christians are then grafted into Christ body and soul, as members of the head; for their souls become temples of the Spirit, while their bodies also participate in the life of the Son of God, albeit still in an imperfect and limited way, until the day of the glorious resurrection, when this participation will be full. In them Christ, the Just One, becomes the supreme principle of action:

> From the physical-intellectual-moral conjunction of man with Christ, through whom Christ becomes the head, the faithful the members . . . , we come to understand the value of some solemn formulas used in the divine Scriptures. . . . To be in Jesus Christ is to say to be inserted in him like the branch in the vine, and says [Saint Paul[56]]: *ex ipso* that is *ex Deo*, because this incorporation is the work of the Most Holy Trinity and is attributed to the Father, from whom proceeds the Word and with it the Word all that unites itself to the Word and forms a body with him. . . . To generate in Christ is the same as to incorporate, to insert into Christ. And it is said *to* generate, because Christ becoming the supreme principle of work . . . , man thus becomes a new person. . . . Having renewed his personality . . . , he is like a seed from which the whole of human nature and all that is made for it must be renewed, since, having obtained the end, . . . the means cannot be lacking, and the principal must pull the accessory to himself; therefore, in the renewal of the upper part of man he rightly sees the Apostle the renewal of the whole human world and . . . of all things. . . . This was the eternal great plan of God, for which also allowed the fall of the first man. . . .[57] And he says in *ipso*, because in Christ are all incorporated and forming with him one body, of which he is the head and the life-giving spirit; because . . . Christ being not only God, but still man, and the humanity of Christ being necessarily composed of soul and body, he is consequently rector, head and life no less than souls than of the bodies of men. . . . Therefore, Saint Paul also in the present time calls the bodies of Christian members of Christ.[58]

53. See 2 Cor 5:17; Rev 21:9.
54. See Isa 43:19.
55. Eph 1:9–10.
56. See 1 Cor 1:30.
57. See Eph 1:9–10.
58. Rosmini, *Introduzione al Vangelo*, 213–15.

Full justice is full union with the Father in Christ, and Christ himself asks the gift of this union to the Father for his disciples. Full union with the Father in Christ must therefore also be the deepest desire of every Christian. In one of the conferences held by Rosmini and his confreres in the first communities of the Istituto della Cartià, the founder says as he reflects on the desire for justice:

> In the desire for justice, it is better to be insatiable, and however much our desires go beyond all limits, God will grant them, because those who hunger and thirst will be satisfied: it is the word of Christ. May hearts be grafted onto a deep noble desire for justice. God loves telling us: *qui sanctus est sanctificetur adhuc, qui justus est justificetur adhuc*. It is fitting, therefore, that those who profess the Christian religion should strive with every effort to make the seed of justice, which Christ hid in his heart with his first grace, flourish and bear fruit. The Christian is encouraged to ask for this righteousness, for whatever he asks in the name of Christ, will be given: "Whatsoever ye give to the Father in my name, he will give it to you." Notice, "whatsoever." Therefore, if I were to ask God with fervent and uninterrupted prayers for the highest degree of justice, I would rise to this, because his promise is not restricted, knows no boundary, but whatever is asked of him in the name of Christ will be obtained from his infinite kindness. . . . At this thought, the disciple may be encouraged to ask to wear only the white insignia of a justice that knows no limits. Christ asked the Father on our behalf for the grace to unite us closely, and to form one with him, as he is joined, and holds the same nature as the Father. So, if we are called to such a sublime union, should we not make every effort to acquire justice, without which no one pleases Christ, justice that makes us similar to him? It is therefore appropriate to be tireless at this point so that we may acquire so much justice to say with the Apostle: I live but no longer I, it is Jesus Christ who lives in me.[59]

Living union with the Father in Christ, however, also means entering into a mystery of love that far surpasses any capacity for understanding on the part of man. Sometimes the ways of God's righteousness are difficult for man himself to accept, and they pass through suffering and pain. However, it is precisely in the awareness of this mystery that man can accept with faith even the trials of life, aware that union with the Father in Christ is that which conquers evil in man himself and in the world, and that the way of

---

59. Rosmini, "Conferenze spirituali," 183.

justice, however impervious and sometimes crucified, is that from which all good comes with the grace of Christ himself:

> It is true that man can be said to be just if he does not consider only what he has by nature, but united to Christ with what he has received by grace. . . . Moreover, man incorporated into Christ is just of the righteousness that Christ communicates to him. Now, first of all, the Christian has a thousand reasons that persuade him never to complain about the evils he suffers; so that we do not need to struggle to justify in his eyes the providence that in everything and without ceasing he blesses and adores. . . . Wherefore there is none on earth who can deserve the name of righteous, except the true Christian; and this just man is the one who highly professes and declares ignorance of his own righteousness, which he considers as something most hidden in the hand of God.[60] That if justice were expressly revealed to him, still, he would not consider himself to deserve exemption from earthly evils, because he knows too well, that he cannot attribute to himself that justice, but that it comes to him from Christ . . . concorporated with his patient Redeemer; remaining in him until the root of evil lives here below.[61]

Suffering, in fact, comes to man not so much from contingent realities, but ultimately more profoundly from the disorder created in the world by sin, which has precluded man, made for good, from his full realization. In union with Christ, through the gift of grace, the door of the road that leads to the Father's house is reopened and the person rediscovers communion with God, in a progressive journey that already gives a foretaste in this life of full union, full justice, full realization that will take place at the final resurrection, at the end of time.[62]

Conclusions

Taking an overview of what has been said, I think we can grasp a substantial basic unity in the passages taken from the various works of Rosmini, outlining in the discourse a logical path, and at the same time an ascetic-mystical path. Christ's original righteousness resides in his union with the Father, in the Trinity, and in eternity. It is a fruitful union, which is at the origin of creation, and in a special way of man, created in the image and likeness

---

60. *Sunt justi atque sapiente set opera eorum in manu dei.* See Qoh 9:1.
61. Rosmini, *Th*, 166–67.
62. See Rosmini, *Th*, 177.

of God. Man's justice, a response to the gift of life and grace, consequently consists in adherence to God's plan. In a creature endowed with intelligence and will, such as a person, this is then realized in obedience, which is the free and intelligent adherence of the whole person to God through his own supreme active principle: the intelligent will or loving intelligence, in which all the powers of man, physical, intellectual and moral/spiritual, find their full realization in a personal yes.

Sin is the negation of this personal yes, the yes entrusted to the freedom of man. But if the disobedience of sin has had the power to break man's union with God and the harmony between creation and Creator, obedience is the way of redemption. The task of mending the wound of man's no to God, if entrusted solely to the forces of a humanity sick and weakened by sin, would be impossible.

For this reason, God becomes man, and through the human-divine yes of the Son to the Father reconciles the fracture and offers man the moral, ontological, and theological way to return to lost communion. It is the way of Christ's justice, obedient justice, in which God gives himself to man in the highest degree and man responds in the greatest degree to God's gift. It is a moral model of life, since Christ, as a man, lived communion with the Father to the fullest in loving obedience to his plan.

At the same time, it is a gift of grace, which truly heals in Christ the wound produced in man by sin. Indeed, it is Christ himself who lives in the baptized person through the gift of the Spirit: "I have been crucified with Christ; yet I live, no longer I, but Christ lives in me; insofar as I now live in the flesh, I live by faith in the Son of God who has loved me and given himself up for me" (Gal 2:20). This is why Christ says of himself: "I am the way and the truth and the life" (John 14:6). Christ is the way, inasmuch as he lived and showed as man the path through which man can realize in himself, concretely, in history, the Father's plan. It is truth inasmuch as in him there appears, alive and actual, in the Rosminian sense of "dynamically in action," the original and final plan of the Father for man and the world. Finally, it is life, inasmuch as it accompanies man beyond the confines of his finitude and unites him to himself with the gift of grace. Christ thus leads man beyond the threshold of the finite, which no human effort can make him cross, but through which man enters, by the power of grace, into the fullness of life, living as a son in the Son, to use again a Rosminian expression, "becoming embodied" in God, abandoning himself totally to him.

We ask ourselves then, at this point, what can be, in the light of what has been said, Rosminian contributions useful to the spirituality of the twenty-first century. The man of the second millennium has at his disposal "many goods,"[63] and yet he often does not know how and for what purpose to use them. Sometimes he tends to get excited about experiences, collective or individual, which on closer inspection often turn out to be rather poor if not trivial, and that common opinion, not a little influenced by the means of mass communication, strives, without really succeeding, to clothe with a somewhat unprovable depth and value. On the other hand, he feels, and this is palpably perceptible in our days, the lacerating need to give depth and consistency to life. This need, when it is not anesthetized by the palliative of the moment, produces phenomena and poignant testimonies of humanity that cries out its thirst for truth and goodness.

Rosmini's invitation, yesterday as today, is not to respond to this yearning by closing oneself in unreal or surreal worlds, but rather to listen courageously and reflectively to it. Rosmini's invitation is to look around and look inside without fear.

His century had imprisoned man, claiming to be the creator of truth. A truth, however, that in order not to be recognized as coming from other than itself, had been turned into an idol of a despotic and cruelly impersonal nature. Rosmini invited the men of his time (and I think he also invites those of our time) not to fall into this trap, but rather to let themselves be questioned by the truth, by its infinite, immutable, and eternal nature.

This is the meaning of his going back to the origins of man's own capacity to know, to understand, in this light, the value of feeling, intelligence and freedom in the natural experience of the finite and in supernatural relationship to the infinite. "To become oneself," "to recognize one's being in his own order," "to do the will of the Father in the obedience of the Son," are basically ways of describing not a life of convicts chained to oars, but rather of personal subjects constantly open to the unpredictability of the relationship with the other by oneself.

Every day the Captain calls his sailor to advise him, and every day the good sailor returns to knock on the door of the cockpit, to be admitted and study the route and, if God the Creator brings him his nautical chart, that of the infinite, man learns to read it, as far as he can, bringing with him his sextant and his compass. He knocks wondering how it is possible for him to feel, know, and love the infinite sea despite having such a limited horizon. And in the echo of the infinite, even in its limitations, he recognizes the voice of God, who calls him to open himself to his gift of communion. God, who places himself freely at his side, makes himself his travelling companion, shares with him, as far as it is possible for man to understand them, his plans, and above all gives him his own life and opens to him the doors of

---

63. See Luke 12:16–21.

eternity. All entrusted to his yes, made possible by God himself, but nevertheless left free, and therefore never to be taken for granted.

Bibliography

Bozzetti, Giuseppe. "Natura umana e persona nell'educazione rosminiana." In *Opere complete. Saggi—Scritti inediti—Opere minori—Recensioni*, edited by Michele Federico Sciacca, 3:3377–83. Milan: Marzorati, 1966.

Capograssi, Giuseppe. *Il diritto secondo Rosmini*. Edited by Mario D'Addio and Enrico Vidal. Vol. 4 of *Opere*. Milan: Giuffrè, 1959.

Colombo, Giacomo. *Bilancio della teologia del secolo XX*. 4 vols. Rome: Città Nuova, 1970.

De Giorgi, Fulvio. *Rosmini e il suo tempo. L'educazione dell'uomo moderno tra riforma della filosofia e rinnovamento della Chiesa (1797-1833)*. Brescia, It.: Morcelliana, 2003.

Lorizio, Giuseppe. "Il Cristocentrismo." In *Eschaton e storia nel pensiero di Antonio Rosmini*, 247–70. Brescia, It.: Morcelliana, 1988.

Quacquarelli, Antonio. *La lezione patristica di Antonio Rosmini*. Stresa, It.: Città Nuova, 1980.

Rosmini, Antonio. *Antropologia in servizio della scienza morale*. Edited by François Evain. ENC 24. Rome: Città Nuova, 1981.

———. *Antropologia soprannaturale*. Edited by Umberto Muratore. 2 vols. ENC 39–40. Rome: Città Nuova, 1973.

———. "Conferenze spirituali della prima comunità religiosa dell'Istituto della carità al Sacro Monte Calvario di Domodossola. 1830–1831." In *Massime di perfezione cristiana*, edited by Alfeo Valle, ENC 49, 177–221. Rome: Città Nuova, 1976.

———. *Costituzioni dell'Istituto della Carità*. Edited by Dino Sartori. ENC 50. Rome: Città Nuova, 1996.

———. *Directorium Spiritus. Monita pietatis seu Fundamenta Constitutionum*. 3 vols. Unpublished. https://www.rosmini.it/objects/Pagina.asp?ID=680.

———. *Introduzione al Vangelo secondo Giovanni*. Edited by Maria A. Raschini. Rome: Città Nuova, 2002.

———. "Lettera al Conte Giulio Padulli." In *Epistolario Ascetico di Antonio Rosmini*, 1:315–16. Rome: Senato, 1911.

———. "Lettera a Madre Maria Geltrude Cerutti, Superiora al Monastero di Arona." In *Epistolario Ascetico di Antonio Rosmini*, 3:143–46. Rome: Senato, 1913.

———. "Maniera di recitare utilmente i salmi." In *Operette spirituali*, edited by Alfeo Valle, ENC 48, 127–84. Rome: Città Nuova, 1985.

———. "Lo spirito dell'Istituto della Carità." In *Operette spirituali*, edited by Alfeo Valle, ENC 48, 15–99. Rome: Città Nuova, 1985.

———. *Storia dell'amore*. Edited by Umberto Muratore and Alfeo Valle. ENC 52. Rome: Città Nuova, 2002.

———. *Teodicea*. Edited by Umberto Muratore. ENC 22. Rome: Città Nuova, 1977.

Part 5

Rosmini's *Suspended Middle* (and the Comparable Social Theory of Radical Orthodoxy's *Suspended Middle*): Possible Juridical Implications

19

Consuetude and Neuroscience?

Elements for an Affective Reading of Rosmini's Thought

PAOLO HERITIER

Enunciation of the Affective Reading of Law in Rosmini: The Person Is the Right Subsisting in Law

THIS PAPER STARTS FROM a hypothesis: that a reading of Rosmini's thought can show a significant legal philosophical actuality. I will attempt, albeit in brief allusive hints, to indicate how and why it is interesting in interpreting the contemporaneity and evolution of law.

Elsewhere it will be a question of verifying whether this hypothesis can constitute a real line of interpretation of Rosmini's philosophy of law, which in the legal philosophical field seems to me to have been excessively reduced to the general theory of law, sometimes forgetting the link between anthropology, theodicy, and other aspects of Rosmini's impressive production, and the philosophy of law. The interest of Rosminian philosophical juridical thought does not consist in highlighting a particular aspect or concept within it, starting from an ideological position (for example, analyzing its "liberal" perspective in relation to the concepts of freedom and property) or other, but in detecting the properly interdisciplinary nature of its conception of the person as a right subsisting in law.[1] Capograssi effectively points this out, in indicating how the specific feature of Rosmini's philosophy of law consists in indicating the individual as a person, and the person not so much as the foundation of law, as theories of human rights maintain,[2] instead taking one further step, even perhaps, paradoxically anticipating the problems they show in the era of globalization: If the whole of Rosmini's juridical thought is that the individual is a person, "the person himself, as an individual life force, as a 'supreme activity by his nature' (I, para. 52) as an absolute but individual activity of the individual, it is the right subsisting in law," as Rosmini wrote.[3] That is to say, the relevance of Rosminian theory of law consists in providing an anthropological and moral response to the problem of the universal foundation of human rights, showing how they must be thought of in a shared anthropological conception. In this sense, starting from Rosminian analysis can be useful to face this contemporary challenge.

To maintain that the person is the foundation of the legal system is to affirm that the law is a Kelsenian system of norms that, from the outside, appears to be founded on the person; Rosmini's position is at the same time more radical and more coherent, making it possible to recover and dissolve the tension between positive and customary law, so to speak, from within the person as a right subsisting in law, making it possible to overcome the dualism between state and individual prevailing in the contemporary, post-Kantian debate: the person is not the *foundation of* law, but *is* the law itself, in its factual dimension. The anthropological significance of juridical knowledge, already implicit in Vico's juxtaposition, is taken up here.

We could perhaps say that the person is the *source* of law, but the social dimension of his destination makes the device more complex and articulated and here there is no possibility of already configuring the results of the analysis, but simply of indicating some perspectives considered interesting for further developments.

The reading of Capograssi seems to me to indicate precisely the relevance of Rosmini, as well as the actuality of Vico, configuring a potentially fruitful interdisciplinary field of studies[4] around the evolutions of legal

1. Rosmini, *Filosofia del diritto* (Philosophy of law) 2, para. 52.
2. For a Rosminian reading of the theme of human rights, see Petrillo, *Lezione di Antonio Rosmini-Serbati*.
3. Capograssi, *Attualità e inattualità*, 29.
4. Allow me here to recall the most recent works in the pedagogical and juridical field by Bellelli, who, after specifying the affective turn in metaphysics as an essential element for the reading of Rosminian thought (Bellelli, *Etica originaria*), approached the juridical-philosophical and political-philosophical themes, grasping the Vico-Rosmini

philosophy in the contemporary world, to be discussed starting from the resumption of authors now forgotten by the debate.

The novelty of Rosmini's juridical conception therefore lies in the identification between law and person, which is described with extreme precision, without denying the ontological and anthropological context to which it necessarily refers. The person is a source, both activity and sovereignty: in a description that appears evocative and at the same time rigorous, Capograssi enunciates its scope: in a long quotation, in fact, the person is placed beyond the separation of objective and subjective law.

> Being the power from which life flows in all its manifestations, it gathers within itself reality, the very source of all human realities; and since the appearance of the eternal and the divine in empirical reality, the affirmation of the infinite willed by the subject in his own impulse of love, gathers in itself the indeclinable necessity of the moral destination of life and in short, the very source of all moral necessities, of truth and of the values of life. At this point there is both the only activity and the only truly original authority of the life of the concrete: the person, this kind of magic ring of the infinite and the empirical, is, as such, activity and sovereignty: activity because it is life itself that moves and organizes itself in all its concrete needs, and sovereignty because it is the affirmation of life as truth, that is, of its infinite destination. Consequently, the person is the right subsisting in law, because in the person truth and life, eternal and feeling, value and fact are blocked: for him to realize one's life is to fulfil an infinite duty in which all the duties of life are summarized. And so, to use the precise language of jurists, objective law and subjective law coincide in it: the affirmation of one's life as a tendency to happiness is the affirmation of life as absolute law.[5]

The relevant point that Capograssi grasps, and poses at the same time as a problem and criticism of contemporary positivistic notions, is precisely the place of this coincidence (of fact and value, eternal and feeling, truth and life, objective law and subjective law, justice and force, command and obedience). The person is the junction around which these dichotomies revolve, which merge into the concrete life of the person as the first, only,

---

connection: Bellelli, *Percorsi storici*. Allow me also to recall my own work: Heritier, "Provvedenza vichiana," in which I try to focus on Vico's relevance for legal culture, following Capograssi.

5. Capograssi, *Attualità e inattualità*, 29–30.

original "appearance of law as such in the world"[6] from which freedom is founded, as the source of rights.

Habit and Affective Neuroscience: Two Lines for an Innovative Reading of Rosmini's Philosophical and Legal Anthropology?

Precisely on the basis of this unitary conception of the person at the source of the conception of law, a theory can be initiated that tries to re-propose an anthropology in the contemporary debate that is both philosophical and juridical, able to go beyond the proposal of neo constitutionalism, understood as a synthesis of natural law and juris positivism, positivization of the minimum contents of natural law. The project appears impressive, but the breadth of the horizon called into question by Rosmini in his work places it as a research objective to be (re-pursued). While the debate following the Second World War has, in fact, consolidated the resumption of natural law issues following the scandal of the Holocaust in a theory of human rights, it is precisely the recent events of the twenty-first century that have shown how the utopia of a universal liberal democracy, a dream of the developed West, proves to be only one of the conceptions that are confronted on the global scene, which is characterized as the confrontation between different cultures and religions to be connected in a common intercultural perspective, if we want to avoid the conflict of civilizations on the horizon. In this sense, some of Rosmini's intuitions can be interpreted in a different framework from his original cultural and political situation, obviously without understanding the actuality of his thought as a system waiting to be realized, but as a reflection that intends to make law and anthropology coincide, and perhaps able to offer ideas able to hold together a non-reductionist anthropological perspective of the person with a concrete analysis of the reality of the legal phenomenon and its evolution. In this article, far from wanting to offer a reading of Rosmini's legal theory, I would just like to mention two aspects of his thought that, perhaps surprisingly, can be reread starting from current problems: the notion of habit and the relationship with neuroscience, articulating along these two lines the conception of the person as a right subsisting in law. These references are intended only to offer some starting points to coordinate the legal perspective with anthropology and psychology, in particular, of Rosmini's viewpoint.

The attempt is part of a broader attempt to decline an affective reading of Rosmini's thought, indicating its link with the deontology of Sequeri's

---

6. Capograssi, *Attualità e inattualità*, 31.

foundation[7] and the affective turn in metaphysics, in the reading that Bellelli provides in terms of a new phase of Rosminian studies.[8] In this sense, some aspects of the contemporary debate, not only juridical, but philosophical and theological, can offer reading grids to reconfigure Rosmini's contribution: in the paper I will allude to some junctions that seem promising to me, including the recovery of the category of habit and the theme of the affective foundation of neuroscience. Finally, I will allude to the need to rethink the problem of obedience to law in an anthropological key, starting from the theme of Jesus's faith as an articulation of a relationship between obedience and faith, which must also be rethought in an anthropological rather than systematic theological key[9] and susceptible to a juridical philosophical relevance.

I would not, however, have had the courage to start from the analysis of the theme of "custom" in Rosmini if I had not found a reference in Felice Battaglia, who claims, in his philosophical juridical approach, the influence of Savigny on Rosmini.

The starting point, already taken up, by Capograssi in his work *Attualità e inattualità di Rosmini* appears germane to understanding Rosmini's relevance in denouncing the contemporary reductionist misery into which law has fallen; therefore, the sense of an approach to the theme of custom[10] starting from Rosmini.

Law today, in its configuration as a system of norms, in a certain sense appears to be orphaned of that link between freedom and responsibility, which sinks into the Greek-Christian roots of its history from the patrimony of Roman law. The practice of law is facing an epochal battle against the scientist reductionism that intends to eliminate the figure of the human, of the person as a right subsisting in law, to replace it with something equally absolutely technical, even within the teaching of law and the faculties, sorry, of the "departments" of law: which can be indicated by the return of the ghost of the robot judge and of the "algorithmic decisions" in the legal philosophical imaginary, already placed at the origins of *juridical cybernetics*.[11] The idea that today there is a secularization of law, a loss of the ritual and anthropological character of law, is thus spreading in parallel with the

---

7. See Sequeri, *Deontologia del Fondamento*. More broadly, Sequeri, *Sensibile e l'inatteso*.

8. See Bellelli, *Etica originaria*.

9. Starting from Canobbio, *La fede di Gesù*. For a review of this subject, see Comi, *Fede di Gesù*.

10. For an in-depth analysis on the theme of rethinking the custom today, see Bombelli and Heritier, *Volti molteplici della consuetudine*.

11. On the subject, see Carleo, *Decisione robotica*.

digital configuration of social life, represented as apparently "technological" and "neutral." The secularization of the juridical presents itself as the analogous and logical continuation, the actualization of the secularization of theology and the reduction of that anthropological nucleus guarded by the right to something else, technical,[12] assumed at the same time as original and destinal. It seems to me that this is the risk against which Rosmini's philosophy of law can defend us, if we analyze the meaning of his idea, already mentioned, of the person as a right subsisting in law.

The incipit of Capograssi in *Il diritto secondo Rosmini* seems to me to be of great interest. Today Rosmini does not appear to be very presentable in the general cultural climate of juris positivist or pragmatic-utilitarian of a department of law. Students would not be able to understand the intention, the problem is part of what we could call, to use a Rosminian analogy, adapted and transposed from the church to the university, the "second wound," the expulsion of the cultural and historical contents of the Christian and Catholic philosophical tradition from the collective imagination and its reduction to the new challenges of neuroscience, of artificial intelligence, the economic system and the calculation of utilities, devoid of an anthropological reference.

Capograssi observes how there are obstacles in understanding Rosmini's philosophy of law: first, its excessive clarity, its language, its chain of deductions that today risks being paradoxically complicated, following the fact that Rosmini, reflecting on law, is aware of meditating on a relational, anthropological trait, which he characterizes with reference to the Christian symbolic universe: law is something "on which man's life, destiny, fortune and very existence depend. And therefore, every position or conclusion is dominated by a present and vigilant charity, which identifies with his thought. Especially in the philosophy of law it is seen with every clarity. Instead, we meditate without charity."[13] This seems to me to be the general problem of juridical pedagogy, the absence of a charitable, affective, simply relational dimension, and the prevalence of the dimension of cognition and rationality.[14]

One of the places, by way of example, in which Rosminian thought can be developed in a direction aimed at criticizing the juris positivistic and realistic foundation of the legal system in crisis of contemporary liberal democracies is certainly the notion of the foundation of law.

We come briefly to an association that I propose, although without having the opportunity to analyze it due to its complexity, simply presenting

12. Irti and Severino, *Dialogo*.
13. Capograssi, *Attualità e inattualità*, 21.
14. On the problem of juridical pedagogy, again Bellelli, *Percorsi storici*.

its interest: that between the fundamental feeling and a non-Rosminian concept such as Kelsen's fundamental norm.

This association, even if simply evoked, will allow me to express the meaning of the reversal between law and custom that I propose as one of the interpretative figures of Rosminian juridical thought from which to move to show its relevance.

The fundamental feeling or perception is that triple awareness of spirit, body and idea of being that, according to Prini, already anticipates the phenomenological idea of the own body.[15] Without being able to enter into the theme of the articulation between fundamental feeling and fundamental perception,[16] not reducible to a mere relationship between percipient and perceived, the latter is, as Piemontese points out, "the *objectified* fundamental feeling: known, no longer only felt, as mine, constituting me"[17]: to be understood in reference to the fundamental feeling in its function, even if animal, from the point of view of anthropology, but always referable to the act by which the human subject subsists.

Without being able to refer here to the "affective" reading of fundamental sentiment and its role in Rosmini's thought made by Bellelli, as just specified in footnote 15, but simply indicating how the affective turn in metaphysics is the premise of an affective turn to be implemented in law, I note how the Modenese theologian, in the text already cited and following Sequeri's affective turn, specified how "at the time of Rosmini, what was lacking was already the conviction of the need to be able to bring every moral choice back to a universal law. Today we are dealing with the effects

---

15. Prini, *Introduzione a Rosmini*, 92. For Bellelli, the analysis of the link between the fundamental sentiment is the hermeneutic operation that he intends to perform in his work (Bellelli, *Etica originaria*, 81, 98–99). The identification of the centrality of the "law of syntheticism" (104–5), the centrality of the identification of affection in reading the notion of fundamental feeling and the "third" dimension of the moral being (137–39), also with reference to the natural law (227) and the natural light (246), converge to indicate the connection, of extraordinary interest and relevance (289–97), between the third kind of reality, the moral form, the fundamental feeling and the "bastard thought" of the *Chora*, the object of analysis today, of theologians such as Sequeri and of jurists such as Mario Ricca, as well as the object of research that involves me directly and that is linked to the subject of the article (even if in its breadth and complexity it cannot be pursued here, but only indicated as the problematic background that supports the indications provided). See Sequeri, *Sensibile e l'inatteso*; Ricca, "Sussidiarietà orizzontale e dinamica."

16. I refer to De Lucia, *Essere e soggetto*, 43: "Rosmini, in the mature phase of his thought, calls 'fundamental feeling' that triple warning (of his own spirit, of his own body and of the idea of being), which at a young age he had called 'conscience.'" For context, see from 37.

17. Piemontese, *Dottrina del sentimento fondamentale*, 155.

of a moral reflection that has failed to do this: the fragmentation of the subject. In this research, in the dialogue with postmodernity, it seems more appropriate to start from consciousness as 'reflection' than from consciousness as 'law.'"[18] In a certain sense, my reference to custom and the shift from the fundamental norm to freedom intends to represent the juridical equivalent of what is indicated as an objective in theory and morality by Sequeri and Bellelli's affective reading of Rosmini's thought.

If affection can be the cornerstone of a new metaphysics aimed at indicating the ontological scope of Sequerian sensitivity for meaning[19] where, in Rosminian terms, the capacities of affection constitute the passage from external operations to practical judgments and where metaphysics is profiled at the same time as pro-affection (exteriority-real being) and self-affection (sensitivity fundamental feeling), affection becomes "the connection between the fundamental feeling, the idea of being and judgment."[20] Therefore,

> the fundamental sentiment has a structuring role in the ontology of affection inasmuch as it configures the affection of the will in the impression and expression of the components of the judgment of conscience as a speculative judgment (also with the fundamental intellectual sentiment) of a practical judgment (from which and to which affections come and arrive) in the order of moral good and of real and ideal being. The anthropological pervasiveness of the moral law can be grasped mainly starting from the conscience and within the dynamisms of conscience the specificity proper to the affection is decisive for grasping the ontological, metaphysical, and phenomenological value of conscience itself.[21]

Without being able to explore the topic further, it is evident that the crucial point consists in indicating a fundamental anthropological component of the role of the person as a right subsisting in law, where the resumption of the concept of affection is the starting point for rethinking the link between justice and law, between conscience and law. It is a complex theoretical task, but in my opinion relevant to indicate the possible relevance of the conception of the Rosminian person in the observable contemporary evolution of the juridical phenomenon.

---

18. Bellelli, *Etica originaria*, 114.
19. See Sequeri, *Ritrattazioni del simbolico*.
20. Bellelli, *Etica originaria*, 138.
21. Bellelli, *Etica originaria*, 139.

I return a little abruptly to another lexicon, to the completely different use of the concept of *fundamental* in Kelsen, starting from the aesthetic reading of his theory on *Grund Norm*,[22] read in continuity with the two previous concepts. What does Kelsen do when he has to say what pure law, the pure theory of law, is: he constructs a hierarchy of norms (which is still the one substantially accepted as a current theory of the sources of law), at whose summit, at least in one of the many versions formulated by Kelsen, he places a syllogism that is precisely that of the fundamental norm as an unplaced, but only presupposed norm. It is a syllogism that leads us to justify the reason for our obedience to the law, a syllogism that we should all have thought, where the fundamental norm is a thought that replaces in a logical key the foundation of society in the social pact of natural law. It is precisely in this connection that the analysis of fundamental sentiment and the fundamental norm in parallel seems interesting to me. At the top of the whole positivistic conception of law there is a thought, a syllogism that then, skipping decades of general theoretical debates, is substantially, with Hart, reduced to a custom, in technical language to a rule of recognition.[23] What is the logic of this debate that goes from Kelsen to Hart and reaches today? The idea that all in all the problem of obedience to the state and law is not a theoretical problem, when it is practiced by everyone in the same way, is obvious, and therefore does not create a problem from the theoretical point of view. For fifty years the general theorists of law have moved forward, simplifying the debate, following this guideline. Today, however, we are in a situation in which this evidence no longer appears to be shared, in the face of a crisis of liberal democracy. The evidence of obedience to law and the rule of law in its traditional form is lacking and here, in my opinion, and the relevance of Rosmini's theory of law and his conception of the person as a right subsisting in law starting from the critique *à la* Böckenförde returns.[24]

The role of affection in understanding the fundamental feeling as an alternative solution to the fundamental norm as the only logical foundation of law therefore appears to be a path to be configured that can prove useful to dissolve the opposition between positive law and customary perspective without resolving the latter in a mere recognition of the customs of a people or a culture. This opens the need for the reconfiguration of a theory of custom worthy of the theory of moral form and juridical chorology.[25]

---

22. Heritier, "Legal Liturgies."
23. Chiassoni, "Tre buoni filosofi."
24. Böckenförde, *Stato, Costituzione, democrazia*.
25. On the subject of chorology, see n15.

As a side note, to understand the meaning of the reference to custom in this context: when I think of custom, I refer to something dynamic, a term that also interested Rosmini, that is, not to an idea of a mythical thought of the past that is always repeated in the same way, but something that has to do with the social dimension, constructive, social interaction. I say this using the words of a great contemporary romanist, Filippo Gallo, who combines *interpretatio* and custom. After all, Gallo argues, "in the reality of things, the link between legal interpretation and the customary formation of law has never failed. Nevertheless, the awareness of the same, which, as we have said, had already been lost in the Roman age, has continued to be so in the subsequent Roman tradition and still is so in our legal science."[26] In reality, however, interpretation and custom have the same matrix as a form of reception of a position that spreads in an environment, that is to say, as Gallo notes, "A jurist's new interpretation of a text, meeting the favor of other jurists and associates in general, is received and consolidated in the social environment."[27] In short, legal interpretation and custom have the same dynamic as to their origin. The Roman *interpretatio* created law only through the reception, and, to the extent that this happens, by the social environment. Here is also the explanation of the fact—although the point should be adequately analyzed and argued—that Hart speaks of custom replacing it with Kelsen's fundamental norm: custom is present in the legal system at the moment of its foundation, but also throughout its evolution, even if Hart would never admit such a circumstance.

And here, then, the observation about the customary nature of interpretation[28] allows me to project all this on Rosminian theory through a quote from Felice Battaglia. Battaglia is defending Rosmini from accusations of logicism and abstractness, and refers to historical experience: the enunciation of the supreme law of the legal order from which all laws derive belongs to the moral order, through truth and the original reference to the person. Precisely this process, although not merely the fruit of conventions, requires proof of historical experience, where foundation and evolution meet "as the form and matter in the specific of a process, which touches society and consequently the person, indeed persons in their events, each various and contingent."[29] And then the historical and theoretical sources of Rosmini's reasoning are specified:

26. Gallo, *Interpretazione e formazione consuetudinaria*, 7.
27. Gallo, *Interpretazione e formazione consuetudinaria*, 3.
28. On the topic see Zorzetto, *Consuetudine giuridica*; more generally see Bombelli and Heritier, *Volti molteplici della consuetudine*.
29. Battaglia, *Filosofia del diritto*, 28.

if we go to verify the lines of the historical process mentioned, we must agree that Rosmini relies on the model of historicism *à la* Savigny. The law, born as a custom, matures through the work of jurisprudence, that is to say, through the elaboration that experts can make of it, and then, in a further phase, it passes from oral or vocal forms to writings, to customs collected and put in writing. It is only in this last phase that the judges appear to rework what is very improperly called law. The law, if anything, is evident from the repeated and confirmed judgments, which are placed alongside custom, a double source of law. The law in the technical sense is different, it involves a very advanced society, even if it has serious drawbacks, in the sense that, having established a lasting connection between the norm and the legislator, it can generate the idea that the only normative source is the dictate of the legislator, himself the law. The *formula jus quia iussum* is the sad experience of tyranny. If we seek the origin of these views, there is no doubt that they are due to the work of Savigny, to the meditation of evolution among two exemplary peoples, the Roman and the Anglo-Saxon often recalled by the author.[30]

Here, in this long and articulated quotation, Battaglia puts forward the idea that Rosmini's conception based on Savigny, but, it seems to me, also on Vico's theory of Roman law on the other hand, is substantially customary, if we interpret the custom in a dynamic sense, if we do not crystallize it within a natural law model already excessively positivist natural law model,[31] but we indicate its relationship with evolution and history, not separated from the temporal explanation of the foundation (also starting from its link with the dynamics of interpretation, previously indicated in relation to Gallo's reading of Roman law and the theme of *mores*).

This is precisely why I hypothesize that Rosmini's relevance in the theory of contemporary law can be based on a customary and interpretative conception of law, the connection of which I already seem to grasp in the quotation of Battaglia, but which shows how at the center of this conception the person can be identified as a "right subsisting in law," "essence of law," "intellectual subject inasmuch as it contains a supreme active principle informed by the light of reason."[32]

This reading referring to the centrality of the person tells us two aspects of contemporary law. Today those who complete the legislative

30. Battaglia, *Filosofia del diritto*, 28.
31. For example, see the perspective of Finnis, *Legge naturale*.
32. Rosmini, *Filosofia del diritto*, paras. 49 and 51.

process, after the affirmation of legal realism and the accentuation of the role of jurisprudence in the concrete and daily administration of the law, is the judge who interprets the law in the solution of the case, there is no need to disturb the debate on the subject to support it. Here the person who acts is, today, above all the judge.[33]

On the other hand, on the other hand, the return of souverainism[34] tends to identify the person not with the assembly, but with the emblem in the juridical aesthetic sense,[35] of power: the sovereign, the body of the sovereign.

And as if here we fall back into the first wound of the church identified by Rosmini, not referring to the church, but, laicized, it is referable to the state: the idea that the person, and therefore the subsisting human law/right is the judge or the sovereign, completely detaching itself from the relationship with the people, as if contemporary law had taken up a theory of the elites that forgets the relationship of the person with the people through the reference to formation and evolution of custom. And here it seems to me the democratic reality, which certainly does not forget the central role of the aristocracies in the formation of the juridical, of Rosmini's conception of the person as a right subsisting in law indicates, in his extension of the theory of rights to every person, exactly a criticism of this "wound" of the contemporary state (and culture). It is, of course, a starting point that deserves much more analysis, however, it identifies in Rosmini an author to be taken up and proposed again to interpret the contemporary evolution of law, in a direction that, if not complete, appears at least original: precisely starting from the relevance of the affective dimension of the fundamental feeling and the moral form of being; in this theoretical place that stands on the border between law and theory of conscience it seems interesting to me to provide a reading of Rosmini's anthropological and legal thought.

I would therefore like to move on to another point, referring to anthropology and in particular the relationship between anthropology and neuroscience, in a critical sense with respect to a certain anthropological reductionism. Here too, as in the juridical field, Rosmini's thought seems to me current in proposing a theory of anthropology and non-reductionist psychology at the same time. In a text by Leonardo Paris, presented at a conference on Rosmini, about the relationship between neuroscience and fundamental feeling, the author, an expert on the link between neuroscience and theology, shows us how the proto-self, that is to say Damasio's

---

33. For this thesis it seems sufficient to refer to Dworkin, *Diritti presi sul serio*.
34. See Valditara, *Sovranismo*.
35. See Heritier, *Estetica giuridica*.

recent theory of affective neuroscience[36]—to which I would add the contribution of Panksepp, and which I connect to Sequeri's affective turn in metaphysics[37]—represents the core of the underlying feeling that constitutes consciousness. Speaking of the relationship between the animal and man, Paris notes, "What we perceive as stable is not the outside, but our own body, and in particular a series of biochemical parameters and enteroceptive maps, that is, related to the perception of internal organs,"[38] enteroceptive maps that result from the oldest part of our brain[39] in a series of integrative nuclei of the brainstem, "constituting, so to speak, the blank sheet with respect to which we can then perceive the colors and traits of what happens around us."[40] Affective neuroscience, therefore, versus cognitive neuroscience, which makes the "Cartesian error,"[41] shows the relevance of the oldest part of our brain and cortex. After having explained the topic impeccably, Paris then, however, refers to the theme of fundamental feeling: "a 'fundamental feeling of oneself' is identified here that differs from what Rosmini proposed in that it is placed at an exclusively biological and animal level. It is not so much the brain that is the protagonist as the body; it is the body, the concreteness of the flesh that guarantees the brain the solid basis on which to build the sense of self and, starting from here, the support for the higher psychic functions."[42] Paris believes in other words that contemporary neuroscience goes against Rosmini and he is certainly right if we refer to cognitive neuroscience. On this point, precisely on the basis of the concept of habit mentioned, I contrast instead the idea that affective neuroscience on the one hand and the affective turn in Sequerian metaphysics on the other, show how an affective foundation can be provided to the fundamental feeling, following the perspective indicated by Bellelli. Certainly, here the discourse extends, becomes difficult to control, and would require a more in-depth study: it can only be configured as a research hypothesis to be pursued in Rosminian studies, aimed at holding together an affective conception of law, psychology, and metaphysics. I only quote, to indicate the fruitfulness of the theme, a text by Fulvio De Giorgi, *La scienza del cuore*, in which, recalling a note of Rosminian principles, in the paragraph "Dalla sclerocardia a una *scientia mentis et cordis,*" the author

36. See Damasio, *Il sé viene.*
37. Precisely in relation to the theme of chorology: see the texts cited in n15.
38. Paris, "Dimensione antropo-teologica," 76.
39. Biven and Panksepp, *Archeologia della mente.*
40. Paris, "Dimensione antropo-teologica," 77.
41. See Damasio, *Errore di Cartesio.*
42. Paris, *Dimensione antropo-teologica*, 77.

specifies: "The heart is the seat of affections: a *wise heart* therefore means the complex or the source of affections in conformity with wisdom. This is the true estimate of things."[43] If we relate what I tried to say earlier between the connection with interpretation and custom, we could say that the heart, that is, the spirit of the law, is that which precedes the letter of the law, just as custom precedes the law. The heart is the seat of affections: we could find confirmation of all this in a paragraph entitled "La moralità della facoltà del libero conoscere si propaga agli affetti dell'animo e alle operazioni esteriori" (The morality of the faculty of free knowledge spreads to the affections of the soul and to external operations), in the first part of the *Filosofia del diritto* (Philosophy of law). In that central point of the philosophy of law, in which Rosmini, analyzing the affections of the soul, notes how, in reaction to the relationship with the object, it is a question of a

> wonderful union of the different parts of man, of this being so multiple and so one. Give me a *voluntary judgment* that will produce me an opinion of the goodness of an object I perceive. Quicker than an electric spark an affection starts from the judgment that rises in my soul, without any other work of will, and that affection, all spiritual as it is, nevertheless makes the beating of my heart more frequent, colors my face with love, and moves it with a smile, and finally produces in my members themselves an agitation, which all express the same affection, and it seems that they want to help me as it were, so that I may either come into possession of the good loved if I do not possess it, or if I do possess it, enjoy and delight in it.[44]

In this passage from *Philosophy of Law*, in my opinion, Rosmini expresses this line of affective and customary reading of law and of the conception of the human person as a right subsisting in law, aimed at keeping together perception, and custom, in a moral, affective and foundational figure of being.

This is perhaps the starting point for an analysis of his juridical philosophical history. Undoubtedly, one could, at least, continue at length in the series of quotes related to the point. Also during the conference from which I took the quotation from Paris, Fernando Bellelli, speaking of affection, with reference to Sequeri, notes how "it is the imprinting on the real being of the subject of the real structure of objective being"[45] and connects Sequeri's "sensitivity to sense" as a metaphysical criterion and phenomenological

---

43. De Giorgi, *Sienza del cuore*, quoting Rosmini, *PMS*, 340n.
44. Rosmini, *Filosofia del diritto*, 1:118.
45. Bellelli, "'Polis' forma dei legami," 26.

question, to that of original sin, reconstructing from Saint Paul's view of the phenomenology of the flesh the opposition between *soma* and *sarx*:

> It is necessary to develop an anthropology of the fact that the Word became flesh and did not become *a burden*, to destroy *soma* with the resurrection of his true body. The (Western) Christian tradition seems too afraid of the presumed danger of the flesh-*sarx*, in a real anthropological pessimism that risks being a lack of faith in the Creator's ability to be stronger than the forces of evil, as well as debasing the principle of the Incarnation of the *Verbum caro* and of the theological-salvific criterion of the *caro salutis cardo* Rosmini did not have this fear, as he had the anthropological confidence that man created by God is all good, and therefore the flesh, understood as pro-affection, before being a temptress and a cause that leads out of the truth, first of all, gives the ontology of truth.[46]

This further aspect aimed at bringing together anthropology, psychology, theology and law in a conception of the divine reliable *à la* Sequeri, and of the human capable of corresponding to this reliability, seems to me the fulcrum of a reading that is at the same time an anthropological, juridical and theological philosophical conception of Rosmini.

On the level of the importance of this anthropological, psychological and juridical junction in contemporary culture, we can also refer to other authors, even in a completely different context, who seem to converge on this non-pessimistic anthropology. I am thinking of an author like Hayek, who, when referring to spontaneous order, makes it start from a sensory order[47] that certainly has a family resemblance to affection—no more than this, moving from a theoretical context concerning the connection between the sensory order and the completely different custom—and with the theme of fundamental feeling. I am thinking, however, above all of Vico, however, when, from the anthropological point of view, referring to the Vichian invention of the animal man, of the beast, of the giant who is about to become man, the first divine fable is built, the invention of Jupiter, king and father of men and gods (*Iovis omnia plena*), an invention from which all religions descend, and also law as a social order, which derives from it.[48] It might seem that Rosmini does not agree with this Vichian idea, but the criticism could also be extended to the authors I mentioned earlier, placing them in contrast with Rosmini. He writes in *Philosophy of Law*, precisely with regard to Vico,

46. Bellelli, "'Polis' forma dei legami," 28.
47. See Hayek, *L'ordine sensoriale*.
48. Vico, *Scienza Nuova*, 919–21.

except that he believed it necessary to ascend first from the concept of order to the demonstration of the existence of an infinite mind author of the eternal truths, and then deduce the notion of natural honesty from there, placing it in the contemplation and love of this perfect and infinite being where the eternal truths are contained. It harms Vico—here we come to the theoretical point—to have believed it necessary to deduce an eternal eternity from an eternal order of things, when truth precedes and order follows, so that he should rather have deduced an eternal order from an eternal truth, that being simple and this manifold.[49]

The point is that here Rosmini refers not to the Vico of *Nuova Scienza*, but to the Vico of *De Uno* and therefore ideally does not refer to the passage in *Nuova Scienza* in which the first poets and theologians invent the divinity. In my opinion this criticism of Rosmini, although it is absolutely precise and refers to the comparison and confusion between social order and truth of *De Uno*, does not apply to the doctrine of *Nuova Scienza* and this anthropological aspect concerning the religious origin of the human. And this is exactly the core of the Vico Rosmini report and of this inversion. My hypothesis to be verified is therefore that in reality the affective turn in metaphysics, the deontology of the foundation, and also the customary interpretation of the law founded on the person as a right subsisting in law subsisting in Rosmini is to be found in the sense of an articulation of the two directions, from order to truth and from truth to order, within which the same problem of the relationship between multiple and one evoked above can be inserted in the indication of the centrality, to this anthropological and juridical of the moral form of being.

The last point of the paper on which I have only one suggestion to make, conclusive and concerning the anthropological relevance for *philosophy of law and the theme of trust*[50] of Christology and the topic of faith, is the connection of all this reconstruction of different themes with the theme of the faith of Jesus, and of the distinction between faith in Jesus and the faith of Jesus. I refer here to an article that Piero Coda dedicates to the reconstruction of the theme in Saint Thomas and that seems to me very clear, perhaps clearer than the criticism or interpretation that Antonio Comi addresses to him in his book dedicated to the question.[51] Coda, having completed the analysis of Jesus's faith in Saint Thomas, expresses himself in these terms: "While the experience of obedience brings Jesus much closer

---

49. Rosmini, *Filosofia del diritto*, 2:143–44, sect. 10, "Principio dell'ordine nella mente divina" (Principle of order in the divine mind).

50. On the subject of trust in the law, recently, see Greco, *Legge della fiducia*.

51. See Comi, *Fede di Gesù*.

to us, knowing something of God, thanks to Jesus, brings us a little closer to Jesus. In this sense, although Jesus has a knowledge of God that is and remains unique, both insofar as he is the Incarnate Word and because his human nature is perfect and filled with the fullness of grace, he himself, as man, has had, in the deepest possible way, the experience that we live through faith."[52] In this position it seems very clear to me how Coda reads the theme of Jesus's faith in a relational and affective sense. He refers to the interpretation of the anthropological and theological meaning of Jesus's lived experience on the cross as "something analogous to humanly lived experience as extreme absolute naked faith."[53] It seems to me, that I can to say conclusively in the face of a whole series of horizons that would now open up, that this attempt at a sketchy reading of the theme of custom as present in Rosmini, is in a certain sense relative to the criticism of Kelsen and his conception of the fundamental norm and therefore also to a certain way of reading the question of faith in Jesus for the philosophy of law: that is to say, it is linked to emphasizing the centrality of obedience as the fundamental point for understanding the experience of law in the positivistic conception of law. It seems to me that both in Kelsen and in Thomas the theme of custom, of the affective turn in metaphysics, of the faith of Jesus, inserts the juridical theological centrality of the relevance of faith, and not of obedience, in understanding the theme of law. And I believe that precisely this element, which in some way Sequeri with his *Dio affidabile* on trust in the reliability of the divine places in theological reflection can represent a starting point in the interpretation of Rosmini's theory of law and of the person as a right subsisting in law.[54] Holding together the conception of habit and the contribution of affective neuroscience in relation to Sequeri's affective interpretation of metaphysics and Bellelli's reading of the theme of moral conscience in Rosmini raises the question about a fiducial foundation of law and the state after the juridical nihilism of the twentieth century. This may (perhaps) consist of the (new) actuality of Rosmini's thought.

Bibliography

Battaglia, Felice. *La filosofia del diritto in Rosmini*. Rome: Giuffrè, 1977.
Bellelli, Fernando. *Etica originaria e assoluto affettivo. La coscienza e il superamento della modernità nella teologia filosofica di Antonio Rosmini*. Milan: Vita e Pensiero, 2014.

52. Coda, "Fede di Gesù?," 523.
53. Coda, "Fede di Gesù?," 526.
54. Sequeri, *Dio affidabile*, 77.

———. *Percorsi storici della pedagogia giuridica. Vico, Rosmini e la* dignitas hominis. Rome: Aracne, 2020.

———. "La 'polis' forma dei legami di libertà tra coscienza personale e coscienza civile: Rosmini e la postmodernità." *Quaderni di Synaxis* 6 (2016) 15–28. Catania, It.: Grafiser, 2016.

Biven, Lucy, and Jaak Panksepp. *Archeologia della mente. Origini neuroevolutive delle emozioni umane.* Edited and translated by Andrea Clarici and Antonio Alcaro. Milan: Raffaello Cortina, 2014.

Böckenförde, Ernst-W. *Stato, Costituzione, democrazia.* Milan: Giuffrè, 2006.

Bombelli, Giovanni, and Paolo Heritier, eds. *I volti molteplici della consuetudine.* 2 vols. Milan: Mimesis, 2022–2023.

Canobbio, Giacomo, ed. *La fede di Gesù. Atti del convegno (Trento, 27–28 May 1998).* Bologna: EDB, 2000.

Capograssi, Giuseppe. *Attualità e inattualità di Rosmini.* Edited by Vincenzo Lattanzi. Rome: Fondazione Nazionale Giuseppe Capograssi and Centro Internazionale di Studi Rosminiani, 2001.

Carleo, Alessandro, ed. *Decisione robotica.* Bologna: Mulino, 2019.

Chiassoni, Pierluigi. "Tre buoni filosofi contro i cattivi costumi (Giurisprudenza analitica contro i cattivi costumi)." In *La consuetudine giuridica. Teoria, storia, ambiti disciplinari*, edited by Silvia Zorzetto, 63–108. Pisa: Ets, 2008.

Coda, Piero. "Fede di Gesù? Una *quaestio disputata* ancora attuale a partire dalla risposta di Tommaso d'Aquino." *Lateranum* 3 (2014) 511–32.

Comi, Giuseppe. *La fede di Gesù.* Assisi: Cittadella, 2017.

Damasio, Antonio. *L'errore di Cartesio. Emozione, ragione e cervello umano.* Milan: Adelphi 1995.

———. *Il sé viene alla mente. La costruzione del cervello cosciente.* Milan: Adelphi, 2012.

De Giorgi, Fulvio. *La scienza del cuore. Spiritualità e cultura religiosa in Antonio Rosmini.* Bologna: Mulino, 1995.

De Lucia, Paolo. *Essere e soggetto. Rosmini e la fondazione dell'antropologia ontologica.* Pavia, It.: Bonomi, 1999.

Dworkin, Ronald. *I diritti presi sul serio.* Translated by Federico Oriana. Bologna: Mulino, 2010.

Finnis, John. *Legge naturale e diritti naturali.* Edited by Francesco Viola. Turin: Giappichelli, 1996.

Gallo, Filippo. *Interpretazione e formazione consuetudinaria del diritto. Lezioni di diritto romano.* Turin: Giappichelli, 1993.

Greco, Tommaso. *La legge della fiducia.* Rome: Laterza, 2021.

Hayek, Friedrich A. von. *L'ordine sensoriale. I fondamenti della psicologia teorica.* Translated by Lina Gallina. Milan: Società aperta, 2021.

Heritier, Paolo. *Estetica giuridica.* 2 vols. Turin: Giappichelli, 2012.

———. "Legal Liturgies: The Aesthetic Foundations of Positive Law" *Polemos* 8 (2014) 137–52.

———. "Provvedenza vichiana e metodo clinico legale della Terzietà." *Teoria e Critica della Regolazione Sociale* 1 (2018) 117–42.

Irti, Natalino, and Emanuele Severino. *Dialogo su diritto e tecnica.* Rome: Laterza, 2001.

Paris, Leonardo. "Dimensione antropo-teologica determinata dalle neuroscienze." *Quaderni di Synaxis* 6 (2016) 73–85.

Petrillo, Francesco. *La lezione di Antonio Rosmini-Serbati. Principi giuridici fondamentali e diritti umani*. Chieti, It.: Solfanelli, 2012.

Piemontese, Filippo. *La dottrina del sentimento fondamentale nella filosofia di A. Rosmini*. Milan: Marzorati, 1967.

Prini, Pietro. *Introduzione a Rosmini*. Rome: Laterza, 1997.

Ricca, Mario. "Sussidiarietà orizzontale e dinamica degli spazi sociali, ipotesi per una corologia giuridica." *Science and Peace. Rivista del Centro Interdisciplinare per la Pace* 22 (2014) 1–65. www.scienzaepace.unipi.it.

Rosmini, Antonio. *Filosofia del diritto*. Edited by Michele Nicoletti and Francesco Ghia. 4 vols. ENC 27, 27/A, 28, 28/A. Rome: Città Nuova, 2013.

———. *Principi della scienza morale*. Edited by Umberto Muratore. ENC 23. Rome: Città Nuova, 1990.

Sequeri, Pierangelo. *Deontologia del Fondamento*. Turin: Giappichelli, 2020.

———. *Il Dio affidabile*. Brescia, It.: Queriniana, 1996.

———. *Ritrattazioni del simbolico. Logica dell'essere performativo e teologia*. Assisi: Cittadella, 2012.

———. *Il sensibile e l'inatteso. Lezioni di estetica teologica*. Brescia, It.: Queriniana, 2016.

Valditara, Giuseppe. *Sovranismo. Una speranza per la democrazia*. Milan: Book Time, 2017.

Vico, Giambattista. *La Scienza Nuova. Le tre edizioni del 1725, 1730 e 1744*. Milan: Bompiani, 2012.

Zorzetto, Silvia, ed. *La consuetudine giuridica. Teoria, storia, ambiti disciplinari*. Pisa: ETS, 2008.

20

Philosophy and Theology of Law

Rethinking the Legal Systems in the Light of Rosmini's Ideas

MARIO CIOFFI

Introductory Note

A PHILOSOPHER AND AN innovative theologian, Antonio Rosmini was also a master of wisdom and holiness and a witness of intellectual charity. Underpinning his theoresis is "the manifold wisdom of God" (Eph 3:10), which was behind the thinking of Augustine, who had valued both science as *cognitio naturalis* capable of leading to the humanity of Christ, and wisdom as *cognitio intellectualis* capable of leading to his divinity. Rosmini adopted the *intellectum valde ama*, which combines without confusing them, science and wisdom in the pleromatic unity of distinctions, synthesized in man as *imago Dei*, ontological foundation of the person who knows, wants, and loves. The basis of all of Rosmini's practical philosophy is the essential objectivity of the *ordo amoris*, according to which no law is authentically such if it is unjust. He also followed the Pauline exhortation, *Omnia autem probate, quod bonum est tenete* (1 Thess 5:21), as a premise for an epistemology based on the organic intelligence of reality which, with its synthetic capacity to understand the whole, makes it possible to reconstruct the sciences in their unity and overcome the fragmentation of knowledge. After recovering the ontological foundations of Catholic philosophy, Rosmini restored and updated Catholic philosophy with the best of modern thought, proposing it once again as a *system of truth*. Fighting errors, condensing truth in a system, providing a philosophy that could be a solid basis for the sciences and of which theology could avail itself, were the special purposes to which his doctrine was directed, characterized by unity and totality and by the method of freedom of philosophizing and conciliation of sentences.[1] Mediating between ancient philosophy, of which he attested the objective basis, and the modern philosophy, of which he ensured the values in the light of perennial principles, Rosmini healed the fracture between tradition and modernity, and gathering the fragments of truth present in the discarded thinkers, sought new veins of the one truth, without ever departing from the *ordo amoris* of Augustine and the *bonum commune* of Thomas Aquinas.[2]

Introduction: Philosophy, Theology, Religion

To remedy the failures of sensism, subjectivism, and the secularization of thought, Rosmini undertook a reform of philosophy capable of regenerating society through the "restoration of all the other sciences, mainly of morals, where every decorum and every honor of humanity lies,"[3] a reform that was the result of the "good courage that frees philosophy from unnecessary restrictions and unjust constraints, and that is born in the mind of those who begin to philosophize moved by the *love of truth*."[4]

Kantianism had separated reason and faith, relegating the latter to the private sphere and excluding it from the ranks of the sciences. It was therefore necessary to have a philosophy capable of "respecting faith as that which accomplishes what she (philosophy) lacks and revering it as her superior."[5] For Rosmini, the relationship between reason and faith was of positive and fruitful agreement: the former does not surpass the postulates of the latter and finds in it the means for total understanding of reality; the priority of faith does not mortify reason; it does not empty its philosophical and demonstrative itinerary. Faith is independent of reason, "but it is

---

1. Rosmini, *IP*, 15–108.

2. For a broad profile of Rosmini's thought, see my work, Cioffi, *Rosmini filosofo di frontiera*.

3. Rosmini, *IP*, 31.

4. Rosmini, *IP*, 49.

5. Rosmini, *IP*, 325.

not consequently hostile to philosophy,"⁶ which "is reasoning, and nothing but reasoning and is not established on any authority, neither divine, nor human."⁷ Faith and science are two distinct forms of knowledge that synthesize in a single truth.

In addition to science, philosophy is also wisdom, a means of practice: "Vain is a philosophy that does not tend to the improvement of man."⁸ True science cannot be separated from virtue, so that the state of mind most suited to the study of philosophy is "that man practice virtue, as, in the order of a higher science and wisdom; it is written: 'My son, you who desire wisdom, preserve justice, and God will give it to you.'"⁹ Wisdom is accomplished only when the truth known in the idea is freely assented and loved by man and passes into action, reforming it in a virtuous sense. Philosophy cannot solve the total problem of man, nor make him wise, not even of the wisdom alone "which in the light of nature can be seen as conceived,"¹⁰ for the imbalance between the ideal and the real makes science incomplete and perfect virtue impossible. Only Christ overcame the human limitation that prevented the accomplishment of wisdom: he, *eternal wisdom*, "revealed Himself, and implemented knowledge in humanity,"¹¹ making it possible for natural science to fulfil itself in the supernatural. The revelation of the Trinitarian mystery solves the problem of the one-many and becomes the foundation of ontological speculation.

Rosmini's contribution to theology was considerable, also in the updating of the language used, which remained mired in Scholasticism. Theology is a science that completes natural knowledge and offers philosophy answers to otherwise unsolvable questions, but not action and worship, *a life lived*, which belongs to practice and lives on a supernatural principle.¹² Philosopher of being and theologian of charity, Rosmini synthesized the truthful-contemplative moment with the charitable one or the recognition of being, love that is justice, fidelity to the order of being and "form to which all the virtues are reduced."¹³ If the truth contemplated is willed and loved as good, man practically adheres to the norm and rises to morality, "being

---

6. Rosmini, *IP*, 83.
7. Rosmini, *IP*, 91.
8. Rosmini, *IP*, 319.
9. Rosmini, *IP*, 145.
10. Rosmini, *IP*, 166.
11. Rosmini, *IP*, 160.
12. See Rosmini, *SA*, 1:54.
13. Rosmini, *T*, 949. See Cioffi, "Essere come amore."

as it is loved is the moral form,"[14] sublimated in charity which is "the ultimate form of morality,"[15] the perfect fulfillment of justice and "the execution and substantiation of truth."[16] Truth and charity are different concepts, "but each of them includes the other,"[17] and in "charity exercised in *truth* truly consists the work of Christian wisdom."[18] Being is "a current and most perfect act of love,"[19] essentially communicative, which assimilates the lover to the beloved:

> In the imperfect acts of love that fall within the experience of man, we recognize an effort that the lover makes to transform himself into the beloved ... such an effort in the nature of love ... in an infinite being ... can never be imperfect, it must always obtain all its effect: the act of love must be completed and quiet, in the end, attained. The lover must therefore have taken the form of the beloved. And if the lover is at this point the beloved, the subject himself must subsist for himself beloved, which is the last conceivable reality and perfect stillness of being.[20]

Starting from the intelligence ignited by the natural light of reason, Rosmini arrives at God-Love. Man by nature aspires to "joining the limitless Being by loving knowledge,"[21] and this "vital feeling that leads to being"[22] inclines him to happiness, which "is really fulfilled in complete holiness."[23] Rosmini wrote: "Briefly, our system begins with the divine and ends with God.... The light of reason as a moral principle tells man what he must do, shows him where to go ... : it is the map, it is not the chariot, not the ship, not the winds that carry, pull, push ..., that actually make the journey."[24]

The journey is "the work not of the idea, but of the other light of supernatural reason, the work of the Word of God."[25]

---

14. Rosmini, *T*, 1026.
15. Rosmini, *T*, 1007.
16. Rosmini, *IP*, 184.
17. Rosmini, *IP*, 181.
18. Rosmini, *IP*, 183.
19. Rosmini, *T*, 1084.
20. Rosmini, *T*, 1085.
21. Rosmini, *T*, 269.
22. Rosmini, *T*, 1091.
23. Rosmini, *T*, 1092.
24. Rosmini, *PMS*, 304–5.
25. Rosmini, *IP*, 159. See Cioffi et al., *Percorso rosminiano dall'intelligenza all'amore*.

PART 5

Justice, Law, Society

Rosmini aimed at a society based on justice and law, with the person at the center, and where order and freedom could coexist. Moreover, wanting to restore to the law the dignity of a science based on justice, he prepared a juridical philosophy[26] as a science of social justice. Law is unthinkable detached from philosophy, and Rosmini, at the beginning of *Philosophy of Law (Filosofia del diritto)*, reported the words of Atticus to Marcus Antonius in Cicero's *De legibus*: "Therefore, you think that the discipline of the law is to be drawn from the edict of the praetor, as many today wish, and not from the twelve tables, as the elders wished; but all from inner philosophy."[27]

Philosophy of Law is a work closely linked to the overall thinking of the author, characterized by the concepts of *unity* and *totality*, proper to philosophy directed to true science.[28] At its base is the person, reduced by false doctrines to the merely sensitive or subjectivist dimension: "We want to complete this man so miserably diminished,"[29] wrote Rosmini. Since "the subject of every right is always the human individual,"[30] man is the fundamental datum from which to begin the scientific study of law, founded on *the moral being*, which is the very truth of being, "the steadfast foundation of all the science of law"[31] and the essential goal of every society. Human relations have a moral nature because they are informed by the *ideal being* that is common to all men and constitutes the social bond of humanity; so Rosmini considered a true and authentic expression of the essence of the law "Cicero's declaration, worthy of the light of Christian times, that 'the foundation of law is found in the inclination that we have from nature to the love of our fellows.'"[32] In order for law to exist, which is the real beginning of human actions, there must be intelligence and will, essential for giving solid foundations to civil life. The person is the foundation of the political community as a society of persons: "In order for there to be society, it is necessary that there be intelligence: moreover, society presupposes law, justice,

---

26. See Cioffi: *Persona e diritto* and *Diritto come giustizia*.
27. Rosmini, *PL*, 1:70.
28. Rosmini, *IP*, 201.
29. Rosmini, *PY*, 17–18.
30. Rosmini, *PL*, 1:106.
31. Rosmini, *PL*, 1:154.
32. Rosmini, *PL*, 2:243.

and moral virtues."[33] Since "the social bond is opposed to the bond of sovereignty," it follows that "the society by its very nature excludes servitude."[34]

There is society only if each person is an end and never a means, so that it is not the person who is a function of the community, but vice versa, since "the reason for all social occurrences is found in man, an element of society."[35]

Since the human person has in his nature all the constitutive elements of law,[36] he "is the subsisting right, the essence of law."[37] Synthesis of utility and justice, law is not an abstraction but the person himself as the concrete substance of morality, freedom, and measure of the social order.[38] As a living right protected by the moral law that imposes respect for it, informed by the ideal being and created free, the person is sacred and inviolable and "can submit to nothing but the truth."[39] It is an end that can never be reduced to means, and God himself "disposes men with great reverence."[40] The person has three fundamental rights of nature and reason, three key privileges that are inalienable, inviolable, and common to all men: the right to truth, virtue, and happiness, "from which flows his excellence, his dignity and his supremacy.... Any attempt to strip man of truth, or virtue, or happiness is a violation of the formal law that is the person."[41]

By embodying it in the person, Rosmini brings the law to its zenith from a theological perspective where divine reason creates an *extra-social law* prior to any legislation, which cannot be renounced even when man becomes part of society. Incorporated in the ideal order and in living and concrete reality, an expression of justice that is its essence and form and theologically founded, the law enjoys the character of objectivity. It arises "from the moral duty not to harm the person"[42] and can exist only within justice, which is "akin to religion and which constitutes its supreme sanction."[43] The law "is a moral thing."[44] And, if deprived of ethics, it is re-

---

33. Rosmini, *Pp*, 241–42.
34. Rosmini, *Pp*, 197.
35. Rosmini, *Pp*, 452.
36. See Rosmini, *PL*, 1:178.
37. Rosmini, *PL*, 2:26.
38. See Cioffi et al., "Persona-diritto sussistente nel sintetismo."
39. Rosmini, *PL*, 2:225.
40. Rosmini, *PL*, 3:152.
41. Rosmini, *PL*, 2:34.
42. Rosmini, *PL*, 2:163.
43. Rosmini, *CSJ*, 231.
44. Rosmini, *CSJ*, 147.

duced to mere force and loses the dignity of an entity founded on justice. If the command not to harm that comes from being is violated and an attempt made to undermine or suppress the right embodied in being, it gives off a flash of theological light the moment it is violated:

> When brute force oppresses the man who has the law on his side, it excites an extraordinary interest in other men: his right seems to shine with unusual splendor: it triumphs, because it escapes the action of violence as an immortal entity, inaccessible to all material force that cannot even touch it, all its efforts remaining excluded from that high and spiritual sphere in which law dwells.[45]

The violation of the law manifests in the injured person that *juridical resentment* proper to the intelligent nature, spurred to resentment "whenever they believe that injustice has been done to them, so that injustice can be said to be a wound to the moral entity."[46] The person is microcosmic beauty,[47] the beginning and the end that reflects the structure of being, and the confusion between means and ends is the premise for any abuse of man, who can be saved only if brought back to the ontological dimension of the person: "If the person is saved, the man is saved; if the person perishes, the man perishes."[48] Without ontologically founded personal dignity, man remains closed in the subjectivism that binds him to nature and is liable to all wickedness. To harm the person is to damage a subsistence, to harm nature is to damage a condition of that subsistence.

Theocracy and Social Christianity

In *Philosophy of Law* Rosmini dwelt on the society "which God wanted to form with his human creatures on this earth, and which we call *theocracy*."[49] He knew that the word *theocracy* was problematic for many, "but woe betide me," he wrote, "if I too begin to flatter this century rather than to reason with it, as I have resolved to do."[50] A theocratic society is the only one that

---

45. Rosmini, *PL*, 1:173.
46. Rosmini, *Pp*, 680.
47. See Rosmini, *T*, 1141.
48. Rosmini, *Introduzione del Vangelo* (a commentary to the introduction of the Gospel of John), 243.
49. Rosmini, *PL*, 3:131–32.
50. Rosmini, *PL*, 3:130. See Cioffi, "Ragionare col secolo."

"exists for itself as *a society of law* independently of the work of man,"[51] and it is necessary and indispensable, together with the domestic and the civil society for the perfect organization of the human race. Belonging to this unique society, which welcomes God and man within itself, allows the person to relate to the infinite being, which constitutes and guarantees his rights through the moral law that imposes respect for them. In a truly universal society, God must also find a place, since his exclusion would entail, for society itself, the risk of an unjust end.[52]

It is an ecclesiological and juridical fact that God has a right of lordship over society attributable to the creative act, a divine supremacy[53] that excludes all dominion of man over man. The relationship that man has with God in theocratic society is "of utmost servitude," which He reciprocates "with a relationship of utmost friendship,"[54] a relationship, therefore, of both juridical lordship and charity. The Catholic Church is for Rosmini "the society of the sublimated human race,"[55] and its supremacy is understood by him not in an authoritarian sense, but as an offer of an ethical patrimony and a horizon of meaning aimed at eradicating selfishness and injustice from other societies. Scripture itself can be the source of positive law only through philosophical and cultural mediations.

Christianity has saved human societies by reforming their customs, and it has done so by addressing individuals and not the masses, because only healed individuals can in turn heal society. Rosmini sees in mankind an essentially personal and individual end,[56] and all that is born in the nations "is already present in the bud, in the minds of the individuals who compose these nations."[57] Since the gospel has eliminated from society the noble element that degenerates into despotism, "in the midst of Christianity, an eminently social religion, mere lordships cannot last long."[58] Consequently, "the society of servitude and lordship is not a true society," because the Legislator of humanity, "intending to unite all men in a fully universal society, completely excluded the concept of dominion and lordship . . . , preserving all domination to God alone."[59] Christianity, "ably raising the

---

51. Rosmini, *PL*, 4:226.
52. See Rosmini, *Pp*, 174.
53. See Rosmini, *PL*, 3:850.
54. Rosmini, *PL*, 3:278.
55. Rosmini, *PL*, 3:231.
56. Rosmini, *Pp*, 346.
57. Rosmini, *Pp*, 452.
58. Rosmini, *Pp*, 308n.
59. Rosmini, *Pp*, 182–84.

law over the *fact*, took away this unjust domination of the world,"[60] and "he led men to that important separation between the modality of rights and the rights themselves: separation that alone leads to the perfect idea of civil government."[61]

It is a factual truth that "what is right and conforms to the spirit of the Christian religion is also more useful in general to the Christian principle."[62] As an actor in the redemption of politics and in the progressive affirmation of the values of the person, Christianity was the author of the first drafts of a natural-rational scientific law, erroneously considered the work of the Enlightenment and not the gradual product of the good news.

> This divine religion has restored and increased in man the three elements that form the *subject of rights*, which are activity, intelligence, and morality. . . . Who does not understand from this how the institution of Christian society must have influenced all other societies, especially the domestic and the civil, making new rights appear in them, almost out of thin air, drawing them with creative power and ascertaining the uncertain, even if only by improving their roots, that is, by admiring and almost creating in man the *subject of rights*? . . . Christianity not only highlighted the rights already due to man, together with human dignity, recreating the subjects suited to being invested with them; but also ensured that they were respected . . . together with those who wanted to observe that respect. . . . Christianity forced man to respect the law in the most gentle and only effective way, by making people want to respect it. In a word, it improved the will of man: the law from then on found respect. Thus, the realization of human rights was made possible: hence, these had a value.[63]

For Rosmini "the theoretical and practical principle of justice exists in humanity; it was placed there by Christianity, which alone possesses the theoretical principle in the truth it teaches, and the practical principle in the grace with which it supports the will."[64] By teaching humility to all, rulers and governed, "the Gospel revealed the true social principle,"[65] a government humbled under the unchanging eternal justice common to all societies.

---

60. Rosmini, *PL*, 3:133–34.
61. Rosmini, *PL*, 4:311. See Mercadante, *Regolamento della modalità*.
62. Rosmini, *FW*, 209.
63. Rosmini, *PL*, 3:136.
64. Rosmini, *PL*, 4:433.
65. Rosmini, *Sull'unità d'Italia* (About the unity of Italy), 262.

Even the supreme political power must submit to justice, the founding value of Rosminian constitutionalism, but this can only happen when "there is uniformity of national thinking about the laws of social justice,"[66] the result of a "long, public, free discussion," until "the language of each one becomes the single language of all."[67]

Convinced that only a fully universal and just society can curb despotism, Rosmini demystified the state, considered omnipotent, infallible, and the only source of law:

> In order to chop at the roots of despotism, years ago I published *Philosophy of Law* where I began to defend all the natural and rational rights of man against the invasions and usurpations of civil society whatever form they take; to establish the authority of an inviolable, indelible and inscribable extra-social right superior to all positive provisions, and to restrict civil government within its just boundaries, demonstrating that it has no authority whatsoever over the value of any human right, has no other authority than to determine the modalities, always except for the entire value of the same. This doctrine reduced to practice destroys all social despotism.[68]

In the person, the seat of the "divine," there is a law born before society and the state, a law that is an ethical limit to the legislator: "The moral law and the juridical law are always reduced ultimately to God, as in his first source and in his essential seat."[69]

Prophetic Ideas

Born ahead of his time, Rosmini was not understood by many of his contemporaries, to whom he brought truths often unintelligible even to men of the church, mired in the language of "perennial philosophy" and not yet ready for doctrines and practices that, while referring to ancient ecclesiastical traditions, were decidedly innovative and daring. He was critical of the illusion of being able to escape the challenges of modernity and deeply committed to the dialogue between faith and culture, the agreement between philosophy and life, and new ways of rooting Christianity, also on the

---

66. Rosmini, *PL*, 4:433.
67. Rosmini, *PL*, 4:435.
68. Rosmini, *CSJ*, 64–65.
69. Rosmini, *PL*, 2:9n2.

model of the patristic era, where "science and holiness were born from each other united, and science contained holiness in its viscera."[70]

Today Rosmini is particularly appreciated for the practical-social values marshalled in the unity of the person and the identification of rules and principles for applying morality to the area of law, draft constitutions based on social justice and the attempt to reconstruct politics as a human science governed by law and justice: "Only if directed to the achievement of the moral good, can politics participate in the nobility of law, and be sanctified by it. . . . Any principle of law is an excellent rule to follow in politics."[71] Aiming at a society where everyone can freely exercise their rights within the confines of the moral law, Rosmini looks to a "true and healthy liberalism" resolved "in a harmonious reconciliation between private freedoms and the authority of the government, so that under the firmest authority the exercise of the greatest possible legal freedom is preserved for everyone."[72] He also indicated how to establish the art of governing according to the principle of *political wisdom*:

> The central government must be strong, and at the same time all those governed must enjoy greater freedom. It is essential to distinguish what belongs to the strength of the Government, and not to the freedom of the governed, and what belongs to the freedom of the governed, and not to the strength of the Government: to yield nothing of this, and to usurp nothing of that: here lies one of the main and most difficult parts of political wisdom.[73]

Convinced that "the greatest benefit that can be done to man is not to *give* him goodness, but to make him the author of this goodness"[74] advocate of the *regulation of the modality of rights* as a function proper to society and the state[75] and of competition and the free market, Rosmini anticipated the *principle of subsidiarity*: the government must only "establish laws, courts, legal procedure so made that with greater speed, with minimum spending, with the minimum inconvenience, and with the utmost righteousness justice is rendered to all."[76] He placed justice, which is "a principle, an idea,"

---

70. Rosmini, *FW*, 90.
71. Rosmini, *PL*, 4:607.
72. Rosmini, *Saggio sul comunismo* (Essay on communism), 21.
73. Rosmini, "Della libertà d'insegnamento" (About the freedom of teaching), 218.
74. Rosmini, *T*, 242.
75. See Rosmini, *PL*, 4:248, 443–44; and *Pp*, 672–73.
76. Rosmini, *PL*, 2:459.

above utility, which is "a consequence, a fact"[77]: "Politicality seeks utility, but true and accomplished utility arises from justice applied rigorously to its last consequences, to all social adversities."[78] He knows that evil is unavoidable, that the perfect society is unrealizable because man is not perfect and that laws cannot promote all good and prevent all evil, he has been able to distinguish between *perfectionism*, the utopia that ignores "the great principle of *the limitation of things*,"[79] and perfectibility. He reorganized the state by placing a limit to its preeminence in personal freedom: it is merely a juridical person equal to the others and with functions of service only, and the questions between private individuals and between them and the institutions "must be decided by the same principles of universal justice."[80] He anticipated personalism and devoted himself to the concrete recognition of the natural rights of man, proper to each and equal in all, and which "are not merely qualities inherent in the nature of the individual, but *moral relations* between several individuals, resulting from common human nature."[81] Of an unconventional nature, human rights are inviolable, not questionable or challengeable, and guaranteed by a special *political tribunal*, which precedes modern constitutional courts.[82] Rosmini did not limit himself to showing the ideal of justice naturally present in conscience, but prepared the means to concretize it: only in this way is the constitution "no longer a written paper without a voice, it is given life and speech."[83] On the ecclesiological side, he anticipated by more than a century, against every custom of the past, the public confession of the faults of the church, denouncing with piety and filial love that which obscured the face of his beloved Mother, disfigured by awful wounds. What he wanted was to reform the state, but he also wanted to update the church: only if removed from political subjection and restored to the freedom and poverty of the origins, would she, thus regenerated, be able to worthily carry out her mission as supreme guarantor of universal justice. These and other insights, such as the appreciation of the laity, the renewal of the clergy, the awakening of the liturgical spirit, would be fundamental chapters of the Second Vatican Council.[84]

77. Rosmini, *PL*, 1:56–7.
78. Rosmini, *Pp*, 669n4.
79. Rosmini, *Pp*, 137.
80. Rosmini, *PL*, 2:444.
81. Rosmini, *PL*, 2:234.
82. On Rosmini's constitutional projects see my report presented in the Campidoglio during the inaugural meeting of the UGCI National Conference, held in Rome in Dec. 2008: Cioffi, "Figure di costituenti." See also Cioffi, "Costituzionalismo albertino."
83. Rosmini, *CSJ*, 235.
84. See Muratore, *Profezia per la Chiesa*.

The fight against despotism, the limitation of power, personal freedom and social justice were Rosmini's fundamental concerns, which are capable of giving answers to today's prevarications of politics over law and utility over politics and to the various forms of ungovernability that affect every society, from the family to the global. The precedence and primacy of the person over society and the state, its coincidence with the law, are the premises for its inviolability in every situation. Founding law on being, which is stronger than man's creations, gives it objective bases and subtracts it from abstract and arbitrary constructions, which are revealed to be mere formula. As an essential right and the realization of freedom in law, an irreducible end by means, the person is the basis of a just society, where everyone can realize their own freedom and fulfillment and where the individual and the state are equally subject to the same one law. Rosmini's entire practical philosophy rests on a single basic theme: the person and their value, and hence the warning not to expect a free society from those who cancel individual freedom,[85] to avoid subverting the degrees of dignity of being by bending the truth to suit one's own designs, and the invitation to lower the peaks of pride and self-sufficiency and adhere to being, which is truth and love.

Distinguishing the essence from the inessential, the necessary from the superfluous, is the supreme principle of every government of the world, and on this principle revolves the real, intellectual and moral universe:

> In the entire universe there are only two entities, one minister of supreme mercy, the other minister of supreme justice. This divine intention in creating, maintaining, governing things shines everywhere, and demonstrates and teaches what the first principle of all government is. And this is a *cosmic* law, of both the moral world and of the physical . . . a law that preserves everything that forms part of the universal order, and everything perishes when trying to disturb it: a law that confirms the words of a sublime thinker: "The principles of Christianity are none other than the laws of the world deified."[86]

The law of justice and love, which relies solely on the power of truth and evangelical meekness, will lead society to complete justice, the charity that is the essence of morality and the complete fulfillment of the law.

> This is the time *of national egoism*: it is indulging in this egoism, it grows, invades everything, believes it can do everything, becomes irritated and angry at any objection, refuses all restraint. And yet this restraint is necessary, and it will come from the law

85. See Rosmini, *Saggio sul comunismo*, 31.
86. Rosmini, *Pp*, 152.

of universal justice proper to theocratic society, and from the progress of universal charity preached unceasingly by Christ's Church. Theocratic society does not want to destroy civil society, but wants to draw from it the vice of selfishness that deforms it, making it unjust.... Civil society remains to perfect itself, enlarging itself, by befriending the universal society, the perfect theocratic society, in order to draw complete justice and purge itself of every spirit of injustice. To pave the way for such a happy rejuvenation of nations we avoided determining precisely the end within which civil society must be held with its government, "the regulation of the mode of rights." It is a small seed, but we consign it to the logic of the time and to the charity of Christians . . . : the future may bear fruit.[87]

Bibliography

Cioffi, Mario. "Il costituzionalismo albertino e il costituzionalismo rosminiano." In *Rosmini politico. Tra unità e federalismo*, edited by Gianni Picenardi, 123–58. Stresa, It.: Rosminiane, 2011.

———. *Il diritto come giustizia e amore nella filosofia di Rosmini*. Biblioteca di studi rosminiani. Stresa, It.: Rosminiane, 2012.

———. "L'essere come amore nella filosofia morale di Antonio Rosmini." *Rivista Rosminiana* 3-4 (2021) 295–314.

———. "Figure di costituenti. Antonio Rosmini." In *Valori costituzionali. Per i sessanta anni della Costituzione Italiana*, edited by Francesco D'Agostino, 47–68. Milan: Giuffrè, 2010.

———. "La persona-diritto sussistente nel sintetismo dell'essere." In *Antonio Rosmini teologo, giurista, filosofo, educatore*, edited by Pasquale Stanzione, 127–55. Salerno, It.: UGCI, 2002.

———. *Persona e diritto in Rosmini*. Biblioteca di studi rosminiani. Stresa, It.: Rosminiane, 2005.

———. "Ragionare col secolo senza adularlo. La lezione di Antonio Rosmini." *Iustitia* 2 (2020) 30–51. https://www.iustitiaugci.org/wp-content/uploads/2020/09/220-Cioffi.pdf.

———. *Rosmini filosofo di frontiera*. Florence: Città di Vita, 2001.

Cioffi, Mario, et al. *Il percorso rosminiano dall'intelligenza all'amore; Antonio Rosmini: Truth, Reason, Faith*. Edited by Umberto Muratore. Stresa, It.: Rosminiane, 2009.

Mercadante, Francesco. *Il regolamento della modalità dei diritti. Contenuto e limiti della funzione sociale secondo Rosmini*. Milan: Giuffrè, 1981.

Muratore, Umberto, ed. *Una profezia per la Chiesa. Antonio Rosmini verso il Vaticano II*. Panzano in Chianti, It.: Feeria-Comunità di San Leolino, 2009.

Rosmini Antonio. *Antropologia soprannaturale*. Edited by Umberto Muratore. 2 vols. ENC 39–40. Rome: Città Nuova, 1983.

---

87. Rosmini, *PL*, 4:642–43.

———. "La Costituzione secondo la giustizia sociale." In *Scritti Politici*, edited by Umberto Muratore, 39–245. Stresa, It.: Rosminiane, 2010.

———. "Della libertà d'insegnamento." In *Opuscoli politici*, edited by Gianfreda Marconi, ENC 37, 183–239. Rome: Città Nuova, 1978.

———. *Delle cinque piaghe della Santa Chiesa*. Edited by Alfeo Valle. ENC 56. Rome: Città Nuova, 1988.

———. *Filosofia del diritto*. Edited by Michele Nicoletti and Francesco Ghia. 4 vols. ENC 27, 27/A, 28, 28/A. Rome: Città Nuova, 2013.

———. *Filosofia della politica*. Edited by Sergio Cotta. Milan: Rusconi, 1985.

———. *Introduzione alla filosofia*. Edited by Pier P. Ottonello. ENC 2. Rome: Città Nuova, 1979.

———. *L'introduzione del Vangelo secondo Giovanni commentata*. Edited by Samuele F. Tadini. ENC 41. Rome: Città Nuova, 2009.

———. *Principi della scienza morale*. Edited by Umberto Muratore. ENC 23. Rome: Città Nuova, 1999.

———. *Psicologia*. 10 vols. Milan: Hoepli, 1887.

———. *Saggio sul comunismo e sul socialismo*. Rome: Talete, 2008.

———. "Sull'unità d'Italia." In *Scritti Politici*, edited by Umberto Muratore, 249–265. Stresa, It.: Rosminiane, 2010.

———. *Teodicea*. Edited by Umberto Muratore. ENC 22. Rome: Città Nuova, 1977.

———. *Teosofia*. Edited by Samuele F. Tadini. Milan: Bompiani, 2011.

21

Antonio Rosmini: Ascetic and Mystic

VITO NARDIN

He Shines in a Mystical Light

THE TITLE OF THIS paper is not mine, it is taken from Father Clemente Rebora, Rosminian poet and priest, who died in Stresa in 1957. The pages published in the Rosminian monthly *Charitas* in November 1955 are entitled "Antonio Rosmini, Ascetic and Mystic" *(Antonio Rosmini, asceta e mistico)*. Indeed, Rebora wrote, "He, as sovereign cognoscente and thinker elevated to divine understanding, essentially lived in reality, wholly practical and not a dreamer, a true ascetic because he was truly mystical, and he was therefore still a very broad and truthful experimenter of human experience." Then he added, "He, one of the most excellent mystics, had not exceptional manifestations, apart from living totally and perseveringly as one of the most exuberant members of the Mystical Body."[1]

His articles were later published as a book on the occasion of the bicentenary celebrations of Rosmini's birth.[2]

---

1. Rebora, *Rosmini*, 200.
2. See Rebora, *Rosmini*.

Recently, in 2016, there was an important reference to this publication. In *Nuovo Dizionario di Mistica*, we read certain items that are important, at least for us: *Antonio Rosmini, Angelina Lanza, passività.*

The pages of the *Nuovo Dizionario Mistica* concerning Angelina Lanza were written by the Sicilian theologian Don Massimo Naro, those on Rosmini by Don Alberto Neglia, a Carmelite brother, author of a book on Rosminian ecclesiology, *Laici senza complessi*. Alberto Neglia considers mainly the passivity and the indifference of charity. He mentions among his sources the pages that shine with mystical inspiration. These are *Massime di perfezione* (Maxims of Christian perfection), *La dottrina della carità*, and *Epistolario ascetico* (Ascetical epistolary).

From the first pages of the authoritative and important *Nuovo Dizionario Mistica*, previously mentioned, we find mention of "passivity," which is then defined as follows:

> The idea of mystical passivity goes back to a phrase by Dionysius the Areopagite [Ed.: also quoted by Rosmini] that speaks of the soul and which, through a supernatural influence, not only knows but experiences divine things (*non solum discens sed patiens divina*, according to a medieval translation). St. Thomas Aquinas explains this phrase by saying that the soul "is not only in the state of one who receives the knowledge of divine things, but also of one who, loving them, unites himself to them with affection." Thus, positive experience is placed in the field of affect because this tends towards objects in their reality while intelligence stops at one's own knowledge.[3]

This is an authoritative and welcome confirmation, since Rosmini adopted passivity as a source of his rules of behavior, from which indifference derives, that is the detachment from any preferable activity, a condition for full willingness to embrace God's will.[4]

The origin of this concept is to be found in Saint Augustine's writings. This is the opinion of Fulberto Cayré, speaking of the effects of grace.

The ideal, again according to Saint Augustine, will be that of the perfect Christian, docile without reservations regarding the impulse of the Holy Spirit. The first condition of this *docility* to grace is *faith*, not, however,

---

3. Borriello et al., *Nuovo Dizionario di Mistica*, 1709.

4. See Rosmini, *Directorium spiritus*, 1:106–7: "Since therefore grace does not destroy nature but perfects it, natural reason should minister to faith as the natural bent of the will ministers to charity" (see Saint Thomas Aquinas, *Sum* I, q. 1, art. 8, ad sec.m). The text of *Directorium spiritus* by Rosmini, in three volumes, is available online: https://www.rosmini.it/objects/Pagina.asp?ID=680. Saint Thomas is mentioned in the *Directorium spiritus* sixteen times.

any faith, but a supernatural faith, combined with a most sincere *humility* (it is God who is the truth and principle of all the good that man can accomplish) to a full *trust* (requisite of the prayer that implores the grace), in a luminous *intelligence* of God, at least practical, which is necessary to direct the *conduct*, and, finally, to a great *purity* of heart, without which it is it is even impossible to have the aforementioned knowledge of God. It is on the basis of such prescripts that man is really placed in a condition to fruitfully receive divine inspirations. Here is the essence of what could be called Augustinian "passivity." However, we must never forget that this passivity itself is a principle of action, it is an active passivity, given that we can use this verbal antithesis. Faith submits man to God only to make him act *per charitatem*. . . . Inner activity has its completion in works, whatever they are, guided by the Holy Spirit.[5]

We could say that all the effects of Rosmini's ascetic and mystical spirituality are to be found in the spiritual theology of Thomas Aquinas. As an example, given the nature of this paper, I will simply mention the quotations of Thomas Aquinas that Rosmini includes in *Directorium spiritus*, which he wrote prior to setting out the *Constitutions of the Institute of Charity (Costituzioni dell'Istituto della Carità)*. With regard to his considerations on Thomas Aquinas's *Summa Teologica*, Rosmini says:

> The truths, the offices, the means, the history, the prayers, and the feelings are the five main sectors into which the Christian's library could be conveniently divided. I. The truths. The *Roman Catechism* and the *Diocesan Catechism*, the *Summa* of Saint Thomas (an eminent work for its content and method), the *Ritual*, the *Ceremonial*, the *Pontifical*, etc. The *Opera* of Benedict XIV. The *Proceedings* of the Church of Milan. The Compendium of theological doctrine of Crupfel (for the method).[6]

Rosmini Ascetic and Master of Ascetiscism (the "Shadowed" Ascetic Profile)

The pamphlet entitled *Maxims of Christian Perfection* is generally considered the fundamental text regarding his asceticism. It was reprinted many times, translated into various languages and commented by many experts.

---

5. Cayrè, *Patrologia e Storia*, 726. In a note it is specified: "Passivity means, in this case, an aptitude for receiving (pati), rather than inaction, as is sometimes understood."
6. Rosmini, *Directorium spiritus*, 17.

The celebrated theologian Hans Urs von Balthasar, in the introduction to a new edition in the German language of *Maxims of Christian Perfection*, translated into Italian by the Rosminian father Pierluigi Giroli, wrote in 1964:

> [Antonio Rosmini] has left to his sons and daughters a brief, perhaps even too brief, summary of his spirituality, the *Maxims of Christian Perfection*, which are now published for the third time in German, in correspondence with the 34th Italian edition. Franz Xavier Kraus, to whom we must be grateful for the fine, comprehensive appreciation of Rosmini (in German) described this work as "A small but precious book that, with simple language but ironclad logic and penetrating eloquence, presents the everlasting principles of spiritual life, perhaps the shortest and most beautiful compendium that ascetic literature has ever offered."[7]

In the six maxims it is possible to identify both the ascetic purpose and the mystical dimension, in differing proportions. For example, the ascetic indication of the fifth maxim on *acknowledging one's own nothingness* leaves no room for pride, or for laziness: "Lastly, they will lead a life of constant occupation, so as never to lose the least moment of time."[8] Everyone recognizes that Rosmini, who wrote these word, also put them into practice. Clemente Rebora also took this commitment to heart, with a special vow.

The sixth maxim refers to this generous commitment and ranks it with what is called "the spirit of intelligence"[9] in neatly arranging the actions of the day. We find here twenty-five "instructions" that mark the personal path in the church, in the family and in society. The Christian, quickened by the grace and strengthened by the gifts of the Holy Spirit, is encouraged not to flee from the world, but to sanctify the world. The maxims are completed by three more lessons, the last of which deals with the order of prayer. Here is eloquent proof of the convergence, in Rosmini, of the *lex operandi* with the *lex orandi*.

The *Constitutions of the Institute of Charity* are his ascetic masterpiece destined for the brothers of the institute. They were written during the Lenten and Easter seasons of 1828, a period of illumination that we could call mystical, in the tranquility of the Domodossola Sacred Mountain. A chapter on ascetism refers to the period of the novitiate.

---

7. Giroli, "Traduzione," 258.
8. Rosmini, *Massime di perfezione cristiana*, 34.
9. Rosmini, *Massime di perfezione cristiana*, 34.

I feel it necessary to point out at least three ascetic recommendations: prayer, disciplinary balance, true poverty of spirit.

1. Rosmini wrote, "I will not prescribe much communal prayer, except for an entire hour of mediation, due to the apostolic efforts that may come to pass."[10]

    It is interesting to mention the type of prayer recommended to all the Rosminian brother in rule 11.

    > The first and most solid exercise of piety consists in striving to do more perfectly every day with the grace of our Lord Jesus Christ, all that one must do according to one's state and rank, ever better and more intimately uniting one's life with God our Lord, so that this is nothing but a continuous homage and offering to the divine majesty.[11]

2. The purpose of all the charity and balance of Rosmini the ascetic is well expressed in this instruction: "As far as corporal penitence is concerned, I remind you that this Institute does not generally prescribe any, so that the strength thus preserved can be employed in charity towards God and one's neighbor; and in the more precise observance of the *Constitution*."[12]

We cannot avoid mentioning the enormous quantity of letters he wrote. The *Ascetical Epistolary (Epistolario ascetico)*, published 1911–12 in four volumes, contains 1501. The alphabetic index of the subjects, that is of the topics dealt with, in the fourth volume, covers no less than 180 pages. It is a genuine dictionary of Rosminian asceticism and mysticism.

With regard to our topic it is opportune to mention one of the first. On February 18, 1815, writing to his cousin Leonardo Rosmini in Padova, he made the following prediction: in his life dedicated to God, he will be cast aside by men, but not by God, who choose "the most vile and despicable according to the world."[13] He transcribes on this matter a tercet that he had already composed in a sonnet:

> Yes, already the stone that every man holds inept
> For every work, burnished and cleaned,

---

10. Rosmini, *Costituzione dell'Istituto della Carità* (The constitutions of the Institute of Charity), para. 496.

11. *Regole dell'Istituto della Carità*, para. 11.

12. Rosmini, *Costituzione dell'Istituto della Carità*, para. 223nD.2.

13. Rosmini, *Epistolario ascetico*, 1:24.

Was elected as a column for your temple.[14]

Recently, but two hundred years from then, a new statue of Rosmini has been erected in Stresa, in the parish church, where he often prayed and where his funeral was celebrated. It stands not in a niche, nor above the altar, nor on a pillar or in front of a column, but on top of a column, in the center of a chapel that was specially refurbished. The prediction of 1815 has come true, also visually. Rosmini, previously despised, is now a chosen one, a saint, a column of the church.

With regard to the *Ascetic Epistolary*, Clemente Rebora, scholar, uses a particularly eloquent image. The ink on Rosmini's pen marks the page, but from that page fresh streams of sanctity spring forth,[15] spreading mystical light. They are:

> letters pervaded by wisdom and supernatural beauty, flowing with healthy and holy water, springing—in newness of life—from the depths of the Christian and Catholic tradition, purifying the sediments and the most secret meanders of human anguish: and it is salient water to what is eternal. Such a reading first surprises, then edifies (in the proper sense of the word) the spirit, so often disconcerted today: faith and hope and charity are unexpectedly reinvigorated and restored: a vital transport awakens, full of certainty and abandonment, towards God, and Christ and his church; and the person feels strengthened and encouraged to fulfill himself in unity in the All-good, and to integrate himself in the unanimity of the brothers. Then it is natural to think: "A good man out of the good treasure of his heart bringeth forth that which is good." (Matt, 12:22)[16]

The Mystic Christian (We Observe the Divine Sculptor at Work)

Today the attention we pay to the mystical Rosmini is legitimate, as we will see. It is a mysticism that is still relevant today. Indeed, in our times, "the twenty-first century will either be mystical, or it will not," according to an aphorism attributed to Karl Rahner. We read these words in a book

---

14. Rosmini, *Epistolario ascetico*, 1:24.

15. See Rosmini, *Directorium spiritus*, 1:154: "1st Holiness is ascribed to everything pertaining to God. (Saint Thomas Aquinas, *Part II, Quæst.* 36, article 1)."

16. Rebora, *Rosmini*, 217.

dedicated to all the mystical forms, written with the same title by Jean Vernette.[17] Rosmini is also a mystic, according to many authors, who I will now quote.

This item in the *Nuovo Dizionario di Mistica* is signed by Luigi Borriello:

> In the fourth century Dionigi Areopagita in his pamphlet *Theologia mystica* uses this expression, adding a clarification: this mysterious knowledge of God constitutes the apex of the Christian experience, in the sense of a "*suffering*" the divine Transcendent.... Only much later, in the sixteenth and seventeenth centuries, did attention shift to the subjective conditions of the direct and passive experience of the presence of God in the soul and in particular, to the modalities of mystical contemplation and to mixed or para-psychological that can occur in it.[18]

Balthasar adds: "An experience not only notional, but existential of the divine."[19] The spiritual life, in its mystical dimension, can also be defined thus: "It is experience of the Spirit, therefore it is experience of faith. All Christians, without distinction, are called to this experience which fulfils the Christian life as an anticipation of the future life."[20] Specifically, it is necessary to stress the following aspect: "The mystic always emphasizes the ascendancy of the self-revalation of God over the human search, of grace over any human merits, of the kingdom, compared to the seed that dies and grows in the earth, whether the farmer sleeps or watches over it" (see Mark 4:26–29).[21] Once again, the following emphasis is of central importance: "The mystic refers to a knowledge lived, that is a concrete knowledge of life, a knowledge of love, which is the substrate of the mystic life."[22] The shortest definition of a mystic, generally attributed to Bonaventura, is: *Cognitio Dei experimentalis* (experimental knowledge-awareness of God).[23]

It is therefore necessary to acknowledge that Christ is not simply an object of faith, but rather the presence of a personal reality that enters the life of the Christian, who, in turn, finds in this presence the principle and the foundation of his being and his actions.[24]

---

17. See Vernette, *XXI secolo*.
18. Borriello et al., *Nuovo dizionario di Mistica*, 1467.
19. Borriello et al., *Nuovo dizionario di Mistica*, 1468.
20. Borriello et al., *Nuovo dizionario di Mistica*, 1470.
21. Borriello, "Esperienza mistica."
22. Borriello et al., *Nuovo Dizionario di Mistica*, 1472.
23. S. Bonaventura, in *Sent.* III, D. 35, q. 2, co.
24. Borriello et al., *Nuovo Dizionario di Mistica*, 1473.

The fullness of the theme of the Christian mystic is then explored in the *Nuova Dizionario di Mistica* in twelve characterizing traits, which, obviously, it is not possible to describe here. The last of these quotations, nevertheless, is also particularly worthy of our attention and I will quote it:

> The mysticism described so far is not a reality detached from history, but is placed through the mystic in the very heart of history as a concrete testimony of a living and true God. The mystic, therefore, is not a spirit sated with himself, closed in on himself to escape from the human assembly and remain in sterile solitude. On the contrary, he is open to others in the communication of love; indeed, he lives on the streets in solidarity with other men: he shares their aspirations, their joys, their pains to build the heavenly city with them and narrate, here and now, the marvels that God is working in him (see John 1:1–3) and in human history. On the roads of the world, the mystic, like the Risen One at Emmaus, becomes a travel companion of men to make his mystical life a humble service of mediation between the Savior and humanity.[25]

The Rosminian Doctrine on Mystic Theology

We find in a chapter dealing with mystic theology, explored in nine articles, in book 1 of *Supernatural Anthropology (Antropologia soprannaturale)*,[26] where Rosmini deals with *confini della dottrina filosofica e della teologica* (boundaries of philosophical and theological doctrine), chapter 6, "Della teologica mistica."[27]

Rosmini distinguishes between the exterior revelation, common to all, and the interior one, for those to whom grace is given.

> Now this inner revelation is all made up of feelings, of perceptions; but just as we have the faculty of reflecting on all the feelings we experience, so we can also reflect on this, and observe (at least up to a certain point) what happens in us in that

---

25. Borriello et al., *Nuovo Dizionario di Mistica*, 1478.

26. That the Rosminian conception of the relationship between nature and grace is inspired by that of Saint Thomas can also be seen in this previously quoted passage from Rosmini, *Directorium spiritus*, 1:106–7: "Since therefore grace does not destroy nature but perfects it, natural reason should minister to faith as the natural bent of the will ministers to charity" (see Saint Thomas Aquinas, *Sum* I, q. 1, art. 8, ad sec.m).

27. Rosmini, *SA*, 1:227. For an overall view of these aspects, see Bellelli: *Metodica di Rosmini*; *Il divino nell'uomo*; *Pedagogia del sapere*; *Nuzialità trinitaria*.

supernatural communication, especially at times of special, and current graces, and put these observations into words, order them into science, and this is the mystical theology they call doctrinal, while communication with God Himself they call experimental and it too can truly be called science, because God is a an object knowable in Himself, and therefore, unlike other things, to feel Him, as we have said, is to know Him, and indeed there is no other true thing about Him than to feel Him. Hence the difference between revealed or common theology and mystical or secret theology is sufficiently seen: they are like the two parts of the knowledge that men of God can have in this life.[28]

Rosmini further explores the interior revelation, focusing on the topic of fundamental, supernatural feeling, the experience that introduces a communication that transcends the merely human one:

Of the language understood by a few or by only one. Now the feeling of grace, the deiform feeling is completely distinct from any other; and it is as distinct as God is distinct from all created things. Therefore, whoever does not have this feeling, this perception cannot have the corresponding idea: consequently, even if words were found and instituted to signify those feelings and perceptions, they would have no positive value for those who had not received and experienced those feelings within themselves. This explains what Saint Paul says he heard during his well-known abduction, "the arcane words which men are not permitted to pronounce," which means words that man cannot use, because they would be unintelligible, since men do not have the ideas corresponding to them; because they did not feel those feelings to which those ideas refer, since as the Apostle says "neither eye saw, nor ear heard, nor entered the heart of man" what pertains to future glory.[29]

---

28. Rosmini, SA, 1:227–28.

29. Rosmini, SA, 1:228–29. With regard to the relational dimension of this aspect, see the next passage (Rosmini, SA, 1:231): "Of the Society of Saints. John describes it with these words: 'What we have seen and heard we proclaim now to you, so that you too may have fellowship with us; for our fellowship is with the Father and with his Son, Jesus Christ' (1 John 1: 3). Here, the bond by which men associate themselves with the Father and with his Word is that by which men also associate with one another; the same charity binds them to God, and to one another, precisely because associating and being bound to one another is nothing other than finding all alike in this, that is, in being associated with God. God being the form and therefore Himself the simplest node common to all in which all are simplified and unified. Of which effect the principle is faith. This is what Saint John means, in the aforementioned words, with which he promises to preach Christ precisely so that by then receiving the faith they can have

Since the experience of grace is profoundly spiritual, reflection on it requires that whoever carries it out has certain characteristics, regarding which Rosmini says:

> *Of the qualities of the perfect theologian.* Hence, the reason the fathers teach that one who does not combine the sanctity of life and the experience of eternal truths with study can never be a perfect theologian. Because without this, man could not understand all this part of the secret and most sublime theology of which we are speaking. Other sciences can be known without the goodness of life, that of supernatural and divine things not; because of this a large and the best part arises from the experience that man has of God, who does not communicate Himself to one who does not make himself worthy.[30]

A very illuminating page on Rosminian doctrine, relating to mystic theology, is to be found in the answer to a question from the Rosminian Sisters of Divine Providence in England, in which the practical application of synthesism of the three forms of being in the interaction between the three forms of charity—corporal (real being), intellectual (ideal being), and spiritual (moral being)—is suggested:

> How can one unite in practice the spirit of contemplation with an active life in works of charity? The union of holy contemplation with the exercise of works of charity is the intention of our Institute; and therefore, we must not be satisfied until we have obtained from God the light to join these two things in us: . . . there is no teacher who can teach us such a sublime science, except that Jesus Christ who itself showed a very perfect example of this. Because this science does not consist in anything other than in intimate union with Jesus Christ, in a union that is as effective as possible. And he by his mercy has already prepared the means in his Church, even before we were born or even knew how to desire it. . . . We read of certain holy people, who while they seemed all busy on the outside, they conversed internally with their God and Creator; and this conversation did not prevent them, on the contrary it helped them to do better what they did outside, just as vice versa, what they did outside did not dissuade them from that internal affectionate conversation.[31]

---

together with him that secret and wholly spiritual society and communication that only believers have together."

30. Rosmini, *SA*, 1:231–32. In dealing with these topics, Rosmini quotes the Saints Clement of Alexandria, Augustine, and Cyril of Alessandria.

31. Letter dated Sept. 24, 1850, in Rosmini, *Epistolario ascetico*, 3:638–39, 641.

Some Examples of the Mystic Life

I will give a few significant examples.

The eucharistic celebrations that saw him attentive and absorbed. Saint Giovanni Bosco, when visiting Stresa, gave a particular attestation, saying that he had never seen a priest celebrate Holy Mass with the same devotion as Rosmini.[32]

His esteem for the eucharistic sacrifice is expressed in an elegy. It is not difficult to find the the binomial *culmen et fons* of the constitution of the Second Vatican Ecumenical Council *Sacrosanctum Concilium*: the concept of the culmination is present at various times, such as that of the source:

> If one looks at the excellence and sublimity of this divine sacrifice, it is such that even in Heaven there is no more august act of worship. For this, the earthly Jerusalem competes with the heavenly; nor can the choirs of angels mind descending from the empyrean to assist the priest in the divine mysteries. . . . Here is a copious source of living waters! Here every piety can quench its thirst. Here is angelic bread! Even superhuman devotion can be nourished in full abundance of Him. What is lacking here of the great, the holy, the sweet, the beneficent, the merciful and the soul-stirring that one should seek or find something religious, pious, useful and good, something beautiful, rich and sublime that is not already eminently in this, which is the source of all holiness, grace, love, beauty and magnanimity.[33]

See Rosmini, *Directorium spiritus*, 1:95: "(on the contemplative and active life) Saint Thomas Aquinas, *La verità*, quest. XI, art. 4." And see Rosmini, *Directorium spiritus* 2:5: "The operations of the active virtues are, so to speak, preparations and predispositions for the contemplative virtues. Therefore, the end of man is to arrive at the contemplation of the truth. (Saint Thomas Aquinas, *Contra Gentiles*, II, 83)."

32. See Rosmini, *Directorium spiritus* 3:38: "In the meditation of the Supper, Christ aims to show true love: 'Total union with the loved object'; therefore this most divine Sacrament is called *Sacramentum amoris*, because it is a sacrament of union, and Saint Thomas teaches that Christ showed greater love in the Supper than on the Cross, because the Passion occurred through separation, but this Sacrament is realized through a total union with us, like food with the person who eats it."

33. Rosmini, *Dell'educazione cristiana*, 136. See Rosmini, *Directorium spiritus*, 1:142: "Among the Jewish people there were four feasts linked together: 1st that of the *trumpets*, which replies to the first test, and was an invitation to the feast of atonement. 2nd that of *atonement*, a day of confession. 3rd that of the *tabernacles* on the second illuminative way. 4th that of the *Collect* in the third unitive way. (See Saint Thomas, Book I, *Quæst. CII*, IV, ad 10m.)" and Rosmini, *Directorium spiritus*, 1:156: "Saint Thomas Aquinas chapters II, III, Q. CLXXXVI, art. 3 compare *alms* to the Sacrifice and the voluntary poverty of the holocaust, which is more perfect."

Still a newly ordained priest, he wrote a mystic poem entitled *Affetti spirituali*.[34] It is certainly autobiographical and deserves a special comment. It is an itinerary with forty dimensions of union with God expressed with the same number of verbs. The first part is in harmony with the well-known *Istruzioni* of Saint Columba:

> Let me look, contemplate and desire only you, only love you and only wait for you with the most ardent desire. Deign, beloved Savior, to show yourself to we who knock, because knowing you, we love only you, we desire only you, we think continuously only of you, and meditate on your words day and night.[35]

Rosmini seems to echo Saint Columba:

> O how sweet it is to converse with God,
> To speak about God, only satisfying God . . .
> Only hoping for God, only delighting in God . . .
> And pleasing God alone, suffering for God,
> Only finding contentment in God,
> Only wanting God and always being with God.[36]

In the second part Rosmini draws on the final page of the *Itinerario della mente in Dio* by Saint Bonaventura, "May every affection of the heart be integrally transformed and transferred to God."[37]

> And, while enraptured and transformed through God
> With God and in God, offer God to God,
> With everlasting glory and honor of God.
> Oh God, what joy and what sweetness is God.[38]

Finally, the testimony of Father Francesco Paoli, who was close to him for twenty-five years.

> His mind was in continual oration, also because from a very young age the presence of God had become a habit and almost a necessity. All his studies and thoughts were turned to God:

---

34. See Rosmini, *Directorium spiritus*, 1:12: "La regola degli affetti. "Charity truly concerns one's neighbor, but not as its principal object, since its principal object is only God: in fact, charity loves nothing in its neighbor except God. (Saint Thomas, *Quæst. X, La verità*, art. VII, ad 7.m.)"

35. Saint Columba, "Istruzioni, Sulla compunzione," as cited in Conferenza episcopale italiana, *Liturgia*, 4:340.

36. Nardin, *Amore mio dammi l'amore*, 32.

37. Saint Bonaventura, *Mistica sapienza rivelata*, 5/1:312–13; see the liturgical memorial of July 15.

38. Nardin, *Amore mio dammi l'amore*, 32.

either because God was the immediate object of his studies, or because he saw and observed every other object in the light that comes from God, and he studied every other thing to know and better know God and his heart. His every act and affection began and ended in God, because it was either adoration or love of God, or universal charity for all humanity.[39]

The fact that from childhood he cultivated his union with God is also testified by the fact that he was seen to "kneel and devoutly pray on the threshold of the church of Madonna di Loreto every time he passed it on his way to school."[40]

Among the practices of piety he preferred *silent prayer*: an hour of meditation to purify the soul. He formulated some intentions of purification in short prayers and noted them on the final pages of his prayer book, *Jesu Christi Passio*. There are seventy of them and, as we say, you are spoiled for choice. I will mention only the first and the last, as examples of *passive prayer*, that is entrusted to Jesus, and therefore liturgical: "Father, just as your divine Son would pray in me, so I want to pray to you. . . . I ask of you what that heart (of Jesus Christ) wants me to ask."[41] The *mystic passivity* that unites him to God in Christ is evident.

Rosmini Acknowledged Ascetic and Mystic

In addition to the words we gathered directly from him, it is opportune to add a taste of the studies on this topic, which we can consider almost "new" with regard to the figure of Rosmini.

Among the many authors, let's read some sentences from the works of Father Giuseppe Bozzetti, the provost general of the Istituto della Carità from 1935 to 1956. He left many writings on the asceticism and mysticism of Rosmini: "Asceticism is not a unique privilege; asceticism is for all, because Christians are called to God to cultivate their soul. The method may

---

39. Paoli, *Antonio Rosmini*, 97. See Rosmini, *Directorium spiritus*, 1:44: "With regard to the studies, the author of the *Imitation of Christ* (bk. 1, ch. 3; bk. 3, chs. 1–4) writes very well: 'The prayer by Saint Thomas before study is a fine one, it begins: 'O ineffable creator, who from the treasures of your wisdom'"; and Rosmini, *Directorium spiritus*, 1:97: "To ask for the opposite virtues, a beautiful prayer is that of Saint Thomas Aquinas which begins like this: 'Grant me, o merciful God, to ardently desire what is pleasing to you . . .'"

40. Rosmini, *Directorium spiritus*, 1:19.

41. Rosmini, *Jesu Christi passio*.

differ, the essential purpose is one."[42] On other pages he advises how to avoid individualistic mysticism.

Here is the fundamental point of Rosminian asceticism. "Perfect love drives man to seek union with God and therefore leads him to want to do the will of God, and to enact all the good that God wants from him and that he shows to the world."[43] The five directives of Rosminian piety will be of help to us.

Father Bozzetti reports, among the *Discorsi della carità*, the fourth, dedicated to the queen of virtues. Many commentators agree with him in finding all the elements of true, full-blown mysticism.

Accepting and rephrasing the words of Bozzetti (and others) in commenting Rosmini's *Discorsi sulla carità*[44] we can say that it is truly a wide-ranging and magnificent canticle, harmoniously composed. Anyone who is capable of penetrating the significance has an unmistakable impression of having become intimate with God. It is a profound and elevated exploration of a heart enthralled by love,[45] an expression inundated with balance and transport by the fullness of the human spirit that sinks and is absorbed into an adoring and contemplating expropriation of self by the Trinitarian love that seizes the human soul. It is necessary to read the text repeatedly; it is necessary to read with lengthy pauses for meditation in order enjoy every expression and the unfolding of the enveloping and sweeping force of Charity, the same Charity that is as strong as it is gently caring, cradling the desire of the person until they subside into the absolute. We could say that here lies the most compelling and enthralling nucleus of the beating heart of Rosmini's spirituality, ascetic and mystic at the same time: and this because we no longer perceiving Rosmini, but rather a stronger power, that expresses and communicates itself through him, which is the grace of that crucified and resurrected Love that transfigured[46] and elevated

---

42. Bozzetti, "Tra noi e Dio," 1:450.
43. Bozzetti, "Tra noi e Dio," 1:428.
44. See Rosmini, *Dottrina della carità*.
45. See Rosmini, *Directorium spiritus*, 3:37: "Nella Meditazione dell'amor di Dio considers that: 'Love, according to the Areopagite, is the desire for what is good and beautiful', and according to Aristotle's rule imparted by St. Thomas Aquinas 'if that which is simple recalls what is simple, if what is greater recalls what is greater, and what is highest recalls what is highest, and if what is good and beautiful is to be loved, what is good and beautiful in the highest degree and infinitely, this means God, we must love Him infinitely.'"
46. See Rosmini, *Directorium spiritus*, 1:112: "Ad II. Being too sad, and being depressed because of some disturbance or defect, must be considered a more serious imperfection than the defect itself: in such a state of prostration we must have total trust in the Lord that our vow will be fulfilled for his mercy. In fact, since it is written

his soul and all his person—hovering more so each day in that clear sky of celestial bliss (until the *Nunc dimittis* on his deathbed: worship, be silent, enjoy)—through the events of his "Roman mission" in 1848–49, episodes that involved for him and others the banning of his best-known and most important works (which post mortem became essential reference texts) but also the general "prosecution" of all his works by the Congregation of the Index,[47] lasting five years, with the terrible risk of a disastrous outcome; a prosecution that concluded with the solemn *Dimittantur* of 1854 (and still controversial, finally arriving at the conclusively clarifying Doctrinal Note of 2001, "passing" through the *Post Obitum* of 1887).

The Mystic Life in *A Commentary on the Introduction to the Gospel of John* (*L'introduzione del Vangelo Secondo Giovanni*)

In 2002, Maria Adelaide Raschini wrote the preface to the work *A Commentary on the Introduction to the Gospel of John* by Rosmini. The references to Rosmini the mystic are explicit, precious and numerous.

> Every day, moment by moment, everything required the most careful patience and holy trust from him. . . . Rosmini is alone, but he is alone with God: and therefore, he has within himself a superhuman strength which, overcoming his own physical fragility, makes him a victor of the spirit, to the point of allowing him an inner peace that no violence or human malice can touch.[48]
>
> It appears to our eyes as the fruit of a miraculous spiritual elevation above the miseries of the world: it is the manifestation of an inner freedom untouched by events, the most painful and mortifying for a man of good will and the highest intelligence.[49]

---

that '. . . the just fall seven times a day . . .' (Prov 24:16), never neglect (however wrong you may be) the resolution to do well, indeed show yourself strong against adversity, knowing that God often permits this, so that you recognize your weakness, and can be fully convinced that you need God's help in everything, and that you cannot do any good on your own: therefore, you must pray continuously, and never stop. All this says St. Thomas in the pamphlet 64."

47. Translator's note: Established by Pope Pius V with the Apostolic Constitution *In Apostolicae* of Apr. 14, 1571. The Congregation of the Index was charged with examining texts potentially harmful to the spiritual life of the faithful. The expression *mettere all'Indice* derives from the name of the Sacra Congregazione dell'Indice and has been translated as "to ban."

48. Rosmini, *Introduzione del Vangelo*, 7.

49. Rosmini, *Introduzione del Vangelo*, 10.

With regard to the manuscript:

> This work seems to be dictated by a voice that knows no discontinuity or dissonance.... A miracle of inner strength is reflected externally in the drafting and structure—almost painted—of the pages, as if by magic also graphically resumed without alterations of any kind after ten years, and generously flowed from the mind of a genius of the meditating spirit on the highest truths of Christianity.[50]

On the basis of the criterion of synthesis, a permanent characteristic of Rosminian thought, "it allows for judgments which, not without reason, attribute to the work a theological, but also a philosophical character, a strong mystical and at the same time ascetic imprint, a historical and at the same time philological flavor, biblical interest and exegetics."[51]

Other important reports were gathered by Professor Raschini, under the title *Dall'Aquila giovannea prende ala il genio cristiano di Rosmini*[52]:

> We must reaffirm the emergence of a constant mystical dimension; and this accords well with a dominant feeling of asceticism which involves the intellectual soul, not only to testify, so to speak, and even to "verify" its presence, but also to attest to its intimate, radical relationship with the Word, the foremost object of the comment.[53]

"We must repeat that Rosmini . . . is the only one truly capable of clearly representing the strength of the faith and the power of the intellect that come together in the light of the divine Word. . . . The 'thinking big' . . . characterizes him as a reformed and modern Father of the Church."[54] This attribution comes from Antonio Quacquarelli, who, as Maria Adelaide Raschini reports, writes that Rosmini "is an author to be studied in order to understand the contributions of Patristics to nineteenth-century theology. I refer to the movement known as neopatristic, to which Möhler, Rosmini and Newman belong."[55]

I would add that the same appreciation is to be found in paragraph 38 of the study by the International Theological Commission, published on March 2, 2018.

50. Rosmini, *Introduzione del Vangelo*, 10.
51. Rosmini, *Introduzione del Vangelo*, 15.
52. Rosmini, *Introduzione del Vangelo*, 17.
53. Rosmini, *Introduzione del Vangelo*, 18.
54. Rosmini, *Introduzione del Vangelo*, 20.
55. Rosmini, *Introduzione del Vangelo*, 20n15.

In 2019 Monsignor Bruno Forte also dedicated a study to *La Bibbia dei Filosofi*. Chapter 6, dedicated to John the Evangelist, has the subtitle "Rosmini and the Trinitarian Ontology." Here is part of the conclusion:

> In the light of Rosmini's comment on the Prologue of the Fourth Gospel we note the correspondence with the most important ethic fundamental to his Trinitarian ontology: recognizing in practice what is known speculatively means acknowledging in the mystery of reality the living imprint of that God of love which was recognized in the contemplation of the mind enlightened by faith, and is translated into the invitation to adore everything and welcome the event of the Trinitarian gift of self, weaving relationships of communion and peace with everything and everyone. In the great house of the world stands the eternal abode of the Trinitarian mystery of God, who envelops everything, and in everything asks to be recognized and loved as the purpose and meaning of everything. "The universe could not find completion in anything other than God, that is, the manifestation of the glory of God, which glory is his holiness and his beatitude, in a word, his perfect and absolute Being one and triune.[56]

The Cardinal Gianfranco Ravasi, on the occasion of the beatification, November 18, 2007, in an article for the daily newspaper *Il sole 24ore* expressed his appreciation no less than four times for the mystic dimension of Rosmini. "Apart from the science, there is a real world, that often escapes the eyes of the scientists and the philosophers; and in this world live most of mankind, who do not live only for science."[57]

Last year, Professor Fulvio De Giorgi published a massive volume *La scuola italiana di spiritualità. Da Rosmini a Montini*. It includes no less than twenty-three studies previously carried out on this topic, many of them on Rosmini. The characteristics of this school are: Catholic reform of the Church, christocentricity, totality and triniformity of charity, primacy of the word and of the liturgy, critical acceptance of modernity, refusal of statolatry, pedagogical demands and positive education, dialogue, humanism, emphasizing the formation of awareness.

"The two principal names are those of the layman Manzoni and the priest Rosmini,"[58] together with others. "It reached the Vatican II of which it

---

56. Forte, *Bibbia dei Filosofi*, 60.

57. A consideration also taken up in Rosmini's work "Degli studi dell'Autore" (On the author's studies). For the report of the intervention, see Ravasi, "Prefazione."

58. De Giorgi, *Scuola italiana di spiritualità*, 13.

was not so much a forerunner or a premise, as a spiritual root."[59] A root not only spiritual in a generic sense, but also with a mystic note.

It "is a school that I call Italian school of spirituality, in its authentic mystic and charitable timbre, having deep roots and long being part of the history of spirituality."[60] I am reminded of the image of the wide river that does not make a noise, compared with the tumbling brook.

It is a beguiling theory, especially for we Rosminians. To find confirmation a question seems fair: Would Pope Paul VI have been the same great pope that we had, and would the Second Vatican Ecumenical Council have been the same if no one had studied Rosmini in the decades that preceded the council? A legitimate answer leads us to believe that, while the initiator of the movement was Rosmini, the disciples and those who carried it forward, not only Pope Paul VI, would not have been the same if they had not taken on at least some of the characteristics of this school.

De Giorgi seems to state precisely this.

Our interest turns also to finding traces of the mystic dimension. Once again in the introduction he writes, "We could ask: the rule of passivity involved a cold, austere, aristocratic spirituality, completely ascetic and not at all mystic, excessively regulated by the mind and not warmed by the heart?"[61] De Giorgi answers with three chapters that confirm in Rosmini "the dimension of beauty, the centrality of the heart and the totality of love."[62] This choice is confirmed when examining the five Rosminian directives of *piety*: the universality of prayer, one's own sanctification, intelligence in piety, the offer of one's own blood, the eucharistic blessing.

De Giorgi insists once again: "To contradict anyone who denies an authentic mystical dimension or experience om Rosmini there are some pages that I would call almost astounding."[63] Among these, he too mentions the great discourse on charity, "true mystic peak of Rosminian spirituality."[64] In confirmation of what I said at the beginning, with regard to Clemente Rebora, he describes him as "a passionate, acute and brilliant interpreter of Rosminian mysticism."[65]

In this regard, it enhances what Rebora wrote about Rosmini: "He translated unity and totality into asceticism and they consist in his

---

59. De Giorgi, *Scuola italiana di spiritualità*, 13.
60. De Giorgi, *Suola italiana di spiritualità*, 14.
61. De Giorgi, *Scuola italiana di spiritualità*, 25–26.
62. De Giorgi, *Scuola italiana di spiritualità*, 26.
63. De Giorgi, *Scuola italiana di spiritualità*, 28.
64. De Giorgi, *Scuola italiana di spiritualità*, 95.
65. De Giorgi, *Scuola italiana di spiritualità*, 124.

mysticism, which marks the decisive abandonment to the deiform action of God-Charity: personally in the soul and unanimously in the Mystical Body of the Church."[66]

Conclusions

Given the theme of the convention from which this paper is taken, it is opportune to conclude with a reference to the conclusion of the note of the Congregation for the Doctrine of the Faith, of July 1, 2001.

> It must also be affirmed that the speculative and intellectual enterprise of Antonio Rosmini, characterized by great courage and daring, which at times bordered on a risky rashness, especially in some of his formulations, where he was trying to offer new possibilities to Catholic doctrine in the face of the challenges of modern thought, was undertaken in a spiritual and apostolic horizon that was honoured even by his staunch enemies, and found expression in the kind of works that led to the founding of the Istituto della Carità and the Suore Figlie della Divina Provvidenza.[67]

On the occasion of the audience granted by Pope Francis to the delegates of the general congregation, together with two Rosminian nuns and two members, a document was delivered with the main pronouncements of the Popes on Rosmini. It begins with Pius VII on April 1, 1823; Pius VIII on May 15, 1829; Gregory XVI on September 20, 1839, approving the institute and including praise for the Rosmini that we know; Pius IX on July 3, 1854, on the occasion of the *Dimittantur*; Leo XIII, indirectly, in the letter of the archbishops of Milan, Turinm and Vercelli dated January 25, 1882; John XXIII in 1962 during his spiritual exercises; Paul VI on various occasions; John Paul I; John Paul II on various occasions, in the encyclical letter *Fides et Ratio*; Benedict XVI on various occasions and on November 18, 2007; Pope Francis on various occasions, with reference to his reading of the book *The Five Wounds of the Holy Church (Delle cinque piaghe della Santa Chiesa)*, a copy of which I sent to him in December 2013.

An explicit reference by John Paul II to the ascetic and mystic Rosmini is to be found in the message to the delegates of the general congregation of September 26, 1998.

---

66. Rebora, *Rosmini*, 136.
67. Congregazione per la Dottrina della Fede, "Nota sul valore," para. 9.

> In the midst of the chaos of his time, Antonio Rosmini understood that there could be no liberation from Christ, but only a liberation through Christ and for Christ: this intuition inspired his entire life and work and is at the center of his many writings that are both scientific and religious, philosophical and mystical.[68]

And again: his "mysticism of the Cross led him to a profound devotion towards the woman who kneels at the foot of the Cross, Our Lady of Sorrows."[69]

Benedict XVI, at the Angelus of the solemnity of All Saints in 2010 said, "Holiness, imprinting Christ in oneself, is the purpose of the Christian's life. The Blessed Antonio Rosmini wrote: 'The Word had imprinted itself on the souls of the disciples with its sensitivity . . . and with his words . . . he had given his disciples that grace . . . with which the soul immediately perceives the Word.'"[70] Pope Francis, in particular, on July 26, 2014, in the Palatine Chapel in the Royal Palace of Caserta, speaking to the priests of the diocese, used a bold expression:

> And the Lord says: "go here, go there, do this . . ." encouraging that creativity that cost the Saints so highly. Think of the Blessed Antonio Rosmini, who wrote *The Five Wounds of the Holy Church*, he was a creative critic, because he prayed. He wrote that the Holy Spirit spoke, for this reason he was sent to the spiritual prison, that is to his own home: he could not speak, he could not teach, he could not write, his books were banned. Today he is Blessed![71]

I will conclude with two expressions from Pope Pius IX: "Praise be to God, who occasionally sends these men for the good of his Church."[72]

"Not only is he a good Catholic, but a saint: God employs the saints to make truth triumph."[73] Adding then, that he knows Rosmini and his goodness well, and that it was Rosmini himself who took care to be very close to him in Gaeta. Pius IX said that Rosmini was an extremely erudite, obedient, and exemplary person, to the point where, in his opinion, it would be possible to sing his praises with just three superlative adjectives (most erudite, most obedient, most exemplary).[74] He had good reason to say that Rosmini

68. De Giorgi, "Santa Sede-Rosmini."
69. De Giorgi, "Santa Sede-Rosmini."
70. Rosmini, *SA*, 1:256–66.
71. Francis, "Vista Pastorale a Caserta"; meeting with the priests of the diocese, speech made in Palatine Chapel in the Royal Palace of Caserta on Saturday, July 26, 2014.
72. Paoli, *Della Vita*, 1:517, ch. 31, para. 2.
73. Pagani and Rossi, *Vita di Antonio Rosmini*, 2:680.
74. See Paoli, *Della Vita*, and see Pagani and Rossi, *Vita di Antonio Rosmini*. On the

was most obedient. On November 18, 1848, he wrote to Monsignor Stella, "I beg you, at an opportune moment, to place me at the feet of His Holiness, and to tell him that for any eventuality, I am at your disposal, my person and my blood, which I would consider myself lucky to shed for him, and I only ask him to bless me."[75]

On November 18, 1832, he began to write *The Five Wounds of the Holy Church*; on November 18, 1848, as we have seen, he was ready to shed his blood for the pope; on November 18, 2007, he was proclaimed blessed.

Bibliography

Balthasar, Hans Urs von. "Geleitwort" [Foreword]. In *Leitsätze für Christen*, by Antonio Rosmini, translated by Hans Urs von Balthasar, 5–12. Einsiedeln, Switz.: Johannes, 1964.

Bellelli, Fernando, ed. *La metodica di Rosmini tra filosofia, teologia e pedagogia. Prospettive interdisciplinari*. Milan: Mimesis, 2022.

———. *Nuzialità trinitaria: relazione e identità. Rosmini e il fondamento simbolico dell'umano*. Panzano in Chianti, It.: Feeria-Comunità di San Leolino, 2017.

———. *Il divino nell'uomo e l'umano nella rivelazione*. Rosminianesimo teologico. Milan: Mimesis, 2017.

———. *Pedagogia del sapere di Dio. Una prospettiva storico-culturale*. Rosminianesimo teologico. Milan: Mimesis, 2019.

Bonaventura. *La mistica sapienza rivelata dallo Spirito Santo*. In *Opera Omnia*, translated by Silvana Martignoni et al., 5/1:312–3. Rome: Città Nuova, 1993.

Borriello, Luigi. "Esperienza mistica." Scrutatio, n.d. https://www.scrutatio.it/DizionarioTeologico//articolo//2347/esperienza-mistica.

Borriello, Luigi, et al., eds. *Nuovo Dizionario di Mistica*. Vatican City: Vaticana, 2016.

Bozzetti, Giuseppe. "Tra noi e Dio." In *Opere complete*, edited by Michele F. Sciacca, 1:375–488. Milan: Marzorati, 1966.

Cayrè, Fulberto. *Patrologia e Storia della Teologia*. Rome: Soc. S. Giovanni Evangelista, 1936.

Conferenza episcopale italiana. *Liturgia delle ore secondo il rito romano*. 4 vols. Rome: Libreria Vaticana, 1989.

Congregazione per la Dottrina della Fede (Congregation for the doctrine of the faith). "Nota sul valore dei decreti dottrinali concernenti il pensiero e le opere del Reverendo Sacerdote Antonio Rosmini-Serbati" [On the force of the doctrinal

---

topic of obedience, see also the words of Rosmini in *Directorium spiritus*, 1:47: "Obedience and the natural passage from common life to religious life. With this virtue one can easily reach the others; the vow of obedience, says Saint Thomas Aquinas (II–IIæ, Q. 186, art. 8), embraces the other vows, but cannot be exchanged for them. In fact, although the priests are bound to observe chastity and poverty by vow, nevertheless even these vows are under obedience; to which belongs the observance of many other virtues, besides chastity and poverty."

75. Letter to Monsignor Stella in Rome dated Nov. 18, 1848, in Rosmini, *Epistolario ascetico*, 3:462.

decrees concerning the thought and work of Father Antonio Rosmini-Serbati]. Vatican, July 1, 2001. https://www.vatican.va/roman_curia/congregations/cfaith/documents/rc_con_cfaith_doc_20010701_rosmini_it.html.

De Giorgi, Fulvio. "Santa Sede-Rosmini: le piaghe e la libertà." *Il Regno* 14 (2001) 445.

———. *La scuola italiana di spiritualità. Da Rosmini a Montini*. Brescia, It.: Morcelliana, 2020.

De Giorgi, Fulvio, and Lorenzo Prezzi. "Antonio Rosmini Serbati (1797–1855). Riabilitato un credente legittimato il sistema." *Il Regno* 14 (2001). https://www.rosmini.it/Resource/Causa/Articoli%20Stampa/2001%2007%20Il%20Regno%20Attualit%C3%A0.pdf.

Forte, Bruno. *La Bibbia dei Filosofi. Il Grande Codice e il pensiero dell'Occidente*. Brescia, It.: Morcelliana, 2019.

Francis, Pope. "Vista Pastorale a Caserta" [Pastoral visit to Caserta]. Vatican, July 26, 2014. https://www.vatican.va/content/francesco/it/speeches/2014/july/documents/papa-francesco_20140726_clero-caserta.pdf.

Giroli, Pierluigi. "Traduzione dell'Introduzione alle *Massime di perfezione cristiana* di Hans Urs von Balthasar" [Italian translation of the introduction to *Massime di perfezione cristiana* of Hans Urs von Balthasar]. *Charitas. Bollettino Rosminiano* (Oct. 2010) 257–60; (Nov. 2010) 290–94.

Nardin, Vito, ed. *Amore mio dammi l'amore. Coroncina di Giaculatorie di Antonio Rosmini*. Stresa, It.: Rosminiane Sodalitas, 1999.

Neglia, Alberto. *Laici senza complessi. Intuizioni profetiche di Antonio Rosmini*. Messina, It.: ESUR, 1988.

Pagani, Giambattista, and Guido Rossi. *La vita di Antonio Rosmini scritta da un sacerdote dell'Istituto della carità, riveduta ed aggiornata dal prof. Guido Rossi*. 2 vols. Rovereto, It.: Manfrini, 1959.

Paoli, Francesco. *Antonio Rosmini. Virtù quotidiane*. Verona: Fede e Cultura, 2007.

———. *Della Vita di Antonio Rosmini-Serbati*. 2 vols. Rovereto, It.: Grigoletti, 1854.

Ravasi, Gianfranco. "Prefazione." In *Il beato Antonio Rosmini patrono della Pop-Theology*, by Antonio Staglianò, Pop-Theology 7, 7–12. Rosolini, It.: Santocono, 2021.

Rebora, Clemente. *Rosmini*. Edited by Alfeo Valle. Rovereto, It.: Longo, 1996.

Regole dell'Istituto della Carità. Rome: Curia Generalizia dell'Istituto della Carità, 1994.

Rosmini, Antonio. *Antropologia soprannaturale*. Edited by Umberto Muratore. 2 vols. ENC 39–40. Rome: Città Nuova, 1983.

———. *Costituzione dell'Istituto della Carità*. Edited by Dino Sartori. ENC 50. Rome: Città Nuova, 1996.

———. "Degli studi dell'Autore." In *Introduzione alla filosofia*, edited by Pier P. Ottonello, ENC 2, 13–194. Rome: Città Nuova, 1979.

———. *Dell'educazione cristiana*. Edited by Lino Prenna. ENC 31. Rome: Città Nuova, 1994.

———. *Directorium spiritus*. 3 vols. Unpublished. https://www.rosmini.it/objects/Pagina.asp?ID=680.

———. *La dottrina della carità*. Edited by Giuseppe Bozzetti. Domodossola, It.: Sodalitas, 1931.

———. *Epistolario ascetico*. 4 vols. Rome: Tipografia del Senato, 1912.

———. *L'Introduzione del Vangelo secondo Giovanni commentata*. Edited by Annalisa Capuzzi. Rome: Città Nuova, 2002.

———. *Jesu Christi passio. Preghiere e Pensieri*. Domodossola, It.: Sodalitas, 1942.

———. *Massime di perfezione cristiana*. Edited by Suor Maria Michela Riva. Stresa, It.: Rosminiane, 2020.

———. *Massime di perfezione cristiana*. Edited by Alfeo Valle. ENC 49. Rome: Città Nuova, 1976.

Vernette, Jean. *Il XXI secolo o sarà mistico o non sarà*. Rome: OCD, 2005.

22

Rosminian Suggestions on Ecclesiology

ALESSANDRO ANDREINI

The "Other Treaty"

THE TWO INTRODUCTORY TEXTS to Antonio Rosmini's best-known work, *The Five Wounds of the Holy Church (Delle cinque piaghe della Santa Chiesa)*, constitute, in their colloquial and essential form, an authentic masterpiece of practical theology. They were written about seventeen years apart: the first, coeval with the drafting of the text and entitled *Some Preliminary Words Necessary to Read (Alcune parole preliminari necessarie a leggersi)*, bears the date of November 13, 1832. The second, entitled *Warning (Avvertimento)*, presumably dates back to June–July 1849: intended as a premise for a possible second edition, it briefly illustrates the most significant changes made to what Rosmini calls an *operetta* (a minor work). In fact, these are two short texts that, despite their temporal distance, complement each other and offer precious indications for a church that intends to set out on a synodal path. What is particularly striking is the flat, colloquial style with which Rosmini reports, in the first case, his own inner considerations about the appropriateness of writing a text of this nature, in the second, the objections that have been presented to him and to which he tries to give an answer.

It is in *Avvertimento*, moreover, that Rosmini reveals the plan to continue the work of criticism carried out in this volume by drafting an "other treatise," in fact never realized, with which to offer the indispensable *pars construens* to be flanked by that *destruens* accomplished so far. Intending, in fact, to respond to the criticism according to which, "describing the present pains of the Church, to make them stand out more, he often instituted a comparison between the condition in which the Church finds herself today and that in which she found herself when charity flourished most ardently in the Christian people,"[1] of having thought of indicating as a "universal remedy" for the evils of the church "the ancient ecclesiastical discipline," he reiterates that this was in no way his intention. And that, if anything, it would not be a question of looking back, but forward because "discipline cannot be completely immutable, indeed it is appropriate that it be adapted to the circumstances of the times." And he concludes: "The purpose of the work was simply to point out the calamities of the Church: of the remedies he barely touches what the connection of the discourse requires it: according to his design they should form the subject of another treatise."[2]

Reserving the right to return immediately to other crucial elements of this precious introductory material to the *Five Wounds*, it is worthwhile, we believe, to underline that Rosmini's project included a work in the form of a couple that unfortunately remained unfinished. And that in any case confirms the breadth of vision and the spiritual and intellectual openness that Rosmini always cultivated and that, after all, constituted the guidelines of his ecclesial commitment. It is no coincidence, in fact, that for the Blessed there has been talk of a true and proper "spirituality of reform" that aimed at "a self-reform of the Catholic Church, internal reform and from within, with the harmonious collaboration of both the teaching Church and the learner Church (to use the categories of the time)."[3] A particularly precious perspective precisely for our time in which we are increasingly aware of the inadequacy of closed and prepackaged systems, incapable of reading the complexity and dynamism of contemporary reality in the heart of the epochal change of this beginning of the third millennium.

---

1. Rosmini, *FW*, 18. The present essay simply limits itself to drawing some ecclesiological ideas from this text, without claiming to be able to offer a more precise interpretation in the context of Rosmini's thought.
2. Rosmini, *Cinque piaghe*, 18.
3. De Giorgi, "Rosmini e la riforma," 13; see Nadalini, "Antonio Rosmini."

PART 5

Writing in Edification

Rosmini's own spirituality of reform and his passion for an *ecclesia semper reformanda* constitute a decisive and far from obvious perspective. And it is very appropriate that we wanted to define it as a "spirituality" because precisely concerns Rosmini's basic orientation. A crucial trait, a conviction that informs, in fact, the entire work of the Blessed Rosmini: the act of faith in a church that is the wounded body of Christ, suffering and even disfigured, but always and more than ever in the process of healing since it is inhabited by what Rosmini himself defines "a force that is outside the sphere of human events, an infinite force, which repairs her losses, which restores her life when it fails."[4]

It is in this framework, and in the awareness of participating fully and effectively in the journey of the church, that Rosmini reflects and writes; and he does so, as he points out, "in edification and not in destruction": "Finally the author invokes the indulgence of readers for defects that still remain in his writing, instantly begging their charity to interpret his words in common sense, since he wanted to write in edification, and not in destruction: he wanted to unite and not divide. All that he said he submitted to the judgment of the Church with those sentiments that are expressed in the words that precede the operetta."[5]

This is a key dimension: in relation to the unstoppable process of healing of the church in which he knows he is included, there are only two possible perspectives: that of those who build and that of those who demolish. Just as Jesus had predicted when speaking of the mission of the good shepherd as opposed to that of the mercenary who is a thief: "A thief comes only to steal and slaughter and destroy; I came so that they might have life and have it more abundantly." (John 10:10). Nor is it certainly a coincidence that the first objection expressed and immediately resolved in the *preliminary words* is precisely that linked to the fact of having no jurisdiction, that is, of not taking on the very ministry of pastor entrusted to the successors of the apostles and to all ordinaries: "Or does he not have anything reckless to occupy his thought, not to write about it, when every concern of the church of God belongs by right to the Pastors of the same? And is not the detection of their wounds a lack of respect for the Pastors themselves, who either did not know these wounds, or did not remedy them?"[6]

---

4. Rosmini, *FW*, 20.
5. Rosmini, *FW*, 21, para. 1.
6. Rosmini, *FW*, 102, para. 58.

Objection to which Rosmini responds by affirming that even the lay person has the right to meditate on the evils of the church "where to do so he is moved by the lively zeal of the good of her, and of the glory of God," and returning to reiterate, with a moving insistence, his own personal motivation: "It seemed to me, examining myself, as far as man can be assured of himself, that all my meditations should proceed from no other source."[7]

Writing constructively, therefore, and not destructively, offering, in fact, an extraordinary criterion of practical discernment: this is what Rosmini himself suggests, inviting readers to "interpret his words with common sense." It is impossible to deal with such profound and decisive issues without sharing the basic conviction that we are really all in the same boat—this is the strong expression used by Pope Francis to launch the strong and urgent appeal to fraternity—and that only starting from this awareness can we contribute to building and union.[8]

The "Synodal" Method

That Rosmini bases his reflections on this fundamental conviction is confirmed by a second very significant element that emerges from these introductory pages. We could call it—it is the purview in which the church is trying to place itself under the impulse, once again, of the magisterium of Pope Francis—a sort of "synodal" method.[9] In truth, it is a practice proper to the whole scientific world; the need to submit one's statements and conclusions to the scrutiny of other experts in the field and thus reach a shared and more authoritative validation—a process, moreover, strongly destabilized in our time dominated by artfully built suspicion and fake news. The unintended circumstance, explains Rosmini, that this treatise, which ended up in the hands of booksellers, was published "against the will of the author" and disseminated in various editions quickly produced reactions and criticisms from readers. An incident that, in Rosmini's eyes, becomes rather an opportunity: "This incident brought the author nothing less than a real advantage. Some pious and learned ecclesiastics, to whom he declares himself grateful, made sensible observations to him, and to show how much he appreciated them, it was resolved to make this new edition, in which he proceeded to diligently amend all those places which were indicated to him as worthy of amendment."[10]

7. Rosmini, *FW*, 21, para. 1.
8. See Francis, "Address of His Holiness" (speech given in Dubai).
9. See Melloni, *Sinodalità*.
10. Rosmini, *FW*, 17–8.

There follow, as we mentioned, a series of examples of the corrections that Rosmini made to the text starting from the observations received. In the first place, after the response to the misinterpretation of his work as praise for the world of the past, to which we will return, came the clarification concerning the use of Latin and not the vernacular in the liturgy. Moreover, the more complex question of the involvement of the laity in the election of bishops, where Rosmini explicitly refers to the "synodal" practice: "It was said that the author wanted to attribute to the people the election of bishops: how false such a belief is demonstrated by itself in Chapter 4, in which he never expresses any other desire, except that the people can in such elections give their free and pious witness to the candidates, according to the spirit of the Church."[11]

Particularly striking is the concluding reference to the "spirit of the Church," once again the awareness of taking part in a long and fruitful process of reform that includes listening to what the Spirit is saying to the churches also through the mouth of the last believer. A conviction that Rosmini reiterates broadly and punctually in the letter to Canon Giuseppe Gatti dated June 8, 1848, one of the three letters that he attaches to the *Five Wounds* precisely to reiterate precisely his thoughts regarding the *sensus fidelium* and the baptismal priesthood of all believers:

> The simple Christian nevertheless enjoys a mystical and private priesthood that gives him a special dignity and power, and a sense of spiritual things. Therefore, not only the hierarchical, and the nonhierarchical clergy, but also the Christian people have certain rights of their own; there is a freedom of the clergy, there is a freedom of the people within those boundaries that were prescribed by sacred tradition and by the laws of the Church: all are free in Jesus Christ.[12]

One cannot fail to notice the insistence on what is, to all intents and purposes, the key word of the reform according to Rosmini, namely the exercise of freedom: a freedom, as has been acutely highlighted, which is intimately connected with the challenge of education and to which we will return.[13]

---

11. Rosmini, *FW*, 19.

12. Rosmini, *FW*, 305.

13. See Nadalini, "Antonio Rosmini," 326–28; see also F. Traniello, *Società religiosa*, and De Giorgi, *Rosmini e suo tempo*.

The Concept of "Accommodation"

The third crucial emphasis contained in the two premises is that relating to accommodation, in the sense of settlement, mutual agreement. Rosmini refers to it, as we have mentioned, to respond to the objection that depicted his treatise as a criticism of the early church, of which the church of his time—and ours—had lost the enthusiasm and disruptive force. In fact, the Blessed Rosmini strongly rejects a reading that he seems to perceive as a serious misunderstanding if not as a total incomprehension of his own thought and positions. As for the suspicion that he wants to re-propose the ancient ecclesiastical discipline as a universal remedy for the present evils of the church, Rosmini responds decisively: "He never had this thought: he recognizes in modern discipline the work of that same divine wisdom that dictated the ancient, and knows that discipline cannot be completely immutable, indeed it is appropriate that it be adapted to the circumstances of the times, which the Church does according to what the Holy Spirit, who continually assists her, suggests to her."[14]

The Holy Spirit is at work in the church of all times. He assists and enlightens her so that she can constantly respond to the circumstances of the time with no less truth and effectiveness. This is a crucial point of Rosmini's entire reflection, in fact the true and indispensable theological foundation of freedom that we have already indicated is an eminent characteristic of the church and her reform. The church is free because she knows that she is faithful to the Holy Spirit who guides her and not corseted in the forms that history has gradually impelled her to assume and which have grown old. The church is free to the extent that she is not opposed to that continuous development which is the only guarantee for remaining faithful to the essential.

One cannot fail to recall here the analogous considerations of Saint John Henry Newman in his decisive essay on the *Development of Christian Doctrine*, the text that represented the turning point in his progressive approach to Catholicism. It is a well-known study, just as the relationships that linked Newman and Rosmini, in fact contemporaries and singularly close in their human and spiritual journey, are well known. It is said, says Newman, that the water of a stream is clearer at its source. In reality, he immediately adds, it is an observation, however evocative, that cannot be applied "to the history of a philosophy or sect, which, on the contrary is more equable, purer and stronger when its bed has become deep and broad and full."[15] At first, the water of that idea or belief will still taste like the earth

---

14. Rosmini, *FW*, 18.
15. Newman, *Development of Christian Doctrine*, 38.

from which it springs. And it will indeed be the very obstacles, the hardships that it must overcome as it flows that make it purer and more transparent. In short, Newman concludes, "In a higher world it is otherwise; but, here below *to live is to change*, and to be perfect is to have changed often."[16]

Accommodation is not a diminution, but a growth, not a loss, but a gain, the true gain of Christ's disciples who do not live barricaded to defend an ancient and rigid truth, but rather alive and active in the world entrusted also to their care and certain that Christian greatness is not behind, but before them and that the fruitfulness and beauty of Christianity are still to be discovered.[17]

Five Horizons for a Liberated Church

The lack of freedom is indeed the crucial evil that Rosmini identifies in his treatise on the church. A very serious if not chronic disorder that he traces back to the profound influence that the feudal system has exercised for centuries on the entire structure of the Christian community, pushing it to assume forms and traditions that it struggles to overcome even today.[18] This, after all, is "the great work that still remains to be done in Rome"[19] of which Rosmini speaks at the beginning of the discussion of the fifth plague, the *servitude of ecclesiastical goods*, where he formulates for the first time clearly and explicitly the accusation of feudalism as the true cause of the evils of the church. Precisely those barbarians whom providence used to bring down the Roman Empire and avenge the persecutions against Christians, precisely they ended up introducing "feudalism which extinguished the freedom of the church herself, so that all her evils came about. For, to tell the truth, the influx of riches would not have been sufficient to plunge the clergy into that trough that we saw; nor would they have had such a miserable effect by misplacing the temporal domains, if they had been independent."[20]

And it is to the bishop of Rome—continues Rosmini—that Providence itself has entrusted this work of liberation, since he is the only one to have preserved at least in part that freedom of which the rest of the body of the church has been deprived: "On the contrary, God used sovereignty

---

16. Newman, *Development of Christian Doctrine*, 38.

17. See, in this regard, the provocative and stimulating thesis of Dominique Collin in her recent volume *Cristianesimo non esiste ancora*.

18. See Nadalini, "Antonio Rosmini," 328; see also Galantino, "Riformismo rosminiano."

19. Rosmini, *FW*, 264, para. 129.

20. Rosmini, *FW*, 263–64, para. 129.

to keep the freedom of the Apostolic See inviolate, so that at least the head might live safe from universal servitude, and the free head then make the members free in due time, which is the great work that still remains to be done in Rome."[21]

Rosmini himself offers here a sort of rapid overview of the entire treatise by explaining the direct derivation of each plague from the feudal system, the story of a slave church, but which is already walking towards its own liberation by the very fact of having become aware of its evil. An authentic and moving hymn to freedom that deserves to be briefly retraced in order to grasp the power and acuteness of Rosmini's vision and the inevitability of the process that it put in place.

It was the feudal system—the Blessed Rosmini argues—a mixture of lordship and vassalage transferred within the ecclesial structure, that produced the first plague of division between the clergy and the people in the exercise of divine worship, suffocating that creative freedom of the liturgy of the church to which its Founder entrusted the power to continually build and form his community. Again, it was the feudal system itself that introduced the division within the clergy and gave rise to that distinction between low and high clergy which, Rosmini writes, "replacing the relationship of father and son, that tied it, with that of lord and subject that unties it," has ended up producing the second plague of the "neglected education of the Cleric." And just as the feudal lords soon began to contend for power and clash with each other, so the descendants of the apostles continued—but evil is ancient, if one thinks of how many times Jesus's friends have revealed their ambitions that are anything but evangelical—"forgetting fraternity, mindful of lordly jealousy, yes, on their own account than on behalf of the prince, to whose vassalage they belonged," they ended up being isolated both from the people and from their confreres and friends. Equally evident is the feudal origin of the fourth and fifth plagues, produced at the moment in which the church, "so exhausted of forces that she does not even know how to preserve and defend the appointment of her own pastors" ended up entrusting their protection and responsibility to the temporal power and failing the six maxims that had always presided over the possession and management of goods.[22]

The solution that Rosmini suggests for the elimination of the fifth plague and the progressive healing of the others is drastic. Evoking the failure of Pope Paschal II and declaring his enthusiasm for the new Pope Pius IX, "a pontiff who seems destined to renew our age and to give the church

---

21. Rosmini, *FW*, 263–64, para. 129.
22. All the above quotations are from para. 130; see Rosmini, *FW*, 264–65.

that new impulse that will push for new paths to a course as unexpected as wonderful and glorious," Rosmini really seems to dream of the advent of a pope who courageously returns to the church, disfigured but not annihilated, its free poverty and its poor freedom.

We are reminded of the literary transposition of the anxiety of reform of the church realized by Italo Alighiero Chiusano in his novel *L'Ordalia*. The unforgettable author of *Konradin* recalls another crucial, but no less disastrous moment, of this laborious process of reform, when, at the turn of the year one thousand, with the ascent to the papal throne of Sylvester II and with the very young Otto III at the head of the empire, it seemed that the dream of so many might come true, that is the *renovatio imperii* which, through a new agreement between the papacy and the empire, was supposed to establish a universal order in which both renounced their ancient territorial claims in favour of a peaceful and supportive world. A project that, unfortunately, with the resurgence of internal struggles in Rome, the reopening of old polemics between the papacy and the empire, the premature end of Otto III (1002), was destined to fail, in fact, the *renovatio imperii* remained in the aspirations of medieval consciences a living ideal, but, in fact, unrealizable.[23]

After all, the Christian adventure is the following of a risen Crucified One and is always called upon to repeat that unspeakable paradox of a fire lit, then extinguished, then irresistibly lit again. To resort to an image dear to another great Catholic novelist, the Englishman J. R. R. Tolkien, the Christian faith resembles the art of those who light signal fires: beacons always new and different, lit in contexts and with materials never identical, which develop flames of colours or shades different from each other, but which make the same, joyful announcement run from one hill to another, from the top of one mountain to another, endlessly. This is how the incendiary matter that is the word of God runs. Rosmini lit one of these fires, robust and vigorous, from which we have all had the grace to see ours lit, if possible. May it be so until the end of history!

Bibliography

Chiusano, Italo A. *L'Ordalia*. Rome: Castelvecchi, 2013.
Collin, Dominique. *Il cristianesimo non esiste ancora*. Translated by Gloria Romagnoli. Brescia, It.: Queriniana, 2020.
Community of San Leolino. *Italo Alghiero Chiusano. La scrittura tra visibile e invisibile*. Panzano in Chianti, It.: Feeria-Comunità di San Leolino, 2014.
De Giorgi, Fulvio. *Rosmini e il suo tempo*. Brescia, It.: Morcelliana, 2003.

23. See Community of San Leolino, *Italo Alghiero Chiusano*.

———. "Rosmini e la riforma della Chiesa." *Notes et documents* 27 (2013) 11–18.
Francis, Pope. "Address of His Holiness." Vatican, Feb. 4, 2019. https://www.vatican.va/content/francesco/en/speeches/2019/february/documents/papa-francesco_20190204_emiratiarabi-incontrointerreligioso.html.
Galantino, Nunzio. "Il riformismo rosminiano e la sua condanna." In *Rosmini e Gioberti. Pensatori Europei*, edited by Giuseppe Beschin and Luca Cristellon, 325–42. Brescia, It.: Morcelliana, 2003.
Melloni, Alberto, ed. *Sinodalità. Istruzioni per l'uso*. Bologna: EDB, 2021.
Nadalini, Emanuele. "Antonio Rosmini: A Passion for the *Ecclesia Semper Reformanda*." *Rosmini Studies* 4 (2017) 325–34.
Newman, John H. *An Essay on Development of Christian Doctrine*. London: Toovey, 1845.
Rosmini, Antonio. *Delle cinque piaghe della Santa Chiesa*. Cinisello Balsamo, It.: San Paolo, 1997.
Traniello, Francesco. *Società religiosa e società civile in Rosmini*. Bologna: Mulino, 1966.

23

Spiritual Theology of Desire and Intellectual Charity in Antonio Rosmini

WILLIAM ABBRUZZESE

The Founding Desire of Spiritual Life

SPEAKING OF THE SPIRITUAL theology of desire is like dealing with the entire Rosminian philosophical opus, because the theology of desire remains the basis of its entire intellectual and spiritual process, halfway between philosophical and theological argumentation and living and teaching the way to be in relation to the Lord Jesus in the Trinity.

In the various works or letters the term *desire* is often used in a generic way to mean an affection or the possibility of a visit or the solution of a problem. This does not detract from the little that we have described, because it is a term that denotes a profound spiritual depth capable of intersecting the structure of man with his idea of being understood and the gift of grace received from God.[1]

---

1. The definition and its development can be traced in Rosmini, "Società ed suo fine" (Society and its purpose)," in particular 190–91, 341–42, 344.

Surely the spiritual operettas offer us the first principle to grasp something of the Rosminian proposal that finds its most real originality in the simplicity of living desire. Rosmini describes it thus: "To desire only and infinitely to please God, that is, to be just."[2]

It seems to us a qualifying path of spiritual theology capable of illuminating man's present existence, since it was concretely lived by Rosmini as a correct correspondence rather than as a restitution of what was offered. We would go so far as to say that desire is the face of a research that has its "innate" foundations in man. The gratuity of God's love leaves such an indelible mark, as to cause in it an openness of a structural nature, and this cannot be identified only in a choice of the subject but is an integral and structuring part of it.

In this perception of God and in a real involvement it is possible to trace an effective holiness that is an explication of goodness, beauty, unity and truth, profoundly divine characteristics that man receives starting from the encounter with Jesus.[3] Structurally we perceive a void that the gravity of original sin has left, a nostalgia that is not something sentimental but a reality in which the ego of all times finds itself. The power of baptism consists in this emptiness a name and a consistency. Desire is nothing more than nostalgia for the stars, for something greater than ourselves without however falling into subjectivism for its own sake. In fact, it is part of a possible commonality because man determines himself as a person precisely starting from his being in relationship with God. Rosmini writes: "Desire is that rational appetite which arises in an intelligent being when he judges that it is good for himself to have or enjoy something that he does not have or does not enjoy, and which he learns it is possible to have or to enjoy."[4] The term of comparison for our ego is not an object but an objective subject that comes to meet man. In Rosmini's texts the theme fits into the entire philosophical system in which he develops the triadic nature of being and at the same time in the profound interaction of the three modalities. Ideality, reality, and morality/spirituality are in the background of our discourse on desire, which therefore assumes moral and spiritual connotations and offers

---

2. Rosmini, *Massime di perfezione cristiana* (Maxims of Christian perfection), 37.

3. We cannot forget the strong provocations of Jesus on the "being good" of man. "As he was setting out on a journey, a man ran up, knelt down before him, and asked him, 'Good teacher, what must I do to inherit eternal life?' Jesus answered him, 'Why do you call me good? No one is good but God alone'" (Mark 10:17–18); "If you then, who are wicked, know how to give good gifts to your children, how much more will the Father in heaven give the holy Spirit to those who ask him?" (Luke 11:13).

4. Rosmini, "Società ed suo fine," 341. In order to correctly interpret the desire, it is advisable to keep an article of Bellelli in the background, "Importanza degli ordini."

us the possibility of considering Rosminian spirituality as an act with solid theological foundations. Generally, the nineteenth century is considered the period of devotionalism. Here, as in other situations, while remaining faithful to the language and considerations that his time offers him, Rosmini manages to identify a *unicum*, an originality.

This emptiness is generative in that it moves man towards an object-subject that completes him not in a subordination but in a concrete participatory correlation.

The fact remains that the desire is always and only of something else and of the other. In this regard, Jacques Lacan offers us an analysis of the articulated preposition *of*: our desire is of the other in the sense that we desire the other from us; something already possessed cannot be desirable. The analysis does not stop at a first interpretative possibility but glimpses a second: the desire concerns the Other. Lacan capitalizes the word to differentiate it from the other as proximate. This analysis shows how, according to the "law of desire," acting is the regulator of our own behavior. Our desire is for the other to the extent that we are led to aspire to what others aspire to, fashions, lifestyles, the future. We are led by Lacan to value not only the question "What do I want?" but "What do others want from me?" If desire desires us, can human desire be the same desire that God has for man?

Hegel too, in *Phenomenology of Spirit*, gave reflective substance to that feeling, understanding how fundamental the process of mutual recognition is for our lives. In order to be recognized, one surrenders part of one's freedom, becoming servant and master in a process of self-awareness. The human being, Lacan observes, is not only governed by the desire to know but also by the irrepressible desire to ignore. Because truth is secret, pause, interruption, silence, and it is in the emptiness of the word that thought is allowed to breathe, which however can only emerge in the place of continuous confrontation with those who know how to listen.[5]

In Rosmini's thought there is an engaging whole. The detail is its expression. When this concerns man, it is possible to perceive a spark of God precisely in his desiring being. Being between fullness and lack, between the "already" and the "not yet." Concentration on the particular without a fruitful attention to the universal does not give reason for beauty, individual originality. The search for the good "does not stop at an ideal plan, but descends to a concrete level, and reaches the strength of an experimental fact."[6] Only in this way is it possible to give voice to desire without falling

---

5. See Lacan, "Sovversione del soggetto" and *Seminario*, bk. 20, p. 5.
6. Velocci, *Esperienza religiosa*, 301.

into devotional trivialization more inclined to the repetition of formulas than to the dialogical openness of one's being to God.

Desire animates a trusting disposition towards the encounter with God; the way of passivity of Ignatian memory.[7] The third maxim of Christian perfection according to the Blessed Rosmini was: "To remain perfectly at peace as to all that is ordained by God in regard to the Church of Jesus Christ, working for the Church in obedience to the divine will."[8]

Desire not only leads to an active search for encounter but also to passivity as we have learned from the Lacanian proposal. Confirmation of our interpretation is the fourth maxim that brings with it the warm invitation to greater trust in God's benevolent desire. Desiring passivity is the remedy for those anxieties that bring confusion and not sanctification.[9] In a letter to Maria Geltrude Cerutti dated November 9, 1846, Rosmini states:

> For this reason, it is my feeling that it can do no good to your soul to be solicitous to know definitively the step of the ladder to which it can have reached through the goodness of the Lord: it is enough that the Lord knows it. He knows it truthfully, and we, who need not know it, can too be deceived. Therefore, instead of turning our thoughts too much on ourselves, let us keep this thought directed and wholly understood in our Lord himself, the sure way by which to move our steps, and the effective truth and life of our life, the good of all our good. In short, we love and we seek nothing else, we do not seek even what may come of our love for us, content to love, I say, to love Jesus only in himself, and in all his brothers.[10]

---

7. "It is therefore necessary to be indifferent to created things, in all that is permitted to the freedom of our free will, and is not forbidden to it; so that for our part, we desire no more health than disease, wealth than poverty, honor than dishonor, long life than short, and so in everything else" (Ignatius of Loyola, *Esercizi spirituali*, 103).

8. Rosmini, *Massime di perfezione cristiana*, 45.

9. "The Christian must therefore enjoy perfect tranquility and maintain full joy, resting entirely in his Lord, however much events may seem contrary to the good of the Church itself; without, however, refraining from groaning and supplicating that his will take place in heaven as well as on earth, that is, that men on earth practice his holy law of charity like the saints in heaven. The Christian must therefore banish from his heart restlessness, and every kind of anxiety and solicitude, and also that which at times seems to have as its aim the sole good of the Church of Jesus Christ; and much less should he rashly flatter himself that he can remedy those evils, before he sees the will of the Lord manifest in this"; and again: "No one is necessary to the divine Redeemer for the glorification of his Church, which consists in redemption from the slavery of sin, in which all men are equal; and only by his gratuitous mercy, he assumes those among the redeemed, which pleases him" (Rosmini, *Massime di perfezione cristiana*, 45).

10. Rosmini, *Epistolario ascetico* (Ascetical epistolary) 3, para. 994.

The love for God that is consequential to desire, related to the ideality of being and of the same Trini-form Grace inherent in the structure of man, is the *incipit* for an industriousness with a Christic mold towards one's neighbor, leaving it to the encounter with Providence to propose feasible paths of realization. The life of prayer lived by Rosmini is a way of sanctification and the cornerstone of all his life, both spiritual and intellectual, where one *forms* the other, in a "gymnastics of the spirit."[11] What might seem trivial is actually a profound sign of originality. The center lies in the relationship with his Lord: a concise "place" and cornerstone of all his actions which he expounded in the lesson on the first maxim "not loving . . . other than to be dearer to God than ever possible, keeping this for his only good and always never asking for it."[12]

Through the comparison with Lacan, it is possible to reach a further understanding of Rosmini's work that can be defined as intellectual charity.[13]

> Until God shows me what I should do, or that he wants me to work with respect to charity towards my neighbors, I must love the common life, hidden, quiet and perfective of myself. . . . I must not, therefore, move from myself arbitrarily, and from such a presumption to undertakings for the benefit of others, however good in themselves, since I do not know how to choose those that are useful on the whole, nor do I have the strength in myself to carry them out, nor are they worth anything to my purpose if they are not in conformity with the divine will. I must therefore conform to the will of my heavenly Father, also

---

11. Rosmini, *Manuale dell'Esercitatore* (Handbook for spiritual teachers), 42. The embers are so important but to become fire need some attention that allows them to develop; so it is with desire. See Pagani and Rossi, *Vita di Antonio Rosmini*, and Paoli, *Antonio Rosmini*. These biographies describe the deep spiritual experience of Rosmini, helping us to understand him.

12. Rosmini, *Massime di perfezione cristiana*, 37.

13. Ottonello writes: "Intellectual charity is nothing other than the exercise of the spirit of intelligence, which also requires the philosophical foundation of the entire universe of sciences as it is enmity of the 'empty knowledge' or 'naked knowledge,' inasmuch as, if this alone were reduced, that is, to its intellectualistic or rationalistic or nominalistic partializations, intelligence would remain mutilated and would be consumed in the sterility of its multiple reductionisms, thus precluding its most proper fulfillment and its fullness, which makes it the very principle of all asceticism and therefore in the supreme way of Christian asceticism, that is, in so far as it is actualized as the 'spiritual intelligence of truth' that clears 'the heart of all the cares and constraints that prevent directing the whole mind and all life in God in charity' (Ottonello, "Rosmini e carità intellettuale," 340).

in the *way* of exercising charity towards my neighbor, in order to find perfect justice.[14]

It is clear that Rosmini has allowed himself to be shaped by desire and by charity itself in its universal tension, seeking with the intellect and its rational progress and with action, ways of sanctification for himself and for all men.[15]

Justice is not only the ability to share equally what is due to each but, spiritually, it is the attitude of profound gratitude that we address to God for all that he does for us.[16] The main way to assume a form of desiring justice is the continuous contemplation of the Crucified One, from whom Rosmini believes that all justice is given for man, in order to grant his salvation. For Rosmini it is not in fact a simple sign but it is the expression of total love, capable of giving concreteness to man's desire in the activity of Good. Only the latter, in fact, satisfies him and fills him precisely in his imperfections. "The justice of God is the Crucified One, who spreads his arms to understand all humanity and save them on the wood of the Cross."[17]

God's desire for man expressed in his will is the spark promoting the human volitional and rational process, finally capable of recognizing the traces of the divine presence in history and open to the "blessed enjoyment of the same Divinity"[18] because it is illuminated by it.

Desire and Intellectual Charity

The lines of development of spiritual desire that innervate Rosmini's entire work of intellectual charity can be glimpsed in the testamentary triptych that he gave from his deathbed to his friend Manzoni: "Be silent, enjoy, adore."[19] In our progress, the scheme is only functional to understanding:

14. Rosmini, *Manuale dell'esercitatore*, 161.

15. It is necessary to remember the purpose of the Istituto della Carità, which is none other than the sanctification of its members. During the nineteenth century many congregations were born with particular charitable purposes. Here it is possible to trace a subtle originality on the part of Rosmini and an enhancement of that passivity, expression not of laxity but a starting point to carry out the work of God in the sole desire to please him and him alone. For an overview of the flourishing of congregations in the nineteenth century see De Giorgi, "Congregazioni religiose dell'Ottocento"; Goffi, *Ottocento*; Pazzaglia, *Chiesa e prospettive educative*; Sani, *Chiesa, educazione*; Velocci, *Crisi e rinascita della spiritualità*.

16. See Paoli, *Antonio Rosmini*, 55.

17. Abbruzzese, *Carità intellettuale*, 87.

18. Rosmini, *Operette Spirituali* (Minor spiritual works), 38.

19. Pagani and Rossi, *Vita di Antonio Rosmini*, 2:505.

in the spiritual man meticulous separation is not possible because man is always and only one.

Silence, in Rosminian simplicity is the space of listening necessary so that the other can speak and find acceptance. The summit of this way of life is the sacrifice of one's ideas. Spiritual characterization becomes passivity, which is not idleness or proud negligence but is a real impetus for a balanced and, therefore, wise life.

Enjoying is the possibility of living not prey to events, but knowing that we are guarded by Providence. What he has to say in lesson 4 on the third spiritual maxim is interesting:

> The Christian must, therefore, enjoy perfect tranquillity, and maintain full joy, resting entirely in the Lord, however much events may seem contrary to the good of the Church herself; without however avoiding groaning and supplication, that his will be done in heaven as on earth, that is, that men may practice on earth his holy law of charity as do the saints in heaven.[20]

Rosminian enjoyment does not indicate mirth or exemption from every problem but is born of an inner trust in the One who is the guardian of the life of each and every one of us. In prayer he intercepts and trusts the divine way of seeing, his judgment, without letting himself be ensnared by human judgment.

Adoring is what in the intellectual sphere Rosmini calls "inobjectification," transporting oneself into the other by oneself who is not an object but a Subject. We believe that this is the consequence of an active ability to make space in itself, as evidenced by the line of silence.

The introduction of the three lines enclosed in the three words allows us to see how in Rosmini's texts desire is not something ephemeral but is structurally linked to the experience of the person and at the same time it is a promoter of the operation of charity such as intellectual charity.

Silence: The Desire between Passivity and Supply

Rosminian asceticism is entirely oriented to the awareness that "God arranges all things gently."[21] To understand his work and respond to it, it is necessary to implement that attitude of passivity aimed at making room for the Other by allowing oneself to be instructed, thus fulfilling the desire for

---

20. Rosmini, *Operette Spirituali*, 45.
21. Rosmini, *Epistolario ascetico* 1, para. 74.

sanctification which is none other than a corresponding communion.²² This procedure is not the result of devotions but of a careful reading of the sacred texts and of the actualization that some charismatic figures have made of which Rosmini had knowledge.²³

Desire is involvement available to God's action, thus leading man to recognize the seeds of Grace and to work patiently so that they bear fruits of sanctification.²⁴ To be silent is not to withdraw but it is "space for." Man is created and finds happiness in his encounter with the other by himself and this is made possible only if he knows how to keep quiet, precisely, make room.²⁵

Desire as a "thrust" makes the encounter with Grace possible, without which the intellect, not being informed, cannot give the necessary coordinates to the will so that it can get involved. Silence is an intermediate space. The psychoanalyst Donald Winnicott observing the child gives us an interesting fact about the creative involvement of man in life and also in the life of grace.²⁶ In play, an intermediate area between the subjective and the objective, man discovers and enriches himself. In our case, frace favors in him the maturation of those potential seeds of virtue in an intellectual-volitional awareness. For Winnicott, creativity is the encounter that the individual has with reality. The same, in the perception that man has of it, places him in the situation that life is always worth living and in any case.²⁷

Desire thus becomes that game capable of involving man in finding ways of accepting divine grace and, therefore, of sanctification.²⁸ Man discovers the beauty of fulfillment when he makes himself available to the relationship with the other enriching and determining the total involvement

---

22. See Velocci, *Esperienza religiosa*, 125–26.

23. See De Giorgi, *Scienza del cuore*. The historian De Giorgi tracks some significant encounters that influenced Antonio Rosmini, highlighting the extent to which they characterized Italian spirituality of the nineteenth century, in line with spiritualities from other countries, which were also influential in Italy. See De Giorgi, *Scuola italiana di spiritualità*.

24. Zovatto, "'Charitas' intellettuale rosminiana."

25. Baggio, "Rosmini e 'carità intellettuale,'" 46–47.

26. Donald Woods Winnicott was born in Plymouth, England, on Apr. 7, 1896, and died in London on Jan. 28, 1971. He was a pediatrician and psychoanalyst whose works increased psychoanalytic knowledge by identifying particular interpretative paths for contemporary man.

27. See Winnicott, *Gioco e realtà*.

28. "Conform yourself with your will to the ideal being, or be it in the light of reason.... Recognize by your practical strength this or that entity, according to the extent of its entity directly conceived by you" (Rosmini, *PMS*, 181).

of himself in a loving position, so as to give up his freedom.[29] It is what is called "inobjectification" in which the subject knows something as an entity in itself, that is, he knows it as its object, and "with having it present he makes an act that has a peculiar nature, . . . quite different from any other generation of acts, and this act consists in transporting oneself with thought into the entity that is present to it."[30] There is a cognitive progression in the movement towards the other, there is a beginning and an objective attraction that moves and challenges desire, leading it to formulate morally identifiable choices.[31]

Paradoxically, therefore, the exit from the ego forces the self to say something to and about itself: it is the principle of human solidarity that remains a given fact. The experience of sin upsets this order which the Incarnation of Christ shows to be something original from creation. Therefore, inobjectification is not only a gnoseological question but involves man's own morality. The good of the latter does not lie in the same but in its concreteness, something to be sought and filled with. Entering into the search might seem like a loss, but in reality, what seems so becomes a gain, as Saint Paul teaches us.[32]

When we formulate this type of analysis, we must pay attention to details because they give man himself a new look, capable of recognizing the divine presence that in its activation of an attractive tendency causes him to let himself be carried away by the desireful reality.

Rosminian asceticism is the fruit of an experience that can be traced first in the experience and then in his entire opus. He offers his life in the concreteness of time, between joys and failures.

In addition to the fact of inobjectification and more deeply in the Rosminian spiritual proposal, a particular aspect of desire is grasped, namely the offering of one's own blood. The contemplation of the crucifix remains of fundamental importance, in which Rosmini captures the act of love capable of constantly involving man in an imitative way.[33]

In fact, it offers the possibility of being disciples: one is not an apostle without having been a student of a love that reaches depth, that involves the enemy and which Rosmini also experienced within the church itself.

---

29. Muratore, *Conoscere Rosmini*, 75.
30. Rosmini, *T*, para. 867.
31. See Rosmini, *T*, paras. 869–73, 875–77, 890–99.
32. "I consider them so much rubbish, that I may gain Christ" (Phil 3: 8).
33. See Rosmini, *Operette spirituali*, 82.

The intellect of man who reads and seeks the truth thus places itself in an attitude of absolute indifference: a mystical death for a fruitful resurrection faithful to intellectual charity.

In his "On the Author's Studies" *(Discorso sugli studi dell'autore)* (1850) Rosmini observed that "beyond science, therefore, there is a real world, which often escapes the eyes of scientists and philosophers; And in this world lives largely man, who does not live by science alone."[34] There is a transcendent horizon that leads man to desire that the encounter in his reality take place in a fruitful dialogue to be built, preserved and loved, "abdicating from opinion and conviction," in order to be obedient to God and to the church he loved so much.[35]

Enjoyment

In *The Constitutions of the Institute of Charity (Costituzioni dell'Istituto della Carità)* we read a passage in which Rosmini expresses his considerations about the eucharistic blessing. It does not take on the contours of a simple devotional practice, however important, but is the condition of possibility of our Christian witness:

> Since from the blessing of the Eucharistic bread derive all other blessings and customs, our longing for everything to be blessed and consecrated to God, and to arouse this desire in all the faithful, so that from all things in this world they may profit for piety and praise God and our Lord. Let them also teach them that all things of this world, animate and inanimate, come from the body and blood of him made present through the priest, sanctified and ordered to the worship of the Lord; and thus ordered, they are made profitable for the health of body and soul according to divine goodness; so that in all things praise and glory may be given to Christ who dwells under the Eucharistic species, and that all the faithful may remain incorporated into him with the food of life, and that everything may be united in him.[36]

A specific trait of Rosminian ascetics emerges from this text: the value of the Eucharist. The blessing that comes from it becomes a desire for joy, the only one capable of giving a glimpse of Good and constantly seeking it in every situation of life. Everything was created by God and, we could

---

34. Rosmini, *IP*, 117.

35. Antonelli, *Ascesi cristiana*, 81.

36. Rosmini, *Costituzioni dell'Istituto della Carità* (The constitutions of the Institute of Charity), para. 764.

say, everything is his. Man, himself is the summit of creation, which has been entrusted to him, therefore he is called upon to guard creation as a blessing for him. Here lies the secret of that joy which has as its expression the so-called indifference, which is a dwelling in the divine embrace, since God constantly knows how to become providence for each one of us. The human gaze is called to overcome sensible experience by moving forward in the reading of divine providence. Everything is an opportunity to encounter God because "everything is grace."[37]

In the Eucharist Jesus takes everything into himself and, with his own life, offers it to the Father from whom every blessing on the whole world comes. It turns out, therefore, that the blessing that comes from the Eucharist gives man the capacity to be a blessing for others. For Rosmini, blessing always indicates a growth in holiness of man, who in turn becomes a beneficial presence for others and "it is clear that the saint becomes a factor of growth already in the context of his services to society."[38]

Worship

The desire that becomes adoration first of all becomes recognition of one's own nothingness, eliminating that presumption that makes the individual ego judge of everything and that leads it to conceive itself, and not the love of God, as necessary for salvation.

Rosmini, to counter the instinctive human pride—instinctive pride as a residue of concupiscence, which disfigures the original goodness of the natural feeling of just self-esteem as a creature related to, with and for God—proposed a serious work of vigilance and mortification. He wrote to Father Guglielmo Agar in 1854:

> And yet man cannot completely overcome this subjective feeling of his own strength by punishing him alone, if at the same time he does not find a way to give birth in himself to another feeling more powerful (though sometimes deeply unconscious) and supernatural that entirely wins his games and that natural feeling.[39]

To adore is to desire the gift of holiness in a real abandonment to the divine work: there is a profound relationality to be lived concretely.

---

37. Bernanos, *Romanzi*, 805.
38. Muratore, *Antonio Rosmini*, 42.
39. Rosmini, *Epistolario ascetico* 4, para. 1430.

The intellect, as a gift of grace, is the pivot of the moral life of man because by glimpsing the divine will it is capable of giving the human will the decision-making force necessary to do good, that is, the same will of God. Desire becomes the describable form of an imperceptible but profoundly real and visible passage in its concrete choice and at the end of its maturation process. In this dynamic it is possible to speak of participatory and at the same time desirable correlation.

There is a particular place where this union happens: the heart, which Rosmini prefers. The response to a provocation made by Don Paolo Orsi in January 1827 on what formative preference to have with respect to the heart or mind is curious; from it we can deduce, in terms of the implication of spiritual doctrine, the metaphysical-theological primality of the moral form of being over the other two (that is, the real form and the ideal form). Rosmini wrote:

> Dearest friend. You would like to know what I think of that question: whether it is worse to have a very good ingenuity accompanied by a very evil heart, or a very weak ingenuity accompanied by an excellent heart. You already know that my answer to this question is yours. The main reasons are as follows. 1st Talent is a gift, and the use of talent is our business. Now talent for itself does not help us to use it well, indeed it can try to use it badly. The heart, on the contrary, inclines us to use the talent we have well. The dowry of the heart is therefore more valuable, because it is the one that disposes to do well the operations that are ours; virtue, in short, from which alone praise can come to man, as of his own thing. 2nd Talent does not make us happy, if it is used badly. The heart, on the contrary, inclines us to virtue, and thus also helps us to obtain happiness. Experience offers us continuous and illustrious proof of this in human history. Solomon, Origen, Tertullian, not to mention the pride of Greek philosophers or other nations, were made unhappy by their talents. 3rd. Jesus Christ never praised the gifts of ingenuity, but always those of the heart. 4th. The ingenuity is also proper to the devil, that is, to the most evil creature. Not so the heart. 5th. Men love the beautiful heart more than the ingenuity. So even in the world great wives are esteemed as dangerous, and they usually have many enemies. Those who have a beautiful heart are loved by all.[40]

The heart is the seat of authentic discernment because it is the place of encounter between the human and divine will in an important dialogic

---

40. Rosmini, *Epistolario ascetico* 1, para. 56.

exchange: it is the occurrence of an inobjectification of communion. Faith itself "results from two elements: the *incipient divine perception* and the *assent* of our will, with which alone the act of faith is accomplished."[41] The human will in dialogue with the divine one always seeks to recognize the true good and to desire it despite sin having undermined the whole of man.

In the work "On Christian Education" *(Dell'educazione cristiana)* Rosmini writes very profound pages on the Eucharist from which it is possible to derive how intellectual research nourishes desire. He wrote:

> Here is an abundant source of living waters! Here all piety can quench its thirst. Here is angelic bread! Any superhuman devotion can be nourished in full abundance by him. What is lacking here that is great, that lacks holy, sweet, beneficial, merciful, and moving? What outside of this can one seek or find religious, pious, and useful, and good, and beautiful, and rich and sublime, which already in this eminently is not, where the source is of all holiness, grace, love, beauty and nobility?[42]
>
> Therefore, let those who love to be in perfect devotion think that they hear the Mass well, and that they savour this divine sacrifice worthily.[43]

In the eucharistic sacrament we can find a synthesis between the offering of Jesus's life to the Father for every man and woman and the offering of the life of the disciple who, imitating Christ, desires the good and only the good for himself is for others. Starting from this, the intellect is invited to clothe itself with that desirable affection capable of moving the will to achieve good.

Conclusion

The path identified in the three lines given by the testamentary words has highlighted how much desire is deeply inherent in man, making him capable of being a seeker of fullness. At the same time, intellectual charity is not a work in itself, but the result of justice (which is redemptive justification in the biblical-christological-soteriological sense) that asks us to render to God what is God's, in the awareness of belonging to a human community called to live divine charity in relating to him simply and daily.

---

41. Rosmini, *SA*, 1:127.
42. Rosmini, "Dell'educazione cristiana" (On Christian Eeducation), para. 219.
43. Rosmini, "Dell'educazione cristiana," para. 222.

Desire has its own versatility depending on where the analytical study intercepts it. It is possible to speak of desire for God, of human desire, to use it for something generic or to discover its depth. It is strongly inherent in human dynamics, and its outward thrust makes man capable of passion by helping him, in his moral/spiritual being, to give light to the correlation between being ideal intuited but shapeless and colorless with the real being with which man tells himself and grasps the other by himself.

Desire is part of the structure of man: through the human will it remains linked to the search for the good for man that the incarnation of Christ has shown to be in God but becomes a promoter of paths of intellectual charity until reaching the maximum of charity highlighted by Rosmini as spiritual charity. Desire is capable of transforming charitable thought into continuous charity so that all men may know the loving goodness of God.

We also see how much desire is not only pushed towards the Other, but also silence in itself, so that we can implement that participatory correlation not only in an ideal way but also, and in this case in a particular way, real (in full synthesistic logic). The Other, like the Lord, comes to meet man. Intellectual charity itself is not something properly of man but a gift given by divine Charity which knows how to set in motion that intellectual process capable of offering educational paths and not only of human emancipation. The latter, precisely because it is a work of charity, cannot be isolated from God and valued only from the subjective human point of view, since man's fulfillment lies precisely in the participatory correlation with his Creator whose perfect image is Jesus. Precisely for this reason desire becomes imitation and intellectual charity is placed at the service of this attitude on the part of man. An imitation that is not given by vainglory or sterile heroism but by the awareness of the gift of fullness to which desire by its nature tends and that intellectual charity *iuxta propria principia* tells and conveys. Intellectual charity involves the intellect of man by showing the attractive beauty of the object or subjective object, as God (who is not a thing) who in turn places the will to take significant steps even when choices are made that cross the wounds of suffering but that make man capable of imitating that sacrifice of the cross always present in the eucharistic sacrament, gift of loving communion in which man can find the taste for seeking and the way of imitation as the highest form of justice, thus assuming that style of intellectual charity aimed at giving ground to the desire inherent in man, as a nostalgia for God.

PART 5

Bibliography

Abbruzzese, William. *La carità intellettuale in Antonio Rosmini*. Rome: City News, 2019.
Antonelli, Maria T. *L'ascesi cristiana in Antonio Rosmini*. Stresa, It.: Rosminiane, 1999.
Baggio, Antonio M. "Rosmini e la 'carità intellettuale.'" *Città Nuova* 20 (1998) 46–47.
Bellelli, Fernando. "L'importanza degli ordini di intellezione e degli ordini di riflessione nella pedagogia rosminiana: analisi storico-culturale di un vuoto della letteratura critica" [The importance of the orders of intellection and of the orders of reflection in Rosmini's pedagogy: historical-cultural analysis of a void of critical literature]. *Rivista di storia dell'educazione* 7 (2020) 83–97.
Bernanos, Georges. *Romanzi*. Translated by Paola Messori. Milan: Mondadori, 1998.
De Giorgi, Fulvio. "Le congregazioni religiose dell'Ottocento e il problema dell'educazione nel processo di modernizzazione in Italia." *Annali di storia dell'educazione e delle istituzioni scolastiche* 1 (1994) 169–205.
———. *La scienza del cuore. Spiritualità e cultura religiosa in Antonio Rosmini*. Bologna: Mulino, 1995.
———. *La scuola italiana di spiritualità. Da Rosmini a Montini*. Brescia, It.: Morcelliana, 2020.
Goffi, Tullio. *L'Ottocento*. Bologna: EDB, 2015.
Ignatius of Loyola. *Esercizi spirituali*. Cinisello Balsamo, It.: San Paolo, 1995.
Lacan, Jacques. *Il Seminario*. Turin: Einaudi, 1983.
———. "Sovversione del soggetto e dialettica del desiderio nell'inconscio freudiano." In *Scritti*, by Jacques Lacan, edited by Giacomo B. Contri, 2:795–831. Turin: Einaudi, 1974.
Muratore, Umberto. *Conoscere Rosmini. Vita, pensiero, spiritualità*. Stresa, It.: Rosminiane, 2012.
Ottonello, Pier P. "Rosmini e la carità intellettuale." *Città di vita* 52 (1997) 340.
Pagani, Giambattista, and Guido Rossi. *Vita di Antonio Rosmini*. Rovereto, It.: Manfrini, 1959.
Paoli, Francesco. *Antonio Rosmini. Virtù quotidiane*. Edited by Maria M. Riva. Verona: Faith & Culture, 2007.
Pazzaglia, Luciano, ed. *Chiesa e prospettive educative in Italia tra Restaurazione e Unificazione*. Brescia, It.: Scuola, 1994.
Rosmini, Antonio. *Antropologia soprannaturale*. Edited by Umberto Muratore. 2 vols. ENC 39–40. Rome: Città Nuova, 1983.
———. *Costituzioni dell'Istituto della Carità*. Edited by Dino Sartori. ENC 50. Rome: Città Nuova, 1996.
———. "Dell'educazione cristiana." In *Scritti pedagogici*, edited by Lino Prenna, ENC 31, 33–186. Stresa, It.: Rosminiane, 2009.
———. *Dio è amore. Pagine scelte*. Edited by Umberto Muratore. Milan: Paoline, 1993.
———. *Epistolario ascetico*. Turin: UTET, 1914.
———. *Introduzione alla filosofia*. Edited by Pier P. Ottonello. ENC 2. Rome: Città Nuova, 1979.
———. *Manuale dell'Esercitatore*. Edited by François Evain. ENC 51. Rome: Città Nuova, 1987.
———. *Massime di perfezione cristiana*. Edited by Alfeo Valle. ENC 49. Rome: Città Nuova, 1976.

———. *Operette Spirituali*. Edited by Alfeo Valle. ENC 48. Rome: Città Nuova 1985.
———. *Principi della scienza morale*. Edited by Umberto Muratore. ENC 23. Rome: Città Nuova, 1990.
———. "La società ed il suo fine." In *Filosofia della politica*, edited by Mario D'Addio, 123–563. Milan: Marzorati, 1972.
———. *Teosofia*. Edited by Samuele F. Tadini. Milan: Bompiani, 2011.
Sani, Roberto, ed. *Chiesa, educazione e società nella Lombardia del primo Ottocento. Gli Istituti religiosi tra impegno educativo e nuove forme di apostolato (1815–1860)*. Milan: Centro Ambrosiano, 1996.
Velocci, Giovanni. *Crisi e rinascita della spiritualità. Dal Sette all'Ottocento*. Rome: Studium, 1982.
———. *L'esperienza religiosa di Antonio Rosmini*. Milan: Àncora, 1971.
Winnicott, Donald W. *Gioco e realtà*. Translated by Livia Tabanelli. Rome: Armando, 2020.
Zovatto, Pietro. "La 'charitas' intellettuale rosminiana." *Catholic School* 118 (1990) 553–82.

24

Conclusion

FERNANDO BELLELLI

IN THESE CONCLUDING REMARKS, I would like to indicate possible lines of research for the development of the path taken, with specific attention to what are, in my view, the fundamental elements of Antonio Rosmini with regard to the key coordinates of the comparison with his *Suspended Middle* and the *Suspended Middle* of J. Milbank and radical orthodoxy movement.

I have already had the opportunity, in previous research, to explore the works of Rosmini, from both the theological science and the humanistic science standpoints; above all analyzing the topic of human dignity in the Rosminian opus, I brought to light the existence in it of the religious anthropology of freedom of conscience. In order to highlight this religious anthropology of the freedom of conscience, it was necessary to first introduce a further device present in Rosminian thought, which I have called *synthesism within synthesism* and that I explore in the essay in this volume. Central to this device, and for the deployment of its potential was *cognition*.[1] Synthesism within synthesism is essential to understand how the various orders of *affection, intellection, volition, cognition,* and *reflection*

---

1. This, and its orders, are what takes shape to the extent that an intellectual affection is about to become a volition, which, uniting in turn precisely with cognition, becomes a judgment, which can be and/or become practical, speculative, and/or speculative judgment of a practical judgment, of which the second order of reflection of the latter is the emergence of the conscience. See on this topic Bellelli, "Importanza degli ordini."

are connected. The *affections* correspond to the real form of being, the *intellections* to the real form, the *volitions* to the moral form. Each of the orders of *affections*, *intellections*, and *volitions* passes to the next according to this modality: an affection passes from the first to the second degree of affection because it interacts with a volition that restores to the orders of affections the first affection through a cognition that generates the volition of the reflection on the intellection. The evolution of the orders of *affections*, *intellections*, and *cognitions*, in increasing stages of awareness reflected by the ontological conscience, from one order to another of the orders of reflection expresses the *synthesism within synthesism*. The *synthesism within synthesism* in its pedagogical, political and juridical meaning is at the same time connected with and distinguished by its ethical meaning, as I show in the following explications.

Ethics for Rosmini consists in the science of the honest good:

> Now, the goodness of man, and not of his things, is called *moral goodness*, and that quality of the human will, for which man is good, is called *moral good, honest good*; and Ethics deals with this good. Ethics, therefore, is a science that deals with the *honest good*.[2]

> Then, Ethics is divided into three parts: The first deals with the *nature of the honest good*, and is called General Ethics, because it does not derive from any of those habits or special acts in which the honest good transfuses almost divided into parts, but it speaks of that good that all habits and all acts must have equally to be honest. The second deals with *the ways of the honest good*, and it is called *Special Ethics*, because it considers the habits and special acts that are part of it. The third deals with *the excellence of the honest good*, and it is called *Eudemonological Ethics*, because the excellence of the honest good is found only in seeing intelligent and volitive nature perfect and happy.[3]

Also in the *Compendium of Ethics (Compendio di etica)*, a work divided into three parts, Rosmini deals with what he describes in these brief contents:

In the first part, in which he adds the scientific definition of the honest good, he first gives—together with the rules for recognizing the moral condition of the actions and of the various states of man[4]—the three ele-

---

2. "Prefazione," in Rosmini, *Compendio di etica* (Compendium of ethics), 29, para. 3.
3. Prefazione," in Rosmini, *Compendio di etica*, 32, para. 10.
4. "First, there is a general rule which includes all the others, and which is like the principle of moral logic: *it is the following: The moral good results from the union of three elements, will, norm, relationship. If only one of these elements is missing, the moral order*

ments of the honest good, which are: the will, the law, and the relationship between the law and the will.

In the second part, on special ethics, he deals with the ways of honest good, describing them as *offici*[5] *morali* (good intercessions or mediations), "moral habits" (virtues[6] and vices), relating them to each other, also in order to determine the means by which man becomes virtuous: it is precisely before this question that Rosmini, emphasizing that there are means independent from the individual for becoming virtuous, shows the insufficiency of natural ethics, which requires a supernatural (otherwise also known as theological ethics of truth). He deals with this topic even more masterfully in *Logica*.

In the third part he deals with the excellence of the honest good, which is so for those who practice virtuously, also and in particular through supernatural perfection, which ensures that happiness and bliss (expressive of the *duplex ordo* between natural happiness and supernatural bliss) are never miserable (while evil is).

Rosmini did not simply write *Compendium of Ethics*, he also wrote *History of Ethics (Storia dell'Etica)*, a minor work still not sufficiently appreciated. Rosmini wrote other works of a similar nature on complementary topics: in particular the voluminous and better-known *Saggio storico critico sulle categorie*, the *Storia comparativa e critica de' sistemi intorno al principio della morale*, and *Frammento di una storia filosofica della società civile*.[7]

---

cannot come about; there can be neither good nor evil. Therefore, the moral order must be judged to exist, when it is ascertained that all three of those elements are found in the fact: then the moral good can be judged to exist, when the relationship between the will and the law is one of conformity: then it can be judged that there is moral evil when the relationship between the will and the law is one of dissimilarity" (Rosmini, Compendio di etica, para. 160).

5. "We call '*officio*' that action which is exercised towards an intellectual entity in accordance with its moral requirement" (Rosmini, *Compendio di etica*, para. 255).

6. "Therefore, considered in its unity, virtue is that quality which makes the will good, and therefore which makes man, the human person, good . . . and is defined as: *An absolute preponderance of the will towards the first and eternal law (which includes all others) and a universal and constant purpose to operate in accordance with and in reverence thereof*" (Rosmini, *Compendio di etica*, para. 514).

7. The *Frammento* includes nos. 1805 to 1824 of *Filosofia del diritto*. (See Rosmini, "Frammento.") This work and those indicated in the previous notes of a historical nature should be compared with Rosmini's *Storia dell'amore* and *Frammenti di una storia*. If on the one hand Rosmini lived in a cultural era in which historical studies had not yet seen the breakthrough of the historical-critical method, and therefore did not master the epistemological registers of the historical sciences that have been elaborated subsequently, on the other hand he shows an acumen proper to the positive historical sciences that can well be combined with theological reflection on history, as is emblematically documented in his *Teodicea*. Also on this point, which has been and is much

For Rosmini the history of ethics went hand in hand with the assimilation over the centuries of the principle of morality, both disciplines (ethics and moral science) configurable in their epistemological accuracy only through a reciprocal and complementary delimitation of their pertinent sectors, not without the centrality of the natural and supernatural theological, without which it is not possible for ethics and moral science to grasp both the intrinsic reasons for their own limitation and the possibility of determining the effective overcoming and exceeding complement of this limit in the total and absolutely free self-communication of the divine present in nature.[8]

The correlation between the definition of "ethics" and the definition of "morals" in Rosmini can be seen when comparing the above definition with the following definition of "morals."

> Now, it must be understood that morality is neither the ideal nor the real, but the union between them (this mystical kiss, so to speak, of two forms that become complete when they are joined); and it will be easy to see that the systems which reduce morality either only to the order of real things, or merely to the order of ideal things, are excluded, that is, they exclude the elements necessary to form the moral essence and therefore do damage in their falseness.[9]

Here is the definition of honest good given by Rosmini, since the honest good is one of the cardinal principles of his conception of ethics.

> 30. If therefore the natural tendency of the will moves towards the entity in proportion to its degrees of being; and if the perfection of this act consists in joining and going to its object, according to how the object itself is naturally proportionate to it; it follows that the act of volition will be good, when it does not reject any entity, any degree of being, but tends towards all, unites with all, and the more it unites with the entities, the more they will have of the being, which is its natural object. 31 Therefore, the *moral quality* of the will, its good, its evil, is not something that the will can have considered by itself, but consists in its external relations, in the real relations that it forms in one way or another, with the entities that are the object of thought. 32. If we call *order of being* the distribution of being

---

studied by various schools and currents of thought, I take the liberty of referring again to Bellelli, *Percorsi storici*.

8. See Rosmini, *Del divino nella natura* (On the divine in nature).

9. See Rosmini, "Storia comparativa e critica," 188–89. For an overview of morals and morality in the Rosminian opus see Bergamaschi, *Grande dizionario antologico*, 3:164.

itself in the various entities that can fall into cognition; in that case we will say, that the act of the will will be good when it, in its affection, retains the *order of being*. 33. We call *affection* the way in which the will unites itself with its objects, that is, with known entities. Wherefore, the good of the will and its acts consists in distributing its affection to the various known entities in proportion and according to the order of their entity. 34. And since the good of the will is called honest good; Therefore, the honest good consists in this, that the order of the affection of the will corresponds to the order of being, the very object of that power and its acts.[10]

Part 1: Rosmini's Purification of the Scotist Aporias of Phenomenology (between Analogy and Paradox) and the Division of Being: Metaphysics and Ontology

One of the purposes of the convention and the publication of the proceedings is to illustrate the possibility of understanding the purification made by Rosmini's thought—an intrinsic part of it—from the reductionism implicit in Scotus's solution, thus providing the hermeneutics of this purification as a Rosminian critical anticipator of the aporias of phenomenology. Thomas Aquinas and Edith Stein are Rosmini's privileged interlocutors in this sense, revealing these aspects of his thinking, together with Henri de Lubac and Hans Urs von Balthasar. On the question of the paradox, the Vico-Rosmini relationship is fruitful, on the question of the analogy the Thomas Aquinas-Rosmini connection, while on their conjugation, the Rosmini-Balthasar relationship on the matter of "christological analogy" of the *universale concretum* of the *Verbum caro* to the *maior dissimilitudo* between the *fides Christi* and the absence of faith of the creature elevated by grace to the divine sonship.[11]

Contemporaneous to *Theosophy (Teosofia)*,[12] that is in the last years of Rosmini's life, apart from the work *The Theological Language (Il linguaggio teologico)*, is *Logic (Logica)*. With respect to the sheer size of *Theosophy*, that

10. Rosmini, *Compendio di etica*, paras. 30–34, *et seq*.: "This definition of the honest good must be carefully pondered. It supposes a fact to be detected in human nature with that psychological observation which notices and observes what happens in man; and this fact is that the will can give its affection to any entity, and also has a natural disposition to give it; which demonstrates that the entity as an entity is its natural object" (para. 35).

11. An attempt at this is to be found in my book *Cristocentrismo e storia*.

12. See, in particular, bk. 5 on dialectics.

of *Logic*, although considerable, is decidedly minor. The most recent Rosminian studies, based in part on the application of the historical-cultural method, consider important not only a diachronic approach to the entire Rosminian opus, but also a synchronic approach which, in the specific case, can be given by comparing *Logic* and *Theosophy* with regard to the anthropology of the triadic and Trinitarian synthesism of the three forms of being focused on the moral form. In the following sections of *Logic* we can find what can be considered one of the most inherently significant for drawing on the synthesis of Rosminian thought. It is important to give a brief explanation with the aim of showing the importance of their collocation in this research. Paragraph 1164 gives the overall epistemological horizon of the Rosminian theoresis, focusing on the confines of the human mind within its possible concrete collocation of having only natural enlightenment, both natural and supernatural enlightenment having enlightenment *in statu viae* or in the condition of the *visio beatifica* that Rosmini calls in state of *terminus*.

> It is better then, when dealing with the confines of the human mind, to distinguish the two states in which human nature can be found, in the one given only by natural enlightenment, in the other with a twofold enlightenment, the natural and the supernatural, which differs in the present state from what it will be in the state of terminus. However, it is possible to see something in common on the borders of the human mind, in whatever state man finds himself.[13]

In the following paragraph 1165 of *Logic* among the conceptual elements that Rosmini uses in describing the triadic and Trinitarian synthesism of the three forms of being from the *logical* standpoint as a theoretical discipline in the terms of *formal reason, real reason* and *moral reason*, he intends to emphasize the following: *human superintelligence*, power, which is not precisely a *power* but rather a *function* of reason; the unknowability of the supreme moral reason for man according to nature, except in a *negative* and *virtual* modality. By *human superintelligence* as a *function* of reason we must understand the anthropological possibility of the act of faith as a structure of human nature created in grace: the predisposition of confines of the human mind to be illuminated by the supernatural is an ontological predisposition of the structure of the human being, precisely created with the possibility that its eventual self-damnation can be redeemed by the salvation of God. It must be noted that Rosmini does not respond to *theological rationalism* with *fideism*, but is rather able to clearly show all the

13. See Rosmini, *Logica* (Logic), para. 1164.

philosophical reasons that lead man to knowingly determine the awareness of his structural ontological limit, leaving to human and divine freedom the imponderable nature of the respective decisions: divine decision by provident human freedom is ultimately unpredictable, in the sense of the Rosminian divine *Theodicy (Teodicea)*. The distinction between power and function is not to be seen nominatively, since it indicates that in human nature there are faculties that transcend and exceed all its powers: the function of human superintelligence, which leads the freedom of the person as a right subsisting in law to accept the christological-Trinitarian revelation co-generates, together with the work of supernatural grace, what Rosmini calls real and proper supernatural powers,[14] which are the theological virtues.

14. It reads directly from Rosmini: "Then, when it is done in adults, the very act of mutation that arises in man when he first begins to have the supernatural power created in him by grace, by this power already obtained, must be distinguished. The passage that man makes from not having grace to having it, from not having to having in himself that supernatural power which with the first operation of grace in man is born and created: this marvelous passage is not observable in us, because it is not even sensitive. Marvelous as this proposition may seem, it will not prove incredible to anyone who observes that it depends on a general law to which feeling is subject: which is this that one cannot feel the act by which we begin to exist with that act by which we are naturalized, that is, we take nature or essence: just as it cannot be felt that by which our nature is undone, either we lay down our very life or (if it could happen) we cancel ourselves. Therefore, the child cannot feel the act in which he is conceived and begins to be, because he is not yet in that act; and he needs to already be to hear. In the same way, the act of dying cannot be sensible, because it is nothing but an undoing, an annulment of our power to feel animal; which is not to use this power, but to put it down. And truly in an instant in which we felt we would not have died yet, we would not have yet done the act of dying: this act of dying is not done before we are dead, and before it is done it cannot be felt, and when he is made today, we are no longer sensitive beings, and therefore we cannot hear him. This is also confirmed by experience in what happens in accidents in which the power to feel suddenly ceases in a part of the body; for this happens without pain: and the apoplectic finds himself half dead without himself knowing how this happened to him: but on the other hand, it seems clear that the ceasing to feel is not feeling: on the contrary, it would be a contradiction if it were. And this observation of the accident is notable in that it proves insensitive to us not only the cessation of the entire power of feeling, but also of a part of it: and certainly, that part which ceases in ceasing is not felt: although may the other party remaining resent it at that termination. The same is true of increasing sensory power: this growth is not a matter of any sense, and therefore our body grows, strengthens itself, or heals itself without us knowing how; although after grown, strengthened, healed we enjoy the growth, strength, and health. Let us now apply this law of feeling to the supernatural power created in us by divine action. With the divine action a new power is created in us: this power begins to exist in us, when it did not exist before; and she is an element, a part of our essence. Therefore, according to the law set forth, this first effect of grace in us must necessarily be insensitive, because grace acts, as we said, in a creative way, it does nothing but create, which places a new power within us, which magnifies our essence. Of the act, therefore, of this mutation we cannot have any consciousness, because we have no feeling of it. The same can be proved by considering the nature of each power. I

Natural theology allows man, in Rosmini's opinion, to know the supreme moral reason in a negative and non-virtual manner. The negative ideas are, in fact, substantially all ascribable to the negative idea of the essence of God, that man can form through the sole exercise of his natural enlightenment. The effectiveness of the virtual knowledge[15] of the supreme moral reason is, on the other hand, the prerogative of the superhuman intelligence informed by supernatural power of divine grace, and it belongs to the man in whom the natural knowledge and the supernatural knowledge interact to lead man in *in statu viae*[16] to the final state of the *visio beatifica*. This is Rosmini's *suspended middle*—absolute moral reason as the *function* to reveal the divine and supernatural nature of Trinity. In that dynamic phenomenology is purified from Scotist reductionism, because the anthropological moral reason, as it is shown in the next paragraph, is *virtual* and not absolute.

---

have demonstrated that every power is a first act; for example, the power to feel is a first feeling which, when modified, changes in the second acts which are called acts towards the first which is called power. Now the effect of grace is to produce in us a new power of feeling, a first feeling. Now if this feeling is first; if before him there is no other sense of its kind, and all sensations start from him as from the beginning; it is evident that before that first act is produced there can be no sense of that kind. Therefore, that action of grace with which supernatural power is generated in us, or the first supernatural feeling is not sensible, nor can it be the object of our awareness" (Rosmini, SA, 1:94). About this topic see Canu, *Pensare la fede*.

15. On the meaning of the virtuality of knowledge in relation to the work of supernatural grace see this passage: "Morality, therefore, is impossible for the natural forces of man, at least for that part which concerns God: and as the private universe of God is without principle, without support, it cannot even be conceived; thus the severed moral virtue of that respect which regards God is cut off from its capital part, it is dead, it is nothing by itself. Because finally all love towards creatures must actually terminate in God in order to be perfect, and must terminate in God virtually, they must at least not contradict the love of God if they are not to be crimes" (Rosmini, SA, 1:86).

16. Rosmini expresses himself thus (in terms of Trinitarian nuptiality) on the *virtual* proper to faith: "In that negative concept of God also the positive news of God is virtually contained: and grace inclines and makes man very eager to penetrate those mysterious and hidden truths, of which the discovery of which takes so long for him: this man touched by the action of grace has become the beloved 'who is behind the wall, and who eagerly looks through the windows, and gazes at the openings of the gates.' Grace shows him some faint light, some particle of the infinite beauties that are veiled and hidden from him" (Rosmini, SA, 1:97).

CONCLUSION

Part 2: Rosmini's Trinitarian Ontology and His Suspended Middle: The Primality of the Moral Form of Being in the Synthesism with the Real and Ideal Forms

The second part of this volume rereads this description, highlighting the implications of this perspective in as far as it is based on the synthesism of the three forms of being, markedly in the primality (which is not primacy) of the moral form as a metaphysical-theoretical-speculative chorological criterion of Rosmini's philosophical-theological thought, both in the natural order and the supernatural order of being (triadic creature and revealed Trinitarian). In other words, the possible focus to be explored is that Rosmini's *suspended middle* is the synthesistic consideration of the moral form of being, which implies and fosters the affective turn of metaphysics (see P. Sequeri), Rosmini's *suspended middle* could fruitfully interact with the analogous *suspended middle* of radical orthodoxy.

In one of the most significant passages of *Logic*, a work written towards the end of Rosmini's life and to be interpreted as a compass with which to understand his entire opus, the author offers one of the most successful syntheses of his thought on synthesism and its application:

> It is therefore necessary to consider that there are three supreme, categorically different reasons, which we will call the *formal reason*, the *real reason* and the *moral reason*. The supreme formal reason is given by man in the idea of being and it is the commencement of all formal logic.
>
> This then is what makes known also the *real reasons* and the *moral reasons*. But, of the real reasons, the *supreme* is not given by nature to man, because this is the reality of God himself, and man cannot perceive the reality of God by nature. So, since he has on the one hand *the formal supreme reason* and in it the power to know all the real reasons, also the supreme, if it were given to him, which is to say that he knows everything that was communicated to his sentiment; consequently, he has the faculty to realize his limit, that is to realize that it is not given to him to know all that can be known; and so he gathers faculty and having to be beyond, something unknown to him. Now if this impulse, with which the human mind guesses that there is something beyond what is all that it knows, we will call it *human superintelligence*, manifestly we will see, that this is not precisely a *power* but rather a *function* of reason, so that this comparing the field of the possible that is given to it in the idea, to the field of the real given in sentiment, sees that that infinitely exceeds this, and the in that part of reality that it can touch there

is no supreme reason, that is *the real being for its essence*, which can only be a type of every reality, and therefore also the reason of all finite realities. With regard then to the supreme moral reason, this lies in the essential and total order of being: because being thus intrinsically ordered is in itself good to all the Wills that know it. Now man in the idea possesses this order *virtually*, but does not implement it before the thought, except in the real being. Of this real being he knows a part *positively* with sentiment, and that part which by nature knows in this way, belongs to the finite being; with the function of the human superintelligence, it knows *negatively* and confusedly the infinite real being, in which only the supreme moral reason is implemented, since there is the essential and total order of the being. Therefore, according to nature, man cannot know the supreme moral reason, except in a negative and virtual way. Thus, the moral is imperfect in its implementation. There are, then, two maximum limits for human intelligence: the first is that of not being able to know the *supreme real reason*, and therefore not to be able to have a sole material criterion for all the realities, so we have had to establish that every *specific perception* of reality, is a criterion for that species of which that perception assumes the type; second that of knowing only virtually the supreme moral reason.[17]

Since man knows the maximum limits of his intelligence (first, that he does not fully possess the totality and globality of the real form of being; second, that he knows only negatively and virtually the totality and globality of the moral form of being), starting from the natural impossibility of perfectly implementing the morality of being, he can reach the peak of natural *fulfillment* possible in the mortal life.

> 1166. But since man knows the *supreme formal reason* and with this knows only two limits; then he aspires to extend himself in infinity and desires a state in which these anxieties cease.
>
> However, when man has come to understand clearly that these limitations cannot be removed in the present life, he acquires this necessity, and thus finds that satisfaction of his intelligence, which in mortal life is possible.[18]

Up to this point we have given the necessarily brief and essential framework of the collocation of Rosminian ethics of education within his opus, formation of ethics within the moral form of being, exploring and explaining the Rosminian religious anthropology of freedom of conscience,

17. Rosmini, *Logica*, para. 1165.
18. Rosmini, *Logica*, para. 1166.

inspired by the criteria presented here and summarized in the "synthesism within synthesism" orders of affection, intellection, volition, cognition, and reflection. For Rosmini the question of ethics is inseparably connected to the question of education: its ethics is always generative and cause/effect of education, and his idea of education is always ethical-moral.

The view of the structure of the ethics of education in Rosmini can, in effect, serve as an overall epistemological criterion for outlining the interdisciplinary perspectives of Rosmini's method, between philosophy, theology, and pedagogy. In the light of this, at this point I would like to offer some possible keys to reading the contributions of the five sections into which the volume is divided and finally some possible lines of development of the overall perspective that has been outlined and expressed in the concert of all the contributions; possible lines of research orbiting around performativity, both as a possible summary and significant figure and perspective of the current scientific debate in pedagogy, and as potentially very useful to make the importance of the usability of Rosmini's training ethics appreciated in a pertinent and adequate way, precisely in the present inter-multi-trans-disciplinary scientific debate on pedagogy, politics, and law.

Anthropology, both philosophical and theological (Rosmini would say supernatural), is the overall thread that runs through the inter-multi-trans-disciplinary themes of this entire volume. Ethics of education, which, in the moral reason, as theorized by Antonio Rosmini is compatible with the theological ethics of truth elaborated by P. Sequeri,[19] and it constitutes the *fil rouge* of each and all the contributions present in the two sections: a *fil rouge* that I will now illustrate.

In order to enframe *Logic* and the method of the supreme principle of the Rosminian methodology, I think it is essential to briefly offer a classification of what Rosmini defines as logic—including the principle of moral logic—and method. In fact, to understand the specifics of the methodology, it is necessary to understand where it stands in relation to the method, just as to understand the specifics of the method it is necessary to understand where it stands in relation to logic, within which moral logic is in turn to be placed. If we are to comprehend Rosmini's pedagogical-political-juridical-ethic of education it is very important and useful to highlight these connections, because the interlacing and the weave of them makes it possible to semanticize what Rosmini intended by what we can call the performativity of his pedagogical-political-juridical-ethic of education.

We will begin from *Logic*. It is necessary to say that Rosmini wrote this work contemporaneously with *Theosophy* and *Theological Language* in the

---

19. See Sequeri: *Fede e la giustizia*; "Metafisica e ordine del senso."

last years of his life. These works, in particular the first two, should be read together, because the contain not only a summary of Rosmini's thought, but also his interpretative key, including that of the diachronic evolution through which he refined and perfected his entire system of thought. With regard to the definition of logic, Rosmini spoke first in general terms, polishing more definitions as he revised and reread his *New Essay Concerning the Origin of Ideas (Nuovo Saggio sull'origine delle idee)*[20]:

> 64. What is thinking?—By this word we usually understand all the acts of the intellectual faculties. But not all are subject to art, since quite a few of them escape the free manipulation of the human will, such as those, which are posed and determined by nature itself. In order therefore to know and ascertain what the proper object of Logic is, it is convenient, by separating the necessary acts of thought, to define and retain those others which can be the object of art. Now the intellectual faculties are reduced to two main ones, intellect, and reason. The acts of the Intellect belong to nature alone, those over which art presides can only be found among the acts of Reason. Let me better explain this concept. 65. The intuition of being is what constitutes the Intellect (Ideol. 481–484). Intellect is act, habit, and power in several respects. It is act, because there is a primitive and natural intuition of the indeterminate being (Ideol. 413–472), which never ceases in the intellectual soul, and makes it so. It is a habit in that the being is present to the soul without confusing itself with it, and therefore is not the soul, but is possessed by the soul. Finally, it is power, in that from the essential and immanent act by which the soul sees the indeterminate being, others arise, with which it intuits the being endowed with more or less determinations, and thus the Intellect it can be defined as: "the power to intuit ideas." It is clear that the primitive act of the intellect is given by nature and is not subject to art. 66. Likewise, all subsequent intellectual acts, as regards the way in which they are emitted, are as necessary as the first, and are virtually contained in the first. And yet not even these, to be expressed in one way rather than another, require acquired skill, nor are they the object of any art, because the way of intuiting is simple and determined by nature. 67. The general power of applying being is called Reason. 68. This is not an act, but a pure power that follows the act of primitive intuition, because with it man applies being (Ideol. 338, 481). Under this expression "applying

---

20. When Rosmini refers to "Ideologia" he means the work generally entitled *Nuovo Saggio sull'origine delle idee.*

being" we understand any use of the intelligence, after the first intuition. Reason means this use of intelligence, and reasoning, the set of operations of reason linked to one of its ends.[21]

From the text we can derive the centrality of the Rosminian theoresis on the act, also with regard to logic. Another aspect to which it is opportune to draw attention is the fact that Rosmini, immediately, when dealing with logic, considers it both as an application of being depending on the act of primitive intuition, and as an exercise of reason which is the reasoning proper to the art. Exploring specifically this characteristic of logic as an art, Rosmini presents the following definitions:

> 69. Does reasoning or making use of reason require an acquired ability of man, and can this be greater or lesser? In other words, can reasoning be the subject of an art? We distinguish the two main functions of Reason. Reason inasmuch as it applies the idea of being to feeling, exercises that function which is called Perception. Reason, insofar as it applies the idea of being to objects already thought of, exercises that function which is called Reflection. The first of these two functions, that is perception, is necessary in itself and cannot be an object of art, although what precedes it may depend on art for its preparation and condition. Hence it may very well depend on man's industry, skill, or art to acquire these rather than those perceptions and to make them more alive and perfect for himself with the best application of sensory organs or instruments. But with regard to the second function, that is, reflection, this is the one that most depends on man's will and ability, because reflection can be guided by the will in very different ways and with very different results. And yet the good use of this is the proper object of the art of thinking. I say "the proper object" because it is certainly true that what precedes and prepares certain perceptions and intuitions can depend on the voluntary activity and ability of man, but this itself falls under the domain of reflection, for only for the use of this man can voluntarily prepare himself and his attention, as well as prepare external things, for which preparations he has rather these perceptions and these intuitions than those. 70. With these observations we can perfect the definition of the Logical Art. Because in this way the boundaries within which thinking can be an object of art remain fixed. It is therefore the logical art: "the Art of reflecting." 71. If the rules according to which this art proceeds are collected, formulated, and distributed in an

---

21. Rosmini, *Logica*, paras. 63–68.

appropriate order, we have the science of this art, which is logic. Logic therefore is "the science of the art of thinking" (Def. 2); i.e.: "Logic is the science of the art of directing reflection" (Def. 3).[22]

From the substantial elaboration of the cited text, it is clearly evident that for Rosmini logic, by applying the two main functions of reason, i.e., what is called perception and what is called reflection, in particular with regard to the latter, highlights that logic, in its scientific definition, has an intrinsic artistic component, and that this expressly consists in the ability to appropriately formulate and distribute orders, in particular orders of reflection. Given that in Rosminian elaboration "everything holds together," it seems to me important to reiterate the centrality of the notion of order, as I have previously presented it by describing the "synthesism within synthesism" of the orders of affection, intellection, volition, cognition, and reflection-judgment.

Part 3: Rosmini's Suspended Middle (and the Comparable Social Theory of Radical Orthodoxy's Suspended Middle): Possible Pedagogical Implications

Within synthesism as a fundamental theoretical structure of the aforementioned *suspended middle*, in Rosmini's thought we can identify the "synthesism in and of the synthesism" of the orders of *affection* (real being), *intellection* (ideal being), *volition* (moral being), *cognition*, and *reflection* within the founding theory of the metaphysical-affective-symbolic structure of the believing conscience, as a speculative judgment of a practical nature, at least of the second order of reflection. A possible educational-communicative application of this Rosminian approach is the pop theology of A. Staglianò. The possible link in pedagogical terms between Rosmini

---

22. Rosmini, *Logica*, paras. 69–71. As regards the boundaries of logic, in a series of passages Rosmini offers an admirable synthesis of all the disciplinary knowledge in which he has ventured with his encyclopedic production: "From this definition it can be seen that other sciences similar to it were frequently confused with logic. Some deceived by the etymology of the word, believed that in Logic we should be dealing with Reason in all respects. But the doctrine about the nature of Reason in the subjective sense, that is, as the 'principle and power of reasoning' belongs to Psychology, which is the first part of Metaphysics; the doctrine about the nature of Reason in an objective sense, that is, as 'the object in which the acts of power terminate,' belongs to Ideology and to Theosophy, which is the second part of Metaphysics. Logic therefore must restrict itself to considering 'the exercise of Reason', and properly 'the Art of this exercise,' by which reasoning is conducted in the best way, and to the best rational end" (Rosmini, *Logica*, para. 72).

and radical orthodoxy could be Rosminian *juridical pedagogy as philosophical and juridical discipline*, both consequent to and deriving from the conception of the person as a right subsisting in law and relationship and the criticism and the overcoming of individualism proposed by radical orthodoxy.

The scientific-experimental nature of the rationality of logic, as a science of the art of reflecting and directing reflection, contains in a nutshell not only the principle of moral logic, but also the empirical-observational dimension of the supreme principle of the methodology. In support and reinforcement of what this, it is also worth dwelling on the description that Rosmini offers of the origin of logic.

Indeed, on this subject, Rosmini says, including the fact that science perfects the habit and the art of reasoning:

> 73. Now how did human ingenuity come to discover and compose logic as a science? Reason passes to its acts spontaneously, when it has the material for them, and some stimulus that moves it to them. And yet there is an aptitude to reason naturally, and to reason rightly; because everything that is not right is contrary to nature. This instinctive attitude was called Natural Logic. But in this denomination the word Logic does not yet indicate either an art or a science, but a simple disposition. 74. Reason exists equally in all men; because rationality is of the essence of man. But the ability to reason powerfully and correctly is not given by nature equally to everyone, but to some more and some less; and hence the diversity of wits concerning reasoning ability. Since this attitude is distributed by nature to men in different measures, it can neither be taught nor learned. But every man begins his culture from that measure of reasoning aptitude which he has received. 75. The reasoning aptitude can then be cultivated and increased with the exercise of reasoning, and with logical science. And with the exercise of reasoning, one acquires the habit of using one's reason promptly, with ease, with pleasure, and with certainty; which constitutes the art of reasoning. 76. Art belongs to action, for here we are dealing with an active habit, science belongs to speculation. Even if a man speculatively knew all the precepts of painting and thus had the knowledge of it, he would not be able to exercise the painter's art for this reason, he would not have the art. On the other hand, one can possess art and not science. The rope dancer possesses that art, without needing to know the muscles he moves while dancing, or the laws of movement and balance.[23]

23. Rosmini, *Logica*, paras. 73–76.

CONCLUSION

In these sections Rosmini expressly uses the term *action*, and not *act*, precisely to differentiate action from deed according to this denotation: the deed belongs to speculation, art as a science of nature mainly belongs to action.[24] There is therefore, for Rosmini, a scientific nature proper to speculation and a scientific nature proper to art as action. Reflection on art as action allows him to explain how the art itself of reasoning is perfected in those who have acquired the logical science.

> 77. Formed with the exercise of the Art of reasoning, how did science withdraw from it? Through reflection on art. Suppose the art of reasoning has reached its perfection in a man: one would have the ideal reasoner in him. Reflecting on the manner in which he reasons, and analyzing the different reasonings that he makes, one would find that certain norms and certain forms were constant in them. Collecting all these norms, reducing them to brief propositions, ordering them according to the scientific method and demonstrating their necessity, would be the same as composing the Science of the Art of Reasoning. But since the perfect reasoner that we have imagined is not found among men, it is fitting that the philosopher collect the said norms by observing and analyzing the reasonings of many different reasoners among those who come closest to perfection, verifying them all evidence of the first principle, and thus deducing them a priori. For the question immediately arises: how do we know that a man is a just reasoner? How, that a discourse proceeds straight? This cannot be deduced from observation; which is indeed a critical judgment on the reasoning observed. All this must therefore be drawn from natural intelligence, that is, with the two powers of intellect and reason, in which human intelligence is summed up. We saw that the intellect offers the light, which contains virtually every knowable thing and makes it possible to distinguish the true and the false, and that reason applies it to what falls into sense and thought. Therefore, if one wants to know whether a reasoning (which is something that falls into thought) is right, it should be noted whether it is a right application of being. Now man knows that this application is right, if all that reasoning contains is virtually contained in the same being which is the evident and non-refutable light. The possibility of detecting all this lies in reason itself, that is, in the

---

24. On this aspect of the action the references and possible connections between the thinking of Rosmini and that of Maurice Blondel and Vincenzo La Via are clear, although still relatively unexplored and not adequately developed; see Bellelli, "Rosmini e Blondel"; La Via, *Coscienza e libertà*.

virtue of applying being, which is a deducing in act what is contained in potentiality in indeterminate being. Reason therefore gives man the faculty of knowing whether what is proposed to him as information deduced from being is truly such: and if it is such, it declares the reasoning to be correct, if not, not correct, but erroneous. Logic therefore as a science is found, after the existence of logic as an art, partly with observation, partly with the immediate use of natural intelligence. 78. Having explained how Logic is formed through reflection and philosophical meditation, let's see how science perfects the aptitude and the Art of reasoning. The Will is a power capable of moving and directing the other powers of man and among these also that of reflecting. But it takes from the intelligence the norms and ends according to which it moves and directs the other powers. Therefore, if the intelligence knows the norms according to which right reasoning proceeds, the Will makes use of this science to move and direct reason. Therefore, the aptitude and the art itself of reasoning is perfected in men who have learned the science of logic.[25]

25. Rosmini, *Logica*, paras. 77–78. With regard to the limits, the special offices and the division of *Logica* Rosmini said: "79. Logic, therefore, as a science, 1st does not give man the light of the Intellect; 2nd it does not give him Reason, or the power to reason; 3rd it does not give him the instinct and aptitude to reason; 4th does not give him the primitive quantity of this attitude. These four things are gifts of nature; 5th it does not give him that increase and improvement of aptitude which is acquired with practice, and which the Art of reasoning produces. But logic as a science adds a new improvement to this natural and habitual aptitude, and ensures its exercise, as this depends on the activity and direction of the human will. 80. And therefore the definition of the Logic is better clarified. Because from what we said, it appears that 'it is that science which collects and arranges in an orderly manner the norms, according to which reflection, proceeding in any kind of reasoning, reaches the truth and avoids error' (Def. 4). 81. The acts of reason, which depend on man's Will and ability, are ordered to two general purposes, according to which the acts themselves can be divided into two kinds: 1st some of them have the purpose of presenting for consideration of the mind the truths; 2nd some consist in the assents that man gives or denies to the truths that are presented to him. 82. Therefore logic has two special offices: 1st that of offering man the norms according to which reason can present truths to man; 2nd that of proposing the norms according to which man must give assent to the truths. 83. To these two parts of the Logic, it is advisable to add a third, which teaches us to judge whether what is presented before the thought is the truth or not. To make this judgment, it is advisable to resort to the idea of being, which is the primitive truth and seat of evidence. Hence the division already mentioned above, according to which Logic embraces: I. the theory of judging of the true and the false, or rather of the Criterion; II. the theory of reasoning; III. the assent theory. We will collect these three theories in three books in reverse order, so that the exposition proceeds from easy to difficult. The first book, therefore, will be of Assents and of the norms according to which they must be given or rejected; the second book, of Reasoning and of the norms according to which one must

CONCLUSION

The sections on logic presented here highlight the synthesistic dimension of Rosminian logic, in which all three of the forms of being operate, including the idea of being, the perception, both intellective and sensible, judgment to be applied through virtue to being. Logic, as an art of reflection develops in an ordered way the orders of reflection, which include the orders of affection, of intellection, of volition, of cognition, and of reflection-judgment.

> Considering, in a synthesistic perspective and from the standpoint of the primality of the moral form of being, Logic as a habit and art of reasoning perfected by those who have learned the science of logic, it is possible to arrive at the specification through which Rosmini sets out the principle of Moral Logic, which he defines thus: 160. When then, in a given state or act of man, will there be moral good? And on the contrary, when will there be evil? What rules will find us making a right judgment about it? First, there is a general rule which includes all the others, and which is like the *commencement of moral logic*; it is the following. *The moral good results from the union of three elements, will, norm, relationship. If only one of these elements is missing, the moral order cannot come true; there can be neither good nor evil. Therefore: the moral order will have to be judged to exist, when it will be ascertained that all three of those elements are found in the fact: then the moral good will have to be judged to exist, when the relationship between the will and the law is one of conformity: then he will have to judge that there is moral evil when the relationship between the will and the law is one of dissimilarity.*[26]

Where does the connection between logic, the principle of moral logic, and method lie? Precisely in the relationship between the will and the law/norm, inasmuch as it is an element of both the principle of moral logic and of method as an order conferred on the various mental operations finalized in the efficacy and the effectiveness of the reasoning. For Rosmini, as we have seen in particular in his definition of order, the connection-relationship is structural to order. These passages between logic, moral logic, and method lead us to methodology. Method, in fact, is *demonstrative* (which includes the *probative*, the *apologetic*, and the *polemical*), *inventive* (which includes

---

conduct oneself; the third book, of the first truth or of the Criterion, with which one tests the reasoning and its conclusions" (Rosmini, *Logica*, paras. 79–83).

26. "This principle is self-evident. But in order to apply it correctly, it is advisable to resort to some special rules, which teach us to verify the existence of each of those three elements. Let's see what they might be" (Rosmini, *Logica*, para. 161). From paras. 162 to 250 Rosmini illustrates these rules in detail.

the *deductive*, the *critical*, the *hermeneutic*, and more), and *didascalic* (which includes the *doctrinal*, insofar as one wants to make the truth known to the mind, and the educative since it intends to persuade the mind to adhere interiorly and profoundly to the known truth).

> 750. By the word Method we intend the order that is given to the various operations of the mind necessary to the purpose of reasoning, if it is to be achieved. From this definition we can see, first that the aim of the Method is not simply any intention of the man who reasons, but that which is *proper to* the reasoning itself and that always seeks the truth. Second, that the intention of reasoning can be considered in a more general or a more specific way, and however, if we want to classify the methods according to their aims, there are many, as many as the intentions of reasoning can possibly be, and the more or less general Methods, according to the more or less general intentions. Third, the aforementioned methods, the *demonstrative*, the *inventive* and the *didascalic*, are thus distinct from the more general intentions, and however each of them includes within it more special methods, since the demonstrative includes the probative, the apologetic and the polemical, according to whether it is intended to give direct proof of the truth, or to defend it against the objections, or disprove the errors. The inventive method includes the *experimental* and the *educative* according to whether the intention is to make the truth known to the mind, or to persuade and vividly imprint it on the soul. Fourth, if methods are to be classified not by their intent, but by the *different order* in which the operations of the mind from which they result occur, they admit other classifications, among which that of the *analytic* or *resolutive* and *synthetic* or compositional method is well-known. 751. Now, since there is no single reasoning that proceeds in a wholly analytical, or wholly synthetic way, the way that is synthesis and analysis operate equally in the Demonstrative method, in the Inventive and in the Didascalic methods; therefore, we will mention the Analysis and the Synthesis before dealing with these three special methods.[27]

---

27. Rosmini, *Logica*, paras. 750–51. A little further on we read: "Method of nature, principle and foundation of all methods 755. Now before coming to special methods, it is necessary to seek whether there is an eminent principle from which all the rules of those methods descend as consequences. And this lofty principle which presides over and directs every method with its light is certainly there, and it is none other than the very immutable nature of human understanding. This has, so to speak, a mechanism of its own: the laws of this mechanism are fixed, unalterable, and the mind cannot move except by taking those steps and following that path which is determined by said laws.

CONCLUSION

Furthermore, it should be noted in particular that also with regard to method Rosmini highlights the importance of the order and of the different orders, through which the modalities with which the operations of the mind are carried out are classified. The analytic-resolutive method in fact, is the classification of the orders of operations of the mind, which starts from the complex to arrive at the simple, it breaks down the ideas of the concepts into other elementary concepts; on the other hand, the synthetic or compositional method, which goes from the simple to the complex, is the one with which the parts or elements are united in the whole to which they belong, considering the whole composed by them both with respect to itself and with respect to the its parts.

What is the correlation between method and methodology? It can be said that methodology is a particular application of method, both analytical and synthetic, through which the child, and in general every person, through the "artistic" *action*, is enabled to correctly exercise method as an "order that it is given to the various operations of the mind necessary for the proper intention of reasoning, in order to achieve it."[28] This aptitude occurs precisely through the supreme principle of methodology which, as mentioned in a number of the contributions in this volume, Rosmini defines

---

So it is that the art of moving the human mind is reduced to helping it, so that it quickly and surely takes those steps that are preestablished by its nature, according to a fixed order. 756. And this art is the method considered as a habit: then the science of the method is reduced to determining and describing the natural order of these steps, which the mind must do successively according to its nature, to arrive at some intention that proposes and which is proper to it. There is therefore a method of nature, which is like an exemplar of the method of art. 757. Therefore, if man finds a suitable way to stimulate and help his mind to take its natural steps quickly and safely, he has the method. If then he stimulates or excites his mind to an order of operations different from that of nature, this kicks back, being impossible for it to obey the will and the ignorance of those who claim to guide it, and that man labors with vain thought as it envelops, and stumbles in errors and finds darkness instead of light. This is not a method, although man may believe it and call it such. And this sinister effect depends on the universal principle, that in all kinds of things man consumes himself in his own impotence whenever he presumes to dictate laws to nature, instead of following those imposed on him by the Creator. If the expert of the medical art puts all his study into knowing and docilely following the unalterable laws of the functions and operations of the healthy and sick living body, and takes advantage of them for the conservation or restoration of health, he works with skill and often attains his end. If by neglecting the study of those laws, through ignorance he opposes them, and flatters himself that he can do artificially what only natural forces, aided by a prudent regime, can do, the healing art no longer exists, and due to this lack of art human lives are sacrificed. It is a question of regulating the running waters so that they do not desert the fields. By operating according to the laws which govern the course of the waters, the end will be attained, otherwise, the waters deaf to your arbitrary prescriptions will cause greater damage" (Rosmini, *Logica*, paras. 755–57).

28. Rosmini, *Logica*, para. 750.

in his essential formulation as follows: "Represent to the mind of the child (and it can be said of man in general) primarily the objects that belong to the first order of insights; then the objects that belong to the second order of insights; then those of the third and so on."[29] Rosmini directly indicates the intellections and its orders; however, as has been shown, he does not give (order of) intellection without (order of) affection, just as the complete fruition of the orders of intellect is not synthetistically exercised without the affective intellection synthesizing from the relative order of the ideal form of being to the relative order of the moral form of being through will (and its order).

Additionally, in order to proceed from one order of intellection to another, the logical-methodological-"artistic" application of the method of the methodology requires that from the volition (and its relative order) derived from the intellection (and its relative order) reaches, through the passage of cognition, the synthesis completeness of the order in question through the reflection that produces the moral judgment. And it is precisely on this last passage that the relationship between the principle of moral logic and the supreme principle of methodology is evident.

The inclusion of the content obtained from this synthetic restitution of the survey on the relationship between method and methodology in Rosmini, "introduced" into the exemplary bibliography offered in the first passage of this conclusion, allows us to grasp *in nuce*, in particular, the inter-multi-disciplinary nature of the performative probed from a Rosminian perspective. From this point of view, in fact, Rosmini's *Philosophy of Politics (Filosofia della politica)*—in both its metaphysical[30] and in its theological[31] dimension, and, therefore, its *teletic* dimension—is the *medium*

---

29. Rosmini, RPMAE, paras. 78–80.

30. See Armellini, *Rosmini politico e storiografia*.

31. On the importance of theology, which is inherent in the fourth aim of philosophy, Rosmini expresses himself thus: "If the Theologian renounces philosophy, either he will have to leave out the deepest questions and leave science imperfect, or if he nevertheless wants to place himself within them, he will not succeed in resolving them, if not perhaps in a very imperfect or false way, hence he will be blamed by true philosophers, mocked by others, with discredit on the sacred discipline.... Philosophy then, by its very nature friend and faithful handmaid of Theology, if it is repudiated by the latter and driven away from its company, does not cease to live, especially in our times, which according to the sentence of Pope Pius VIII want men to be guided to goodness and to faith itself by reason; but unfortunately that will happen as it happens to a girl abandoned by her parents and guardians, who sells to those she meets her honesty and decorum, in order to eat. And what marvel that Philosophy, as we see everywhere, degenerates into that superb rationalism, which today aspires to be alone, banishing all revealed Theology? It is therefore desirable that thought be directed to recomposing and reestablishing a system of Philosophy, which true and sound and sufficiently complete, can be received

CONCLUSION

quid between ethics, pedagogy, and law (as well as the *medium quid* for economics), precisely in the overall sense—and can be systematized in the sense of the ethics of education—of Rosminian *teletics*:

> A special branch of ethics, which can be considered almost a summary of it, is that which deals with moral perfection. It will be articulated in a doctrine of the "human archetype" (*teletics*), a doctrine of the actions with which to conform to the archetype ("ethics"). . . . That discipline which is called here *teletics* "was never attempted"—Rosmini notes—"at least, not in a systematic manner."[32]

Part 4: Rosmini's Suspended Middle (and the Comparable Social Theory of Radical Orthodoxy's Suspended Middle): Possible Political Implications

The heart of Rosmini's theology, philosophy, and meta-politics is his theory of fulfillment, closely linked to his conception of *cognition*.[33] *Teletics*, which Rosmini did not fully and systematically explain, finds in performativity

---

by theological science as its auxiliary, and that these two branches of knowledge are reunited in that unity to which they were born, and in which they mutually benefit, both flourishing for the benefit of mankind" (Rosmini, "Degli studi dell'Autore," 40–43). The connection between philosophy and theology is realized through the relationship between religion and morals, as I indicated in the third chapter: "The communications that God makes to man both through external revelation and through internal grace; and the duties corresponding to them on the part of man, give increase and fulfillment to religion. Such is the notion of religion: now let us begin to see briefly what is the relationship that links morality together, whose principle is the recognition of truth in universal; and religion, whose principle is the recognition of the Supreme Being" (Rosmini, *Filosofia del diritto* [Philosophy of law], 1:161).

32. Pagani, "Rosmini e l'organismo," 150. For the most comprehensive illustration of these aspects, see my forthcoming publications.

33. The role of contentment and cognition and their relationship is exemplified in this passage from Rosmini, *T*, para. 9: "We must imagine all this universe, and especially all that happens in the human race, its multiplication, the division into different peoples, the dispersion of these peoples over the whole face of the earth, and subsequently their mutual relations, their wars, their emulations, and their friendships, the union of many into one, and the division of one into many, especially then the history of the Jewish people led by God with particular providence, to make it a little model of what was later to be all mankind. I say, we must imagine all this universe, both physical and moral, as a great and sacred book opened by God before the eyes of men and not written inside, if not all of questions and difficulties proposed to human intelligence for resolution, so that with the to investigate its resolutions and responses, it may increase in *knowledge* and *fulfillment*."

one of its possible points for reflection—in an original connection between politics, ethics, pedagogy, law, and economy—on the "human archetype" between philosophical anthropology and theological anthropology. For Rosmini, one of the key passages, in a negative sense, of *Storia dell'Etica* (which I dealt with in the introduction) was that in which an unwarranted overlapping/substitution of the political economy with (moral) philosophy occurred. Rosmini dealt with this aspect also when he described the aims of philosophy, in particular when he dealt with the third aim, which is to provide a philosophy that can be a solid basis for the sciences:

> Since therefore the bodily sense, which does not comprehend the truth, was proclaimed the only trustworthy teacher, the only faithful guide of men, and they (men) believed this even though it carried Contradiction within it, Morality, Law and everything else of an eternal nature perished together with the Truth in the opinion of the hallucinated and politics became an aleatory art, in which men gambled and bet themselves and their dearest things on the two dice of cunning and brute force. And according to this doctrine the new generations were educated in sensual wisdom. The voluptuousness of the senses became, as it had to become, the aim of the sciences and of the pedagogical art, and so that the latter, consuming substance, did not consume itself too quickly, the science of political economy was given as a counterweight (also this science in itself fine and very useful, thus corrupting itself), so that we Italians learned from Melchiorre Gioja to reduce our morals! Nor do we want to scrutinize here what instinct induced the sensists to preserve this name of Morals with such solicitude, when it seemed that the name of Political Economy should suffice for them, since, since there should remain only this single science, it seems that for single science has no need of two names.[34]

In this quotation, Rosmini's theoretical position is quite clear: morals and political economy are two distinct disciplines and this is due to the need to correct the error of sensism, according to which the bodily sense comprehended the truth, an error of sensism that attributes to political economics that which is proper to morality. For Rosmini, in fact, it is not the bodily sense (which has its original structure in the *affection*) that comprehends the truth, but rather the *intellection* which, through abstraction, synthesizes with the *affection* and with the respective orders, and also synthesizes with the *will*, the *cognition*, and the *reflection-judgment* (Rosmini distinguished, within the *practical reason*, the faculty to abstract and the faculty to think).

34. Rosmini, "Degli studi dell'Autore," para. 15.

CONCLUSION

The synthesism within synthesism that also, and in particular in this curatorship, has been explored in its epistemological-pedagogical foundation, with specific attention for the *affection* of *cognition*, could constitute a valid speculative structure containing *in nuce* the implicit and possible elaboration of an ontoprismatic[35] theory of the performative, through which, in fact, Rosmini saw sensism deconstructed and reconstructed *antelitteram*, thanks to the interaction between his theory of fulfillment and his original theoresis and epistemology on and of *cognition* (and its orders) which, through the focus on *affection* (and its orders) can be considered the fulcrum of the "synthesism within the synthesism" of Rosmini's methodology (and of his method).

Both the pluri-disciplinary vastness of Rosmini's thought and the complexity of the scientific operation of effectively "transposing" Rosmini's thought (within and beyond the "Rosminian question") necessarily mean that such an enterprise can only be successfully carried out through research conducted symphonically by a range of multidisciplinary experts. The aim of the conference—of which the present curatorship is a restitution relating to the interdisciplinary perspectives on Rosmini's methodology between philosophy, theology, and pedagogy, starting from the ethics of education—was to contribute to developing precisely this perspective of work and research.

The theory of (anti-perfectionistic) fulfillment in Rosmini focuses on the synthesistic interaction of the three societies: the domestic-parental society, the civil society, and the ecclesial society. This part of the volume highlights these aspects from multiple points of view. Should the desired dialogue between Rosmini's thought and the (social theory of) radical orthodoxy come about, the focus could be the comparison between the theory of (anti-perfectionistic) fulfillment of, and in, the three societies identified by Rosmini and ecclesiology as social theology in Milbank and in the radical orthodoxy movement.

Part 5 Rosmini's Suspended Middle (and the Comparable Social Theory of Radical Orthodoxy's Suspended Middle): Possible Juridical Implications

Furthermore, in the research I have carried out, I have had the opportunity to apply multiple scientific registers in an inter- and trans-disciplinary way, including the delineation of an unprecedented epistemological interaction

---

35. On ontoprismatism in Rosmini see Tadini, "Rosmini e nuova metafisica."

between the historical-cultural method and the analysis of the corpora. Indeed, in the light of the centrality of the theme of language, even theological, in Rosmini's thought it emerged that the interaction that he outlines epistemologically between the philosophical sciences, the pedagogical sciences, the juridical sciences, the political sciences, and the theological sciences determines, also with regard to the specific content of each of these disciplines, the need for inter- and transdisciplinary insights. In other words, in order to understand what ethics and education represent for Rosmini, it is necessary, for example, to consider in his philosophy of law (both as a work and as a discipline) the relationship between the discipline and ethics itself, just as (always in the philosophy of law) it is necessary to carry out the same operation with regard to the conception and definition of education. Likewise, always among the results of the research I previously carried out, it is necessary to take up another acquisition achieved and corroborated in Rosmini's research: that is Rosmini's attention to language, and his original linguistic elaboration and production needs to be suitably interpreted in the light of the fact that the Italian in which he writes is not our contemporary language, but that of the scholars of his time. On the other hand, it was Alessandro Manzoni, a close friend of Rosmini and a great admirer of his all-round genius, and a writer who with his work contributed in a decisive way to give life to current Italian, who urged him to use an Italian closer to his own literary style.[36]

The philosophical value of the application of digital technologies to the linguistic analysis of Rosmini's thought proves fruitful precisely on the theme of the ethics of education (just as it has already shown itself useful with regard to legal pedagogy), as it is in this philosophical theme that the references and epistemological connections between philosophy itself and pedagogy, law, politics and theology are significant.[37] Moreover, these

36. It is necessary to enter the language used by Rosmini to understand his thought but, at the same time, it is difficult, both for the concepts expressed, that his linguistic creativity allows him to express in an original and brilliant way, and for the precise lexical and stylistic choices. However, once the considerable initial obstacle has been overcome, the reader can realize for himself the fruitfulness of Rosmini's linguistic choices and the reasons for his choice not to fully accept the exhortation of his friend Manzoni. On the question of the language used, see Brugiatelli, *Problema filosofico del linguaggio*, and Muscherà, *Manzoni filosofo*; on the friendship between Rosmini and Manzoni, which produced a fruitful exchange of letters, the correspondence between the two collected and annotated by Bonola: *Carteggio*. The permanent tension that is created in particular on the theme of language between Rosmini and Manzoni is particularly interesting even today and will stimulate insights, unprecedented understandings and re-understandings of Rosmini's thought, also with the aim of understanding it faithfully and correctly and of creatively placing it in this sense in dialogue with contemporary ideas, in this case philosophical.

37. I analyzed the *corpora*, with historical-cultural comparison in Bellelli, *Percorsi*

references and connections can only be grasped once the connections of meanings having terminologically different signifiers in Rosmini's work has been identified. Rosmini distinguishes ethics, seen as a science of the honest good, from morality, seen as a triadic-Trinitarian synthesis relationship of good (the "mystical kiss") with an intelligent nature that wants it. In this sense, the orders of reflection—and particularly the second order of reflection, proper to a speculative judgment on the morality of the practical judgment which constitutes the rise of the reflected moral conscience—are generative of the formation of human rights.

One of the most effectively brief and descriptive passages of the generative dynamic of the formation of human rights is the following.

> Classification of the rights according to the order of reflection of the human mind. 1005. Primarily it is necessary to distinguish the *first order rights*, that is the ones that man acquires with the use of his *natural freedom*, and not with the acquired, that is not with the exercise of another right already acquired. Thus the occupation of an unoccupied piece of land occurs with an act of *natural freedom*, which does not consider any other previously acquired right. 1006. Next come the *second order rights*, that is those which are acquired without first order rights having been already formed. For example, I cannot acquire lien on movable or immovable property unless there is an owner of that property who grants me lien; this owner must be in possession of a previous right of ownership, a first order right with respect to the lien that I purchase. 1007. *Third order rights* then follow, that is rights that require the existence of second order rights. Such would be the right that the owner of the property would acquire if I unduly sold or destroyed the property; the right of compensation, which presupposes the right of lien before it, just as the right of lien presupposes the right of ownership of the property in question. 1008. It is clear that the various orders of right do not end here, and that there can be fourth or fifth orders, and even more if wished, and that all these orders must be based on the same formula, which says: Any right belongs to a higher order than those rights on which it is founded, and which are the condition of its existence. 1009. This is the hierarchy of human rights: and has its reason in the limited nature of human activity, which with its acts modifies itself, and grows, and takes advantage of its previous acts to make new ones. 1010 It has its reason mainly in the special human activity of the intelligence

storici, and in the forthcoming monograph on *juridical pedagogy* from the perspective of philosophy of law.

which, subject to a similar law, likewise performs acts that are distributed in as many orders, which we call *orders of reflection*. (2) 1011. Now, the distribution of the rights according to the hierarchy of said orders of reflection is not a useless thing: it is rather a very useful classification. Anyone who begins to write a philosophical history of rights will see the truth of this.[38]

Since for Rosmini the person is a a right subsisting in law, the formation of these rights is the formation of the person and their dignity: in Rosmini's theory, the centrality of the orders of reflection is crucial for understanding the ethical value of the formation of rights. Rosmini's *ethics of education* (and the *integrated theory of human dignity and juridical pedagogy* linked to it) is based on the original conception of the relationship between science and honest good that is ethics and philosophy of law, a relationship that turns on his conception of freedom.

In this sense it is necessary to avoid falling into the trap of thinking that Rosmini's philosophy of law depends in a negative and unfavorable sense on his moral philosophy: for Rosmini the law is, to all intents and purposes, independent and constitutes a discipline with its own criteria and epistemological canons, just as his moral philosophy is among the most successful moral philosophies that reject and deny every form of moralism, including that religiously connoted. The interaction between Rosmini's philosophy of law and moral philosophy, which turns on his idea of freedom, conceives both disciplines as an exercise of freedom and of liberties (in their respective orders).

The origin of law and rights in Rosmini's thought is generated by the orders of reflection as illustrated in the aforementioned "synthesism within and of synthesism." This is the juridical declination of Rosmini's *suspended middle* consisting in the synthesized consideration of the *moral form of being*. The relationship between law and right, in the multidisciplinary consideration of Rosmini's *Philosophy of Law*, is recognized as co-original. Expressly Rosmini—with Vico—argues and effectively maintains that respect for the genesis and orderly development of the orders of reflection makes it possible to clearly distinguish false rights *from* true rights. This perspective allows us to identify the focus on the desirable development of dialogue and comparison in particular between Rosmini's philosophical-legal thought and the (*social theory* of) radical orthodoxy: the comparison—in the perspective of *juridical pedagogy as juridical discipline*—between these two aspects: (1) Rosmini's genesis and development, in the perspective of the deontology of the

---

38. Rosmini, *Filosofia del diritto* 2, paras. 1005–11. I already dealt with this topic in Bellelli, *Importanza degli ordini*.

foundation of P. Sequeri and the legal aesthetics of P. Heritier, of the orders of reflection—in the "synthesism in and of synthesism"—as constitutive both of the (original metaphysical-affective-symbolic structure of) consciousness (believer) and of law and rights; (2) Milbank perspectives of these arguments starting from his *Revisionist Account of Natural Law and Natural Right* and *On the Division of Rights* (including his *Against Human Rights: Liberty in the Western Tradition*).

Bibliography

Armellini, Paolo. *Rosmini politico e la storiografia del Novecento*. Rome: Aracne, 2008.

Bellelli, Fernando. *Cristocentrismo e storia. L'uso dell'analogia nella cristologia di H. U. von Balthasar*. Monographic issue of *Divus Thomas* 1 (2008).

———. "L'importanza degli ordini di intellezione e degli ordini di riflessione nella pedagogia rosminiana: analisi storico-culturale di un vuoto della letteratura critica." *Rivista di Storia dell'Educazione* 1 (2020) 85–99.

———. *Percorsi storici della pedagogia giuridica. Vico, Rosmini e la* dignitas hominis. Rome: Aracne, 2020.

———. "Rosmini e Blondel interpreti di Aristotele." *Rosmini Studies* 5 (2018) 141–58.

Bergamaschi, Cirillo, ed. *Grande dizionario antologico del pensiero di Antonio Rosmini*. 4 vols. Rome: Città Nuova, 2001.

Bonola, Giulio, ed. *Carteggio tra Alessandro Manzoni e Antonio Rosmini*. Stresa, It.: Rosminiane Sodalitas, 1996.

Brugiatelli, Vereno. *Il problema filosofico del linguaggio in Antonio Rosmini*. Bologna: EDB, 2000.

Canu, Giammaria. *Pensare la fede nell'orizzonte della salvezza. Una teologia fondamentale ispirata ad Antonio Rosmini*. Rome: Città Nuova, 2020.

La Via, Vincenzo. *Coscienza e libertà. Rosmini e l'assoluto realismo*. Edited by Biagio G. Muscherà. Vol. 1 of *Saggi rosminiani e altri scritti*. Milan: Mimesis, 2020.

Muscherà, Biagio. *Manzoni filosofo: l'invenzione della parola. In dialogo con Antonio Rosmini*. Milan: Jaca, 2019.

Pagani, Paolo. "Rosmini e l'organismo delle scienze." In *Profezia e attualità di Antonio Rosmini*, edited by Fernando Bellelli and Giovanna Gabbi, 123–77. Stresa: Rosminiane Sodalitas, 2016.

Rosmini, Antonio. *Antropologia soprannaturale*. Edited by Umberto Muratore. 2 vols. ENC 39–40. Rome: Città Nuova, 1983.

———. *Compendio di etica e breve storia di essa*. Edited by Maria Manganelli. ENC 29. Rome: Città Nuova, 1998.

———. "Degli studi dell'Autore." In *Introduzione alla filosofia*, edited by Pier P. Ottonello, ENC 2, 13–194. Rome: Città Nuova, 1979.

———. *Del divino nella natura*. Edited by Pier P. Ottonello. ENC 20. Rome: Città Nuova, 1991.

———. "Del principio supremo della Metodica." In *Scritti pedagogici*, edited by Fernando Bellelli, ENC 32, 37–364. Rome: Città Nuova, 2019.

———. *Filosofia del diritto*. Edited by Michele Nicoletti and Francesco Ghia. 4 vols. ENC 27, 27/A, 28, 28/A. Rome: Città Nuova, 2013.

———. *Frammenti di una storia dell'empietà* [Fragments of a history of impiety]. Edited by Samuele F. Tadini. ENC 55. Rome: Città Nuova, 2019.

———. "Frammento." In *Filosofia del diritto*, edited by Michele Nicoletti and Francesco Ghia, ENC 28/A, 305–12. Rome: Città Nuova, 2015.

———. *Logica*. Edited by Vincenzo Sala. ENC 8. Rome: Città Nuova, 1984.

———. *Nuovo Saggio sull'origine delle idee*. Edited by Gaetano Messina. 3 vols. ENC 3–5. Rome: Città Nuova, 2003–2004.

———. *Saggio storico critico sulle categorie*. Edited by Pier P. Ottonello. ENC 19. Rome: Città Nuova, 1997.

———. "Storia comparativa e critica de' sistemi intorno al principio della morale." In *Principi della scienza morale*, edited by Umberto Muratore, ENC 23, 161–459. Rome: Città Nuova, 1990.

———. *Storia dell'amore*. Edited by Alfeo Valle and Umberto Muratore. ENC 52. Rome: Città Nuova, 2002.

———. *Teodicea*. Edited by Umberto Muratore. ENC 22. Rome: Città Nuova, 1977.

———. *Teosofia*. Edited by Samuele F. Tadini. Milan: Bompiani, 2011.

Sequeri, Pierangelo. *La fede e la giustizia degli affetti. Teologia fondamentale della forma cristiana*. Siena: Cantagalli, 2020.

———. "Metafisica e ordine del senso." *Teologia* 36 (2011) 159–71.

Tadini, Samuele Francesco. "Rosmini e la nuova metafisica ontoprismatica: un dialogo possibile con l'ontologia analitica." In *Ontologia, fenomenologia e nuovo umanesimo. Rosmini ri-generativo*, edited by Fernando Bellelli and Emanuele Pili, 59–75. Rome: Città Nuova, 2016.

Afterword

A Rosminian Future?

It is a pleasure and honor to supply this afterword to such a stimulating and comprehensive set of essays concerning the thought of Antonio Rosmini.

It has often been asked who might be the nearest to the equivalent of a modern Aquinas. As the authors of these essays tend to suggest, Rosmini's claim is arguably the strongest. He was, of course, actually a Catholic, unlike other claimants to that title; he was a saint and activist as well as a scholar, and his written output was on a scale of prodigality to rival if not surpass that of his scholastic forebears: touching on almost every aspect of philosophy and theology and extending beyond that to politics, law, history, logic and mathematics. He also remains more obviously within the scope of classic Christian orthodoxy than other great modern Christian synthesisers like Hegel, Schelling, and Soloviev.

Much more fundamentally, he contrived to take account of what might be valid in modernity without in any way betraying Christian tradition, but rather by deepening its fundamental insights with respect to both metaphysics and political understanding.

It is surely no accident that it was an Italian who managed to do this, since the stance of Italy and perhaps the Latin world in general is significantly different from that of the European north that has been more culturally dominant in modern times (with France naturally caught somewhere in the middle). Italy was the first country to foreshadow the modern in the mode of Renaissance humanism, and yet this current itself remained rooted in the classical and medieval past. Often its mode of later "Enlightenment" remained in continuity with this legacy and accordingly less departed from a Christian horizon.

At times, this can make it appear to northerners that we are dealing with a strange hybridity of the traditional and the modern, as in the case of the sociohistorical thought of Giambattista Vico or the economic thought of Antonio Genovesi; and yet from a different vantage the synthesizing and mediating character of much Italian thought can tend to challenge oversharp antitheses between past and present and to insist on more fundamental continuities that have to do with a sustained Western inheritance. The idea that modern subjectivist, expressivist, and liberal thought has really escaped this purview can then appear as an illusion, especially when this thought is more distilled, sifted, and tempered.

This is not at all to say that the typical mark of Italian thought is compromise: on the contrary, from Bruno to Agamben it often exhibits a startling originality that is nonetheless perhaps precisely to do with its unexpected fusions of the deeply buried with the novel and arriving.

This is especially true of Rosmini, as the authors of this collection so well bring out. Faced with modern empiricism, rationalism, and idealism, Rosmini tended to shift subjective foundationalism towards a relational personalism and a phenomenological intentionality more compatible with Christian realism, but also moving the latter further away from an impersonal residue of paganism. He also realized the degree to which a "turn to the subject" had always been implied by a synthesizing philosophy that refuses either a naturalistic monism or a naturalistic atomism. The mixture of the one and the many, upon which his gaze remained always fixed, is not accessible to us outside the example of personal and subjective judgment.

For this reason, Rosmini was able patiently to learn from the modern epistemological focus and yet to realize that this focus itself is not alien to the most fundamental ontological outlook. Being that is both unified and plural is naturally also Being that contains both an ineffably real and an expressively ideal dimension, assuming the existence of spiritual creatures.

Thus, for Rosmini, we need to advance beyond a perspective that seeks to make either the objectively real or the subjectively ideal all-governing. They can be united only by pragmatic action, and yet he resists pragmatism as a third philosophy also. Instead, he insists that reality is always a triple interplay between the real, the ideal, and the performative. None of these three powers immanently prevails over the others, because all are rooted in transcendence. Yet thanks to the Christian revelation we can understand even this transcendence not as a unity that ultimately obliterates the pertinence of the personal, but itself as a perfectly realized triadicity, an infinite *perichoresis* of the three ontological potencies.

In this manner Rosmini's response to the modern was actually to increase the Christian character of philosophy as such. With extraordinary ingenuity he suggested that only the Trinitarian outlook is able to give a rigorous account of just how Being is divisible if, unlike a genus, it can only ever add further modes of existence to itself, always thereby threatening either monism or ontological disintegration. But the revelation of the Trinity suggests that infinite Being as such is ordered and relational and so in a certain sense pre-distributed as both including and included, or containing and contained. More finite and participatory modes of this order then become imaginable.

Not only is this clue to the resolution of our natural perplexity itself revealed, it is also the case, as the above authors suggest, that all our active participations in the divine triune life, including our daily spontaneity and intellectual speculations, besides our moral actions, involve both the anticipation and the actual descent of grace, because the integrating and beautiful completion of any single thing, deed, or relation is already a spiritual return to God. Without this integrating gratuity it would be lacking in truth.

Thus, indeed, Rosmini's Trinitarian ontology occupies a "middle" that is suspended between a natural ground that we cannot adequately fathom and a supernatural height we cannot adequately reach. It is thereby a philosophy of faith, but also all the more rigorously one of reason, as Rosmini's astonishing resolution of so many inherited aporias demonstrates.

The synthesizing third moment of action, which is also the descent of grace, pertains in all three realms of the existential, the speculative, and the ethical, ensuring that truth is always available only through love. All the same, the centrality of action, upon which this volume again and again insists, implies that moral, spiritual, legal, and political performance are less for Rosmini the application of theory than they are its completion in practice. In a sense it is the social life of the polity and above all that of the church that is his fulfilled metaphysics, very much in keeping with the mystic civility so characteristic of Italian humanist tradition.

In the case of politics and jurisprudence, just as he qualified but integrated epistemology, so he qualified but integrated liberalism. The liberty of the individual must be paramount, but this cannot be divorced from relationality or a working social consensus as to virtue. Rosmini's constitutionalism was indeed less a formal one mediating between random differences than a substantive and even Trinitarian one insisting on a balance between inherited situational real factors, ideal aspiration, and their practical mingling and integration.

Equivalently, the real sovereign and forceful political power had to be "an-archically" subject to ideal law, just as the divine Father, the ultimate origin, is still exhaustively the expression of the Son as Logos. The human spiritual task, participating in that of the Holy Spirit, is to interpret and apply the law with local appropriateness and effective resolution.

In politics then, Rosmini's liberalism involved a relational constitutionalism and not a dogmatic insistence on the same pattern of formal democracy for everyone in all circumstances—for all that he was an admirer of the work of the American founders. Everywhere we need effective unification, wise advice, and the consent of the governed, besides reasonable individual freedom, but just how this is to be achieved can validly vary.

There may be much wisdom here for us today, as we now tend to oscillate between an over-dogmatic and precise liberalism on the one hand and a resigned and essentially defeated "realism" on the other. Rosmini the legal, political, and ecclesial thinker would tend to remind us that we cannot, as Christians, abandon as henceforwards globally irrelevant a deeper Christian personalist legacy, older than Enlightenment, however precarious it may have become.

The same personalism, in the mode of Trinitarian ontology, suggests that in the future we need to respond to secularity with a more specifically Christian philosophy that will also have a Christological dimension. Yet curiously or not, this more Christian philosophy incorporates more than in the past the Renaissance-rooted dimension of modernity that insists upon the place of unique individual self-expression and shifting patterns of negotiated relationality and perspective.

In complex but surely successful ways that owe something to Neoplatonism as well as to Christian thought, Rosmini showed that the most fundamental categories of reality involve a conscious, subjective, and committed dimension. Rather like F. W. J. Schelling, he was able to outflank Kant (a thinker perhaps alien to the inherited Italian focus on the cosmos as well as the city) by insisting that the subjective is not so much a barrier in the face of the infinitely real as the key to it, since itself incorporated within it.

It is clear that Rosmini refused Hegel's more rationalistic version of this insight, but questions remains as to his proximity to Schelling and to Schelling's Russian heirs like Soloviev. Rosmini's three powers are surely akin to those of Schelling, who was less an idealist than a kind of "spiritual realist" who wished to balance and integrate the real and the ideal through action, which in his case he took to be most of all the action of art. And Rosmini's own construal of their inextricable relational inter-involvement in terms of the grammatical model of the predication of a subject by an object and their judged fusion is deeply akin to intuitions already present in Schelling but taken much further by the Russians.

All these thinkers seem now to belong to our twenty-first-century future as we more and more realize, in the face of the crisis of our human relation with nature, that the anti-metaphysical bias of twentieth-century thought was only *one* possible development of nineteenth-century intimations and not really the most revolutionary ones. After all, the practitioners of artistic modernism were often much more interested in Bradley, Bergson, and Florenskij than they were in Heidegger, Frege, or Wittgenstein.

Yet in comparison with kindred nineteenth-century spirits, some questions arise in relation to Rosmini: the future may be his, but he shares the future also with others. Notably, his sense that we fully encounter Being as such existentially rather than intellectually was deficient, and his account of our conscious grasp of "ideal being" was too aprioristic. Superior here was Schelling's sense that our intellectual life is just as historical, contingent, and emergent as that of "real" nature, with the consequence that the arrival of objective truth depends all the more upon the third moment of action—surely Rosmini's most interesting and real intentional thrust.

In this context we can wonder whether there was some validity to the Catholic Vincenzo Gioberti's contemporary critique of Rosmini's "ideal being" and insistence, rather like Eckhart, that Being itself is God in whom we directly participate. It has often, right up to the present, been objected that Gioberti is thereby the more dangerously "ontologist" a thinker, such that we can see Rosmini's ideal being as inserting a cautious "phenomenological" barrier between us and God, thereby sustaining more sense of an independent "pure nature" and of the sheer extrinsic gratuity of revelation.

But as for, I think, the majority report of the above authors, this tends to dilute the radical synthesizing of Rosmini's "suspended middle," which the core of his Trinitarian ontology sustains, in many ways overriding the dubiously aprioristic account of ideal being. The latter concurs with his endorsement of a Scotist univocity of being and yet *just that* tends to encourage the wrong sort of "ontologism" in the sense of suggesting an identical divine and human access to absolute truths and excellencies.

The same Scotism in Rosmini goes along with a much more deliberative and voluntarist account of the divine distribution of Being, which threatens to render the spontaneous and participative Trinitarian account of this distribution redundant. And yet, as the authors here say, it is manifestly obvious that Rosmini does not really intend such a Scotist reductionism, if he has devoted so many thousands of words to his Trinitarian metaphysical innovations.

There is a sense in which Gioberti's mode of ontologism, though more directly radical, is also more orthodox. We do indeed always live and see and act only in God, but in a partial, analogical, and anagogical manner that is true to Augustine's *real* doctrine of illumination, which did not deny sensory mediation and which is echoed by Aquinas. This same mode of ontologism is, I submit, also more interestingly phenomenological, insofar as our experience is always engaged in speculation and this experience can never be complete or "reduced" as it can be in the Scotist perspective, which was essentially retained by Husserl and Heidegger.

The more that the Scotist, aprioristic, and epistemological residue is removed from Rosmini therefore, the more, as already said, everything comes to depend upon the third moment of engaged action, for which there are no pre-written rules. It is for this reason that Giovanni Gentile was probably right to say that Gioberti had a stronger modern sense of natural and human action as actually creative than did Rosmini. Nonetheless, this insight is not essentially alien to his Trinitarian ontology, but rather required by it: for the third, judging moment of affirming a predication or proposition by or for (or by and for) a subject is necessarily creative: it is *adding* the unanticipated and so altogether new, just as it is both making and disclosing a new *linkage,* a new bond, hitherto unknown to the real.

So the human future, if there is to be one, belongs to Rosmini, if also to other kindred thinkers. But perhaps to Rosmini most of all, since he elaborated in the most detail a "grammatical" Trinitarian ontology in its inseparable theoretical and practical dimensions.

JOHN MILBANK
Southwell, Nottinghamshire, United Kingdom

Index

Abbruzzese, William, 32, 412, 417n17
Abécassis, Éliette, 84n36
Adler, Alfred, 222n13
Adorno, Theodor W., 108n5, 177
Agamben, Giorgio, 306, 306n12, 307n13, 458
Agar, Guglielmo, 422
Ales Bello, Angela, 93, 93n4, 93n5, 96, 96n12, 243n45, 247n60
Alighieri, Dante, 151, 305
Anders, Günther, 177, 177n47
Andreini, Alessandro, 31, 402
Angelini, Giuseppe, 111n13
Anselm of Aosta, 28, 50, 51, 107
Antonelli, Maria T., 421n35
Aporti, Ferrante, 192
Aquinas, Thomas, 204n17
Archer, Margareth S., 108n8
Arendt, Hanna, 202n9
Areopagita, Dionigi, 385
Argenio, Antonella, 108n6
Aristotle, 17n34, 279, 282, 287, 295, 392n45
Armellini, Paolo, 277n15, 448n30
Atticus, 368
Augé, Marc, 170n12
Augustine (Agostino d'Ippona or Aurelio Agostino), 18n34, 23, 24, 27n48, 92, 119, 146, 162n53, 173, 176, 178, 199, 199n3, 201, 201n8, 202, 202n10, 203n13, 204, 205, 205nn20–21, 206, 207, 207nn26–27, 208, 208n31, 209, 209nn32–34, 282, 284, 294, 328, 364, 365, 380, 388n30, 461

Bachelard, Gaston, 84n36
Badiou, Alain, 105n2
Baggio, Alberto, 108n7, 162n51
Baggio, Antonio M., 419n25
Balthasar, Hans Urs von, 21, 105n1, 177, 382, 385, 432
Barth, Karl, 120
Barzaghi, Guiseppe, 5n6, 6, 6n8, 15, 19n37
Bataille, Georges, 105n2
Bateson, Gregory, 214n5, 230n22
Battaglia, Felice, 304, 349, 354, 354n29, 355, 355n30
Bearzot, Cinzia, 109n9
Beccaria, Cesare, 305
Bellelli, Fernando, 1nn1–2, 9nn14–15, 13n28, 32n56, 93n3, 96, 96n13, 107n4, 158n32, 199n1, 218n9, 220n10, 230n23, 252, 252n1, 253nn3–6, 253nn8–9, 254n11, 256n15, 256n17, 257n20, 263n34, 264n37, 266n44, 276, 346n4, 347n4, 349n8, 350n14, 351n15, 352, 352n18, 352nn20–21, 357, 358, 358n45, 359n46, 386n27, 413n4, 428, 428n1, 431n7, 443n24, 452n37, 454n38

INDEX

Benedict XVI, Pope (Ratzinger, Joseph/ Benedetto), 120, 120n12, 129, 129nn34–35, 130, 130nn36–37, 130n39, 136, 137n11, 397, 398
Benetollo, Ottorino V., 199n4
Bennardo, Michele, 203n13
Bergamaschi, Cirillo, 2n3, 3n3, 214n6, 431n9
Bergonzoni, Filippo, 29n51
Bergson, Henri, 92, 461
Bernanos, Georges, 422n37
Bernays, Paul, 75
Berti, Domenico, 177, 183
Beschin, Giuseppe, 158, 158n29, 246n57
Biven, Lucy, 357n39
Blondel, Maurice, 30n52, 126, 126n28, 443n24
Bobbio, Norberto, 281n30
Böckenförde, Ernst-W., 353, 353n24
Boethius, 156
Bollnow, Otto, 111n12
Bombelli, Giovanni, 349n9, 354n28
Bonafede, Giulio, 17n34
Bonaventura, 17n34, 385, 385n23, 390, 390n37
Bonhoeffer, Dietrich, 143, 173, 173n27
Bonola, Giulio, 452n36
Borriello, Luigi, 380n3, 385, 385nn18–22, 385n24, 386n25
Bosco, Giovanni, 195, 196, 389
Bozzetti, Giuseppe, 321, 321n3, 322, 322nn4–6, 391, 392, 392nn42–43
Bradley, Francis Herbert, 461
Brancaforte, Antonio, 14n29, 77n10, 78, 78nn13–14, 82, 82n29
Brugiatelli, Vereno, 157n27, 452n36
Brunello, Bruno, 53n49
Bruno, Giordano, 305, 309, 458
Bruzzone, Daniele, 221n12
Buganza, Jacob, 24, 198, 201n7
Buroni, Giuseppe, 76n7, 82, 82n27
Byung-chul Han, 170n9

Cacciari, Massimo, 109n9
Cady Stanton, Elizabeth, 84n35
Callini, Daniele, 84n36

Campanella, Tommaso, 305, 309
Campanini, Giorgio, 24n46
Canetti, Elias, 169
Canobbio, Giacomo, 349n9
Cantone, Raffaele, 109n9
Cantor, Georg, 75
Canu, Giammaria, 23, 166, 171n18, 174n30, 435n14
Canullo, Carla, 213n4
Capelle-Dumont, Philippe, 128n31
Capograssi, Giuseppe, 274, 275n3, 284, 284n42, 322, 323n7, 346, 346n3, 347, 347nn4–5, 348n6, 349, 350, 350n13
Carleo, Alessandro, 349n11
Carlini, Armando, 304
Cartabia, Marta, 109n9
Carulli, Antonio, 84n36
Casalino, Giandomenico, 84n36
Castelli, Enrico, 277, 299n2
Cat, Philip, 80, 80n21
Catuogno, Lorena, 131n40, 142n33, 156n16
Cavazza, Gianpietro, 108n8
Cayré, Fulberto, 380, 381n5
Cerutti, Maria Geltrude, 320, 415
Chiassoni, Pierluigi, 353n23
Chiusano, Italo A., 410
Chomsky, Noam, 266n41
Cicero, 282, 295, 368
Cioffi, Mario, 30, 364, 365n2, 366n13, 367n25, 368n26, 369n38, 370n50, 375n82
Claverini, Corrado, 299n1
Cleary, Denis, 273, 276, 276n13
Clement of Alexandria, 282, 388n30
Coccia, Emanuele, 84n36
Coda, Piero, 21, 22, 23, 125n26, 133, 146n49, 360, 361n52, 361n53
Cole, Thomas, 293
Collin, Dominique, 174, 408n17
Colombo, Giacomo, 326n15
Columba, Saint, 390, 390n35
Comi, Giuseppe, 349n9, 360n51
Congar, Yves M. J., 22, 84n35, 141
Corradetti, Daniele, 84n36
Cotta, Sergio, 276, 276n7
Couture, Thomas, 293

Cravero, Domenico, 25, 212, 231n23
Croce, Benedetto, 304, 305
Cubeddu, Raimondo, 276n14
Cullmann, Oscar, 84n35
Cuoco, Vincenzo, 305
Cusinato, Guido, 105n1, 110n11, 227n20
Cyril of Alessandria, 388n30

Da Vinci, Leonardo, 305
D'Addio, Mario, 276, 276n9, 276nn11–12
D'Agostino, Francesco, 111n13
Damasio, Antonio, 357n36, 357n41
Dante, 151, 305
Darwin, Charles, 254n10
Davidson, Thomas, 2n3
De Giorgi, Fulvio, 23, 23n45, 24, 26n48, 30n52, 31, 32, 32n55, 139, 140n26, 147n51, 183, 199n4, 253n5, 256n15, 322, 323, 323nn7–8, 357, 358n43, 395, 395n58, 396, 396nn59–65, 398nn68–69, 403n3, 406n13, 417n15, 419n23
De Lubac, Henri, 22, 126, 126n28, 432
De Lucia, Paolo, 301n4, 304n8, 314n23, 351n16
De Luise, Fulvia, 111n13
De Sanctis, Francesco, 305
De Sutter, Laurent, 84n36
de Tocqueville, Alexis, 26
Del Noce, Augusto, 305
Demandt, Alexander, 290n1
Demaria, Tommaso, 22, 22n44
Derrida, Jacques, 97, 97n15, 177
Descartes, René, 117
Di Bari, Cosimo, 266n43
Di Giovanni, Piero, 314, 314n23
Dionysius the Areopagite, 380
Dombrowski, Daniel A., 82n25
Donà, Massimo, 15, 22n43, 59
Donati, Pierpaolo, 108n8
Dossi, Michele, 30n53, 150, 150n1
Duns Scotus, 14, 17n34, 18n34
Dupuy, Jean-Pierre, 230n22
Dworkin, Ronald, 356n33

Eckhart, Meister, 461
Esposito, Roberto, 299, 299n1, 305, 306, 307n13, 308, 309, 309nn17–18, 310, 310nn19–20, 312, 314
Eusebi, Luciano, 109n9
Evain, François, 175n40
Evola, Julius, 84n36

Fabella, Virginia, 84n35
Fabro, Cornelio, 126, 127n30
Ferrara, Luca, 307n13
Ferrari, Massimo, 305n10, 307n14
Ferraris, Maurizio, 42n2, 45n19, 76n5
Ferronato, Marta, 26, 273, 274n2, 279n22
Fichte, Johann Gottlieb, 42
Filangieri, Gaetano, 314
Finnis, John, 355n31
Fizzotti, Eugenio, 221n12
Florenskij, Pavel, 461
Fornari, Pier L., 26n47
Forte, Bruno, 125, 126n27, 395, 395n56
Forti, Gabrio, 109n9
Fraisopi, Fausto, 76n5
Francesco, Pope (Francis, Pope), 21, 30n54, 129, 129n32, 133, 133nn1–2, 134, 134nn3–5, 135, 135nn6–8, 136nn9–10, 137, 137nn11–14, 138, 138nn16–19, 139, 139nn20–23, 139n25, 140, 140n28, 141, 141n29, 142, 142n32, 142n36, 144, 144n43, 145, 145n45, 146, 147, 147n50, 148n55, 175n35, 397, 398, 398n71, 405, 405n8
Frankl, Viktor Emil, 23, 25, 213, 213n2, 221–28, 221n12, 223nn15–16, 225nn17–18, 226n19, 229
Frege, Gottlob, 75, 461
Freud, Sigmund, 225, 253n10
Froebel, Friedrich, 190
Fromm, Erich, 105n2

Gabbi, Giovanna, 230n23, 253n9
Gadaleta, Ludovico A., 275n5
Galantino, Nunzio, 408n18
Galati, Domenico, 253n8

INDEX

Galilei, Galileo, 309
Gallo, Filippo, 354, 354nn26–27, 355
Galluzzi, Mario, 253n8
Galvani, Martina, 16n32, 25, 26n47, 93n3, 96n11, 234, 247n60, 263n34
Garin, Eugenio, 307, 307n14
Gennari, Mario, 264n35
Genovesi, Antonio, 314, 458
Gentile, Giovanni, 59, 63, 191, 301, 301n4, 304, 305, 307, 307n14, 309, 310, 310n20, 311, 311n21, 312, 462
Gentili, Dario, 305n11
Ghia, Francesco, 30n53, 277, 277n16
Ghigi, Nicoletta, 241n35, 243n47, 244, 244n49, 264, 265n38
Giammusso, Salvatore, 111n12
Giannini, Gianluca, 84n36
Giannini, Giorgio, 246n57
Gibbon, Edward, 289, 297
Gilbert, Paul, 213n4
Gilson, Étienne, 126, 126nn28–29
Gioberti, Vincenzo, 51, 303, 304, 304n9, 305, 308, 308n15, 309, 311, 312, 461, 462
Gioia (Gioja), Melchiorre, 321, 450
Giovetti, Paola, 221n12
Giroli, Pierluigi, 28, 319, 382, 382n7
Givone, Sergio, 84n36
Gödel, Kurt, 75
Goffi, Tullio, 417n15
Gogarten, Friedrich, 84n35
Gramsci, Antonio, 305
Grandis, Giancarlo, 221n11
Gray, Carlo, 53n49
Greco, Tommaso, 360n50
Gregory XVI, Pope, 300n3, 397
Guardini, Romano, 177
Gutiérrez, Gustavo, 84n35
Guzzo, Augusto, 304

Hayek, Friedrich A. von, 359n47
Hegel, Georg Wilhelm Friedrich, 42, 63, 92, 123, 225, 414, 457, 460
Heidegger, Martin, 92, 128, 128n31, 129n33, 168, 171n14, 173n28, 461, 462

Heim, Michael R., 84n36
Hemmerle, Klaus, 22, 125n26
Henry of Ghent, 18n34
Heraclitus, 63
Herbart, Johann Friedrich, 190, 192
Heritier, Paolo, 17, 19, 20, 29, 30, 111n13, 345, 349n10, 353n22, 354n28, 356n35, 455
Holste, Lukas, 320
Horkheimer, Max, 108n5
Husserl, Edmund, 91, 96, 96n13, 227n21, 241, 462

Ignatius of Loyola, 415n7
Incampo, Antonio, 84n36
Indellicato, Rosa, 199n2, 202n11, 202n12, 203n13
Irenaeus of Lyons, 146
Irti, Natalino, 109n9, 350n12

Jaja, Donato, 301
Jaspers, Karl, 168
Jerome, Saint, 293
John Paul I, Pope, 397
John Paul II, Pope, 130, 135, 138, 138n15, 397
John the Evangelist, 146
John XXIII, Pope, 397
Jungmann, Josef A., 84n35

Kant, Immanuel, 42, 301, 460
Kelsen, Hans, 353, 354, 361
Knitter, Paul F., 84n35
Kraus, Franz Xavier, 382
Krienke, Markus, 307n13
Krienke, Paul F., 76n5

La Via, Vincenzo, 14, 16, 16n30, 76n7, 77n10, 82, 82n28, 253n6, 443n24
Lacan, Jacques, 170n11, 414, 414n5
Lakeland, Paul, 84n35
Lanfranchi, Rachele, 183n1
Langella, Simona, 314n23
Lanza, Angelina, 380
Laprune, Ollé-, 30n52
Le Corbusier, Charles-Édouard Jeanneret, 169

466

INDEX

Lenti, Marina, 84n36
Lentiampa Shenge, Adrien, 111n13
Leo XIII, Pope, 115, 397
Leopardi, Giacomo, 305
Liermann, Christiane, 27, 289
Livy, 295
Locke, John, 26
Lonegran, Bernard, 131, 131n40
Lorizio, Giuseppe, 129n33, 173n26, 174, 174n34, 177, 326n14
Losacco, Luigi, 247n60
Luhmann, Niklas, 227n21, 228n21
Lukas, Elisabeth, 222n12
Luminais, Évariste-Vital, 293

Machiavelli, Niccoló, 285, 292, 305, 309
Macrobius, 295
Maine de Biran (François-Pierre-Gontier de Biran), 92
Makarenko, Anton, 191
Malusa, Luciano, 27, 28n49, 298, 299n2, 300n3, 302n6, 304nn8–9, 308n16, 314n23
Mamiani, Terenzio, 308, 308n16
Manganaro, Patrizia, 93n3
Mantovani, Mauro, 22n44
Manzoni, Alessandro, 32, 417, 452n36
Marchetto, Michele, 93n3
Marconi, Gianfreda, 199n1
Marianelli, Massimiliano, 160n40
Maritain, Jacques, 31
Martino, Marco, 161n48
Maslow, Abraham H., 227
Mastracchio, Francesca, 221n11
McFague, Sallie, 84n35
Melando Granados, Tomás I., 84n36
Melloni, Alberto, 405n9
Melville, Herman, 63
Mercadante, Francesco, 372n61
Merleau-Ponty, Maurice, 92
Metz, Johann B., 84n35
Milani, "Don" Lorenzo, 22, 196
Milbank, John, 10n19, 16, 17, 17n33, 18, 18n36, 428, 451, 455, 462
Mina di Sospiro, Guido, 84n36
Mondin, Battista, 76n5
Moltmann, Jürgen, 84n35
Montessori, Maria, 196

Morin, Edgar, 177, 213n3
Mounier, Emmanuel, 177, 177n46
Muratore, Umberto, 15, 41, 375n84, 420n29, 422n38
Muscherà, Biagio G., 266n42, 307n13, 452n36

Nadalini, Emanuele, 403n3, 406n13, 408n18
Nardin, Vito, 30, 31, 379, 390n36, 390n38
Naro, Massimo, 380
Necker de Saussure, Albertine-Adrienne, 186
Neglia, Alberto, 380
Neri, Filippo, 31
Newman, John Henry, 92, 135, 139, 146, 407–8, 407n15, 408n16
Nicolas of Cusa, 92
Nicoletti, Michele, 277, 277n16
Nietzsche, Friedrich, 105n2, 168, 174
Nobile, Mauro, 93n3
Nothomb, Amélie, 84n36
Nussbaum, Martha, 108n8

Oppy, Graham, 82n25
Orecchia, Rinaldo, 277, 277n18, 303n7
Origen of Alexandria, 423
Otto III, Pope, 410
Ottonello, Pier P., 199n3, 416n13

Pagani, Giambattista, 3n3, 398nn73–74, 416n11, 417n19
Pagani, Paolo, 449n32
Pagazzi, Giovanni C., 21n42
Paglia, Vincenzo, 109n9
Panero, Marco, 199n4
Pangallo, Mario, 253n8
Panksepp, Jack, 357, 357n39
Paoli, Francesco, 42, 185, 275, 390, 391n39, 398n72, 398n74, 416n11, 417n16
Pareyson, Luigi, 114, 177n48
Paris, Leonardo, 356, 357, 357n38, 357n40, 357n42
Parisi, Vincenzo, 307n13
Pascal, Blaise, 92, 177, 177n46, 178, 178n51

Paschal II, Pope, 409
Pasolini, Pier Paolo, 305
Paul, Saint, 29n52
Paul VI, Pope (Giovanni Battista Montini), 26n48, 29n52, 30n52, 31, 32, 135, 136, 141n30, 396, 397
Pazzaglia, Luciano, 417n15
Peratoner, Alberto, 16, 18, 89
Perniola, Mario, 105n2
Petrillo, Francesco, 346n2
Piaget, Jean, 265
Piemontese, Filippo, 351, 351n17
Pili, Emanuele, 22, 23, 93n3, 142n35, 150, 152n4, 153n9, 155n14, 157n25, 158n31, 162n53, 262n33, 263n34
Pillay, Gerald J., 139n24
Pirandello, Luigi, 63
Pius V, Pope, 393n47
Pius VII, Pope, 397
Pius VIII, Pope, 43, 83, 397, 448n31
Pius IX, Pope, 397, 398, 409
Plato, 5n5, 200, 201, 201n7, 282, 295
Plotinus, 123, 201, 201n7
Plutarch, 295
Polycarp of Smyrna, 146
Porcarelli, Andrea, 199n4
Porphyry, 201
Prandini, Riccardo, 108n8
Prenna, Lino, 199n1
Preziosi, Francesco, 230n23
Prini, Pietro, 351, 351n15
Procopius (Procopio), 294
Przywara, Erich, 94

Quacquarelli, Antonio, 320, 320n2, 394

Rahner, Karl, 84n35, 166n1, 384
Raschini, Maria Adelaide, 199n3, 393, 394
Ratzinger, Joseph. *See* Benedict XVI, Pope (Ratzinger, Joseph/Benedetto)
Ravasi, Gianfranco, 395, 395n57
Rawls, John, 130

Rebora, Clemente, 173n29, 379, 379nn1–2, 382, 384, 384n16, 396, 397n66
Renik, Salomon, 84n36
Repole, Roberto, 178, 178n49
Ricca, Mario, 351n15
Rich, Adrienne, 110n10
Ricoeur, Paul, 111n13
Rilke, M. Rainer, 173n29
Rinaldi, Raffaele, 84n36
Rizzardi, Mario, 265n40
Rossi, Guido, 398nn73–74, 416n11, 417n19
Rousseau, Jean-Jacques, 92, 184, 189, 190
Rousselot, Pierre, 105n1
Russell, Bertrand, 75

Saccon, Alessandra, 45n18
Sala, Vincenzo, 111n13
Sallust, 295
Salvioli, Marco, 5n6, 10n19, 16n31, 16n32, 18n35
Sani, Roberto, 417n15
Sanna, Gian Luca, 307n13
Sapienza, Piero, 199n4, 200n5, 204n17, 208n30
Savigny, Friedrich Carl von, 355
Scansani, Stefano, 84n36
Scheler, Max, 105n1, 107n4, 227
Schelling, Friedrich Wilhelm Joseph, 129n33, 190, 457, 460, 461
Schillebeeckx, Edward, 84n35
Sciacca, Michele Federico, 22, 157n23, 158, 158n30, 170n10, 214n6, 299n2, 304
Seneca, 282, 295
Sequeri, Pierangelo, 15, 17, 19, 20, 20n40, 29n51, 103, 108n8, 111n13, 261n27, 349n7, 351n15, 352n19, 357, 358, 361, 361n54, 438, 438n19, 455
Severino, Emanuele, 350n12
Siegel, Daniel, 230n22
Silvestrini, Emilio, 199n4
Simmel, Georg, 84n36
Sismondi, Jean Charles Léonard Simonde de, 294

468

INDEX

Sloterdijk, Peter, 23, 167–70, 168n3, 169nn4–7, 170n8, 170n13, 174, 174nn31–32, 176, 177
Smerilli, Elettra, 305n11
Socrates, 282
Sola, Giancarla, 252n2, 264n35
Solari, Gioele, 276n7
Soloviev (Solovyov), Vladimir, 457, 460
Sombart, Werner, 84n36
Spaventa, Bertrando, 59, 301, 301n4, 311
Staglianò, Antonio, 13n27, 21, 114, 119n11, 125n26, 130n38, 131n40, 441
Stefanini, Luigi, 158, 304
Stein, Edith, 16, 16n32, 18, 23, 25, 26, 93–94, 93n5, 94n6, 96, 96n11, 234, 239–50, 239nn25–27, 240nn28–32, 241nn33–34, 241n36, 242nn37–38, 242nn40–41, 243nn42–43, 243n46, 244n48, 244n50, 245nn51–53, 246nn54–56, 250nn74–75, 264, 265n39, 432
Stella, Aldo, 264n36
Stoppani, Antonio, 253n8
Suarez, Francisco, 282
Supiot, Alain, 111n13
Sylvester II, Pope, 410
Sylvestre, Jospeh-Noél, 293

Tacitus, 294, 295
Tadini, Samuele Francesco, 2n3, 10, 10n20, 15–16, 41n1, 74, 74nn1–2, 75n3, 76n6, 77nn8–9, 77n11, 79n18, 80n20, 81n24, 82n26, 160, 160n45, 201n7, 260n26, 451n35
Taylor, Charles, 174
Teilhard de Chardin, Pierre, 126, 126n28
Terenti (Terentia), 29n52
Tertullian, 423
Theobald, Christoph, 131n41
Thomas Aquinas, 1n1, 14, 16, 16n32, 18, 19, 24, 28, 31, 51, 77n8, 92, 94, 115, 116, 122n15, 129, 130n37, 148n54, 156, 199n4, 200, 204n17, 208n30, 265n39, 282, 286n49, 333n43, 361, 365, 380, 380n4, 381, 384n15, 386n26, 389nn31–33, 390n34, 391n39, 392n45, 393n46, 399n74, 432, 457, 461
Thucydides, 295
Tillich, Paul, 84n35
Tolkien, John R. R., 410
Tommaseo, Nicolò, 184, 184n2
Torres, Sergio, 84n35
Traniello, Francesco, 406n13
Tronti, Mario, 305

Ulpianus, Domitius, 109
Unamuno, Miguel de, 176, 177n46

Valditara, Giuseppe, 356n34
Valla, Lorenzo, 307n14
Valle, Alfeo, 147n51
Vanini, Cesare, 309
Varro, Marcus Terentius, 295
Varzi, Achille C., 42n2
Vattimo, Gianni, 171n14, 177, 305
Vecchiet, Cristian, 96, 96n13, 265n39
Velocci, Giovanni, 414n6, 417n15, 419n22
Vernette, Jean, 385, 385n17
Vettorello, Luca, 307n13
Vico, Giambattista, 29, 305, 314, 346, 347n4, 355, 359, 359n48, 360, 458
Vigna, Carmelo, 90n1
Vimercati, Emanuele, 109n9
Violante, Luciano, 109n9
Virgil, 293

Wagner, Richard, 174
Wallon, Henri, 265
Washington, Joseph R., 84n35
Waterhouse, John William, 293
Watson, Terence, 273, 276, 276n13
Winnicott, Donald W., 419, 419nn26–27
Wittgenstein, Ludwig, 461
Wolterstorff, Nicholas, 111n13

Xenophon, 295

Zanardi, Stefania, 300n3, 314n23
Zangwill, Nick, 84n36
Zanoni, Elena, 253n8

Zorzetto, Silvia, 354n28
Zovatto, Pietro, 419n24

www.ingramcontent.com/pod-product-compliance
Lightning Source LLC
Chambersburg PA
CBHW052046290426
44111CB00011B/1636